# THE UNITED STATES
# IN THE WORLD ARENA

AMERICAN PROJECT SERIES
Center for International Studies

MASSACHUSETTS INSTITUTE OF TECHNOLOGY

# THE UNITED STATES IN THE WORLD ARENA

## AN ESSAY IN RECENT HISTORY

# W. W. ROSTOW

HARPER & BROTHERS, PUBLISHERS, NEW YORK

THE UNITED STATES IN THE WORLD ARENA

*To*
*Peter and Ann*

Books from the Center for International Studies

PUBLISHED BY HARPER & BROTHERS

A Proposal: Key to an Effective Foreign Policy
  by M. F. Millikan and W. W. Rostow, 1957
Forging a New Sword: A Study of the Department of Defense
  by William R. Kintner, with Joseph I. Coffey and Raymond J. Albright, 1958
The American Style: Essays in Value and Performance
  edited by Elting E. Morison, 1958
Postwar Economic Trends in the United States
  edited by Ralph E. Freeman, 1960
The United States in the World Arena
  by W. W. Rostow, 1960
The Question of Government Spending: Public Needs and Private Wants
  by Francis M. Bator, 1960

OTHER BOOKS FROM THE CENTER FOR INTERNATIONAL STUDIES

The Dynamics of Soviet Society
  by W. W. Rostow, Alfred Levin, and others. Norton, 1953; Mentor Books, 1954
Soviet Education for Science and Technology
  by Alexander G. Korol. Technology Press of MIT and Wiley, 1957
The Economics of Communist Eastern Europe
  by Nicholas Spulber. Technology Press of MIT and Wiley, 1957
The Structure of the East German Economy
  by Wolfgang F. Stolper. Harvard, 1960
The Prospects for Communist China
  by W. W. Rostow and others. Technology Press of MIT and Wiley, 1954
China's Gross National Product and Social Accounts: 1950-1957
  by William W. Hollister. Free Press, 1958
The Chinese Family in the Communist Revolution and A Chinese Village in
    Early Communist Transition
  by C. K. Yang. Technology Press of MIT and Harvard, 1959
Scratches on Our Minds: American Images of China and India
  by Harold R. Isaacs. John Day, 1958
Changing Images of America: A Study of Indian Students' Perceptions
  by George V. Coelho. Free Press, 1958

*Moscow and the Communist Party of India*
  by John H. Kautsky. Technology Press of MIT and Wiley, 1956

*Industrial Change in India:* Industrial Growth, Capital Requirements, and Technological Change, 1937-1955
  by George Rosen. Free Press, 1958

*Industrial Growth in South India:* Case Studies in Economic Development
  by George B. Baldwin. Free Press, 1959

*Indonesian's Economic Stabilization and Development*
  by Benjamin Higgins. Institute of Pacific Relations, 1957

*Financing Economic Development:* The Indonesian Case
  by Douglas S. Paauw. Free Press, 1959

*Overseas Chinese Nationalism:* The Genesis of the Pan-Chinese Government in Indonesia, 1900-1916
  by Lea Everard Williams. Free Press, 1959

*The Religion of Java*
  by Clifford Geertz. Free Press, 1960

*Handbook for Industry Studies*
  by Everett E. Hagen. Free Press, 1958

*The Japanese Factory:* Aspects of Its Social Organization
  by James C. Abegglen. Free Press, 1958

*Bloc Politics in the United Nations*
  by Thomas Hovet, Jr. Harvard, 1960

*The Passing of Traditional Society:* Modernizing the Middle East
  by Daniel Lerner, with Lucille W. Pevsner. Co-sponsored by the Bureau of Applied Social Research, Columbia University. Free Press, 1958

# CONTENTS

## Book Three
## THE TRUMAN-STALIN DUEL
### Part I    The New Challenge

### Part II    The Slide into Cold War

### Part III    The American Counteroffensive

### Part IV    The Watershed of the Early 1950's

## Book Four
## THE EISENHOWER ADMINISTRATION
## AND ITS CRISIS
### Part I    Introduction

### Part II    The New Communist Offensive

### Part III    The Eisenhower First Term

### Part IV    The Crisis of 1956-1958

Book Five

## PROSPECTS AND PROBLEMS

*Part I   Introduction*

Book Six

## THE AMERICAN AGENDA

# PREFACE

This book is part of the American Project conducted at the Center for International Studies, Massachusetts Intitute of Technology, in 1955-1958 under a grant from the Carnegie Corporation. Its subject matter has been the interplay between American society and the world of which it is a part with special reference to military and foreign policy. The first acknowledgement is, therefore, to the Carnegie Corporation which, in the old-fashioned tradition of high-risk banking, encouraged us to investigate problems the embrace many areas of fact and cut across the formal disciplines which fragment our intellectual life.

In writing this book many men and women have contributed generously from their personal experience or from their own investigations touching upon one or another aspect of the subject matter. I should like particularly to thank the following: Frederick Anderson, Katherine Arnow, Max Ascoli, Francis Bator, Lee Benson, Richard M. Bissell, Jr., Donald Blackmer, Lincoln Bloomfield, John Blum, Robert Bowie, Chester Bowles, William Bundy, John Burchard, James Cross, Trevor Dupuy, Richard Eckaus, Frank Elliott, John Fischer, Jerome Frank, Max Freedman, Ralph Freeman, David Gleicher, Paul Hammond, Frederick Holborn, Samuel Huntington, Morris Janowitz, Gordon Jensen, Suzanne Keller, George Kennan, Albert Kervyn, Charles Kindleberger, Clyde Kluckhohn, Henry Kissinger, Roy Lampson, Eric Larrabee, Daniel Lerner, Martin Lichterman, George Lincoln, Richard McAdoo, William Marvel, Edward Mason, Edward Mayer, Max Millikan, Elting Morison, Samuel E. Morison, Harry Murray, Robert Osgood, Talcott Parsons, Stefan Possony, David Potter, Harry Ransom, John Rae, David Riesman, Arnold Rivkin, Eugene Rostow, Paul Samuelson, Werner Schilling, Arthur Schlesinger, Sr., Arthur Schlesinger, Jr., Arthur Singer, Julius Stratton, Ordway Tead, Leon Trilling, Earl Voss, Jerome Weisner, Rudolf Winnacker, and Jerrold Zacharias.

I have been supported even more directly by those who, in one way or another, were associated directly with the Project: by Raymond Bauer, who provided a searching analysis of the concept of the mass communications society; by Denis Brogan, who surveyed changes in the American scene over the long span of his personal experience; by Afred D. Chandler, Jr., who contributed the preliminary findings of his research on the evolution of American business administration; by Lewis Dexter, who conducted an original investigation, based on intensive interviews, into Congressional attitudes and procedures in handling military policy; by Nancy Boardman Eddy, who studied American public opinion in foreign affairs; by Roger Hagan, who served as both critic and aide in putting the final version of the book to bed; by Richard Hughes who, in the midst of a demanding business career, never failed to respond as consultant and critic from the beginning to the end of the enterprise; by Helen Kangeiser, who examined the social themes and attitudes which suffuse recent American literature; by William Kintner and Joseph Coffey who, while on active duty in the Army, not only found the time to write they own book on the Pentagon as part of this project (*Forging a New Sword*) but also meticulously criticized various drafts of this book; by Roland Mitchell, who made many helpful suggestions on early drafts and investigated the evolution of post-1945 research and development within the government; by Peter Ogloblin, who investigated in detail the sequence of the Korean War and prepared much useful background material on recent military affairs; by Gregory Rochlin, who studied the evolution of Eisenhower's concept and method of administration; by Jeanette Clarvoe Tierney, who tracked out the evolution of the Middle East Crisis of 1956.

Responsibility for the final judgments expressed rests, of course, wholly with the author.

The enterprise was sustained throughout by the good cheer, readiness to meet extraordinary demands, and high competence of the secretaries who served at various stages: Carol Anderson, Mabel Cooper, Susan Cort, Rosemary Parkins, and Lucinda Pye.

A quite special debt is owed to Miss Harriet Peet. Out of her long experience as teacher she wrote, within this Project, a book entitled *The Creative Individual: A Study of New Patterns in American Education,* which I trust will soon be published. From this work she organized and made available a helpful critical bibliography of the vast contemporary literature on the problems of education in the United States. In addition, she gave unflagging encouragement and critical suggestions of the most pertinent and usable kind. Her mixture of wisdom and enthusiasm, as well as her substantive contribution, have been a major source of strength.

Richard Hatch served as sounding board, adviser, critic, and editor throughout. Page by page, line by line, he worked over this book in the long final stage of its editing. To the extent that its ideas prove communicable, the reader is deeply in his debt. The author's debt to him is incalculable, bringing as he did a mixture of editorial virtuosity, comradeship, and ruthless dedication to the large purposes this book aims to serve. Few men can have given so much of themselves to another's book.

The substance of this book incorporates at every point the views of my wife, Elspeth Davies Rostow, without whose active collaboration this job would not have been undertaken. She is herself an American historian whose professional qualifications range from social to diplomatic history. For three and a half years a dialogue has proceeded out of which, in effect, the main themes of this book emerged. It was at her urging, for example, that I brought to bear what insights economic history could afford and the concept of stages of growth took shape; and the concept of the national style and its components owes much to her. Were it not for her excessive scruple, she would appear as co-author.

*September 1959*                                    W. W. Rostow

# INTRODUCTION

This book is one man's effort to define where his society has come from; where it stands; what dangers it confronts; and in which directions lie an appropriate response.

The origins of this book lie in the receding past. In 1943-1945 I was an officer assigned to work in the British Air Ministry, a privileged observer and minor participant in the air war as it came to its climax in Europe. The difference between British and American styles in the planning and execution of military operations was evident even to the least perceptive and most preoccupied observer.

These reflections on the link between the inner nature of societies and the way they handle the problems they confront came again to mind when, after a year in the Department of State, I found myself in the fall of 1946 a teacher of American history at Oxford. One task of the visiting professor is to deliver an inaugural lecture. I chose then to consider, in a paper called "The American Diplomatic Revolution," the position on the world scene the United States was likely to adopt in coming years and how the nation's performance would be strengthened and weakened by forces imbedded in American history, values, and institutions.

In the decade that followed, while pursuing my profession as economic historian, I was also called upon from time to time to participate in public affairs and to write about them. In 1947-1949 I worked as special assistant to the Executive Secretary of the Economic Commission for Europe, in Geneva; and over the period 1951-1954 I undertook within the Center for International Studies at MIT to study the evolution of the Soviet Union and Communist China and to form views on what an appropriate American policy toward the Communist Bloc might be. In addition I gave some time to the question of American policy toward the underdeveloped areas.

Every experience of military and foreign policy—as student or participant—strengthened the judgment that the nation's fate would be determined in coming decades less by the actions of our enemies than by the courses of action we proved capable or incapable of generating from our own society. Out of this conviction, I accepted the invitation in the spring of 1955 to take charge of a study of American society in relation to world affairs at the Center for International Studies. This enterprise, in which a number of scholars have taken part, yielded the series of books, monographs, and essays listed in Appendix B.

My own major task has been to grapple directly with these central issues: how has the nature and evolution of our life at home affected the nation's military and foreign policy performance, notably over the past quarter-century; what foreseeable problems on the world scene must the United States solve in order to protect its interests; what must the nation do to solve those problems while maintaining the quality of the domestic society?

These issues embrace the sweep of the nation's history, the complex diplomatic and military events of recent times, the nature and problems of contemporary American society, and the rapidly moving forces in the world outside. How were these mammoth areas of fact to be brought into focus?

In part the solution I have chosen is historical. The book begins by tracing the interplay between domestic and external affairs in the century and a half before the Second World War; it considers then, in greater detail, the war years and the evolution of American society and its external policy under the two postwar administrations; and it closes by peering ahead and offering prescription.

In facing new circumstances which require new courses of action, it is often useful to look back and to order the experience through which we have passed. This is not because history repeats itself. While patterns of events reminiscent of the past often recur, history is treacherous as a literal guide to the present. It is, in fact, a major conclusion of this book that American policy has gone astray in recent years because the American view of current circumstance was too strongly controlled by memories of the preceding crisis. The virtue of the historical method is more limited and general: to help men and nations to understand how they have come to the point at which they stand and, thus, to deal more rationally with what they face. As Sir Lewis Namier says in his essay on *History*:

> On the practical side history should help man to master the past immanent both in his person and in his social setting, and induce in him a fuller understanding of the present through a heightened awareness of what is, or is not, peculiar to his own age. Knowledge and understanding are required before any reasonable endeavour can be made to direct and control; and man, despite a thousand dismal failures and though more and more depressed by his own creations, can never abandon the attempt to navigate the seas of destiny, and resign himself to drifting in them: he therefore tries to gain a better

comprehension of the circumstances in which he is set and of his own ways of acting.

The historical method, however, was only a partial answer to the problem posed in this book. There are many ways of telling the story of recent times. The shape of this book was finally determined by three concepts which are its recurrent themes: the national style, the national interest, and the stages of economic growth. Each requires a preliminary word.

The concept of the national style is a way of describing how the United States has typically gone about solving its problems. The ultimate motivating forces of nations—like those of the human beings who make them up—are complex and elusive. The recurrent pattern of a nation's performance, however, is more accessible to study and to description. Once the main elements in a national style are established one can consider how, out of the interplay of men and their environment, a national style slowly changes.

A national style expresses itself in many dimensions: in the way a nation's family life is conducted, its poems and novels are written, its humor is expressed. Here the central concern is with the American style in the conduct of organized affairs, public and private. In this sense the concept of a national style serves to link the way Americans have dealt with problems at home, which have been their main preoccupation, and the way they have dealt with the peculiar problems of war and diplomacy.

The national interest is the conception which nations apply in trying to influence the world environment to their advantage. The national interest figures here in two distinct ways. What Americans believed the national interest to be has strongly affected how we have behaved on the world scene. Thus, as a matter of fact and history, various conceptions of the national interest have an important place in the story. In addition, however, the questions posed in this study required that in the end I face the task of prescription. I was thus confronted with the problem of passing judgment on the wisdom and efficacy of various courses of action—past, present, and future. This, in turn, meant that I had to bring to bear a concept of the national interest I believe to be correct. The problem of personal judgment is inescapable for the historian and social scientist; for personal judgment will always shape the narration and analysis of human events. The author's duty is not to seek or pretend to have achieved some absolute level of objectivity; his duty is to make clear what his standards of judgment are. To this end Appendix A sets out briefly the definition of the national interest which is brought to bear throughout this book, and the reader may wish to acquaint himself with that view forthwith.

One aspect of this definition of the national interest should be particularly noted. It takes its start from the task of preserving an external environment for the nation which will permit the domestic society to preserve its chosen basic qualities. On this view the problem of power and its use is linked to the problem of the good life as Americans have conceived it. The consideration of domestic and foreign national objectives is thus related.

The third basic theme which recurs throughout this book is the concept of stages of growth. Out of my work as an economic historian there has gradually emerged a way of analyzing societies as they move from relatively primitive agricultural status through the gradations of growth, modernization, and high levels of consumption. The stages of growth are used here as a framework within which to describe both the evolution of American society and the evolutions of the major nations and regions of the world which constitute the nation's external environment. The ultimate test of this concept comes in the book's final chapters, where it is used to illuminate the problems foreseeably to be confronted by the United States and other nations in the world arena.

Although they are derived from the study of economic history, these stages are ways of talking about whole societies, not merely about their economies. There is no implication in them that economic factors uniquely determine the shape of societies or their policies; nor is it implied that economic motives dominate human behavior. People and the societies they construct are viewed as complex interacting phenomena, in which no single motive or sector enjoys primacy.

Each of these concepts evolved independently out of different aspects of my work. In the course of writing this book, however, certain relations among them have emerged. The ruling concept of the national interest in various periods of American history is related, for example, to the national style; the national style is seen to change partly in response to the stages of growth through which the nation has passed; the stages of growth turn out to be a useful tool in defining the changing problems of power in the world arena which the nation has confronted in seeking to protect the national interest. The reader will find, in short, that these themes, enunciated and used to illuminate basic elements in the nation's history in the first three chapters, flow contrapuntally through the book until, in Book Six, they are all brought to bear on the nation's foreseeable problems.

In terms of these three concepts the book's final theme can be broadly rephrased in the form of this question: How must the national style change in order to protect the national interest in a world where power is being rapidly diffused? And, in substantial part, the concept of the stages of growth is used to define the issues on which the answer depends.

This is, then, a long essay on recent American history rather than a conventional narrative. In its original draft it was, in fact, considerably longer.

Book One, "A Prologue: Variations on Three Themes," is a summary of a much more extended introduction covering the pre-1940 period. The author was prevailed upon radically to cut this portion of the text, a process of deletion and editing which delayed the publication of this book for a year. The full original introduction has been reproduced as a working paper of the Project under the title, "The Making of Modern America."

Why this emphasis on the period before 1940? The reason is simply this: the contemporary meaning and relevance of each of the three basic concepts used in this book flow directly from their relation to the long sweep of the past. A national style is a deeply rooted phenomenon; and one must look far back to understand why nations perform as they currently do. Although it is one of the final conclusions of the book that the American style is in process of change, I felt that it was essential to establish the historic base from which change is now taking place. Similarly, the nation's current difficulties in defining and communicating the nature of the national interest require that one begin, at the latest, with Washington's Farewell Address. Finally, the usefulness of the concept of stages of growth as applied to American contemporary society flows from the possibility of viewing the whole pattern of the nation's domestic evolution—in many ways unique—as a version of universal modern experience.

There is a fourth notion that suffuses this book and effects its contours at many points: no matter how persistent and powerful impersonal forces are in shaping history, history unfolds within limits which leave a substantial place for the individual. After the event it is always possible to argue the inevitability of a given historical sequence; but the range within which the accident of human personality operates is so great that history is, before the event, never inevitable. Thus individuals figure in this story more substantially than might be expected in an analytic essay; and the book's final prescriptions on the process of innovation are strongly colored by the proposition that history is tolerant of the individual if he avoids the larger illusions of grandeur.

Like a great many men of my generation I have been privileged to participate in and to observe closely certain phases of the nation's diplomatic and military performance. At a few points—notably in the account of our war and immediate postwar experience—I have drawn on personal knowledge. In dealing with more recent years, however, I have relied on material in the public domain. This reticence is not only a matter of taste; it reflects as well the view that the passage of some time is necessary before one can place in decent perspective the very small sector of public affairs one has known well.

An effort to assess events as close to hand as those of the Roosevelt, Truman, and Eisenhower years is, of course, extremely difficult. And, with so many possibilities for error, there is little satisfaction in passing critical judgment with the benefit of hindsight on the decisions of the dedicated and hardworking men who, as best they could, have confronted in positions of responsibility the flow of difficult problems of the past two decades. I have often thought, as this account of an inadequate national performance moved on, of Dexter Perkins' rule of thumb, in his *Popular Government and Foreign Policy*: "The Abbe Sieyes, that ingenious and flexible Frenchman of the period of the French Revolution, was once asked what he had done during those stirring years of convulsion. 'I have survived,' was his reply. Precisely so. The first test of a regime is its capacity to perpetuate itself."

If, then, a reliable perspective is so difficult to achieve and the nation still stands in continuity with its past, why should this effort have been made? The answer is that the problems we confront in a world caught up in a nuclear arms race and in violent revolutionary change require of us a better national performance than we have yet been able to achieve. That we have thus far survived is no guarantee that we shall continue to survive.

And these words are not a conventional rhetoric. The United States, brought out of its own dynamics to a state of relatively bland comfort, stands, in the most literal meaning of the phrase, in mortal peril.

The performance required of us now and foreseeably demands a heightened sense of where in our recent experience we have succeeded and where we have failed; a heightened sense of the dangers and possibilities that confront us; a heightened sense of dedication to the community of nationhood and of humanity. These are the ends this book aims to serve.

BOOK ONE

# A PROLOGUE:
# VARIATIONS ON THREE THEMES

# A PROLOGUE:
# VARIATIONS ON THREE THEMES

## 1. Introduction

In the spring of 1940 opinion polls indicated, as they had for some time, that two thirds of the American public believed it was more important to keep out of war than to aid Britain; by September less than half of the American public held this view; and by January 1941 70 per cent were prepared to aid Britain at the risk of war. The German victory in the West, climaxed by the fall of France in June 1940, brought about a change in American public opinion and in public policy which the nation's most influential political leader of the twentieth century had tried but failed to bring about since at least 1937. By every index, a substantial majority of Americans came at last to the view that the avoidance of British defeat was sufficiently in the American interest to justify the risk of war. On the basis of that shift in public opinion the presidential campaign of 1940 was fought and the groundwork laid for Lend-Lease and accelerated rearmament. And it is essentially with this transition in American opinion and policy that the body of this book takes its start.

To understand what followed down to the summer of 1958 requires, however, that one look beneath the surface of this reversal of isolationism. For the American performance from 1940 to 1958 was influenced not merely by the flow of external events and problems which were, over this interval, accepted as part of the national agenda. The American performance was influenced even more profoundly by habits of mind and action which determined how these events and problems were handled, and by concepts of the national interest which determined how they were perceived. Moreover, at every stage, the American performance on the world scene was influenced by the intrusion of imperatives arising from the dynamics of domestic life.

On the eve of the Second World War the United States was overwhelmingly taken up with domestic problems. And the nation was dealing with them by institutional processes and in human style wholly consonant with the American past. The problems centered on an intractable depression that yielded still, in 1939, some 17 per cent of the working force unemployed. The New Deal, which nominally dominated the political scene, was wrestling pragmatically with this problem and also pressing forward, with waning force, to install in American society a series of structural reforms. Since about 1936 a bipartisan conservative coalition had formed which argued the danger and inappropriateness of its methods and which succeeded in bringing the drive toward a welfare state to a virtual halt.

Meanwhile, the gathering power of the Axis forced the issue of foreign policy toward the center of national politics and posed for Americans the question of what their interests were on the international scene. Down to the summer of 1940 Franklin Roosevelt had lost, at almost every stage, a dour set of guerrilla engagements with Congress in which he had sought to free his hands to permit the American weight to be exercised in such ways as might forestall the gathering struggle in Eurasia. The nation remained, on balance, acutely isolationist, committed to a policy of nonengagement.

American diplomats and the American military reflected the state of the society they aimed to protect. The diplomats were, in effect, passive observers of the scene, understanding better or worse the forces at work and the dangers they raised for the United States, but essentially impotent. Similarly, the military, left between the wars with inadequate resources, having fallen behind in research and development except at a few germinal points, were obsessed with their own weaknesses, without either a plan or a consensus as to what should be done. No better and no worse than the society of which they were a part, they had operated the processes of diplomacy and the military establishment between the wars within the narrow constraints their society had imposed upon them.

Beneath the surface of these public conflicts over domestic and foreign policy—and the distracted state of diplomacy and military policy—the United States was a rich society which in the 1920's had translated its industrial maturity into a new phase of high mass consumption and rapid growth, based on the trek to surburbia, the mass diffusion of the automobile, and the diffusion of a flow of durable consumers goods which provided some compensation for the lack of service which went with a high income democratic society which had also decided virtually to halt the flow of immigrants. But it had proved impossible during the 1930's to resume this process of diffusion, interrupted at an intermediate point by the Great Depression. The key to full employment was not found; and the nation contented itself with the kind of satisfaction that welfare policies could offer, combined with a partial recovery from the pit of depression.

On the world scene, however, the 1930's had not been a stagnant interval. Germany and Japan had driven their economies back to full employment on the basis of rearmament, a phase which strengthened the technological maturity of Germany and brought Japan for the first time to at least adequate mastery of the technology which underlay modern warfare. And Stalin's Five Year Plans had brought Russia toward a similar historical point. The world of power and of industrial potential was radically different in 1939 from what it had been even a decade before. Processes of industrialization launched in the nineteenth century had thus yielded by 1940 irreversible changes in the distribution of power and in the problem of protecting the interest of the United States.

The two decades that followed the outbreak of the Second World War brought further radical change for the United States in every dimension. The national style was stretched to encompass a pace of innovation never before required of Americans. A concept of the national interest was overwhelmingly accepted which committed the nation to a policy of alliance beyond the Western Hemisphere in protection of its own interests. Between them these changes transformed diplomacy and the diplomat, military policy and the American soldier. Meanwhile the domestic life was thrown into a new balance by the reachievement of full employment during and after the Second World War. The pattern of growth of the 1920's was resumed in a new and modified version. But the most important modification— a radical and sustained rise in the birth rate—came, by the late 1950's, to pose new central problems for domestic life which set limits on the nation's ability to bring to bear its weight beyond its shores. And on the world scene, too, the march of technology and growth yielded in the 1950's a quite revolutionary result, with the emergence of nuclear weapons, the spread of industrialization to China and Eastern Europe, and its gathering momentum throughout the whole southern half of the world.

The narrative that follows deals with the American response to the challenges posed by the Axis and by international communism in these terms from, roughly, the summer of 1940 to the summer of 1958.

The character of the nation's response was, however, rooted in American history just as the character of the challenges was rooted in forces long in their generation within the world arena which the United States confronted. The purpose of the prologue that follows is to identify, in a series of short chapters, the principal historical forces which continued to color the American performance beyond the watershed of mid-1940. These chapters are organized around the three interwoven concepts which give order to this book: the stages of growth, the national style, and the national interest.

## 2. The Stages of American Economic Growth

A LUCKY VERSION OF A COMMON PATTERN

The economic evolution of the United States from the 1780's to the present can be viewed as a special version of a general experience. Like many other societies, the United States gradually formed up the preconditions for sustained growth; moved through a clearly marked take-off into industrialization in the two decades before the Civil War; concentrated for two further generations in extending the tricks of modern technology to the bulk of its resources; and then came to devote its efforts (and to reshape its mores) around the task of diffusing to the mass of American citizens the high consumption which a thoroughly modernized industrial system can provide in a rich society.

In terms of the process of economic growth the United States belongs among a small group of lucky nations, notably Canada, Australia, and New Zealand. The luck of this group has consisted in two related facts, one technical and the other cultural. Technically, the United States enjoyed a balance between population and natural resources which permitted a relatively high standard of welfare even in preindustrial days. Culturally, these nations, building substantially on foundations derived from a Britain already in transition toward modernization, have not had to overcome to the same degree as the older societies the heavy weight of a traditional society: a low productivity, labor-intensive agriculture; a fuedal system of land ownership; an hierarchial social organization built around rigid castes; a system of values inappropriate to modern economic activity; and the powerful regional political interests connected with such societies which have systematically obstructed the process of modernization in many parts of the world. Almost all the struggle and pain of uprooting and transforming such arrangements the bulk of the nation was spared—although the South has known them all and borne the consequences.

THE COMPLETION OF PRECONDITIONS AND TAKE-OFF

Nevertheless, it took some time for the United States to build up the preconditions for an industrial society. There was a threshold to be overcome. The threshold consisted on the one hand in the need to create a domestic transport system which would make the United States a reasonably unified national market and, on the other hand, in the need to find an economic setting in which industrialization would be profitable despite the high attraction of exploiting the nation's rich natural resources in agriculture and raw materials. Between 1790 and 1860 both thresholds were surmounted. The Middle

West was linked to the Northeast first by roads and waterways and then by railways; and the building of the railways themselves merged with the development of a modern textile industry in New England to give the United States a solid industrial base on the eve of the Civil War, with real momentum in modern coal, iron, and heavy engineering industry sectors.

Industry acquired a less secure base in the South; but the South acquired some modern industry in the pre-Civil War decades and was also a confident, prosperous, and physically expanding agricultural empire in the 1850's.

### THE DRIVE TO MATURITY

After the Civil War, the South, in a state of chaos, had slowly to reform its structure and gradually to make the preconditions for a regional take-off, which was solidly begun only some seventy years after Appomatox. But the nation as a whole moved on after 1865, with accelerated momentum, in a drive to industrial maturity.

Steel launched this great expansion, and railway steel remained an important category of use; but in these decades, mass-produced lighter engineering products came into their own: agricultural equipment, the typewriter, and those two almost universal harbingers of the age of durable consumers goods —the sewing-machine and the bicycle. Above all, with the railways mainly laid by the 1880's, the nation became a unified Continental market with powerful incentives within it to organize production and distribution in vast centralized bureaucratized units.

Much in this industrial surge was based on radical improvements in the metal-working machine tool, which comes as close to being a correct symbol for the second phase of industrial growth as the railway is for the first. And, by the 1890's, electricity, chemical, and automobile industries, which were to play an extremely important role in the third phase, were commercially in being, the first two rooted in new and expanding fields of science and technology.

### THE CHOICES OF AMERICA AT MATURITY

Like other societies which have come to technological maturity, the United States faced a problem of choice and balance as among the three directions which a technologically mature society can take: to expand its power on the world scene; to soften the harshnesses of industrialization through the devices of the welfare state; to elevate the standard of mass consumption. All three manifestations of maturity are reflected in the American performance during the first two decades of the twentieth century.

As indicated in Chapter 4, the United States began to consider a new role in the world arena, centered around the doctrines of Captain Mahan and the

Large View, which transcended the precepts of Washington's Farewell Address and the terms of the Monroe Doctrine. In the Progressive Era, significant steps were taken to discipline the powers of industry in terms of larger human and social objectives rooted in the American version of the democratic creed. By 1916 the income tax was installed; the Sherman Act had been given some substance, with labor afforded a limited exemption from its provisions; a Federal Trade Commission operated, as well as a Federal Reserve System; and, in certain of the States, even more direct interventions of the political process into the economy occurred.

On balance, however, the United States opted rather wholeheartedly to use its technological maturity not in pursuit of world power or to provide increased leisure or social security but to expand the level of private consumption.

### THE FOUNDATIONS OF THE AGE OF HIGH MASS CONSUMPTION

The shift in the American economy from the central task of extending modern technique to the continent's resources to the expansion of private consumption into new ranges was based not only on a rise in real income but also on an equally profound change in the character of the American working force. Between 1900 and 1940, while the total labor force increased 40 per cent, semi-skilled workers increased by 98 per cent, professional persons by 112 per cent, and white collar workers by 134 per cent. Meanwhile, farmers declined by 13 per cent.

Thus American society was not merely increasingly urban but also increasingly made up of persons in white- and blue-collar jobs. It was this population, knowledgeable in the ways and the potentials of a modern industrial structure, which in the 1920's set up an effective demand for the transformation of the United States into a society dominated at the margin by the process of suburbanization, by the diffusion on a mass basis of the automobile and of durable consumers goods of all kinds. The American economy helped both to stimulate and to respond to this demand. And it was this process of economic and social transformation which provided the basis for the boom of the 1920's, the impetus of which derived from the building of houses and roads; the spread of the radio, the icebox, and the other electric-powered gadgets; and, above all, from the flivver and all it symbolized.

### THE GREAT DEPRESSION AND THE NEW DEAL

Both at home and abroad the prosperity of the 1920's took place in a setting of credit institutions (and agricultural depression) which made its structure exceedingly fragile. And the depression after 1929 went to abnormal depths because these institutions were progressively shattered. Moreover, it proved difficult to reachieve full employment in a setting where growth had come to depend on the extension of mass consumption without government intervention on a scale which no responsible American politicians were then prepared to contemplate.

The business cycle had been present over the whole of the nation's life; but it had been accepted as a rhythm outside the scope of public policy to correct —even though the fortunes of American politicians had been intimately tied to that rhythm.

From the first decade of the twentieth century an increasing amount of research on the business cycle had been proceeding on an orderly academic basis, with suggestive, if occasionally odd, proposals from the nonprofessional wings; but it had yielded no coherent general view of the dynamics of the economy and no persuasive concepts for public policy. There was no consensus, no framework of accepted ideas and institutions, within which Americans could bring the national gift for operational vigor effectively to bear on a major depression. The theories that were brought to bear both by Hoover and by the New Deal on the problem of recovery were an extremely confused mixture.

Hoover was committed to the doctrine that the economy would right itself, as it had often done in the past, if its central processes and private institutions were not tampered with and if the government helped from the sidelines with a posture of confidence supplemented by advances of credit to cushion the impact of deflation on certain major business institutions. As compared to some in his Cabinet (notably, Mellon), Hoover was an activist, as indeed he had been during his period as Secretary of Commerce; but he feared that the occasion of depression would be used by reformers unsympathetic to capitalism as he understood its institutions and working mechanisms to make radical change in the nation's economic and social life and in its values. In these circumstances it was inevitable that Hoover's posture would appear negative and the actions undertaken by the national government late and inadequate.

THE NEW DEAL

Frustrated by this ideological semiparalysis, the nation responded positively to Franklin Roosevelt's statement in 1933 that he recognized the existence of a major national crisis and proposed to act with vigor and confidence in the face of it. So far as unemployment was concerned, he lacked a program, notably since he had campaigned on the principle of a balanced budget; and his program was vague in other directions as well. In a deeper sense, however, the concept of a program of action had quite concrete meaning given Roosevelt's administrative method; for he gathered around him in the Executive Branch—and released in the Congressional Branch—every variety of activist.

There was no national plan; but there was a competitive contest to apply every partial insight or national experience which seemed relevant to the nation's crisis. Roosevelt's first term is a climactic bringing together—an orchestration—of men, ideas, and policies formed over the previous half-century's national debate, study, experiment, and experience.

The New Deal broadly combined the mood and heritage of the Progressives and that of the War Industries Board of 1917-1918. Looked at closely, however, one can detect more particular elements: from the Grangers and bimetallists to labor leaders; from the disciples of Veblen and Wesley Mitchell to those of Irving Fisher; from social workers to bankers. Men who learned how to operate in the setting of state capitals, who had operated in Wall Street, who had never operated before outside a college campus and academic politics, who had never before held a job—all were put to work side by side in the feverish setting of Washington in 1933. Roosevelt released and organized in the New Deal the national gift for action in the face of palpable problems guided by *ad hoc* theories of limited generality.

In two specific respects the New Deal can be regarded as a major success of the national style. Leaving the problem of massive unemployment aside, the nation made a series of limited, specific innovations, each with a substantial history of prior thought, debate, and, in some cases, state-level experiment behind it. This was so with respect to farm policy, social security legislation, banking and securities legislation, the Tennessee Valley Authority, and even the enlargement of labor's rights to organize and bargain collectively. Behind what sometimes appeared the hasty and casual labors of the Executive Branch and the Congress were men with long-accumulated knowledge and concrete particular purposes which were shared by substantial constituencies and backed by serious staff work. It is for that reason that so much of the legislation passed in a flood during the first New Deal phase proved, with minor modification, acceptable in the subsequent generation. The New Deal altered the balance of power between the Federal Government and the private markets and among the major social groups competing for shares in the national income along lines that conformed to powerful trends of thought and feeling which—the depression of 1929-1933 having occurred—could have been further frustrated only at increasing danger to the society's stability.

Technically, the New Deal performed successfully a second task. It strengthened the institutional foundations of the economy in such a way that it was likely to be less vulnerable to a cyclical downturn. The government became committed automatically to cushion declines in farm incomes as well as income losses due to unemployment; the banking structure was given an adequate insurance basis; and the capital markets were put under rules and a surveillance that were to prove wholesome. The institutional floors within the

United States which had caved in during the decline of 1929-1932 were not only repaired; they were also strengthened. The measures that accomplished their repair were also, of course, measures of reform; and as such they involved the alteration or extension of familiar institutions or the creation of institutions long canvassed. Here too, then, the New Deal was at home with its problems, and it could draw on concepts, men, and experience directly relevant.

With respect to the problem of recovery policy there was no equivalent body of experience or consensus. In his 1933 mood of mixed determination and profound intellectual uncertainty Roosevelt reached back to the last great national crisis the nation had faced, the First World War, and created the National Recovery Administration on analogy with the War Industries Board. Its underlying conception—that price stability and wage increases achieved by negotiation would stimulate recovery—was incorrect, tending to raise costs without in fact increasing the level of effective demand. The NRA absorbed and dissipated in the course of 1933 a good deal of the nation's initial emotional response to the new President's mood and probably slowed down the process of recovery. It was removed from the scene by the Supreme Court in 1935, leaving behind the Wagner Act and a substantial additional heritage of reform but otherwise only relief that the way was cleared for a more rational and effective approach to revival. Gradually, however, out of the maze of debate and experiment it did emerge that the central task was to increase effective demand; and the national budget was used in various ways to this end. The powers of government were never used, however, on a scale and with a conviction capable of bringing the economy back to full employment.

As the 1930's wore on, government and private economic institutions appeared to settle into a kind of acceptance of substantial unemployment as a way of life. With no clear understanding of the deflationary impact of current government policies, and with 14 per cent still unemployed, leaders in and out of Washington appeared to panic in 1937 at a modest tendency of prices to rise; and the nation plunged into a sharp recession from which it had not fully recovered by September 1938. It took the war—and the war in its most desperate stage (1942-1943)—to make the nation rediscover its full economic potential and to alter the dour expectations on which private investment decisions in the 1930's appear to have been made.

THE DEPRESSION, THE NATIONAL STYLE, AND THE NATIONAL INTEREST

The New Deal exercise in employment policy—a problem requiring radical innovation in a short period of time—thus saw the American style yield a quite mediocre result.

American society was, however, sufficiently unified on essentials and sufficiently resilient to carry the burden of chronic unemployment without fracture; and the existence of a high level of unemployment at the outbreak of the Second World War made the relative burden of the war economy light since increased military output could come substantially from increased employment rather than decreased consumption. If one were to apply merely the criteria of domestic performance to the American experience of the Great Depression, one might say that this shocking affair was successfully weathered and the American style vindicated; for out of the New Deal experience, the Second World War, the growth of conceptual knowledge, and a gathering popular conviction that severe unemployment was unnecessary, there emerged a remarkable postwar consensus both as to the character of the employment problem and the techniques for dealing with it by public policy in a political democracy.

But from at least 1917 forward an assessment of American domestic policy has an extra dimension; for the manner of solving or failing to solve domestic problems came increasingly to affect the world environment of American society and, ultimately, the American national interest. From this perspective, in all its many ramified consequences throughout the world and back on to the United States, the confusions of the Hoover and Roosevelt administrations in dealing with the problem of unemployment proved costly. The national style failed to grip and to solve promptly a problem in radical innovation.

### 3. The Evolution of the National Style

THE HERITAGE OF THE SEVENTEENTH AND EIGHTEETH CENTURIES

The initial content of the American style—that is, the typically American way of dealing with the nation's environment—was determined by the colonial links to Britain. Notably, it was determined by the profound American connection with nonconformist Britain of the seventeenth century. The imperatives and opportunities of a wild but ample land early asserted themselves, however, transforming initially transplanted attitudes and institutions. In the eighteenth century, the colonies could produce men as peculiarly American as Benjamin Franklin, Thomas Jefferson, and Eli Whitney; and foreign travelers could begin their catalogue of American traits, many of which remain recognizable down to the present. But a truly distinctive American style did not emerge until the surge over the Appalachians began in earnest after 1815 and the generation of Founding Fathers passed from the scene.

The nation that was founded in the late eighteenth century was formed, then, by a society in transition, a society still strongly molded by the British connection but also touched in every dimension by features unique to a North American life which had been working its effect for a century and a half.

The style which took shape betwen, let us say, 1815 and 1900 had these three components: a nationalism and sense of community achieved by explicit commitment to particular ideal concepts of social and political organization; a day-to-day life challenged and dominated by the extraordinarily rich potentials of the American scene; and a sequence of national life the continuity and success of which appeared progressively to validate the initial commitments in the nation's culture and values. Taken together, these elements permitted innovation generally to take the form of a sequence of relatively minor, piecemeal, compromise adaptations of a stable basic structure.

## THE UNIFYING FUNCTION OF AMERICAN IDEALS

The nation's initial commitment to a creed in the Declaration of Independence, and to a political procedure in the Constitution, took on a cumulative power as the nineteenth century unfolded. These ideal national goals and the institutions shrewdly built to give them a degree of working vitality were the essential device for unifying a society otherwise fragmented by acute individualism, regionalism, and race.

The commitment to govern by methods which left maximum individual freedom and to organize social life on the explicit principle of equality of opportunity not only gave content to American nationhood, but also, perhaps more important, served as the essential solvent, the source of compromise, the common meeting-place, in a society otherwise dedicated to the proposition that its affairs should be conducted by vigorous conflict and competition among individual, group, and regional interests.

In the end, the rationale of the Civil War was articulated by Lincoln in terms of a national unity to be maintained by commitment to these initial values and institutions; and this commitment, progressively reinforced by the nation's experience in the nineteenth century and after, played an essential role in the nation's relations with the external world.

## THE OPERATOR'S WAY WITH IDEAS

Counterpoised against the society's active commitment to great ideal goals was the character of American life in the nineteenth century: a life of hard, absorbing, material pursuits executed substantially on the basis of individual initiative and conducted to individual advantage. But men sought in the adventure of the American economy not only material advantage but also the sense of power, achievement, and status in the community elsewhere granted by a more complex scale of values.

On balance, there was little in American life that encouraged the care and contemplation required in the more abstract intellectual pursuits. At his best, the American came to be knowledgeable and wise about the nature of the physical world and about how human life was really conducted: but he remained close to the facts and processes with which he lived. As an intellectual, the American was an empiricist; as a philosopher, he was a rather literal pragmatist, loosely generalizing the situations and experiences his round of life made real.

## CONTINUITY, SUCCESS, AND THE AD HOC FORMULA

How in the nineteenth century was the gap bridged between a heightened reliance on idealism to define and maintain a sense of nation and community and a heightened reliance on the vigorous interplay of individual, regional, and group interests to do the day's work? How was the gap bridged between a concentration of effort on particular chores perceived in terms of low-order abstraction and the rich but somewhat disorderly kit-bag of higher abstractions into which Americans reached for their general organizing principles.

The answer appears to be that the nation built its style around the task of solving problems. Americans were content to leave implicit the moral and philosophic ambiguities which flowed from the method of compromised conflict and experiment. Relatively little attention in formal thought or articulation was given to the common-law formulae which emerged from these ardent living processes because of two massive facts: first, the extraordinary continuity of the American experience over the nineteenth century; second, that as a national society the United States was a distinct success. Men are more inclined to examine with intellectual refinement a complex system of which they are a part which is confronted with radically new problems, or which is failing, than a going concern. And when toward the close of the nineteenth century some Americans became more reflective and articulate about their society, they tended to elevate "life, experience, process, growth, function" over "logic, abstraction, deduction, mathematics, and mechanics."[1] Holmes' dictum embraced more of the national style than the law: "The life of the law has not been logic; it has been experience."

But the intellectual content of a process is immensely complex. It involves many factors interacting over time. The normal forms of rigorous logical exposition can grip only elements within the process and are likely to give them a more rigid and static cast than, in fact, they have; the number of unknowns is likely to be greater than the number of equations that can usefully be formulated. Men successfully operate processes by accumulating experience, feeling, and judgment; by sensing recurrent patterns rather than by isolating clear-cut, logical connections of cause and effect. This is how good captains of sailing vessels have worked, good politicians, good businessmen. This was the typical American style in operating and developing the nation's society in the nineteenth century.

Its success, however, was dependent on two conditions which are, to a degree, alternative. First, the problems confronted must be in their essence relatively familiar, and thus capable of solution by only moderately radical innovation on the basis of existing principles or institutions. Second, there must be sufficient time for the experimental exploration of possible solutions and the osmotic process of accepting change. The more the time permitted, the greater the workability of a technique of problem-solving by empirical experiment.

It was, therefore, in the less radical orders of innovation—in science, industry, and politics—that the nation excelled. Or, put another way, the American style which emerged from the nineteenth century was least effective when it confronted issues which required prompt and radical innovation.

THE NATIONAL STYLE: 1900-1940

Although the national style as it developed in the nineteenth century was still recognizable in its main contours on the eve of the Second World War, the changes in the nation's domestic life and in its relations to the world over this period brought change in each of its three major dimensions.

With respect to nationalism, American ideals maintained their unifying function, but they were brought to bear around a new range of domestic issues. On the one hand, the nation's old concept of freedom of opportunity served as the ultimate foundation for the Progressive Era and the New Deal, the state being invoked to redress the distorting balances created by the drive to industrial maturity. On the other hand, those who resisted the new intrusions of the state on the private economy substantially identified the nation's ideals with the maintenance of a system of private enterprise, with maximum individual and corporate freedom.

In addition to this contrapuntal application of the nation's ideals in the continuing domestic debate, American nationalism began to assume more conventional dimensions. The Spanish-American War, the pre-1914 adventures in diplomacy beyond the Western Hemisphere, and the searching experience of the First World War and its aftermath put the nation's old ideal image of itself on the world scene to the test. At every point there was a clash between the imperatives of behavior as a more or less conventional world power and the old popular but inaccurate image of a nation uniquely free of the European power taint; and on the eve of the Second World War, as indicated in Chapter 4, this unresolved clash left the United States in a stage of acute self-imposed isolationism in which a desire to protect the nation merged with a sense that only isolationism could protect the special virtues of American domestic society.

In the philosophical dimension of the national style, these years saw a decisive transition from an agrarian to an industrial pragmatism. The nation's life at home was still caught up overwhelmingly in material problems; but these problems had increasingly become problems of large-scale industry and government rather than those of frontier and rural life. Moreover, the drama of American industrialization and the forces that it set in motion produced refinements of thought and reflection—in harmony with or in protest against what was taking place—which were new to America at least since the initial generation of eighteenth-century gentlemen had passed from the scene. In philosophy, there were Peirce, James, Dewey, and their followers. In science, there were Millikan and Michelson; and in industry (notably electricity, chemicals, and aviation) as well as the universities there were new men who carried forward the old empirical, experimental tradition at higher levels of sophistication.

And in the 1930's, in both the natural and social sciences, a generation began to emerge which reacted explicitly against the empirical tradition. It was increasingly prepared to meet Europeans on the highest level of scientific abstraction that Western society had attained. The maturing of the American society had, by 1940, thus altered in degree the conception of the American as merely a shrewd investigator and vigorous manipulator of fact and concrete situation.

These decades saw the beginnings of change in still another dimension of the national style: process and continuity in the old nineteenth-century patterns no longer seemed to be enough, and a simple automatic optimism about progress harder to justify. Whether viewed from an isolationist or an internationalist perspective, the American performance at Versailles had clearly failed. Similarly, at home, the Great Depression constituted a break in continuity for which there was no equivalent since the Civil War.

But these were changes at the margins of American life. The United States in the 1930's had not abandoned its old commitments and was, on the whole, dealing with its environment in a style which, in many directions, still reflected the characteristics which the Tocqueville had defined a century earlier. The nation's commitment to strive for a group of ideal solutions by a distinctive constitutional process persisted and, in the end, remained the core of national unity. Although the balance between government and the private sectors of the society had altered, the United States remained a society dominated by its domestic material pursuits and the values of individual striving and performance that went with them. The nation's dominant philosophic cast was still pragmatic, although its level of sophistication and scientific virtuosity had increased.

And so, although the national style had significantly shifted in its content and balance in the two generations which had passed since the Spanish-American War, when the nation finally turned in 1940 to deal with the problem posed by the aggression of Hitler and the Japanese militarists, it did so in ways resonant with the nation's past.

### 4. The Evolution of the Concept of the National Interest

THE NATIONAL STYLE AND THE NATIONAL INTEREST

The special character of the United States as a national community raised, immediately upon the nation's founding, the following problem: how should the sense of ideological commitment and mission built into American nationhood and the national style be related to the abiding imperatives of special national interest and national power? How should the new democracy, unique in its local geography and in its distance from the seats of major power, as well as in its political organization and conception, deal with the international interest of a nation state living in a world of competing sovereignties?

This was not a wholly new question even in 1788. First thoughts on a distinctively American interest had been stirred during the third quarter of the eighteenth century as the sense of communal identity grew and the colonies sought to define a new status for themselves within the British Empire. The Revolution itself had been fought partly as a colonial revolt in the name of independence and freedom, partly through a wholly conventional balance of power alliance with France; and the Constitution had been drawn up and accepted in part because of external threats to the nation's physical integrity and to its ability to protect its economic interests in conventional diplomatic negotiations.

And then in the 1790's the nation faced a peculiarly searching test in defining its relation to the Revolutionary and Napoleonic Wars, mingling as they did the worlds of national power and political concept. Despite American remoteness from the major theaters of conflict, these wars pervaded both the American economy and American political life, bringing with them a sequence of disruption and trouble, from Citizen Genêt and the Alien and Sedition Acts to the Embargo and the War of 1812.

What was the American interest in the outcome of these wars? Should that interest be determined by an assessment of their ideological content? By memories of past assistance from the French? By revulsion from the excesses of the French Revolution and a continued sense of racial and cultural connection with the British Isles? By the impact of the belligerents' actions on special economic or regional interests? Or was there a distinctive American national interest that transcended trans-Atlantic ties of race, ideology, gratitude, or memory—and even short-run economic advantage?

WASHINGTON'S RESOLUTION

In his Farewell Address Washington spoke of these matters in the context of a general theme which embraced domestic as well as foreign policy. In the early portion of his statement he considered the dangers of party faction within the United States and, particularly, the danger of developing parties rooted in competing regional interests. He saw this danger compounded if regional domestic party strife were to converge with distinctive foreign policy positions, with each party tied in sentiment and interest to a major European power—a real enough danger in the 1790's.

Washington's objective was, then, to strengthen the precarious sense of nationhood and the barely achieved structural unity afforded by the Constitutional system. His method was to define on the domestic scene an area of national interest beyond region and party, and to define a distinctive American interest in relation to the world. He sought to limit the sphere in which Americans would act abroad in terms of the essentially universal ideals out of which the nation was constructed.

In his military assessment Washington asserted that, in the short run, the American nation could be protected by its own strength combined, as opportunity required and offered, with that of other powers whose interests temporarily converged with those of the United States; and he sensed that in the long run the rise in American military potential, relative to others, if translated into a reasonably substantial defensive force at readiness, with a well-trained professional group at its core, could cope with whatever threats might arise.

Washington did not deny or ignore the reality of the American commitment to a distinctive set of values in political and social life. He spoke movingly of the nation's attachment to liberty. But he counseled that the nation's ideological commitment was likely to be fruitful only to the extent that the nation exploited the military possibility of a security achieved and maintained without taking up fixed positions in the European power struggle, working out its ideological destiny within its own expanding borders.

The cumulative myth of American isolation was, however, quite different from Washington's thoughtful prescription for the way American foreign policy should evolve. A gap emerged between the concept of a virtuous isolated America uniquely free of enmeshment in wicked balance-of-power politics and the way American relations to the world were actually conducted. The nation practiced balance-of-power politics abroad just as it did at home in party politics conducted on a continental basis; and when military force was used in the nineteenth century it was used for relatively clear and limited political and geographic ends, not for unlimited crusade in the pursuit of ideal absolutes.

## POWER AND IDEOLOGY IN NINETEENTH-CENTURY DIPLOMACY

The framework created by Washington was, thus, successfully elaborated by his successors into a working process of diplomacy. The essence of this process was that the United States exploited the major power conflicts of Europe in order to advance direct American interests. In effect the United States scavenged on the fringes of the world arena of power to acquire the Louisiana territory and Alaska; to assert successfully its special position in the Western Hemisphere through the Monroe Doctrine; and to acquire in the Far East the favorable trading position its merchants sought.

But the acceptance in working American diplomacy of power politics and the reality within it of an American national interest did not end the problems of reconciling American diplomacy and American ideals. The issue of a kind of liberation doctrine with respect to Greece and other current victims of the Holy Alliance arose, for example, between Monroe and John Quincy Adams. And between them also arose the question of whether the American view of Latin America depended not merely on the maintenance of the independence of those States but also on their development as recognizable democracies in American terms. An American representative to Japan in the 1850's felt free to underline the difference between association with the United States as an equal and the danger of British and Russian imperialism. America, in its view of the world, did not abandon its old sense of democratic mission and destiny. It used that conception as a rationale for a purposeful, even ruthless, expansion of American power over the face of the continent; as a rationale for the Monroe Doctrine, and even for its incursions into the Western Pacific. But this happy combination of a sense of virtue and the pursuit of specific national interests depended on two transient circumstances: first, a world arena which, in effect, could be kept in order by the British Fleet; and second, an American role within it which did not extend far beyond the limits defined by Washington and John Quincy Adams. As the nineteenth century came to a close, both conditions were being violated.

## THE NEW WORLD ARENA

The nineteenth-century arena of effective power that Britain held in balance consisted mainly of Western and Central Europe and the maritime fringes of Asia, the Middle East, and Africa. Russia lurched from one side of its Eurasian cage to the other, first to the west, then to the east; but in the nineteenth century it could be held within that cage with reasonable economy of force, as the Crimean and Russo-Japanese Wars indicated. And the Western Hemisphere emerged as a special sphere, closely related to, but still separated from, the major power game by the Monroe Doctrine and by the complex implicit understanding with Britain which gave it vitality.

In the three decades after the Civil War the four great northern areas— Germany, Japan, Russia, and the United States—whose coming to technological maturity was to determine the world's balance of power in the first half of the twentieth century were at stages which did not lead to major aggression. After the Franco-Prussian War, Germany settled down under Bismarck to consolidate its political position and to move from the remarkable take-off into economic maturity. Japan, after the Meiji restoration, took about a decade to consolidate the preconditions for take-off, and, less dramatically than Germany, moved into the first stages of sustained economic growth. Russia also slowly completed its preconditions and, from the 1890's forward, moved into a take-off bearing a family resemblance to that of the United States a half-century earlier.

The twentieth-century arena, clearly beginning to form up in the latter decades of the nineteenth century, assumed, then, this form. Stretching east from Britain were new major industrial powers in Germany, Russia, and Japan, with Germany the most advanced among them. In the face of this phenomenon, Britain and France were moving uncertainly toward coalition, with Britain also beginning to look west across the Atlantic for further support. And, poised uncertainly on the rim of the world arena, groping to define a position consistent both with its tradition and with its new sense of world status, was the enormous young giant, the United States, its economic maturity achieved.

But the sweep of industrialization across northern Eurasia was not uniform. Eastern Europe and China did not move into take-off. They were still caught up in the early, turbulent, transitional phases of the preconditions; and they were to provide peculiar difficulty.

Why should this have been so? Each of these two regions, if attached to any major power, had the geographic location, population, and long-run potential capable of shifting radically the Eurasian power balance; but, lagging behind their neighbors in the growth sequence, they lacked the political coherence and economic strength to defend themselves.

In the end, it was the relative weakness of Eastern Europe and China when flanked by industrially mature societies—their vulnerability to military, political, and economic intrusion in their protracted stage of preconditions—which provided the occasion for the great armed struggles of the first half of the twentieth century.

But in the 1890's the implications of the differential stages of growth in a competitive world arena were still latent. Despite occasional gunfire from the Yalu to Cuba, from South Africa to Manila Bay, it was not too difficult to view the world as still held in balance by a British relationship to Eurasia which prevented any one power or coalition from dominating or threatening to dominate that area.

## INTIMATIONS OF CHANGE IN AMERICAN POLICIES: 1880-1900

While forces in the world arena began to stir in these new directions and the foundations of the existing balance of power were being altered by the spreading process of industrialization, the United States remained primarily absorbed in bringing its continental economy to technological maturity. However, as with other sectors of the nation's life, diplomacy and military affairs were marked by a series of events in the 1880's and 1890's which forecast the break-up of the nineteenth-century pattern of American performance. There was, for example the Samoan affair, in which the United States was willing to assert its rights in the Islands; the annexation of Hawaii, executed in 1898 after five years of acute vacillation; and then the Cuban insurrection and the American reaction to it, leading to the Spanish-American War.

To the diplomatic incidents in the Pacific and Caribbean can be added the early suggestion of a possible new American relationship to Britain, resulting from the rise of Germany. The vigor with which the German consular and naval units played the game in Samoa in 1889 for the first time defined Germany as a potential threat to American interests; and although negotiations ended the affair in reasonably good order, the flare-up left some memories in the United States which (along with the Kaiser's current intervention) may have helped permit a peaceful resolution of the quite serious Anglo-American quarrel of 1895.

## MAHAN AND MAHANISM

More significant, perhaps, than these harbingers of a new American diplomatic stance was the emergence of the doctrines of Captain Mahan and of Americans who took his views seriously.

The principle elements in Mahan's thought can be rearranged and summarized in the following sequence:

1. The balance of the world's power lies in the land mass of Eurasia; and it is subject to unending competitive struggle among nation states.

2. Although the balance of world power hinges on the control of Eurasian land, the control over the sea approaches to Eurasia has been and can be a decisive factor, as the history of many nations, most notably Britain, demonstrates.

3. In the end, naval power consists in the ability to win and to hold total dominance at sea, which, in turn, requires a naval force in being capable of

meeting and defeating any likely concentration of counterforce. A naval power must, therefore, maintain as a concentrated tactical unit at readiness an adequate fleet of capital ships with adequate underlying support.

4. Support for such a force includes forward bases, coaling stations, a merchant fleet adequate for overseas supply, and, perhaps, certain territories whose friendship is assured at a time of crisis. It follows, therefore, that a naval power should be prepared actively to develop an empire as well as a substantial foreign trade and pool of commercial shipping.

5. The United States stood at a moment in its history and in its relation to the geography of world power when its full-scale development as a naval power was urgent.

6. The pursuit in times of peace of the prerequisites for naval power would have the following ancillary advantages: the challenge of commercial and imperial competition would maintain the vigor of the nation; acceptance of responsibility for Christianizing and modernizing the societies of native peoples within the empire would constitute a worthy and elevating moral exercise; and the whole enterprise would be commercially profitable.

Before 1900, at a time when the Germans had still not moved seriously toward continental dominance, and when the Japanese had not yet defeated the Russian fleet, it was difficult to dramatize the underlying shifts in power within the Eurasian land mass that were taking place; and it would have been even more difficult to make Americans accept consciously the notion that the build-up of naval strength was ultimately required in order that American influence be exerted not merely defensively in the Atlantic and the Pacific but also on the structure of power within Eurasia. In Mahan's own writing the full significance of propositions 1 and 2 were thus obscured and slighted; for, if they were taken seriously, what was called for was not an exuberant American effort to assert itself unilaterally on the world scene but an expansion in its total military power—Army as well as Navy—in alignment with those other nations which shared its interest in avoiding a dominant concentration of power on the Eurasian land mass.

Mahan was, it is true, steadily an advocate of Anglo-American understanding, and later, as the First World War approached, he helped articulate the nature of the American power interests in its outcome; but, generally speaking, propositions 3 through 6 became detached from 1 and 2, leaving Mahan, in his net influence, mainly a propagandist for the expansion of the American Navy and its forward bases, for the creation of the Isthmian Canal, and for the concentration of the battle fleet.

Projected out into national policy the comfortable ambiguities left in the exposition of Mahan and his followers had an important consequence. Whereas the technical requirements of the American strategic position called for the rapid development of the concepts and attitudes of alliance, the new doctrine was shaped to fit the mood of national assertiveness which welled up toward the end of the nineteenth century—the mood embraced in the concept of the Large View.

## THE RISE AND DECLINE OF THE LARGE VIEW

Although Mahanism was to remain a powerful strand in American thought and in the American performance down to and beyond the Second World War, the advocates of the Large View did not immediately win the day in the United States. The issues of foreign policy and military administration which arose during and after the Spanish-American War did not dominate national thought in the early years of the century. The underlying humane and hopeful activities of the Progressive movement clashed with Mahan's dour perception that the armed struggle of rival powers was an unavoidable feature of international life which the United States must come to accept. The nation went along with the Spanish-American War; and it voted in 1900, in effect, to keep the Philippines. And the nation went along, too, with the inexpensive and romantic exercises in gobal foreign policy conducted by Theodore Roosevelt. But the new concept of America as a world power, and a serious concern for the skill and organization of the American military and diplomatic establishments, were confined to a relatively small group of Easterners—in political terms, mainly to one wing of the Republican party.

Down to 1914, building a Navy, fighting the Spanish-American War, administering the Philippines, and dabbling in the great power politics of Europe and Asia—in the Open Door notes, at Portsmouth, and Algeciras—constituted the main strands of an enlarged but still narrow national experience on the world scene. Although there was much that might have been learned, the nation could accept this experience almost as an observer, without altering in any fundamental way its outlook on the world arena or its basic priority for domestic tasks and problems; and, as the first decade of the century wore on, even as an observer the nation became bored.

## THE WILSON CRUSADE AND ITS FAILURE

In 1912 the nation elected a president who acknowledged his lack of experience in foreign affairs and whose New Freedom was a wholly domestic program. Wilson's general view of foreign policy was dominated by a conviction that America was great and creative only when it was true to its highest ideals; that, in a sense, the values of the Progressive program at home were a sufficient basis for the nation's foreign relations. Bryan, his Secretary of State, was a confirmed anti-imperialist whose view of the American destiny as a moral force on the world scene, disassociated from the politics of power, paralleled

Wilson's. If Wilson had a positive operating foreign policy, it was initially one which looked to arbitration treaties, increased trade, and a general American posture of benignity on the world scene rather than to the harsh clarity of Mahan's concepts of the world power system. Wilson had viewed the Spanish-American War as a legitimate manifestation of American idealism but deplored efforts to capitalize on victory for lesser American purposes.

In formal pronouncements Wilson sought to disassociate himself from the imperialist positions and attitudes built up under the two previous administrations. But the imperatives of the American position in Latin America were not so easily denied by an administration which bore the full weight of day-to-day responsibility. American commitments were in fact maintained or extended under Wilson in Nicaragua, Haiti, and the Dominican Republic; and Wilson countenanced, as well, the punitive mission against Pancho Villa. The conflict between Wilson's aspirations for the projection of American ideals on the world scene and the political realities was evident before 1917. Caught in this dilemma, he foreshadowed the conception of democratic crusader which he was later to seize as the ultimate solvent: he would "teach the South American republics to elect good men."

When it came time to go to war and then to make peace, Wilson formulated the American position in terms which almost wholly bypassed the power concepts developed by the Large View group in the two prewar decades, and which bypassed as well the concepts which some of his closest advisers brought to their assessment of the situation in Europe and the American interest in it.

The United States, in fact, went to war in 1917 because unrestricted German submarine warfare challenged the historic neutral claim to freedom of the seas and because it threatened Anglo-American control of the Atlantic and the Allied position on the European Continent. German policy simultaneously heightened the case for supporting actively the Allies and weakened the purely nationalist case for continued neutrality. The balance of opinion tipped sufficiently in favor of belligerence to make a declaration of war possible if not overwhelmingly popular.

But Wilson did not present the war as an American struggle to preserve American power interests either in the Atlantic or on the European mainland. He characterized it as a crusade to make the world safe for democracy. Reaching deep into the American past and into his own previous formulation of its meaning, he evoked the sense of ideological mission toward Europe and the world which had always been latent in the American view, which had found many outlets in missionary work and in the private expression of Americans, but which had been suppressed or rigidly limited in the nation's formal diplomatic behavior. And when Wilson came to the peace table he again evaded the issues of power and the problem of linking them in an orderly way to moral principle. He nailed his own and the nation's flag to a formulation of a postwar world in terms of the high abstract principles rooted in the American creed and in an interpretation of that creed which only partially reflected the American national experience.

The two new conceptions which related America to the world—the Large View and the crusade for world order—came into mortal combat in Wilson's struggle with the Republican leadership in the Senate; and, in a major tragedy for the United States and the World, they both foundered. On any objective reckoning, a reconciliation of Wilson's and Lodge's views of the appropriate postwar role for the United States on the world scene should have proved compatible. More than that, the evidence on the balance of political opinion in 1920 is that the nation was prepared to accept an increase in its responsibilities which transcended this hemisphere. While the League in itself was not an issue capable of swinging the election of 1920 to the Democrats, there was nothing in the balance of opinion in both parties that would have precluded American entrance if Wilson and Lodge had not exercised their powers of leadership as they did. In the upshot, however, the views represented by both Lodge and by Wilson were largely lost. Borah with his neo-isolationism, was, for the time, victor over both.

## THE ILLUSORY EQUILIBRIUM: 1920-1931

Despite the apparently isolationist decision of the election of 1920, the United States did not wholly withdraw from the world scene. It remained active over a range of key international issues.

The Nine Power Treaty of 1921, by defining and confirming the *status quo*, apparently clarified the relations of the major powers to each other and to China in the Far East, formally internationalizing the Open Door. The Washington Naval Treaty of 1922 (and the short-lived London Treaty of 1930) settled the terms on which the victorious Allied powers (Britain, France, Japan, and the U.S.) would live together without a naval armaments race. The Dawes and Young Plans (1924 and 1929, respectively) kept the tangled flows of international capital, reparations, and war debts moving without complete breakdown. Kellogg, goaded on by Borah from the Senate and by Nicholas Murray Butler and James Shotwell from New York, initiated the Pact of Paris (1928) outlawing war as an instrument of national policy.

Formally, then, the United States operated as a major power on each of the principal overt issues of the period: the balance of power in northeast Asia, the level of armaments, the post-Versailles status of Germany, and the keeping of international peace. Down to 1929, at least, it appeared that the nation had emerged successfully from the First World War and its aftermath. It had asserted its freedom of action, disavowed Wilson and the League of Nations, and made a separate peace; but it had, nevertheless, played a role of leadership and dignity on the world scene. As Stimson has said of the nation's position when he took office under Hoover:

> The country had defied reality in 1920; nine years later there had come no punishment for this folly, and the people were thus more confirmed than ever in their determination to avoid foreign entanglements. Narrowly considered, American foreign relations between 1920 and 1929 had been highly successful.[1]

It took the sequence of international crises from 1931 to 1939 to demonstrate that the mixture of isolationist concept and limited diplomatic intervention in Eurasia which characterized American policy in the decade after 1920 was an illusory solution to the nation's foreign policy problem.

### THE PROCESS OF DISINTEGRATION

First, in Japan and then in Germany the worldwide depression broke the prestige and power of those moderates who had been prepared to compress their national interests within the limits of the post-1919 settlement. Simultaneously, by creating grave internal problems within the United States, Britain, and France, the depression weakened the energy and cohesion with which, individually and together, they confronted the new challenges. For the extremists in Germany and Japan (and for Mussolini as well) the depression both cleared the path to more ambitious policies at home and weakened effective opposition abroad.

For the United States the first and decisive foreign policy test came in 1931-1933. In September 1931 the Japanese army proceeded to occupy key areas in South Manchuria in flagrant violation of the Kellogg Pact, the Nine Power Treaty, and the older American commitment to the Open Door. The State Department under Stimson was fully alive to the implications of the Japanese action and notably to the fact that the stature and meaning of the postwar treaty and collective security arrangements as a whole were at stake. After several months in which the power of the Japanese moderates over policy was tested and found to be ineffective, the government confronted the question of what the United States should do in the face of this primitive act of defiance. President Hoover consistently took the view that the United States had no interests in Asia justifying the use of force or the risk that it might have to be used. He rejected any action, military or economic, that could conceivably embroil the United States in an Asian war.

The interplay between Hoover's firm refusal to contemplate the use of force and Stimson's awareness of what was at stake for the United States and the world in the Far East yielded a curious result. The powers of the Western world, in this matter clearly following the American lead, condemned and refused to recognize as legal an act proclaimed both as immoral and dangerous to a "system of orderly development by the law of nations"; but—also following the American lead—they refused to apply their military or even their economic strength to preserve that system at a vital point. The diplomacy of 1931-1933—the reiteration of high moral principles without the will to face risk or undertake sacrifice in their support—invited aggression. It both opened the gates to German (and Italian) aggression and set in motion the long slow process of defining the interests and principles around which the United States and the West later rallied for their desperate effort at self-preservation in the Second World War.

In the dreadful sequence in the West of 1935-1938—Ethiopia, Spain, the Rhineland, Austria, and Czechoslovakia—at no one point did the nation's formal obligations force it to take a clean-cut position as it did when the Japanese invaded Manchuria in September 1931. The Congress, in a sense, had purposefully guaranteed that this would be so in the Neutrality Acts of 1935-1937. There was not even an occasion for enunciating a moral position equivalent to Stimson's nonrecognition to which the nation could later repair. The United States, having made a separate peace after the First World War, and having tied its hands in the Neutrality Acts, left the task of holding together the world created by Versailles up to Britain and France—both split and weakened in the aftermath of the First World War, in part by the fact of American abstention.

SOME REASONS FOR FAILURE

The following appear to have been the major underlying ingredients in the peculiarly intractable American isolationism of the 1930's.

1. The discrediting of both the Large View and Wilson's policy in the period 1918-1920. Theodore Roosevelt's education of the American people in the period 1901-1908 had not prepared them fully for the sacrifices of full-scale involvement in Eurasia; Wilson's idealism had not prepared them for the harsh realities of international politics and power. In the face of the challenge of 1917 the nation had accepted the costs of war and had stretched to the limit of its aspiration in backing initially a Wilsonian settlement; but the tough bargaining and detailed issues of power and politics which arose at Versailles did not fit the nation's Wilsonian vision of what peace would be like and were distinctly a shock. Even the Large View, with its distorted naval ingredient, had not fully prepared the nation for the serious, sustained commitments to the European Continent demanded by the French and implied by membership in the League of Nations.

2. The sustained prosperity of the American economy in the 1920's combined with the nation's deceptive diplomatic successes confirmed the notion of an America capable of maintaining virtue and world authority without effort, sacrifice, or sustained involvement in the affairs of Eurasia. To Americans of the 1920's Theodore Roosevelt and Wilson seemed, in retrospect, archaic crusaders. The men who ran the nation came honestly to believe that, if the United States concentrated on business, the rest of its interests would take care of themselves with minimal applications of either force or idealism to the world scene.

3. The shock of depression weakened the faith of the men who had made national policy since 1920; and after the election of 1932 it threw them on the defensive. The New Deal challenged their stature in the community and the institutions and modes of life to which they were attached. They were forced into opposition under circumstances not conducive to a sense of national, let alone international, responsibility; and with them there temporarily disappeared from authority men of the stamp of Root, Hughes, and Stimson, who had tempered the isolationist winds of the 1920's.

4. Although headed by a man much of whose formative political experience down to 1920 had been in military and foreign affairs, the New Deal was a coalition primarily built around issues of domestic policy. Many of the younger men who worked within it had never known the world before 1914. Their minds were focused on issues of domestic reform and recovery; and they believed the First World War a product of European power rivalries in which the United States had no legitimate interest and from participation in which it should have abstained. They were uninterested in issues of international power and military affairs, regarding them as somehow associated with the conservative mind. In many ways the young reformer of the 1930's was a more purposeful throwback to the Wilsonian Democrats of 1912-1916. More important, New Deal domestic support hinged on Congressmen and constituencies representing areas and minority groups that were distinctly isolationist. In short, the New Deal was an awkward set of personalities and a difficult political grouping from which to mount a sustained internationalist effort in the 1930's.

Thus, just as the Republicans of the 1920's had moved away from the concepts and precepts of the Large View, the influence of Wilson on the Democrats had waned by the 1930's. Although their concept of the nation's life and institutions might differ from that of the isolationist Republicans of the 1920's, many New Dealers, their minds filled with large domestic hopes and plans and struggles, and observing the disorderly state of Eurasia in the late 1930's, would have been prepared to echo Herbert Hoover's retrospective statement that it "was not isolationism"; it was a belief that "somewhere, somehow, there must be an abiding place for law and a sanctuary for civilization."[2]

Here, then, was the old sense of moral superiority and world mission, never absent since the nation's founding, having failed in Wilson's great projection, having fallen back to empty moralizing (in, for example, the Kellogg-Briand Pact), now turned in on itself defensively and in desperation as the Axis moved to dominate a Eurasia where the values of civilization appeared to be dead or dying. There is a sense in which the United States regarded itself as an innocent violated by the First World War and now belatedly protecting itself from its own ardors and a wicked world by a chastity belt of Neutrality Acts.

## 5. The Evolution of the American Diplomat and Soldier

The diplomat and the soldier have been the instruments for executing the national interest as it was conceived at various stages in the sweep of modern history. Their manner of operation, however, reflected the changing content of the national style of a society which moved from its initial agricultural and trading base to full industrial maturity.

### THE DIPLOMAT IN THE NINETEENTH CENTURY

The ease with which American interests could be protected in the world arena of the nineteenth century was reflected in the scale of American diplomatic operations. Two clerks worked for Livingston when he tried to manage foreign affairs under the Articles of Confederation; a Chief Clerk with seven subordinates served John Quincy Adams; and the staff of the Department of State numbered less than a hundred as late as the turn of the century.

As the century wore on, the number of missions abroad increased, and the number of incoming and outgoing messages. The typewriter superseded the painfully transcribed and copied dispatch; wireless, for many purposes, the seapouch; but there was a true continuity in the Department of State's business. For the most part, it handled a steady flow of two-way communications concerning the commercial and other private problems in which American citizens traveling or conducting business abroad become involved; and it noted and filed the endless flow of dispatches forwarded by those on foreign service, describing the state of things in the parts of the world to which they were assigned.

Down to the First World War (and even to 1939), the great acts of foreign policy—the issues which get into the books on diplomatic history—were so few and far between that they were handled personally by the

Secretary of State, usually in intimate consultation with the President; or they were directly handled by the President himself. At the most, each administration of the nineteenth century is associated with only two or three such major diplomatic affairs, usually in the form of a negotiated treaty, but twice (the Monroe Doctrine and the Open Door) a unilaterally enunciated statement of American policy.

Under such circumstances the average among those drawn into the professional work of foreign affairs was unlikely to represent the highest levels of ability or vigor in American life. The professional's day-to-day jobs were basically clerical or social in character. And many men were apparently strongly influenced to enter the Foreign Service by a desire to live abroad for a time. Down to the Root Reforms of 1905-1906, appointments were generally a highly political affair.

In 1794 John Quincy Adams defined the role of the American diplomat as follows: "It is our duty to remain the peaceful and silent though sorrowful spectators of the European scene."[1] Sorrowful or not, the American representative abroad had to become the detached analyst of a set of relationships which it was the interest of his nation intermittently to exploit while avoiding sustained involvement.

The skills demanded of the American diplomat were, then, skills untypical of the American style as it was formed in the course of the nineteenth century; for his profession demanded patience, detached observation, reflection, restraint, and a degree of cosmopolitanism. The good American diplomat could be neither a moralist in articulation nor an activist in spirit. In the eighteenth century, when many American leaders were still intimately bound up with the culture and manners of Europe, Americans with such skills emerged rather naturally from the center of affairs; but as time passed, the man of diplomacy became increasingly untypical, a transition symbolized by the shift of the Adamses—from John to Henry—from the center to the margins of American life. Nevertheless, American life had the resource, variety, and resilience to man an effective diplomacy over the century and a quarter after independence of Britain was asserted.

THE MILITARY TRADITION IN THE NINETEENTH CENTURY

Although in both substance and professional style there is a real continuity in the American diplomatic tradition from Franklin and John Adams to Cleveland and Olney, that tradition caught up the lives of only a handful of Americans, for many of whom diplomacy represented merely a transient or partial interest and concern. The professional military tradition is a different matter. It was institutionalized at West Point and Annapolis and, before the century was over, at Leavenworth and Newport. It touched, if it did not dominate, the consciousness of many more Americans through the real if dilute ties of the regulars to the state militia; and it suffused the full-time career of a good many men and structured the lives of their families. It was closer to the nation's consciousness than diplomacy if for no other reason than that war brings many nonprofessionals under arms whereas knowledge of diplomacy remains vicarious for all but the professional, and a consciousness of diplomacy and its functions is confined to a few.

Not many Americans have passed through boyhood without identifying themselves at one time or another with passages and figures from the nation's military saga; there can have been only a few who dreamed their dreams of glory as Secretary of State.

Despite these links to the society, the American military tradition was created in a nation which concerned itself only sporadically with war, against an undertow of persistent national prejudices. The prejudice against a substantial standing army, as a danger to the democratic state, for example, went deep, having been inherited from the seventeenth-century struggle and transformation in Britain. Moreover, the European concept of a professional military career, ancillary to inherited social status, did not easily fit the American scene except to a degree in the ante-bellum South. And above all, the major positive challenges to American life lay in the material development of the Continent, not in service to the state. Many Americans, in diverse walks of life, did dedicate their working careers in the nineteenth century to values and objectives which transcended material advantage. Still, "Duty, Honor, Country" were not conventional touchstones in this era.

Nevertheless, the attractions of a military career were sufficiently powerful elements in the society's life to draw a substantial corps of professionals steadily into the Army and the Navy. Moreover, these professionals reflected in their mode of operations the underlying characteristics of the national style. The American military were, for example, persistently strong in operations, weak in military intelligence and higher planning, and profligate in logistical support.

But these were national variations within a profession rooted deeply in an international tradition. Washington had been a British soldier in his time; Steuben strongly left the imprint of German eighteenth-century experience; and the cast of West Point in its formative stage reflected French thought and practice. And this continuity persisted throughout the nineteenth century despite the operational bent of the American professional's interests and his generally scant knowledge of history and the world beyond American shores. It persisted mainly because the fundamental concepts taught American soldiers derived from a common foundation of experience and doctrine; and to some extent also because relatively few men of influence—notably, the two Mahans, Delafield, Upton, Luce, and Sims—maintained touch with the evolution of military affairs outside the nation.

Despite the wide area of concept, organization, and manners shared between American and other military men, there was much distinctive in the American military tradition by the end of the nineteenth century. After Washington it was a tradition virtually devoid of high-level strategic thought about the nation's military position in the world. Captain Mahan, when he emerged, was not only unique; both he and the Navy agreed that he had probably chosen the wrong profession. Sims spoke for generations of American military men—and, indeed, for the whole society of which he was a part—when he wrote to his wife concerning his assignment to the Naval War College in 1911, following a mild scandal: "It may even be that things will blow over to such an extent that I may get some duty I would like better—something in closer touch with practice and less on the theoretical side."[2] The best American military man was, *par excellence*, an able engineer, with a firm grasp on the basic principles of battle, a gift for applying them effectively under the confused conditions of the field, a quality of courage and resilience in the face of the unexpected problem, and a special flair for the bold outflanking maneuver. Both symbolically and in fact he was a man of the age of railways and of gadgeteering that immediately followed the railway age. The vicissitudes of Stephen Luce in founding the Naval War College accurately catch the predominant biases and interests of the post-Civil War naval man, the professional in general, and of the nation.

> It was the transition period of our navy, when we were pressing from wooden ships to iron and steel; from sails to steam; from simple engines to complicated machinery and electricity. The majority of officers on shore duty were engaged with inspection of steel, powder, guns, engines. It seemed as if every one was eager to be identified in some way with the building of the new navy. "Thus mental activity," says Mahan referring to this period, "was not directed toward the management of ships in battle, to the planning of naval campaigns, to the study of strategic and tactical problems nor even to the secondary matters connected with warlike operations at sea." It was therefore natural that the idea of going to school was to most officers absurd.[3]

But the predominant biases and interests were already undergoing change in the 1880's; for the Naval War College was established just as the new graduate schools took hold at Johns Hopkins and elsewhere.

THE EVOLUTION OF PROFESSIONAL DIPLOMACY: 1900-1941

Reflecting changes in the nation's outlook and style which had been gathering force in the latter decades of the nineteenth century, American diplomacy and military affairs began to move toward a new maturity after 1900. Elihu

Root is the father of the modern Department of State as well as of the modern American Army. His reforms in 1905-1906 usefully mark the moment when the modern American professional diplomatic tradition was founded. Its subsequent development lagged behind the rise in *de facto* American power on the world scene. Nevertheless, the Department of State and its Foreign Service was a quite different institution on the eve of Pearl Harbor from what it had been when Hay despatched the Open Door notes.

The Foreign Service came to be based on a Civil Service merit system, and a few of the universities began systematically to train young men for diplomacy. The process of maturing was carried forward by the experience of the First World War. The tangled issues arising in its early stages from American neutrality were, on the whole, well handled, the Department of State being the President's diplomatic instrument for these narrow purposes. When, however, the United States became a belligerent and then assumed major responsibility for the making of peace, Wilson looked elsewhere for his staff work. A special group under Colonel House was created in 1917 to prepare for the Peace Conference; and the Secretary of State, Lansing, acquiesced in this arrangement, which basically divorced the Department of State from the peace-making process.

The First World War and its immediate aftermath did not, then, significantly develop the Department of State as an instrument of staff work or planning in foreign policy. It did, however, expand the cumulative professional experience of the Department in the technical business of modern diplomacy, and the nation's withdrawal of commitment after 1920 brought the level of the nation's problems and responsibilities in foreign affairs back to the low, but rising, level of the State Department's competence. Perhaps the most important positive effect of the First World War and its aftermath on the development of American diplomacy was to draw into the Department a new generation of able men whose imagination was caught by the Foreign Service and who concluded from the events of 1914-1920 that the American role in foreign affairs would eventually expand. And in the postwar decade Hughes and Stimson carried forward in the Root tradition. From 1920 to 1933, within the narrow limits of American foreign policy, the professional Service developed steadily in stature.

With the Roosevelt administration there began to operate forces which were radically to alter the role of the Department of State and the American diplomatic tradition.

Unlike his three immediate predecessors, Roosevelt was actively interested in the details of diplomacy as well as in broad foreign policy positions. He was unwilling to delegate day-to-day operations to the same degree as Harding, Coolidge, and Hoover; and, like Wilson, he was not prepared to regard the

Secretary of State as his sole agent in foreign affairs.

There is no doubt that Franklin Roosevelt regarded Hull as responsible advisor over only a limited area of foreign policy and the Foreign Service as an instrument of limited usefulness to him. It was Hull's position in relation to the Senate that mainly commended him to the President. This was an important link and increasingly important as the diplomacy of the Second World War came to its climax; but the truly revolutionary factor which progressively affected the role of the Department of State was that the United States began to throw into the world power balance its military, economic, political, and psychological weight.

In early 1941 the United States began military and economic negotiations with the British. By the time of Pearl Harbor or shortly thereafter the Department of State was surrounded by a Treasury pressing hard distinctive lines of foreign policy, the Lend-Lease Administration, the Board of Economic Warfare, and a White House group headed by Harry Hopkins. In addition, those charged with war production and shipping responsibilities had their hands on important levers of foreign policy which they often used with vigor on their own initiative. Moreover, within the Department of State the Foreign Service (of some eight hundred men) was all but engulfed by men on temporary appointment who were doing special jobs arising from the war effort.

The coordination of this sprawling new foreign affairs empire lay uniquely in the President's hands. Although the Department of State itself expanded greatly in the course of war years, and its personnel shared many of the adventures and enterprises of the time, its monopoly position under the President was broken, never to be regained in the postwar decade.

Looking back from the early days of the Second World War, the American diplomatic tradition can be seen to have developed in three phases. The first embraced the first century or so of the nation's life. Then the nation's foreign policy business was handled personally by the Secretary of State with the President in a series of well-spaced treaty negotiations or pronouncements while the day-to-day business of American diplomacy remained almost wholly consular. In the second phase, down to the Second World War, the scale of American involvement in the diplomacy of Eurasia expanded, and an American diplomatic corps emerged after 1905. Except during the First World War and its aftermath, however, this corps represented a nation which refused to admit that it had persistent major interests beyond the Western Hemisphere; and, in consequence, the American diplomatic style between the wars was more nearly that of an observant wary minor power, with no bargaining instruments to bring to bear, than that of a major power. With the fall of France in 1940 and the British demonstration of military viability in the autumn, the United States turned to the task of bringing its assets to bear in relation to its interests on a worldwide basis; and thus was launched the third and truly revolutionary phase of the American diplomatic tradition.

## THE EVOLUTION OF THE AMERICAN MILITARY: 1900-1941

Surveying the administrative debacle of the American Army in the Spanish-American War, Root, influenced both by the German military example and by his own experience as a corporation lawyer, sought to create an Army General Staff; and in achieving the passage of the General Staff Act of 1903 Root won at least limited victory.

The Navy, after long controversy, adopted in 1915 a different plan, more nearly in harmony with the nineteenth-century tradition, which left large powers with the Bureau Chiefs, and the civilian secretary with more ambiguous authority than in the Army. Nevertheless, both services moved toward a new maturity in organization during the pre-1914 decade.

In the First World War the United States played at the margin a decisive role in the Allied offensive in 1918; but at the time of the Armistice the American forces had not been brought to full planned strength and their military experience was still limited. It would have been in the offensives of 1919 that the American Army would have operated in distinctive army groups; a serious Allied strategic air offensive, possibly commanded by an American, would have been mounted; and fully trained and American-equipped forces would have been at their effective peak. The Armistice came, in short, at an intermediate stage of the American build-up.

The First World War did, indeed, give the United States and its professional military an extensive experience of the problems of large-scale coalition warfare far from American bases. It trained the American Navy in the problems of convoy in the face of submarines. It gave the ground forces an extensive experience of modern logistics and staff work; and it introduced the American military to two innovations—the tank and the military aircraft—as well as developing distinctive American methods and doctrines of artillery employment. But the formal return to isolationism after 1920 appeared to deny the continued relevance of the First World War experience in coalition continental warfare.

At a deeper level, the First World War left its permanent marks on a few key professional soldiers. Thus, when the problem of world war recurred, a high degree of continuity with the earlier experience was built into American military leaders and, through them, into American military institutions. There was a greater linkage between the two world wars than the interwar hiatus would suggest.

Nevertheless, the interwar years were a difficult period for the American military. They were allocated by the nation far less in men and resources than was required if they were to remain prepared to play promptly a major role on the world scene; and the energies of the professionals were largely dissipated, year after year, in making a losing case for the enlargement of their funds.

In these circumstances, they did only an indifferent job of building into the permanent military establishment the lessons of the First World War and of keeping up with a military technology still in the process of rapid evolution.

Some work did, indeed, go forward within the services on the key problems of innovation. An Army Industrial College was set up to work on problems and plans for industrial mobilization, reflecting the possibility of a second total national military effort. The ground forces moved on to a supply system based on motor transport; and, after some vacillation, the tank was finally woven into a sound conceptual structure of armored divisions. Important experimental work went forward on chemical warfare and in antiaircraft; and the American artilleryman maintained the foundations for his primacy at rapid movement and concentrated fire. But this work was conducted with inadequate resources and against much bureaucratic resistance—often by a few men dedicated to their private insight at apparent cost to their professional careers.

In the Navy there were three major directions for innovation each of which was to have major significance in the Second World War: naval aviation, the technique of amphibious landings, and the development of supply techniques for the Pacific Fleet which permitted sustained operations at vast distances from major bases. In the Navy as well as the Army, however, policy was dominated not by the requirements for innovation but by the conservative weight of preserving in being a limited and essentially static establishment—in this period one built on the capital ship, to which most naval minds turned with comfort after what was hoped was a transient concentration on convoy and antisubmarine problems in the First World War.

The First World War was regarded as a transient experience because the Navy, like the nation, did not accept the concept of a permanent American interest in the balance of power on the Eurasian land mass. If that lesson had been drawn from Mahan and the First World War—as well it might—the permanence and priority of the problems of convoying, amphibious landings, and antisubmarine warfare would have logically followed. But the Navy returned to a purer concept of sea power and focused its attention on the balance between Japanese and American capital ships.

The one inescapable problem of military innovation during the interwar years was air power where, amidst interminable controversy, a degree of momentum was maintained. Between 1919 and 1934, there were fifteen public hearings concerning the appropriate role of air power in the American armed forces—a running battle foreshadowing many of the decisive issues of policy and organization during and after the Second World War.

Administratively the air force was established at the level of an army corps, without independent intelligence or planning prerogatives. Tactically what emerged was the decision that some air units would work intimately and directly with ground commands at the corps level or lower; but that self-contained general headquarters air force units might aid the ground battle by indirect support some distance from the battlefield, operating within an over-all ground support plan. With respect to strategic bombing, the Air Corps was permitted to develop a long-range bomber and bombardment doctrine—a task to which in the 1930's the air force devoted in many respects its best men and talents, straining Army directives to the limit; but at higher levels the future of strategic bombing was left unsettled, and air force activities in this direction were partly rationalized as an effort to defend the United States against naval attack. The issue of precision attack on industrial installations versus area attack on morale was tipped towards the former by a technical rather than a doctrinal decision; that is, through the Air Corps' adoption of the Norden bomb sight and its concentration on a daylight heavy bomber. The Navy kept to itself a wide range of air functions; and within the Navy a more muted battle, parallel to that proceeding on the national scene, went forward between the advocates of carriers and those of conventional capital ships. Spurred by the danger of air force competition, by the dramatic test sinkings of naval vessels from the air in 1921-1923, and by their own aviation enthusiasts, the Navy, despite its devotion to the doctrine that the capital ship would remain the center of effective naval power, laid the foundations for carrier warfare and produced a fighting carrier force capable of stemming the Japanese in the Coral Sea and before Midway in 1942. In the end, however, no relevant military planning could proceed in a nation which formally defined its objectives merely in terms of a return to the Monroe Doctrine and of a policy of defense of the American continent. Even when joint Army and Navy planning began, after Munich, in November 1938, the basic terms of reference set for professionals were based on isolationist assumptions—although, at last, at lowest priority, they were permitted to contemplate the possibility of war in Asia and Europe, but not both simultaneously.

Like the nation, the military were thus dragged slowly from isolationism by the march of events in the face of a succession of palpable crises, for each of which the degree of prior preparation proved grossly inadequate. This lack of preparation extended from the ruling concepts of the national interest, through war-planning, the state of military technology, to a grossly inadequate order of battle.

Fortunately, the American professional tradition as of 1939 was adequate for the war the United States was about to fight. Its leadership was guided by certain relevant lessons from the experience of coalition in 1917-1918; it recruited a reasonable sample of able men from the society; it indoctrinated them in the values of the society as well as in the disciplined requirements of their profession; it managed to select from them those most capable of command in war; it incorporated strategic concepts of operations and a tactical style well suited to the national temper; it developed a respect for logistics and a skill in supply which merged with the capabilities of the society, the tasks of bringing American power to bear, and the needs of celerity in combat. Down through the Second World War persistent weaknesses in intelligence, research and development, and in higher military thought and planning could be borne without disaster, given the stage of history and of war-making in which the United States was caught up; for in the first half of the twentieth century the United States was, in fact, the strategic reserve of the West; and its allies twice provided sufficient time for the nation not only to mobilize its skills and resources but also to divest itself of the wishful illusion that its interests did not extend to the balance of power on the Eurasian mainland.

# BOOK ONE

*Notes*

CHAPTER 2. The Stages of American Economic Growth

1. *Historical Statistics of the United States, 1789-1945*, Washington, D.C., Govt. Printing Office, 1949, p. 65.

CHAPTER 3. The Evolution of the National Style

1. M. White, *Social Thought in America*, Boston, Beacon, 1957, pp. 12-13.

CHAPTER 4. The Evolution of the Concept of the National Interest

1. H. L. Stimson and McGeorge Bundy, *On Active Service in Peace and War*, New York, Harper, 1948, p. 159.

2. *The Memoirs of Herbert Hoover: The Cabinet and the Presidency*, New York, Macmillan, 1952, pp. 377-378, quoted in Dulles, *op. cit.*, p. 108. Note also Harry Hopkins' 1939 speech at Grinnell College quoted in R. E. Sherwood, *Roosevelt and Hopkins*, New York, Harper, 1948, pp. 19-21, notably the following passage, p. 21:

"With the world situation the way it is today, almost a mad house, with hate and fear sweeping the world; with this nation almost the last stronghold of Democracy; with the American people determined to maintain that Democracy, the kind of government that we have is extremely important, and it is the one thing in America that is important."

CHAPTER 5. The Evolution of the American Diplomat and Soldier

1. Quoted, S. F. Bemis, *John Quincy Adams*, New York, Knopf, 1949, p. 364.

2. E. E. Morison, *Admiral Sims and the Modern American Navy*, Boston, Houghton Mifflin, 1942, p. 289.

3. A. Gleaves, *Life and Letters of Stephen B. Luce, Founding of the Naval War College*, New York, C. P. Putmans', 1925, p. 173.

# THE SECOND WORLD WAR

# PART I

# A PERSPECTIVE

## 6. *The National Style and the National Interest in the Second World War*

The Second World War was a direct challenge to the national style and to the American concept of the national interest as they had evolved by the 1940's.

The commitment to the principle of individual freedom was tested by the need to organize something like half the national output in a communal effort. The commitment to assume responsibility for the democratic principle on the world scene was tested both by the exigencies of dealing with Communist allies and administering liberated areas and by the aspiration to create a democratic structure for the postwar world. The old style of vigorous operational pragmatism was tested by the racing succession of new and difficult problems of production and training, transport and combat; while the newer national virtuosity in the higher reaches of theory was tested by the need to develop and apply under forced draft the emerging knowledge of atomic energy and electronics. The nation's sense of confidence, with its automatic assumption of success, was tested by a plunge into war in the form of a major national catastrophe followed by almost a year of American and Allied retreat and setback. And specific issues, familiar from the past, came to a head. In China—what price the Open Door? In Eastern Europe—what price self-determination? Which military strategy—a Mahanist sweeping of the Western Pacific or, once again, strategic reserve to Western Europe? Should the national failure of 1920 and after be acknowledged; and, if so, what kind of an international political and economic system should be created, and how deep and expensive should the American commitment to it be?

But the Second World War was not merely a replaying, with variations, of old themes; it was also the prelude to a new national experience. The war left in its wake a defeated Germany, Italy, and Japan, an enfeebled Western

Europe, a Britain almost bankrupt. The Soviet Union, having been accepted and succored as an ally, fought its way into Eastern and Central Europe and then pressed out into a world of broken and disrupted states. Japan, having moved into the colonial empires of the Pacific and into China, and having demonstrated the ability of Asians to develop and apply the instruments of modern warfare, left in the wake of its defeat an accelerating Asian surge toward independence and modernization; and there was a Communist force in China capable of moving from its northern bases to victory. Above all, the exigencies of war having yielded the long range bomber, radar, atomic weapons, and the German V-2, the making of war was permanently and radically transformed and, with it, the problem of American security.

It is, therefore, in a dual perspective—as a measure of the American nation in the 1940's and as harbinger of problems the nation would subsequently confront—that the Second World War is examined here.

## 7. *The Washington Scene: Policy, Methods, and Men*

THE MOOD

In atmosphere and spirit Washington during the Second World War represented a unique passage in American history. Never before had the energies of so many Americans representing so many interests, talents, and points of view been brought into play in a single enterprise. In part this result flowed simply from the magnitude of the national effort required and the extraordinary unity of the nation after the attack on Pearl Harbor. The primitive challenge of the Japanese assault, followed by Hitler's declaration of war, made the fighting of the Second World War an unambiguous affair into which all but a tiny minority of Americans could throw themselves without inner reservation. On many domestic issues New Dealers and businessmen found themselves, in mutual surprise, working side by side without conflict—a human process that helped remove some of the scars of earlier domestic battles and prepare the way for the widening domestic consensus of the postwar years.

In part the mood of Washington resulted from Franklin Roosevelt's methods of administration. He tended to allocate overlapping responsibility to a number of government institutions and agencies, and he encouraged them to compete for his ear, reserving all major decisions to himself. Moreover, despite an ability to develop and sustain strong personal dislikes, Roosevelt's taste in human beings was catholic. So long as men were energetic in pursuit of an objective that fitted somewhere in the moving mosaic of his policy, he was not generally inclined to insist that they conform in detail to his own views and prejudices. Until he acted on a particular major issue, Roosevelt kept a wide range of alternatives open and permitted (if, indeed, he did not actively encourage) the unconcealed clash of their advocacy. Thus men representing an extremely wide spectrum of American life and opinion held posts of responsibility in the wartime Administration, had their way, and influenced to a degree the course of the nation's policy.

If the pace of innovation rather than merely formal order is judged a legitimate criterion for good administration, Franklin Roosevelt was a remarkably successful administrator.

## THE CIVIL-MILITARY BALANCE

One specific aspect of wartime administration deserves special note—the primacy of military considerations in the making of foreign policy. This circumstance was only to a very minor extent, if indeed at all, the consequence of an attempt by the military to impose on civil policy its influence and power.[1] The lack of balance in American policy during the Second World War was a product of Roosevelt's policies and administrative methods and of the historic asymmetry between the status of soldier and diplomat in the American government.

Roosevelt conducted policy in such a way as to give virtually overriding priority to urgent short-run military considerations. As nearly as one can reconstruct his mind, there were four principal reasons for such a course. First, at home the criterion of total victory was a unifying concept. Second, there was the hope that a narrow military approach to the war would convince Stalin that the West was not maneuvering for postwar power positions and thus maximize the chances of firm Big Three unity as a foundation for the peace. Third, this approach seemed to simplify allied as well as domestic politics in the short run. The formula of unconditional surrender was, in part, designed both to assure the world that there would be no further dealings with men tainted with fascism[2] and to project the notion of the post-surrender period as a political clean slate where all would start afresh. Fourth, the history of the First World War and its aftermath was read as indicating that the Allies had made a mistake in not carrying war into the heart of Germany and pressing the fact of defeat indelibly on German minds.

In general, then, Roosevelt's policy of making his wartime decisions in terms of the overriding military criterion of early victory and minimum American casualties was designed not merely to give his soldiers a relatively free hand in making current military decisions but also to simplify his political problem in dealing both with an American public which lacked a clear and firm consensus concerning the long-run American interest and with allies anxious that the United States make (or avoid making) specific and explicit postwar commitments.

So far as postwar commitments were concerned, the politically safest issues were those concerned with the erection of a worldwide structure to maintain the peace. As the war proceeded, it was clear that Americans regarded their rejection of the League of Nations as a historical error and now looked to participation in an international organization for peace after the war; but consensus on this point concealed ambiguity or conflict on issues of substance.

It would have been extremely difficult to develop during the war itself a more precise consensus concerning the nature of the American interest and the difficult problems its implementation was likely to confront in the postwar period. It was easier to concentrate on tactical victory in the field and on the formal organization of stable peace than on its substance as defined in terms of particular areas and responsibilities. From the choice of this easier course flowed, in part, the problems and crises of the postwar world.

### SOLDIER AND CIVILIAN IN WARTIME ADMINISTRATION

The military bias in American policy—as made by civilians—was reinforced by the marked increase in the influence of the professional military in government. It was inevitable that the war should elevate the status of the professional military within the Executive Branch. It gave to a group of key officers a widened experience and enlarged authority; and, as the military establishment grew by a factor of forty between 1939 and 1945, the military professionals maintained at every stage the key posts of command and authority. This was not true in quite the same way for civilians drawn into major wartime posts. The capital represented by their experience and rank was, in bureaucratic terms, diffused.

To a substantial extent the diffusion of civilian authority in wartime Washington arose from the nature of the administrative process and could not have been prevented. To a degree, however, the process was accentuated by Roosevelt's administrative method. When Roosevelt found a branch of the government inadequate for his purposes, he rarely sought to reform it to his needs; instead, he bypassed it or put it under competitive pressure by creating an overlapping instrument. In some instances the method worked well; but it was costly to the American interest at one point—in the Department of State.

It would, of course, have been impossible to assign all wartime foreign policy functions to the Department of State. Many were temporary in character, required very large staffs for their discharge, and would have grossly distorted the State Department if taken on. More than that, training in the interwar Foreign Service had not adequately prepared men for forward planning in terms of large national objectives and for the execution at American initiative of a series of operations designed to realize them. As McCloy notes:[3]

> The isolationism of the 1920-1940 period had produced a vacuum of political objectives. The State Department did not have, indeed, it was not encouraged

to have, any political aims in the world. More thinking along political lines was being done and being asserted in the Munitions Buildings—this was before the era of the Pentagon—than in the old State Building.[3]

Nevertheless, the Department of State might have been used more intensively than Roosevelt used it as an instrument of policy-making and coordination, and the war might have served as an occasion to strengthen it for the long pull. It contained the only permanent corps of civil servants dedicated to the conduct of foreign policy; and the postwar balance between military and civil elements in the Executive Branch would depend partly on whether that corps grew in stature from its wartime experience and responsibilities. As it was, the members of the Foreign Service were left relatively in a backwater during the war; and so, when it came to the question of occupying the defeated nations after the war, the posts not merely of formal command but also of administration and policy-making in the field fell to military men rather than to civilians. In Washington as well the voice of the Pentagon was stronger than that of the State Department in the making of immediate postwar policy; and those who took major civil responsibility in postwar foreign policy tended to be drawn not from the Foreign Service but from other agencies which had played a part in the war effort.

Similarly, Roosevelt's method of operating with the military services unnecessarily weakened the civilian heads of the military departments. Roosevelt dealt directly with Marshall, King, and Arnold, often bypassing Stimson, Knox, and their civilian subordinates. He was, in fact, an operating Commander-in-Chief as well as an operating Secretary of State.

It is wholly understandable that in the American system of government a strong President should conduct affairs at a time of life-and-death conflict as Roosevelt did. The President is the only politically responsible officer in the Executive Branch of the government, and only he can have a unified vision of the extraordinarily complex range of factors relevant to the making of a politically viable national policy. Nevertheless, Roosevelt's administrative method during the Second World War contributed to a disproportionate weakening of the civilian elements in American military administration at a time when larger forces were weakening the relative stature of civilian agencies charged with foreign policy responsibilities.

## FOUR KEY MEN

Despite the relative rise of the military as a day-to-day force in the making of national policy, there was an underlying unity in the essentials of American policy which transcended even the extraordinary power of the President. That unity proceeded from a broadly common outlook shared among the President, his principal aides, and the men brought forward by his aides. Aside from the

President, the three major figures who shaped wartime policy were Hull, Stimson, and Marshall.

Hull was a southern lawyer and a Democratic politician, rooted in the Tennessee hills. His formative years in the Congress were spent fighting for the income tax; as early as 1916 he became associated with the concept of liberalized trade as an instrument for peace. Wilson's defeat over the League was a major personal as well as political event for Hull; and at the Department of State during the Second World War he aimed to achieve a postwar world in the Wilsonian image while avoiding Wilson's failure to carry with him on a nonpartisan basis a preponderance in the Senate. A cautious, shrewd politician attached to Wilsonian objectives, Hull, despite the dilute wartime authority of the Department of State, left more of a mark on events of long-lasting significance—for example, policy toward Germany, Poland, and the United Nations—than is often credited.

Stimson was a New York Republican, indelibly marked by the memory and tradition of Theodore Roosevelt and, especially, of Root. Nevertheless, for him too the permanent reversal of interwar American isolationism was a central objective of wartime planning for the postwar. Although the Democratic defeat in 1920 did not have the personal meaning for him that it had for Cordell Hull and Franklin Roosevelt, he had come to know intimately the costs of interwar isolationism as Hoover's Secretary of State; and in accepting the post of Secretary of War under Roosevelt in 1940 he committed the climactic years of his life to the struggle for internationalism in the United States. And (unlike Hull) he was able to bring into his department a phalanx of younger men—Patterson, McCloy, Lovett, and others—who shared his values and objectives, imparting to his position a strength beyond the power of his own considerable personality and influence.

If Hull was an American version of an Edwardian British Liberal, Stimson was more nearly an Edwardian British Conservative. Closer to Mahan and conditioned by the formative national experience of governing the Philippines, Stimson was more comfortable with the instruments of military power than Hull. But he carried over into international affairs the ethical code of an Anglo-Saxon gentlemen and a Yale man, which, in the end, was not so very far from Wilson's Presbyterianism.

For both Hull and Stimson, then, the great job of wartime foreign policy and planning was to ensure that the nation would not again revert to isolationism; and their somewhat different ideological commitments—tempered in Hull's case by a professional sense of American politics, in Stimson's by a sensitivity to the problem of military power—tended to bring them to similar positions on at least three of the great (closely interwoven) wartime issues:

the priority to be accorded the setting up of the United Nations, dealings with the Soviet Union, and policy toward Germany.

Marshall was carrying forward a related but distinct tradition. Pershing was for him roughly what Root was for Stimson, Wilson for Hull. His formative experience had been as a staff officer in France during the First World War, including responsibility for the remarkably complex set of troop movements required to mount the decisive Meuse-Argonne offensive of the autumn of 1918. He had seen American ground forces brought to bear in Europe and learned something of the problem of intimate wartime alliance; and he had also seen in March's dealing with Pershing how difficult a relationship could develop between Washington and the field. In his time, Marshall avoided March's relative impotence as Chief of Staff in the headquarters town. Above all, Marshall fully accepted the concept of civilian control as it had emerged in the pre-1914 decade under Root's initiative. That concept permitted the professional soldier a close and influential partnership with the responsible political officer but required that he hold himself in tight rein politically, outside that relationship. Marshall's commitment to the Root-Pershing formula may have been strengthened by a long-drawn-out feud with Douglas MacArthur, who by instinct, family history, and personality was of a more assertive school. Sent by MacArthur, despite protest, from a long-sought field command to the Illinois National Guard in 1933, Marshall came to know a number of influential Democratic politicians, preparing the way for his remarkable relations with Congress.[4]

Marshall was thus well prepared to serve as Chief of Staff to a strong President; to build quickly a powerful and effective higher military staff, capable of directing a global war; and to work with allies in a setting of Congressional confidence. The men who rose to posts of high responsibility under Marshall reflected his experience and his conception. Although the strategy of Europe first had much to commend it on any objective assessment of Axis strength and its threat, the coalition policy it required came easier to Marshall than to many other American military men. The elevation of Eisenhower, for example, reflected an intimate knowledge of the difficulties of Allied operations and the need for unified theater command executed with tact and minimum ego. And close around him, in the Operations Division of the War Department, Marshall built a command post through which passed the best staff brains of an Army generation, including a sprinkling of men from West Point who had experienced some British training as Rhodes Scholars.

Roosevelt, Hull, Stimson, and Marshall were, of course, by no means the only characters on the stage. There was the rude but capable Admiral King, presiding over his air-admirals, enjoying the definitive victory of carrier over battleship. There was General Arnold, a kind of instinctive administrative genius, driving the air effort forward with a double goal: the nation's victory in war and an independent air force in the postwar. There was Harry Hopkins, converted suddenly into a shrewd, hard-driving, single-minded instrument of coalition warfare. There was Morgenthau and his somewhat overactive Treasury staff, leaving a trail of controversy and, occasionally, an imprint on many aspects of postwar policy, most notably on German policy and the Bretton Woods institutions. There was William Donovan, weaving with extraordinary imagination Americans from every part of the society into the beginnings of mature organizations for intelligence and covert operations. There was the complex struggle over how to deal with Nationalist China, involving several military parties, but centered in a clash between two extraordinary men, Stilwell and Chennault. And, on most major issues, echelons of ardent, determined bureaucrats sitting at an endless sequence of interdepartmental committee meetings, their names lost in the archives, managed nevertheless to leave their individual marks on the course of events.

In the end, however, the President—half a Commander-in-Chief, with a strong naval bias, half a sobered, cautious Wilsonian statesman—dominated the enterprise. And the patterns of thought which he brought to the wartime issues of policy were by and large shared and reinforced by Hull, Stimson, and Marshall. What bound these four men together was, ultimately, that their minds had been formed in the first two decades of the twentieth century, when the nation was moving out on to the world scene. Each had shared in important aspects of that national experience; each had become convinced that the fate of the nation was to assume greater international responsibilities—that there was to be no return to isolation. For them the Second World War was not a dramatic operational incident—as it was for, say, Harry Hopkins; it was the resumption of national experience along paths that fitted their expectations as well as their memories.

What emerged was a policy colored systematically by two principles: a virtually overriding priority for those immediate actions judged by the military most conducive to the effectiveness of current military operations; and a concentration of effort and attention on the erection of institutions for long-term collective international action which would embrace both the United States and the Soviet Union. Their effort was more or less consciously designed to succeed where Wilson had failed.

But Wilson failed in two respects, closely related, perhaps, but separable. He failed to build an effective domestic political consensus capable of carrying the nation into the League of Nations; and he failed to relate the specific issues of power involved in peacemaking to the large principles of international order and organization he espoused. He failed to understand, or, at least, to project, an understanding that an effective world organization must be built on and intimately related to an underlying structure of effective power. In a sense the story of America in the Second World War is the story of men who succeeded in correcting the first of Wilson's failures but fell victim to a new version of the second.

The roots of this failure lay, however, not simply in a national style given to solving urgent problems *ad hoc*; not simply in confusion about the character of the national interest in Eurasia or about how to deal with Stalin. This failure also derived from the shape of the battle and the ambiguous victory it yielded.

## 8. *The Shape of the Battle*

SIX ESSENTIAL DEFENSIVE VICTORIES

The Second World War proceeded from an effort by the three Axis powers to gain undisputed control of the Eurasian mainland (ultimately including Africa, the Middle East, and Southeast Asia) by exploiting, in the first instance, the vulnerability to external attack and subversion of China on the one hand and of Eastern Europe on the other. On this view, the Second World War began with the Japanese seizure of Manchuria in 1931 and moved into its decisive phase when Russia was successfully neutralized by Hitler's division of Eastern Europe with Stalin in August 1939.

The war took initial form in a series of Axis offensives. Its final shape derived from the successful Allied checking of those offensives. The outcome was thus prefigured in the following sequence of Allied defensive victories:

1. Chinese Nationalist and Chinese Communist resistance survived every attempt of the Japanese to eliminate it in their sweeping 1937-1939 offensive.

2. The Battle of Britain, September 1940, maintained British daylight air supremacy over Britain and the Channel and led Hitler to abandon his plan to invade England and, instead, to turn on Russia.

3. The American naval victories in the battles of the Coral Sea and Midway, May-June 1942, halted the extension of Japanese power and prevented a disruption of the Allied strategy of primacy to the defeat of Germany.

4. The defensive victory in October 1942 by Montgomery over Rommel, climaxing two years of British effort undertaken at the peak of relative Axis strength in 1940, prevented German domination of the Middle East and, coupled with the Allied landings in North Africa, laid the basis for Montgomery's drive from El Alamein and for the joint victory of forces from east and west at Tunis. (There was no more farsighted decision of the war than Churchill's dispatch of armored forces to the Middle East in the summer of 1940, when German invasion of Britain appeared to threaten at any moment.)

5. The holding by the Russians of the Voronezh-Stalingrad line in the

summer and autumn of 1942 permitted the Soviet Union to remain a force in being on the Eurasian mainland and, in the context of Lend-Lease, the increasing weight of air attack on Germany, and the Mediterranean offensives, to launch and sustain the Red Army offensive of 1943.

6. The desperate precision air attacks on rapidly expanding German fighter production in the last half of 1943 checked the expansion of German air strength and permitted decisive Allied air supremacy over western and central Europe to be gained in February 1944.

The Battle of Britain stands in a special category. Its loss might well have confirmed both the Soviet Union and the United States in their then detached position, forestalled the formation of an Allied coalition, and led to a negotiated settlement with the Axis in a position of virtual domination in Eurasia. But all six engagements were defensive successes on which were mounted the Allied offensives which determined the outcome of the war.

Victory was won, then, by a coalition representing essentially a group of island powers off the Eurasian mainland (Great Britain, the United States, Canada, Australia, and New Zealand) in alliance with exiled elements from the continent (France, Poland, Norway) and with the unconquered powers on the Eurasian mainland—Russia, the large but mainly passive Nationalist and Communist forces in China, and the European underground forces.

### THE EXPANDING AMERICAN ROLE IN THE COALITION

For the United States the Second World War repeated military history. Ill-prepared, confronted by a mounting crisis, the nation finally faced and defined its immediate tasks, executed them with vigor and operational ingenuity, and in the end—given time, distance, allies, and the limited power of weapons—shared in a total victory in the field.

The American position in the Allied coalition in Europe was successively that of a virtually impotent and self-isolated observer of the scene, a major nonbelligerent source of supply, a junior partner in the field, and then, finally, the senior partner in the coalition on the western fighting fronts. In Asia the United States throughout was the principal active Allied force, assisted by British strength mounted from India and by elements of Chinese resistance.

The stages in which the United States assumed its increasingly responsible functions may be marked off roughly as follows:

*September 1939 to October 1940.* Operating under the September 8, 1939 Presidential declaration of a state of limited national emergency, the nation increased its degree of preparedness on a restricted and essentially isolationist basis, adopting no clear strategy with respect to the European war except to modify the Neutrality Act to permit cash-and-carry trade with the belligerents.

As the German offensive of May-June 1940 succeeded, the President, acting virtually alone and risking political disaster for himself should Britain fall, used his powers to assist Britain by releasing small arms, ammunition, field artillery, and aircraft and by the destroyer-bases deal (September 3, 1940). The Selective Service Act became law September 16, 1940.

The President even at the nadir of Allied misfortune in June 1940 looked to the survival of Britain and to the defeat of the Axis by an alliance in which the United States would participate. The military planners, influenced by an acute sense of current American weakness, faulty intelligence appreciations of British-German relative air and naval capabilities, and, to a degree, by deep confusion concerning the long-run character of American interests, resisted action which would dissipate American resources in support of Britain and which would commit the United States to deal with the full weight of Axis power in the near future.

The President evidently felt himself caught in a domestic political position of the greatest delicacy, in which he would risk the whole structure of arrangements to strengthen the Allies if he were to seek Congressional approval for full American engagement at American initiative. He did not accept minority advice (notably Stimson's and Morgenthau's) to assert strongly the American interest in Axis defeat and to rally the nation for a maximum effort to avoid the passage of Western Eurasia into the hands of a hostile power. Instead, the formal rationale for his initiatives was expressed in conventional Mahanist terms, reasonably acceptable to isolationists as well as interventionists: namely, that it was contrary to American continental interests to see the British fleet pass into the hands of a hostile power.[1] The nation, whatever its sympathies with the Allied cause, was by no means united in the view that American interests required not merely the survival of the British Navy as part of the Atlantic shield but also the defeat of the Axis on the Eurasian mainland; and the professionals were acutely aware that the current level of American strength in being was grossly inadequate even to implement the Monroe Doctrine in the event of German victory over Britain.

*October 1940-December 1941.* With the emergent British defensive success in the Battle of Britain and the re-election of President Roosevelt, the United States moved into a position of limited active overt support for the Allied cause, the decisive step being Lend-Lease (March 11, 1941), which permitted an invaluable expansion both in basic capacity and in current production of military end-products.

In addition, the United States in effect undertook limited naval war in the Atlantic, landing troops in Iceland on July 8, 1941, permitting a shoot-at-sight policy from September 11, and modifying the Neutrality Act on November 17 to permit American merchantmen to carry supplies to the

Allies. On August 12 the Selective Service Act was extended by a majority of one vote in the House of Representatives. Lend-Lease was extended to the Soviet Union soon after the German invasion of Russia. From the Japanese occupation of Southern Indo-China (July 24) and the prompt freezing of Japanese assets in the United States (July 26), American-Japanese relations moved into a stage of acute crisis.

Starting at the end of January 1941, *de facto* Allied planning for the defeat of the Axis began. The priority of German over Japanese defeat was accepted, being confirmed at the Atlantic Charter Conference of August 11-12, 1941. This uneasy period—of active commitment to the Allied cause fully sanctioned by the Congress in its Lend-Lease vote but without military engagement at American initiative—ended with the attack on Pearl Harbor.

*December 1941-November 1942.* A period of rapid American mobilization, during most of which the Allies suffered severe setbacks throughout the world. The Axis offensives were finally held at points short of breakthrough. With Montgomery's victory at El Alamein (October 23), with Guadalcanal at last firmly held (*circa* November 15), with the Anglo-American landings in Northwest Africa (November 8), and the Russian counteroffensive before Stalingrad in November-December, a turning point was achieved and the base for Allied attack established.

*November 1942-February 1944.* In the Pacific the offensive against Japan was launched in July 1943 and thereafter sustained until Japanese surrender.

In Europe the Allied counteroffensive, against the background of heavy attrition of German forces and Russian forward movement on the eastern front, was gradually developed via air power and the Mediterranean campaigns to the point where the direct assault on the Western European mainland could at last be undertaken. This stage was concluded in the final week of February 1944, when daylight air supremacy over central Germany was established, guaranteeing full air control of the Normandy beachheads in June and permitting the use of the Anglo-American air forces to support the ground offensive with the attack on German oil and transport facilities.

*February 1944-May 1945.* The defeat of Germany accomplished after the Western Allies failed to seek a decision in 1944, thus permitting Soviet forces to hold the territory of Poland, and much land further to the west, at V-E Day.

*May 1945-August 1945.* Victory against Japan completed by the virtually complete destruction of Japanese sea power climaxed by the dropping of atomic bombs on Hiroshima and Nagasaki, while the Soviet Union moved into a commanding position in Manchuria.

The moment of American assumption of the role of senior partner in Europe can clearly be dated from January and February 1944, although American forces engaged in Western Europe were outnumbered by the British until some time after D-Day. With the movement of General Eisenhower's headquarters to Britain in preparation for OVERLORD, and the rapid build-up of American forces for the invasion, the central fact became apparent that the United States, which up to that time had been distinctly the junior partner in the Allied enterprise in Western Europe and (to a lesser degree) in the Mediterranean, was assuming unambiguous primacy in the Allied effort. This position was reinforced by the success of the American air forces in achieving daylight air supremacy over Germany in February 1944.

## A MAHANIST VICTORY

Such was roughly the framework of the Second World War. It left the United States unchallenged leader of a coalition which dominated the seas, Western Europe to the Elbe, and the colonial empires of Western European states; but it left the fate of Central and Eastern Europe and of China not merely unsettled but already dangerously embroiled with Communist power.

At the beginning of 1943, at Casablanca, Admiral King had said:

> In the European theater Russia was most advantageously placed for dealing with Germany in view of her geographic position and manpower; in the Pacific, China bore a similar relation to the Japanese. It should be our basic policy to provide the manpower resources of Russia and China with the necessary equipment to enable them to fight.[2]

The American role, as it emerged, was not as insular and naval as King's 1943 Mahanist prescription for victory. American ground forces were engaged as well as the Navy; and American battles were fought deep within Eurasia as well as on the island approaches. But the timing of the American build-up and the instinct to conserve American lives converged with ambiguities about the conditions for postwar peace to grant the nation only a dilute Mahanist victory.

## THREE DECISIVE AREAS OF WARTIME EXPERIENCE

The military history of the Allies in the Second World War is an enormous and still growing literature, and it is not the purpose here to summarize that literature in its own terms. Here the relevant question is limited and arbitrary: For good or ill, what experiences and developments of the Second World War significantly influenced the evolution of the American security position in the postwar decade and appear still to exercise an enduring imprint on the American security position?

In this perspective, there appear to be three military characteristics of the Second World War which deserve particular attention: first, the linking of military technology to the full resources and potentialities of modern science, notably in the new or rapidly developing areas of atomic energy, electronics, and jet and rocket propulsion; second, the development of the weapons, concepts, and organizations required for strategic bombing; third, the experience of organizing and leading coalition warfare with Eurasian allies. In these respects the Second World War moved on with hardly a break into postwar problems and events.

These were by no means the only major military consequences of the Second World War for the United States. The American Navy underwent a thoroughgoing transformation between Pearl Harbor and V-J Day. The carrier replaced the battleship as the core of a newly built and rebuilt fleet; a major submarine force was built and acquired experience and virtuosity in the Pacific; remarkable innovations were made in combined operations; the technique of island-hopping was created and applied. The United States, after its successful offensive against the Japanese in the Pacific, emerged unquestionably as the first naval power of the world. In 1945 the United States also had under arms 91 Army and 6 Marine divisions. Americans had fought in African deserts, on tropical islands, and in the cold of a European winter. The American Army and Navy experience was not merely a matter of scale and the variety of operational problems faced and surmounted in the field. In every branch of staff work—personnel, logistics, planning, and even intelligence—the two older services matured, emerging with a confidence on the world scene new in the national military experience.

The three chapters that follow examine, then, three facets of the American experience in the Second World War important—but not uniquely important—for the postwar military performance of the nation.

# PART II

# THE MILITARY EXPERIENCE:
# THREE DIMENSIONS OF INNOVATION

## 9. Science, Technology, and War

During the Second World War military practice became linked as never before to the world of science and technology. This special and hitherto remote world was, of its own intellectual momentum, entering an almost explosive stage of growth at the end of the 1930's. The problem of innovation and the society's capacity to generate creative intellectual performance and to organize it for public purposes thus became central to the maintenance of the national interest. Here, in the most concrete way, was a test of whether the national style was capable of yielding a performance which would protect the national interest.

The emergence of the problem of military innovation at the highest levels of American public life suddenly heightened the importance of questions hitherto of secondary concern in the society. What was the relation between basic science, technology, and military strength? What kinds of men were most effective in military innovation? How should they be organized and their thoughts related to national policy as a whole?

Although these questions entered American public life during the Second World War, their importance was heightened rather than diminished by events after 1945. It is worth while, therefore, to look at the experience of innovation during the Second World War not merely as part of the national saga but in the light of these persistent underlying questions.

### THE SOURCES OF INVENTION

The relationship between basic science and technology and the development of new military instruments stems from the character of science and technology itself.

The history of a given branch of technology is reasonably consistent and shapely. From some new (or occasionally long-familiar) proposition in fundamental science there is an initial breakthrough in the form of a method or tool for solving a practical problem, *i.e.*, an invention. As men seek to bring the invention into economical and efficient operation refinements are made; and after it is first applied and diffused into the production process refinements continue. Some of these refinements represent major improvements essential to the further development of the whole branch of technology; but usually the sequence of refinements tends to add less and less to the productivity of the original insight.

Over a period of time, then, one can conceive of the history of a given branch of technology as an arc, not necessarily smooth, but reflecting diminishing returns to man's inventiveness in any particular direction once a basic workable concept is crystallized.

At a given moment in time the bank of technology available to society is made up of many branches: some new, with their practical possibilities hardly yet realized; some young and fruitful, with new possibilities emerging in many directions simultaneously; some mature and slowly developing along fairly predictable paths; some old and virtually stagnant. It is from this whole heterogeneous bank of inherited science and technology that the peculiar requirements of war can be met.

Along the arcs of technological evolution one can distinguish at least four levels from which military applications have been developed in recent times. The first level represents the application to military technology of relatively new fundamental science. The rapid evolution of atomic energy engineering from the demonstration of fission by Hahn and Strassman, expounded by Niels Bohr in Washington on January 26, 1939, to the explosion of the first atomic bomb on July 16, 1945 is the most dramatic of these progressions from fundamental science to military operations.[1]

Second, there are areas of technology where the foundations in fundamental science are well laid but where the practical possibilities are at a stage of rapid productive elaboration. The field of modern electronics is the most familiar of this second category.

Third, there are applications for military purposes to be drawn from mature but still developing technological fields; for example, the steady improvement in power and efficiency of liquid and air-cooled airplane engines during the Second World War was based on slow but important progress in the technology of internal combustion.

Fourth, there are imaginative applications of long-familiar technical devices to particular situations. The low level altimeter used in the RAF raid on the German dams in May 1943 (the convergent beams of two searchlights) illustrates this kind of homely ingenuity which has always had a high place in military affairs.

In short, new military technology has been drawn from the full spectrum ranging from new breakthroughs in fundamental science down to old scientific and engineering capital.

### THE CONTRASTING EXPERIENCE OF THE FIRST AND SECOND WORLD WARS

The wars of the past two centuries, excepting the Second World War, have tended to involve the application of relatively mature science and technology rather than younger unfolding branches of technology or derivations from new fundamental science itself. Excepting aircraft, for example, the technology of the First World War was based mainly on a rather unimaginative application of relatively mature fields—the internal combustion engine, telephonic and telegraphic communication, etc. Even poison gas represented the application of long-familiar working technology rather than the opening of new fields of chemistry; and Ernest Swinton's brilliant perception of the tank was the bringing together of altogether familiar, even pedestrian, technological elements to solve a practical problem in the field rather than a significant scientific or engineering achievement. Despite the aircraft, the tank, and other new developments, ". . . the First World War was fought with the weapons that existed at its outset."[2] The most operationally effective innovation of the First World War was probably the large-scale use of artillery, based on mass production methods of a relatively low technical order.[3]

The experience of the Second World War was distinctive in three respects. First, military technology became linked to one area of science virtually at the level of fundamental science—atomic physics. Second, military technology became linked to several areas of rapidly developing technology based on known but incompletely elaborated scientific principles, notably electronics, rockets, and jet turbines. In all of these areas major new engineering (rather than fundamental scientific) breakthroughs were in the process of developing in the interwar years; and military technology both became enmeshed with them during the Second World War and accelerated their unfolding practical possibilities under forced draft wartime development.

The third characteristic of the Second World War as a scientific and engineering experience was simply that the scale on which first-rate minds were mobilized exceeded anything in past experience; and this yielded a flow of technological developments derived from all levels of science and technology and applied over the full range of military activity on a unique scale. Like modern industry, modern warmaking came to build into its institutional structure the process of purposeful invention and innovation; and thus, in

quite new ways and on a quite new scale, a partnership was launched between
the professional military men and the men of science and engineering.

### THE QUALITIES OF SCIENTIST AND ENGINEER

The assets scientists can bring to the process of innovation are, generally,
first-rate minds, the existing capital of fundamental science and technology,
and, above all, a cast of mind professionally dedicated to discovering new
truth. Academics are by trade, or should be, inventors and innovators. "Science
is novelty, and change."[4]

In the spectrum between pure theorists and practical operating engineers,
what kind of men, with what sort of training, were most productive? The
record gives no unambiguous answer except to suggest that under the conditions and motivations of war the qualities of the first-rate theorist often
proved transferable to practical invention; and that many essential practical
developments were made, and perhaps only could have been made, by men
whose professional life and training had been in the areas of fundamental
scientific thought rather than in applied engineering.

If there is any interim conclusion to be drawn in this area it is that the
character of normal professional interest and experience, as between theory
and practice, is vastly less important to the contribution a scientist is likely
to make than his intellectual quality. As the historian of the American
scientific effort in the Second World War has said:

> The first requisite of a satisfactory organization of science for war is that it
> must attract first-rate scientists. One outstanding man will succeed where
> ten mediocrities will simply fumble.[5]

### THE ORGANIZATION OF AMERICAN SCIENCE IN THE SECOND WORLD WAR

The scientific and engineering challenge of the Second World War involved
several major administrative and organizational problems. It was necessary
that American scientists and engineers capable of creative invention be mobilized on a sufficient scale to cope with the range of major problems where
they might be of significant use. It was necessary that the administration of
the effort be in the hands of men able to command the respect of first-rate
scientists and able to establish a setting which would foster creative effort.
Although the effort of the scientists had to be geared closely to the full
bureaucratic machinery of the war effort, their work had to be conducted
in an atmosphere of sufficient intellectual freedom that their creative talents
not be frustrated. "Really striking movements away from the crowd will not
occur once in a thousand years in a tight bureaucracy."[6] But the men directing the scientific effort had to be close to the war effort as well as their
scientists, for without intimate practical knowledge proper priorities could

not be set within the total scientific effort. Finally, administrative arrangements had to be created to guarantee that the results of scientific invention be transferred from laboratories to effective field operations with minimum delay.

A number of different factors converged to fulfill these conditions reasonably well in the mobilization of American scientists during the Second World War.

In the first instance, the German offensives of 1940 appeared to represent—notably in armored tactics and the use of air power in ground support—startling military innovations which would have to be met and defeated should the United States become involved against Germany. Hitler's blitzkrieg in 1940 had a look of inventiveness about it—although its instruments were to be quickly outmoded. It served to accelerate the pace of military innovation within both the British and American military establishments.

Beyond the actual German field performance of 1940 it was regarded as possible, if not likely, that the Germans had a head start in the development of atomic weapons, given the history of the first successful experiment with fission. Albert Einstein's famous letter to President Roosevelt was sent on August 2, 1939; and it warned of the possibility that Nazi Germany might be the first to produce atomic weapons. The first meeting of an advisory Committee on Uranium was held as early as October 1939. Even aside from the ominous stirrings of atomic energy, German science was highly regarded; and it was assumed—wrongly as it turned out—that Hitler would effectively mobilize this German asset.[7]

A second factor was the initiative assumed by a group of men who not only represented the accepted leadership of American science and technology but who had also believed, virtually from the outset of the Second World War, that the United States would and should play an active part in it. When Hitler swept across France, Bush, Conant, Compton, Tolman, and Jewett were not merely prepared to take the initiative in mobilizing American science; they had for some time informally considered the appropriate form for such effort and had in hand a concrete plan of organization ready for presentation to the White House. Their quality and prestige permitted them to select and to recruit first-rate men from the whole terrain of American science and engineering.

A third factor was that Roosevelt and key figures in his administration—notably Stimson and Harvey Bundy—were by temperament and experience sympathetic to scientists and the possibilities of innovation in military technology; and there were men scattered through the wartime military establishment (professionals and others) prepared to grasp and to apply what the scientists might offer. More than that, Roosevelt permitted the National

Defense Research Committee to be set up as an independent unit linked to the President directly. In the bureaucratic jungle of Washington the right of Presidential access, when wielded by strong personalities, gave the scientists great leverage in dealing with the military services and with other powerful institutions.[8]

This structure left a remarkable range of administrative freedom to the scientists themselves and permitted the administration of scientists to be conducted to the maximum possible by their own kind rather than by military men or other professional administrators.

### THE SCALE OF THE EFFORT

The scale of wartime research and development is difficult to calculate due to the number of administrative units involved and the impossibility under wartime circumstances of drawing a firm line between research and development on the one hand and production on the other. The order of magnitude of the effort is suggested by the fact that something like $500 million was spent in the period 1940-1945, beyond the $2 billion allocated to the development and production of atomic weapons.[9] The diversity of the effort is suggested by the fact that OSRD operated with nineteen divisions and two special panels.[10]

Most work proceeded under dispersed contracts which left men to work as civilians, under familiar conditions, often in their home university or industrial plant. The two great exceptions to the dispersed contract system were the radar laboratory organized at M.I.T., and the various laboratories and plants of the Manhattan District.[11] The concentration of talents at M.I.T. and Los Alamos—each laboratory ended the war with staffs of about four thousand—permitted a wider range of interchange, within the limits of security, generating a rare degree of concentration of creative effort, and, in human terms, high morale.

### ELEMENTS OF PRODUCTIVE DISORGANIZATION

The success of the American scientific effort appears to have hinged in part on a purposeful violation of normal administrative procedures.

As one reads accounts of the scientists in World War II it is evident that many among them operated not merely as inventors but also as innovators, salesmen, demonstrators, and mass production engineers. In the end, the lines between pure research and quantity production in field operations had to be drawn. But in making the transition from laboratory to effective performance in the field many scientists themselves took active responsibility in the transitional effort. Moreover, the success in cutting the time between invention and application appears to have hinged on the scientists overseeing personally the many stages which constitute the essential transition.[12]

The second violation of conventional bureaucratic procedure stems from the quasi-independent status of the NDRC and its ability to vend some of its products in what was almost an open market. If a new idea or device did not attract immediate attention and support from, say, the Army, the scientists were in a position to approach the Navy or the Air Force, or even the British. It was, for example, with British rather than American backing that the powerful explosive RDX was brought to a stage of tolerable stability, after which the hitherto skeptical and unhelpful American services put it eagerly to use.

Finally, the American wartime effort was substantially strengthened in more direct ways by intimate collaboration with the scientists of Britain and the Empire. The tie to Britain was established by NDRC in the summer of 1940. The British scientific effort had been launched earlier than the American; and in the decisive field of radar the British had put on a major accelerated effort at the highest level of scientific quality from the end of 1934, having accurately calculated that a fully elaborated radar system was essential for the air defense of Great Britain. Out of this effort came the resonant cavity magnatron.[13]

THE WARTIME SCIENTIFIC EFFORT IN PERSPECTIVE

The American wartime effort in the development of new military technology was not an unequivocal success. Certain areas proved relatively barren, overwhelmed in memory by the striking achievements in atomic weapons, radar, and the proximity fuse. There was wasted and misplaced effort. There was a chronic clash of bureaucratic and scientific minds. As with many wartime institutions, by 1945 the NDRC began to assume many of the heavy rigidities of an old-line government agency. Nevertheless, the major challenges were met to a degree which could not have been anticipated on the basis of past American experience and past American performance. The elements for a creative response were, of course, present in American society, but that they would be brought together in quite so successful a way was by no means inevitable. There was a President respectful of ideas and men of ideas and given to administrative methods which encouraged innovation. There were men in the military establishment prepared to press through even disruptive technological change. There was a group of scientist-administrators of high intellectual quality respected by the men of first-class creative talent, respected by industry, quite capable of dealing with the military and civil bureaucracy on even terms or better; and this group was given its head. There was an emerging younger generation of first-class American basic scientists plus the stiffening presence of older European scientists, arrived as refugees, motivated profoundly to fight the war.[14] There was the interwar heritage of research and development in electrical, chemical, and aircraft industries. And above all, there was a moment of national crisis in which, for the time, virtually all interests tended to converge. From all these flowed a performance which both exploited the potentially creative elements in the national style and strengthened them.

The postwar military research and development effort was squarely built on the men, experiences, and, to a high degree, on the intellectual breakthroughs of the war years. But the problem of a continuing technological race in arms had a dimension which did not greatly concern the architects of the wartime effort. In a sustained effort the nation's job was not only to create new weapons but also to maintain and develop the sources from which they flowed. Fundamental science and scientists—and a social setting and educational system capable of creating them—thus took on in the postwar years a new significance for the nation's security.

## 10. The Development of Strategic Air Power

The Second World War shifted air power from a peripheral to a central role in military practice and strategy.

From the 1600 Air Corps officers of 1938 there was built up by March 1944 a force of 2,411,000 persons (plus 422,000 civilians), representing 31 per cent of United States Army forces.[1] Within the Navy the personnel in aviation (including Marines) rose in the same period from a handful to over 500,000—more than 15 per cent of peak mobilized naval strength.[2]

Key to this transition was the development between 1941 and 1945 of a mature strategic bombing force within the Air Corps. The transformation of a handful of four-engined bomber aircraft, a precision bombsight, a commitment to operate in daylight, and ardent hopes for the future of air power as the principal basis of the nation's security is a story of the national style at work on an urgent and inescapable task of innovation.

### THE EMERGENCE OF AIR PLANS AND DOCTRINE: 1941

Substantially, the transformation began on July 9, 1941, when President Roosevelt requested the Secretaries of War and Navy to prepare for him an estimate of the American armament production level required to defeat Germany and Italy. In executing this request the Army Air Corps developed a document known as AWPD/1 (that is, the first product of the Air War Plans Division). This proved to be, in both scale and doctrine, the rude foundations for the building of the modern American air force.

So far as American war planning was concerned, the President's request climaxed a series of discussions which had been pursued over the previous six months with the British designed to yield an Allied strategy for the defeat of the Axis. In the course of these discussions the role of air power had arisen in a quite particular form.

In early 1941 the British, then fighting virtually alone against Germany and Italy, were exceedingly skeptical that a direct assault on the European mainland could be mounted across the Channel. Matching their own resources, even backed by Lend-Lease, against those of an Axis-dominated Continent, the British leaned instinctively toward the indirect pattern by which they had brought down Napoleon rather than to another grueling sustained continental struggle such as had decimated a British generation in bringing down Kaiser Wilhelm. During the planning phase of early 1941 the British thus viewed the war against Germany as a series of peripheral operations to be combined with very heavy bombardment of German cities designed ultimately to break German morale. In British thought the RAF Bomber Command assumed many of the historic attritional functions of naval power and economic blockade against an entrenched continental enemy. In this setting the British made in 1941 most serious commitments to build a massive fleet of night bombers capable of conducting heavy raids against German urban concentrations.[3]

American Army leaders were skeptical from the beginning that war in Europe could be won in this fashion; and they insisted from the time joint planning began that at some stage a direct assault on the Continent across the Channel would have to be contemplated. American ground force planning, in response to the President's July 9 request, proceeded on this assumption, leaving the issues between the Allies (and, to some lesser extent, between American air and ground commanders) to be decided at a later time.

Against the background of these joint planning discussions, the Army Air Corps seized with both hands the possibilities opened to it by the President's request. By a series of piratical initiatives (which violated its formal status as a technical branch of the Army) the Air Corps emerged from this exercise not only having captured a major share of the nation's war production but also having created an independent basis for intelligence and planning of bombing operations.[4]

AWPD/1 took its shape from an attempt to answer one question: the destruction by air power of which industries would render Germany incapable of continuing to fight a war? Implicit in this question was the view that, if the enemy's will to resist could be broken, it would be broken by denying him the technical means for conducting operations in the field rather than by damage to civilian installations and to civilian morale.[5] In American planning in 1941 area bombing designed to affect civilian morale was envisaged as useful, if at all, only in the final stage of a war when the war industry structure of the enemy had been cleanly cut through by sustained precision bombing.

A second initial American Air Force conception was implicit in this formulation of the problem; namely, that the task of the precision bombing force was to attack systematically a limited number of whole enemy industries rather than to attack large or important targets in many industries. The old military principle of concentration of effort was thus built into American Air Force planning from the beginning. The target systems hastily selected in AWDP/1 are shown in Table 1:[6]

TABLE 1. AWDP/1 TARGET SYSTEMS

|  | Number of Targets | Target System |
|---|---|---|
| Intermediate objectives: | 30 | Aircraft and light-metal industries |
| Primary objectives: | 50 | Electric power plants |
|  | 47 | Transportation centers |
|  | 27 | Petroleum and synthetic oil industries |
|  | 154 |  |

AWDP/1 was for its time a sound planning document, incorporating hitherto uncrystallized but long-developing Air Corps prejudices and faith plus the instinctive good sense of men with civil as well as military experience who had been brought by happy accident into the arena of higher planning.[7]

The formulation and the later acceptance of AWDP/1 by Stimson and Marshall with one stroke virtually converted the Army Air Corps into an arm of the American military coequal with the ground forces and the Navy. The scale of the air forces envisaged and approved, combined with the experience of producing AWDP/1 and the subsequent development of Air Corps intelligence and staff units, gave the Air Corps the essentials for independent growth.

THE OPERATIONAL CRISIS OF 1943 AND ITS RESOLUTION

AWDP/1 had settled broadly the scale and composition of American air forces; it established a strategy; and it suggested a tentative group of target objectives for the air forces in Europe. But it was a long while between August 1941, when the plan was completed, and the spring of 1944, when the American air forces approached their planned peak strength. Over this interval they had to make their way step by step, caught up in an active unfolding war, a war of ground and naval as well as air operations, and a war of alliance, in which the British were initially not merely senior partner but also vastly more experienced and committed to a distinctively different bombing doctrine. The imprint of AWDP/1 was never quite lost; but it faded in the face of the concrete issues of strategy and tactics which emerged in Europe.

The first American heavy bombing operation in Europe was an attack by twelve aricraft, August 17, 1942, on the marshalling yards at Rouen, a target chosen as a nursery exercise, within short-range fighter protection. From that time operations expanded, but they were confined to nearby targets in occupied Western Europe and were in many respects training missions to give the Eighth Air Force knowledge of the problem of bombing accurately in European weather against targets defended by anti-aircraft guns and fighter planes. The forces assembled in Britain and available for strategic bombing grew slowly, for heavy bombers were diverted to support ground operations in Africa and the Mediterranean after the November landings in North Africa. The strategic mission and target systems for American air operations were broadly confirmed in the directive of the Casablanca Conference of January 21, 1943, which formally included as top priority the attack on submarine installations. This virtually overriding priority had already been accepted in October 1942, when the Battle of the Atlantic was going badly, despite grave skepticism that bombing could achieve any significant result against submarine installations. The Air Corps accepted this priority because it could not argue that it was yet capable of doing anything more useful, given its inability to penetrate deeply into Germany.

The high-level decision at Casablanca, however, in no way solved the real problems the Eighth Air Force confronted in Europe in 1943. These problems were:

1. Although the Air Force in Europe built up rapidly in the course of 1943, it was for the first six months of the year too small to undertake sustained operations of the kind envisaged in AWDP/1 or the Casablanca directive except virtually ineffective attacks against submarine yards and pens and a scattering of operations against accessible targets in the west without major significance to the German war effort.

2. The German single-engine fighter force, under extremely rapid expansion, demonstrated that it could inflict casualties against unescorted bombers too heavy to be sustained as a regular feature of American Air Force operations.

3. European weather afforded relatively too few days in which weather over bases and over targets was predictably clear enough to sustain a program of daylight precision bombing on a major scale.

As these limitations in the American position revealed themselves, RAF capabilities to attack built-up urban areas at night developed rapidly. The American difficulties down to mid-1943 appeared to confirm British suspicion that the American air effort was misguided.

In the light of their successes at Hamburg in July 1943 and the subsequently heavy attacks on Berlin, the British steadily urged the American forces to join them in the night bombing effort in the hope that such blows might end the war in a kind of Wagnerian cataclysm centered on German civilian morale. The British successes came at precisely the point when American daylight penetrations of Germany were being conducted in the face of extremely severe losses. The British pressure continued down to the American successes of January 11, and especially of late February 1944. Churchill, however, steadily held back, sensitive to the deep attachment and commitment of the Americans to their own air power doctrines and the possible long-run costs to the Anglo-American alliance of forcing a decision.[8]

British pressure was resisted at high and low levels while the American air forces struggled to create the conditions which would make their effort effective. The development of the long-range fighter was accelerated; the bomber's defensive capabilities were strengthened by chin-turrets, tighter formations, and other devices; area bombing in daylight with radar was introduced to permit bad weather days over target areas to be used; and methods for dealing with poor weather conditions on take-off were introduced. But only time could bring the build-up of the long-range fighters which were needed if Germany were to be effectively attacked by daylight; and the superiority of American long-range fighters over German short-range fighters could by no means be guaranteed in advance.

The American Air Force thus faced in mid-1943 a most painful choice: the choice of postponing by perhaps six months (until long-range fighters were available) the precision attack on objectives in Germany, while the German fighter defense forces doubled; or of attacking German targets without fighter support, with exceedingly high losses.

The American Air Force decided that, despite its evident limitations and the promise of more bombers and long-range fighters toward early 1944, it would proceed immediately with precision bombing attacks deep in Germany.[9] More than any other man, Major General Frederick L. Anderson, then chief of Eighth Air Force Bomber Command, was responsible for that decision—although many both in the United States and in Europe shared in shaping and executing it.

The modern American Air Force as a fighting establishment—rather than a small body of dedicated pilots, production plans, and untested convictions —emerged directly from the crisis imposed by the need to make this choice, a crisis which can be dated from July to December 1943. A generation of leaders, a firm operational doctrine, a set of mature staff concepts, and a fighting style crystallized over these decisive months. The character of the modern American Air Force cannot be understood outside the context of that experience.

Between July and December 1943 some sixteen attacks were delivered against the German aircraft and anti-friction bearing industries.[10] These were mainly mounted from Britain; but a few were carried out by the Fifteenth Air Force, which was mainly engaged in support of ground force operations in the Mediterranean theater. Forty-six thousand tons of bombs were dropped on aircraft factories in these crucial six months: a mere 20 per cent of the total American effort during this period, and only one-third of one per cent of the total bombing effort of the American air forces in the Second World War in Europe.[11] These few attacks were, however, of immense importance. German single-engine fighter production, which had risen from less than 400 in January 1943 to 1050 in July, was down to less than 600 by December, a decline caused by direct bomb damage combined with the effects of dispersal induced by the fear of further damage. In the absence of bombing attacks the figure by December might well have been of the order of 2000 per month. Table 2 lists the monthly figures for 1943.

TABLE. 2. GERMAN SINGLE-ENGINE FIGHTER AIRCRAFT ACCEPTANCES, 1943

| January | 381 | July | 1050 |
|---|---|---|---|
| February | 725 | August | 914 |
| March | 819 | September | 853 |
| April | 790 | October | 955 |
| May | 847 | November | 775 |
| June | 957 | December | 560 |

Beyond the loss of about three months' output of German fighter aircraft, the unexpected success of these few gallant, costly missions led the Germans to disperse their production at a crucial stage of the war. This dispersal was conducted with energy and success; but its timing was disastrous to German interests. At just the period when German fighter production was beginning to recover from the 1943 attacks the American Air Force made its bid for daylight air supremacy over Germany, backed at last by an effective long-range fighter, the P-51, available in quantity.[12] Exploiting a remarkable sequence of clear days in the European winter, the American air forces attacked the aircraft and bearing industries of Germany in great force on February 20-25, 1944, following a plan which had been developed and held in readiness for many months. On the night of February 19 the attack was ordered on the assumption that it might cost one hundred or more American bombers and their crews. General Spaatz made this extremely difficult command decision knowing that either the Americans had to act on their air force concepts, and take their losses, or admit they had been wrong. And he was fully aware of the repercussions on the Air Force of the loss of 60 bombers in a single raid in October 1943. The losses on February 20 were only 22. And, following fundamental military principle, the breakthrough was driven home day after day, despite the strain on the crews (and the understandable resistance of their commanders), until normal winter weather again closed in on February 26.

German sources indicate that 75 per cent of the buildings in the aircraft plants were damaged or destroyed and German bearing production driven down to about 50 per cent of peak output. But this was a military victory for the American Air Force, not a victory over German production capabilities. The German loss of aircraft production was of some possible military significance; the loss of bearing production—already outmoded as target system by 1944, given the imminence of D-Day—was virtually none. The attack of February 1944 was important because the German fighter force was tactically defeated in the air in close and bitter battle; and it never again recovered major capabilities for sustained defensive operations in daylight. This tactical defeat took the form of the progressive loss of experienced pilots at a greater rate than in the American fighter force; and, partly due to later attacks on oil and its effects on pilot training, this loss could never again be made good by the Germans.[13]

Thus the strategic attacks on fighter production in 1943 may well have succeeded in containing the German fighter force at a size which permitted the close tactical victory of February 1944. Precision bombing was the instrument and the occasion by which the equivalent of the Battle of Britain was won by the Air Corps over Germany; but the formal victory was tactical and took the form of a subsequent supremacy of American fighter aircraft, which permitted freedom to the daylight bombers at acceptable cost. American bomber forces continued to suffer losses, sometimes heavy losses; but never again was their ability to sustain significant operations throughout Europe in question. The indispensable foundation for OVERLORD—Allied air supremacy over the Continent, assumed from the beginning—was at last established.[14]

### THE EXPLOITATION OF THE BREAKTHROUGH: 1944-1945

Before the Big Week in February had ended, the American air staff in Europe was already formulating its plan for the exploitation of the strategic breakthrough achieved over Germany; and the proposed program was presented to General Eisenhower for approval as early as March 5. Its choice was to attack German oil production as the maximum support which strategic air power could give to the impending OVERLORD operation, and also to exploit the last glimmering chance that air power in itself might bring a decision in the war against Germany.

The decision to attack oil was opposed by Air Marshals Tedder and Leigh-Mallory, who at this stage were, respectively, Deputy to General Eisenhower as Comander of SHAEF and Chief of the Allied Expeditionary Air Force (AEAF). They put forward an alternative plan for the use of air power before D-Day. This aimed to create a "transport desert" in Western Europe behind the proposed area of landing through the attack on Western European freight marshalling yards.[15]

The American bomber staffs, supported by important elements in the RAF, opposed this doctrine. They proposed a mixture of attack on oil combined with highly selective attack on transport targets in Western Europe (notably bridges), and with the bombing of ammunition, fuel, and ordnance dumps and other concentrations of German ground force strength. The choice as seen in the air staffs was, then, between an attack on selected transport and other tactical targets designed to interdict the battlefield and weaken German field strength plus an attack on oil versus virtually total concentration on marshalling yards.

This choice never came clearly to Eisenhower in the form in which it was argued at the level of his staffs. He made his decision on March 26, 1944, in terms of the issue as argued in his presence by Tedder and Spaatz. Although Spaatz expressed skepticism of Tedder's transport conception he decided that is would be inappropriate for him, the commander of a heavy bomber force, to put forward a tactical program. In this he was certainly moved by a desire to ease to the maximum Eisenhower's command problem by not actively intervening in an area where he had no formal responsibility. More than that, he may have wished to avoid the American air forces taking initiative—in the area of tactical support—where it did not have responsibility and thus risking the charge that it did not fully meet all of the responsible commanders' requests for D-Day support. Tedder was pleased to argue his case in terms of transport versus oil rather than to argue the merits of bridges versus marshalling yards, where he may have sensed his ground was weak. Eisenhower was thus forced to make his decision in terms of false alternatives, a fate often reserved for those who rely too heavily on the workings of formal chains of command to define the choices available for executive decision.

Eisenhower chose to support Tedder's marshalling yard plan on the ground that it promised some results in the immediate context of achieving a lodgment on the French coast—which was Eisenhower's grave responsibility—whereas the attack on oil could guarantee no such immediate tactical effects, on the estimates then available of German oil stocks. In concession to General Spaatz's view, however, and to the fear that the German fighter force would recover if not engeged in the air—which only attack on first-rate German targets would guarantee—two good weather days before D-Day were allotted to oil targets.

Those who advocated a selective attack on bridges as a means of interdicting the battlefield did not, however, give up, despite Eisenhower's decision of March 26. Their formal grounds were that Tedder claimed that six hundred sorties were required to take out a bridge whereas the experience in Italy seemed to indicate sixty would suffice. The case was pressed for an experimental attack. It was finally made on May 7 under the most inauspicious conditions. A handful of fighter-bombers were allotted by Leigh-Mallory to the experiment rather than the full heavy bomber force (divided in groups of sixty) which had been proposed. Nevertheless, the attack was immensely successful. On May 8 the Allied leaders in London studied with fascination a striking photograph of the bridge at Vernon lying at the bottom of the Seine, having been deposited there by the attack of less than ten P-47s. This success led to acceptance of a systematic attack on the Seine-Loire bridges which had been advocated in the American air staff from early in 1944.

The attack on oil was similarly brought about through the back door. On April 5, breaking loose from a formal injunction on which Tedder had insisted to attack marshalling yards, even in the Mediteranean area, the Fifteenth Air Force in effect brought oil back on the target list by attacking all the marshalling yards at Ploesti including the railway sidings alongside the refineries.[16] For the first time—there had been two previous American attacks —really serious damage was done to the Ploesti oil targets. And against this background, when the first of the two attacks promised to Spaatz by Eisenhower was carried out in Central Germany (May 12), the German response was so evidently one of distress that oil at last became an accepted target system, some three weeks before D-Day.

Despite these diversions, the American air forces achieved three solid results in the course of 1944. First, they won and held daylight air supremacy over Germany. Second, they did sufficient damage to the German transport system— by a mixture of efficient and wasteful means—to contribute significantly to the success of OVERLORD and the subsequent exploitation on the ground of that lodgement. Third, in the attacks on oil they virtually grounded the German air forces and enforced a high degree of immobility on the German ground forces, which helped make possible the rapid movements of General Patton's Third Army as well at the other ground force actions which led to victory in the East as well as the West.

The victory over the German air force in daylight was a peculiarly American victory, shared by the bombers and long-range fighters. The attacks on transport were shared by the RAF, whose heavy bombers carried, in fact, a high proportion of the tonnage involved, and by the British and American light bombers and fighter-bombers, the latter immensely effective in close support attacks once the ground forces were engaged after D-Day. The attack on oil was shared by the RAF Bomber Command, whose great weight in attack was, in several cases, immensely effective.[17]

THE EUROPEAN ANTICLIMAX

The American bomber forces in Europe reached by the middle of 1944 a strength and capability of which American airmen had long dreamed. But the scope and timing of the European war was such that these capabilities could not be fully employed.

It is possible to speculate, of course, that the war might have been won in Europe in the course of 1944 if three conditions had been met:

1. Oil had been attacked from March forward on absolute priority by the American and British heavy bomber forces.

2. Allied diplomacy had offered to dissident, anti-Hitler Germans some formula other than unconditional surrender.[18]

3. General Eisenhower had either enforced on Montgomery his wish that the port of Antwerp be promptly cleared after its capture on September 4, 1944, or had thrown his limited paratroop units, oil supplies, and transport facilities behind either Montgomery or Patton at that time.[19] The combination of these conditions (or, perhaps, either the first or third with the second) appears, with the benefit of hindsight, at least to raise a question with which historians can wrestle when so minded and to raise issues of principle worth re-examination as of possible future relevance to soldiers and politicians. It is certainly arguable that the delay in attacking oil on an overriding priority basis and the failure to give dissident Germans a reasonable political basis for action were costly to Western interests. It is also arguable that the war would have been ended earlier if Eisenhower had faced down Montgomery promptly on the issue of Antwerp or if supplies had not been split between the northern and southern wings of the Allied attack. But, aside from the possibility of a 1944 decision to which the attack on oil might have contributed, the Second World War in Europe did not offer the air forces the means for employing their maximum capabilities.

There is little doubt, of course, that if both eastern and western ground forces were halted on the rim of Germany, Germany could have been hammered to defeat by the Allied air forces with their capabilities of 1944-1945 and assuming an offer to the Germans short of unconditional surrender. Given the limited degree of understanding and communication between the Soviet Union and the West, this solution was never seriously considered. The political context of the war, including the commitment to unconditional surrender, demanded the most rapid possible occupation of German territory by ground forces. And, above all, the existence of the war against Japan argued for the most rapid denouement possible to the European War.

Under these circumstances the heavy bomber forces simply ran out of worthwhile targets. Oil was beaten down and held to some 25 per cent of peak production. The German transport system was chopped to ribbons.

German war production in all categories disintegrated progressively from the late summer of 1944. Many useful attacks designed to keep oil production low and the German rail system disrupted were indeed made by the air forces. But so long as there were men in the field obeying orders from Hitler and his chain of command, there were enough guns and ammunition in being and in tactical dumps inaccessible to strategic bombers for costly ground warfare to continue. The bombers struggled to be useful, and their commanders felt deeply the irony of a situation where, at peak strength, they were unemployable except on second-rate, indecisive targets and make-work jobs. It was in this setting of frustration that shattering but unnecessary attacks were made on Dresden and Chemnitz in the final days of the war in Europe.

One major consequence of this situation was that those charged with the higher direction of the war did not fully appreciate the potential capabilities of the European air forces (as of the end of 1944 and early 1945) as an instrument against Japan or as a bargaining counter in negotiations with the Soviet union, notably at Yalta. The American bombing forces made their great contribution to the war in Europe before they had achieved their full strength; and the tonnage of bombs dropped that most mattered was only a small proportion of the totals dropped.[20]

THE JAPANESE CLIMAX

If, in a sense, air strength was redundant in Europe toward the close of that phase of the war, so ground and naval strength were redundant in the climactic phase of the war against Japan.

As early as February 1944 sober military thought in Tokyo recognized the inevitability of Japanese defeat. The existence of significant political pressure for a negotiated ending to the war against the United States was evident in July, shortly after the American success at Saipan, when the regime of General Tojo fell. In October the desperate Japanese effort in Leyte Gulf failed. The air attacks on Japan, which began seriously from the Marianas toward the end of November 1944, struck against an economy which, even at its peak strength, could not have borne the weight which the United States was mounting against it.

Bombing attacks on the home islands of Japan, from November 1944 until March 9, 1945, were conducted at high level and in daylight mainly against precision targets in the aircraft industry. On March 9, under the direction of General LeMay, who had been transferred from Europe, the direction of attack was shifted; and the four principal Japanese cities were attacked at night by the B-29s from medium altitudes (7,000 as opposed to 30,000 feet). In a period of ten days Tokyo, Nahoya, Osaka, and Kobe were heavily hit by incendiary raids; and attacks continued not merely against urban areas but also against military and transport targets, including the disruption of Japanese coastal shipping by mine-laying.

By July 1945 Japanese industrial production was perhaps one-third of its peak output in 1944, due not merely to the effect of bombing but also to the decimation of Japanese transport by the Navy, notably by the submarines. There was grave doubt in Tokyo that such production as remained could be moved successfully in support of the ground forces in case of invasion. This enormous and general effect was achieved with vastly less bomb tonnage dropped than in the case of Germany. A total of about 161,000 tons of bombs was dropped on the home islands of Japan as opposed to 1,420,000 tons on Germany. Japan was not only a less substantial and resilient war economy than that of Germany but it was also less strongly defended by antiaircraft and fighters; it was more concentrated; and it was more vulnerable to incendiary attack.

Although the form of attack decided upon by LeMay was highly effective in both its material effects and its consequences for mass morale, the problem of bringing Japan to its knees through air power was primarily a political problem. That is, it required not merely that the United States present to the Japanese leaders a vision of inevitable defeat but also that the United States, without violating basic long-term American interests, conduct its diplomacy so as to ease the domestic political task of those who had long wished to disengage Japan from the war. The success of the atomic attacks on Hiroshima and Nagasaki finally sufficed to break the political power of those in Japan who wished to hold out until Japan was conquered on the home islands.

In ending the war against Japan the United States was inhibited by two weaknesses. First, the power represented by the American Air Forces at the close of 1944 and in early 1945 was seriously underestimated by the senior officers and staffs of the Army and Navy. Second, the United States lacked a concept of its long-range national interests around which it might have modified its approach to the Japanese political situation in such a way as to induce a surrender which would also be compatible with the American interest. The issue of a more political approach to the Japanese surrender had been raised and argued in Washington, initially by Stimson and Grew, from February 1945 forward.[21] In the end a warning was given to the Japanese at Potsdam and some concession was made on the issue of the Japanese Emperor.

There were understandable reasons for the awkwardness of the United States in dealing with the politics of surrender—both in Germany and in Japan. Behind these difficulties lay not merely the formal commitment to unconditional surrender, and the political situations and vested interests built around it over the war years, but also a deeper problem. The United States lacked any clear touchstones of national interest to apply to the long-run future of Germany and Japan except that they became democracies; and this ambiguity converged with the parochial interest of the military in maintaining a situation where the defeat of the enemy in the field was the overriding criterion for all decisions. For the military, unconditional surrender cleared civil policy and interests out of the way of the strictly military task until "victory" was won. It also permitted the military to apply almost technocratic formulae to the conduct of war on the assumption that the postwar world began neatly from the moment of final and complete surrender. The relation between the politics of surrender and the conduct of war was never maturely developed in the American government during the Second World War despite the fruitful precedent of Wilson's Fourteen Points, a precedent which was by and large misread by those charged with the conduct of World War II; and this relation lay at the heart of the problem of using air power as a decisive independent instrument of war.

## AMERICAN STRATEGIC BOMBING IN PERSPECTIVE

The story of strategic air power in the Second World War is to be viewed in one dimension as a remarkable example of the national style at work. The nation made a massive commitment to the physical instruments required for daylight precision attack without carefully thinking through how, and, indeed, whether, such operations could prove possible. It trained its air crews for such operations; and a substantial proportion of the total American war production effort was committed to strategic bombing at a time when intelligence and planning preparations were almost nonexistent.

Then came actual contact with the problem. Once operationally engaged, the naïveté of prewar conceptions was vividly revealed; but the energy, confidence, and ingenuity of the nation came into play and, step by step, a tolerable solution was fashioned. By the end of the war a strategic bombing force had been created, its working procedures, doctrines, and staff work institutionalized. This act of pragmatic innovation depended, however, on a tolerable amount of time. Time was needed to revise ideas, methods, and instruments in the light of unfolding combat reality and to bring the weight of American industrial power to bear. But success depended equally on the willingness of many individual men—professionals like Anderson and LeMay, amateurs like Hughes and Hitchcock—to take lonely risky decisions in the face of organized bureaucracy, and to live by the Chinese proverb on General Anderson's desk throughout the war: "There are some orders of the Emperor which must be disobeyed." Out of this communal act of innovation, undertaken in a time of crisis, came a new institution—the Strategic Air Command.

Furthermore, the Second World War had yielded not only a new means for delivering weapons but also a new weapon—the atomic bomb. And the event raised as many questions as it answered:

1. The bomb evidently sufficed to administer the *coup de grâce* to a Japan whose allies had unconditionally surrendered, whose navy and merchant

marine were decimated, whose major cities were in ashes, whose industries were functioning at about one-third capacity, and most of whose politicians had been seeking a formula for ending the war for almost a year. But under what military and political conditions would atomic attack from the air prove decisive against a less battered and more resilient foe?

2. Although ethical doubts were raised in many minds before and after the atomic attack on Japan, by and large the case for the use of atomic weapons was strong in the American and Western value system, given the history of Japanese aggression, the Potsdam warning and its apparently flat rejection, and the millions of lives at stake—Japanese as well as American—should invasion be undertaken. But under what future conditions would the nation's values as incorporated in its political processes permit the use of these weapons; and by what means would American security needs be met under such moral and political limitations?

3. Neither the bomb nor its means of delivery lay outside the capabilities of many nations; here were weapons capable of bringing major destruction into the heart of the United States. What of the nation's security—and what of the military meaning of weapons of mass destruction—when other states possessed them?

These three great issues confronted the nation from the day that atomic weapons and their means of delivery over long distances became a reality. In ending the war against Japan the United States thus launched itself into an era where it faced problems of military security more searching and difficult, and less susceptible of solution by traditional American formulae and instinct, than any it had faced before. Around these issues a good deal of the postwar debate on the American security problem would arise. That debate was to reveal that an American capability to attack a potential enemy with atomic weapons delivered from long-range bombers was not a sufficient basis for the nation's security; but it was also to reveal that this capability was a minimum condition for national security, at least until supplanted by mobile, accurate, long-range missiles. To maintain this condition required, however, something new in the national experience: a major military establishment— a long-range bomber force—at instant battle readiness, day in, day out, through years of peace. The creation of this establishment—an interim, limited, but essential instrument of the nation's security—was the contribution of the strategic bombing experience of the Second World War.

## 11.  The Wartime Experience of Military Alliance

The innovational experiences of the Second World War foreshadowed not only the technological arms race and the cold-war role of the strategic Air

Command; they also embraced experiences of military alliance, West and East, which foreshadowed major areas of American success and failure in the postwar years.

THE BASIS OF THE WESTERN ALLIANCE

The geographic inevitability of American alliance arrangements was reflected as early as 1939 in Rainbow Plans 2 and 5, formulated at a time of national isolation. When prewar military planners defined the framework of operations required to meet the Axis threat in the Western Pacific or on the European continent, that framework was instinctively one of alliance. In 1941, when the nation accepted its stake in Allied victory and began to act short of war, alliance arrangements were the first order of business; and when Japan attacked in December, caving in or rendering precarious the whole structure of Allied positions in the Western Pacific and Southeast Asia, suddenly Australia became a key ally.[1] Like the historic position of Britain in relation to the European continent, the American island position in relation to a potentially more powerful Eurasia required that the United States work with others when the domination of that continental area by a single power threatened to come to pass.

The emergence of the Anglo-American alliance in 1941-1942 was, however, the outcome not merely of geography but also of British policy. From the outbreak of war—and certainly from Churchill's entrance into Chamberlain's cabinet—British eyes turned to Washington. In the short run the British counted ultimately on active American participation to convert their ability to survive in 1940 into clean-cut Allied victory. For the long run the Anglo-American tie came during the Second World War to be widely and explicitly accepted as the foundation of Britain's continuing world position. And many British wartime concessions to American views were made with this long-run interest in mind.

In 1940-1941, however, the British were extremely sensitive to the danger of appearing to force the American hand. Churchill, especially, was aware of the complexities of American domestic politics and of the precarious transition, in the American mind and in American politics, from the isolation of 1939 to the active, but incomplete, commitment to Allied victory of 1941. But having examined the brutal arithmetic of power, the British knew in their hearts that the job could not be finished with American tools alone. While continuing in the battle on the terms permitted by American politics, they counted for victory not merely on a continuing flow of American supplies but also, in the end, on active American military engagement. The Japanese attack on Pearl Harbor, followed promptly by Hitler's and Mussolini's declarations of war against the United States, were a vindication of British calculations concerning the historical forces at work as well as a culmination of British hopes.

While the fact of alliance was the product of geography and British policy, its form and content flowed from the human interplay of Churchill and Roosevelt. Their formal exchanges were initiated by Roosevelt on September 9, 1939, after Churchill entered the Chamberlain government as First Lord of the Admiralty. Their relationship was never crystallized into an Allied War Council or otherwise formalized. They undoubtedly sensed that they could do more as two unique individuals, exploiting the flexibility of their essentially common-law powers and the accident of their overlapping if not identical outlook on the future, than they could by creating a quasi-constitutional arrangement. They corresponded, they met together with their advisers, expanding or contracting their company (including Stalin and Chiang Kai-shek) as occasion demanded. Beneath their level, however, grew up a formidable Allied machinery of negotiation.

### THE ORGANIZATION OF THE WESTERN ALLIANCE

At the working level the Anglo-American alliance began with a series of visits designed to fulfill a necessary cold-blooded American purpose. The British received in 1940 a flow of American military and civilian observers whose task it was to assess whether or not Britain was likely to stay effectively in the war. As early as the summer of 1940, however, acting on the optimistic assumption that Britain would survive and the alliance would come to life, British and American scientists made their first arrangements for full collaboration. Systematic joint staff work between the United States and Britain began on a wider basis early in 1941 and was climaxed by the meeting at Placentia Bay in August. In the course of 1941 detailed operational understandings were reached not only in executing the Lend-Lease arrangements and in war production generally but also in coordinating British and American naval operations in the Atlantic. When Pearl Harbor was attacked, the working foundations for a formal Anglo-American military alliance had been well laid:

> Its operational detail was . . . tried and tested before its obligations and principles were defined or avowed; its bricks were . . . made and cemented before there was any agreed design for the complete edifice.[2]

Less than a week after Pearl Harbor Churchill left for Washington on the battle cruiser *Duke of York*. The discussions which followed not only defined the strategy for the defeat of Germany but also set up the formal machinery of alliance. The conduct of war within the framework of agreement reached by Roosevelt and Churchill lay in the Combined Chiefs of Staff, made up of the heads of the three services in each country. A combined Secretariat was set up in Washington, and representatives of the Chiefs of Staff met weekly. The principle of pooling resources and allocating them in terms of an agreed strategy was adopted, to be executed by the Munitions Assignment Board, a Combined Shipping Adjustment Board, and a Combined Raw Materials Board. And, above all, it was agreed that the war would be fought tactically as a joint operation, not merely by two nations working under an agreed strategy.

### ALLIANCE IN THE FIELD

The first major experience of joint operations in the field was in the landings at North Africa and in the subsequent campaign to clear the Germans from the southern shore of the Mediterranean.[3] The pattern of Allied organization set there left marks which can be seen throughout the Second World War and, indeed, down to the present.

Two principles applied in North Africa represented painfully acquired lessons of alliance from the First World War.[4] In each theater there was a single commander responsible to the combined Chiefs of Staff; under him, however, national formations were to fight in large units, of army size if possible.[5]

Despite the fact that the British carried the main weight of the African operation, Churchill surrendered the over-all command to an American—a pattern that was to persist.[6]

In formal structure the Allied commands in Europe were generally characterized by the following key elements:

A single theater commander; an Allied headquarters staff attached to the theater commander in which British, American, and other Allied officers were woven into each staff section; a naval theater commander who in all European cases was British; generally, a single theater air commander for tactical operations;[7] direct access of two major ground force commanders—one British, one American—to the supreme commander, the device of a single ground force chief under the theater commander having been rejected, except for the initial assault period in Normandy.

### EISENHOWER AS DIRECTOR OF AN ALLIED STAFF

Despite the difficulties into which the British-American ground forces ran in the autumn and winter campaign in Northwest Africa, and despite Eisenhower's awkward experience with French politics, the early months of this experiment in Allied command were judged successful. Thereafter the patterns created by Eisenhower remained relatively fixed for the duration of the war.[8]

As an organizer and leader of an international staff General Eisenhower was successful. His success stemmed not only from the high premium he attached to the maintenance of Allied harmony but also from his conception of the requirements of a modern executive. His analysis of the modern general's task, with appropriate modification, also describes a widespread American view of the changing character of executive responsibility in other fields of activity—a view of institutionalized leadership later reflected in Eisenhower's conduct of the Office of President.

> The military methods and machinery for making and waging war have become so extraordinarily complex and intricate that high commanders must have gargantuan staffs for control and direction. . . . But personal characteristics are more important than ever before in warfare. The reasons for this are simple. It was not a matter of great moment if a Wellington happened to be a crusty, unapproachable individual who found one of his chief delights in penning sarcastic quips to the War Office. He was the single head, who saw the whole battlefield and directed operations through a small administrative staff and a few aides and orderlies. As long as he had the stamina and the courage to make decisions and to stand by them, and as long as his tactical skill met the requirements of his particular time and conditions, he was a great commander. But the teams and staffs through which the modern commander absorbs information and exercises his authority must be a beautifully interlocked, smooth-working mechanism. Ideally, the whole should be practically a single mind; consequently misfits defeat the purpose of the command organization essential to supply and control of the vast land, air, sea, and logistical forces that must be brought to bear as a unity against the enemy.[9]

Here, fully formed, is a romantic conception of bureaucratized leadership, where smooth-working teams, made up of men whose egos are well disciplined, will pose the alternatives, out of orderly staff processes, for executive decision. This was a conception alien and inappropriate to the lonely choices of either Roosevelt or Churchill at the apex or to those of a Patton, Montgomery, or Bradley in the field. It was, within limits, a useful conception, however, for an intermediate Allied staff headquarters.

In addition to the suitability of his personality and his nonassertive conception of administration, Eisenhower exhibited one special quality which made him an admirable director of an Allied staff. He understood the delicacy of the British transition from senior to junior partner in the European theater, and he made that transition as easy as it could humanly be made for the British. He never forgot the role of the British in 1940, their tactful treatment of Americans entering the European theater in 1942 as relative amateurs, the sustained human sacrifice and self-discipline of the British public. The British felt and appreciated this dimension of sensibility.

Although the arrangements for joint operations were a notable administrative and political success, they did not, of course, end allied friction. The historians of both Bradley's and Montgomery's armies evoke vividly the mood of suspicion, competition, and dissidence which was bound to be generated in the field under circumstances where the normal dislike of higher headquarters was compounded by its Allied character. More serious, however, was the dilution of strategic decision which arose from the imperatives of the alliance as judged by Eisenhower. His vacillation over Antwerp, his decision to split supplies and paratroopers between Patton and Montgomery in the late summer of 1944, and his decision on the use of air power before D-Day—in face of the controversy between Tedder and Spaatz—were profoundly colored both by extramilitary considerations and by Eisenhower's conception of executive decision as a form of arbitration among subordinates bearing the direct weight of operational responsibility.

### TWO NATIONAL STYLES AT WORK

The operation of Allied headquarters was an interesting comparative test of British and American methods of staff training and organization. Despite significant exceptions, there is little doubt that the British in the Second World War exhibited greater skill and maturity in higher staff operations than did Americans. The roots for this widely noted national distinction lay in several circumstances.

By and large the British then placed a higher premium on staff work than did Americans; and they probably assigned to staff jobs abler men and women —although this judgment must be impressionistic. Without question, however, a British higher education, on the average, left its product distinctly better prepared to draft terse, coherent staff papers and to debate them effectively in committees than an equivalent American education. On issues of any importance, moreover, the British government had a unified and clear position which was effectively communicated to British staff men, down to quite low levels, where it was stoutly and consistently defended within the Allied Staffs. On many such matters there was no clear United States governmental position; and if a decision had been arrived at in Washington, it was unlikely to be communicated far down in the American chain of command. On issues where no explicit guidelines had been laid down by the British government the British tended to have an instinctive and fairly uniform sense of the national interest, including its political dimensions; whereas the American national interest was a matter of unresolved political debate, if not of private personal opinion.

The upshot was that Americans often felt themselves at something of a disadvantage within the joint staffs, facing, virtually as a detached group of individuals, a united and purposeful phalanx on major issues of policy.

But in most day-to-day circumstances there was no touchstone for correct action except that which would advance the common military cause; and, in consequence, there emerged a joint human effort which transcended national feeling and which suffused Allied enterprises at many points with harmony. And, even when national differences arose, some participants came to respect the difference of interest and view which characterized each party and emerged with a more profound understanding of the long-term problem of joint Anglo-American action. For some the experience of Allied operations was an exercise in coming to understand another nation for the first time; and it yielded a new objectivity toward their own.

## THE IMPRINT OF SHAEF

Leaving aside the question of whether the balancing of national viewpoints led to something less than the wisest military decisions—and, perhaps, even lengthened the European war—there is no doubt that the experience of combined Allied headquarters, notably of SHAEF, had a long-term and constructive effect on American relations with Western Europe. It gave institutional form to the concept of an American stake in the West Eurasian balance of power. It was from this experience that NATO emerged in 1948-1949 and SHAPE in 1951.

SHAEF contributed to the civil as well as to the military organization of postwar Western Europe. The branch of SHAEF charged with civil affairs in liberated territories—G-5—started an impressive family line of international economic committees and organizations. G-5 began the task of European reconstruction in the summer of 1944. From the time, roughly, that Paris was captured (late in August), SHAEF was faced with urgent problems of food and fuel supply, of transport rehabilitation, of the repair of electric power lines.

The British and American officers in SHAEF had to deal intimately with French, Belgian, and Dutch civil agencies. They had to fight for shipping and resources; and they had to allocate the scarce imported supplies on which they could lay their hands. As they worked together they began to look further ahead in the process of reconstruction. Out of their emergency operations emerged three postwar European institutions: The European Coal Organization, the European Central Inland Transport Organziation, and the Emergency Economic Committee for Europe. In turn, their maturing experience and limited, but real, successes in dealing on a communal basis with European problems of reconstruction after V-E Day led on directly to the notion of organizing European (or Western European) recovery on a more permanent unified basis.

## ALLIANCE IN THE EAST

In Asia no such wholesome consequences of the Allied wartime experience emerged. The relatively sterile outcome there proceeded directly from two causes: first, a failure of Anglo-American understanding concerning military and political policy in Asia; second, an inability of American policy to adapt to the fact that, in China and elsewhere, it was dealing with unstable transitional societies—somewhere between traditional and modern status—to which the methods of alliance appropriate in Western Europe could not successfully be applied.

The British and Americans never generated in the Far East a unified strategic conception. The British tended to regard the American preoccupation with Japan as a necessary evil draining resources away from the European theater, where the major issues—Asian as well as European—would be settled. Even where Britain's Empire stake appeared most direct, and its prestige was engaged by responsibility for leadership in an Allied command—in Mountbatten's Southeast Asia command—British wartime policy was desultory. North of the Kra Peninsula in Malaya the British had a naval and commerical policy of limited liability. The British had no clear China policy beyond the interest to reoccupy Hong Kong and Singapore and resume old commercial connections with China. They recognized clearly the weaknesses of Chiang Kai-shek and the unlikelihood that Nationalist China would, in fact, emerge as one of the four major powers at the end of the war; but Churchill gave Roosevelt a relatively free hand in shaping Anglo-American diplomacy at the highest level, essentially leaving China as an American headache. And American China policy was an incompatible amalgam of sentimental, moral, and diplomatic commitment to the Chinese mainland combined with a military policy directed mainly toward the Japanese islands and the control of the Western Pacific waters. The consequences of this situation during the Second World War were mainly political and diplomatic rather than military and are, therefore, not dealt with here. Certain military dimensions of the alliance in Asia—and their consequences—are, however, worth noting briefly.

The results were mixed.[10] The Southeast Asia Command was by and large frustrating to those Americans who were stationed within it. It undertook no major operations, and it left no substantial constructive heritage either in its institutional arrangements or in men's minds.

In Australia and, to a lesser extent, in New Zealand, the American experience was mainly bilateral; the Americans and Australians, evidently sharing a sense of common danger more urgent than London's and a more or less common response to it, had to learn to work together. In this case the Second World War yielded a significant long-term result. Australia and New Zealand came to look to the United States as their major source of military security; and the experience of common staff work, in this case, founded in similar, if not identical, strategic concepts, was later institutionalized via the ANZUS Pact.

The wartime experience of alliance with China was, of course, a major American failure. The United States was here caught up with a nation in the midst of a disruptive revolutionary process and civil war. The United States did not fully face these facts in making a wartime China policy; and, in addition, there was an immense gap between long-run American diplomatic policy toward China and short-run military policy in the Pacific War.

### THE ALLIANCES IN PERSPECTIVE

In terms of American history, the alliance exercises of the Second World War carried forward conceptions latent in earlier national experiences. They translated into working reality two dreams of earlier American generations. In Europe the American-led offensive of 1944-1945 fulfilled, in a sense, the frustrated plans for the offensive of 1919, in which the United States would have played a mature role. In Asia, the war against Japan, in alliance with Nationalist China, fulfilled the national image encapsulated in the Open Door notes and lifted, to a degree, the widespread burden of guilt that developed after 1931.

In general the American experience of alliance was constructive when two conditions were satisfied: there was a shared strategic conception between the United States and its ally which could be translated into agreed common enterprises; and the ally was sufficiently well organized to assume and discharge real, even if limited, responsibilities. Despite important cross-purposes in Europe between the United States and Britain, both of these conditions were broadly satisfied; and they were satisfied as well in American dealings with Australia and New Zealand on a lesser range of issues. The first condition was not satisfied, however, in the SEAC area; and in the case of United States-China relations, neither condition was satisfied.

In all its dimensions the nation's experience of alliances during the Second World War helped create patterns of both success and of failure that were to persist in the postwar years.

## 12. A Military Balance Sheet for the Second World War

The revolutionary impact of the Second World War on the military position of the United States can be arrayed as a kind of balance sheet. The wartime experience contributed to the nation a set of strengths which transcended the defeat of its immediate enemies; but it also revealed or accentuated a set of weaknesses in the nation's postwar security position.

The long-run security position of the nation was strengthened by the possession of four distinct assets. First, the wartime revolution in military technology left the United States with the most advanced military machine in the world, equipped uniquely with atomic weapons and capable of holding in check the Soviet ground forces which otherwise could have enabled the Soviet Union to dominate the postwar scene. Second, the nation had developed a strategic air force which could deliver the new weapons against any potential enemy, a capability no other nation could match in the immediate postwar years. Third, the nation had a corps of mature, skilled, confident professional military men to whom the experiences of the war had imparted a new vision of the nation's worldwide problems and responsibilities. Fourth, the nation had made the transition from the status of self-isolated observer of the world scene to that of operational leadership in a worldwide military coalition, learning in the process the problems and responsibilities of successful leadership in a joint theater of operation.

But for each of these accretions to the nation's military potential there was a related debit.

Atomic weapons and the new military technology were sufficient to prevent Soviet ground forces from proceeding to conquer western Eurasia; but they left the United States and its allies open to forms and degrees of limited aggression with which atomic weapons could not directly cope and under circumstances where the moral values and political institutions of the West did not permit retaliation in the form of direct assault on the Soviet bases of Communist aggression. In the longer run the monopoly position of the United States in 1945 was bound to be transient. There was no reason why reasonably mature industrial societies could not develop sufficient atomic weapons and delivery capabilities to threaten the United States with major destruction and loss of life; and when that inevitably occurred, the problem of national security would have new dimensions. The strategic meaning of the ocean approaches to the United States would be radically altered; the power of the new weapons and the possibility that they could strike directly against the United States would virtually eliminate the cushion of time which historically had played so great a role in protecting the nation; and, finally, the scale of damage which even a limited number of the new weapons could achieve if delivered with reasonable accuracy would diminish the military significance of American primacy in basic industrial potential. In both the long and the short run, then, the real effect of the new weapons was to increase the importance of nonmilitary measures for the protection of the national interest.

Moreover, the new weapons accentuated an old American weakness in the pursuit of national security: their existence put a premium on anticipating problems before they became major crises. If major war were to come, the United States would risk outright defeat if it had achieved at the outbreak only a degree of preparedness equivalent to that of 1917 or 1941. And an unaccustomed degree of anticipation was required in American foreign policy as a whole if the possibility of war itself was to be minimized; for major war could now assume a life-and-death meaning for the United States. In short, the new technology made dangerous as well as inappropriate many of the nation's traditional ways of thinking about its security problem and much in the national style.

What was true of atomic weapons and the new technology in general was true quite specifically of the American strategic bomber force. Linked to atomic weapons, American long-range bombing capabilities gave the nation in the immediate postwar years, when its atomic weapon monopoly still held, an indispensable shield at a time of virtual ground force and naval disarmament. But strategic air power was a weapon of limited capabilities for the paradoxical reason that, if used, its capabilities for destruction were radically disproportionate to the objective sought. Morality and politics in the United States and the western world permitted its use only under life-and-death circumstances; and the armory of Communist methods permitted forms of aggression which could not be judged to create such circumstances. Beyond that, the maintenance of a Strategic Air Comand capable of efficient wartime operation at a moment's notice placed on the United States unique new requirements: the requirement of full battle preparedness for a major military formation at a time of peace; and the even more difficult requirement of recruiting and holding within the armed forces at a time of peace highly trained technicians capable of handling the increasingly complex and expensive instruments of delivery and defense.

There were two sides even to the third military asset derived from the Second World War. The rise of the professional American military in technical skill, confidence, and vision added a major element to the nation's strength; but this accretion was not matched by an equivalent development of civilians and civilian institutions in the formulation and execution of foreign policy. This unbalanced national development encouraged the traditional American tendency to deal with a security threat by strictly military means and to separate sharply civil from military lines of action. Although military men undertook, generally with distinction, specific tasks in civil diplomacy in the postwar years, the rise of the professional military as a group could not fill the partial vacuum left by the inadequate preparedness and organization of the civil side of foreign policy.

Finally, the experience of coalition. It provided the foundation for the civil and military measures which successfully checked Soviet efforts to expand to the west in the postwar decade; but the very success of the concept of the regional military alliance in Europe led the United States to apply it in areas and under conditions where it did not solve the fundamental problems on which American security came to rest, notably in the underdeveloped parts of the world.

The Second World War was fought, then, under circumstances and in a manner not only consistent in many dimensions with the abortive experience in 1917-1918 but also consonant with the long sweep of American history and the national style; that is, as the vigorous pragmatic response to a set of concrete problems undertaken only when acute crisis had arisen and solved over a considerable period of time by means which yielded both substantial institutions and relatively fixed patterns of thought. But the course of the war and its consequences projected the United States into a new set of relations to the world for which the national military experience was substantially inappropriate and for which the apparent lessons of the Second World War offered incomplete and, in some cases, misleading lines of guidance for future policy.

# PART III

# THE DIPLOMACY OF WAR
# AND PEACEMAKING

### 13. *Diplomatic Expediency, World Order, and the National Interest*

The character of American wartime diplomacy was determined by the inadequacy of the synthesis of Mahanist and Wilsonian views which, in effect, dominated American policy during the Second World War. An unfortunate legacy of the Mahanist vision was that it left the nation without a clear sense of the strategic meaning and priority of Eastern Europe and China for the American interest. The memory of Wilson—and his influence—led both to a separation of the planning of postwar institutions from the concrete issues of postwar power and to a disproportionate emphasis on the creation of these institutions.

Under such circumstances—when the most prevalent abstractions did not clarify events and suggest unambiguous courses of action—the vacuum was bound to be filled by the imperatives of battle and of diplomatic convenience. Expediency—mainly military, but political and diplomatic as well—in the end governed day-to-day decisions; while, for the long run, the nation looked to the undoing of the error of 1920 by creating and joining in a new world order. Neither the narrow pragmatism of expediency nor the high aspirations of the global blueprints could prevent a third major struggle for dominance in Eurasia from succeeding promptly to the second.

In examining how the prevailing concept of the national interest shaped the principal diplomatic decisions of the war years it is necessary, therefore, to seek the answer to these further questions: What decisions were taken which determined the shape and problems of the postwar world? And, specifically, how and why did wartime diplomacy lead on to the Cold War?

## 14. France

VICHY AND DE GAULLE

The first major test of American wartime diplomacy came with respect to the French; and, over the whole period 1940-1944, American relations with France were the subject of an active national debate[1] precipitated by the fall of France, the Armistice of 1940, the creation of the Vichy regime, and the emergence of De Gaulle.

Once the fundamental French decision was made to accept the Armistice, the arrangement of affairs had something to command it on all sides. In 1940 Britain made virtually irreversible commitments to De Gaulle and the Free French movement. The British permitted his famous broadcast of June 8, 1940, formed up French units within the British military establishment, and recognized the skeletal government which De Gaulle created. On this side of the Atlantic, the Department of State recognized the regime at Vichy, and, although shaken by Weygand's dismissal in November 1941, the American policy of recognition persisted down to Pearl Harbor and into the phase of American participation.

The French nation emerged, in Langer's phrase, with "eggs in two baskets": the British had in London an ally capable of assisting in the development of intelligence sources and an underground movement on the Continent, minor accretions to Allied military strength; the United States could use Vichy as a source of intelligence and perhaps exert a marginal influence in stiffening Vichy backs against Berlin. In addition, the North African economic agreement of February 1941 permitted American intelligence to operate somewhat more effectively in that strategic area than would otherwise have been possible, with Weygand, the local commander, exploiting his relations with the United States to strengthen the national bargaining position of France against Germany and looking forward to ultimate Allied victory.

While tactically useful, this Anglo-American arrangement did not relieve the United States from the necessity for further consideration of the future of De Gaulle and of the wisdom of its link to Vichy.

The public debate centered on these issues proceeded in terms of liberal and conservative views projected out from the politics and values of American life. The formal diplomatic position, however, was limited to the simple proposition that after the war the French people should have the opportunity to choose their political leadership by democratic means. As in other areas where this concept was applied, it was corrupted by short-run developments and political decisions required by the conduct of military operations. In fact, American policy toward France was settled by two expedient military decisions which decided the running ideological debate among the civilians successively in different directions.

## THE DECISION IN NORTH AFRICA: 1942

In the course of 1942, when the invasion of North Africa was planned, the following issue was faced: What kind of political policy toward the French in North Africa would minimize French resistance and Anglo-American casualties?

Examined more than a decade after the event, there is much pure farce in the political handling of the North African invasion: the inaccurate estimate that it mattered greatly that American (rather than British) forces dominate the landings; the extreme opportunism of Darlan and others, who made their moves on the basis of relative strength on the spot rather than in terms of deep moral, legal, or ideological attachments; the hasty last-minute integration of military and political plans; and so on.

It is not the purpose here either to rehearse the story in detail or to make a fresh evaluation of the wisdom of the nation's part in it. There are, however, two characteristics of the political decisions made that are worth noting. First, every important political decision was made by the military in terms of what would prove militarily expedient. At no point were political factors judged worthy of military cost. Second, the priority of military expediency converged with a tendency to what might be called diplomatic expediency. That is, the diplomats sought men with whom they could talk and negotiate and who could act on the existing structure of power and administration if agreements were reached. Under the post-Armistice circumstances such men were bound to be part of the Vichy administration. Thus normal diplomatic techniques and biases created an automatic tendency to throw American weight behind the *status quo*—and to do so under circumstances which were abnormal and bound to change rapidly.

During 1942 there was abundant evidence that public opinion in France was rapidly crystallizing around De Gaulle and the Free French as the agreed symbol of resistance. In North Africa public opinion may have been somewhat less strongly for De Gaulle, although he was emerging there as well as the symbol of resurgent France. In any case, the organized resistance groups with whom the United States mainly worked at the time were dominated by men whose links in law and sentiment were to Petain rather than to De Gaulle. It was inevitable that, in bringing about a transformation of the whole North African situation by military action, the United States had to choose between enforcing a radical political transformation along Gaullist lines, consistent with trends in France and probably with local public opinion as well, or associating the United States politically with the Vichy forces believed to wield immediate military and administrative power on the spot. The latter course was chosen.

On the whole the evidence now is that in virtually all French minds in North Africa the decisive issue was whether the Allied invasion would be successful and that, within tolerable limits including an important role for De Gaulle, the local French would have accommodated themselves to whatever political setting the Allies had proposed once Allied military strength had been effectively asserted in the area. American policy-makers were overly impressed with the operational significance of the French cultural attachment to legalism. The French generals and administrators in North Africa—like other human beings—were not martyrs, but patriots and opportunists in varying proportions.

Whether it was necessary to appease Vichy in order to achieve American purposes in North Africa is, of course, debatable. What is clear is that the outcome was colored not merely by military expediency but also by that form of diplomatic expediency which seeks to deal with the man on the spot rather than to try to shape a new political conformation from elements possibly harder to find and harder to evaluate but more consonant with the long-run national interest.

## DECISION IN FRANCE: 1944

The same dual criteria of expediency determined that the United States—in violation of its formal policy of assuring the French postwar free choice—should in 1944 virtually install De Gaulle as the immediate postwar ruler of France.

In June 1943, following De Gaulle's arrival on May 30, the French National Liberation Committee was set up in Algiers. This grouping, in which the Free French merged with noncollaborationist French resistance elements, was designed not merely to unite French forces but also to provide a diplomatic formula which would permit the United States and Britain to come together on French policy.[2] Within the committee a number of Frenchmen worked effectively to focus their leaders' minds on future problems and possibilities rather than past tragedies and current rivalry for status. Washington was reluctant to grant this committee "recognition" and chronically uneasy about the rise of De Gaulle's authority within it at Giraud's expense. Giraud proved an extremely limited political figure who, sensing his awkward status, resigned with dignity on November 8, 1943, leaving the field clear for dominance by De Gaulle.

Despite recurring Anglo-American difficulties with the Committee and with De Gaulle, as D-Day approached in 1944, De Gaulle, in effect, came to speak not only for the Committee but also for all effective French political and military forces outside of France; and intelligence from France itself strongly confirmed the unique symbolic prestige which had been gathering about him over the past two years.

The President and the Department of State still refused to grant formal recognition; but the exigencies of *Overlord* determined that the Allies would recognize De Gaulle as the political and military voice of France at the time of the landings, eliminating any realistic alternative to recognition of the Committee as a provisional French government.

The process of converting an American diplomatic formula for postponement into *de facto* recognition is vividly described by Eisenhower in his *Crusade for Europe:*

> One of our final visitors was General De Gaulle, with whom some disagreement developed, involving the actual timing and nature of pronouncements to be made to the French population immediately upon landing. General De Gaulle wanted to be clearly and definitely recognized by both the Allied governments as the ruler of France. . . .
>
> President Roosevelt was flatly opposed to giving General De Gaulle this specific and particular type of recognition. The President then, as always, made a great point of his insistence that sovereignty in France resided in the people, that the Allies were not entering France in order to force upon the population a particular government or a particular ruler.
>
> The attempt to work out a plan satisfactory to De Gaulle and still remain within the limits fixed by our governments fell largely to the lot of our headquarters and occasioned a great deal of worry because we were depending on considerable assistance from the insurrectionists in France. They were known to be particularly numerous in the Brittany area and in the hills and mountains of southeast France. An open clash with De Gaulle on this matter would hurt us immeasurably and would result in bitter recrimination and unnecessary loss of life.
>
> The staff thought the argument was, in a sense, academic. It was considered that, in the initial stages of the operation at least, De Gaulle would represent the only authority that could produce any kind of French coordination and unification and that no harm would result from giving him the kind of recognition he sought. He would merely be placed on notice that once the country was liberated the freely expressed will of the French people would determine their own government and leader. We had already, with the consent of our government, accepted De Gaulle's representative, General Koenig, as the commander of the French Forces of the Interior, who was serving as a direct subordinate of mine in the Allied organization.
>
> We particularly desired De Gaulle to participate with me in broadcasting on D-Day to the French people so that the population, avoiding uprisings and useless sacrifice at non-critical points, would still be instantly ready to help us where help was needed.[3]

Thus, just as the operational requirements of invasion as judged by the military determined that De Gaulle should be thrust aside in North Africa in 1942, they led to his installation as head of the French state in 1944, a fact confirmed by Britain and the United States in October. Even this final step had its military component: the military desire to relinquish administrative responsibility for the widening liberated area that could be regarded as a secure Zone of the Interior helped force Washington's still somewhat reluctant hand.

## POLICY TOWARD FRANCE IN PERSPECTIVE

With hindsight there are many legitimate questions that can be raised concerning this sequence in American policy toward France. Given the turbulent, obscure circumstances of war, it can be argued that, by and large, it met the nation's interests. The American goals were to reconcile a political policy that would minimize casualties with the emergence after the war of a democratic France as strong and united as its history and capabilities would permit. These aims were, on the whole, achieved.

The manner of their achievement, however, strengthened bad habits in American thought. American policy refused systematically to recognize that the American impact on postwar France would consist in good part of the cumulative result of the short-run decisions taken during the war. The clean distinction between war and peace—so vivid in Washington thought and pronouncements—was a false one. The emergence of a reasonable result in policy toward France was not the consequence of American political planning or American attachment to the principle that the French people must be given a chance to choose their own government after the war. It came about because *Overlord* required the cooperation of the French underground and the French people; because De Gaulle was judged in 1944 a political figure who could evoke that response; and, ultimately, because Frenchmen themselves—including De Gaulle—desired overwhelmingly a return to democratic government.

Although the French story ended reasonably well, it had a special significance. The American handling of the North African invasion was, in a sense, the first major American appearance operating on the stage of Eurasian politics since Versailles. It came at a time when the peoples of the world regarded the American President as a figure sympathetic to progress and an opponent of political reactionaries. Franklin Roosevelt was regarded as a worthy successor of Wilson; and he raised men's hopes as had no political figure since 1919. It was something of a shock to those whose view of international affairs was dominated by the canons of Western liberalism to see that American weight could even briefly be thrown behind a reactionary *status quo*, that expediency could so easily triumph over evident long-run principle. And this image of the nation was strengthened to a degree by American wartime policy in Italy and, later, in China.

To state this is to state a fact, not to pass a judgment. Washington faced difficult, narrow, intractable choices in conducting international politics in the midst of a desperate war. It is possible to argue that American short-run policy was less imaginative, more expedient, less attuned to long-run American interests and aspirations than necessary; but it is clear that expedient compromises had to be made. It is also clear, however, that the world looked peculiarly to the United States for the enunciation of its postwar goals and aspirations. The fact that American short-run policy was governed so strongly by military and diplomatic expediency—in part because long-run objectives were so vaguely defined and incapable of providing useful touchstones for practical current decisions—began to project a new and confused image of the nation's purposes on the world scene. At its roots this confused image—of an expedient America supporting the *status quo* in opposition to groups whose objectives more nearly conformed with American ideals—was legitimate; for it stemmed from unreconciled strands in American character and thought which played their part in American policy from the days of the North African invasion forward.

## 15. Germany

### THE ISSUES

The confusion between expedient decisions in relation to the French and long-run objectives led directly to the enunciation of a general policy of unconditional surrender at Casablanca in January 1943. This notion, which separated sharply the states of war and peace, set the framework for the consideration of postwar policy toward Germany,[1] which involved issues at three distinct levels.

First, there was a range of what might be called administrative issues: the drafting of an agreed instrument of surrender, the marking out of zones of occupation for the victorious Allied armies, and the training of a corps of men to administer the German occupation at a working level. Second, there were problems of immediate postwar policy: how should the Nazis be dealt with; how should the civil population in general be treated politically and socially; what standard of welfare should be permitted the German people in the early occupation period, and what responsibility should the occupation forces assume for it; what reparations should be extracted from Germany on behalf of those nations which had been the victims of German aggression? Third, there was the issue of what kind of long-run policy toward Germany in relation to the Soviet Union and Eastern Europe would maximize the possibilities of keeping the peace.

UNITY OR SCHISM

The issue of unity or dismemberment was evidently the most important single problem of German policy, once the possibility had been opened by Roosevelt's enunciation and Churchill's and Stalin's reluctant acceptance of the doctrine of unconditional surrender. The possibility of dismemberment, examined in the course of the State Department's forward planning in 1942, was first formally raised within the alliance in conversations between Eden and the President in March 1943; and dismemberment as a positive objective remained a possibility in Roosevelt's mind down to his death, and in American policy down to Potsdam. In a curious, back-handed way it was confirmed as Big Three policy at Yalta, with, however, the Soviets maintaining a freedom of action they subsequently exercised formally to oppose dismemberment.

Hopkin's notes on the initial Eden-Roosevelt discussion give the persistent flavor of the President's thought:[2]

> Eden said that . . . he was sure that . . . Stalin has a deep-seated distrust of the Germans and that he will insist that Germany be broken up into a number of states. The President said he hoped we would not use the methods discussed at Versailles and also promoted by Clemenceau to arbitrarily divide Germany, but thought that we should encourage the differences and ambitions that will spring up within Germany for a Separatist Movement, and, in effect, approve of a division which represents German public opinion.
>
> I [Hopkins] asked what they would do if that spontaneous desire did not spring up and both the President and Eden agreed that, under any circumstances, Germany must be divided into several states, one of which must, over all circumstances, be Prussia. The Prussians cannot be permitted to dominate all Germany.[2]

From the beginning of discussions on Germany's future those at the staff level within the Department of State (and their advisers drawn from outside the government) opposed dismemberment despite Roosevelt's and Welles' advocacy. As early as 1942 they took and held a view paraphrased as follows by Mosely:

> Certain members of the Advisory Committee and the expert staff itself were skeptical of the effectiveness of dismemberment as a means of preventing future German aggression and believed that the United States would not be willing in the long run to impose and maintain dismemberment by force. They also pointed out that dismemberment would prepare the ground for rallying all Germans against the victorious Powers, would discredit all attempts to develop a democratic regime and spirit in Germany, and would render the economic problem of German livelihood absolutely unmanageable. They foresaw that the Germans would strive in every way to undo partition through playing off the victorious Powers against each other, and would thus increase greatly the dangers of a postwar falling-out among the victors.[3]

They sought to meet the substance of the alternative view by advocating a form of unified German government with strong decentralized federalist features.

When Hull went to Moscow in 1943 he was inclined to sympathize with the Department of State staff position, but he confined himself to indicating that there were differing unresolved views in the American government.[4] The issue was referred for inter-Allied negotiation to the European Advisory Commission, which was set up as the result of the Moscow conference to develop agreed Allied policy for a defeated Germany.

A few weeks later, in November 1943, when the Big Three met at Teheran, the weight of top-level British and American policy was thrown quite explicitly toward one form or another of dismemberment; and at Yalta, in February 1945, the instrument of surrender drafted by the three governments stated that steps would be taken for the "complete disarmament, demilitarization, and the dismemberment of Germany as they deem requisite for future peace and security." However, Stalin in his "Proclamation to the People" of May 8, 1945 declared that "the Soviet Union does not intend to dismember or destroy Germany."

At a high level, then, as the war ended, the situation was as follows. Although Roosevelt's death had eliminated the strongest advocate of this position, the United States government was still split on the issue of dismemberment. There was an equivalent muddled situation in British policy, although at least some in London, skeptical that Churchill could bring about German unity, already explicitly looked forward to a split of Germany east and west along the line of the Soviet zone of occupation. There was no agreed British-American policy. The Soviets had gained freedom of action— for propaganda as well as diplomatic purposes—by formally detaching themselves from the tentative Yalta agreement for a form of dismemberment. Thus the Allies entered the postwar period with the single most important issue unsettled in their negotiations.

## EXPEDIENCY TAKES OVER

Lacking any agreed long-term conception, the short-run administrative arrangements negotiated for the occupation of Germany assumed a decisive importance; and they, of course, had a built-in bias toward the division of Germany since it had been agreed at the Moscow conference of Foreign Ministers in October 1943 that the three major Allies would jointly formulate and accept the unconditional surrender of Germany, that they would each initially occupy a zone in Germany, and that control machinery for the joint machinery of Germany would be set up.

To settle precisely the arrangement of these matters was the major task of the European Advisory Commission created by the decisions of the Moscow conference. Its work formally began on January 14, 1944. The lines of zonal division between the Soviet Union and the West were settled without great difficulty, as was the question of joint occupation of Berlin. So far as the instrument of surrender was concerned, SHAEF in the end did not use the detailed substantive instrument drafted in the EAC, which reflected the cumulative result of high level negotiations on the long-run future of Germany, but preferred and obtained the right to use an instrument at once vaguer on political grounds and more narrowly military. Finally, the arrangements for a Control Council of the occupying powers to be set up in Berlin was, once again, negotiated in principle without difficulty.

It was clear to those in the EAC that success in achieving an agreement on occupation measures in no sense settled the substantive issues of German policy; and in mid-August 1944 the issues which still had to be settled were laid before the President by Winant in a lengthy cable here paraphrased by Mosely:

> He urged that every effort be made on the American side to go forward to negotiate the widest possible measure of agreed policies to be enforced jointly by the future occupying Powers. It was not enough to set up the machinery of joint Allied administration; every effort should be made to work out agreed Allied policies which this machinery should carry into effect. Mr. Winant went on to point out that the Russian need for material aid in repairing the vast destruction in the Soviet Union was bound to make the Soviet Government particularly eager to receive reparations deliveries from Germany on a large scale. Since the major part of German industry was located in the western zones, the Allies must try to work out, in advance, a reparations policy which would satisfy a part of the Soviet demands without involving an undue burden for the United States. He urged that Washington hasten the formulation of a reparations policy and then bend every effort toward reaching the earliest possible agreement with its Allies while the war was still in progress. He warned that it would be almost impossible to achieve such an agreement after the close of hostilities and that if no agreement had been reached on reparation the proposed system for the joint control in Germany would break down. Rivalry for control over Germany he said, would rapidly follow. He urged that the United States consider ways of helping the recovery of the Soviet economy, such assistance to be linked to the achievement of a satisfactory settlement of the problem of German reparations and of the most important political issues between the two Governments.[5]

## "HARD" OR "SOFT" POLICIES OF OCCUPATION?

The timing of Winant's cable was determined not only by the rhythm of negotiation in the EAC but also by the emergence in August 1944 of the famous controversy over the Morgenthau Plan. Briefly, Morgenthau argued for a restructuring of the German economy in such a way as to eliminate or reduce its heavy industry component and throw the Germans back upon agriculture and light industry for a safe modest livelihood; and he brought his pressure to a remarkable climax in September at Quebec, where Roosevelt and Churchill initialed a proposal for converting Germany "into a country primarily agricultural and pastoral in its character." Eden was as furious with Churchill as Stimson and Hull were with Roosevelt. In the United States an acute controversy concerning the Quebec decision developed promptly within the Executive Branch and, to a degree, in public discussion. By early October Roosevelt concluded that he had made a grave error, withdrew his support from Morgenthau, and adopted a policy of wait-and-see with respect to German policy.[6]

Lacking high policy decisions, the machinery of planning ground along nevertheless. On September 23, 1944, Eisenhower as Allied commander had received a draft interim directive, never cleared with the Combined Chiefs of Staff, on how to deal with Germany and Germans immediately after defeat—the famous JCS 1067. This instruction contained—evidently unresolved—both "hard" and "soft" elements, and, like many products of interdepartmental committees, was subject to alternative interpretations, leaving it open to those with operational responsibility to make the choice most congenial to their outlook. By early 1945 this directive required revision, and the "hard" elements in the early version were somewhat softened in the January revision of JCS 1067; but the Treasury view remained alive to a degree in the financial annex, which was not fully agreed in Washington until February. More significant in this revision was the controversy on the relative powers of the Allied Control Council and the zonal commanders. The instinctive reaction of the military was to reserve maximum authority for the American zonal commanders, while the State Department pressed to enlarge the authority of the Control Council as a possible administrative instrument for moving toward a German unity that was progressively receding into the background as the armies moved in from east and west and high-level diplomacy with respect to Eastern Europe evolved along the schismatic lines which were to make the determination of Germany's postwar fate a function of other issues.

## AN UNRESOLVED DEBATE

The central fact about American policy toward postwar Germany was that, although the issues were approached in terms of long-run problems and objectives, the debate on them was never resolved. The result was a state of ambiguity in which the military authorities charged with the conduct of the latter stages of the war and the immediate postwar occupation made the key decisions. Thus the postwar status of Germany emerged from a succession of expedient decisions rather than from a set of agreed objectives founded in a concept of the nation's abiding interest in Western Eurasia.

The debate within the American government on the issue of Germany's future turned on two matters. Should a unified Germany be restored or should Germany be dismembered? Should a purposeful long-run effort be made so to reduce Germany's industrial capabilities as to eliminate the possibility of Germany again developing significant military power?

Those who argued for dismemberment felt that the root of Europe's problem lay, in a sense, in the wrong turning of the revolution of 1848: that is, in the defeat of liberalism by nationalism, leading to a Germany unified under Prussia which, given its resources and geographical location, had the potentiality of threatening to dominate the whole continent.

Those who argued against dismemberment felt that a split would give the German people a powerful and effective focus for a policy of revenge which would maximize both the chances of a resurgent and aggressive Germany in the future and the likelihood of a dangerous competition among the wartime allies for German favors.

Similarly, those who argued for the elimination of German heavy industry felt that such a course would be technically possible and decisive to the preservation of the peace; while those who argued against such proposals held that, given German war damage and the world's acute postwar requirements for German industrial output, they were not technically feasible, and that, once again, an issue which would focus German nationalism at its worst would be given to the German people for the long run.

The debate as a whole stemmed from the notion that the victors might perform certain operations on the German state which would guarantee the peace and thus leave the United States without a permanent substantial commitment to maintain the European balance of power. It is understandable that, with the second bloody war against Germany in a generation coming to a close, men should think of the German problem in terms of certain pathological features in Germany's political and economic organization and hope that peace could be assured by their elimination. Nevertheless, there was a mixture of evasiveness and lack of historical perspective in the narrow and technocratic approach to German policy. Although the American failure to join the League of Nations had come widely to be recognized as a historic error, the nation did not explore the full implications of the post-1919 American failure to guarantee the independence of Eastern Europe and to give effective military guarantees to the French concerning German rearmament; and the relationship between future Soviet power and the nature of a German solution was not systematically considered, although it was, of course, not far from the surface of many American minds.

If there was an operating consensus in Washington, it was centered on the hope that there would be reached in the postwar world a general accord between the Soviet Union, Britain, and the United States; and that within the framework of this accord—which would assure the peace and avoid power rivalries in Europe and elsewhere—the Germans would be severely punished, disarmed for a substantial period if not permanently, possibly dismembered, and allowed to revive economically at a slower pace than Germany's victims.

There is no doubt that the implicit fundamental assumption behind the narrow American approach to German policy was that somehow a power struggle in Europe between the Soviet Union and the West would be avoided.

## 16. Poland

### GERMANY AND POLAND

While British and American military and diplomatic bureaucrats were wrestling with the German problem in terms of the details of administrative organization and of "hard" and "soft" occupation policies, the fate of post-war Germany was being settled in discussions among Churchill, Stalin, and Roosevelt which were ostensibly concerned with other matters and which came to center in a quite particular way on Poland. It is only a mild exaggeration to say that history decreed the split of Germany as a by-product of the struggle over Poland—as Poland had often been split as a by-product of the struggle between Germany and Russia.

The wartime effort to structure the postwar world moved to a climax in the course of three conferences: the Churchill-Stalin exchanges in Moscow in October 1944, the Yalta Conference in February 1945, and the Potsdam Conference in July 1945.

In a sense, the least well-known of these meetings—that of Churchill and Stalin in October 1944—was the most important. It exposed the heart of the issue of postwar organization of Europe and, given the subsequent course of American policy, it went far toward determining the outcome.

The subject of the Churchill-Stalin dialogue was Eastern Europe and the principles which would govern its postwar status. On the evening of Churchill's arrival in Moscow (October 9), he laid before Stalin his fateful proportional distribution of Anglo-Russian interest and influence in Eastern Europe:

> The moment was apt for business, so I said, 'Let us settle about our affairs in the Balkans. Your armies are in Rumania and Bulgaria. We have interests, missions, and agents there. Don't let us get at cross-purposes in small ways. So far as Britain and Russia are concerned, how would it do for you to have

ninety per cent of the say in Rumania, for us to have ninety per cent of the say in Greece, and go fifty-fifty about Yugoslavia?' While this was being translated I wrote out on a half-sheet of paper:

| | |
|---|---|
| Rumania | |
| Russia | 90% |
| The others | 10% |
| | |
| Greece | |
| Great Britain | 90% |
| (in accord with the United States) | |
| Russia | 10% |
| | |
| Yugoslavia | 50-50% |
| Hungary | 50-50% |
| Bulgaria | |
| Russia | 75% |
| The others | 25% |

I pushed this across to Stalin, who had by then heard the translation. There was a slight pause. Then he took his blue pencil and made a large tick upon it, and he passed it back to us. It was all settled in no more time than it takes to set down.

Of course, we had long and anxiously considered our point, and were only dealing with immediate war-time arrangements. All larger questions were reserved on both sides for what we then hoped would be a peace table when the war was won.[1]

In Churchill's mind there were clearly quite contradictory lines of thought. On the one hand, his percentages were designed to reflect degrees of legitimate long-run interest as between Britain and Russia in the areas concerned, and many centuries of history, in fact and in Churchill's mind, lay behind them. On the other hand, Churchill insisted that he regarded this proportioning of power only as a framework for immediate postwar action, not as a definitive settlement. As he cabled to his cabinet colleagues on October 12:

> It must be emphasized that this broad disclosure of Soviet and British feelings in the countries mentioned above is only an interim guide for the immediate wartime future, and will be surveyed by the Great Powers when they meet at the armistice or peace table to make a general settlement of Europe.[2]

In what way could these somewhat contradictory notions be reconciled? The answer lay in the question of Poland. It was Poland rather than Germany which was the center of the discussion about Europe's future at Moscow and at Yalta and, in a sense, also at Potsdam.

If Poland, like Rumania and Bulgaria, were to be fully dominated by Moscow, then there would be a continuous belt of Soviet political, military, and economic domination from the Curzon line to the western borders of the Soviet Zone in Germany. The split of Europe would be an accomplished fact from the beginning. If, however, Poland were to be in narrow security terms friendly with the Soviet Union but politically independent, then the possibility of a continuous Soviet bloc would be broken; a principle and precedent for the handling of Eastern Germany along Western democratic lines (despite Soviet occupation) might be established; and Moscow would have to look to the Western Allies for negotiations which would neutralize Germany as a future threat against the Soviet Union. On the disposition of Poland hinged the question of whether Moscow would or would not be in a position to threaten the whole European balance of power in the postwar.

What was involved in the Polish question, then, was not merely a fundamental ideological principle—free elections; not merely a testing ground for Moscow's intentions towards its allies in the postwar period; but also, strategically, a decisive piece of territory—the territory, in fact, whose invasion by Germany had convinced Britain and France to undertake a desperate Second World War. Churchill's proportions in the Balkans merely cleared the way for a show-down on Poland and the European power balance.

THE POLISH QUESTION: JUNE 1941-OCTOBER 1944

The Big Three negotiations on Poland of 1944-1945 took place against a long painful background of Russo-Polish history and in a specific setting of acute difficulty over Poland which began shortly after the German attack on the Soviet Union in June 1941.[3]

As a result of the Hitler-Stalin Pact, Russia had in 1939 occupied about half the area of Poland as then constituted. About 190,000 Polish officers and men were captured and held as Soviet prisoners; and about a million Poles were deported into Soviet forced labor from eastern Poland. This fourth partition of Poland, with its attendant brutality, led to acutely anti-Soviet attitudes within the Polish government in exile in London. Nevertheless, even before the German attack on the Soviet Union, the Polish Prime Minister in London, Sikorski, had begun to look to a Polish-Soviet rapprochement on the dual assumption that in the end Stalin would have to fight Hitler and that Polish independence from Moscow was not an issue on which the Western Allies would go to war with Stalin.

Thus, under active British pressure, but with some awareness that such was the only realistic course open, the Polish Government in London negotiated a treaty with Moscow in July 1941, reopened diplomatic relations, and began to order its affairs as an ally of a sort.

From these early negotiations in the summer of 1941 the touchstone of Polish-Soviet relations was taken by the Poles to be the question of Polish boundaries. The Poles sought to return to the pre-1939 boundaries, incorporated in the 1921 Treaty of Riga. Although the Riga line was short of maximum Polish claims to the east, it had been negotiated in the wake of a Soviet military set-back in a period of evident Soviet weakness. The Russians, with British acquiescence, left the way open in 1941 for a postwar return to the Curzon line, some distance to the west.

Churchill refused to accept the Polish view on the frontier question. He felt, in the raw calculus of war, that the Soviet Union was earning the right to a more advantageous western frontier than the Treaty of Riga provided; and in 1941-1944 he placed a high premium on establishing a basis in Big Three accord for a general postwar settlement into which an independent democratic Poland might fit in a new relation of understanding, if not of friendship, with Moscow. Churchill's position thus sharply separated the question of Polish boundaries from the question of Polish political independence. He urged the Poles to accept promptly a territorial settlement based on the Curzon Line in the east, with compensation from Germany in the west, and on this basis to move into working alliance with Moscow as the recognized government of Poland—thus establishing as a fact, in the heat of war, Polish political independence.

The Poles, by and large, refused to accept this distinction. They made the question of the boundaries the sole test of Soviet intentions and of Western support. In their hearts many Poles believed that the only serious basis for an independent Poland would be the military defeat of the Soviet Union by the Western Allies or its diplomatic equivalent, that any other formula was unrealistic, and that any concessions to Moscow were pointless.

Against this background of history and of outlook, Polish relations went well neither with Stalin nor with Churchill. General Anders was (probably) maneuvered by Stalin into withdrawing a large part of the Polish Army from Russia in 1942. Although the position of his army in Russia was awkward, even painful, the London government perceived the diplomatic advantage of having a substantial independent Polish army on the Eastern Front since it virtually guaranteed a form of Soviet recognition of the London government. In 1943 the attenuated Polish-Soviet diplomatic relations were broken over the question of the Katyn massacre. At Teheran, Churchill formally broached with Stalin the notion of a double westward shift in the Polish borders, forcing the hand of the Polish Government in London; but he was unable to persuade the Poles to reopen diplomatic relations with Moscow on this basis. And in the course of 1944 Moscow began to develop an essentially Communist Polish government in Russia, the so-called Lublin Committee, which had been first organized as far back as December 1941.

Thus by October 1944 the Polish question could be fought out only on the question of the democratic constitution of a future Polish government;

and this issue had been corrupted to a degree by Stalin's progressively more overt commitment to the Lublin Poles.

On October 11, 1944, in Moscow, Churchill drafted a letter to Stalin in order to clarify the thought underlying his Balkan percentages. This letter was never sent; but it is, perhaps, the most clear and explicit expression both of the considerations in Churchill's mind at this stage and of the fundamental issues of statesmanship confronted by the West. It is worth quoting in some detail:

> Moscow, October 11, 1944
>
> I deem it profoundly important that Britain and Russia should have a common policy in the Balkans which is also acceptable to the United States. The fact that Britain and Russia have a twenty-year alliance makes it especially important for us to be in broad accord and to work together easily and trustfully and for a long time. I realize that nothing we can do here can be more than preliminary to the final decisions we shall have to take when all three of us are gathered together at the table of victory. Nevertheless, I hope that we may reach understandings, and in some cases agreements, which will help us through immediate emergencies, and will afford a solid foundation for long-enduring world peace.
>
> These percentages which I have put down are no more than a method by which in our thoughts we can see how near we are together, and then decide upon the necessary steps to bring us into full agreement. As I said, they would be considered crude, and even callous, if they were exposed to the scrutiny of the Foreign Offices and diplomats all over the world. Therefore they could not be the basis of any public document, certainly not at the present time. They might, however, be a good guide for the conduct of our affairs. If we manage these affairs well we shall perhaps prevent several civil wars and much bloodshed and strife in the small countries concerned. Our broad principle should be to let every country have the form of government which its people desire. We certainly do not wish to force on any Balkan State monarchic or republican institutions. We have however established certain relations of faithfulness with the Kings of Greece and Yugoslavia. They have sought our shelter from the Nazi foe, and we think that when normal tranquility is re-established and the enemy has been driven out the peoples of these countries should have a free and fair chance of choosing. It might even be that Commissioners of the three Great Powers should be stationed there at the time of the elections so as to see that the people have a genuine free choice. There are good precedents for this.
>
> However, besides the institutional question there exists in all these countries the ideological issue between totalitarian forms of government and those we call free enterprise controlled by universal suffrage. We are very glad that you have declared yourselves against trying to change by force or by Communist propaganda the established systems in the various Balkan countries. Let them work out their own fortunes during the years that lie ahead. One thing how-

ever we cannot allow—Fascism or Nazism in any of their forms, which give to the toiling masses neither the securities offered by your system nor those offered by ours, but, on the contrary, lead to the build-up of tyrannies at home and aggression abroad. In principle, I feel that Great Britain and Russia should feel easy about the internal government of these countries, and not worry about them or interfere with them once conditions of tranquility have been restored after this terrible blood-bath which they, and indeed we, have all been through.

It is from this point of view that I have sought to adumbrate the degrees of interest which each of us takes in these countries with the full assent of the other, and subject to the approval of the United States, which may go far away for a long time and then come back again unexepectedly with gigantic strength.

In writing to you, with your experience and wisdom, I do not need to go through a lot of arguments. Hitler has tried to exploit the fear of an aggressive, proselyting Communism which exists throughout Western Europe, and he is being decisively beaten to the ground. But, as you know well, this fear exists in every country, because, whatever the merits of our different systems, no country wishes to go through the bloody revolution which will certainly be necessary in nearly every case before so drastic a change could be made in the life, habits, and outlook of their society. We feel we were right in interpreting your dissolution of the Comintern as a decision by the Soviet Government not to interfere in the internal political affairs of other countries. The more this can be established in people's minds the smoother everything will go. We, on the other hand, and I am sure the United States as well, have governments which stand on very broad bases, where privilege and class are under continual scrutiny and correction. We have the feeling that, viewed from afar and on a grand scale, the differences between our systems will tend to get smaller, and the great common ground which we share of making life richer and happier for the mass of the people is growing every year. Probably if there were peace for fifty years the differences which now might cause much grave troubles to the world would become matters for academic discussion.

At this point, Mr. Stalin, I want to impress upon you the great desire there is in the heart of Britain for a long, stable friendship and cooperation between our two countries, and that with the United States we shall be able to keep the world engine on the rails.[4]

Essentially, then, Churchill was asking the Soviet Union to separate sharply its legitimate national security interests in the structure of Europe from its Bolshevik interest in imposing on other states forms of governments similar to that in the Soviet Union. He was asking the Soviet Union to play a powerful role in Europe as a major military power, but to apply a strict self-discipline in ideological matters. In short, he was asking Stalin to behave as a Russian, not as a Communist. Churchill foresaw that the possibility of postwar Big Three accord hinged on such behavior; and from October 1944 to the day he left Potsdam as a defeated politician his central purpose was to induce the United States to use its full military power—before demobilization—to force Stalin to opt for this choice as the best alternative realistically open to him.

It is clear that Stalin did not share Churchill's vision. He was thinking in terms of the most immediate and concrete issues of short-run power, in which security issues and the extension of Moscow's domain through subservient Communist grouping were inextricably mixed. On October 22 Churchill included in a cable to Roosevelt the following summary of the final discussion:

> Later, at my request, Stalin saw Mikolajczyk and had an hour and a half's very friendly talk. Stalin promised to help him, and Mikolajczyk promised to form and conduct a Government thoroughly friendly to the Russians. He explained his plan, but Stalin made it clear that the Lublin Poles must have the majority.
>
> After the Kremlin dinner we put it bluntly to Stalin that unless Milkolajczyk had fifty-fifty plus himself the Western World would not be convinced that the transaction was *bona fide* and would not believe that an independent Polish Government had been set up. Stalin at first replied he would be content with fifty-fifty, but rapidly corrected himself to a worse figure. Meanwhile, Eden took the same line with Molotov, who seemed more comprehending. I do not think the composition of the Government will prove an insuperable obstacle if all else is settled. Mikolajczyk had previously explained to me that there might be one announcement to save the prestige of the Lublin Government and a different arrangement among the Poles behind the scenes. . . .
>
> We also discussed informally the future partition of Germany. U. J. [Uncle Joe] wants Poland, Czechoslovakia, and Hungary to form a realm of independent, anti-Nazi, pro-Russian states, the first two of which might join together. Contrary to his previously expressed view, he would be glad to see Vienna the capital of a federation of South German States, including Austria, Bavaria, Wurttemberg, and Baden. As you know, the idea of Vienna becoming the capital of a large Danubian federation has always been attractive to me, though I should prefer to add Hungary, to which U. J. is strongly opposed.
>
> As to Prussia, U. J. wished the Ruhr and the Saar detached and put out of action and probably under international control, and a separate state formed in the Rhineland. He would also like the internationalization of the Kiel Canal. I am not opposed to this line of thought. However, you may be sure that we came to no fixed conclusions pending the triple meeting.[5]

It was evident that Stalin intended to press Moscow's influence hard in Warsaw and elsewhere, and that he looked to a fragmentation of power in Central Europe. Although the issue of intimate Communist control was explicitly raised only in the references to the Lublin group, Soviet behavior in Eastern Europe toward the end of 1944 made it reasonably clear that Stalin's policy was to extend Moscow's power as far west and in as intimate a form as Western opposition permitted. The exchanges provided no grounds for believing that Stalin had accepted the posture of a major military power "easy and unworried" about the internal governments of European states; and this was not because of Stalin's ideological devotion to communism but because the Eastern European Communists (except Tito) were reliable agents of Moscow's authority. Stalin had long since converted the international Communist movement into an instrument of his personal power; and it was to the maximum feasible extension of that power that he looked.

While Churchill and Stalin were indecisively exchanging views and forming *de facto* agreements on these matters, Roosevelt was in Washington. In October the presidential campaign was moving to a climax, and Hull resigned. Concrete issues of the postwar were emerging in the wake of advancing armies all over Europe. It was the reality and inescapable quality of these issues—and most notably the issue raised by the Red Army's advance into Poland—which had led to the Churchill-Stalin meeting; but it was impossible, given the American electoral process, for Roosevelt to attend. Preoccupied with other matters, his first instinct was "to avoid all semblance of American participation or even interest in the Moscow meetings by sending vague messages to Churchill and to Stalin merely wishing them good luck."[6] Hopkins stopped the dispatch of a cable which would, in effect, have permitted Churchill to speak for the United States as well as Britain; and, as the result of this intervention, Roosevelt explicitly informed Stalin and Churchill that pending the Big Three meeting which was already planned to follow upon the American election he reserved full freedom of action on all matters discussed. But the pattern of Churchill's percentages bit deep in Stalin's mind; and, whatever formal freedom of action the United States reserved, the October meeting of Churchill and Stalin left a permanent mark on events, subsequently inhibiting American as well as British diplomacy.

YALTA

At Yalta many issues were discussed: the terms and timing of Soviet entrance into the war against Japan, the organizational structure of the United Nations, the role of France in the occupation of Germany and in the negotiation of a German settlement, the principle of German dismemberment, German reparations, and the procedures for joint occupation. But it was Poland that dominated the proceedings, Churchill reports:

> Poland was discussed at no fewer than seven of the eight plenary meetings of the Yalta Conference, and the British record contains an interchange on this topic of nearly eighteen thousand words between Stalin, Roosevelt, and myself.[7]

Despite a series of Anglo-American diplomatic difficulties and cross-purposes in the months preceding the Yalta Conference—most notably over Greece—Roosevelt and Churchill worked together effectively during the meetings. In terms of their overlapping, but not identical, vision of the problem, they achieved a remarkable success; for they committed Stalin to the principle of early free elections in Poland and prevented a prompt movement of the Lublin Government to domination in Warsaw. Moreover, the Yalta communique contained the famous passage:

> To foster the conditions in which the liberated peoples may exercise these rights, the three governments will jointly assist the people in any European liberated state or former Axis satellite state in Europe where in their judgment conditions require (a) to establish conditions of internal peace; (b) to carry out emergency measures for the relief of distressed people; (c) to form interim governmental authorities broadly representative of all democratic elements in the population and pledged to the earliest possible establishment through free elections of governments responsive to the will of the people; and (d) to facilitate where necessary the holding of such elections.[8]

It was evident that only strong and united insistence by Roosevelt and Churchill had achieved the statement of these points so obviously contrary to Communist ambition and practice. That statement provided as clear a basis for further Anglo-American policy in Europe as diplomacy could afford. If Poland was to be politically free, then the balance of power in Europe would remain clearly beyond Moscow's grasp, and Germany could be dealt with in terms of a continuing common interest among the wartime allies to avoid a resurgent Germany. If Poland passed under Communist domination and became an active instrument of Soviet power, then the Soviet zone of occupation assumed a new, different, and more sinister role, the European balance of power was endangered for the West, and the competition for Germany between two power blocs—of which the opponents of dismemberment had warned since 1942—was inevitable. At Yalta the latter possibility was forestalled and the door held open for a German settlement in the spirit of Big Three unity.

It is impossible to read the memoirs and transcripts of Yalta, to reconstruct the time and place and personages, the intimate human by-play, the toasts and gestures, without understanding the sense of achievement and confidence that Churchill and Roosevelt brought back to their peoples. It was at Yalta that the hard-headed Hopkins passed a note to Roosevelt saying: "The Russians have given so much at this conference that I don't think we should let them down";[9] and, given Anglo-American objectives and the American top-level military view of prospects in the war against Japan, this was the case.

There were also ample grounds for concern in the light of the Yalta discussions. There was the insistent unresolved Soviet demand for $10 billion in German reparations. There was the dour struggle over Poland, with the limited opportunities afforded for direct Anglo-American contact with Poland

and the awkward problems posed by the new Polish boundaries. There was a haze of ambiguity both about the future of Germany and about the future Soviet role in the Far East during, and especially after, the war with Japan. And—perhaps for Stalin as much as for Churchill—there was the great question mark—the United States.

Roosevelt was evidently a very tired and quite possibly failing man; and, as Churchill rightly characterized it, he had made a "momentous"—but false —prediction about his country at the first Yalta session: namely, that, although the United States would take all reasonable steps to preserve peace, it would not keep a large army in Europe, and its occupation of Germany could be envisaged for only two years. This image of foreseeable American withdrawal from the European arena, reinforced by the evident possibility that Roosevelt himself might soon be removed from the scene, stirred Soviet hopes and British fears, giving to the Yalta agreements as a whole an interim, transitory character. The adversaries were merely sparring, awaiting a later test of strength.

On the face of it, Yalta moved the Western vision of the postwar world a step closer to reality. That vision failed because in 1945-1946 Britain and the United States were not prepared to make its achievement a life-or-death objective. Although the possibility of a free democratic Europe back to the Curzon line, a Europe kept at peace by Big Three security accords, was not definitely lost until a later time, the seeds of this failure can be detected beneath the surface at Yalta. They lay in the difference between Churchill's and Roosevelt's approach to the question of Eastern Europe. The two men were united in pressing the issue of a free Poland, but their reasoning differed in degree. To Churchill—but not necessarily the British Foreign Office—Eastern Europe mattered in itself. He understood in his bones the power structure of the European continent. He knew that a Soviet Union which commanded the territory between the Curzon Line and the Elbe would immediately succeed to Hitler, the Kaiser, Napoleon, and the long line of those who, by threatening the European balance of power, threatened British survival. For Churchill the outcome in Poland meant virtually the difference between victory and stalemate—if not defeat—in the Second World War. To Americans the issue of Poland was important, but in a vaguer, less visceral way. When he thought of Poland, Roosevelt thought less of the European balance of power than of more general questions: could the Soviet word be trusted; could Big Three accord be maintained; and, above all, could the United Nations work? He thought also of Polish voting blocs in American cities, and of the sentimental but still real aura of American responsibility that followed Wilson's role in creating the independent states of Eastern Europe after the First

World War. To Churchill Poland was crucial; to Roosevelt it was important, but not serious.

The death knell of Western hopes for the postwar can be read in this passage from the Department of State's position paper on Poland prepared for Yalta; for that document accurately reflected the lack of conviction in American minds that Poland mattered greatly to the American interest:

Briefing Book Paper:    RECONSTRUCTION OF POLAND AND THE BALKANS:
                        AMERICAN INTERESTS AND SOVIET ATTITUDE

1.   Interests of the United States:   political

. . . It now seems clear that the Soviet Union will exert predominant political influence over the areas in question. While this Government probably would not want to oppose itself to such a political configuration, neither would it desire to see American influence in this part of the world completely nullified.[10]

Of one stage at Yalta, Churchill reports as follows:

The President was now anxious to end the discussion. "Poland," he remarked, "has been a source of trouble for over five hundred years."

"All the more," I answered, "must we do what we can to put an end to these troubles." We then adjourned.[11]

Roosevelt was expressing a typical American view, as postwar diplomacy toward Poland under Truman and Eisenhower was to reveal. The underlying difference in sense of priority and urgency implicit in this Anglo-American exchange was soon to have its consequences.

YALTA TO POTSDAM

On February 27, 1945, the day when Churchill was defending the Yalta accord before the House of Commons, Vyshinsky, then First Deputy Commissar of Soviet Foreign Affairs, ordered King Michael of Rumania to dismiss the government he had formed; and on March 2 a Soviet-dominated regime took over, backed by Soviet military force. Churchill, hamstrung by the percentages agreed at the October 1944 conference in Moscow, felt unable to do more than protest weakly; but, more than ever, the importance of Poland rose in his mind.

In the United States as well, uneasiness about the Yalta decisions and future relations with Moscow grew rapidly in the first few weeks of March. In part this uneasiness derived from the voting procedures agreed for the United Nations, which were made known on March 5. Both the veto in the Security Council and the multiple votes granted in the Soviet Union were defensible, but the rationale for them was not well presented. More important, what was going on in Rumania was as disturbing in the United States as it was in Great Britain; and then it became known that Molotov did not

plan to come to the San Francisco Conference, which increased public uneasiness and confirmed within the government the impression that the United
Nations did not enjoy in the minds of the Soviet leaders the importance
attached to it by Americans. Finally, against this background, a most serious
deadlock developed among the British, Russian, and American negotiators in
Moscow who had been assigned at Yalta the task of agreeing on the composition of a Provisional Polish Government. Molotov simply sat tight in the face
of British and American pressure, urging that the Lublin government should
represent Poland at the United Nations Conference and stalling all efforts to
enlarge its composition to include non-Communist elements.

In the light of the events and negotiations of the previous seven months,
the troubles over Poland were recognized by both Roosevelt and by Churchill
as a matter of first importance. From March 8 to April 11—the day before
Roosevelt died—the Polish issue was the subject of numerous exchanges
among Churchill, Roosevelt, and Stalin. Roosevelt and Churchill sought to
force the entrance of democratic elements into the government. Stalin, holding the trump card of the Red Army's presence in Poland, kept the negotiations going on the basis of minimum modification in the Lublin base. Each
day that passed gave the Lublin government the possibility of strengthening
its hold on the country.

Although London and Washington moved together on the Polish question,
the underlying difference in emphasis and priority persisted. Soviet and Western armies were moving rapidly across the face of Germany. Issues rose as to
how this climactic campaign should be conducted and whether Western
military strength and dispositions should be used to maximize the diplomatic
bargaining position of the West vis-à-vis Moscow. The first such question
arose toward the end of March and concerned Eisenhower's plan for the final
offensive against Germany. Eisenhower wished to detach the Ninth Army from
the Twenty-First (Montgomery's) Army group and thrust hard across the
south of Germany to minimize the possibilities of a last-ditch German re-
doubt being formed up. Churchill argued strongly for maintaining momentum
in the North, for leaving the Ninth U.S. Army Group with Montgomery, and
for getting the Western forces into Berlin before the arrival of Soviet troops.
Churchill believed that it mattered greatly that Western forces shake Soviet
hands as far east as possible; and he was angered that Eisenhower had determined the shape of the final offensive and communicated it to Stalin without
consulting either the British members of his staff or those politically responsible for British and American policy. Eisenhower and the American military
in Washington made their decision on tactical grounds, their view being that
Berlin no longer mattered militarily or politically.

It was at this stage, in the gathering gloom of the post-Yalta situation, that

Roosevelt died. Roosevelt had shared Churchill's anxiety and concern with the development of Soviet attitudes ever since the Yalta conference; but, whereas Churchill had felt that the issue must be put to the test as soon as possible or all would be lost in Poland and elsewhere, Roosevelt had argued for patience in applying presure on Stalin and had seemed less eager for an early showdown.

Roosevelt's mixture of deep concern and reluctance to force the issue of Western-Soviet relations is illustrated clearly by two of his last communications with Churchill.

> We shall have to consider most carefully the implications of Stalin's attitude [on Poland] and what is to be our next step. I shall, of course, take no action of any kind nor make any statement without consulting you, and I know you will do the same. (April 11)[12]

> We must be firm however, and our course thus far is correct. (April 12)[13]

It was evident in the exchanges with Roosevelt during the President's last two weeks that Churchill was anxious to use the full weight that the Allies could then bring to bear on Moscow—including the American military weight that Roosevelt had stated at Yalta would be gone from Europe in two years— to make sure that the diplomatic commitments made by Stalin at Yalta would be honored.

Within a week of assuming office, Truman was plunged fully into the problem of Allied relations with the Soviet Union and had assumed a position consistent with the hardening mood of Roosevelt in his final weeks. Specifically, Truman faced the question of Poland and whether or not the military disposition of British and American forces should be used in the effort to make the Yalta agreements stick.

On April 18 Truman received from Churchill a cable urging that the Allied armies hold their positions as far east as possible until the diplomatic position was clarified. On April 20 Harriman, in Washington from Moscow to brief the new President, explained the general character of the difficulties which had developed with Moscow and the unresolved issue of a balanced interim Polish government. On April 23 Truman reviewed with his principal diplomatic and military advisers the whole question of relations with the Soviet Union; and later that afternoon he handed to Molotov an extremely strong message to be transmitted to Stalin, insisting that the Yalta decision on Poland be carried out, bluntly insisting to Molotov that the Soviet Union was acting in violation of the Yalta accord. Truman reports that exchange as ending:

" 'I have never been talked to like that in my life,' Molotov said.

"I told him, 'Carry out your agreements and you won't get talked to like this.' "[14]

When this message failed to yield results, Truman sent Hopkins to Moscow on May 23 in an effort to end the impasse with the Soviet Union on the question of Poland and to clear up other issues which threatened the United Nations organization and the joint occupation of Germany. Within their limits, these initiatives succeeded. Hopkins got Stalin to agree that a Polish government of national unity be formed, including Mikolajczyk as Vice-Premier, with three additional ministries granted to non-Lublin Poles acceptable to Great Britain and the United States. With this (and several lesser) concessions, the ground was cleared for the Big Three meeting at Potsdam.

At Potsdam the recognition of the reorganized Polish Provisional Government (granted by the United States on July 5) was confirmed; and agreement was made to hold free and unfettered elections on the basis of universal suffrage and secret ballot, with guarantees of access to the world press to report events before and during the elections.

In a sense, then, Truman's diplomacy on Poland in the first four months of his administration appeared to have moved the Polish question forward in terms of the Yalta agreement. However, in the year and a half following Potsdam, Moscow-dominated Communists took over Poland in successive stages, climaxed by the rigged election of February 1947; and in the autumn of 1947 Mikolajczyk, long since rendered politically impotent, fled the country to avoid arrest.

The story of this American and British failure belongs to the postwar years, but its roots can be detected in the radical differences of Churchillian and American attitudes in the spring of 1945. On May 12 Churchill dispatched the following cable to Truman:

> I am profoundly concerned about the European situation. I learn that half the American Air Force in Europe has already begun to move to the Pacific theatre. The newspapers are full of the great movements of the American armies out of Europe. Our armies also are, under previous arrangements, likely to undergo a marked reduction. The Canadian Army will certainly leave. The French are weak and difficult to deal with. Anyone can see that in a very short space of time our armed power on the Continent will have vanished, except for moderate forces to hold down Germany.
>
> Meanwhile what is to happen about Russia? I have always worked for friendship with Russia, but, like you, I feel deep anxiety because of their mis-interpretation of the Yalta decisions, their attitude towards Poland, their overwhelming influence in the Balkans, excepting Greece, the difficulties they make about Vienna, the combination of Russian power and the territories under their control or occupied, coupled with the Communist technique in so many other countries, and above all their power to maintain very large armies in the field for a long time. What will be the position in a year or two,

when the British and American Armies have melted and the French has not yet been formed on any major scale, when we may have a handful of divisions, mostly French, and when Russia may choose to keep two or three hundred on active service?

An iron curtain is drawn down upon their front. We do not know what is going on behind. There seems little doubt that the whole of the regions east of the line Lubeck-Trieste-Corfu will soon be completely in their hands. To this must be added the further enormous area conquered by the American armies between Eisenach and the Elbe, which will, I suppose, in a few weeks be occupied, when the Americans retreat, by the Russian power. All kinds of arrangements will have to be made by General Eisenhower to prevent another immense flight of the German population westward as this enormous Muscovite advance into the center of Europe takes place. And then the curtain will descend again to a very large extent, if not entirely. Thus a broad band of many hundreds of miles of Russian-occupied territory will isolate us from Poland.

Meanwhile the attention of our peoples will be occupied in inflicting severities upon Germany, which is ruined and prostrate, and it would be open to the Russians in a very short time to advance if they chose to the waters of the North Sea and the Atlantic.

Surely it is vital now to come to an understanding with Russia, or see where we are with her, before we weaken our armies mortally or retire to the zones of occupation. This can only be done by a personal meeting. I should be most grateful for your opinion and advice. Of course we may take the view that Russia will behave impeccably, and no doubt that offers the most convenient solution. To sum up, this issue of a settlement with Russia before our strength has gone seems to me to dwarf all others.[15]

Truman's *Memoirs*, besides reflecting the priority then accorded the Japanese war and a neo-Wilsonian view of the United Nations as a substitute for power politics, exhibit his lack of conviction that Eastern Europe really mattered.

I was trying to be extremely careful not to get us mixed up in a Balkan turmoil. The Balkans had long been a source of trouble and war. I believed that if the political situation in the Balkans could be adjusted so that Hungary, Yugoslavia, Rumania and Bulgaria, as well as Poland and Austria, could all have governments of their own people's choosing, with no outside interference, this would help us in our plans for peace.

I did not want to become involved in the Balkans in a way that could lead us into another world conflict. In any case, I was anxious to get the Russians into the war against Japan as soon as possible, thus saving the lives of countless Americans.

Churchill, on the other hand, was always anxious to do what he could to save British control of the Eastern Mediterranean area in order to maintain Great Britain's influence in Greece, Egypt, and the Middle East. I could not blame Churchill for the position he took. Had I been in his place, I might probably have been inclined to do as he wanted to do.

General Marshall and I, in discussing each military phase, agreed that if we were to win the peace after winning the war, we had to have Russian help. I was trying to get Churchill in a frame of mind to forget the old power politics and get a United Nations organization to work.[16]

For Churchill the European balance of power—that is, the meaning of victory—was at stake in Poland; for Americans—as Hopkins explained to Stalin—"Poland was only a symbol."[17]

All of these differences in history and perspective lay behind Truman's insistence on June 12 that the Allied troops withdraw to the agreed zones of occupation despite Churchill's final plea that they hold their forward positions until Stalin moved on the Polish and other unresolved questions. Truman was urged to take this course by both the American professional military and by Stimson.

In the case of the military in the field, Eisenhower consistently took the view he expressed in April, ". . . I do not quite understand why the Prime Minister has been so determined to intermingle political and military considerations."[18] At no stage did anyone take the trouble to explain to Eisenhower the strategic significance of the Polish question and the state of the Moscow negotiation; and he had ample tactical reasons for getting his troops neatly back to agreed zonal areas.

Behind Eisenhower, and close to Truman, there were Marshall and Stimson. Operationally their minds were fixed on the forthcoming offensive against Japan, the difficulty of which was grossly overrated. Beyond that, these men and their staffs did not share Churchill's view of the decisive importance of Poland. In Truman's important meeting with his advisers on April 23, immediately before his interview with Molotov, Stimson counseled caution on Poland:

> Mr. Stimson then said he would like to know how far the Russian reaction to a strong position on Poland would go. He said he thought that the Russians perhaps were being more realistic than we were in regard to their own security.[19]

And deeper thoughts, whether right or wrong, lay behind this view. Whereas Churchill felt clear in his mind that only a show of Anglo-American force and determination would persuade Stalin to seek security by collective means and forego total political domination in the areas held by the Red Army, those responsible for the American military establishment were unwilling to face a showdown until a longer test had been made of Soviet intentions and of the possibility of living with the Russians in Europe and elsewhere without the tension of an unending test of strength. Stimson felt, in a sense, that if the Russians were being admitted into the club of world powers—to him a kind of international Skull and Bones—they ought to be treated like gentlemen; and that, for a trial period at least, it should be assumed that they were pressing their interests within limits that ultimately respected the rules of the Big Three game. And in the Control Council in Berlin, from the very beginning, Eisenhower, Clay, and their staff made extraordinary efforts at human and national reconciliation.

It is still too soon to say that this display of patience and human decency failed to leave an important mark on history through its impact on Soviet military leaders and on the Soviet technicians and bureaucrats who staffed the Control Council in Berlin. At the minimum, it permitted the United States in 1947 to turn to the struggle against the Soviet Union in good conscience, without moral grounds for self-reproach. But when all this is said, it still remains true that the American military and their civil leadership failed to appreciate the significance for the American interest of the disposition of Poland (and Eastern Europe generally); and that, in insisting on a clean separation of military from political policy, they contributed substantially to the split of Germany and Europe and to the onset of the Cold War.

Down to Potsdam the differences in perspective between London and Washington were probably not decisive; that is, even with hindsight, it is hard to see that the maintenance of Western forces east of the zonal lines could have achieved more on Poland than did Hopkins' negotiation with Stalin. London and Washington had chosen to fight the Polish issue on the question of the composition of the interim Polish government; and on this they gained apparently important concessions in the summer of 1945. If the issue had been fought on the question of a prompt free election, the result might have been different; and, after all, at Yalta Stalin had said a free election might be possible in a month. But that course had been long since ruled out. Moreover, both Churchill and Truman felt inhibited by the Churchill-Stalin percentages of October 1944 from forcing the issue of the Yalta Declaration elsewhere in Eastern Europe.

It was in the year and a half after Potsdam rather than in the nine months before that Poland and a European settlement in the Western interest were lost. What this wartime phase revealed was that those responsible for American policy lacked conceptions of national interest and objective capable of avoiding a split of Germany and the European continent on the Elbe.

With the failure promptly and decisively to enforce the Yalta decision in Poland, the arena of negotiation shifted to Berlin and the question of German unity. Although valiant efforts were made by the American negotiators, by the spring of 1946 that initiative too had failed; and in the year that followed, the concept of a desperate continuing struggle along the boundary of a split Germany and Europe was accepted on all sides. All the wartime debates—on "hard" versus "soft" policies toward Germany, on unity versus dismemberment—were lost in the mists. They could have mattered only if American policy had been determined to enforce on Stalin as his best option a politically free Europe held secure by collective arrangements; and Poland was the area for the showdown. At no one point in Washington was such a conception formulated, not even by those who wisely warned of the dangers of German and European schism. Lacking adequate concepts and policies, the tactical arrangements for the occupation of a defeated Germany set the terms for the great continental struggle which persists down to the present.

## 17. Asia

### ASIA AND THE NATIONAL INTEREST

In Asia as in Europe the conduct of the Second World War and the underlying concepts which helped shape its course compromised the possibility of maintaining the Eurasian balance of power to Western advantage in the postwar years. Although the results in the two Eurasian theaters were similar, the sources of failure in Asia were somewhat different from those in Europe.

In Europe the United States was fighting Germany for the second time, and fighting once again as the ally of Britain and of those elements on the continent capable of resisting German hegemony. More than that, the United States had available what it believed to be the lessons of the First World War and its aftermath; and from unconditional surrender (Casablanca) to reparations in kind (Potsdam) American decisions were strongly colored by an effort to avoid repeating what were regarded as mistakes of 1917-1920.

The war in the Pacific was at once both a newer and more traditional national experience. The nation had never fought a major war in Asia; but positive American concepts of national interest in Asia were older than any linking the United States actively to Europe. Those concepts, however, reflected two views of the American interest which had never been clearly related to each other in American thought or policy. One view assumed an American interest that the balance of power in the whole Asian arena, including the Chinese mainland, not fall into the hands of a single power potentially or actually hostile to the United States. Certain of Mahan's writings supported this view, and it was ultimately the rational basis for the policy of an Open Door in China. It was in terms of some such view that Theodore Roosevelt wielded his influence in the Portsmouth negotiations of 1905.

The second view asserted an American interest that the nation's own naval strength be capable of controlling the sea approaches to the United States against any other naval power in the Pacific. It was essentially on this latter doctrine that the American Navy had taken its stand between the two wars and on which it had based its war planning in the interwar years.

The two doctrines of naval and mainland interests could be linked in a single formulation: the achievement of hegemony on the mainland of Eurasia, either East or West, would give to any single power a military potential, including a naval potential, sufficient to threaten the American control of the sea approaches to the American continent. Twice in a generation the German threat to continued control of the Atlantic by Anglo-American forces made such a formulation in regard to Europe persuasive in the American mind. However, the link was made in Europe not in obedience to a logical theory of the national interest but in reaction to a crisis situation; and the crisis in Asia arose in a form which did not link the American theories of mainland and naval interest.

The United States demonstrated in the decade after 1931 that it did not judge the question of who controlled the China mainland a matter of major national interest. The nation's commitment to the Open Door in China proved weak when put to the test. The United States failed to aid China effectively at any time from the Japanese invasion of Manchuria to Pearl Harbor. Whereas the United States had revealed in 1917 and again in 1940-1941 an innate sense that it was threatened if a single power threatened to control the Western Eurasian mainland, the American behavior toward China in the pre-Pearl Harbor decade indicated that there was no equivalent sense of American interest on the eastern Eurasian mainland.

The relative American complacency concerning the Asian mainland had its foundations in several particular circumstances. In the interwar period only Japan appeared to threaten the balance of power in Asia, both by creating a navy potentially hostile to the United States and by actually using its strength to build a dominating mainland position. The Soviet Union was apparently so passive or even defensive after the Chinese Communist debacle in 1927 that American thinking attached little importance to the Russian role in the Asian balance of power. The result of the total concentration of American thought on the apparent menace in Japan was a persistent obscurity in the American definition of its Asian mainland interests.

Equally important, the United States failed to sense the character and pace of the Asian revolution against colonialism and the long-run meaning for American interests of the passionate desire of the Asians to modernize their societies and to create strong dignified national states. In consequence, those areas embracing more than a billion citizens of the world, with their populations growing rapidly, were underrated in their importance to the American interest despite the growing evidence that in a not too distant future their political and military orientation would matter greatly to the United States.

Roosevelt was, of course, aware of the profound currents stirring in Asia. And this awareness was reflected to some extent in his sporadic initiatives during the war against continued colonialism. For example, he and Hull steadily made known their view that India should receive its independence. Roosevelt several times expressed opposition to a return to French colonial rule in Indochina, but he failed to take any action to prevent the return of French troops.

Only at the abstract level of United Nations institutions and pronouncements and in its direct relations with the Philippines did the United States generate unambiguous policies. On the whole, American wartime policy leaned toward an acceleration of the movement toward independence; but Roosevelt's instinct that the United States should reckon with a new nationalist momentum in Asia, the Middle East, and Africa was never made a major criterion of the American interest or developed into workable policies. Looking at the Asian mainland, with its limited military potential, unformed national politics, and social backwardness, the easy and convenient short-run course during the war was to regard Japan as the sole American problem of major significance and to leave the rest of Asia policy for the future.

The upshot was the following:

1. The war against Japan was conducted as if the total military defeat of Japan were the sole national objective.

2. Policy toward China was almost wholly limited to inducing a maximum contribution from China toward the military defeat of Japan.

3. A policy of elevating the international stature of Nationalist China and of aiding China in an effort to achieve postwar integrity was pursued in high diplomacy; but the United States did not devote the thought, energy, and resources necessary to assure the maximum possibility that those goals would be achieved.

4. In Indochina, Indonesia, and elsewhere in Asia the significance for American interests of the pace of the Asian revolution was sensed; but the nation did not formulate policies capable of avoiding costly postwar schisms within the non-Communist world and awkward American postures toward them—most notably, of course, in Indochina.

### THE CHINA PROBLEM

When the Chinese Nationalists fell back on Chungking, they were cut off from their major source of strength, the coastal cities, and the government had to make terms with the local authorities in Szechwan. The morale of the Kuomintang deteriorated as frustrated men, including some generals, turned to enterprises of private power intrigue and financial advantage; and the Nationalist armies, incapable of dealing head-on with the Japanese threat, jockeyed to hold territory from the expanding Communist movement in the North. Chiang Kai-shek, frustrated and oppressed in his narrow circle, fell back in reliance on men personally attached to him, many of whom were of limited competence and integrity, and he lost the banners and spirit of the Chinese national revolution which he had managed to carry forward against grave internal and external difficulties in the decade after 1928.[1]

The Nationalists evidently needed the most careful and sustained support in every dimension if they were to emerge as the effective leaders of China and as a major force on the world scene.

## STILWELL'S MISSION

But in Washington, even in terms of military priority, Chiang's problems were judged a "poor third," after the claims of the war against Germany and the direct assault on Japan.[2] Nevertheless, the United States opened a route of supply to Chungking via air lift and, later, the Burma Road; and it assigned in General Stilwell a remarkable officer to assist in making the Chinese Nationalists a more effective fighting force. If ever a job required a soldier and diplomat, it was that assigned to Stilwell. In fact, a reasonable case can be made out for the impossibility of this assignment—that is, the impossibility of exercising Stillwell's functions as Chief of Staff to Chiang within the tangled web of politics that enmeshed the whole Nationalist military establishment.

In retrospect three things are clear. First, Stilwell lacked diplomatic and human tact in his immensely complex relations with Chiang. Second, Stilwell's task, strictly within the context of the Second World War, was not sympathetically understood and backed in Washington outside the War Department. Third, the problem of military reform of Chiang's armies and his administration for the future role the United States had staked out for him in China and on the world scene was not given the attention and the priority it deserved.

Stilwell's wartime mission was the forerunner of a type of mixed political-military problem—the problem of helping underdeveloped nations make the transition to modern status within the orbit of the democratic world—of which the United States was to see much in the postwar years. The American wartime performance revealed both a lack of awareness of the importance of the task in the American interest and an inability to use the American margin of influence effectively by a mixture of military and political means. If the United States attached serious importance in its own interest to the emergence of a strong China unified under the Nationalists, then the mission assigned to a dedicated professional soldier should have been backed strongly by civil policy in Washington and first-rate civilians on the China scene. As it was, when the complex crisis over Stilwell came to a head in October 1944, Roosevelt was satisfied to settle for Chiang's continued resistance in the war, at a low ebb of effectiveness, and the continuation of a political and military apparatus that made the future of the Nationalist government in postwar China doubtful indeed.

## A "LIMITED COMMITMENT"

With Stilwell's withdrawal from China, Stimson notes: "China became . . . a definitely limited commitment."[3] The Nationalists could not be salvaged without radical changes in political and military organization and in their domestic policy; and Chiang for a variety of personal and historical reasons was incapable of carrying out these changes on his own initiative with the personnel he commanded. Although Wedemeyer made a gallant and not wholly unsuccessful effort to reform the Chinese armies, Stilwell's successors operated in a diplomatic relation to Chiang rather than in the operational intimacy which Stilwell attempted. They could not get at the roots of Chiang's military and administrative problem except by persuasion, exhortation, and sporadic exercise of the bargaining position offered by the American flow of supplies. To have been effective, the American influence would have had to be exerted through a prolonged commitment of policy and men; but after Stilwell's failure this was never again seriously attempted.

The relative priority the United States attached to the question of China's future was tested at the level of high diplomacy at Yalta and more generally in the planning of the final stage of the assault on Japan. At Yalta Stalin demanded that Russia assume generally in the Far East its position as of the period immediately before the Russo-Japanese war of 1904-1905. In the light of expected American casualties in the assault on Japan and the believed strength of the Japanese army in Manchuria, the Western Allies agreed to this position in two major respects at China's expense. Soviet "pre-eminent interests" in the Chinese Eastern Railway, including the right to transport troops through Manchuria to Port Arthur were granted; and, in the Liaotung Peninsula, the internationalization of the commercial port of Dairen and the Soviet lease of Port Arthur as a naval base were agreed. What the United States salvaged for Chiang at Yalta, and the Nationalists confirmed in the Sino-Soviet Agreement of August 1945, was formal diplomatic recognition of their international status.

Specifically, the Chinese Nationalists received from the 1945 agreement a positive Soviet commitment to friendship, including recognition of both their major power status and their authority in China. Discounting the professions of assistance and friendship, the Kuomintang hoped that the Soviets would honor its other commitments: to avoid interference in China's internal affairs and to deny military supplies to the Chinese Communists, to respect China's full sovereignty in Manchuria and forego interference with the internal affairs of Sinkiang, to return the Chinese Eastern Railway to China after thirty years without compensation, and to withdraw Soviet troops from Manchuria within three months after Japan's capitulation.

Given the poor state of military intelligence and judgment concerning the course that effective Japanese resistance would take,[4] there is a wholly understandable short-run military case for the choice made at Yalta. There was, moreover, the possibility of Soviet *de facto* seizure of the positions it wanted in Manchuria, outside international agreement, by a declaration of war against Japan and military occupation—although as late as September 1944 Stalin was formally prepared to agree to leave the war against Japan wholly to the United States and Britain.[5] It was not at Yalta or on any other diplomatic occasion that the Chinese Nationalist cause was lost. The American positions at Yalta did, however, reveal the relative priority accorded to short- and long-range American interests when they conflicted—a conflict which at least conceivably might have been resolved by a more mature assessment of the American air and naval potential combined with appropriate diplomacy in ending the Japanese war.

A final question arises: Why did the United States not engage Japanese military strength on the mainland and occupy Manchuria in the process, thus foreclosing the possibility of a Soviet assertion of legitimate interest and offering the maximum chance that the Nationalists could assert their authority in the face of the Communists throughout China in the postwar period?

The simple answer is that every canon of American military doctrine called for a concentration of such ground, air, and naval strength as was available in the Pacific against the heart of the enemy's position in Japan. From this view the most urgent military task in China was to keep the Nationalists in being and, if possible, to open for them a secure land route of supply. And even the latter objective was long postponed by the general shortage of landing craft, which prevented the amphibious operations in northern Burma originally planned for early 1944. A linking of the Chinese armies to the American flow of supplies (and possibly to American troops) in East China south of Canton was planned for August 15, 1945; and the operation was almost complete when Japan surrendered. As Feis notes:

> Both the Chinese and the American military organizations in China had to face the problems of dealing with a beaten Japanese army and an unbeaten Chinese Communist army sooner than they had figured. The American government did not have the time on which it had counted to make up its mind as to what military support to give the Chinese government after the end of the war.[6]

## THE NATURE OF THE AMERICAN FAILURE

If it was, in fact, the American interest to see in the postwar a unified non-Communist China capable of preventing a disintegration in the Asian balance of power, three steps were necessary. First, the military and political administration of the Nationalists had to be improved and their domestic policy had to be developed along lines capable of meeting the Chinese Communist military and political challenge. Second, a Soviet extension of power in the Far East, and notably the possibility of Soviet linkage with the Chinese Communists in Manchuria and North China, had to be prevented. Third, the United States had to be in a position to assert its interest in the orientation of the mainland and especially of its decisive industrial base, Manchuria. Those objectives were not attained during the Second World War.

It is by no means certain that they could have been attained under any likely circumstances; but, as things in fact happened, the possibility of their attainment was compromised because in American thought and operations the mainland of Asia was a third priority theater in which political as well as military decisions were made overwhelmingly in terms of short-run military considerations.[7] Stilwell's line of approach, instead of being backed and articulated into a total military-civil American policy in China, was rejected in the interest of short-run harmony. The character of the Chinese Revolution and the objectives of the two sides in the Chinese Civil War were misinterpreted or only dimly perceived. Faulty military intelligence on the military strength and resilience of the Japanese under likely post V-E Day circumstances converged with an extreme priority for minimizing casualties, even at the cost of American long-run interests, to give Soviet participation in the Pacific war a false importance. The monolithic character of military planning for the defeat of Japan—as well as a misjudgment of the time required for Japan's defeat—ruled out the assertion of American ground force strength on the mainland.

In short, whether or not Nationalist China was salvageable in the terms in which China's future was conceived during the Second World War by American leaders, it is clear that American conceptions and priorities during the war did not lead to actions which would have maximized that possibility.

### 18. Planning the Postwar Institutions

THE AMERICAN PERSPECTIVES ON THE UNITED NATIONS

While the diplomatic issues of Eurasia—from France to China—were woven intimately into the course of urgent military events imposing their own imperatives, the governments were permitted for a time to contemplate the structural arrangements for the postwar world in terms of long-run principle and aspiration.

Work on postwar policy began immediately after the outbreak of war, in September 1939, and proceeded steadily forward at an exploratory staff level.[1]

After Pearl Harbor these efforts expanded. An Advisory Committee on Postwar Foreign Policy was created at the end of December 1941, including several prominent public figures as well as high officials in the Department of State; and it went to work in February 1942.

In the course of 1943 Roosevelt and Churchill exchanged views on the essential features of a world security organization; and at Moscow and Teheran, in October-November, the three major powers sketched the broad outlines of the United Nations. These were formalized at Dumbarton Oaks in August-September 1944; and at American insistence China was associated with the scheme as a major power in the first week in October.

The issues of substance were, from the beginning, few and relatively simple.

First, it was agreed that the organization would rest on continued negotiated accord among the Big Three, a conscious effort to extend into peace a successful wartime coalition. Put another way, it was not envisaged at any stage that the United Nations would be an instrument for dealing with problems of conflict among the major powers should they fall out. The concentration of authority in the Security Council flowed from this conception, as did the veto power.

Second, after canvassing at length and sympathetically the concept of building the organization on regional foundations, it was finally agreed to concentrate its powers in centralized institutions.

Third, it was agreed that in the Assembly—and the economic and social agencies related to it—there would be an ample and free forum for the smaller nations to express their views and formulate resolutions on the basis of majority vote although action arising from such votes could not override a nation's sovereignty.

Within this area of rough agreement, each of the major powers brought to the discussion a distinct perspective.

The Soviet position systematically reflected a low estimate of the importance of the United Nations organization as compared to other, more substantive postwar issues. It reflected both an intent to maintain in the United Nations maximum authority for the Big Three in determining issues to be dealt with and in the making of decisions and an acute consciousness of the minority position of the Soviet Union on a world basis, from which flowed both Moscow's insistence on multiple votes for the Soviet Union in the Assembly and a chronic effort to minimize the powers of the Assembly. In short, it is evident that Stalin, looking toward the postwar, viewed the power relations among the Big Three as the central question. The Soviet objective was to wring, from Big Three negotiations and the interplay of raw power, positions of maximum Soviet advantage on the basis of territory occupied by the Red

Army while minimizing the possibility of mobilizing within the UN anti-Soviet strength outside the Big Three context.

Churchill also regarded the question of the United Nations organization as of less importance than the actual geographical power relations which emerged from the wartime course of events; and he looked at the structure and organization of the United Nations as part and parcel of the balance of power problem. Churchill, in seeking an American-backed showdown with Stalin, was in no way inhibited by fear of what such a showdown might mean for the new United Nations organization. In his mind such an organization could reflect only underlying power realities; and he wanted those realities to be as favorable to the West as the united will and strength of the Anglo-American coalition in 1945 would permit.

The American view of the United Nations was sharply different from that of either Stalin or Churchill. Historical, ideological, and practical considerations converged to elevate in American minds the importance of the creation of a United Nations organization embracing both the Soviet Union and the United States. Americans hoped that if Moscow could be induced to enter the organization, somehow, by that fact, power politics could be eliminated from the world scene as a major factor. And, perhaps also, Roosevelt and Hull may have feared that the alternative to Soviet participation was not a United Nations without the Soviet Union but, if the proposal for a universal organization failed, a United States withdrawn into isolation once again.

What is certain is the official American view that the United Nations would be a substitute for power politics. On November 18, 1943, reporting to a joint session of Congress upon his return from Moscow, Hull said there would be no longer any need "for spheres of influence, for alliances, for balance of power or any other of the special arrangements through which, in the unhappy past, the nations strove to safeguard their security or to promote their interests.[2] And, in what he regarded as the climactic effort of his life—bringing along the Senate—Hull defined three "pivotal questions": "The first was to keep Russia solidly in the international movement. The second was to develop an alert and informed public opinion in support of the program proposed. And the third was to keep the entire undertaking out of domestic politics."[3] These were the overriding themes and perspectives which distinguished the American from the British and Soviet approach to the setting up of a world organization.

Two powerful practical judgments—one short-run and military, the other long-run and political—reinforced the American effort to ensure the peace by building an organization based on continued Big Three accord. The first was that the final stage of the Japanese war would be a major, costly affair. Time after time, the Joint Chiefs of Staff applied their influence on American wartime diplomacy in the direction of minimizing conflict with Moscow and maximizing the chance of a Soviet contribution to the Japanese war. The second was Roosevelt's judgment that the American people would prove incapable of sustaining armed forces abroad for any substantial period after war. These considerations exercised pressure on American diplomacy to seek both immediate and long-run solutions which would minimize conflict with Moscow.

Thus the story of American policy toward the United Nations during the Second World War is, essentially, the story of American-Soviet relations seen from one perspective.

### HULL AND VANDENBERG

The settlement of the United Nations question began in earnest in the spring of 1944. Starting on April 25, Hull met regularly with an evenly balanced group of eight Democratic and Republican senators to lay the political foundations for American entrance into the United Nations. Their meetings continued down to May 29, but the relationship between the Department of State and the Senate leadership then established was maintained down through the San Francisco Conference of 1945.

In its essence the relationship reduced to a dialogue between Vandenberg and Hull, which can be followed in detail in their respective *Private Papers* and *Memoirs*.[4] Vandenberg was the central figure, because he symbolized and effectively commanded precisely that marginal group in the nation which reluctantly but definitely shifted from old isolationist positions under the impact of the war experience. For Vandenberg the process had begun on the night of March 8, 1941, when, against his judgment and his vote, the Senate had passed the Lend-Lease legislation. He wrote in his diary:

> If we stand *any* show, it will be from pursuing this new, revolutionary foreign policy to the last limit with swiftest speed. I shall vote hereafter accordingly —but *only* because the Senate, on this historic night, has committed America to these illimitable obligations. . . . Our Fate is *now* inseverably linked with that of Europe, Asia, and Africa. We have deliberately chosen to 'sit in' on the most gigantic speculation since Time began.[5]

As a good American he could not for long take a negative, reluctant attitude towards so great and adventurous a "speculation," however much he disapproved it. At the Mackinac Conference in the summer of 1943 he led in shifting the base of the Republican Party toward an internationalist position. With Vandenberg and all he represented positively associated with his policies, Hull clearly could carry not merely an overwhelming majority of the nation but also a decisive majority in the Senate. And this fact was recognized by all hands.

The domestic and international negotiations which led to the setting up of the United Nations centered essentially on three issues: the relation of the organization to the peace settlement, the scope of the veto power, and the range of discussion and initial membership to be permitted in the Assembly.

### POLAND AND THE PEACE

When substantive discussions between Hull and the Senators began on May 2, 1944, "one of the Senators said he desired to know whether we should have a good or a bad peace agreement before he could commit himself finally to an agency to keep the peace."[6] And this issue remained paramount, in different forms, over the following year.

Vandenberg, who first raised the matter, put it as follows after the first round of discussions of May 11:

> The chief difference of opinion, up to date, if any, rotates round the *timing*. I have taken the position that, no matter how acceptable this program for a new League might be, everything depends upon the kind of peace—whether it is a *just* peace—which this new international organization will implement. We are all disturbed by Russia's unilateral announcements from time to time as to what she intends to do, for example, with Poland and the other Baltic States; and by Churchill's constant reiteration of restoring the British Empire intact. The *peace* will create a new *status quo* in the world. The new "League" will defend this new *status quo*. It is my position that the United States cannot subscribe to this defense, no matter how hedged about, unless and until we know more about what the new *status quo* will be. It is my argument that we should go ahead and perfect a plan for collective security; but that we should make it wholly contingent upon a *just* peace. Therefore, in my view, the new "League" must be *contingent* upon the *character* of the *peace*.[7]

Hull argued in reply that, if the United Nations were ever to be set up, decisions had to be made and negotiations pursued while the war alliance existed; and that all would be lost if the issue were postponed to the postwar, after the peace treaties were signed. And, more subtly, he urged that the simultaneous negotiation of an international organization and the peace treaties would permit "beneficial and softening" doctrines and policies to be brought to bear on the latter.[8] In the end Vandenberg permitted and even positively supported Hull's negotiations for the world organization, but he urged on Hull that, if the organization was to prove politically acceptable, it was important to achieve settlements the American people would regard as just; and, to a degree, he reserved his freedom of action.

After the Dumbarton Oaks Conferences (and the 1944 election), Vandenberg turned with full attention to the problem posed by the nature of American aspirations and the facts of world power. No American political statement of the war years put the issue more clearly than his speech in the Senate of January 10, 1945, on the eve of Yalta.

Vandenberg isolated the conflict between the broad principles of collective security incorporated, on the one hand, in American hopes and in the concept of a world organization and, on the other, in the unilateral pursuit of national interests and security by the Soviet Union, and, to a degree, by Britain. Neither Churchill nor Stalin drew back from asserting uniquely national points of view and interests; and they were evidently not perturbed by the fear of Allied disunity. Vandenberg called for a similar candor on the part of the United States.

He pointed out that the Allies had to choose between alternative ways of living in the postwar world. One way would be based on exclusive individual action in which each nation tried to look out for itself; the other would be one where, on the basis of joint action,

> We undertake to look out for each other. . . . The first way is the old way which has twice taken us to Europe's interminable battlefields within a quarter of a century. The second way is the new way in which we must make our choice. I think we must make it wholly plain to our major allies that they, too, must make their choice.[9]

Then, in a climactic passage, Vandenberg said:

> Russia's unilateral plan appears to contemplate the engulfment, directly or indirectly, of a surrounding circle of buffer states, contrary to our conception of what we thought we were fighting for in respect to the rights of small nations and a just peace. Russia's announced reason is her insistent purpose never again to be at the mercy of another German tyranny. That is a perfectly understandable reason. The alternative is collective security. . . . Which is better in the long view, from a purely selfish Russian standpoint: To forcefully surround herself with a cordon of unwillingly controlled or partitioned states, thus affronting the opinions of mankind . . . or to win the priceless asset of world confidence in her by embracing the alternative, namely, full and whole-hearted organization. . . . Well—at that point, Russia, or others like her, in equally honest candor has a perfect right to reply, "Where is there any such alternative reliance until we know what the United States will do?". . .
>
> I propose that we meet this problem conclusively and at once. There is no reason to wait. America has this same self-interest in permanently, conclusively and effectively disarming Germany and Japan. . . . I knew of no reason why a hard-and-fast treaty between the major allies should not be signed today to achieve this dependable end.[10]

The Vandenberg proposal for a major power military pact permanently to neutralize Japan and Germany was not immediately accepted—although Byrnes presented such a proposal for a German Pact in the spring of 1946.

It was clear in the post-Yalta period that Vandenberg's (and the nation's) position had an important ambiguity. At Yalta the Western Allies succeeded in writing into the agreement the formula of free elections for Eastern Europe, thus superficially undoing the Churchill-Stalin proportional distribution of Eastern Europe in October 1944. In a sense, also, the agreement on German occupation and the principles that would govern it had removed, for the immediate future, the question of Germany's emerging as an independent danger to the Soviet Union. The ambiguity present in Vandenberg's speech and in the American position was this: What sanctions was the United States prepared to apply if the Soviet Union persisted on a unilateral course in Eastern Europe? Would the United States withdraw into isolation and refuse to join the international organization as a gesture of pique against its allies' unilateral behavior? Or would the United States be prepared to use force to make the Yalta agreements stick?

As the unsatisfactory aspects of the Polish settlement became clear early in 1945, Vandenberg—peculiarly sensitive to this issue because of the important bloc of Polish-Americans in his electorate—reflected the fatal flaw in the American position.

> The desperately important question now is "what can we do about it?" Manifestly America will not go to war with Russia to settle such an issue—particularly when the President of the United States has endorsed the settlement. In the final analysis, we could not afford to upset our postwar peace plans on account of this issue. Yet I do not want to surrender to this decision insofar as we have any practical means at our disposal to continue to fight it. It seems to me that the best *practical* hope remaining to us is in my proposal that the new Peace League shall have a right to review all these interim decisions.[11]

Neither Vandenberg nor any other responsible American politician was prepared to envision the serious threat of force to make Yalta stick; and this was, almost certainly, the only policy that would have made it stick. And behind the American inhibition lay a lack of clarity concerning the strategic meaning of Eastern Europe and, perhaps, a false prejudging of what the American public would support if the choices were clearly put to it.

In the first half of 1945, however, there were, in Vandenberg's phrase, "practical means" still available to continue the fight over Poland; and the issue of Poland pervaded from beginning to end the San Francisco Conference on the United Nations. To the American delegation the immediate context of the Conference was Truman's stiff note to Stalin demanding that he carry out the Yalta decision on Poland; and Hopkins' success in getting Stalin's agreement on the reconstitution of the Polish Provisional Government marked its latter stage. Thus, as of the end of the San Francisco Conference in the last week of June 1945, the issue of freedom for Poland and Eastern Europe had not yet been foreclosed; the incompatibility of a collective security organization with unilaterally determined peace treaties had not been clearly demonstrated; and Vandenberg could wholeheartedly support American entrance into the United Nations.

## THE VETO

With the possibility still open of collective security arrangements among the Big Three as the foundation for peace, the other U.N. issues of controversy proved negotiable. The concept of the major powers exercising a veto in the Security Council produced instinctively in Americans a mixed reaction. Hull ascertained with some care that it would be impossible to get support in the Congress for an organization in which the United States did not reserve to itself a veto power on the right to take up arms; and the memory of Wilson's fight on this issue was fresh in his mind. The veto was, in this sense, a distinct concession to American views. On the other hand, the notion that the Soviet Union would also have a veto power ran counter to instinctive American sympathy and support for the democratic process and a substantial role for the smaller nations. Americans were, in a sense, embarrassed to find that the logical conclusion of the nation's power and its prejudices was that it should find itself advocating a concentration of world power in a rather exclusive club. Hull sought to soften this image. He often explained that the veto would be sparingly applied and then only on the most vital issues of national concern to the major powers; and that, as experience and confidence in major power unity grew, its use would gradually atrophy.

Whatever the American view, it was evident that Soviet diplomacy attached high importance to the veto and wished to maximize its scope. The San Francisco Conference built up to a first-class crisis on the following issue: Should the major powers have the right to veto the placing of an item on the agenda of the Security Council, or should a majority vote in the Security Council suffice to permit consideration of an issue? The emotional resentments of the smaller powers concerning the role of the veto as a whole converged with American ambivalence toward the veto to make this a major matter. It required Hopkins' intervention with Stalin in Moscow on June 6 to settle the affair; and the Conference broke up with a sense—real or imagined—of American victory, permitting Vandenberg—and the American delegation as a whole—to throw its weight behind the Charter with minimum reservation.

## THE SMALL POWERS AND THE ASSEMBLY

Whether the issue of veto over the agenda was in itself important—whether in fact Stalin regarded it as "insignificant"[12]—it is clear that the Soviet position was part of a general effort to limit the role of the smaller powers in the U.N. both at the Assembly level and in the Security Council. Stalin's attitude was frankly given to Hopkins:

> Marshal Stalin then stated that he had no objection to a simple majority being applied in discussions relating to pacific settlement but of course not to any matter involving enforcement action. He said he stressed this aspect because he knew these considerations were raised by the small nations. He had most respect for the small nations [but] it must be admitted there was a tendency among them to exploit and even to create differences between the great powers in hope that they would obtain the backing of one or more of the great powers for their own ends. He said it was a mistake to believe that just because a nation was small it was necessarily innocent. He added that it should not be understood he would only say this in secret since he was quite prepared to tell the little nations this to their faces. He said, after all two world wars had begun over small nations.
>
> Mr. Hopkins said he thought that possibly the difficulties at San Francisco had grown more out of misunderstandings than real differences.
>
> Marshal Stalin continued that certain statesmen were interested in getting hold of the votes of small nations and that this was a dangerous and slippery path since obviously the small nations would like to get great nation support.[13]

It was out of acute awareness that in a conclave including the small nations Moscow, as of 1945, was obviously in a minority that the troublesome issue of membership for Ukraine and Byelorussia arose; and two of the major battles at San Francisco concerned the right of the Assembly to discuss without restriction any issue it chose and to make recommendations to solve problems judged to endanger the peace. Strong American ideological instincts lay behind the nation's support for these positions; but it was also evident that in a world structured as it was at the close of the Second World War a strengthening of the Assembly increased to some degree American influence in the U.N. and reduced that of the Soviet Union. Similarly, in a major move at San Francisco, the American delegation fought through a concept of regional security organizations under the Charter which preserved the continuity of the Monroe Doctrine and the institutions built upon it.

In short, at every point, as the United Nations took on substance, it took on also the reality of power politics. It was clear that neither Moscow nor Washington was prepared to surrender sovereignty in significant measure; and that Moscow sought to minimize, Washington to maximize, within the hard limits of Security Council veto, the fact that in 1945, on a one-country, one-vote basis, they stood in minority and majority positions with respect to world political power.

The emergence of the bare bones of world power through the administrative skin of the United Nations almost certainly strengthened the intent of Moscow to ensure maximum unilateral positions of advantage. Outside the

United Nations, however, the American successes at San Francisco may have disguised for a time the hard fact that the great issues of the postwar were being actually settled elsewhere.

PLANNING THE POSTWAR ECONOMY

In contemplating the postwar world the nations of the West sought not merely to undo the interwar failure of the League of Nations but also to remake an international economy less precarious than that whose collapse after 1929 so powerfully contributed to the political chaos which preceded and helped make possible the Second World War. Like politicians, diplomats, and soldiers, the economists of the Western World assumed during the Second World War that the postwar would bring a recurrence of interwar problems. In making postwar plans they looked for the most part backward rather than forward, seeking to avoid the errors made after 1918 as those errors were subsequently understood. And their prescriptions proved, on the whole, similarly inadequate, leading directly to major initial weaknesses in postwar international economic policy and institutions; but again, as in military and diplomatic affairs, a national commitment was made during the war years to end an isolationist policy and to assume a major responsibility for the international economy. And this deeper national commitment survived shocks and disillusion over the first postwar decade.

In 1941-1945 the United States assumed responsibility for the short-term reconstruction of war-devastated areas through UNRRA; it assumed responsibility for bringing the world closer to the mechanisms of a free international economy through the Bretton Woods institutions and negotiations on trade policy with Britain; and, in fostering the Food and Agricultural Organization and, to a degree, the International Bank for Reconstruction and Development, the nation assumed responsibilities for helping maintain a flow of technical assistance and capital to the underdeveloped areas. Each of these institutions had its own intellectual history, stemming from one insight or another into what was believed to have been previous national and international error.

Concretely, there was a belief that certain situations judged contrary to Anglo-American interests would recur: the danger that hungry and impoverished peoples in war-devastated areas would turn in desperation to nondemocratic politics, as had happened in Russia and in other areas after the First World War; the danger that the world would fall back into policies of commercial and financial autarky of the kind that had developed between the wars and, notably, during the 1930's; and, looking further ahead, some could perceive the possibility of an explosive frustration in the underdeveloped areas arising from hunger and lack of economic progress.

UNRRA, designed to avoid the first danger, was an effort to carry over into the postwar years the spirit of the wartime alliance. As early as November 1943 an agreement was reached in principle to make common provision for the rehabilitation of the poorer and more devastated areas of the world; and, until that organization was broken under the accumulating tensions of the East-West conflict in 1946, it performed effective rehabilitation services in South and Southeast Europe, as well as in part of Russia and in China.

### BRETTON WOODS

UNRRA was, of its nature, a short-term, crisis venture. It was through the Bretton Woods institutions—the International Monetary Fund and the International Bank for Reconstruction and Development—that the world hoped to re-establish a new version of the pre-1914 world economy. To this end the most sophisticated thought of Western economists was devoted.

The story of the Bretton Woods institutions begins with Article VII of the Lend-Lease agreement negotiated between the United States and Great Britain in 1941, signed in February 1942. Article VII did not commit Britain to abandon empire protection; but it did commit the two countries jointly to seek greater freedom of trade in the postwar and to undertake wartime negotiations looking to this end. It was from this commitment, ultimately, that the International Trade Organization and GATT were developed in the postwar years.

With Article VII agreed, able economists both inside and out of government began in the course of 1941 to formulate schemes for a better world.

Although marked national differences ultimately emerged, the Anglo-American economists, sharing the same intellectual tradition, their mature lives having been devoted to examining similar problems, shared a broad view of what was required. They agreed that low tariffs were a good thing; but they understood that more than increasingly free trade was involved in remaking an international economy. Between the wars, at various stages, nations had faced severe balance-of-payments deficits both in general and in terms of specific currencies; and they had been led to institute all manner of nationalist practices to defend their balance of payments against such deficits. Moreover, it was a central fact of the interwar years that London, which down to 1914 had been the world's center for supply of both long-term and short-term capital, had ceased to perform adequately this crucial international function. In fact, between the wars Britain showed a tendency to generate deficits which could be met only by liquidating capital held abroad. Financial power passed substantially to the United States; and the United States, unaware of its new international responsibilities, or unwilling to acknowledge them, had not effectively performed London's old functions. American and British economists looked, therefore, to the creation of an international institution from which nations could borrow on short term, cushioning balance-of-payments deficits and permitting governments to persist in policies of free currency convertibility and relatively free trade despite the inevitable vicissitudes of balance-of-payments deficits. Thus vicious spirals of protective financial and trade policies would be avoided and the foundations maintained for a neo-classical international economy.

In one sense the new international institution was designed to guarantee that the United States, inevitably the largest and most powerful contributor, would this time behave responsibly as the ultimate source of international short-term capital. This, roughly, was the background of thought which ultimately yielded the International Monetary Fund.

The intellectual ancestry of the International Bank was mixed. In part it was designed simply to supplement UNRRA and aid nations in long-term reconstruction projects which promised to yield returns sufficient to justify loans rather than grants.[14] But at Bretton Woods the representatives of the underdeveloped countries threw their weight towards the concept of the Bank as a source of capital for long-term development projects; and this notion was accepted, within the limits of the Bank's resources, its dependence on private capital markets, and its peculiar criteria of "soundness" in judging loan applications.[15]

In a larger sense the International Bank, like the Fund, represented an effort to assure a degree of American responsibility with respect to long-term capital supply. The captious withdrawal of American capital from Europe in 1929 and after had played a memorable part in driving downward the spiral of international depression; and the Bank was designed to supply a more stable flow of (essentially) American capital to the international economy.

So much by way of broad aspiration and conception.

Out of the interplay of argument and negotiation, however, the institutions were so reduced in resources that they were incapable of fulfilling their grand functions. And this failure derived from an American unwillingness to peer ahead, to measure candidly the probable scale of the postwar economic problem, and to commit the nation firmly to deal with it. An aura of false optimism colored the American economic vision of the postwar as it did American diplomatic and military policy.

The question of scale focused during the wartime years on the foreseeable British balance-of-payments problem. Before Lend-Lease the British had run down their capital holdings abroad, sacrificing future income. As the war went on, they acquired enormous debts within the Empire, notably in Egypt and India, which constituted foreseeable claims on the postwar balance of payments; they suffered a progressive loss of export markets, as production was concentrated on military supplies and the United States moved into the trading vacuum; they suffered severe losses in shipping which would take time to make good and would cut into postwar foreign exchange earnings. In addition, the prices of the foodstuffs and raw materials Britain mainly imported had risen during the war disproportionately to the price of manufactures; and, should this relationship persist, Britain might confront markedly worse terms of trade than during the interwar years. Finally, the British public were in a mood to insist that the British economy be operated not only at full employment in the postwar but also with increased provision for human welfare and security. This mood could evidently not be denied by democratic politicians, and it committed Britain somehow to maintain a high level of imports if political crisis was to be avoided.

From the passage of Lend-Lease, British economists and government officials began to turn a portion of their attention to the scale of this foreseeable postwar balance-of-payments problem and to the means for solving it. It was evident that, unless some drastic new effort was made which would supply large dollar credits, Britain would have to protect its postwar balance of payments by all manner of controls over both imports and currency for some years at least. The British proposal for a Clearing Union drafted by Keynes represented a conscious effort to create an institution which would permit Britain to participate from the initial postwar period forward in a relatively free international economy. Keynes' Clearing Union (published in April 1943) would have provided very large initial international credits in the form of drawing rights proportional to each nation's share in international commerce:

> We need an agreed plan for starting off every country after the war with a stock of reserves appropriate to its importance in world commerce, so that without undue anxiety it can set its house in order during the transitional period to full peace-time conditions.[16]

The credits effectively available under Keynes' plan would have been of the order of $25 billion.

In Washington Harry Dexter White, at the Treasury, led the way in formulating an alternative scheme. This was colored by a conservative judgment as to what Congress was likely to support, by an intent to guarantee a very substantial American voice in the administration of the Fund, and by White's passionate personal desire to leave his mark rather than Keynes' on this piece of history. Keynes, one of the most acute minds and strongest spirits of his century, did not subside without a struggle. The negotiations leading up to the formation of the Fund were charged with all manner of personal as well as international cross-currents. But White had all the cards in his hand, given the fact that the United States would inevitably have to supply a high proportion of the initial capital. And at Bretton Woods, in July 1944, it was a modified version of the White Plan that went into effect. It provided $8.8 billion in capital, with drawing rights so limited as to make the Fund usable only in cushioning short-run balance-of-payments deficits and virtually irrelevant to the kind of profound transitional problem Britain (and other nations) would face in the immediate postwar years.

Incorporated in the Fund, however, was a provision which represented an American lesson from the past painfully learned. Nations were permitted to defend their balance of payments when a foreign currency became "scarce." The United States had failed to acknowledge between the wars that creditor as well as debtor nations had responsibilities to the international community; and American tariff policy combined with the irregularity of American capital movements had created between the wars a mild version of the "dollar short-age" that was to obsess the post-1945 world economy. The "scarce-currency" provision in the Bretton Woods Agreements, volunteered at American initia-tive,[17] represented not merely an important concession to the views of other nations but also a frame of mind and level of international understanding among responsible Americans that was to contribute to later more substantial American efforts to set the international economy on its feet.

As with the International Bank—also originally conceived in ambitious terms—the Fund that emerged from the Bretton Woods Conference was essentially a symbolic gesture of the world's will to do better after the Second than after the First World War; but it was, in both scale and in underlying concept, inappropriate even to those postwar problems that were clearly fore-seeable in 1944.

THE TECHNOCRATS SET UP THEIR CLUBS

Most international institutions spring from an effort to solve a problem the existence of which has been forced on the attention of men and governments over a substantial period of time and to the solution of which they believe concerted international action might contribute. There is a certain apparent inevitability about the creation of such institutions, reflecting as they do widely shared ideas and vested interests converging from many directions. The Food and Agricultural Organization of the United Nations is in this respect something of a sport.

In February 1943 Franklin Roosevelt called an international conference to consider the postwar food problem. His announcement took the world of diplomacy and most of the Anglo-American postwar planners by surprise. For a year and a half the latter had been at work on international machinery designed to deal with postwar trade and payments. They had not been fore-warned and they did not understand the origins of Roosevelt's proposal.[18]

The idea for the Hot Springs Conference arose from an instinctive political judgment of Roosevelt linked to the purposeful lobbying of a small dedicated group of food and nutrition experts. Roosevelt thought that it would be wholesome for the first United Nations Conference to be on so universal and relatively uncontroversial a subject as food. The idea had been pressed on him, however, by Mrs. Roosevelt, Wallace, and Winant, who, in turn, had been pressured by a group which, between the wars, had become impressed both with the scope of the world's future food problem (in view of foreseeable population growth) and the potentialities for dealing with it inherent in enlarged dietary knowledge and improved agricultural technology.[19]

Within their limits both the Hot Springs Conference and the FAO which sprang from it were successful. A major postwar issue was dramatized; a competent picture of the world food supply and demand picture—short- and long-term—was drawn; intelligent broad policy resolutions were agreed among the governments; knowledge of the best food policy practices was spread abroad; and an organization was set in motion competent in analysis, in organizing international technical assistance programs, and in perpetuating as an international lobby the world's dedicated experts on food and agriculture and their friends in the various government ministries.

Moreover, the concepts and methods which went into the development of the FAO foreshadowed much in the approach later taken to American Point Four and other postwar technical assistance programs. And, in general, the issues dealt with at Hot Springs and the direct, almost technocratic, approach to the economic problem incorporated in its outlook were to prove more relevant and important in the postwar years than many more sophisticated postwar planners appreciated in 1943.

Something of the same may be said of the group of organizations for European economic cooperation which sprang from the womb of SHAEF (with the American Embassy in London as midwife) as the war drew to a close. European reconstruction required more than American dollars and food; it required the reconstruction of transport and power lines, the rehabilitation of coal mines, the allocation of coal and other scarce materials in terms of both equity and technical priority. As the armies liberated areas in Western Europe in the course of 1944, cooperative effort to deal with these matters began; and the more farsighted experts set about organizing international clubs to handle these specific European household problems which would evidently persist after Allied victory. Three organizations emerged: ECO (European Coal Organization); ECITO (European Central Inland Transport Organization); and a holding company for cooperative work on power, timber, and other bottle-neck problems, EECE (Emergency Economic Committee for Europe). These humble bodies, arising from efforts to solve immediate, palpable war and postwar tasks, were to have important consequences; for their existence, achievements, and believed potentialities contributed to the development of the regional economic organizations of the U.N. in 1946 and to the organizational concept of the Marshall Plan in 1947.

POSTWAR PLANNING IN PERSPECTIVE

The sort of world to which the United States looked forward during the Second World War was essentially the one which in American minds would have been possible had everyone acted more intelligently after November 1918. It was a world in which the United States was an effective member of a universal security organization based on negotiated accord among the major powers; where the major powers, in concert, took steps to ensure that Germany could not arm and threaten the peace for a third time; where international agreement among the major powers assured that nations could choose their own governments by free democratic elections. It was a world in which a democratic France would resume its place as an effective major power, and Nationalist China would at last take on the role implicit for it in the concept of the Open Door. It was a world in which a free and productive international economy, unmarred by acute nationalist practices, strengthened by all manner of cooperative international ventures, would provide the welfare underpinnings to peace and democracy.

In order to achieve all this the United States was prepared to assume major responsibility in the United Nations; undertake occupation commitments for several postwar years, including the stationing abroad of troops; make substantial contributions to the immedate postwar relief and rehabilitation of war-devastated areas; help to set up and modestly to endow international financial and investment institutions; and, above all, leave the concept of isolationism behind once and for all.

As the war years rolled on, in one area after another emerging reality clashed with ideal conception. In these circumstances the general response of American diplomacy was to make emergency arrangements, to play for time, and to try to keep ideal conceptions alive as a goal. This was the pattern in the whole array of conflicts with Moscow: from the question of voting rules in the Security Council to the fate of democracy in Poland the ultimate objective of Big Three unity on major issues was maintained. This was the pattern in China, where the objective of negotiated national unity under Chiang Kai-shek was pursued. This was also the pattern in economic policy, where, after a relatively brief postwar transition had been passed and the new international institutions took hold, it was hoped a free, self-adjusting world economy would emerge.

There were those who argued that the ideal conceptions were unworkable or that they required vastly more American resources and exertion if they were to come to life. But the conceptions for the postwar broadly fitted the believed requirements for fighting the war; and the nation chose to wait and see before abandoning the relatively easy postwar formulae it created during the war years. It required the better part of two years of postwar degeneration in the American and Western position before these formulae were radically modified or abandoned.

# PART IV

# A CONCLUSION

## 19. Wartime Origins of the Cold War

CONTRASTING VISIONS OF THE POSTWAR

The post-1945 struggle for the control of Eurasia arose from a sequence in which two emerging mature powers—Germany and Japan—were defeated in war, leaving a third—Russia—in command of much of the battlefield, while a fourth vast but transitional power—China—became caught up in a civil conflict the course of which was affected by that war and the outcome of which directly affected the interests of major powers.

The roots of the Cold War thus reach far back in modern history. At the latest, the Cold War can be linked directly to the sequence that begins in the decades after 1840 with the opening of China and Japan to Western trade and influence, the unification of Germany, and the freeing of the Russian serfs; it embraces the pattern of industrialization between (say) 1860 and 1914, the First World War, and its aftermath, including the Russian Revolution; and the sequence flows on to the launching of Japanese aggression in the 1930's, the rise of Hitler, and Stalin's pact with Hitler on the eve on the Second World War. All that brought the new powers into the world arena and ruptured the world of 1815 is relevant to the setting of the Cold War.

Narrowly, however, the Cold War can be dated from the time that the Politburo was clear that Stalingrad would hold—roughly from the beginning of 1943. From some such time Moscow returned with vigor to the territorial preoccupations which were at the center of its diplomacy in the period 1939-1941. This shift was manifest in the spirit and tactics of Soviet diplomatic behavior in many areas during the year 1943. Communist doctrines and, perhaps more important, the Bolshevik experience of gaining power in the aftermath of Russian defeat in 1917 converged to make Stalin and his men regard the postwar period as one of great opportunity for the extension of Communist power under control from Moscow. After November 1917 the internal weaknesses and problems of the new Soviet regime were too great to permit Lenin to exploit successfully the disruptive consequences of World War I; Stalin and his colleagues were determined that no trick was to be missed after World War II. But the form, technique, and extent of Moscow's extension of power could not be determined until the character of specific opportunities and the degree of Western resistance had emerged.

In China the political and military response to Japan's incursions on the mainland had been, from 1935 at least, mainly a reflection of the internal conflict for power of the Nationalists and the Chinese Communists. The Communists postured as the advocates of all-out Chinese resistance in order to divert Nationalist military resources from the anti-Communist struggle and to gain political capital as leaders of the steadily rising Chinese nationalist spirit. The Kuomintang aimed to avoid too deep an engagement in war against Japan in order to prevent the Chinese Communists from expanding freely in the Chinese countryside. It is fair to say that down to 1945 the two Chinese factions were mainly controlled in their wartime behavior by what each faction regarded as the certain knowledge that it faced an internal struggle for power—and almost certainly a military struggle—once the Japanese were defeated.

The British too were aware throughout the war, and notably after Britain's survival was assured in 1940, that what was done in the war would affect profoundly the relative power and prestige on the world scene of Britain and the British Empire. This factor entered instinctively—and as a matter of course—into virtually every major decision that Churchill made and into every major position he took in the debates among the three allies.

And the minds of the French, Polish, and other political leaders of occupied areas were even more sharply focused on the postwar world—on the domestic character of postwar restoration and on the international status their countries would enjoy. These considerations constantly influenced, if, indeed, they did not control, their wartime behavior and policies.

There was no equivalent in American thought to this lively awareness that wartime performance would inevitably affect national interests and postwar status whatever formal structure the peace assumed. There was nothing in the American concept of the postwar as concrete as the Soviet aim to maximize its power in Eastern and Central Europe, the desire in China to defeat an opposing political faction, the British purpose to restore the Empire and to hold its own in alliance with the United States as a major power on the world scene, or the exiled and underground European leaders' interests in postwar factional and national position.

American thought about the postwar looked primarily to the organization of a world structure for permanent peace which would avoid the failures of Wilson's effort and the interwar mistakes in general as those failures were then understood. The factor of power was not absent from American considerations, but it took the form of seeking a particular method for the settlement of major power conflicts—private negotiations of agreement among the Big Three.

This overriding American interest in the creation of conditions for world peace—rather than with the details of territorial power[1]—accurately reflected both old American patterns of thought and a fatalistic conviction that American forces could not be kept in Eurasia beyond a few postwar years. Thus the nation did not define or seek systematically to achieve the power position requisite for the achievement of the grand design.

If Big Three unity were to be achieved and held as the basis of postwar organization, it could be accomplished only by making it the most attractive alternative realistically open to Moscow. This meant not merely that Moscow be treated with dignity as an ally; it meant also that Moscow be denied by Western strength and purpose and by geographical positions held by the West the realistic alternative of expanding its power by unilateral action.

This possibility was not finally lost to the West until after the end of the war, roughly during the period from Potsdam (July 1945) to the spring of 1946, when Moscow apparently decided, in the face of American demobilization and the general weakness of the West, that it could do better by pursuing a unilateral rather than a collective power policy. Nevertheless, American wartime attitudes, policies, and decisions contributed to the result.

No man can say with honesty and with confidence, even with all the benefits of hindsight, that it lay within American military and diplomatic capabilities to win the war in Europe in the course of 1944; or to face Stalin down in Poland without major war; or to have so strengthened the Nationalist government in China as to have avoided the Communist victory in the postwar years; or to persuade the American people to support an American occupation of Manchuria. And even if it were possible to establish firmly that these specific possibilities once lay within American grasp, it would be of extremely limited value and interest to do so. But it is possible and useful to examine the frames of mind and the paramount interests which determined decisions which did not maximize the possibility of these results; for frames of mind and interests persist, while the field of action and decision changes unceasingly, never exactly to recur. In this limited perspective it is worth summarizing certain American wartime attitudes and decisions which failed to maximize the possibility of protecting persistent American interests.

THE CONDITIONS FOR BIG THREE UNITY: A HINDSIGHT VIEW

A serviceable American policy in Europe during the Second World War had to answer two questions. How shall the Soviet Union be prevented from dominating Western Eurasia in succession to Germany or in alliance with Germany? How shall Germany be prevented from again threatening to dominate Western Eurasia?

It was clear that, if British, American, and Russian interests in Germany converged, the Big Three commanded sufficient power to rule out a resurgence of a military threat from Germany. In this century Germany has constituted a threat only when permitted by the cross-purposes, weakness, or distraction of Britain and France, Russia, and the United States. It was evident that postwar Britain would have no interest in succeeding to the German wartime position of active dominance on the Continent; and the American interest was certainly not in that direction. How, then, should the Western Allies have proceeded to reconcile the two questions? The answer lay in establishing such a strong a *de facto* position throughout Europe during the war that Moscow would have to negotiate defensively to assure its national security, ruling out in the process the possibility of seeking the dominance of Western Eurasia.

The Western conception of peace was based on a separation of issues of military security from issues of political, social, and economic orientation. Communist doctrine led directly to the contrary principle: namely, that the distinction between political orientation and military control is false, and that security for the major Communist power can lie only in the extension from Moscow of total control over societies. Under these circumstances the task of the West was to force Stalin to look at Germany and Europe as a Russian rather than as a Communist. The Kremlin had to be made to look at Germany as an area to be neutralized rather than as a pawn to be manipulated in its unilateral interest. The Western powers thus had a fundamental vested interest in bringing the war to an end at the earliest stage consistent with Western interests and with Soviet troops as far east as possible; and in establishing Western positions in the east in order to prevent Moscow from achieving total dominance and using Eastern Europe as a military staging area. These objectives would appear to have justified the use of Western military as well as diplomatic bargaining strength both during and after the war so long as their use was compatible with Hitler's defeat.

From such a base of *de facto* dominance of Western Eurasia a long-term foundation for Big Three unity in Europe might have been established. If the best terms available to Moscow were a military neutralization of Germany and Eastern Europe at the cost of the direct exercise of Soviet political and military domination there, then it is possible that Stalin would have opted for a unified policy. More than that, if the West held all of Germany, it is altogether likely that Stalin would have traded the military neutralization of Germany for such direct dominance as his advancing armies permitted him in Eastern Europe.

In the upshot, the war was so fought as to give Moscow the possibility of dominating the whole region from the Soviet border to the Elbe. Moscow lost the Ruhr to the West; but it held a continuous military and political belt running through Poland to the heart of Central Europe; and, above all, since it held in East Germany the key to German unification, it could exercise for the long run a formidable influence over the orientation of all of Germany.

This Soviet position of strength, arising from the course of the war, was not actually consolidated until the postwar years; but it is clear that American thought and policy during the war did not address themselves soberly to preventing its coming about. Wartime policy was dominated by the military requirement of defeating Germany; wartime thought about the postwar future of Europe centered on the problem of preventing the Germans from again undertaking aggression. The problem was not defined as one of forcing the Soviet Union into a position where its interests demanded that it join the Western Allies in a unified policy toward Germany and Europe—although this was the condition for Big Three unity over Germany, and only such unity could create an environment which would leave the Germans no realistic option except a policy of peace. American diplomacy by and large acted on the proposition that if Big Three unity were achieved then the details of a European settlement would fall into place. The truth was that Big Three unity hinged on a particular kind of European settlement—one in which the Soviet Union was forced to bargain away the possibilities of unilateral power to achieve a basis for long-run Russian security in collaboration with the Western powers.

All this is said with hindsight—as if it should have been clear that the Soviet Union would be ambitious for power in Europe after the war, and on the assumption that the postwar struggle for position vis-à-vis the Soviet Union should have been judged inevitable and paramount in American minds. Since wartime American policy in Europe toward the postwar was made neither by knaves nor fools but by men of both political parties representing the best the nation could then mobilize, it is important to reconstruct with sympathy the elements and forces that entered into it and to establish why the perspective now afforded by hindsight was not then self-evident.

BIG THREE UNITY: THE PROBLEM AT THE TIME

First, it is necessary to recall what an enormous enterprise the Second World War was, and how absorbing, even desperate, the battle remained down through the repulse of the German attack in the Ardennes at the close of 1944. The latter half of 1944 was a time when Allied casualties in Europe were still high, flying bombs and rockets were falling on London, and, according to the most responsible military estimates, a mammoth and costly combat on the

Japanese home islands appeared to lie ahead. It is understandable that thought about the postwar would be somewhat obscure and its priority low.

Second, the American military resisted systematically the application of diplomatic and political criteria to their military plans; and Roosevelt supported them. Their overriding criterion for civil policy—when it bore on military plans—was such action as would appear to mininize immediate risk and short-term casualties in the field. From North Africa forward American political decisions were shaped by military expediency; and efforts, notably by Churchill, to interweave Allied military strategy with political objectives were resisted by the American military for reasons different from and independent of those which led American civil leaders to oppose this linkage. The American military resisted the notion that the political consequences of military action or the consequences of political action designed to assist military action could have sufficiently costly consequences for the postwar to justify either any significant modification in military plans or the acceptance of increased military risks or casualties. From the case of Darlan in North Africa to the question of Soviet entrance into the Far Eastern war at Yalta this pattern of military hegemony in wartime policy-making continued.[2]

Third, the behavior of Germany itself since 1917 gave powerful emotional justification to a policy of unconditional surrender and to setting aside the possibility that Germany was inevitably a ground for maneuver between the Soviet Union and the West. Germany's second effort to dominate Europe was attributed by some to the fact that surrender was negotiated in 1917 and that the Germans were not then sufficiently impressed with the fact of defeat in the field. For Americans it was easier to believe this than to believe that the German resurgence was permitted by the willful carelessness and errors of the Allies between the wars, beginning with the American repudiation of Versailles. But there was more than that. Hitler had behaved with such barbarity in Germany, in Western Europe, and in the East, and he had succeeded so well in inducing the German people either to support him or efficiently to do his bidding, that the notion of terms short of unconditional surrender and the notion of competing in any way for German favors, as between the Soviet Union and the West, were deeply abhorrent in simple human terms to most Americans.[3]

It is not at all difficult to understand how sensible decent men faced with the gamble between an unreconstructed Germany maneuvering itself to European hegemony once again as against the Soviet Union using its wartime positions to advance its unilateral interests in Europe would have chosen to accept the latter risk. Nor is it difficult to understand the power in wartime thought about Germany of the notion of the permanent division of Germany into two or more units.

Fourth, American behavior was to a degree colored by the assumption that the Soviet Union was honestly suspicious of the West and of Western intentions; and that therefore a condition for stable Big Three unity was to persuade Moscow that the West sought nothing incompatible with historic Russian security interests and was prepared to treat with the Soviet Union as an equal major power. Here there were complex elements in the triangular relationship of the Big Three. Churchill, having fought the war against Germany from 1939 to 1941, when Stalin was allied to Hitler, felt somewhat less the honest pangs of conscience that afflicted Americans when they contemplated the heavy scale of Russian effort and casualties in the war on the Eastern Front. In one sense Americans felt they owed Stalin something for having failed to open the Second Front in the West in 1942 or 1943. Although Churchill was, as Stalin recognized, a faithful military ally, he was at no stage unclear that Stalin's policy was to maximize Soviet power; and he was, without embarrassment, prepared to press direct British national interests in the face of Stalin's opposition.

All of this straight power-dealing seemed to Americans somehow incompatible with Big Three unity. Churchill and Stalin appeared to assume that, if Big Three unity persisted, at its private core would be a continuing jockeying for national power and position. Roosevelt appeared to seek a different relationship among the Big Three, a relationship less explicitly linked to issues of territorial power. In his efforts to distinguish his interests and motives from those of Churchill, Roosevelt, instead of strengthening the appeal of the Big Three concept, almost certainly confused Stalin about Western purposes.

Fifth, there was a degree of honest doubt as to whether the Russian experience from 1941 to 1945 had or had not wrought a sea-change in Soviet objectives on the world scene. It was argued by some that Russia had undergone great shocks and changes and faced new problems. It was felt that the devastation of Russia and the postwar domestic problems it posed, the experience of acceptance as an equal fighting ally by Britain and the United States, the great national experience of fighting and defeating an invading Teutonic enemy which had required a degree of relaxation in police state controls—all of this would produce a different foreign policy for Moscow after the war, one addressed to long-run peace as the West understood the concept, within which Stalin would be satisfied with a version of the Czarist empire before the Russo-Japanese War. The evidence of Soviet maneuvering in Italy, Eastern Europe, and toward Germany in 1943-1944 all ran in the contrary direction; and such men as Harriman, Deane, and others urged their government to note the somber implications; but the stakes were high enough to lead men who were not naïve to gamble. And, with hindsight, it is extremely easy to underestimate the impact on Roosevelt, Churchill, and their staffs of the manner and terms of negotiation with Stalin at Teheran and at Yalta. It is easy to forget that those on the spot felt that Yalta was truly the performance of three allies. Down to the early months of 1945, experienced and thoughtful men—alive to the possible danger of Soviet postwar aggression —could at least hope that the notion of Big Three unity was not impossible.

These five elements—together, of course, with the domestic political attraction and convenience of not risking a major crisis between the West and Moscow—appear to have determined that the United States would not use its military and political strength to maximize Western *de facto* power in Europe at the end of hostilities. The United States stuck to an unmodified unconditional surrender formula,[4] while Stalin steadily courted the Germans from Stalingrad forward. The United States refused to support Churchill's plea for a drive through the Lubjana Gap, insisting on the invasion of Southern France, even after the Normandy bridgehead was consolidated. The United States did not support Churchill's efforts in 1945 to seek Anglo-American victory in the race for Berlin and Prague or encourage his notion that Western troops withdraw to the agreed occupation areas in Germany only when the Yalta provisions concerning the method of forming the Eastern European government were actually carried out.

As the war in Europe drew to a close in the spring of 1945 and the postwar issues emerged for decision behind advancing armies, the relationship of Soviet objectives to Big Three unity could no longer be suppressed as a major problem for the West. The question came rapidly to a head around the formation of a provisional Polish government and the prompt holding of free elections in Poland. In March and April both Roosevelt and Churchill appeared to be hardened for a fundamental showdown on this issue—although the old American ambiguity about the meaning of Eastern Europe persisted to the end. But Roosevelt's death and Churchill's removal from the scene during the Potsdam conference led, essentially, to a *de facto* acceptance of a split of Europe on the Elbe which proved impossible to eliminate by normal diplomacy, so attractive was it to Moscow as opposed to any alternative compatible with minimum Western interests. The United States continued to separate the pursuit of peace from the maintenance of its strength and bargaining position vis-à-vis Moscow until the collapse of Western Eurasia was imminent in 1947. By that time, however, disintegration had proceeded so far among the Big Three that the recapture of Western strength and bargaining position could proceed only in the context of a Cold War.

# BOOK TWO

## Notes

### CHAPTER 7. The Washington Scene: Policy, Methods, and Men

1. See, especially, J. J. McCloy, *The Challenge to American Foreign Policy*, Cambridge, Harvard Univ. Press, 1953, chap. 2.

2. Robert E. Sherwood, *Roosevelt and Hopkins*, New York, Harper, 1948, p. 697. Undoubtedly his timing of the [unconditional surrender] statement at Casablanca was attributable to the uproar over Darlan and Peyrouton and the liberal fears that this might indicate a willingness to make similar deals with a Goering in Germany or a Matsouka in Japan.

3. J. J. McCloy, *op. cit.*, pp. 36-37.

4. K. T. Marshall, *Together, Annals of an Army Wife*, Atlanta, Ga., Tupper & Love, 1946, pp. 17-18.

### CHAPTER 8. The Shape of the Battle

1. M. Matloff and F. M. Snell (*The United States Army in World War II*), *Strategic Planning for Coalition Warfare, 1941-1942*, Washington, D.C., Govt. Printing Office, 1953, pp. 12-21; R. E. Sherwood, *op. cit.*, pp. 149-151; H. Stimson and M. Bundy, *On Active Service in Peace and War*, New York, Harper, 1948, pp. 345-363.

2. Quoted, R. S. Cline, *Washington Command Post: The Operations Division* (United States Army in World War II), Washington, D.C., Govt. Printing Office, 1951, p. 334.

### CHAPTER 9. Science, Technology, and War

1. J. B. Conant, *Modern Science and Modern Man*, Garden City, N. Y., Doubleday Anchor Books, 1953, pp. 22-24.

2. Vannevar Bush, *Modern Arms and Free Men*, New York, Simon and Schuster, 1949, p. 18.

3. The German statistics appear to show that wounds from artillery in 1916-1918 were 85 per cent of the total recorded as opposed to 8 per cent in the Franco-Prussian War a half-century earlier. T. Wintringham, *The Story of Weapons and Tactics, from Troy to Stalingrad*, Boston, Houghton Mifflin, 1943, p. 169.

4. R. Oppenheimer, "Science as a Way of Life," A. D. Little Memorial Lecture, Massachusetts Institute of Technology, Cambridge, Mass., 1947.

5. J. P. Baxter, *Scientists Against Time*, Boston, Little, Brown, 1946, p. 7.

6. Vannevar Bush, *op. cit.*, p. 11.

7. Baxter, *op. cit.*, p. 26. Patterson attested that the fundamental priority accorded German over Japanese defeat in Anglo-American strategy, when it crystallized in 1941, was colored by the fear of the new weapons that German science might develop in the course of the war.

8. D. Price, *Government and Science, Their Dynamic Relation in American Democracy*, New York, New York Univ. Press, 1954, pp. 44-46.

"But while the National Defense Research Committee could seem to most of its scientists like only a wartime version of their usual committee-style organization, its parent organization, the O.S.R.D., gave it a quite different effect. The President had set up only as recently as 1939 the Executive Office of the President, including an Office for Emergency Management, which was designed to give him greater flexibility in handling emergency agencies in time of war. It was in this Office for Emergency Management that the O.S.R.D. was located. As the head of an independent agency in the O.E.M., Vannevar Bush had every right to go directly to the President on issues involving the use of science and scientists during World War II. A position of direct responsibility to the President was not important mainly in order to let Dr. Bush as head of O.S.R.D. have personal conversations with President Roosevelt. It was much more important to give him the leverage he needed in dealing with the vast network of administrative relationships on which the success of a government agency depends. This is the point that is completely missed by those who think that the ideal position for a scientific agency in government is one of complete separation from the political executive.

"It was this position of direct responsibility to the President, combined with his own personal qualities, that enabled Dr. Bush to deal with military leaders on equal or better than equal terms, in order to push the development of specific weapons in which leading generals were not interested. This position also let him exercise over government policies a vigorous influence that had an important effect on the use of scientists. For example, radar would never have played its timely part in World War II if Dr. Bush had not been able to exercise enough influence with the Selective Service System to protect the younger electronic experts against the operations of the draft. Nor could the whole structure of contractual relations have been maintained had he not been able to persuade the General Accounting Office to relax many of its normal peacetime rules with respect to accounting and contracts. Finally, he had to persuade the Patent Office and the Department of Justice to permit changes in patent policy in order to make industrial corporations more willing to take on the job of weapons development."

9. I. Stewart, *Organizing Scientific Research for the War, The Administrative History of the Office of Scientific Research and Development*, Boston, Little, Brown, 1948, p. 322.

10. On pp. 456-457, Baxter (*op. cit.*) lists the 25 principal nonindustrial and 25 industrial contractors all with contracts with OSRD totaling one million dollars.

11. E. Burchard, *Q.E.D., MIT in World War II*, New York, The Technology Press and John Wiley & Sons, 1948, p. 37.

12. Baxter, *op. cit.*, pp. 247-251.
This was true, for example, of the development of the amphibious vehicle called the DUKW. O.S.R.D. and General Motors had produced and demonstrated (with

the Coast Guard's help) the virtues of the vehicle by December 1942; and a reluctant Armed Service Forces came to perceive its potential importance in amphibious operations. Nevertheless, after the vehicle had been accepted in principle, O.S.R.D. had to maintain responsibility for training crews down to the end of the war, so decisive to its usefulness was the thoroughness of instruction.

13. *Ibid.*, pp. 141-142. The quotation in Baxter's text is from Sir Robert Watson Watt, "Radar in War and in Peace," *Nature*, September 15, 1945, p. 321.

It is often said that the British scientific effort in wartime was more fruitful than the American in basic innovational breakthroughs whereas the American effort was distinguished by the rapid and efficient elaboration of possibilities opened by these breakthroughs and the pressing forward of these elaborations into production. These familiar generalizations are debatable. It is evident that British scientists made the essential breakthroughs in radar and in jet engines, although it is not clear whether these achievements are to be attributed to the basic superiority of British science or to the patent urgency of the British air defense problem. It is also evident that foreign and foreign-trained scientists made the essential intellectual contributions which led to the development of the atomic bomb. Finally, it is undeniable that down to the past twenty years American science has been relatively weak in basic theory as compared to European science. What is in doubt is whether the generation of American scientists (including those foreign-born and foreign-trained) in the United States during and after the Second World War did not in fact match contemporary groups abroad. What can be said with confidence is that the United States benefited in two respects from the British scientific alliance. It benefited by acquiring both basic inventive ideas and the practical experience of field operations which were generally more extensive in British services down through 1943. Second, the scale and intimacy of relations between British and American scientists, by enlarging the community of men concerned with the scientific problems of war, afforded a powerful mutual stimulus to creative effort and undoubtedly increased the net productivity of all concerned.

14. On the role of foreign-born scientists with respect to the atomic bomb see, notably, H. Smythe, *Atomic Energy for Military Purposes, the Official Report on the Development of the Atomic Bomb under the Auspices of the United States Government, 1940-1945*, Princeton, Princeton Univ. Press, 1947, especially pp. 45-54.

## CHAPTER 10. The Development of Strategic Air Power

1. W. F. Craven and J. L. Cate, *The Army Air Forces in World War II*, Washington, D.C., Govt. Printing Office, Vol. 6, p. 32.

2. From A. D. Turnbull and C. Lord, *History of United States Naval Aviation*, New Haven, Yale Univ. Press, 1949, p. 322; and R. Sherrod, *History of Marine Corps Aviation in World War II*, Washington, D.C., Combat Forces Press, 1952, p. 1.

3. For the priority enjoyed by aircraft production in this period see M. M. Postan, *British War Production*, London, Her Majesty's Stationery Office, 1952, especially pp. 313-322.

4. As of June 1941 the Office of the Chief of Air Corps was a minute organization completely dominated by the Army General Staff at the level of strategic planning. Its intelligence requirements were supposed to be met by requests for material from Army Intelligence, G-2, which organization not only was notably incompetent at this stage but also collected and organized its information almost wholly around the criteria of ground warfare. In a mood of conspiratorial secrecy, the Air Corps set up in the early months of 1941 the beginnings of its own intelligence and planning sections under Captain Hansell, a professional Air Corps officer, assisted by a reserve officer, Captain Moss. This organization recruited by June 1941 three additional civilians, one of whom, (later) Colonel Richard D. Hughes, was to become the principal planning officer for strategic bombing in the European theater and the greatest single influence on the selection of target systems and individual targets for attack by American bombing aircraft in the war against Germany. Colonel Hughes was by training a professional British soldier who had served in the Middle East and India from 1917 to 1930, when he moved to St. Louis and became an American citizen. His hard-won sense of the realities of war —and above all, of the need to concentrate attack at carefully chosen points—was an extremely important factor in designing and executing a strategy of attack which partially overcame the inherent tendencies to diffusion of a strategic air force as of 1942-1945. The most important act of this group before drafting AWPD/1 was to acquire through Captain Hansell's private initiative copies of RAF target files and maps which provided an essential degree of independence from ground force intelligence and planning units.

5. In this the British were following the early prophets of air power; but, in fact, their commitment to the bombing of cities arose from their own earlier failures with precision bombing, executed with the inadequate forces available in 1940 and early 1941, combined with a sober assessment of the likely capabilities of the German fighter force to prevent the clean cut air superiority over Germany required for sustained daylight bombing operations of the requisite scale. Here the British were reading the lesson from the reverse side of the coin of their own Battle of Britain victory. Most British air officers believed that short-range fighters had a natural advantage over day bombers or long-range fighters in defending their home territory that could not be overcome. Finally, the British had a clear understanding of the operational meaning of European weather conditions and the limits they were bound to impose on a daylight bomber force committed to precision attack.

From the beginning the American Air Corps stuck to its commitment to precision attack in daylight centering around the B-17 and the Norden bombsight, which had been developed from the original naval model. Initially this was a commitment of faith and ideology, unrelated to any serious knowledge or responsible assessment of the possibilities of making precision bombing an effective instrument in the context of the war against Germany.

6. W. F. Craven and J. L. Cate, *op. cit.*, Vol. I, p. 599. Having extracted from the British target files the names and locations of the 154 targets, American Air Force officers calculated the tonnage of bombs believed required to cut down German production and hold it down to the critical level; and they calculated the number and types of aircraft, required to do the job under assumed attrition rates. Working back from these tonnages and aircraft requirements, there were developed

a training program, a program of manufacture, and a program for building, staffing, and supplying bases.

AWPD/1 predicted with approximate accuracy that, while limited air operations might be begun from Britain as early as April 1942, the American Air Force would not reach maturity and full strength in its operations against Germany until April 1944. It hedged on two points. First, although it assumed that American bombers could operate daylight missions against Germany without fighter support, it suggested that work be begun to develop a heavily armored and armed escort fighter with long-range capabilities; second, although the plan was designed to make possible a decision in the war against Germany through air action, the target systems selected were equally consistent with the use of long-range air power to aid Allied ground armies against Germany by destroying German air capabilities and damaging ground force mobility.

7. The role of civilians in drafting AWPD/1 foreshadowed their importance in the development of strategic bombing plans and in the choice of targets. In ground warfare "the enemy" consists of other ground units; in naval warfare, of other naval vessels. In strategic air war "the enemy" consists of factories, urban areas, transport facilities and other essentially civil installations deep behind the lines. A rational air targets strategy must relate damage to elements in the enemy's economy or society to his ability and will to wage war. Although in the end a military effect is sought, the field of battle is, in a sense, a war economy and its logistical lines of connection to the fighting fronts (for precision bombing), or the whole social system as it relates to military intentions and capabilities (for area bombing). It was natural that professional air officers, trained to fly aircraft and to lead air formations in battle, should turn to civilians for help in the drafting of air war plans.

8. It may be that Churchill's skepticism (see H. H. Ransom, *The Air Corps Act of 1926*, unpublished doctoral dissertation, Princeton University, August 1953, p. 135) about bombing operations designed to achieve a military result through the effects on civilian morale—to which his own air force was committed—played some role in his decision. In the spring of 1944, Churchill again backed the American conception of precision attack on bridges as against the British conception of generalized attack on marshalling yards and railroad facilities, in support of D-Day.

9. Many of the essential elements in this problem are more accurately depicted in W. W. Haines, *Command Decision* (Boston, Little, Brown, 1947), than in the official war histories.

10. The key alliance was between Hughes and an RAF Headquarters Unit called Bomber Operations. This unit was run by a group of younger staff officers fresh from operational experience, who believed that precision attack was not merely vastly more efficient than area bombing but possible to achieve and sustain under European conditions.

The targets for American attack from mid-1943 to early 1944 were determined by a directive of June 10, 1943, issued by the Chief of the British Air Staff, acting for the Combined Chiefs of Staff, interpreting and narrowing the Casablanca target lists. This directive, in fact, represented the wishes of the Eighth Air Force, whose staff, while often at odds with RAF Bomber Command and later with SHAEF and its tactical air force commander, were in close alliance with elements in RAF Headquarters Staff in London. This key directive sanctioned a concentration of effort on German fighter production and the German ball-bearing industry.

In a sense this directive was the first serious target plan of the war. AWPD/1 and the Casablanca directive represented hopes beyond the current capabilities of the American bomber force. The American bombing attacks from August 1942 to July 1943 bore little serious relation to these formal directives. The directive of June 10, 1943, however, was drafted by the air staffs in Europe in the light of actual capabilities and of hopes on which the American operational commanders were prepared to gamble and act. Behind it lay a year's bitter operating experience and the maturing of American air staff work, in which the principles of concentration of effort and of choosing among alternative target systems so as to maximize the direct frontline effect of strategic attack were developed, debated, and made the working basis for intelligence and planning. The concepts and methods developed in Europe in the period 1942-1943 left a lasting imprint on American and to some extent on British air staff work.

The primary objective of the June 10 directive was to decrease the production flow into the German single-engine fighter force, whose growth threatened the possibility of the air supremacy required for OVERLORD as well as the survival in Europe of the American bomber force; but it was decided that attack should also be carried out on one highly concentrated general target system significant for overall war production which barely lay within the tenuous capabilities of the American Air Force, that is, the German anti-friction bearing production.

11. From Statistical Appendix to *Overall Report of United States Strategic Bombing Survey, 1945,* which is also the source of the statistics presented in this chapter.

12. Major Thomas Hitchcock, Assistant Air Attache at the American Embassy in London, was responsible more than any other single person for the successful development, barely in time, of a long-range American fighter. See W. F. Craven and J. L. Cate, *op. cit.,* Vol. 6, pp. 219-220.

13. In both the German and Japanese cases air supremacy appears to have been won by progressive attrition of pilots, in which the winning side gained, day by day, in the relative skill and experience of its pilot establishment, starting from an initial tactical victory. The process was self-reinforcing, as an initial favorable relative loss in planes and skilled pilots led to advantage in the next phase of combat.

14. See especially, D. D. Eisenhower, *Crusade in Europe,* New York, Doubleday & Co., 1948., pp. 46-47.

15. This concept of air support had arisen within Tedder's staff in the course of the Sicilian and Italian campaigns. It had its roots in the following doctrine: precision attack on highly selected targets was wasteful of bombs, and the most efficient use for the heavy bombing force was to attack large target areas such as marshalling yards where generalized attrition against the enemy's transport system might be achieved and bombs would not be "wasted." This somewhat disabused view about bombing capabilities clashed head on with the newly confirmed American sense of confidence that accurate, systematic, and persistent attack on carefully selected targets could yield first-class military results. Evaluation of the results of his attritional strategy conducted by American personnel within Tedder's staff in the Mediterranean had raised grave doubts about this doctrine. Some of those under

his command in the Mediterranean had come to feel that, while generalized damage could be done to marshalling yards, serious military effects in support of the ground forces could be achieved only by cutting and holding out specific lines of supply, mainly by attack on bridges; and this had been demonstrated to be possible at limited cost.

Despite the ambiguous and controversial results of the Mediterranean experience, and the vast difference between the relatively fragile rail systems of Sicily and Italy as compared with the dense and resilient networks of Western Europe, Tedder pressed for a rigid application of his doctrine in Western Europe.

16. Tedder feared—with reason—that the attack on oil might be brought in through the Mediterranean; and he insisted on a concentration of effort on marshalling yards—even when virtually irrelevant to the German war effort and to the allied invasion.

17. At this stage and throughout the summer of 1944 the capabilities achieved by the American air forces were not only dissipated by the two-month delay in attacking oil but also by directives requiring heavy attack on flying-bomb launching sites in the Pas de Calais area, from which, evidently, the Germans were preparing to launch the V-1. These were not merely almost impossible targets to hit with success but they were also vastly redundant, since German production plans never matched the original launching site program.

Air Marshall Harris, long the most effective and vocal opponent of oil and precision attack in general, has acknowledged, after the event, his error in sporting style:

"In the spring of 1944 the Americans began a series of attacks against German synthetic oil plants, and a week after D-Day Bomber Command was directed to take part in the same campaign by attacking the ten synthetic oil plants situated in the Ruhr. At the time, I was altogether opposed to this further diversion, which, as I saw it, would only prolong the respite which the German industrial cities had gained from the use of the bombers in a tactical role; I did not think that we had any right to give up a method of attack which was indisputably doing the enemy enormous harm for the sake of prosecuting a new scheme the success of which was far from assured. In the event, of course, that offensive against oil was a complete success, and it could not have been so without the cooperation of Bomber Command, but I still do not think that it was reasonable, at that time, to expect that the campaign would succeed; what the Allied strategists did was to bet on an outsider, and it happened to win the race."

(See Sir Arthur Harris, *Bomber Offensive*, London, Collins, 1947, p. 220.) The controversy between the American Air staffs and Harris was occasionally sharp, but it was conducted with openness and mutual respect. The controversy over the pre-D-Day transport attacks, fortunately not a strictly British-American affair, left more permanent scars.

18. See notably, Allen W. Dulles, *Germany's Underground*, New York, Macmillan, 1947.

19. See, notably, C. Willmot, *The Struggle for Europe*, New York, Harper, 1952, pp. 477-497; also the remarkable analysis of the problem of Antwerp in R. W. Thompson, *The Eighty-Five Days*, London, Hutchinson, 1957.

20. Tonnage Dropped in Europe by USAAF:

| | Total | On Aircraft Targets | On Oil Targets | Land Transport |
|---|---|---|---|---|
| 1st half | 0 | | | |
| 1942 | | | | |
| 2nd half | 2,003 | 280 | | 468 |
| 1st half | 28,655 | 1,000 | 99 | 3,238 |
| 1943 | | | | |
| 2nd half | 104,434 | 4,639 | 873 | 30,371 |
| 1st half | 379,501 | 24,796 | 20,069 | 123,105 |
| 1944 | | | | |
| 2nd half | 511,160 | 16,703 | 78,372 | 204,616 |
| 1955 | 437,670 | 3,599 | 31,566 | 241,666 |
| (5 months) | | | | |

The two thirds of total tonnage dropped in the last eleven months of the war yielded progressively diminishing returns, except for oil targets and a small proportion of land transport targets.

21. Stimson and Bundy, *op. cit.*, pp. 628-633; also J. J. McCloy, *op. cit.*, pp. 40-43; R. S. Cline, *Washington Command Post*, Washington, D.C., Govt. Printing Office, 1951, pp. 333-351; and, for the evolution of Japanese thought and politics, R. J. C. Butow, *Japan's Decision to Surrender*, Stanford, Cal., Stanford Univ. Press, 1954.

## CHAPTER 11. The Wartime Experience of Military Alliance

1. For the *ad hoc* manner in which the basic decision on Australia was made—but also the long memories and political assumptions which entered into it—see especially, Eisenhower, *op. cit.*, pp. 18-23.

2. W. K. Hancock and M. M. Gowing, *British War Economy*, London, Her Majesty's Stationery Office, 1949, pp. 378-379. For a perceptive account of the developments of 1941, see Hancock and Gowing, Part III. For an American view of this period see J. Winant, *A Letter From Grosvenor Square*, London, Hodder and Stoughton, 1947. Winant's representation of the United States in London over this awkward and delicate period was an important element in that transition. He conveyed to the British people as well as to the government the underlying American sympathy for the British cause, without transgressing the limits of American policy. Another key figure in the Anglo-American alliance at this time was Jean Monnet. Full of fresh practical experience drawn from the Anglo-French effort of 1939-1940, organizing imagination, and zeal for the Allied cause, in a sense Monnet in 1941 taught the British and Americans how to set up their common affairs, although he was by no means alone and sometimes a figure of controversy. For Monnet's role see especially Hancock and Gowing, pp. 181-196; 229-232. The definitive American account of the transitional period is, of course, W. L. Langer and S. E. Gleason, *The Undeclared War, 1940-41*, New York, Harper, 1953.

3. In fact the first formal Allied command was General Wavell's in the Far East. He was placed in charge of the American-British-Dutch forces in Southeast Asia shortly after Pearl Harbor (December 29, 1941). This command area disintegrated promptly under the weight of Japanese attack, to be superseded by other arrangements.

4. It was Marshall, with lively memories of the staff problems of the First World War, who personally enunciated and fought through the principle of unified theater command in the Anglo-American conference in Washington of December 1941. See, especially, Sherwood, *op. cit.*, pp. 455-458; also, Eisenhower, *op. cit.*, p. 18.

"A curious echo from the long ago came to my aid.

For three years, soon after the First World War, I served under one of the most accomplished soldiers of our time, Major General Fox Conner. One of the subjects on which he talked to me most was allied command, its difficulties and its problems. Another was George C. Marshall. Again and again General Conner said to me, 'We cannot escape another great war. When we go into that war it will be in company with allies. Systems of single command will have to be worked out. We must not accept the 'co-ordination' concept under which Foch was compelled to work. We must insist on individual and single responsibility—leaders will have to learn how to overcome nationalistic considerations in the conduct of campaigns. One man who can do it is Marshall—he is close to being a genius.' "

5. Under the pressure of battle this latter principle was occasionally violated, the first substantial violation coming in the first Allied campaign in North Africa. Eisenhower backed Anderson's initial thrust for Tunis with American forces:

"Very early I determined to take whatever additional risks might be involved in weakening our rear in order to strengthen Anderson. Shortage of transport prevented anything but movement by driblets—and the inherent dangers of such reinforcement are understood by the rawest of recruits. There was no lack of advisers to warn me concerning public reaction to 'dissipation' of the American Army! 'How,' I was often asked, 'did Pershing make his reputation in World War I?' What such advisers did not recall was Pershing's famous statement when stark crisis faced the Allies in March 1918. At that time, realizing the size of the stakes, he postponed integration of an American Army and said to Foch, 'Every man, every gun, everything we have is yours to use as you see fit.' I felt that here in Tunisia, on a small scale, we had a glowing opportunity comparable to the crisis of 1918, and I was quite willing to take all criticism if only the Allied forces could turn over Tunis to our people as a New Year's present!" (Eisenhower, *op. cit.*, p. 121.)

6. Eisenhower, *op. cit.*, p. 71. Three major considerations probably influenced Churchill in this move. First, he was aware that over the whole sequence of the Second World War the United States was likely to emerge as a senior partner; and he was prepared to discount the immediate numerical superiority of his own forces in the Mediterranean theatre against the hard fact that the United States, when fully mobilized, would emerge as the major Allied force. This consideration had special point because TORCH, the invasion of North Africa, was in staff terms an off-shoot of BOLERO, the invasion of Western Europe originally planned for 1942 or 1943. An American commander for that decisive operation was always envisaged. Second, the politics of American participation in its first Allied venture in Europe would be eased by the fact that an American commanded the enterprise. This was true at high as well as low levels; for the American military, with their minds set from the beginning on a direct invasion of Western Europe, the acceptance of TORCH was a bitter defeat administered by Churchill (and, in the end, by Roosevelt). This defeat was mitigated to a degree by the fact of American top command. Third, and perhaps most urgent, it was believed that American leadership would ease the political problem of French acceptance of the invasion.

7. The relation of heavy bomber forces to the theater command presented endless problems of channel of authority from the Combined Chiefs which were solved, if at all, on an informal common law basis.

8. Sherwood, *op. cit.*, pp. 677-678. See also, A. Bryant, *The Turn of the Tide*, London, Collins, 1957, Chap. 11, especially pp. 552-556.

The decision to keep Eisenhower at his post, taken at Casablanca, is described by Sherwood as follows:

"For a time there was some doubt whether Eisenhower would remain in supreme command of HUSKY (invasion of Sicily). General Alexander, who outranked him, was now moving into Tunisia from the south with the victorious British forces under the field command of General Montgomery. Here was tough professional competition for Eisenhower at a moment when his own position was most insecure, and I believe he would not have been greatly surprised if he had been put under Alexander or transferred elsewhere. However, he was given the supreme command and a fourth star, which made him equal in rank to his subordinates, Alexander, Cunningham, and Tedder. In announcing this later to the House of Commons, Churchill said, 'I have confidence in General Eisenhower. I regard him as one of the finest men I have ever met.' What weighed most heavily with Churchill and Roosevelt in arriving at this decision, aside from Marshall's persistent faith in Eisenhower, was the tremendous admiration and affection for him of the British officers who had served with him, most importantly Admiral Cunningham, a fighting sailor who was held in very high esteem by the two Naval persons. Thus Eisenhower had achieved his first important victory in the merging of officers of two nations and three services into one effective and harmonious command. After Hopkins returned to Washington from Casablanca he told me that Eisenhower had said to Patton: 'I don't mind if one officer refers to another as that son of a bitch. He's entitled to his own opinion. But the instant I hear of any American officer referring to a brother officer as that *British* son of a bitch, out he goes.' Eisenhower maintained that basic policy with historic success all the way into Berlin where he added the adjective 'Russian' to 'British.' "

9. Eisenhower, *op. cit.*, pp. 74-76.

10. See, for Anglo-American cross-purposes in this theater, Sherwood, *op. cit.*, pp. 771-775; Stimson and Bundy, *op. cit.*, pp. 532-540.

## CHAPTER 14. France

1. The debate on wartime French policy lingered into the postwar years. See, for example, W. L. Langer, *Our Vichy Gamble*, New York, Knopf, 1947; and reviews by L. Gottschalk ("Our Vichy Fumble," *Journal of Modern History*, March 1948) and E. V. Rostow (*World Politics*, April, 1949).

2. See, especially, W. S. Churchill, *The Second World War*, Boston, Houghton Mifflin, Vol. 5, *Closing the Ring* (1951), Chap. 10.

3. Eisenhower, *op. cit.*, pp. 247-248.

## CHAPTER 15. Germany

1. For a detailed account of the evolution of American wartime policy towards Germany, see, P. Y. Hammond, *JCS 1067, Policy for Germany*, New York, Twentieth Century Fund, Study of Civil-Military Relations (preliminary mimeographed edition).

2. R. E. Sherwood, *op. cit.*, p. 711. See also, P. Mosely, "Dismemberment of Germany" and "The Occupation of Germany: New Light on How the Zones were Drawn," *Foreign Affairs*, XXVIII (April and July), 1950, pp. 437-498, 580-604; and H. Feis, *Churchill, Roosevelt, Stalin*, Princeton, Princeton Univ. Press, 1957, especially pp. 124, 221-223, 274-275.

3. P. Mosely, *loc. cit.*, p. 488.

4. *The Memoirs of Cordell Hull*, *op. cit.*, Vol. II, pp. 1286-1288. As Feis (*Churchill, Roosevelt, Stalin*, p. 221) points out, Hull preferred to take the line that partition ". . . might merely create a German national slogan for union."

5. P. Mosely, *loc. cit.*, pp. 595-596.

6. Quoted, P. Y. Hammond, *JCS 1067*, p. 100.
"In regard to your memorandum of September twenty-ninth, I think it is all very well for us to make all kinds of preparations for the treatment of Germany but there are some matters in regard to such treatment that lead me to believe that speed on these matters is not an essential at the present moment. It may be in a week, or it may be in a month, or it may be several months hence. I dislike making detailed plans for a country which we do not yet occupy."

## CHAPTER 16. Poland

1. W. S. Churchill, *op. cit.*, Vol. 6, *Triumph and Tragedy*, 1953, p. 227.

2. *Ibid.*, pp. 234-235.

3. The most complete sources on the diplomacy of the Polish issue during the Second World War are E. J. Rozek, *Allied Wartime Diplomacy: A Pattern in Poland*, New York, Wiley, 1958; and H. Feis, *Churchill, Roosevelt, and Stalin*, Princeton, Princeton Univ. Press, 1957.

4. Churchill, *Triumph and Tragedy*, pp. 231-233. Sherwood (*op. cit.*, p. 852) quotes Churchill at Yalta as presenting his central theme in the following proverb: "The eagle should permit the small birds to sing and care not wherefore they sang."

5. Churchill, *Triumph and Tragedy*, pp. 240-241.

6. R. Sherwood, *op. cit.*, p. 833.

7. Churchill, *Triumph and Tragedy*, p. 365. Byrnes agrees that more time was spent at Yalta on Poland than on any other subject. J. F. Byrnes, *Speaking Frankly*, New York, Harper, 1947, p. 31.

8. *Foreign Relations of the United States, Diplomatic Papers, the Conferences at Malta and Yalta*, 1945, Washington, D.C., Govt. Printing Office, 1955, p. 977.

9. R. Sherwood, *op. cit.*, p. 860.

10. *Foreign Relations . . . Malta and Yalta*, 1945, *op. cit.*, p. 235.

11. W. S. Churchill, *Triumph and Tragedy*, p. 372.

12. *Ibid.*, p. 439.

13. *Ibid.*, p. 454.

14. H. S. Truman, *Memoirs*, Doubleday, Garden City, N. Y., 1955, Vol. I, Year of Decisions, p. 82.

15. W. S. Churchill, *Triumph and Tragedy*, pp. 572-574.

16. H. S. Truman, *op. cit.*, pp. 245-246.

17. Sherwood, *op. cit.*, p. 909.

18. Quoted, Truman, *op. cit.*, p. 215. See also F. C. Pogue, "Why Eisnehower's Forces Stopped at the Elbe," *World Politics*, IV (April, 1952), pp. 356-368.

19. H. S. Truman, *op. cit.*, p. 78.

## CHAPTER 17. Asia

1. For the author's views on this period, at greater length, see *The Prospects of Communist China*, New York, The Technology Press (Massachusetts Institute of Technology) and Wiley, 1954, pp. 8-29.

2. Stimson and Bundy, *op. cit.*, pp. 528.

3. *Ibid.*, p. 539.

4. For an excellent summary of the interplay between U.S. and U.S.S.R. diplomacy in the Far East and an assessment of the motives which determined the U.S. performance, see E. R. May, "The United States, the Soviet Union, and the Far Eastern War," *Pacific Historical Review*, XXIV (May), 1955, pp. 153-174.

5. H. Feis, *op. cit.*, p. 227.

6. *Ibid.*, p. 298.

7. One consequence the American commitment to the Open Door may have had: it may have so committed the nation to the concept of Chinese unity as to make impossible a post-World War II settlement symmetrical with that in Germany and Korea; namely, a split. Although Wedemeyer and other Americans strongly counseled Chiang Kai-shek to consolidate his position in the south before challenging Mao in the north, the United States could not bring itself to use its virtually unlimited bargaining leverage to insist on this course, which, in the upshot, might have proved sensible.

## CHAPTER 18. Planning the Postwar Institutions

1. See, especially, Hull, *Memoirs of Cordell Hull*, New York, Macmillan, 1948, Vol. II, Chaps. 116-122 for a full account of the evolution of American staff work and policy on the United Nations.

2. *Ibid.*, p. 1648.

3. *Ibid.*, p. 1659.

4. See A. H. Vandenberg, Jr., *The Private Papers of Senator Vandenberg*, Boston, Houghton Mifflin, 1952, especially Chaps. 6-11; and Hull, *op. cit.*, Vol. II, Chaps. 119-122.

5. Vandenberg, *op. cit.*, p. 11.

6. Hull, *op. cit.*, Vol. II, p. 1660.

7. Vandenberg, *op. cit.*, p. 96.

8. Hull, *op. cit.*, Vol. II, p. 1661.

9. Vandenberg, *op. cit.*, p. 134.

10. *Ibid.*, pp. 136-137.

11. *Ibid.*, p. 148.

12. Sherwood, *op. cit.*, p. 911.

13. *Ibid.*

14. For earlier and more glamorous American conceptions of the Bank's role see Harrod, *op. cit.*, pp. 539-541.

15. Over the first postwar decade the International Bank operated mainly in terms of the "soundness" of the individual project; that is, its ability directly to yield the revenue which would permit repayment of the loan in hard currencies. This narrow concept was inappropriate to the needs of under-developed areas, the soundness of whose development depended on the contribution of investment to the over-all rate and pattern of growth and whose repayment capacity depended in fact on over-all earning capacity in hard currencies. In the mid-1950's the Bank's criteria began to broaden.

16. Quoted, Harrod, *op. cit.*, p. 527.

17. The meaning of this concession to knowledgeable and sensitive Europeans is reflected in Harrod's reaction (*op. cit.*, pp. 544-545):

"I read on into it, through the scarce currency clause and onwards. I could not believe my eyes or my brain. I read it again and again. I studied some notes by Keynes which I had with me. They did not seem helpful. I was transfixed. This, then, was the big thing. For years we had complained of the United States' attitude as a creditor. For months we had struggled in vain to find some formula which would pin them down to a share of responsibility. Now they had come forward and offered a solution of their own, gratuitously. This was certainly a great event. For it was the first time that they had said in a document, unofficial, it was true, and noncommittal, but still a considered Treasury document, that they would come and accept their full share of responsibility when there was a fundamental disequilibrium of trade. As I sat huddled in my corner, I felt an exhilaration such as only comes once or twice in a lifetime. There were the dishevelled soldiers sprawling over one another in sleep; and here was I, tightly pressed into my corner, holding these little flimsy sheets. One had the urge to wake them all up. 'Here, boys, is great news. Here is an offer which can make things very different for you when the war is over; your lords and masters do not seem to have realized it yet; but they soon will; see for yourselves this paragraph 7; read what it says. I know that you set great store by the Beveridge scheme; but that is only written on a bit of paper; it will all fall to pieces if this country has a bad slump or trade difficulties. Here is the real thing, because it will save us from a slump and make all those Beveridge plans lastingly possible.'"

18. For British confusion and (mainly Keynes') dismay at Roosevelt's announcement, see Harrod, *op. cit.*, p. 554, and E. F. Penrose, *Economic Planning for the Peace*, Princeton: Princeton Univ. Press, 1953, pp. 119-120.

19. The key figures in this amiable cabal were: Sir John Boyd Orr of Britain, Stanley Bruce and F. L. MacDougall of Australia, the latter being the central figure in the maneuvers which led to Roosevelt's acceptance of the idea of an international food meeting.

### CHAPTER 19. Wartime Origins of the Cold War

1. The American interest in certain naval and air bases in the Pacific was, of course, a Mahanist exception to this stance.

2. It is worth quoting, by way of example, F. L. Pogue's conclusion about the much-debated question of entry into Berlin and Prague ("Why Eisenhower's Forces Stopped at the Elbe," *World Politics*, IV [April 1952], p. 368):

"From this evidence, certain conclusions seem to be substantiated. They are: (1) there is no evidence of a political bargain between the Allied leaders whereby the Red Army was to capture Berlin and Prague; (2) the traditional antipathy of U.S. military men to political solutions of questions which can be settled on a military basis is apparent in both cases; (3) there is little evidence that U.S. public opinion in the press or in Congress strongly supported a march on Berlin or Prague—General Eisenhower was usually kept informed of such trends in the United States and there is no material on this question in the SHAEF public information files; (4) all evidence points to the fact that a purely military solution to the problem was sought by General Eisenhower; and (5) on a purely military basis of ending the war in Europe as quickly as possible with the fewest number of casualties, the decision was the proper one."

3. On this point it is worth quoting Feis' thoughtful dissent from the view that the outcome of the war could have been affected by any modification in the terms of surrender for Germany (*Churchill, Roosevelt, Stalin*, Princeton, Princeton Univ. Press, 1957, pp. 357-358):

"What the Germans as a people had to fear most, I think, after this series of interpretations, was not the black terrors of the 'unconditional surrender' formula. It was their own knowledge of the agony they had brought upon the world, and the punishment that might justly be inflicted on them. For the Nazi leaders it was death or prison; for the lesser ones and their associates it was ruin and humiliation. For senior military commanders and staff it was the end of their career and enjoyed power. For other Germans it was foresight of a meager existence in a damaged and occupied country. For almost all there was the frightening possibility of domination by the Russians.

"The maintenance of the unconditional surrender formula, it is my impression, was a minor influence in the fight which the Germans sustained, except perhaps in the very last spell of the war. For what they longed and hoped for was not merely assurance that they would not be oppressed, but a deal with the West which would divide their enemies and allow them to escape penalty and survive as a strong country.

"The real question for the Allies—as distinguished from the tactical one—was what was to be done about Germany and the Germans *after* they submitted. That, in my reading of the record, would not have been decided much differently even though some German group—such as that which made its brave attempt in July 1944—had managed to overthrow Hitler and his crowd and had asked for an earlier peace. The Germans had too much to account for; they were too greatly feared; they had lost the usual rights to justice in a humane society. All that protected them—unconditional surrender or not—was the restraint and tolerance of their enemies and the mutual uneasiness between the West and the Soviet Communist realm."

4. For an able critique of the implications and problems arising from the unconditional surrender formula see, notably, Daniel Lerner, *Sykewar*, New York, George W. Steward, 1949, especially pp. 16-25.

# THE TRUMAN-STALIN DUEL

# PART I

# THE NEW CHALLENGE

## 20. Return to the Defensive

The Second World War ended with the balance of power in Eurasia clearly in the grasp of the United States and forces allied to, or dependent upon, the United States. The reality of American primacy was projected with great psychological force to the world by Japan's surrender in the wake of atomic attack.

In Europe the Western Allies held the Ruhr and the bulk of Germany. They had confirmed at Yalta the Soviet commitment to free elections in Eastern Europe; they had confirmed at Potsdam the Soviet commitment to a Germany to be treated as an economic unit and to be unified by democratic process. In Asia the United States held Japan, and the Nationalists in China had an apparent 3 to 1 advantage in arms over the Chinese Communists as well as the prestige of formal recognition from the Big Three, including explicit guarantees from the Soviet Union of sovereignty and territorial integrity. Underlying the existing political and territorial commitments and positions was the fact of the American monopoly in atomic weapons and the ability to deliver them from the air.

Despite this apparently favorable situation, it was possible even by the time of the surrender ceremonies aboard the *Missouri* to perceive conditions which made the Eurasian balance of power susceptible to the threat of Communist expansion; and there were plain evidences of the Soviet intentions to exploit these conditions in the period from Yalta through Potsdam (that is, January-August 1945).

Although the underlying realities were sensed both inside the government and, to a degree, outside the government as well, those responsible for American policy did not warn the American public that a further desperate struggle for the Eurasian balance of power was imminent—if not already under way. In what appeared to be a mood of national complacency there was pell-mell American demobilization. American political leaders dismantled the military and civil paraphernalia of total war, proceeding on the illusion that the goal of Big Three unity might still be achieved through the negotiation of differences with Stalin by a diplomacy in which the American military potential was not evoked.

In short, from V-J Day to the enunciation of the Truman Doctrine some nineteen months later, the United States acted as if its interests could be protected by a steady retraction of commitment in Eurasia, permitting a concentration of attention and resources on domestic affairs—a mood dramatized and heightened by the issues and the outcome of the Congressional elections of November 1946.

The reversal of American policy and the nation's mood in the two years after V-J Day took place in reaction to Communist policy. The situation created by Stalin's and Mao's efforts to expand their power in the postwar setting came gradually to be regarded as a major threat to the national interest.

To say that American policy was reactive, however, is not quite the whole story; for there was a quite complex interplay between Washington and Moscow. The behavior of each power was determined, in part, by what it judged to be the capabilities and intentions of the other. Moreover, in the immediate postwar years, each was so powerful a force on the world scene that the environment it faced was in part a product of its own past and current actions. For example, American demobilization after V-J Day and the American failure to insist upon the execution of the Yalta provisions in Poland strongly encouraged Moscow to extend its power to the limit in Europe. Thus the situation the United States faced as of, say, the spring of 1947 was in part a consequence of American policy over the two previous years.

When all this is taken into account, it is still fundamentally true that American postwar policy was systematically defensive and reactive. Before examining how that policy unfolded, it is necessary, therefore, to look briefly at the evolution of Communist policy in the immediate postwar years.

### 21. The First Two Stages of Postwar Communist Policy

What was the policy to which the United States and the West defensively responded?

In one sense there has been a complete continuity in Communist foreign policy since the successful defense of Stalingrad. Over the entire period Moscow has actively sought to expand to the maximum the area over which it could exercise authority in Eurasia. And there has been an equal degree of basic continuity in the objectives of the Chinese Communists. Ever since the end of the Long March in 1935 they have steadily looked forward not merely to the achievement of power in China but also to hegemony in Asia and major power status on the world scene.

But such broad objectives are not policies. Policy must be defined not merely in terms of objectives but also in terms of the energy, resources, and methods which are devoted to their achievement. In this operational sense, Communist policy in Europe and Asia passed through three stages between 1945 and 1958.

EUROPE: 1943-MAY 1946. THE SOVIET DECISION TO ESTABLISH THE SATELLITE EMPIRE

This period can be dated roughly from the Soviet defensive victory at Stalingrad to the breakdown of negotiations in the Control Council in Berlin over German economic unity. A fundamental Soviet decision to seize total control in Eastern Europe at the cost of Big Three unity was foreshadowed in the uncompromising tone of Stalin's electoral speech of February 9, 1946, in which he returned to the inevitable conflict between Communist and capitalist worlds as the foundation for the domestic as well as the foreign policy he outlined.

Truman's firmness in forcing the Soviet withdrawal from Iran on March 1946 may have given Stalin pause; but viewing the American performance as a whole, Stalin apparently concluded sometime in the first half of 1946 that it would be safe and profitable openly to ignore his Yalta commitment to free elections in Eastern Europe and his Potsdam commitment to move promptly toward the treatment of Germany as an economic unit. The United States, demobilizing its military strength at an extraordinary rate, was evidently not prepared to make the political disposition of Poland or the issue of German unity an issue of war or peace. Perhaps more important than the fact of demobilization, the American will to assert its interests throughout Eurasia must have seemed feeble. In China the American Marines were used indecisively; and there was evidently no American intent to use its own forces to try to shape the outcome in China. Stalin must have concluded that the United States regarded the area east of the Elbe (as well as China) as regions of secondary concern, worth the expenditure of diplomacy and even money but not military strength. In this setting, he ignored protests over Poland and Eastern Europe generally and permitted a breakdown of key negotiations in the Control Council in Berlin on the issue of German economic unity in May 1946.[1]

The American and Western willingness to accept for the long term the split of Germany and Europe was further underlined in the negotiation of the Italian and satellite treaties in 1946, when, in effect, certain Soviet concessions on the Italian Treaty were traded against a *de facto* recognition of Soviet dominance of the Eastern European states.

EUROPE: MAY 1946-SEPTEMBER 1949. THE FAILURE OF STALIN'S OFFENSIVE TO THE WEST

With his eastern base, in effect, safely within his hands, Stalin looked to the south and west as an area of opportunity. This second, more ambitious period in Soviet policy in Western Eurasia runs approximately from mid-1946 to Stalin's sudden ending of the Berlin blockade in April 1949.

During the summer of 1946 Stalin increased Soviet pressure in Western Eurasia in many directions: against Turkey by diplomacy and threat, in Greece by supporting substantial guerrilla warfare, and in Italy and France by vigorous Communist Party efforts to gain parliamentary power. Meanwhile, the process of consolidating Germany into two organized entities proceeded. In 1947 Stalin responded to the Truman Doctrine and the Marshall Plan by accelerating the movement toward total control in the East, symbolized by the creation of the Cominform in September 1947. He succeeded in Prague (February 1948), but failed in Belgrade, where Tito's defection was announced in June 1948. The Communist effort in Greece proceeded then to collapse, the election in April 1948 saved Italy, and France found a group of center parties capable of governing, if uncertainly, and containing the domestic Communist menace. The deadlock in the Berlin Control Council, already two years old, was dramatized by the Soviet walk-out on March 20, 1948, which set the stage for the blockade which began on March 31.

This phase of Soviet consolidation in Eastern Europe ended with the effort to disengage the West from Berlin which was defeated by the air lift in the winter of 1948-1949. In the West this interacting process yielded the Brussels Pact (February 1948), NATO (March 1949), and the creation (May 1949) of a Federal Republic of Germany, including Berlin, which symbolized and confirmed the Western intent to resist further Soviet expansion.

ASIA: TO DECEMBER 1946. THE PURSUIT OF POWER IN CHINA

There was a basic continuity in Communist policy in China over the decade from the launching of the popular front in China by the Communists, climaxed by the kidnapping of Chiang Kai-shek in 1936 and the Nationalist-Communist Agreement of 1937, to the end of the Marshall mission a decade later. In that period the Chinese Communists sought to expand their power within the framework of truce or limited hostilities with the Nationalists.

In the course of 1946 the negotiations for a truce in China broke down. The Communists—strengthened with Japanese arms furnished in the spring of 1946 by the Soviet Union, with some Soviet weapons, and with Soviet staff assistance—launched an all-out civil war. In 1946 Stalin probably advised against an all-out effort by the Communists to seize power;[2] but once Mao was well started, he was backed by Stalin in 1947-1949, mainly through diversionary operations of the international Communist movement.

ASIA: DECEMBER 1946-JUNE 1951. THE MILITARY SURGE

This stage embraces the Communist victory in China, an upsurge of Communist efforts throughout Asia, and the Korean War. It ended, roughly, with Malik's broadcast in New York on June 23, 1951, announcing Communist willingness to see the Korean War ended by a cease-fire along the 38th Parallel.

In terms of larger strategy, the Communist struggle and victory in the Chinese civil war was the center of a general Communist effort to exploit the weakness of postwar Asia and achieve a definitive victory which would spread through the Middle East and Africa and shift the balance of the world's power radically against the United States and Western Europe.

Communist policy in Asia formally changed in the course of 1947, the new ambitious objectives being enunciated by Zhdanov at the founding meeting of the Cominform in September. Open guerrilla warfare began in Indochina as early as November 1946, in Burma in April 1948, in Malaya in June, and in Indonesia and the Philippines in the autumn. The Indian and Japanese Communist parties, with less scope for guerrilla action, nevertheless sharply increased their militancy in 1948. As victory was won in China in November 1949, Mao's political-military strategy was openly commended by the Cominform to the Communist parties in those areas where guerrilla operations were under way. The meeting of Stalin and Mao early in 1950 undoubtedly confirmed the ambitious Asian strategy and planned its climax in the form of the North Korean invasion of South Korea, which took place at the end of June 1950.

The American and United Nations response to the invasion of South Korea, the landings at Inchon, the march to the Yalu, the Chinese Communist entrance into the war, and the successful U.N. defense against massive Chinese assault in April-May 1951 at the 38th Parallel brought this phase of military and quasi-military Communist effort throughout Asia to a gradual end. Neither Moscow nor Peking was willing to undertake all-out war or even to accept the cost of a continued Korean offensive. And elsewhere the bright Communist hopes of 1946-1947 had dimmed. Nowhere in Asia was Mao's success repeated. Indonesia, Burma, and the Philippines largely overcame their guerrillas. At great cost to Britain, the Malayan guerrillas were contained and driven back. Only in Indochina, where French colonialism offered a seed-bed as fruitful as postwar China, was there real Communist momentum; but Ho Chi-minh was finally forced by Moscow and Peking to settle for half a victory (Geneva, 1954) in the interest of the larger policy of the Communist Bloc which had begun to shape up in Asia from the summer of 1951.

THE TWO STAGES IN PERSPECTIVE

At both ends of Eurasia there was, then, a period of uncertain probing in 1945-1946 which gave way to more ambitious Communist ventures. In both Europe and Asia the Communist decision to proceed was based in part on an assessment of American intentions and capabilities as revealed in the first postwar year. Stalin became convinced that the United States would not oppose with force the full consolidation of the Soviet position in Europe up to the Elbe. Stalin and Mao became convinced that the United States would not oppose with force an all-out Communist effort in China; and Mao, at least, was convinced that, despite his numerical inferiority and despite American support in arms and funds for Chiang, the Nationalists could easily be beaten. And beyond Eastern Europe and China, Stalin and Mao saw in the unsettled state of the postwar world and the weakness of American purpose potentialities for expansion which they judged worth prompt exploitation.

The two efforts were, to a degree, certainly linked. It is probable that the vigorous Communist activities in Europe over the period 1947-1949 (and perhaps even the Berlin blockade itself) were designed to divert American and Western attention and resources from China just as it is certain that this objective (rather than firm hopes for decisive victory) partially motivated the aggressive tactics of the Communist parties throughout Asia in the climactic period of the Chinese Civil War.

The whole of this sequence occurred within the setting of a technological race in weapons stemming from the scientific and engineering breakthroughs of the Second World War. The Soviet Union was initially far behind American military technology in the key areas of atomic energy and electronics; but in a purposeful effort, involving an acute concentration of talent and resources, it proceeded to catch up. From 1945 to 1949 the United States never exploited its monopolistic position in nuclear weapons except as a check on Soviet ground forces. This restraint proceeded from a convergence of two factors: the moral inhibitions of the West, built into political institutions and processes, against initiating war; and the vulnerability of America's Western European allies to occupation by Soviet ground forces in case of major war. After September 1949—the first Soviet atomic explosion—the Soviet possession of atomic weapons became a factor in the world's power policies; and as the arms race proceeded, the existence of Soviet and American capabilities for mutual destruction and their efforts to avoid a position of decisive inferiority at any point in the competitive sequence moved to the center of the stage.

The first two stages of Communist postwar policy posed the central challenges to the Truman Administration. It was Truman who conducted against Stalin the counteroffensive of 1947-1951 which blocked the Communist offensive at both ends of Eurasia, leaving a Western Europe which, in 1952, had gathered economic momentum, weathered the war fears of 1950, and built a substantial common military establishment in NATO. In Korea the negotiations for truce went on; but, except in Indochina, the rest of non-Communist Asia, including the Nationalists on Formosa, recovered at least temporary poise while fighting and diplomacy proceeded in the northern peninsula. The Communists were thus held around the periphery which had emerged from the Second World War; and in the sense that minimum essential American interests were protected without major war, Truman succeeded where the pre-1914 and interwar statesmen of the West had failed.

But while the Korean War was being fought to a standstill, two forces were present on the scene and gathering momentum—the revolution in military technology and the revolution in human and national expectation within the underdeveloped areas. Even before Truman had left office and Stalin died, these new forces were moving toward the center of world affairs. The outlines of a new Communist policy to exploit them were evident as early as October 1952, at the Nineteenth Party Congress; and they dominated the agenda Truman turned over to Eisenhower in December; but this third stage in Communist initiative and Western response belongs with the story of Stalin's and Truman's successors.

# PART II

# THE SLIDE INTO COLD WAR

## 22. American Military Policy: 1945-1947

The military policy of the United States during the first two postwar years was dominated by the process of demobilizing the enormous apparatus built up during the Second World War and by the homeric struggle among the three services to create a new administrative structure for the armed forces, a struggle brought on by the wartime coming-of-age of the Air Corps. The worst of the internecine struggle ended in January 1947, when, acting within redefined terms of reference given by the President, Forrestal and Patterson approved a unification blueprint formulated by General Norstad (Air) and Admiral Sherman, and Truman forwarded these proposals to the Congress.[1] It was formally concluded with the signing of the National Security Act on July 26.

### DEMOBILIZATION

By 1947 the Navy and Air Force were cut to about one-seventh of wartime peak strength, the Army to one-sixteenth. Over-all total military personnel were reduced by mid-1947 to 13 per cent of the mid-1945 peak.[2] But figures alone do not adequately convey the impact of demobilization. Due to the discharge of key trained men, a lack of volunteers, and the need to maintain overhead establishments and noncombat units, the number of combat divisions at readiness was pitifully low. The Air Force reported in December 1946 only two and in June 1947 only 11 groups at combat effectiveness, out of the 52 groups provided as peacetime establishment.[3] The Navy, perhaps less drastically affected than the other two services, was nevertheless stretched thin by a more rapid demobilization of personnel than of base units, which resulted in nominally active units being immobilized for lack of crews.[4]

The basic establishment of the three services remained, of course, vastly larger than ever before in peacetime; and if the United States had been called in 1947 to join combat as a strategic reserve in a long war of alliance, it would have been in a markedly stronger position than it was in either 1917 or 1939. But in terms of the military position faced in this period the Army was in no position to deal with either of the two military dangers in being—the ground forces of the Soviet Union poised in Eastern Germany and the Chinese Communist armies which were beginning to move out from their rural bases in Manchuria and North China.

## THE UNIFICATION STRUGGLE

From V-J Day, if not from some time before, the energies of the professional military were, to a degree hard for civilians to understand, concentrated on the unification question, or, more precisely, on the fate of their respective services within the postwar military establishment. The Second World War was fought on the basis of a unity of military policy achieved through the Joint Chiefs of Staff, who dealt directly with the President. Faced by desperate enemies, forced to negotiate as a unit with purposeful British allies, the Joint Chiefs of Staff arrangement worked reasonably well, a tribute to the acuteness of the circumstances, the sense of responsibility and statesmanship of its membership, and, above all, to the personalities of Roosevelt and Marshall, whose relationship was notably supported, in turn, by Hopkins and Stimson. It was clear, however, that the structure of military organization would have to be radically altered in the postwar if for no other reason than that the Army Air Corps had achieved a *de facto* recognition in 1941 as an arm virtually equal to the ground forces and Navy. As early as November 1943 Marshall commended to his JCS colleagues the notion that postwar planning proceed on the assumption that there would be a single Department of War in the postwar period. And in the spring of 1944, with the military initiative in the hands of the allies, a select House of Representatives committee on postwar military policy set to work.

Given the scale, prestige, and purposefulness of the Air Corps, the realistic choices were only two: to create a single unified military establishment, or to create a third service under some machinery of coordination built around the JCS concept. The Army, including its civilian leaders headed by Stimson, agitated for a simple decision to be taken in principle, with details to be worked out later—a single department of defense within which the three arms of military action would be subsumed and administered in detail from the top by a single chief of staff. The Air Corps on the whole supported the Army but kept open the alternative of a third service department in a looser structure. The Navy's opposition to unification was formally stated in Forrestal's testimony of April 28, 1944, given before the select Congressional committee. Through him the Navy enunciated its disagreement with the Army's concept and presented a case for the continued administrative independence of the Navy.

It was around the Navy's position that the battle was to rage sporadically over the next three years and beyond. The battle was fought within the Pentagon, in the White House, through a variety of friendly and hostile service links between the Pentagon and Congress, and before the bar of public opinion, where extensive efforts were made by all hands to enlist public support for one or another formula. Truman threw his weight initially toward the Army formula, and he insisted throughout on a Department of Defense; but he left a margin for debate and interservice negotiation which was fully exploited.[5] Out of this dialectical process the following issues—many foreshadowed by the Army and Navy debates forty years earlier—emerged as central and were finally resolved according to the indicated formulae.

1. *One service department or three.* The Army advocated a single department, with details of organization to be worked out at a later stage. The Navy advocated a hierarchy of coordinating committees, civil and military, above individual services which would maintain full administrative and operating integrity. Three service departments within a single Department of Defense were finally accepted, with the exact powers of the Secretary of Defense somewhat ambiguous. In addition, a National Security Council, a Central Intelligence Agency, and a National Security Resources Board directly under the President were accepted, following the lines of the Eberstadt (Navy-sponsored) Committee Report.

2. *Equality for the Air Force.* The Army advocated equality within a single department; the Navy opposed. The Air Force emerged as a separate department.

3. *A Chief of Staff of all armed forces.* The Army advocated such a post; the Navy opposed. The Navy won, but in 1949 a full-time chairman for the Joint Chiefs of Staff was accepted. The JCS were assigned the functions of strategic planning and strategic direction of the armed forces and furnished with a staff.

4. *The Marines.* The Army advocated strict limitation of the size of Marine units (lightly armed regiments) and on their role in amphibious operations, with the specific proviso that their functions end at the water line. The Navy opposed. The Marines were granted the right to maintain full divisions, fully armed, with the right of participation in all phases of amphibious operations.

5. *Land-based air operations relating to control of the seas.* The Army advocated transfer to the Air Force of responsibility for antisubmarine warfare, long-range naval reconnaissance, and the protection of shipping by land-based aircraft. The Navy opposed and won total assignment of these responsibilities.[6]

This bureaucratic battle had its roots in deep-seated service loyalties and fears of a most primitive and human kind. It is impossible to regard the men involved as unconcerned with the national interest or, in any normal sense, as unpatriotic. On the other hand, they found it easy to identify the national interest with the course of action most beneficial to the future power and standing of their respective services. There were certainly men in the Army and Air Force who felt about their service as Admiral King did when he said: ". . . if the Navy's welfare is one of the prerequisites to the Nation's welfare—and I sincerely believe that to be the case—any step that is not good for the Navy is not good for the nation."[7]

The Army was concerned to consolidate and perpetuate the enormous prestige and authority it had acquired in the Second World War, symbolized and incorporated in the war and immediate postwar roles of military leadership exercised by Marshall, Eisenhower, and MacArthur. The pattern imposed by Root and Stimson in the first decade of the century had bitten deep in Army conviction and experience; but whatever larger considerations entered into the formulation of its position, the Army judged thoroughgoing unification the best structure for its narrow institutional purpose. The Air Force, confident of the destiny of air power, was prepared to fight hard for thorough unification, as the Army wished; but, when the Navy opposition proved stubborn and effective, it settled relatively cheerfully for an option it had always held open—a tri-service structure, giving the Air Force at last the equality and relative independence it had sought in a generation's bitter struggle. The Navy, sensing a 2-1 West Point–Annapolis struggle (given concreteness by the issues of Marine status and shore-based aircraft), fought with the vigor of an embattled minority, strengthened by a confidence born of its freshly remembered successes in the Pacific.

In sum, the battle over unification was conducted with relatively little thought to the character of the national military problem in the post-1945 period—except for a heated but superficial debate on the meaning and limitations of strategic air power. It was a struggle of bureaucratic politics and of men—not of military ideas.

In the end, Truman and other responsible political figures who would have preferred a more thoroughgoing unification settled for the terms of the 1947 unification act because they felt that to impose something more rigid on men in the mood of the naval officers was likely to cost more in terms of their performance as servants of the state than it was then worth.

## THE UNIFICATION ACT OF 1947 IN PERSPECTIVE

In a larger sense the resolution of the unification battle bore the imprint of persistent national characteristics in political organization. It provided a structure in which there were checks and balances at almost every stage within the military establishment. The effective power of the Secretary of Defense (formally strengthened to a degree in 1949) was left—like that of the President under the Constitution—vague and patently subject to the force of character, qualities of leadership, and administrative style of the man holding the post and of the President who appointed him and who reserved ultimate power of decision. The powers of the three operational chains of command were left great and those of the Chairman of the Joint Chiefs of Staff (and the joint staff serving the Chiefs) left relatively weak, except as the Chairman's leadership, prestige, and influence with the President gave him strength. Independent access to Congress and the public was permitted the three services, guaranteeing that military policy would continue to be a matter of open debate rather than simply a function of negotiation and decision within the Executive Branch. The 1947 move towards unification was, then, a typically messy, subtle affair, fully consonant with the nation's historic suspicion of the effective concentration of power and its tendency to attempt atonement by superficially orderly hierarchies of negotiating committees.

The National Security Act of 1947 appeared to opt, on the whole, for a definition of military missions in terms of the elements rather than in terms of weapons. Roughly, the Army was to maintain the instruments necessary for control over the ground and the Navy over the sea; the Air Force had as its primary mission control of the air and its strategic and tactical exploitation. This approach, congenial to men whose minds and careers were focused on operations with specific weapons, supplied a rationale for leaving with the Navy an air arm, including land-based aircraft required for control of the sea; but it was not extended to giving the Army the aircraft required for control of the land. And, above all, it did not face the issues posed by the potentialities of the new weapons and their foreseeable means of delivery—from cannon and aircraft carriers and via guided and ballistic missiles as well as by land-based aircraft. Nor did it face the issue of air defense. The conceptions brought to bear by the 1947 solution were institutional and narrowly pragmatic, typical of the national style. They did not flow from a conception of the kind of military operations in which the United States might have to engage; nor did they take into account the significance of weapons evidently just over the horizon.

As the Communist threat came to be acknowledged in American policy in 1947 and the Executive Branch formulated plans to deal with it, neither of the alternative concepts of organization and mission debated (nor any combination of them) was to provide useful guidelines for dealing with the spectrum of Communist methods of agression and the relentless pace of the continuing technological revolution in weapons.

The preoccupation of the military with the unification struggle produced a costly hiatus in the formulation of national policy. While the leaders of the American armed forces fought the battle of unification they gave little constructive thought either to the character of the limited, but effective, offensive that communism was mounting against the West or to the kind of contribution which the military might make to meeting it successfully. Moreover, the unification struggle obscured the significance of the long-term military revolution brought about by the technological developments of the Second World War. The assessment which appears in *The Forrestal Diaries* does not appear grossly to overstate the case:

> Until this paralyzing row between the Services on the form of military organization had been settled, it would be impossible to lay down any long-range military plans or policies, to determine properly the size or structure of the military machine to be maintained, or to face with any consistency and forethought the underlying politico-military problems which that machine existed to meet. It is hardly too much to say that the battle over unification . . . delayed the nation for a year or two in grappling with the already dire state of world affairs.[8]

## 23. The Surrender of Eastern Europe: 1945-1946

ACCEPTANCE OF DEFEAT

Against the background of military demobilization and bureaucratic distraction the nation faced the problems of postwar diplomacy. Flowing directly from wartime events and positions, foreign policy centered on well-worn questions: the fate of Eastern Europe, and notably of Poland; schism or unity in Germany; peace, schism, or war in China.

From the Potsdam conference forward, the United States made no serious effort to hold the line in Eastern Europe on the principles negotiated at Yalta and reaffirmed, notably in the case of Poland, at Potsdam. The first volume of Truman's *Memoirs,* covering his first year in office, is full of references to the Polish question; the second volume barely refers to the subsequent fate of that country. From both Byrne's memoirs and *The Forrestal Diaries* the Polish issue virtually disappears after the summer of 1945.

The central fact about American diplomacy in Europe in the immediate aftermath of the Second World War is that Eastern Europe was surrendered to the Soviet Union and the split of Europe on the line of the Elbe was accepted as the more or less legitimate outcome of the Second World War. Why and how did this come about?

STALIN'S SALAMI TACTICS

The first reason for this outcome was that the Soviet technique for takeover in Eastern Europe was designed to minimize the possibility of a clear-cut crisis which might arouse the United States and offer an occasion for a showdown.[1] While the method of takeover varied from country to country, it was generally conducted by slow stages, in each of which the power of non-Communist elements was progressively reduced, a technique later described by Rakosi, Stalin's agent in Hungary, as "salami" tactics.[2] In executing the tactics two Soviet assets were basic—the presence of the Red Army and the initial seizure by Communists of the secret police. Non-Communists were harassed and intimidated, their morale was broken, and the way painstakingly prepared for a final thorough reorganization of the country on the lines of the Soviet Union under Stalin's rule. The job was not completed until 1948.

Stalin's objective, then, was to achieve a slow but steady expansion of direct authority by means which, down to 1948, left open for him an avenue of retreat should the United States make the issue of the violation of the Yalta and Potsdam agreements a question of war or peace; for there is every evidence that Stalin's policy in 1945-1946 was conducted within the firm limitation that it should not involve the Soviet Union in a major war with the United States.

### THE AMERICAN RESPONSE

But the technique of takeover only partly explains the outcome. There were occasions when it was clear to responsible men in Washington that Moscow was systematically violating its wartime commitments at Yalta and Potsdam, some of them sufficiently specific to permit the United States formally to protest through diplomatic channels. The Soviet takeover offered some targets despite its slow staging. Why was it that, having made the question of the democratic process in Eastern Europe a major matter during the war years, the United States in 1945-1946 permitted the whole region to pass under direct Soviet control?

The answer lies in the fact that the United States lacked a conception of its interest in Europe sufficiently clear to make the fate of Eastern Europe a matter for military ultimatum. The United States took a view of Eastern Europe in 1945-1946 parallel to Hoover's view of Manchuria in 1931. It was worth protesting diplomatically against Stalin's course of action and maintaining a *de jure* position of opposition to Communist takeover, but it was not worth risking American blood to prevent the outcome.

Although it is undoubtedly the case that the view of the secondary strategic importance of Eastern Europe was ultimately accountable for the American failure to back its Yalta and Potsdam commitments, three further factors contributed more immediately to the outcome.

First, some of the makers of wartime diplomacy felt unsure in their minds and consciences how seriously the Yalta and Potsdam commitments were to be taken. They wondered if perhaps Stalin might not be justified in believing that the United States had agreed to give him a free hand in Eastern Europe. Neither British nor American diplomacy was ever able wholly to free itself from Churchill's October 1944 percentages, notably as they applied to Bulgaria, Roumania, and Hungary. Allied postwar diplomacy was bemused by the implications of having granted the Soviet Union title to German assets in Eastern Europe. Americans recalled somewhat shamefacedly how grossly the problem of defeating Japan had been overestimated and how ardently the American military had sought Soviet participation in the Far Eastern War. More generally, men wondered if the implication of all that had been done in the war was not really to define spheres of influence on the basis of where the military forces had ended up, and that, somehow, to insist too strongly on the democratic process in Eastern Europe was to seek a reversal of implicit commitments made to a fighting ally. And this attitude may have been strengthened in the post-Potsdam period by the desire to avoid applying the formula of Big Three participation to the Japanese occupation, to Trieste, to the Ruhr, and to other unsettled issues in the non-Communist world. Some may have felt that to fight for freedom in the East would have led to further extensions of Soviet power in the West and in Japan.

The mood of policy-makers in postwar Washington was, then, to some degree colored by ambiguities from the past. Those ambiguities are by no means a complete explanation of the American retreat from Eastern Europe; and in the case of Poland, given the history of wartime negotiation and of hard-won explicit agreements, there was no conceivable ground for ambiguity. But to some extent American diplomacy in 1945-1946 still operated under inhibitions derived from the war.

Second, the extremely rapid demobilization of American military strength in 1945-1946 converged with a turning of the nation's attention to domestic matters to weaken the bases of American diplomacy. It would have taken extremely vigorous executive leadership, backed by a strong, well-presented case, to stem the instinctive and typical American return to the ways and attitudes of peace in the months after V-J Day. It would have required a further suspension of political controversy over domestic issues, already unnaturally extended by a long war. More than that, it would have required a presentation to the public of evidence on the apparent intentions of the Soviet Union which, it was widely believed, might disrupt the efforts to consolidate the institutions of the United Nations and the formal procedures of peacemaking which, in the longer run, were still regarded as the foundations for peace in many American minds. Whether or not the public was prepared for such a shock, it is clear that professional politicians believed it to be unprepared.[3]

A third reason why Truman did not move forcefully on the question of

Eastern Europe—real enough, but difficult to weigh accurately—was that his Secretary of State, Byrnes, took a quite particular view of his task—a view with which Truman was not immediately prepared to cope. Byrnes viewed foreign affairs as a distinct area in which to exercise a large measure of personal command. In part, his attitude may have derived from his own high view of his political status and his limited respect for Truman, but it also may have been connected with a perspective on the role of Secretary of State similar to that which John Foster Dulles was to exhibit in the period 1952-1958. Both Byrnes and Dulles tended to regard the conduct of foreign affairs as primarily a matter of high-level personal negotiation of international agreements. In Byrnes' case this negotiator's frame of mind may have been strengthened by the fact that he would have had to turn to the President to alter the framework within which he operated. Only the President could have altered the pace of demobilization or the basic attitude toward Moscow. And Byrnes was not in a mood to seek the President's help.

Byrnes' central job, as he defined it, came to be the use of the tools of diplomacy to convert the interim wartime arrangements into a stable peace on terms acceptable to the Senate and to the American public without a radical shift from wartime attitudes and without requesting of the President drastic new initiatives. Byrnes' mind, reflecting an abiding legalistic bias in American diplomacy, was concentrated on the four peace treaties: the Bulgarian, Roumanian, Hungarian, and Italian. Poland, in one sense, fell outside his immediate purview because no peace treaty was involved. So far as American diplomacy was concerned, it was in the year between Byrnes' trip to Moscow in December 1945 and the signing of the peace treaties in New York in December 1946 that, in effect, Poland was definitely lost.[4]

### THE END OF THE ROAD IN POLAND

Under maximum pressure on Moscow from Western diplomacy, Mikolajczyk had returned to Poland in mid-1945 as vice-premier only to find the machinery of Communist takeover in high gear.

The Ministry of the Interior was divided in two at the start, with Public Administration (routine bureaucratic matters) under Kiernik, a follower of Mikolajczyk, and Security (secret political police, internal security corps, and militia) under a Communist, Radkiewicz. What was left of the Army was also controlled, at least at the top, by Communists and included many who had served in the Red Army. The third crucial position occupied by the Communists was the Ministry of Regained Territories (the Oder-Neisse region), a separate administration under Gomulka. Since the territory was comparatively rich in industrial and agricultural opportunities, and since a complete resettlement of Poles from the East was called for after the Germans were expelled, ample possibilities for patronage and control were available to Gomulka, who was also at that time Secretary of the Polish Communist Party.

The regime was confronted in the early stages of its rule by the guerrilla operations of some unreconciled members of former underground groups. Later, when the police forces had been organized, the existence of guerrilla bands was exploited as a justification for general repressive measures. After Mikolajczyk's original Peasant Party had been taken over by the Communists, two leaders of the new Polish People's Party, which he then established, were murdered. Mikolajczyk's protests and demands for investigation were taken to exhibit a "lack of confidence in the Minister of Security." A subsequent trial brought a suitable confession from an underground agent.

Mikolajczyk was able to hold a Party congress in January 1946; and he resisted pressure to join the government bloc. Although Mikolajczyk's Polish People's Party (P.S.L.P.) was nominally in the government, delegates were arrested, meetings broken up, and party offices raided. The press continuously denounced Mikolajczyk as a British agent, and the P.S.L.'s own paper rations were cut drastically. In the plebiscite of June 1946—conducted with many irregularities, but more or less on Western election standards—the government announced an anti-government majority of 68 per cent on the one disputed question; but according to Mikolajczyk the result would have been 83 per cent in his favor had there not been arrests and falsification. And there is no doubt that the government figure is an underestimate. It was Mikolajczyk who had urged the Polish People to vote "no" on this issue, which was universally taken to be a test of his strength.

From this time on, the Polish government, frightened by Mikolajczyk's evident grass-roots support, moved quickly under Moscow's guidance. To prepare for the parliamentary elections of January 1947, the western territories, safe under Gomulka's control, were given excessive electoral representation. Mikolajczyk and his followers were incriminated by the confessions of certain political prisoners who asserted they were foreign agents. Two bogus parties were set up to drain off the peasant vote toward Communist-controlled groups, thousands of P.S.L. members were at least temporarily arrested, and "voluntary open voting" took place in many districts. The resulting parliament, overwhelmingly backing the government bloc, passed a new provisional constitution in February 1947.

This, in effect, was the end of the road for Yalta, Potsdam, and Mikolajczyk; but he did not give up the uneven struggle and leave Poland until the fall of 1947, when he was informed of his imminent arrest. The only other "independent" party left in Poland, the satellite Socialist party, completed the operation in 1948, when, in response to a demand for "workers' unity," it merged with the Communists to form a Polish United Workers' Party, purged, in the meantime, of all unreliable elements. By the end of 1948 all effective power was concentrated in this United Party. Poland was an almost completely communized state operating with fully unified police and other controls sensitively under the control of Moscow or those it judged reliable; and so it was to remain for some eight years.

The final interval when Poland might conceivably have been saved was the six months following Mikolajczyk's display of strength in the June 1946 plebiscite. If at that period the United States had made the matter of free Polish elections a fighting issue, it is possible that the Soviet Union, confronted with clear evidence of the Polish popular mood, would have been forced to abide by its Yalta and Potsdam commitments. But the consequences for the whole of Soviet policy in Europe would have been so decisive that probably nothing less than an evident American willingness to go to war would have moved Stalin.

Whatever the possibilities may or may not have been for salvaging a politically free Poland in the latter half of 1946, the weight of American attention was elsewhere—on the treaties, on the rapidly developing split in Germany, on the German assets issue in Austria, on the deteriorating position in Western Europe, on Marshall's failing negotiations in China, on the domestic price level and the question of removing government controls over the economy. If Poland figured in Byrnes' mind, it figured principally in the question of the east German borders. All parties in Poland backed as permanent the new western borders of Poland, which had been given interim status at Potsdam pending a German peace treaty. Moscow, in an effort to strengthen the hand of its agents in Warsaw, also backed as permanent the new boundary. Byrnes, in his Stuttgart speech of September 1946, re-emphasized the American view that the boundary was interim, pending a definitive peace settlement. To many this appeared an effort to appeal to German, as opposed to Polish, opinion, marking, in effect, a decision to hold the line in the West, having largely lost hope of influencing events in the East.

### BYRNES' CHOICE AND THE ALTERNATIVES

Byrnes' method of concentrating one by one on the peace treaty negotiations had the effect of consolidating the emerging split of Europe. As among the treaty problems, he devoted his energies to securing the best deal possible for Italy as part of the West, accepting in return treaties which left Moscow with virtually complete freedom of action in the three satellite areas under negotiation. Over the whole year, starting in about December 1945, there was an awareness in Washington of the trend of events in Eastern Europe but a general hopelessness about it, well reflected in the following entry from *The Forrestal Diaries:*

There was a summary report from Mark F. Ethridge, publisher of the Louisville *Courier Journal*, who had been in Rumania and Bulgaria under State Department auspices; it drew the picture—now familiar to Forrestal if not to the public—of forcible Soviet infiltration and domination. The United States, it said, "is faced with the alternatives of continuing its policy of adherence to the position taken at Yalta and Potsdam or of conceding this area as a Soviet sphere of influence." But as to how the United States could enforce the first alternative, this report, like so many others, was silent.[5]

Byrnes' mood, in the face of these circumstances, is accurately captured in the following contemporary summary:

Secretary Byrnes went to Moscow (December 1945) armed with the report of Mark Ethridge, whose on-the-spot investigation fully confirmed the view that the Groza government in Rumania and the Gheorghiev government in Bulgaria were not broadly representative and were dominated by the Communists. The Bulgarian elections, postponed in August, were held in November, just after Ethridge's visit; boycotted by the opposition parties, they resulted in a sweeping victory for the government bloc, and the U.S. State Department declared that it could not regard them as measuring up to the Yalta principles. Hungary, on the other hand, held an election in November which was comparatively free; as might be expected, since the Hungarians were not enjoying the Soviet occupation, they gave an absolute majority to the anti-Communist Small Landholders Party. It was an experiment which the Soviets would not wish to repeat in Rumania or Bulgaria.

If Byrnes had wanted to take a firm stand on the Yalta Declaration and repeat the previous September's bitter controversy with Molotov, he had plenty of facts to support his case. But he and his advisers were not convinced that non-recognition for an indefinite period would really help to achieve the ends of American policy in the Balkans. Obviously the United States did not intend to back up its view of the Yalta Declaration with force. Without abandoning its principles and policies, it could perhaps support them more effectively while maintaining normal diplomatic relations with the countries in question. In any case, Byrnes was willing to accept a settlement whereby the existing Rumanian and Bulgarian governments would be broadened by token representation for the pro-western opposition parties and would pledge free elections at an early date. The United States and Britain agreed to recognize the governments after the reorganization, to be guided in the case of Rumania by a tripartite U.S.-British-Soviet commission and in that of Bulgaria by the good offices of the Soviet Government, had been effected.

These solutions, although not burying the Yalta principles entirely, unquestionably represented a retreat from the previous American position. The Soviet Government also retreated but traveled a shorter distance to reach the point of compromise than the United States did. The settlements were something of a face-saving device, to enable the great powers to get on with the work of the peace treaties without being further bedeviled by the question of recognition. The Americans and British apparently did not have much real hope that the Moscow agreements on Rumania and Bulgaria would work out any better than had the Yalta agreements on Poland and Yugoslavia which they resembled. They scarcely expected that the "broadened" Rumanian and Bulgarian governments would really hold free elections. If they did not, the world could be told as much, and the actual situation would be no worse than before.[6]

It is clear that the only alternatives considered by Byrnes were nonrecognition or the best face-saving formula he could wring from the peace treaty negotiations.

Was the position in Eastern Europe as incapable of salvage at American initiative as Byrnes' course assumed? Although history cannot be reconstructed retrospectively, two facts are worth noting.

First, where the United States acted strongly in this period, the Soviet Union backed away. At firm American insistence—in diplomatic form, virtually an ultimatum—Stalin withdrew his troops from Northern Iran in March 1946 after exhibiting every sign that he intended to apply the takeover technique to the area occupied by the Soviet Union during the war. Here Truman was clear about the primary character of American interests.

> As I saw it, three things were involved. One was the security of Turkey. Russia had been pressing Turkey for special privileges and for territorial concessions for several months. The Turks had resisted all these demands, but their position would be infinitely more difficult if Russia, or a Russian puppet state, were able to outflank her in the East.
>
> The second problem was the control of Iran's oil reserves. That Russia had an eye on these vast deposits seemed beyond question. If the Russians were to control Iran's oil, either directly or indirectly, the raw-material balance of the world would undergo a serious change, and it would be a serious loss for the economy of the Western world.
>
> What perturbed me most, however, was Russia's callous disregard of the rights of a small nation and of her own solemn promises. International cooperation was impossible if national obligations could be ignored and the U.N. bypassed as if it did not exist.
>
> I talked over all these points with Secretary Byrnes and Admiral Leahy. Then I told Byrnes to send a blunt message to Premier Stalin.[7]

No such effort at a showdown was attempted on the Polish issue. So far as is known, Byrnes never laid the issue of the Polish elections before Truman or requested him to take action equivalent to that taken in Iran.

Second, Byrnes was presented with alternative courses of action and rejected them. Ambassador Lane, in Warsaw, as early as March 1, 1946, wrote to H. Freeman Mathews, Director of the Office of European Affairs in the Department of State, outlining the process of takeover underway and indicating the extremely narrow limits within which, under existing policy directives, he could be effective in ensuring that the Yalta and Potsdam agreements were executed. He concluded:

All of this, of course, boils down in the last analysis to a decision as to what our policy is going to be towards the Soviet Union. My own feeling is that unless we give publicity to what is going on in Poland and other nations in an analogous position, we will not be able to use our influence in these countries either politically or economically. With the withdrawal of the greater part of our armed forces from Europe we have lost one of the few arguments which are effective with a power such as the Soviet Union. In answer to the criticism which would undoubtedly be made that we are courting war with the Soviet Union in making the unpleasant facts known regarding Communist domination of the countries of Eastern Europe (and perhaps later the countries in Western Europe to an even greater extent than at the present time), I should like to say that the American public has a right to know the truth; that unpreparedness nearly cost us the last war, due to the isolationist attitude of a part of the people of the United States; that appeasement will be just as dangerous today as it was at the time of Munich; and that we run much more danger of war if we ignore the dangers of aggression than by honestly facing the facts.[8]

Lane's view was increasingly shared in Washington during 1946, and usually in the form in which he put it: that is, as a need to prepare the public for a general showdown with Stalin rather than far a specific American initiative designed to salvage the Yalta and Potsdam agreements.

At just this period Byrnes was urged to alter his course from another direction. Over the week end of April 20-21, 1946, when he was about to leave for peace treaty negotiations in Paris, he was pressed by Acheson and Clayton (then Undersecretary and Assistant Secretary for Economic Affairs respectively) to consider a negotiating plan along lines different from those which had developed out of the post-Potsdam meetings of the Foreign Ministers. The plan had these elements:

1. The Secretary of State would open the Paris meetings by taking a general initiative covering the whole range of unsettled European issues.

2. He would assert that the United States opposed the formation of exclusive blocs and the split of Europe they would bring about; that, whatever the outcome of his proposals, the American concern with the future of Europe was permanent and not transient; and that the United States was prepared forthwith to make proposals for a European settlement on an all-European basis consistent with the wartime agreements.

3. He would propose formulae consistent with such a general European settlement covering specific issues involved in the treaty negotiations (for example, the control of the Danube) and major issues outside the area of treaty negotiations, notably the unsettled issues in Germany and Austria.

4. He would propose the setting up of a regional U.N. security council to oversee the execution of the settlements arrived at in the treaties as well as in Germany and Austria.

5. He would propose the creation of an all-European economic organization designed to accelerate lagging reconstruction and to achieve greater long-run economic unity in Europe, with subcommissions for fuel and power, trade and transport, finance, the coordination of plans, and so on.

6. He would assert finally, that, should the settlement prove acceptable, the United States Government would back the new economic organization of Europe with substantial economic aid.

The Acheson-Clayton proposal had been initially drafted in the division of the State Department responsible for German-Austrian economic affairs.[9] That division, seeking to carry out the high-level American objectives of achieving economic unity in Germany and a viable independent economy in Austria, became convinced that those objectives were not likely to be achieved if the tendency toward the formation of exclusive blocs in Europe were permitted to proceed unchecked, and that the piecemeal negotiation of the treaties would simply strengthen and confirm that tendency. Germany would be split and it would become an object of competition between East and West; Austria would find economic and political survival difficult as an eastern extension of a western bloc virtually surrounded by Communist states loyal to Moscow.[10]

It was felt that the split of Europe was being accelerated by the judgment of both Soviet and Western European governments that the interest of the United States in the structure of Europe was likely to prove transitory and that, therefore, the Soviet Union had merely to await the progressive withdrawal of the United States before consolidating an Eastern European base, while the Western Europeans increasingly felt that the very best they might look forward to was holding on to the area up to the Elbe and, perhaps, forming a western bloc.

The Acheson-Clayton proposal looked also to the longer run. It reflected the judgment that, if Germany were ever to be united, the legitimate fears of France and the smaller countries of Europe could be allayed only if the whole continent of Europe were so organized that the preponderant economic and political bargaining weight of a united Germany could not be wielded against the lesser European states. Moreover, it was judged—and there was good evidence for this—that the wiser Europeans, including many Germans, read the lesson of the two world wars as proof that the old European state system was no longer viable and that a united Europe was the proper objective for the creative energies of the postwar generation.

The proposal recognized that the Soviet Union had been proceeding in the post-Potsdam period on a unilateral basis in Europe and that the initiative it proposed to Byrnes would cut clean across Stalin's apparent purposes. What then were the chances of success by negotiation with Moscow? The outcome was judged to depend on whether or not the Soviet performance was based on the assumption of future diminished American concern in European affairs. The proposal stated that:

> The U.S.S.R. response to the alternatives of European organization or vigorous U.S. support for the Western bloc cannot be fairly prejudged. [It asserted, further, that the] nature of an alternative to a European organization . . . makes it desirable in the U. S. interest to press for the superior solution, no matter how small the chances of success may initially appear to be. Only after the exhaustion of the line it represents does acceptance of a bloc alternative appear justified.

The proposal did not deal explicitly with the question of political freedom in Eastern Europe, but one of its main purposes was to provide a framework in which the natural East European orientation toward the West could become progressively more effective. In the spring of 1946 Czechoslovakia was still a politically democratic state, the Small Holders Party had not yet been eliminated from power in Hungary, and important democratic elements were still alive in Polish politics. It was felt that the best chance of reversing the evident trend toward complete Soviet consolidation of the area through diplomacy lay in a radical change in the shape which postwar negotiations were assuming —a change based on a United States initiative which would bring to bear "the full weight of its diplomatic power and bargaining position."

This proposal was rejected in April 1946 by both the groups most directly responsible for the Paris Peace Conference. Byrnes and his personal staff rejected it because it did not fit his pattern of treaty-by-treaty piecemeal negotiation—and probably also because Byrnes at that time already planned to test Soviet intentions with his proposal for a fifty-year demilitarization pact in Germany. The senior political officers in the Department of State rejected it ostensibly on the grounds that such an American initiative was calculated to frighten the Soviet Union and obstruct negotiations then underway but probably also because some had already concluded that a Western bloc was the only attainable goal of American diplomacy in Europe.[11]

The existence and rejection of Lane's intervention and the Acheson-Clayton proposal by no means demonstrate that the freedom of Eastern Europe could have been salvaged short of war or military ultimatum in 1946. They do suggest that the resources of an informed and aroused American public opinion were not sought and that the vision of an alternative to schism, backed by American economic resources and full long-term diplomatic commitment, was not brought into play. Both would have required a radical change in the domestic setting within which immediate postwar diplomacy was conducted. The President alone could have brought about such a change; and this Byrnes failed to seek or Truman to initiate.

The treaty negotiations of 1946 thus ran thir course, tidying up the split of Europe except for Germany, where the implications of what was happening in the East were still to be faced.

## 24. The Split of Germany: 1945-1946

POTSDAM

The story of postwar policy toward Germany begins with the Potsdam meeting and its decisions.[1] As it related to Germany, the communique issued on August 2, 1945, contained several elements. In part it proclaimed general principles which were to govern the occupation of each zone in Germany. The principles were to be interpreted and administered by the several occupying powers; but the four-power Control Council in Berlin was to handle all-German issues, and a Council of Foreign Ministers was created to deal, among other matters, with German issues not resolved in Berlin and ultimately with a German unity. The principles covered the elimination of existing military equipment and uniquely military production facilities as well as the democratization of German institutions: the schools and judiciary, local government, and the trade unions. The principles of freedom of speech and assembly and of free elections were proclaimed.

The second set of agreements on Germany related to economic policy and, most specifically, to reparations, and it laid down a number of operating policies. Germany was to be treated as an economic unit, and central German agencies were to be created in economic fields, to operate under the Control Council. Germany was to pay reparations within the general limit of earning for itself a standard of subsistence accommodated to an average European level and within a specific limit of paying out of current exports for current imports. Soviet and Polish reparations were to come from the Soviet Zone; but, in view of heavy Russian war losses, 15 per cent of Western Zone capital equipment removed would be traded against current exports from the Soviet Zone, and an additional 10 per cent would be available as pure reparations to the Soviet Union. A general reparations plan was to be negotiated in the Control Council within six months. Advance reparation deliveries on a limited basis were to be made, pending a general accord, in order to accelerate European recovery.

Diplomatic explorations and technical studies of the reparations problem had been going forward since the Yalta Conference, the negotiations being conducted on the American side mainly under a special group headed by Edwin Pauley. That group was ill-coordinated with other arms of American foreign policy, and there was still no clear American position on reparations formulated at the time of the Potsdam Conference.

At Potsdam, however, the American delegation underwent a vivid experience which clarified its collective mind. Americans saw in Berlin (including the Western zones of Berlin) that, without inter-Allied agreement, the Russians were moving equipment out of factories as fast as their technicians could dismantle it—faster even than the equipment could be properly crated and transported; and it was evident that this process of Soviet seizure was proceeding throughout much of Eastern Europe as well as in Manchuria. American reparations policy quickly focused around the problem of preventing the kind of denuding of West Germany which the Russians were effecting in the East.

Mindful of the Russian war losses, Americans found it hard in July 1945 to put their hearts into protesting what was being done in the Soviet zone even though the hasty unilateral removal of machinery was viewed as inefficient as well as illegal. American effort, therefore, was devoted primarily to limiting the extent of Soviet claims on West German capital equipment and to laying down rules under which it would be impossible for the United States to pour emergency aid into Germany from the West (or finance a German foreign exchange deficit) while current German production was being drained off to the East as reparations. Thus, while Potsdam's general political and economic principles looked to a united four-power policy in Germany, the unilateral principle was strengthened once unilateral action on reparations was accepted as legitimate in the Soviet Zone; and reparations went to the heart of short-run economic and political policy. To a significant degree, then, the initial position from which negotiations were begun accepted a split of Germany.

REPARATIONS

From the Potsdam meetings to April 1946 the question of reparations remained the central issue of four-power diplomacy in Germany, although the larger issues emerged and were gradually clarified.

On December 12, 1945, the Department of State issued a long statement on German economic policy. Its formal purpose was to clarify the principle on which the reparations clauses of Potsdam should be negotiated. Its broader aim, however, was to define the stages whereby the German economy would move from a role of subservience to the needs of other states to recovery and, finally, to resumed economic development when once again German standards of living would be a matter determined by German efforts and efficiency in utilizing German resources. This document symbolized the rapid transition in the post-Potsdam period from a negative to a constructive approach to Germany, a transition which was inevitable given Western values but which was certainly accelerated by a Soviet policy which evidently sought to profit from poverty and frustration in Central and Western Europe.

Although the economists and industrial technicians concentrated in Berlin made valiant efforts to construct an economic plan which would meet the complex Potsdam conditions, the essence of American policy in this period was political. The American purpose was to force at an early stage a clear-cut test of whether or not the Soviet Union was prepared to move promptly toward a united Germany. The architect of this policy, as well as its chief practitioner, was Lucius Clay.

The reparations plan was essentially a definition of the initial complement of industrial equipment necessary to make postwar Germany economically viable if it were effectively unified. The reparations pool would be defined by subtracting this minimum level of industry from capacity actually in Germany. Clay's policy was to work hard and cooperatively with the Russians in getting an agreed level-of-industry plan and then to make actual reparation deliveries hinge on Soviet agreement to treat the German economy as an economic unit. Because of the intimate interconnections between economic and other institutions, it was clear that political and economic unity would come together if they came at all. What appeared a highly remote and often fantastic technicians' game was, in fact, a negotiation to test whether the split of Germany would persist.

The outcome was clean-cut, although its full implications took some time to absorb. A level-of-industry plan was agreed on March 26, 1946, with the American negotiators making every possible concession to meet Soviet demands. Within a month, however, Clay had openly disengaged from the reparations plan on the grounds that the Soviets were clearly unprepared to join in a common program for foreign trade and for the German economy as a whole. Clay's statement in the Coordinating Committee of the Control Council on April 26, 1946 reveals his mind:

> I submit that reparations was only one of the bricks that built the house. If you pull out any of the bricks the house collapses, and it seems to me we have pulled out so many already we are on the verge of collapse. I don't believe we can ever reach a solution on any one of them without reaching a solution on all of them. Certainly the question of the ability to meet the export-import program is tied up definitely with the question of reparations.
>
> Since it has become the practice to quote Potsdam, I would like to quote a part of Potsdam which comes before the part quoted by my Soviet colleague. Paragraph 14 requires that during the occupation Germany shall be treated as a single economic unit. During the year of occupation up to date, I would not think anyone can claim that we have done so. In Paragraph 15 it states that Allied control shall be imposed on the German economy only to the extent necessary to insure during the term of the Control Council the equitable distribution of essential commodities between the several zones, so as to produce a balanced economy throughout Germany, and reduce the need for imports. We have been here a year, but I do not believe that my colleagues would claim that we have accomplished that. And Paragraph 16 shows that

the writers of this protocol foresaw what might happen and required to carry it out the establishment of German administrative machinery to proclaim and assume the administration of these controls. Would my colleagues suggest that we have lived up to this part of Potsdam? I claim that to live up to Potsdam you live up to it in whole and not in its individual parts.[2]

On May 3 Clay stopped advance reparation deliveries from the American Zone—a major turning point in the Cold War.

From this time forward the American position moved steadily toward the unification of the Western zones and the acceptance of a split Germany. This trend was broken only by Marshall's last-ditch effort to negotiate German unity in Moscow in March-April 1947 and, in a sense, by his offer in June 1947 to treat the whole of Europe as an economic unit under the Marshall Plan proposal.

THE CONTROL COUNCIL DRAMA

It is difficult to recapture the mood of the post-Potsdam negotiations in the Berlin Control Council as American hopes came up against the designs of Stalin on the one hand and the fixed positions of the French and British on the other.

Eisenhower and Clay—the former remaining only until November 1945—felt that the Control Council and its negotiations represented a historic occasion to seek a fundamental understanding with the Russians.

> Obstacles, doubts, fears of failure in American-Soviet relations, there were on every side. But the alternative to success seemed so terrifying to contemplate that all of us on occupation duty sought every possible avenue through which progress might be achieved.
>
> Berlin, we were convinced, was an experimental laboratory for the development of international accord. There the West was joined with the East in the task of reorganizing a highly complex economy and re-educating a numerous people to political decency so that Germany, purged of its capacity and will for aggression, might be restored to the family of nations.
>
> If in that endeavor there could be developed friendly ways and means of solving our local differences and problems, a long step forward would be taken toward the friendly settlement of world problems. Overshadowing all goals for us Americans was the contribution we locally might make toward establishing a working partnership between the United States and Russia.[3]

From the beginning, Eisenhower was encouraged by the responsiveness of Zhukov; and between Clay and Sokolovsky, their deputies, there developed a unique relationship of mutual respect and, to a degree, of friendship. This reaching out between American and Russians extended far down into the maze of technical committees into which the Control Council was organized. Although reparations was at the center of high diplomacy in Berlin, there was an interminable array of housekeeping questions which required one form or another of expertise. Neither the Americans nor the Russians involved in this business were professional diplomats. They were, for the most part, technicians, emerging from searching experiences of war, full of national pride, and touched with a human desire to make the peace work. The Berlin Control Council was the most extensive Western contact with the rising second generation of well-trained technicians in Soviet society; and many who shared the experience emerged with a sense that Soviet society had the capability of producing in time a policy easier to live with than Stalin's.

The Control Council quickly established a common law of decorous, dignified debate, a tradition which survived long after the Council had clearly failed in its central mission. On at least one occasion Sokolovsky, furnished by the powerful Soviet political adviser with a conventional diplomatic script full of the increasingly conventional recriminations against the West, did his duty but in a manner that clearly disassociated him from the text. In part, the Control Council style was a carry-over of mutually understood military etiquette as among the military chiefs; in part it reflected a sense of larger mission which, in differing degree, touched men from all four nations.

This mood, of course, had little to do with policy. Policy, on the Soviet side, was determined in Moscow by Stalin. And at no point did Clay and his senior colleagues mistake the human warmth and willingness to compromise among their Russian colleagues for the substance of Soviet policy or Stalin's intent; at no point did they surrender American interests, as they were then understood, in order to get on with the Russians in some vague and general sense. Clay was clear that solid understanding and agreement could come only as between self-respecting nations clear and firm concerning their essential interests.

The human relations which developed between the Americans and Russians in Berlin were watched with mixed feelings by the British and French. The rapprochement raised the possibility of a Soviet-American bilateral agreement which would in effect settle Europe's affairs and reduce all other powers to secondary status. More important, so far as the American hopes in the Control Council were concerned, neither the French nor the British believed then that German unity was a practical or a particularly desirable goal.

The French, having failed to get agreement on the detachment of the Ruhr, sought to delay the revival of German economic and political strength at every stage, sensing that a revived Germany would ultimately overshadow postwar France on the European scene. British policy, on narrower economic grounds, aimed to ensure a more rapid recovery of the British then the German economy, notably in export markets; but, since the costs of British occupation in Germany were high, there was a countervailing interest in making the British zone, which contained the bulk of German industry, a going concern. Neither France nor Britain shared the American anxiety to force a showdown on the issue of German unity, both nations being reasonably content with the split of Europe on the Elbe as representing a tolerable, if not happy, distribution of power between East and West. Given their recent experiences of Germany and their intense domestic preoccupations in the immediate postwar period, their attitudes were wholly understandable—but they were not in harmony with the more ambitious hopes and more ardent mood of Americans caught up in the German problem.

Some British and French undoubtedly shared the sense of promise implicit in the human understanding which briefly flowered in the Control Council. On the whole, however, Clay, in actively seeking an accord with the Russians on the level of industry and then provoking a sharp crisis on the issue of German economic unity, was doubly out of step with his Western colleagues.

Early in 1946 it became evident that Stalin was disturbed at the developing relationship in Berlin, which indeed had within it the seeds of German unity on democratic terms. There were changes in Soviet personnel, and the role of the Soviet Political Adviser was increased. Zhukov was recalled as early as November 1945 and soon isolated in Odessa. Sokolovsky operated with progressively diminished flexibility and freedom for independent action. By the spring of 1946 there was little doubt among the Americans in Berlin that the immediate effort to unify Germany had failed, and that steps to build a unified and viable West Germany as part of the West were urgent.

After the failure of the reparations negotiations in April, the notion of linking the British and American zones began seriously to be considered. On July 20, 1946, a formal offer was made in the Control Council to link the American zone with any other (or all three), and it was accepted by the British on July 30. Aside from aiding German recovery and strengthening the Western bargaining hand vis-à-vis Moscow, the agreement lifted to a degree the pressing financial burden of occupation on London and gave Clay a strong voice in the administration of West German resources. It had rankled among the Americans in Berlin that their authority extended directly only over the wooded hills and farms which mainly characterized the American zone in the south.

The American position taken in the Control Council shared one general limitation of American policy. It sought to test Soviet intentions at a key point; but it incorporated no clear, positive concept of Europe or of the American interest in its structure. German unity was sought in a vacuum, as a goal in itself. Above all, the American view failed to recognize adequately the forces shaping Soviet policy and the extent to which Soviet policy hinged on what Stalin thought the United States would or would not do to enforce agreements he intended to break if violation proved safe.

The American assumption was that Moscow's position was determined by forces essentially independent of the American performance outside Berlin and that the maximum course open to the United States, having honestly reassured the Soviets that the nation's intentions were peaceful, was to accept the split on the Elbe. There was no inkling among the Americans in the Control Council, for example, that the fate of Germany and of their effort to seek its unity might well hinge on whether or not Poland and Eastern Europe were politically free. The reaction in Berlin to the Acheson-Clayton proposal for an American initiative looking to an all-European settlement was that the question of unity or schism in Europe would be settled in Germany and in Berlin. If the Soviets were willing to see a free unified Europe, that fact would emerge in the German negotiations; if not, then a split on the Elbe would be inevitable. There was little awareness that the fate of Germany might hinge on Mikolajczyk's fate in Poland and on what the United States did or failed to do in backing the Yalta and Potsdam commitments in Eastern Europe. And in other respects as well, American policy in postwar Germany was clear, strong, but narrow.

Clay's performance in the eight post-Potsdam months had one important consequence for those charged with making American policy. His effort to seek German unity by negotiation with Russia had been so whole-hearted and conducted with such evident sincerity, and the Soviet unwillingness to proceed seriously toward unity was so patent, that no one who knew the circumstances could feel that a postwar opportunity for accord had been lost for lack of trying in Berlin.

The issue of unity or schism was not, of course, the sole German issue of importance in 1945-1946; nor was it the sole criterion of American policy. The French, for example, exerted the strongest pressure which they could muster to detach the Ruhr by one device or another from Germany, a position resisted in London and Washington. The French, joined by other Western European states, sought urgently an increase in Ruhr coal production for export, a matter that involved both policy in the British zone toward coal production and the question of the equitable proportioning of Ruhr coal between German and Western European needs. There was the issue of reparations deliveries to the Western European states from excess German industrial capacity, which became enmeshed with the negotiation with the Soviets. And there were a host of political and social issues within the American zone of occupation, including the process of denazification, the development of German democratic institutions, and the forms and pace at which Germans would assume limited political control of their country. But under Clay's leadership the issue of unity or schism was kept to the forefront.

The end of the Control Council drama was inevitable. Given the character of Stalin's aims, there was no possibility of achieving unity in Germany by negotiations in Berlin. The bargaining cards for such a purpose were the evocation of the American will and, if necessary its material and military resources to back a settlement consonant with the wartime agreements and the Potsdam commitment to treat Germany as an economic unit. Those cards were not in Clay's hands. Clay had to take the framework of American policy as given; and that policy decreed a split on the Elbe as the best outcome attainable.

## 25. The Emerging Concept of Unity in Western Europe: 1945-1946

### THE HERITAGE OF WARTIME POLICY

In the course of the war American diplomatic positions had to be taken in relation to a number of specific situations on the European continent. In Greece at the end of 1944 and early in 1945 there was the acute problem of installing a new government against Communist opposition. There, in the end, with some considerable American reservation about Churchill's policy, the unique British responsibility was respected. In Italy specific American decisions had to be taken in the context of the Allied Control Commission while hostilities proceeded and, particularly, in connection with the formation of a provisional Italian government. French policy, as a special area of interest and debate, was a feature of the Western scene from the fall of France down through recognition of the Provisional French government in summer of 1944. The evolution of wartime events and negotiations required thought and debate within the government on the nature and limits of American interests in Central and Eastern Europe. But the exigencies of war required no formal decision about liberated areas in the West other than that they return to the *status quo ante*; and it is fair to say that at the end of the war the United States had a less coherent and explicit policy for Western (and Southern) Europe than it had for either Eastern Europe or Germany. The single continuing principle of American policy toward those parts of Europe was that orderly democratic processes be restored.

Relations with Britain represented a different kind of problem. In the course of the war British and American affairs had indeed, as Churchill said, become remarkably mixed up. Joint operations in almost every theater, ultimately guided by the Combined Chiefs of Staff, had produced a military alliance of peculiar intimacy; and Lend-Lease gave this whole arrangement an economic foundation which brought the two nations closer to confederation than to military alliance as hitherto generally understood. At numerous points the combined higher staffs, with intermingled personnel, worked in unity on tasks of war; and generally they worked with success—except in Southeast Asia.

There were many on the British side who looked to a continuation in new forms of this special bilateral relationship and even to the maintenance of combined institutions; but Americans were generally less enthusiastic about perpetuating combined operations, for two reasons. First, in the latter stages of war combined staffs gave to the British a role of relative equality in policy-making which no longer matched the volume of resources supplied by the two nations. The British appeared to gain more than the Americans from pooling. Second, innate British skill at higher staff work and Whitehall's extraordinary unity of purpose gave the British natural advantages in combined enterprises which baffled and frustrated many Americans, who were more at home in line than staff operations and who had to contend with the federalist chaos of Washington behind them.

Nevertheless, Washington considered, for example, whether to proceed directly into a joint occupation of the British and American zones in Germany and whether to maintain as a more or less permanent feature of the postwar world the combined military staff structure. And, although it was envisaged that Lend-Lease as it had operated since 1941 would come to an end, it was implicitly assumed by the British (and by most responsible American officials) that Lend-Lease would be tapered off in such a way as to avoid unnecessary shock to the weakened and distorted British war economy.

With the ending of the war against Japan, however, the United States withdrew from these special intimate links, and Anglo-American relations began to move towards their prewar arms-length pattern. In Germany the zones were separately occupied, and almost immediately there were differences between the British and American approaches to the German problem both within the respective zones and in the Control Council negotiations. Although liaison of a kind never contemplated in the prewar period continued at various working levels, the Combined Chiefs of Staff organization was disbanded, and the two countries quickly developed independent military policies. And, in a famous error, Truman signed without reading Leo Crowley's draft order ending Lend-Lease suddenly on August 21, 1945, dramatizing the process of disengagement which was under way.

In general, American policy operated in Western Europe in the early postwar period on the assumption that the West European countries would recover economically and politically, reassume responsibility for their own protection and for the maintenance of their historic positions of power and authority, and play an important role in the United Nations and other global institutions designed to insure peace and progress. Thus they would permit the United States to fall back, not into isolation, but into a position of diminished responsibility, with the status of more or less conscious strategic reserve with respect to Western Eurasia and benevolent but not costly American participation in worldwide organizations.

At one point after another, as the weakness of the European economy and the political vulnerability of the European states were revealed, the hope for such an American limited disengagement from Europe was demonstrated to be overoptimistic. And so, while step by step the wartime arrangements which bound the United States to Britain and to Western Europe were being dismantled, alternative links were created piecemeal out of specific economic problems, guided by no concept more precise than the American commitment to see economically viable democracies re-emerge in the West.

THE ORIGINS OF ECONOMIC UNITY

Far from the consciousness—or perhaps even the knowledge—of high-level policy-makers, certain new patterns were emerging in economic policy. Out of the arrangements developed in SHAEF to start the Western European liberated areas on the road to recovery came the international coal and transport organizations and the Emergency Economic Committee for Europe, designed to deal with aspects of reconstruction on a regional basis; and the concept of European economic unity latent in these organizations led from the relatively low-level United Nations negotiations of the summer of 1946 to the founding of the Economic Commission for Europe.

The larger issues of 1945-1946, however, were initially handled on an individual country basis.

In Germany the evolution of events led the United States to assume increased responsibility—in the British as well as American zones—over the first postwar year; and it was judged important for the United States to reverse the image left by Roosevelt's wartime estimate of a two-year American occupation limit and to make explicit the nation's intent to maintain a position in Germany—if necessary, indefinitely. In his Stuttgart speech of September 1946 Byrnes pointedly said: "As long as an occupation force is required in Germany, the Army of the United States will be a part of that occupation force."

With respect to Britain, it was evident that the Bretton Woods arrangements were wholly inadequate to see Britain through its postwar economic transition. Negotiations for a British loan began in earnest promptly after the termination of Lend-Lease. With considerable difficulty in the Congress, a transitional loan of $3.75 billion was negotiated in December 1945 in the hope that it would help Britain to maintain its worldwide obligations, notably with respect to European occupation and the orderly liquidation of the sterling balances, and to resume in a reasonable period a free-trade policy harmonious with the concepts and aspirations of Bretton Woods.

Britain was formally committed to undertake convertibility in the summer of 1947; and out of this negotiation came also the last of the essentially warborn international organizations, the ill-fated International Trade Organization.

Major French loans (totaling about $1.2 billion) were also granted. Whereas the British problem was, superficially at least, to ease an acute balance-of-payments problem while Britain recovered its ability to export on an adequate scale, the French problem was presented in terms of Monnet's five-year plan. This plan aimed directly at a fundamental reconstruction of the French economy, which, besides suffering acute war damage, had been weakened by the progressive obsolescence of French industry between the wars.

The Italian treaty negotiations threw onto the United States the principal burden for protecting Italian national positions in the Trieste area and for giving the new republic an opportunity to start life without the burden of accepting not only wartime defeat from the West but also postwar diplomatic defeat from the East. Moreover, it was evident that the Italian economy was in a position that would require protracted economic assistance, and that Italy would not for some time be in a position independently to bear any substantial international burdens.

In Italy and France, moreover, the problem of local communism appeared ominous. The Communists had played in both countries a role of leadership in the resistance. In the immediate postwar they came forward with vigor, rallied to their banners about a quarter of the popular vote, and assumed positions of political or quasi-political authority (notably in the trade unions) which weakened the political life of both countries as the East-West schism in Europe took shape.

In a series of *ad hoc* responses, country by country, the United States extended some $7.5 billion in credits to Western Europe between mid-1945 and the end of 1946;[1] but the crisis there still gathered momentum.

Aside from special, acute problems in virtually every country of Western Europe, the whole region was affected by a world food shortage which left food prices high and threw extraordinary burdens of supply on to the Western Hemisphere, where purchases could be made only in scarce dollars. In Europe itself agricultural output in 1945-1946 was 63 per cent of prewar levels, and it rose in the next harvest season to only 75 per cent. Washington took steps to make food surpluses available; but it was evident that Western Europe would require further massive financial assistance before anything approximating the economic assumptions underlying Bretton Woods or the political assumptions underlying American diplomacy were to be made good.

The depth and seriousness of European economic and political weakness, combined with a gathering sense of Stalin's aggressive intentions, led in many

American minds to a gradual crystallization of a new approach to the European problem in the course of 1946. The process was accelerated by a number of particular formulations. In February 1946 George Kennan's voluminous cable, later to be published in substance under the pseudonym "X," arrived in the Department of State from Moscow—surely one of the most remarkable initiatives of a number-two man when the boss was out of town. On March 5, 1956, Churchill intervened in Western thought with his speech at Fulton, Missouri; and he intervened once again on September 19th in Zurich, where he held up the vision of a United States of Europe. On January 17, 1947, John Foster Dulles, with the backing of Dewey and Vandenberg, supported the concept of an economically unified Germany within an economically unified Europe. At the U.N. Assembly meeting in New York in December 1946 the Economic Commission for Europe was precariously set in motion with curious joint American-Polish sponsorship.

In the first half of 1947, with Marshall at the helm in the Department of State, American policy was at last prepared to make a fundamental approach to a European settlement in terms which faced the hard facts of postwar life—a settlement either on an all-European basis, in cooperation with the Soviet Union, or on a united Western basis if Moscow insisted on unilateral dominance of the East.

## 26. Chinese Civil War: 1945-1946

### THE BACKGROUND OF LATENT CONFLICT

The story of the Communist takeover in China begins not with 1945 but more nearly with the agreement of 1936-1937 between the Communists and the Nationalist government to end open hostilities between themselves and jointly to resist the Japanese invasion. Although Chiang Kai-shek was essentially forced into this agreement, it soon emerged that the situation offered him unique opportunities to act in the name of the nation as its acknowledged leader in a popular cause; and his prestige was perhaps at its highest when he led his country in its resistance against Japan in the years immediately following 1937.[1]

In the course of its first year, certain measures were taken on both sides which appeared to meet the terms of the Nationalist-Communist understanding; but from the making of the agreement in 1937 to the breakdown of negotiations with the KMT at the end of 1946 the Communists refused to place their armed forces under anything like the full control of the Nationalist government. What emerged, then, was a kind of diplomatic accord between two powers—one formally sovereign, the other exercising *de facto* sovereignty within flexible boundaries—to abstain from hostilities with each other and to engage a common enemy. Since each of these adversaries looked ultimately to total authority in China, since their boundaries were ill-defined, and since all the movements of their troops carried implications of enlarged or diminished domestic authority, there were bound to be clashes. These began towards the close of 1938; and in January 1941 chronic mutual suspicion and hostility reached a climax when a headquarters detachment of about 5000 men of the Communist New Fourth Army was decimated while passing through Nationalist-held territory under circumstances not wholly clear down to the present.

When the United States became involved in the Far Eastern war, neither the American government as a whole nor the American people had an adequate sense of the historical depth and purposefulness of the mutual antagonism which underlay the situation in China.

### AMERICAN OBJECTIVES IN CHINA

From the end of 1941 to the end of 1946, when the Chinese civil fight to the finish began, American policy with respect to China had two purposes: to encourage the unification process by American aid; and, mainly by exhortation, to improve the quality and effectiveness of Chiang Kai-shek's political, economic, and military administration. During the war years the American objective was, then, simply to make China a more effective military ally in the war against Japan.

At V-J Day most responsible United States observers judged that Chiang Kai-shek could not achieve the prompt and total reconquest of China with such economic and military assistance as the United States was prepared to grant. It was felt that Chiang, to make good within China his recognized international status as its ruler, would have to enter promptly into political arrangements with the Communists, and then, on the basis of an effective economic, political, and social policy, he would gradually have to win over to his side the Chinese people. The story of postwar China is, in a sense, the story of the failure of both objectives.

### COMMUNIST OBJECTIVES IN CHINA

The failure arose in part because Communist objectives were not universally well understood, despite a variety of warnings including Kennan's cable of April 23, 1945. Kennan's message, evoked by fears that Ambassador Hurley, en route to China, might misunderstand his amiable conversation with Stalin, stated Russian objectives as follows:

> Stalin is of course prepared to affirm the principle of unifying the armed forces of China. He knows that unification is feasible in a practical sense only on conditions which are acceptable to the Chinese Communist Party. . . .
> It would be tragic if our natural anxiety for the support of the Soviet

Union at this juncture, coupled with Stalin's use of words which mean all things to all people and his cautious affability, were to lead us into an undue reliance on Soviet aid or even Soviet acquiescence in the achievement of our long-term objectives in China.[2]

In the immediate postwar period, Soviet, and perhaps even Chinese Communist, estimates of Chiang Kai-shek's military strength were such as to make it unlikely in their judgment that a Chinese Communist victory could be promptly achieved. Moreover, in the aftermath of the extraordinary American victory over Japan neither Moscow nor the Chinese Communist leadership was inclined to challenge American authority in the Far East if the United States had the purpose and will to exercise it. As time passed, however, the effective strength of Chiang was revealed to be less than it initially appeared, American strength in the Pacific was dissipated, and Washington's will to effect a favorable solution in China emerged as highly conditional.

The United States did, however, offer Chiang ample economic and military aid. While the United States was assisting Nationalist China, Soviet assistance was given to Communist China in violation of both inter-Allied and Sino-Soviet diplomatic agreements of 1945. The Soviets delayed Nationalist occupation of Manchuria and assisted the Chinese Communists in infiltrating the countryside of Manchuria, notably during the Red Army withdrawal in the spring of 1946. They turned over to the Chinese Communists stores of Japanese arms and ammunition. There was probably some additional assistance in the form of Soviet-manufactured arms and ammunition and in Soviet military advisers, whose guidance may account for the sharp improvement in Communist staff work noted by observers after 1945.

### THE STAGES OF DEGENERATION

The degeneration of the uneasy armed truce in 1945 into full-scale civil war and Communist victory took place in a series of stages during which the hopes of each side and their appreciation of their own relative capabilities altered.

*V-J Day to the cease-fire agreement of January 10, 1946.* In this period the Communists and the Nationalist government sought to move in on Japanese-held areas. The Nationalist government decided, against Wedemeyer's advice, to occupy Manchuria, as it was legally entitled to do in terms of existing international agreements; and the United States in the end backed Chiang's decision.

Aided by American transport facilities, which rapidly moved about 500,000 men into key areas, the Nationalist government succeeded in installing itself in the major cities of Central, East, and North China. The Communists, meanwhile, made rapid progress in the hinterland of Manchuria and in some rural areas of North China. Although the Soviet occupation of Manchuria limited to some extent the areas the Communists could take over, they received the surrender of many Japanese units and acquired their arms—in violation of agreement with the Nationalist government. Hostilities began as Nationalist troops sought to clear the lines between the cities they held.

Throughout the latter months of 1945 inconclusive diplomatic negotiations were conducted between the Nationalist government and the Communists against a counterpoint of military operations; and Moscow simultaneously explored the possibilities of special bilateral arrangements with the Nationalist government designed to limit or exclude United States influence in China. It was in this degenerating military-diplomatic setting that General Marshall arrived in China in December 1945, seeking the unification of the country by political negotiation. On January 10, 1946, he achieved a cease-fire agreement between the Nationalist government and the Communists. In strictly order-of-battle terms, the Nationalist government at this stage had an advantage in troops roughly equivalent to the relative area of China it held—that is, better than three to one.

*The failure of mediation: January 1946-January 1947.* In the course of 1946 the Nationalist government persisted in its purpose of consolidating its military hold on all of China, including Manchuria; and at the end of the year substantial progress had apparently been registered. Large numbers of troops had been transferred to Manchuria, and, despite Soviet assistance to the Communists in the period of Red Army withdrawal (spring 1946), the major urban centers were held by the Nationalists. Although there was some relative increase in Communists under arms, the Nationalist government had 2,600,000 troops as opposed to a Communist force of perhaps 1,100,000 at the close of 1946. Similarly, despite the Soviet transfer of Japanese arms to the Communists, the Nationalist advantage in rifles was estimated at better than three to one. The military events of 1946 did not, however, damage Communist main strength or alter the Communist hold on important rural areas.

Military action was accompanied by and intimately bound up with a complex series of negotiations sponsored by General Marshall and later aided by Ambassador Stuart. These were designed to establish terms on which might be created a Chinese national government embracing the Kuomintang, the Communists, and so-called Third Force elements. In the first half of 1946 these negotiations appeared to make some progress in the sense that formulae for political and military unification were discussed in detail, compromises were put forward attempting to meet divergent views, and the procedure in general had the trappings, at least, of serious purpose. The negotiations deteriorated from July 1946; and the Chinese National Assembly was convened on November 15 without Communist acquiescence or participation.

There were three fundamental reasons why there could be no effective truce between Chiang's government and the Communists. Both the Kuomintang and the Communists were committed to achieving total power in China. The concept of a continuing political system of mixed fluctuating power which tolerated several parties was understood and acceptable only to a small minority of Chinese politicians, the so-called Third Force, who had neither military strength nor effective political organization. Important and increasingly influential elements in the Kuomintang, including Chiang Kai-shek, saw no possibility of an acceptable solution without complete elimination of Communist military strength; and these elements also believed that it lay within Nationalist capabilities to achieve that end. Finally, the Communists may have been initially prepared to consider a variety of formulae which would give them only minority status in a unified government; but they were never prepared to consider a formula which would deny them control over their own armed forces.

The process of disintegration went on until, in December 1946, General Marshall concluded that no useful purpose could be served by his remaining on the scene. He left China on January 8, 1947.

POSTWAR CHINA: AN AMERICAN DILEMMA

Postwar American policy in China was made in a situation where the nation operated within exceedingly narrow limits. The objective was clear enough: the emergence of a unified China independent of the Soviet Union and moving forward in the democratic process. It was, however, universally agreed by American observers that the Nationalists in 1945 did not have the military, administrative, or political capability for defeating the Communists. Moreover, no politically responsible American of either party was prepared to advocate the use of American military strength on the Chinese mainland to enforce a solution in the American interest. Roughly speaking, four more or less distinctive courses of action were advocated by Americans in these acutely difficult circumstances, the limits of which were recognized by all hands.

1. Wedemeyer proposed in November 1945 that Chiang consolidate his military, administrative, and political position up through north China; and that the United States, Britain, and the Soviet Union establish a trusteeship in Manchuria until the Nationalist government developed a solid ability to assume full control over the area. Chiang rejected this course, and it did not appeal to Washington, anxious to limit direct American commitments in a region of incipient civil war.

2. Hurley (Ambassador in China from September 1944 to November 1945) sought to strengthen the Nationalist Government with economic and mili-

tary aid and advice while looking to the negotiation of national unity with the Chinese Communists on terms favorable to the Nationalists.

3. Marshall's policy in 1946 was essentially the same as Hurley's except that his exceedingly modest hopes for success hinged on a political restructuring of the Nationalist areas and on bringing into the arena of influence Chinese politicians more willing than Chiang to find a *modus vivendi* with the Communists.

4. Finally, a small group of foreign service officers held (notably in the pre-Yalta period when Soviet participation in the Far Eastern war was not yet decided) that the Chinese Communists were bound to win unless the Kuomintang drastically reformed itself; and that, if the Kuomintang did not reform, the only hope of salvaging a China not tied to the Soviet Union was to create an association between the United States and the Communists and to count on the believed nationalist strand in their make-up to yield a situation short of undiluted Soviet influence.[3] These men were, in a sense, seeking, as a last hope, what later might have been called a Titoist China.

Essentially, these were four ways of dealing with the two fundamental facts about postwar China: Chiang's inability to translate a preponderance in military strength into total victory on the mainland, and the American willingness to intervene in China with diplomacy, advice, and money, but not with armed men. Chiang's inability stemmed from weaknesses in administrative structure, political conception, and political policy exacerbated by almost two decades of uninterrupted conflict with the Chinese Communists and the Japanese invader. Stilwell, more than any other American, had sought to get at the roots of these weaknesses; but he was inadequately supported in Washington and he lacked the genius that would have been required even under the best of circumstances to bring about the changes he sought. Stilwell's final report, at the end of his mission, contains the following passage:

> The Kuomintang party, of which he is the leader, was once the expression of genuine nationalistic feeling, but is now an uncertain equilibrium of decadent, competing factions, with neither dynamic principles nor a popular base. Chiang controls by manipulating these factions with an adroit political sense. His seat is insecure. His reluctance to expand military strength, his preoccupation with the security of domestic supremacy, his suspicion of everyone around him, and his increasing emotional instability betrayed a realization of this. He became a hostage of the forces he manipulated.
>
> Nowhere does Clausewitz's dictum that war is only the continuation of politics by other methods apply with more force than it did in CBI.[4]

In the end, the problem of China policy during and immediately after the war was, as Stilwell suggests, both a searching exercise in the relationship between political and military factors and an exercise in making a day-to-day policy which would unite the ideological and power interests which determined the American interest in China.

The American objective derived directly from the Open Door concept, in which American interests in maintaining a China not dominated by any single power had become increasingly encrusted with a friendly missionary attitude toward the Chinese people and an authentic sympathy with the Chinese effort to move toward democracy as well as unity. But the objective could not be achieved on the tangled China scene merely by its high-level assertion or by insisting on the diplomatic acceptance of China as one of the Big Five. Nor, in the end, would the formula of free elections and a democratic constitution suffice, as it might in most European areas, even if actually applied.

Nevertheless, the stakes were so high and the alternative so unattractive that expensive efforts in economic and military aid were attempted, and a flow of advice, mainly unheeded, was forthcoming. From Stilwell's departure, however, no major sustained American effort to get at the fundamental causes of Chiang's military and political impotence was made; and it remains an open question whether Stilwell's formula of American operational control within key elements of the Kuomintang structure could have been made to work.

The alternative to Chiang's reform (leaving aside the formula of an alliance with the Chinese Communists) was the direct use of American military force on the mainland. This approach ran counter to two American inhibitions: against enmeshment on the Asian mainland with "Asian hordes," and against involvement in someone else's civil war. After V-J Day the United States was unprepared to use military force in the making of the peace. And finally, the outcome of direct American military intervention, if not accompanied by a remarkably astute political policy, was questionable.

Both the depth of the nation's trouble with the China question and the intensity of the controversy invoked by the Nationalist defeat had deep roots. Both incorporated a stinging sense of American failure, a sense that here was a situation in which none of the familiar American approaches could work—neither free elections nor economic aid; neither military aid nor the direct use of American force. The most ardent debaters in the controversy held that a bit more democracy, aid, or American force might have turned the trick. The evidence is that the situation of China in the war and immediate postwar years, a complex particular stage in a revolutionary process more than a century old, was not susceptible to successful manipulation by conventional American methods—if, indeed, it lay within the capabilities of any external power to determine the outcome at that late and tangled moment in Chinese history.

In war and postwar China the United States was enmeshed in the politics,

economics, and military affairs of what came to be known after the war as
an underdeveloped area—an area caught up in the complex transition from
a traditional to a modern society, an area politically still not effectively unified
and economically in a pretake-off stage. The average American official did
not understand the situation he confronted in China, and he could not find
and apply the leverage to move it forward in the American interest. The
instinctive formula derived from American life and practice, and from American experience of Europe, simply did not work. A few Americans with China
experience were prepared to plunge into the morass, get hold of a piece of
the problem in its own current and historical terms, and move forward. Some
others without previous China experience exhibited a talent not only for
working with the extraordinary administrative structure that Chiang had
erected but also for playing its game to some constructive purpose. But the
general American reaction was one of moral shock at the state of the Kuomintang and of impotence in dealing with it.

As Marshall returned to Washington early in 1947 to take over the Department of State and help launch the counterattack on Stalin's policy in
Europe, the nation was clearly at the beginning of its education in the dynamics of underdeveloped, aspiring, transitional societies; and it had not made
a very good start.

# PART III

# THE AMERICAN COUNTEROFFENSIVE

## 27. The American Response in Europe: 1947-1952

### THE TRUMAN DOCTRINE

By early 1947 there was a spreading awareness in the United States that a sustained and dangerous program of Moscow-directed military and political pressure on Western Europe was under way. In Greece it took the form of guerrilla warfare managed from Moscow. In Turkey it took the form of diplomatic pressure backed by military threat. In France and Italy it took the form of powerful domestic Communist parties working to disrupt the precarious early stage of economic reconstruction and to destroy the fragile democratic processes set in motion in the latter days of the war. In Germany it was the Soviet aim to delay the economic revival of Germany and to postpone as long as possible the emergence of an effective organized grouping of the three Western zones linked to West Berlin.

On February 21 the First Secretary of the British Embassy brought to the Department of State notes announcing the British decision to end aid to Greece and Turkey. Behind the British action lay the fact that British postwar recovery, despite the American loan of 1945, was proceeding so slowly and with such irreducible commitments to the improvement of welfare that the British lacked the margin of resources required to hold the disruptive forces at work throughout the arc of Western and Southern Europe, where Britain had sought to maintain historic interests and responsibilities.

On March 12 President Truman addressed a joint session of the Houses of Congress, laid before them a proposal for aid to Greece and Turkey, and enunciated the two fundamental principles on which he proposed to base the American response to the mounting Communist threat in Europe. He said:

I believe that it must be the policy of the United States to support free peoples who are resisting attempted subjugation by armed minorities or by outside pressures.

I believe that we must assist free peoples to work out their own destinies in their own way.[1]

The enunciation of the Truman doctrine signified the rejection of the American hope that the United States could stand at a distance from the Eurasian scene, accepting only limited or transient responsibilities there. For the third time in the twentieth century the United States undertook to apply its active weight in order to hold the balance of power in Western Eurasia against forces threatening to dominate that area. It was evident at the time, and it has become increasingly evident since, that Truman's words marked a major turning point in American and world history.[2]

The Truman doctrine did not launch a decisive clash of arms in which "victory" or "unconditional surrender" could serve as meaningful goals. It launched the nation on a still unended duel with limited force, in which all the instruments of power and influence were interwoven: military, political, economic, and psychological. The Truman Doctrine thus opened a new and authentically revolutionary phase in the nation's experience.

### THE MOSCOW CONFERENCE

Two days before Truman's address to the Congress there began in Moscow a conference set against the background of the major power discord on Germany and Austria which had gathered momentum since the first half of 1946. American preparations for that conference had been made with great care, detailed American staff work having proceeded in Washington, Vienna, and Berlin steadily since the previous summer. Despite the apparent intentions of Soviet policy in Europe, Truman and Marshall decided that one last effort at the highest level must be tried before accepting the split of Germany and the continued occupation of Austria as the terms of reference for postwar Europe over, at least, the medium-range future.

The United States went to the Moscow meetings prepared with a range of clear detailed negotiating positions in order to establish whether Soviet objectives were compatible with American interests on the questions of German unity, German disarmament, and the end of Austrian occupation. General Marshall's staff included the ablest and most knowledgeable men who had worked on European problems in the two postwar years; and, although hardened by accumulating experience of Soviet postwar diplomacy, the American delegation was prepared to stretch to the limit to meet legitimate Russian security interests in the structure of Germany and Europe. This mood of searching flexibility was in no sense a sentimental harking back to the wartime alliance. It stemmed from a mature realization of the consequence of failure in Moscow: a split Germany and Europe the reunification of which was difficult if not impossible to perceive through the mists of a dangerous and tense future.

The position taken by the Soviet negotiators was thoroughly unambiguous: Stalin refused to move toward a definitive settlement in Europe. In a conversation[3] toward the end of the conference, Stalin indicated to Marshall that he regarded the negotiation of a German settlement as at only an early stage, and he counseled patience. Stalin's attitude was widely interpreted in the American staff to be that, with things going their way all over Western Europe, it was the Soviet intention to play for time and to exploit Western weaknesses to the limit short of war.

The Americans came home from Moscow firm in the conclusion that the United States should never again negotiate from a base of weakness, and that it was useless to test Soviet intentions before self-evident Western strength and the development of alternatives to Soviet agreement had narrowed the realistic choices open to Moscow to a range of solutions compatible with the American interest.

### THE MARSHALL PLAN

The aid bill for Greece and Turkey, the immediate result of the Truman Doctrine, dealt with only a small piece of the European problem; but in his address to the Congress the President laid before the nation the serious nature of the European situation as a whole. It was clear that the Truman Doctrine committed the nation over a far wider range than the Greek and Turkish issues.

Throughout the late winter and early spring of 1947, while the Moscow Conference was in session, reports poured into the Department of State about the rapid economic disintegration of Western Europe. The winter had been extremely cold; the harvests had been bad; coal was in short supply; dollar reserves were declining rapidly, and only dollars could purchase the food and raw materials needed to supply its industries. The picture of Europe was one of mammoth slow-moving crisis. There was a growing awareness that something big had to be done in Europe to avoid a disaster to the American interest; that a substantial program of economic aid addressed constructively to the problems of economic recovery was required to deal with the multiple threats to the Eurasian power balance.

A convergence of reports from Europe with the conclusions about Stalin's attitude and intentions drawn from the Moscow Conference set the stage for the Marshall Plan.

On April 29, the day after his report to the nation on the failure of the

Moscow Conference, Secretary Marshall instructed the Policy Planning Staff to prepare a general plan for American aid in the reconstruction of Western Europe. The Marshall Plan concept which resulted from that initiative emerged from much hard staff work by professionals in the State Department; but it was also the product of an extraordinary ferment of thought and activity within the civil service, in the Congress, among the leading newspapermen and columnists, and, to a degree, among thoughtful and knowledgeable men and women throughout the country.

Within the Department of State various strands of thought came together, each of which had evolved with its own background of intellectual history and experience since the end of the war.[4] There was George Kennan's somewhat negative but wholesome insistence that, in its relations with Europe, the United States should move only in association with real European efforts to achieve their own salvation. There was Will Clayton's more positive mixture of humanitarianism and an acute sense that the United States could not prosper if the world were a poorhouse. There was a growing acceptance of the conclusion that a solution to the problem of Germany, whether split or unified, could be found only in terms of a unified Europe.

And there was even in being an organization dedicated to European economic cooperation—the Economic Commission for Europe—which in April 1947 had taken over the League of Nations Palais in Geneva, absorbing the three European emergency economic organizations.[5] The ECE was, however, an organization of the United Nations, with Soviet and Eastern European countries as members. Its very existence posed a basic question. Should an effort be made to embrace all of Europe in a new enterprise of reconstruction, or should the lesson of the Moscow Conference be read as indicating that the only realistic alternative for the West was to accept the split and to strengthen the area still outside Stalin's grasp?

### THE DIPLOMACY OF INITIATING THE MARSHALL PLAN

On May 8 Under Secretary of State Acheson spoke in Cleveland, Mississippi, on American economic foreign policy, meeting an engagement originally made by the President. Acheson's speech did not deal sharply with the possibility of enlarged American aid. Nevertheless, it recognized clearly that measures taken by the United States in support of European reconstruction were inadequate to the economic crisis reflected in European balance-of-payments deficits; and it indicated that the United States government was prepared to view European reconstruction in long-run terms. The speech was designed by Truman, Marshall, and Acheson to prepare the way for a major initiative, and it accurately reflected the gathering mood in Washington.

Abroad, the Cleveland speech was widely reported as an important trial balloon.

Marshall's speech a month later was diplomatically more precise. It not only analyzed in some detail the character of the European economic problem but also committed the United States to receive sympathetically a request for additional assistance in terms of a "European program" in which "a number, if not all, European nations" would join. The speech also stated that "any government which maneuvers to block the recovery of other countries cannot expect help from us. Furthermore, governments, political parties, or groups which seek to perpetuate human misery in order to profit therefrom politically or otherwise will encounter the opposition of the United States."[6] However, the way was left open for Eastern Europe and the Soviet Union to join on a cooperative basis in the proposed European enterprise.

The British Foreign Office, prodded by British correspondents in Washington, had been following carefully the build-up of staff work and the mood in Washington which finally yielded Marshall's proposal. British Treasury officials remained more skeptical that anything substantial was in the wind. Bevin, however, proceeded to act on the assumption that Marshall's was a definitive American commitment if Europe was prepared to meet its terms. And it was soon clear that, under Bevin's leadership, Western Europe would respond in concert to the American offer.

On the Western side, over the month after Marshall's speech, there was something of a schism in attitudes toward Eastern European and Soviet participation. In sections of the American government and on the European continent there were those who honestly hoped this final effort to dilute or prevent the split of Europe would succeed; and they were prepared to take the risks with the American Congress of Communist participation in the European reconstruction effort. On the other hand, Bevin and the British Foreign Office (as well as some American officials) were fearful that Stalin would agree and took no pains to create a hospitable atmosphere at Paris for Molotov. Bevin's view was based on the dual judgment that Congressional approval would be impossible for a plan including the Communist states and that the Soviet intentions were so evidently hostile and aggressive toward the West, and their fulfillment depended so directly on Western economic weakness, that honest East-West cooperation in European recovery was a pipe dream.

The question then arose as to whether or not the Soviet Union would permit the Eastern European states to join in the venture. It is evident that when Moscow was first sounded out by Belgrade, Warsaw, and Prague no firm negative decision had been reached in the Kremlin. The Eastern European countries proceeded to exploit this transient ambiguity by indicating willingness to join in the Paris discussion among the European states. They were evidently drawn toward the Marshall Plan for two distinct reasons. First, they badly wanted additional external aid in reconstruction and recovery, which the United States alone could supply. Second, most Eastern European Communists and virtually all non-Communists in positions of responsibility wished to reverse the trend toward absolute unilateral Soviet power within their countries; and they saw in enlarged economic ties with Western Europe a way of achieving this goal. So far as Czechoslovakia was concerned, the development of an all-European arena of action and negotiation appeared a matter of life and death; that is, Benes and Masaryk knew in 1947 that a democratic Czechoslovakia with friendly ties to the East and West would prove impossible to sustain if the split of Europe crystallized. And so Poland, Czechoslovakia, and Yugoslavia reached out toward Marshall's initiative and to the West.

In the end, perhaps at the very last minute,[7] Stalin decided that the risks of entering the plan on terms acceptable to the West were politically too great. It is not difficult to reconstruct Stalin's probable line of thought.

Eastern Europe in the early summer of 1947 had by no means reached full satellite status. A democratic government existed in Prague; in Warsaw all manner of Polish nationalists, inside and outside the Communist Party, had not yet been brought to heel; in Yugoslavia, unknown to the West, Tito was holding firmly to his army, his police, and his party against Soviet pressure and infiltration; and he was stirring the Bulgarian and Hungarian Communists with ideas about a Balkan Communist alliance, quasi-independent of Moscow. Into this situation came the American counteroffensive which, in its economic dimension, had a powerful appeal. Undoubtedly some argued in the Politburo that Soviet presence in the European negotiations, if well handled, could produce a situation and a set of terms which would prove unacceptable to the United States and which would thus disrupt the Plan. This maneuver probably appeared overcomplicated to Stalin; and he opted for total control where it could be achieved rather than dilute influence over a wider area.

Another factor may have entered into Stalin's calculations at about this time. In the spring and summer of 1947 Stalin was probably revaluing upwards the possibility of prompt Communist takeover in China, with all that might imply for the early extension of Communist power in other parts of Asia. A strategy of consolidating firmly what had been gained in Europe and of extending Communist power in Asia may well have been forming up in his mind.

In any case, the withdrawal of Molotov from Paris was carried out in a manner which left Western consciences quite clear that an honest effort had been made and rejected.[8] Although there is still much to be learned about Communist thought and controversy in this matter, it is most unlikely that either Western hopes, Western fears, or Western maneuvers significantly influenced Stalin's clear-cut decision to recall Molotov from Paris.

TWO BASIC POLICY DECISIONS

The character of the Marshall Plan was substantially shaped by two British positions taken in the summer of 1947 when, under the leadership of Oliver Franks, the sixteen Western nations organized a recovery plan and a joint request to the United States for European aid.

The first decision was that aid be allocated among the European countries on the basis of dollar deficits in their balances of payment rather than over-all deficits. This had the immediate effect of increasing the legitimate British claim for assistance, since an expansion in British exports to sterling and other soft-currency areas was already beginning to narrow the gap in its over-all balance of payments. But there was an important international consequence to this technical decision. Britain had acquired substantial debts during the Second World War in India, Egypt, and in other areas where British troops fought and from which British imports were drawn but to which it was impossible during the war to send a normal flow of British exports. The British hope in the postwar was not merely to repay these debts and to maintain London's good name as a debtor, but also to build up through repayment new and expanded lines of trade for the long pull. With American assistance allocated on the basis of dollar deficits it thus became possible for Britain, still in a shaky economic position, to perform as a major capital exporter in the early postwar years.

Thus Britain (and, to a degree, France and Belgium) became intermediaries by which capital flowed to the underdeveloped areas during the Marshall Plan period. Although at the time the attention of economists, civil servants, and the public was concentrated on European recovery in the narrow sense, in a longer perspective the Marshall Plan may be remembered equally as the device by which American aid to Europe permitted a substantial and continuing flow of capital into the underdeveloped areas of the world at a time of profound European economic weakness.

The second major decision of the Marshall Plan's first stage was that the secretariat of the new European organization (Organization for European Economic Cooperation) would be "weak."[9] In 1947 primary British interests were conceived in London to be national economic revival, the preservation of the British Empire, and the revival of Britain as a major power on the world scene. The prevailing British government view was that European unity was a tertiary matter and that too rapid a revival of economic and political strength on the continent might run counter to British interests, as, for example, in the case of German trade rivalry. The British therefore threw their weight strongly against a strong Secretariat within the OEEC; and although they were to a degree opposed by the French and certain other continental states, they succeeded in their effort. Oliver Franks, who had strongly led the initial effort to formulate a European plan, was withdrawn from Paris and sent to Washington as British Ambassador. On the whole the British attitude at this stage was that a European plan was an awkward but necessary way to get the dollar resources required to permit British recovery.

While the United States had a major stake in British revival, the case for a Marshall Plan approach to European recovery lay in the fact that it was on the continent that a loss of Western economic and political strength might lead to a grave degeneration in the Western power position. Britain might have been salvaged by bilateral American action; but the American strategic interest required the generation of friendly political and economic strength from the Channel to the Elbe. But in this matter American diplomacy was unclear and unsure, reflecting, in fact, throughout the postwar period an uncertainty as to whether the United States should take an arm's length Mahanist view of Western Europe, relying essentially on the North Atlantic triangle, or throw its weight fully into the scales on the continent itself, drawing Britain and Canada along. On the question of the OEEC, the British prevailed—and a unique, transient opportunity to build a Western European civil service was lost. The ablest younger men in Western Europe were authentically fired by the vision of a united Europe; but it soon became apparent that the positions of real responsibility and authority would remain within national governments, not in the OEEC Secretariat.

### THE LIMITS AND ACHIEVEMENTS OF THE MARSHALL PLAN

The structural weakness of the OEEC Secretariat converged with other factors to restrict the consequences of the Marshall Plan for the movement toward European unity.

On the American side the notion of European unity had a long history and great attraction. From an early stage in the nation's history, many Americans looked out on the competing sovereignties of Europe, pushing for power restlessly and dangerously, and concluded that peace could come to Europe only if Europeans were to follow the American example of continental unity. More immediately, it was evident to Americans that the failure of Europe to cope with Hitler had in part stemmed from a lack of unity; and, more than that, there was the experience of *de facto* unity in the final phases of the war when an American-led SHAEF managed briefly to make the Western alliance an organizational reality.

On the European side the experience of the Second World War—and of a Europe that had to be rescued from its own failures by the Americans from the West and by the Russians from the East—had convinced many men that the European state system had outlived its usefulness. In the curious polyglot democracy of German concentration camps this was a central theme among those who could exchange views. And after the war, quite apart from the immediate threat of Communist domination, Europeans began to argue that if continental Europe were to maintain the stature and dignity of even a second-rate power—in a world apparently bestrided by Washington and Moscow—European unity would have to be sought. Even more narrowly, some Frenchmen and some Germans saw in the prospect of European unity the only way of ending once and for all the mutually destructive enmity of France and Germany—Frenchmen to tie down a Germany bound to rise to superior strength; Germans to insure their nation against its own worst instincts and most destructive historic ambitions. On both sides of the Atlantic, then, the concept of European unity had a real attraction despite the fact that it also raised grave problems and doubts—most notably in Britain.

But the Marshall Plan initiative posed a problem much more precise than the broad question of European unity. Assuming that unity was the goal, and assuming that joint economic reconstruction was the medium chosen to advance towards it, how should one proceed? The initial basis for the European recovery program was the national reconstruction plans of individual governments. And, indeed, it was clear that so far as economic reconstruction was concerned, the three key issues—the scale and direction of the national investment programs, the scale and character of American aid, and the rate at which sources of non-dollar foodstuffs and raw materials could be generated in areas willing to buy European exports—bore only obliquely on the question of European unity. Barring a drastic opening of dollar markets—and even, perhaps, with such measures—the dollar problem could not be solved by enlarged trade with dollar areas alone.

If the political and strategic goal of unity—rather than merely prompt national recovery—was accepted as a primary objective, there were, indeed, many fields of joint economic action in Western Europe which could have been fruitfully pursued: for example, movement into other countries (notably France) of surplus Italian labor; coordination of national investment plans to permit a high degree of regional specialization and to avoid unnecessary overlapping; the exploitation of the possibilities inherent in the distribution of coal and steel raw materials in Western Europe (later exploited by the Schumann Plan); movement toward common fiscal policies and common standards in tax collection, ultimately an indispensable base for a politically unified Europe; a freeing of intra-European capital flows. While such moves could only marginally assist the process of European economic revival in the short run, they lay at the heart of any serious movement, from the direction of economic policy, toward political unity. In the end, nationally directed recovery plans were given a clear-cut immediate priority.

On the American side initial thought about how to use the Marshall Plan as an instrument for European unity was relatively shallow. The European recovery plan presented at the end of the summer of 1947 was, at American insistence, overlaid with pious but not profoundly felt statements of intent to proceed with customs unions and other enterprises looking toward European unity. The one serious common function allocated to the OEEC in the first instance was the responsibility for making an initial allocation of American funds; and even though the allocation of other people's resources is the easiest issue on which to get international agreement, the United States had to take an increasing hand even in that process as time went on.

On the whole, therefore—because the British opposed it, because the economic requirements of unity did not converge with requirements for prompt recovery, and because the United States was unclear as to how its influence should be applied—the Marshall Plan did not succeed in moving Western Europe radically towards unity.

Nevertheless, the concept of unity was advanced by the Marshall Plan experience. Although the OEEC fulfilled few operating functions, it built up the habit of common consultation among the European states. The whole operation brought together a younger generation of European and American officials in human and operating relations which left a permanent mark on their thinking, cumulative in its results with the wartime experience of intimate alliance. The European officials involved became extremely sophisticated in the problems of each other's economics and politics; they began to think comfortably and operationally in European terms; and, generally with some pain, Europeans were forced to learn something of the intricacies of the American government as, year after year, the Marshall Plan appropriations were brought to the bar of Congress.

Put another way, should a unified Europe emerge as the result of a long historical process, the Marshall Plan experience will be judged to have made important common law contributions to the outcome despite its disappointing immediate results.

As a recovery program, narrowly conceived, the Marshall Plan was, of course, a considerable success. By 1951 industrial production in the Marshall Plan area (including Yugoslavia) was 37 per cent higher than in 1948, 40 per cent higher than in 1938.[10]

In addition, agricultural production revived in Europe and in non-dollar areas; and the dollar gap for the Western European countries diminished.

But it did not disappear, remaining down to 1958 just beneath the surface, covered by American military expenditures in Europe.

The truly revolutionary economic development in post-1945 Europe revealed itself clearly only toward the mid-1950's: namely, the transition of Western Europe into a phase of growth led by durable consumers' goods and services. By the late 1950's Western Europe was seized of the mass automobile, experiencing a version of the American 1920's. This transition accounted for the maintenance of an economic momentum which Western Europe had not seen since 1914. Western Europe was pushed into this stage of growth by a number of forces, including relatively steady full employment and relatively ample demand for European exports from the newer industries: light engineering, electronics, chemicals. But the Marshall Plan, by permitting momentum to be regained without a cut in European consumption or a fundamental change in political, social, and economic institutions, played a major part in bringing about this transition; and, to some imponderable degree, the presence of the American GI and other manifestations of American life almost certainly played an ancillary role.

## THE EFFORT AT MILITARY CONSOLIDATION

The course of events in Europe and Asia did not permit the Marshall Plan to develop in an atmosphere divorced from military concerns. Early in 1948, at the time when the Congress was considering the first Marshall Plan budget, the Civil War in Greece remained at an acute stage, the Communist *coup d'état* in Prague was executed, and the Chinese Communists were attacking Chiang Kai-shek's weak and extended garrison positions in Manchuria. Moreover, tension was developing in Berlin which later resulted in the blockade and the air lift. It was in March 1948 that Truman called unsuccessfully for universal military training but was granted conscription by the Congress.

Reacting to the shock of the Korean War, American policy in Europe took a major turn on September 12, 1950. At a meeting of the Western Foreign Ministers in New York the question of German rearmament was formally introduced by Acheson; and a week later agreement was reached in principle that, while a German national army was excluded, the process of German rearmament on a basis controlled by Britain, France, and the United States would be begun.

Over the three previous years many steps had been taken which brought West Germany into the common enterprises of the Western community. This process accelerated after the London Agreements of June 1, 1948, which led to currency reform in West Germany and provided the fiscal basis for German recovery. Economic progress in Germany was extremely rapid thereafter. The German role in the OEEC and in other forms of European economic negotiation expanded; and the political bargaining leverage of Bonn generally increased as Western plans came increasingly to hinge on West Germany's gathering strength and its loyalty to Western strategy.

In April 1949 West Germany had moved toward sovereignty with the setting up of the Allied High Commission. In the spring of 1949 NATO was forming up and the Berlin blockade was being brought to a close. Western Europe felt a new degree of strength and confidence, having faced down the Russian blockade without resort to war. The vigor of the Western reaction and the poise of the Germans under provocation had given substance to the notion of a North Atlantic Community reaching into the East as far as Berlin. And when the Foreign Ministers Conference on Germany, which followed the ending of the blockade, saw the Russians holding rigidly to positions which foreclosed the possibility of prompt movement toward German unity, the Germans, with their minds fastened on the gathering miracle of German economic recovery, were prepared for a time to continue to postpone unity and to build their political, economic, and diplomatic base on the Western ties. In May 1950 the Schumann Plan conception was launched, designed both to exploit possibilities for increased productivity in the European steel and coal industries and, more important, to bind France and Germany together in ways which would minimize the possibilities of future friction and conflict.

In Europe, then, the spring of 1950 was, relatively, a good time. Recovery, after a mild sag, was regathering momentum; rationing was going off even in Britain; the threat of war in Europe had receded; the American recession of 1949 had reversed itself; and a Western Community was taking shape. Although the ugly split of Germany and Europe remained, and the agenda of unsolved problems remained full, there had been progress since Britain surrendered responsibility for aid to Greece and Turkey three years before.

In this setting, where attention was largely focused on regional problems and developments, and where Asia was regarded as distant and secondary, the Korean War came as a distinct shock.

### REARMAMENT AND GERMANY

The reaction of the United States and of Western Europe to the first stages of the Korean War was to reappraise Soviet intentions and to elevate the possibility that Stalin might be planning a military showdown with the West to which the Korean War was a preliminary diversionary movement. And, even though the fear of imminent attack receded by early autumn, the military vulnerability of Western Europe was more acutely felt than it had been before. The technique of the invasion of South Korea—by a Soviet equipped satellite—had potential European analogies. Moreover, with the first Soviet atomic explosion having taken place in September 1949, the notion grew that an atomic stalemate might develop in which it would be irrational to use American atomic strength as a check on Soviet ground forces; and Western Europe began to think of creating a ground force establishment capable of deterring, if not defeating, a direct assault by the Red Army. In the autumn of 1950 both Western Europe and the United States were thus in a mood to give some substance to NATO as a shield for Western Europe as well as a plate glass window or trip-wire to guarantee immediate American involvement in a Soviet attack.

Against this background the difficult issue of German rearmament was first posed. German rearmament was a military necessity if a sufficient ground force was to be developed in Western Europe to deter the Soviet infantry potential; for Britain, France, Italy, and the United States were, in different ways, under political and economic inhibitions which precluded the development of a sufficient European counterforce without a substantial German contribution.

For Germany the problem was difficult for other reasons. It was believed by some that the arming of West Germany might be regarded as an act sufficiently provocative to bring on war. Others feared it would foreclose the possibility of negotiations for German unity with the Russians. In another direction, it was felt that the revival of militarism might set back the still weak but gathering forces in West Germany which had been working toward the development of democracy at home and a Western orientation abroad. Nevertheless, under Adenauer's guidance, the move was accepted in principle. Adenauer—the incarnation of much in the Germany which had been lost when Prussia came to dominate the Revolution of 1848—believed that the only safe course for Germany was to associate itself inextricably with the West and move toward unity as part of a strong Western European base supported by the United States—a judgment based not merely on an assessment of Germany's limited bilateral bargaining strength vis-à-vis Russia but also on a fear of the course his countrymen might pursue if they once again moved on their own in the arena of European and world power.

Although many Germans were more skeptical than Adenauer of a long-run strategy of unity with Western Europe and the Atlantic world—and less frightened of bilateral negotiation with Moscow—the majority was persuaded to follow Adenauer's lead as a tactic, if for no other reason than that the West still had considerable to offer Germany—and was willing to make the offer—whereas Moscow was evidently not prepared to offer the prize of unity on tolerable political terms. And psychologically West Germans in 1950 were primarily absorbed in the process of economic reconstruction and revival.

It was still some time before they would be prepared to look out on the world and define their destiny on the European and world scenes.

In France, of course, the re-emergence of German military strength set in motion profound instinctive fears, despite the existence of NATO. Partly to diminish those fears, the United States, after searching Congressional and public debate, made the commitment to maintain four divisions in Europe in 1951—a momentous decision in terms of previous American reactions to French requests for guarantee, stretching back to Versailles.

To the British, NATO had several attractive features. The British commitment to the European continent was essentially in naval and air strength; and this fitted British plans and military thought. Moreover, the organization of NATO gave the British great influence through Lord Ismay's role in the Secretary-Generalship and Lord Montgomery's command over the ground forces. As an organization NATO had many of the advantages of SHAEF during the Second World War. Finally, London found satisfaction in the wholehearted manner in which Canada could participate in NATO arrangements. For Canadians an enterprise which attracted the support of the United States, Britain, and France was the optimum setting in which to play an active role on the world scene, given the nature of Canadian social and political life. It is fair to say that NATO, as organized and set in motion in 1949-1952, set up fewer conflicts and strains in London than in any other major capital.

NATO rapidly gathered strength in 1951-1952 as Congress agreed to station the American divisions, Eisenhower built SHAPE, and substantial American aid helped build the "infrastructure," that is, the airfield and communications base of the enterprise. Moreover, Germany appeared to be moving slowly but steadily toward the assumption of responsibility for a major ground force contribution; and generally, the will of Europe to make substantial sacrifice in order to deter Soviet ground force troops seemed beyond question.

By the end of 1952, with the Korean War simmering down into truce negotiations over a narrow range of issues, and with the cast of policy in Moscow and Peking evidently undergoing some change, it was clear that the Lisbon force goals (agreed early in 1952) would not be achieved on schedule. Nevertheless, the West had obviously been stirred by the Korean War to build a vastly more substantial degree of unity and effective military strength than would have seemed possible in the spring of 1950. And, at the existing level of weapons technology and relative delivery capabilities, there seemed to be good sense in supplementing American atomic weapons delivery capabilities with a substantial conventional weapons establishment in Europe. In the course of 1953, however, forces came into play that were to render the NATO of 1950-1952 a transient phenomenon.

## 28. The Political Background of Military Policy: 1947-1950

CONTAINMENT: THE EUROPEAN PATTERN

The political core of American military policy as it evolved from 1947 to 1950 was a doctrine derived from Kennan's cables from Moscow of February 1946, the essence of which was published in *Foreign Affairs* for July 1947.

Kennan's conception of Soviet motivations and intentions did not uniquely determine American policy, but it crystallized and articulated the impressions and judgments which many responsible men had derived from their observation of Soviet behavior over the first postwar years. His analysis emphasized that the United States confronted a long-term challenge, not a short-range Hitlerian military plan. It dramatized the interplay between Moscow's hopes, fears, and actions on the one hand and, on the other, what the United States was as an international force and what it appeared ready to do on a sustained basis. It called for a willingness to meet and to frustrate Soviet aggressive initiatives ranging from politics and diplomacy to limited and major war. It held out a decent hope that, under the experience of protracted frustration, and if American society met the challenge which confronted it by exercising vigorously its historic strengths and virtues, Soviet society might undergo slow but important changes which would in the end make it a force less dangerous to American interests on the world scene.

This long-run frame of mind entered into the formulation of American policy in Europe from 1947 forward. The Truman Doctrine reacted to Moscow's threat to Turkey and to the Communist bid for victory in the Greek civil war. The Marshall Plan offered a foundation for the revival of Western Europe on a democratic basis. American backing for the Brussels Pact of 1948, elaborated a year later in NATO, gave the Europeans heart to proceed with long-term reconstruction despite the presence of overwhelming Soviet ground forces on the Elbe. The vigor, diplomatic poise, and technical and psychological success of the American response to the Berlin blockade via the airlift confirmed the essential short-period effectiveness of the policy of containment in Europe.

If that policy were to have long-term success, it had to embrace the steady performance of three tasks in Europe: first, persuading Moscow that the United States was militarily prepared to deal with further erosion of the Western Eurasian balance of power; second, persuading Moscow that major war would result in Soviet defeat and was therefore an irrational course to contemplate; third, dealing with whatever forms of limited military aggression Moscow might mount without incurring excessive risk of major war.[1] The first task was essentially political and psychological, requiring that American commitments to occupation and policing in Europe be met and that the mantle of the American interest be thrown explicitly over Western Europe and the Mediterranean area, including Tito's Yugoslavia, which defected in 1948 from Soviet control. The second task was to develop and sustain American military strength in being and in reserve capable of defeating the Soviet Union in major war or, at least, of making Soviet victory unobtainable. The third, in the peculiar circumstances of Europe, came down to dealing successfully with the Greek civil war and the airlift.

The American military policy evolved in the period 1947-1950 was designed essentially to deal with the military components of these tasks in Europe, but it did not look far beyond the European scene.

THE FAILURE OF UNIVERSAL MILITARY TRAINING

This regional limitation on American conceptions stemmed from the progressive limitation of Army capabilities. In the course of 1947 the continuing process of demobilization seriously reduced the ground forces stationed at the many points in the world where the United States was diplomatically committed, notably in the areas of occupation: Germany, Austria, Trieste, Japan, and South Korea. The problem came to a head early in 1948 in a form summarized as follows in the *Forrestal Diaries:*[2]

*18 February 1948*                    *Meeting—White House*

. . . General Gruenther made a presentation concerning our available military strength balanced against present and possible commitments:

STRENGTHS—1 FEBRUARY 1948

|  | Actual | Budget Authorization | Congressional Authorization |
|---|---|---|---|
| Army | 552,000 | 560,000 | 669,000 |
| Navy | 476,000 | 526,000 | 664,000 |
| (includes USMC) | 79,000 | 87,000 | 108,000 |
| Air Force | 346,000 | 362,000 | 382,000 |

Deployments of Major Army Elements

Far East: 140,000 against requirement of 180,000. (Includes 20,000 in Korea as of 1 March 1948 against requirement of 40,000. Department of Army has cut Korea allotment to 30,000.)

Eucom: 98,000 against requirement of 116,000. (In addition, 10,000 in Austria and 5,000 in Trieste.)

Zone of Interior (U.S.) operating 155,000 against requirement of 166,000. This figure does not include the General Reserve. The total Army shortage will be 165,000 by the end of 1948. The Navy has an acute personnel shortage now which requires the immobilization of 107 ships, but this condition is expected to improve by July 1. The personnel situation in the Air Force is satisfactory.

Truman and Marshall, surveying this situation and anxious both to dramatize to Moscow and to the world the long-run American intent to be prepared should aggression be initiated and to meet urgent immediate garrison commitments, advocated universal military training.

The proposal was made at a moment of acute tension. On February 24, 1948, the Communist *coup d'état* seized power in Prague. Britain, France, and the Benelux powers gathered to consider measures of collective security, and the concept of their being joined by the United States was set in motion through diplomatic channels. Clay, hitherto a notably cool observer, reported increased tension and an ominous worsening of relations with the Soviets in Berlin.[3] On March 17 the President went personally before the Congress and proclaimed a policy of increased American military strength. Specifically he asked for three measures to strengthen the Western position: the prompt passage of the Marshall plan, the adoption of Universal Military Training, and the temporary re-enactment of Selective Service to keep the armed forces at their authorized strength. Despite the mood of crisis, the military measures were long-run proposals designed to maintain the political weight of deterrence rather than to provide for imminent military engagements. They were projected as a program to keep the peace—not to make war.

## THE NEW AIR ROMANTICISM

But these proposals were cross-cut by the reports of the Finletter and Brewster Committees. These dramatized the growing importance and potentialities of air power; and they advocated a radical expansion in air power which would make the Air Force the preponderant arm of American defense.

The notion that an adequate air striking force, backed by a monopoly in atomic weapons, could deal with the Soviet menace was obviously attractive to the Congress and to the country. In a political democracy, unused to serious sacrifice in times of peace, universal military service is intrinsically unpopular. And reliance on air power fitted other elements in the national style and tradition: the substitution of capital and machinery for manpower, carried to a high point in the Air Force, fitted the nation's industrial character; and the image of American security firmly in the hands of an American Air Force and American weapons suited the national temper, appealing strongly to residual isolationist sentiments.

In Washington of early 1948 the infantryman thus seemed an old-fashioned if not an irrelevant fellow at a moment when the American atomic-weapons monopoly still held. Moreover, he was associated in recent experience with long-drawn wars of alliance and high casualties, and the concept of engagement with the Soviet ground "horde"—raising quasi-Asiatic images in American minds—was instinctively abhorrent. The roots for a policy of deterrence based on a strategic air force and atomic weapons went deep.

Air power romanticism was a natural successor to the naval romaticism which had sprung up a half-century or so earlier; its advocates were in the direct line of the Mahanist proponents of the big navy of the first decade of the century. A preponderant Strategic Air Command—like the Great White Fleet—appeared a device for performing as a world power without getting too deeply enmeshed in the complex, dangerous, interior affairs of Eurasia.

Although Selective Service was re-enacted, Congress regarded a strengthening of the Air Force as an alternative to universal military training and accepted the goal of a seventy-group Air Force advocated in the two Committee reports.[4]

The Congressional decision to rely preponderantly on air power for national defense converged with an equally far-reaching development in the political framework of military policy. The administration decided to set an arbitrary limit on military expenditures. Truman placed a ceiling of about $15 billion on the military budget—a sum defined as "what the country could afford for the long pull." Moreover, in the wake of the defeat of the Communist guerrillas in Greece and of the Soviet blockade of 1949, Truman reinforced it strongly by permitting (or ordering) the Secretary of Defense (Johnson, who succeeded Forrestal at the end of March 1949) to cut back military expenditures sharply, including the cancellation in April 1949 of the Navy's flush-deck carrier, which triggered the most outlandish of the interservice outbreaks of the postwar period.[5] In the year before the Korean War the armed forces lost about 10 per cent of their personnel, the burden being borne disproportionately by the Army.

NCS 68: A SLUGGISH REACTION TO NEW THREATS

It was not difficult for the administration to find reasons for being relatively complacent in mid-1949. The Western European economy had forward momentum, and the Communist political menace from within had been contained in France and Italy. Berlin had been held, and the NATO Treaty went through the Senate in July 1949 by a vote of 82 to 13. Since the United States still held a monopoly in atomic weapons, it was not hard to believe, despite doubts about the capabilities of the B-36 in relation to Soviet fighter and antiaircraft defenses, that the Soviets would continue to respect the American main strength, incorporated in air power, notably if the NATO forward bases, which enormously enhanced delivery capabilities, were built and maintained.

But it was an entirely different matter to remain complacent as the year wore on. In September the first Soviet atomic weapon was exploded. The Chinese Communist government formally took over in Peking on October 1 and immediately proclaimed its intent to seize Formosa by means of an amphibious operation. Mao went to confer with Stalin in December; and throughout Asia the Communist forces, accelerating an offensive developed over the previous two years, pressed hard against the shaky structure of the non-Communist Asian societies. Stirred by these developments, the administration undertook a thoroughgoing reappraisal of the American strategic position, starting formally in January 1950.

This reappraisal resulted in the famous document NSC 68, which received the President's somewhat ambiguous blessing in April.[6] NSC 68 called for a radical increase in military expenditures; depending on the assumptions used, increases of anywhere from $5 billion to $37 billion could be derived from its analysis. It would have provided increased resources not only to deter major war but also to prevent or to deal with limited war and to expand economic aid programs. Although a consensus on some such major change in the level of American effort was achieved between the State and Defense Department working level staffs, the pressure from those concerned about the budget remained heavy. Nevertheless, the machinery of bureaucracy was put to work in the Spring of 1950 to thrash out expanded figures for the next budget presentation, in January 1951, which would meet the terms of the new somber assessment of the nation's position. The Korean War intervened before this definitive process was well started. Thus, although the work of those who initiated NSC 68 served as a foundation for the build-up of force after the attack in South Korea, the alarm they sounded failed to alter the nation's position before June 1950.

### 29. The Military Services and Policy-making: 1947-1950

WHAT KIND OF WAR?

With the underlying political framework for military policy-making derived from a view limited essentially to the European scene, with Congress committed to extreme reliance on strategic air power, and with the Administration determined to maintain a tight rein on military outlays, what was the situation within the armed forces? With what issues did the professional military concern themselves from unification to the attack on South Korea?

Essentially, they debated three questions. For what kind of major war should the nation prepare? What should be the role of each of the services in such a war? And (in the light of answers to the first two questions) how should the arbitrarily limited military budget be split among the services?

Over this period the first question was never clearly answered on an agreed basis by the Joint Chiefs of Staff or by the Secretary of Defense.

Forrestal wrestled endlessly with the problem of defining the kind of war for which the nation should prepare. All his reflections, instincts, and old attachments to the Navy led him to question an excessive reliance on strategic air power; but, as the following notes indicate, his formulation never quite crystallized into a persuasive alternative to that pressed forward by Air Force adherents:

*27 October.* *General Notes on the Question of Naval Air—Air Forces*

1. We now have in existence strategic air forces of great potential power in terms of weight-lifting capacity and range. The unresolved question, however, is whether unescorted big bombers can penetrate to targets that have a vigorous fighter defense.

2. We also have in existence a nucleus of carrier aircraft and in reserve an additional number of carriers which can provide tremendous striking power.

3. Strategic air warfare is the assigned responsibility of the Air Force with the proviso that they are to call upon Naval Air for whatever help Naval Air can provide. It is my opinion that if war came the Air Force itself would immediately, or shortly after the outbreak, realize the diversionary possibilities necessary of the aircraft carrier task forces. . . .

4. No one knows the form and character of any war of the future. War planning—so-called strategic plans—are largely an intellectual exercise in which the planners make the best estimate of the form of a war against possible enemies. But the actions of the enemy must, necessarily, profoundly affect any war planning. If one did not have an enemy, it would be possible to have a perfect plan that could be taken off the shelf for immediate execution, but unfortunately the enemy does not always conform. . . .

5. I do not believe that airpower alone can win a war any more than an Army or naval power can win a war, and I do not believe in the theory that an atomic offensive will extinguish in a week the will to fight. I believe air power will have to be applied massively in order to really destroy the industrial complex of any nation and, in terms of present capabilities, that means air power within fifteen hundred miles of the targets—that means an Army has to be transported to the areas where the airfields exist—that means, in turn, there has to be security of the sea lanes provided by the naval forces to get the Army there. Then, and only then, can the tremendous striking power of air be applied in a decisive—and I repeat decisive—manner.[1]

Forrestal's final paragraph half argues that strategic air attack would be indecisive, half argues that it would be decisive with adequate forward bases. There is no clear distinction here between a major war and a limited engagement—only the unresolved puzzlement of paragraph 4. With this issue unsettled, Forrestal was unable, in good conscience, to organize or discipline the three services or to make the case he instinctively felt for an enlarged military budget.[2]

The Air Force, strengthened by the Finletter and Brewster reports, and heartened by the evident attractiveness to the Congress of the notion that American security could be fully protected by massive delivery capabilities with atomic weapons, proceeded to argue strongly for maximum allocations to the Strategic Air Command. The Navy and the Army insisted that major war could not be won wholly by strategic air power and that a dangerous degree of unbalance would come about in American military preparations if, within the total military resources fixed by the politicians, the Air Force should get too high a total. The Air Force, however, proceeded to plan a level of attack so devastating that, if delivered, it would leave a most limited and ambiguous role for the Army and the Navy in its wake.

It is true that no one, not even the Air Force, was prepared formally to claim that a major war could be won from the air alone; but, on the other hand, the relation of ground and naval arms to the strategic air arm was never thought through and consolidated into a coherent and persuasive concept. Instead, the Army and Navy proceeded to think in terms of a recurrence of some version of World War II, while finding ways also of cutting themselves in on atomic weapons; and, above all, as institutions they sought the maximum strength in being and in reserve they could wring from the bureaucratic and political process. Neither the Army nor the Navy at this stage was prepared to press forward the case for deterring or preparing to deal with limited war.

## MISSIONS AND THE BUDGET

Lacking a more than verbally agreed answer to the first question—the char- acter of a future war—the second and third questions—concerning missions and the budget—led to vigorous interservice debate over a wide front.[3]

On one issue a peculiarly dour and purposeful battle was launched in this period by the Army and the Navy, a battle to disengage the Air Force from monopolistic control of atomic weapons. Each service exploited fully the potential inherent in its right to conduct research and development relevant to its own sphere, the result being that they gave more thought and energy to the military problem at the parochial level—of the atomic cannon and super carrier—than to the question of the nature and limitations of war with atomic weapons and the relation of the three services to such war. Service strategic doctrines tended to follow the battle for new weapons and functions rather than to be the source from which they were derived, the most notable example being the manner in which the Navy's assault on the efficacy of strategic bombing died away with the acceptance of the super carrier.

The conflict among the services was formally resolved by the highly am- biguous concept of "balanced forces." Pressed to a logical conclusion, the notion of "balanced forces" was that the United States had to prepare itself for two kinds of major war. One would be an air war in which the full capabil- ities of the Strategic Air Command would be loosed against the Soviet Union should it initiate war. The other would be a major ground force engagement on the Eurasian continent either in the wake of strategic attack or should the strategic air attack not produce decisive results. This, as nearly as one can make out, is what the notion of "balanced forces" was. It did not contemplate the third possibility—a limited ground force engagement with conventional (and perhaps lesser atomic) weapons which would require maintaining a highly mobile infantry (and Marine) force at combat readiness.

With military and political thinking limited to one form or other of major war, the central problem posed for military planners in 1948 was how to accommodate the claims for the Army and the Navy within the $15 billion limit at a time when Congress had accepted the seventy-group Air Force. The "balanced forces" notion, if it were to be realistically put into effect, called for more than the $15 billion could possibly provide. The controlling fact was thus political—the urge to economize. Neither the Executive Branch nor the Congress was prepared to justify an over-all increase in the military budget in order to keep simultaneously in being and at combat readiness forces capable of fighting two different kinds of major war—an atomic war with air power and a ground force war with conventional weapons; and this was, roughly, what the proopsals of the three services added up to.

The upshot was that, when the Korean War broke out, the United States had in being a Strategic Air Command capable of mounting some 180 heavy bombers and 52 medium bombers over the Soviet Union and Communist China—enough for a devastating strike with atomic weapons at likely levels of penetration and accuracy if NATO forward bases were available, permitting fighter cover; and, with lighter aircraft (including naval and marine forces), first-line bombing strength could probably have been pushed to about 2,000. But the nation's Army and (to a lesser extent) its Navy were merely a thin understrength reserve structure requiring desperate improvisation and pell mell expansion before a large but essentially second-rate enemy on the ground in Eurasia could be held in check.

The American military concentrated, then, on the problem of major war and the role of their respective services within it. Their eyes were focused on the enemy's main strength in the Soviet Union. The tasks in Greece, Berlin, and even NATO (which was initially designed to serve a political and psychological purpose) were regarded as essentially diversionary except to the extent that NATO provided invaluable forward bombing bases. Truman was forced, for example, personally to overrule Vandenberg, then Chief of Air Staff, to release the aircraft necessary for the Berlin airlift, the Air Force resisting vigorously the dissipation of the pool of air strength judged necessary should major war with the Soviet Union come about.[4]

Given the American military tradition, the hard pressure of the fixed military budget, and the difficult problem of assessing the meaning of strategic air power with atomic weapons, all this is understandable. And, indeed, the first task of the professional military was to ensure that Moscow was deterred from using its ground force preponderance by the likelihood, if not the certainty, of defeat by the United States in major war. And this minimum foundation for American security was provided.

## LIMITED WAR

Why did not the military in this period pose more effectively the question of limited war? Why was not a strong and persuasive case made to the President, the public, and the Congress by the military for keeping at combat readiness a ready reserve of infantry with naval support capable of dealing with limited war? Why were the civil war in Greece and the Berlin airlift not recognized as prototypes of the main Communist thrust?

In part, the answer is that the military agreed that a force in being capable of dealing with "brushfire" wars was desirable[5] but, under hard budgetary pressure, accorded the capability to deter or to deal with limited war a relatively low priority. One explanation for that assessment was that by 1949 the possibilities of limited Soviet military aggression which would not be tantamount to major war were pretty well exhausted in Europe. The other is that Washington failed to understand the potentialities in Asia for an extension of the Soviet method used in Greece.

There were also deeper flaws in American reasoning. Washington failed to sense the extent to which Stalin and Mao would regard Communist victory in China not as the occasion for settling down to consolidate the new empire but as a moment of historic Communist opportunity to press on to decisive victory over the West in Asia. Washington also failed to appraise the extent to which the nation's main strength—strategic air power—left open an area of vulnerability not merely to limited wars conducted at one remove by Moscow's agents but also to situations where the imperatives of Western morality and the alliance system to which the United States was deeply committed would make extremely difficult the employment of the nation's main strength. It failed to reckon with the acute vulnerability of American allies which, due to the scale and location of Soviet ground forces, assumed a new dimension after the Soviet Union developed atomic weapon delivery capabilities in 1949.

## THE SHREWD BLOW

In sum, the result of United States military policy as it evolved from 1947 to 1950 was that the Korean War found the United States singularly ill-prepared. Washington had been thinking in terms of deterring major war or winning such a war if it came. Here was a limited war. Washington had been thinking of the Strategic Air Command as its force in being to carry the burden of prompt counterattack. Here was a situation where SAC could be invoked politically only at great and unmeasurable risk, tactically with doubtful effect, and strategically only at the cost of dissipating American main strength in secondary, indecisive operations. Washington had been thinking of war in terms of the employment of Soviet forces. Here were North Koreans on the march, obviously armed and manipulated from Moscow, but not even linked to the Soviet Union by a mutual security pact. Washington had been thinking primarily of Western Eurasia, blanketed by NATO and other formal American commitments. Here was a challenge in Eastern Eurasia in an area outside the announced national defense perimeter, a challenge which the nation was committed to deal with through the untried collective security machinery of the United Nations.

The Communist invasion of South Korea on June 25, 1950, was thus carefully designed to exploit the gaps in American military thought and policy which developed after 1947.

### 30. The Korean War: Its Military And Political Conduct

KEY MILITARY DECISIONS[1]

The Korean War was as bitter and difficult a series of ground force engagements as the United States had ever fought. From June 25, 1950, to July 27, 1953, total American casualties were 137,051. South Korean casualties were about ten times that figure; those of the fourteen members of the United Nations who shared in the fighting were around 13 per cent of the casualties suffered by United States forces.

The climactic engagements of the war occurred in the Spring of 1951, when two massive Chinese Communist offensives were launched, one on April 22, the other on May 16. These were met by a flexible defense designed not to hold fixed positions but to expose masses of enemy troops to artillery fire, the scale, mobility, and control of which were the principal American relative advantage in the field. After initial advances, both Chinese Communist offensives were successfully contained and the Chinese suffered enormous casualties. It is likely that in one week at the peak of the May engagement some 90,000 war casualties were inflicted on the Chinese Communist forces; and the casualty ratio as between Chinese Communist and UN forces was estimated at a five-day peak period as something over 36 to 1.

By early June the organizational integrity of most of the Chinese Communist units engaged had been destroyed, and General Van Fleet, field commander in Korea, believed (and he was almost certainly correct) that with reasonable reinforcements he could drive the Chinese Communist armies back to the neck of the Korean peninsula (roughly, the Pyongyang-Wonsan line). But the decision in Washington was not to proceed north of the 38th Parallel again. On June 17 Van Fleet announced that his counteroffensive back to a line approximating the 38th Parallel was over; and on June 24 Jacob Malik let it be known in a radio broadcast that a cease-fire was negotiable.

Behind the battlefield performance of the American forces lay controlling decisions made in Washington, the most fundamental of which was the decision that full American mobilization was not justified but that it was necessary henceforth to keep in being a greater deterrent force than the budget policy had permitted between 1947 and 1950; that is, having failed to antici-pate the Korean War, American military policy fixed on the problem of pre-venting the recurrence of a similar attack.

In determining the new level of forces, it was reasoned that in major war the American Strategic Air Command would have to be the primary initial weapon of counterattack, and that, in any case, it was beyond the capabilities of Western societies and their economies to maintain in being sufficient ground forces to match those of the Communist world. Therefore, until major war actually broke out a fully mobilized SAC and a partial mobilization of ground and naval forces capable of holding defensively for sufficient time for total mobilization to occur appeared to represent the only rational course for the United States and the West.

The resulting military policy therefore had three guiding objectives: a rapid build-up of NATO forces, including the stationing in Europe of the five infantry divisions to which the United States was committed by treaty; an expansion of all three American services to provide "balanced strength" on a scale that would, this time, really deter Moscow and Peking from further military aggression; and the creation of sufficient resources to contain the Korean aggression. Broadly speaking, the basic military establishment of the United States was somewhat more than doubled between June 1950 and June 1952, when there were some 3,600,000 Americans under arms.[2]

## AN EXERCISE IN LIMITED WAR

Historically, perhaps the most significant military decision of the Korean War was one tacitly shared by the United States and the Soviet Union—not to employ the most powerful weapons at their command.

The United States could have launched strategic air attacks against the Soviet Union and Communist China. It could have seriously damaged the Chinese Communist economy by blockading its coast. Tactically it could have made untenable the Manchurian air bases from which Soviet-built MIG-15s flew their sorties against American bombing attacks within Korea; and, more generally, tactical attacks in Manchuria and the Soviet Far East could have done much more damage to the lines of supply to the Korean front than was accomplished by the heavy close-support bombing and strafing operations that were employed. The Soviet Union probably could have delivered a serious but not decisive atomic assault against a number of major American cities by, say, early 1951. It could centainly have disrupted the American base in Japan both psychologically and politically by delivering a few atomic or even non-atomic bombs there. By submarine, it could certainly have interfered with the amphibious operations undertaken against the North Koreans, the general supply by sea of the United Nations front, and the supply of the American base in Japan.

But both nations refrained from these possible courses of action. The threat of setting in motion a chain of events which might lead to war with atomic weapons decreed, through a subtle, inarticulate process of interplay between Moscow and Washington, that the Korean War be fought essentially as an infantry war within a limited terrain. Thus there underlay the whole conduct of the war the paradox that, despite the failure of both sides to use atomic weapons, the Korean War was distinctly a product of the atomic age.[3]

SOME LESSONS, MAINLY PAINFUL

It follows that, in one sense, the lessons drawn from the war by the American military services were, with a few exceptions, simple, rather old-fashioned lessons:

*Tactical air.* It was found extremely difficult to interdict the flow of food and ammunition to the Chinese Communist ground armies in Korea. The cost of supplying the Communist front was undoubtedly vastly increased by the use of American tactical air forces; but the Chinese Communists were prepared to use manpower as well as railways and motor vehicles to transport their essential supplies; and men carrying packs on their backs over the Korean hills were not satisfactory air targets. Moreover, the conditions of battle only occasionally involved a sustained rate of Communist fire such that an interruption of rail and road lines of supply could affect the weight of attack. The virtually complete air supremacy enjoyed over the battlefield by the UN forces did, of course, permit casualties to be inflicted at relatively low costs and cut down the over-all capability of the Communist forces; but tactical air supremacy was not, in itself, decisive.

*Infantry.* The lavish use of artillery, tactical air power, and modern communications demonstrated that industrial capital could, to an important degree, be successfully substituted for manpower against an Asian land army. But the Korean War emphasized that, in the end, the fundamental qualities of a good infantryman still mattered greatly; and it revealed a series of weaknesses in American training, notably with respect to night fighting.

*The enemy.* Before their collapse the North Korean Army demonstrated that it was capable of handling modern weapons and conducting itself with some skill against a modern Western army.[4] These conclusions were strongly reinforced by the conduct of the Chinese Communist Army. Its higher commanders were judged first class by their American opposite numbers; its officer corps was evidently well trained; the Chinese Communist infantryman was disciplined and thoroughly capable of handling modern artillery and mortars, the latter available in profusion. The principal Chinese Communist weakness appeared to be an inability to sustain a mobile well-organized offensive, due primarily to inadequate communications.

*Brainwashing.* The application to American prisoners of physical and psychological pressure designed to make them acquiesce in treasonable acts posed a new and searching problem for the armed forces.

*Technological innovations.* Essentially, the Korean War was fought with weapons of the latter days of the Second World War;[5] but there were two major areas of innovation: the extensive use of helicopters for front-line supply and the evacuation of wounded, and an improvement in the medical handling of casualties which strikingly increased survival rates over the levels achieved in the Second World War.

THE ARMS RACE GATHERS MOMENTUM

Despite the essentially old-fashioned nature of the Korean War and its battlefield lessons, it was accompanied at home by a process of far-reaching military significance. The decision by Truman, in January 1950, to proceed with the production of a hydrogen bomb coincided with and related closely to the launching of the studies which led to NSC 68. The revolution implicit in the weapons pioneered during the Second World War began to emerge into full reality. Between 1950 and 1953 the consequences for military technology of the atomic-electronics age became clear not merely to scientists but also to responsible men in governments; and the arms race in the new weapons, the means of their delivery, and the means of defense against them took shape and gathered momentum.

Perhaps more important, the ideas which men brought to military policy and planning began actually to reflect the reality of the race that was on. As a counterpoint to the bitter, crude war of infantry and artillery in Korea the scientists and engineers in both the United States and the Soviet Union proceeded to press forward with military instruments which not only altered radically the security problem of each nation (and of all other nations as well) but also reshaped the missions of the services within each military establishment.

## 31.  *The Korean War: Political Decisions, the Debate, and a Summation*

POLITICAL DECISIONS

The demonstration that the United States would not make the honoring of the Soviet commitment to political freedom in its areas of occupation a matter of military importance set the stage not only for the Communist takeover of Eastern Europe but also for the creation in North Korea of a satellite government. A small cadre of Soviet-trained Korean Communists backed by the Red Army proceeded to achieve virtually total control of the Soviet area and to erect institutions along lines virtually identical with those erected in Eastern Europe. The Soviet area of occupation was formally constituted as the People's Democratic Republic of Korea on May 1, 1948.

The only Soviet response to American and United Nations attempts to effect unification of Korea on the basis of free supervised elections was the demand for a withdrawal of occupation forces. Throughout the postwar period Moscow conducted a general diplomatic campaign against the presence of American military force on the Asian continent. Molotov's diplomacy with respect to China in 1945, for example, focused obsessively on the withdrawal of the American Marines.[1] And from an early stage it was evident that Moscow placed a high priority on disengaging American troops from their occupation position in South Korea. When the Korean Communist regime was consolidated and armed, Moscow unilaterally withdrew its occupation forces on December 31, 1948, thus exerting strong diplomatic pressure on the United States to follow suit.

The American decision to withdraw troops from Korea had already been agreed upon by the Joint Chiefs of Staff in September, the American military being anxious to conserve and concentrate scarce ground forces.[2] The United States recognized the newly established Republic of South Korea in January 1949, and on June 29 American troops were withdrawn except for a military mission of some five hundred men stationed there to help administer continuing United States economic and military aid.

The position within Korea, then, was unique among the postwar occupied areas by July 1949 in that, formally, both the occupying powers had withdrawn their formations. The mantle of direct American responsibility had been lifted. Where, then, did Korea fit in terms of American security policy?

The American position was incorporated in two statements made by the Secretary of State early in 1950. The first, on January 12, outlined the national defense perimeter in the Pacific, derived from the virtually unilateral American occupation responsibility for Japan as well as from deeper direct interests. It traced out a defense line (formulated by the JCS) running along the Aleutians to Japan, then to the Ryukyus, thence to the Philippines. The Secretary of State then said:

> So far as the military security of other areas in the Pacific is concerned, it must be clear that no person can guarantee these areas against military attack. But it must also be clear that such a guarantee is hardly sensible or necessary within the realm of practical relationship. Should such an attack occur—one hesitates to say where such an armed attack could come from—the initial reliance must be on the people attacked to resist it and then upon the commitments of the entire civilized world under the Charter of the United Nations, which so far has not proved a weak reed to lean on by any people who are determined to protect their independence against outside aggression.[3]

The second statement, made in March 1950, and reiterating earlier official American pronouncements, was a general warning to Communist China against aggression:

> [The Chinese people] should understand that, whatever happens within their own country, they can only bring grave trouble on themselves and their friends, both in Asia and beyond, if they are led by their new rulers into aggressive or subversive adventures beyond their borders. Such adventures would violate not only every tradition and interest of the Chinese people; they would violate the United Nations Charter. They would violate the peace which the Charter was designed to preserve.
>
>   I say this so that there may be no mistake about the attitude of the United States, no opportunity to distort or twist it, and so that all in China may know who would be responsible for all that such adventures might bring to pass.[4]

The United States was thus committed to defend the integrity of non-Communist areas in Asia on general security grounds; and it was committed quite specifically to react should Chinese Communist troops move across Chinese borders or should Peking seek to extend its power by subversion.

When on Saturday afternoon, June 24 (Washington time), news of the invasion came, the American government responded quickly in terms of this announced policy. Its formal ground was the national commitment to collective security under the United Nations Charter; but uppermost in the minds of American political and diplomatic officials was the need to demonstrate to members of the developing NATO alliance that the United States was prepared to react to Communist military aggression with force and protect the ground invaded. There is no doubt that these considerations were paramount in Truman's decision to intervene with vigor in the Korean War; and it was such general and symbolic considerations—rather than the strategic importance of the area—that underlay the support of a majority of the United Nations for resistance with force.

The American (and Western) reaction to the invasion of South Korea was colored by another and quite separate factor: namely, doubt as to the extent and direction of Communist aggressive intentions. The invasion of South Korea was an exceedingly bold move, involving a degree of risk of major war which the West had believed Stalin unlikely to take. It was necessary now to reappraise Soviet (and Chinese Communist) intentions.

The following question was thus raised: Is the invasion of South Korea a feint, designed to pin down the limited existing American ground forces in preparation for a subsequent attack in Western Europe? At no other time after 1945 was the possibility of general war in Europe taken as seriously as between the end of June and the end of September 1950. The view that the Korean War might prove to be merely an incident in a larger Soviet offensive helped determine the character of the American and Western reaction to it. That reaction was a heightening of security measures on all fronts rather than a concentrated effort in Korea.

The Korean situation required precisely the kinds of force which had been weakened under the policy of the previous three years—infantry, naval strength, and tactical air using conventional weapons. For the Strategic Air Command the Korean War raised the possibility of dissipating the pool of strength husbanded and kept in being to deter Soviet ground forces in Europe and to serve as the prime American instrument of counterattack should major war come. Nevertheless, the four occupation divisions available in Japan were thrown promptly into the battle; forces were dispatched from the United States, and a foothold in South Korea was held. A new program of national defense was formulated and vigorously put into effect. In the course of the Korean War the armed forces were expanded from 1.5 to 3.5 million men; annual military appropriations rose from $12 to $41 billion; foreign aid increased from $4.5 to $7.1 billion.

The remarkable success of MacArthur in the landings at Inchon on September 5, 1950 transformed the military situation and posed a new range of issues. After these landings the North Korean armies were thrown into full retreat and the road to the Yalu was opened. On October 7, 1950, the use of United Nations forces north of the 38th Parallel was authorized by the General Assembly of the United Nations. This decision significantly altered the nature of the United Nations military and political objectives. The purpose was no longer simply to repel invasion. It was to destroy the enemy forces. Moreover, as the enemy forces disintegrated, a further objective came within reach—to consolidate the victory in Korea and provide the military basis for the unification of the country by democratic process, the announced political objective of the United States and, indeed, of the United Nations.

The decision for an enlarged objective was taken despite reservations of three kinds. First, on general grounds, certain members of the United Nations were uneasy with the conversion of a war designed merely to demonstrate resistance to aggression into a war to achieve a positive political objective. Second, certain members of the United Nations, most notably India, believed it possible or likely on the basis of information available early in October that the Chinese Communists would intervene with force if the United Nations forces proceeded to the Manchurian border at the Yalu; and they clearly preferred to avoid a substantial risk of extending the war even if the cost was to be the continued split of Korea. Third, there were technical military objections offered to the manner of United Nations advance. The Eighth Army and X Corps proceeded in two widely separated columns under a command unified only in Tokyo. It was felt that, should the Chinese Communists intervene, this disposition offered the possibility of defeat of the United Nations forces.

Under these circumstances, and wishing to minimize a sense of direct threat to Manchuria from Americans, the JCS proposed a compromise plan of action. They advised that the United Nation forces proceed to the neck of the Korean peninsula, just north of the line Pyongyang-Wonson, and permit only Korean troops to probe beyond.[5] However, when MacArthur chose to permit the whole of his force to proceed into the wide mouth of the North Korean funnel on the grounds that the Korean troops lacked adequate commanders, the JCS accepted MacArthur's tactical decision. Neither the political nor the military figures in Washington were in a mood confidently to overrule the judgment of the man who virtually alone had believed in the probable success of the Inchon landings and who appeared in September-October 1950 to be converting the North Korean aggression into the greatest single political and military victory over communism of the postwar years.

When the Chinese Communists, having succeeded in massing an army inside Korea without detection, launched a major offensive and by the end of December had pushed the United Nations forces back to the 38th Parallel, Washington was faced with a further fundamental decision. Now the aggressor was not merely North Korea, whose forces had been so badly mauled that their total defeat seemed certain, but also Communist China; and the effort which would be required to crush communism in Korea and make possible a united country assumed a new magnitude.

The administration's decision was to return to the original limited objective of preserving South Korea, that is, to defend the line at the 38th Parallel. That line having been successfully held against the spring Chinese Communist offensives, Washington accepted the offer of truce negotiations made by Malik in June.

THE DEBATE

The decision to accept a truce at approximately the 38th Parallel led to the most searching and bitter national debate on foreign policy of the postwar years, coming to a head in the Congressional hearings which followed the removal of MacArthur on April 10, 1951, but echoing down over the next two years and beyond. The debate was formally conducted in terms of the policy to be followed in the face of Chinese Communist aggression in Korea; but it ranged over a wide area of postwar foreign policy and had emotional roots and overtones deriving from the sweep of American history in the Far East and from the tensions and cross-currents of the Cold War as a whole.

The formal position taken by MacArthur in opposition to the administration can be summarized as follows: The entrance of the Chinese Communists into the Korean War was a new act of aggression, creating a new situation in diplomatic terms and a new war. In the face of this situation the United States, as a matter of national pride and principle, should hold to its post-Inchon objective of a military victory in Korea capable of providing for the unity of the country. This victory could be achieved by the following courses of action: the bombing of Manchurian bases, the blockade of the China coast, the use in Korea of elements from the Nationalist Army on Formosa, and a United Nations ground force offensive in Korea backed with major reinforcements. Against the background of the Chinese Communist domestic position these actions would yield decisive defeat for the Chinese Communists in Korea, possibly a major internal crisis favorable to the American interest, and certainly a political and psychological base from which the balance of power in Eastern Eurasia could be easily held; and this could be done without using American troops on the ground inside Chinese borders. In the face of such an American (if not United Nations) offensive Moscow was not likely to enter the Far Eastern war, since Stalin would only go to war on rational grounds when he judged it to his advantage. The United States should be prepared to accept whatever diplomatic costs were necessary and pursue this course of action in the face of whatever defection of allies in Europe and Asia might result.

The administration's reply was essentially as follows. The military mission proposed by MacArthur ran the risk of proving indecisive and involving the United States in a protracted war. Even if the Soviets did not enter the war, it would engage the bulk of American military resources against a secondary enemy; but a war of this kind and on this scale was in fact likely to force Soviet intervention because of the depth of Soviet commitment to the Chinese Communists. Moscow could not afford to appear so unreliable a shield to its satellites. The MacArthur proposals thus risked the possibility of a Third World War which might break out with the bulk of American forces in being committed to fighting the secondary enemy in a secondary theater. In a global perspective the alienation of allies in Western Europe and Asia must be accorded an extremely heavy weight: in the short run, given the importance of European bases to SAC's deterrent power; in the long run, given the importance of NATO and of American relations with Asian powers most unlikely to support the policy MacArthur advocated. If major war should come with the Soviet Union, long-run American interests demanded that it be on grounds accepted by the world as just. Under the existing circumstances the proper course was, therefore, to abandon the idea of unifying Korea by force of arms and to accept a truce which met the terms upon which the Korean action was initially undertaken: namely, a demonstration that military aggression could not succeed.

Acheson summed up the administration's case as follows :

> What this adds up to it seems to me, is that we are being asked to undertake a large risk of general war with China, risk of war with the Soviet Union, and a demonstrable weakening of our collective security system—all of this in return for what?
> In return for measures whose effectiveness in bringing the conflict to an early conclusion are judged doubtful by our responsible military authorities.[6]

The debate embraced another issue never clearly stated by either side—the issue of preventive war. MacArthur sedulously avoided arguing in favor of an American-initiated showdown with the Soviet Union. On the contrary, he put his case on the grounds that Korea could be unified without a general war and without even substantially increased ground force engagement with Communist China. But there were many Americans, frustrated by the whole sequence of postwar Communist actions, who felt that the United States should use the occasion of the Korean War to force a showdown with Moscow and who supported MacArthur for that reason. They felt that, rather than face an endless period of strain marked by a series of costly indecisive crises, it would be better to have it out, cost what it may. Their view was strengthened by the fact that in 1950-1951 Soviet capabilities for delivering nuclear weapons, which would evidently grow rapidly, were still limited. Here was a clear case of Communist aggression. Why not go, at full American strength, to its source? The rise in Soviet delivery capabilities in the following years never again permitted this deep and recurrent American instinct to be put in so nearly a responsible way.

In 1951 the administration, in effect, replied to this argument—despite the fact that it was not thus clearly put—by emphasizing the costs of nuclear war not merely to the United States but also to American allies and by arguing that American and Free World military strength was on the rise. Acheson's summation of the administration's position was that ". . . time is on our side, if we make good use of it."[7]

Behind the remarkably orderly, detailed, well-conducted debate before the Russell Committee in the Senate there lay a long history, a history of conflicts of policy and personality. For MacArthur the debate represented the occasion for releasing an accumulated sense of dissent and frustration which went back to the days of the Second World War and even earlier—the rise of his old rival Marshall to position as wartime Chief of Staff, and of Bradley and his former aide Eisenhower (neither of whom he greatly respected) to eminence; the acute priority given to the European over the Asian theater during the Second World War, and the continued failure of Washington to understand the long-run meaning of Asia, as he saw it, to the American interest; the deference Washington accorded the views of European and Asian allies whom he regarded as decadent, unreliable, or both; the willingness of Washington to accept the fruits of his personal gamble and insight on the Inchon landings but its unwillingness to back his play when he (and Washington) guessed wrong on the intervention of the Chinese Communists; the political character of an administration he had hoped to supersede with his own Republican candidacy in 1944, an ambition still not wholly laid to rest; and, above all, the long expatriate isolation, where he was surrounded by lesser men of limited critical capacity, out of touch with the flow of national life and for five years acting virtually in succession to an absolute Japanese Emperor—all this ended by rude dismissal from high command.

There were equally strong, reciprocal feelings behind the Administration's presentation, including especially the memory of a sequence of recent (as well as ancient) affronts and provocations to established military and civil authority. Out of a mixture of human respect for a unique senior soldier and political expediency the men of the administration had made, in their view, many concessions to MacArthur's sense of status and to his style of operation; but this was the end.

And there was even more of American history latent in the debate. Beyond the recently remembered clashes of policy and personality, MacArthur symbolized that part of American history which, since the early days of the China trade, had looked out over the Pacific to Asia as a region where the American nation could express its enterprise—missionary, commercial, and military— relatively untrammeled with ties to old Europe. And MacArthur's insight was not wholly derived from the past. No figure in American politics since 1945 evoked more memorably the mood and aspiration of contemporary Asia than did MacArthur in certain passages of his address to Congress after he was relieved of command. Marshall and the Truman Administration as a whole stood solidly, on the other hand, for the twentieth-century experience of strategic reserve to Western Europe and of leadership of the Atlantic coalition.

In the immediate context, the administration won its debate with Mac- Arthur on the issue of policy with respect to the Chinese Communist intervention, the turning point, perhaps, being the following colloquy between

Senator MacMahon and MacArthur on May 3, the implications of which MacMahon drove home in subsequent exchanges.

SENATOR MACMAHON: ". . . Now, General, do you think that we are ready to withstand the Russian attack in Western Europe today?

GENERAL MACARTHUR: Senator, I have asked you several times not to involve me in anything except my own area. My concepts on global defense are not what I am here to testify on. I don't pretend to be the authority now on those things.

SENATOR MACMAHON: And so, General, you concede it seems to me by that statement, that the Joint Chiefs of Staff, having access to global intelligence, having made global plans for our defense, may have in that information, and because of that information made decisions contrary to your recommendations which could be sound."[8]

Truman, Marshall, Bradley, and Acheson did indeed convince the majority of the Congress and the public as well that it was wiser in the light of total American interests to seek a settlement at the 38th Parallel rather than take the multiple military and political risks of seeking a decision in Korea by bringing increased military pressure on Communist China in a widened theater of operations.

A SUMMATION

Despite the nation's acceptance of this outcome of the debate—eased by the fact that Malik's cease-fire offer came two days before the close of the hearings—[9]the Korean War and its resolution were a searching, troubling national experience. There were many reasons for this.

First, casualties were heavy and they continued through a period of protracted, often humiliating negotiations, stretching out over two full years.

Second, both contestants in the great debate had been fooled by the Chinese Communists. They had been tempted by the defeat of the North Koreans to unify Korea on the assumption that the Chinese Communists would not enter the war; and, when the Chinese Communists did attack, the United States was not willing to back its play. There was virtually no American for whom this was not a disagreeable experience. Whatever more mature considerations were brought to bear on national policy, it was a simple, universally understandable truth that the nation had gambled, its bluff had been called, and it had not backed its play.

Third, the truce itself and the concept of a costly military engagement merely to demonstrate an abstract principle ran counter to deeply rooted American emotions. Never since the War of 1812 had the United States ended a military engagement on such terms. Fresh from the comfortable but illusory experience of "unconditional surrender" in the Second World War, the nation had responded instinctively in the first instance to MacArthur's call for "victory."

Fourth, and more generally, the Korean War impressed upon the United States the limitations of its power and the complexity of the network of relations with its allies and with its enemies within which it was committed to protect its interest and work out its destiny. This extreme complexity had, in fact, governed the American position since the end of the Second World War; but the other exercises in meeting Communist aggression on a limited basis—Greece, the Berlin airlift, and even the formation of the NATO alliance—had yielded reasonably concrete results at reasonable cost. In Korea the results seemed abstract, and they were inevitably obscured by the great debate. And the costs were certainly high.

In its broad impact, then, the Korean War was an experience in which the United States as a nation was forced to choose consciously among unattractive alternatives; to confront and measure its own limitations. The simple, instinctive reaction consonant with the nation's romantic image of itself and its historical tradition was presented, examined, and rejected.

But this experience of maturity gave no clear constructive leads to further action. The decision to accept a truce at the 38th Parallel was, perhaps, a necessary condition for making an American policy in Asia; but it left that policy still to be made in Japan, Formosa, Indochina, and Southeast Asia generally. And in some respects the consequences of the Korean War were not merely unilluminating but negative. At a period when the development of new weapons and the character of the arms race made urgent the creation of a military policy embracing the possibility of limited war, the old fearful image of Asia as a terrain where the white man might be swallowed up by endless fatalistic hordes was reinforced. Memories from the Korean War certainly weakened the nation in its later approach to the Indochina crisis and in seeking to give substance to SEATO. By its faulty perspective the nation was even denied a sense of the achievement it had wrested from failure.

For there had been achievement—even if limited. The Korean War did more than demonstrate the viability of collective security arrangements backed by American commitments and force. It frustrated an ambitious Communist effort to exploit the victory in China to shift decisively the balance of power in Asia. The American success in avoiding a quick *fait accompli* in South Korea, the year's intensive war that followed, and the fighting stalemate of the period down to the armistice of July 27, 1953, forced a concentration of Communist energies and resources in Korea. In the meanwhile three factors transformed the scene, leaving the Communist position in Asia radically different from what it was when Stalin hopefully launched the invasion of South Korea in June of 1950.

First, non-Communist Asia, excepting the two colonial areas of Malaya and Veitnam, had used this period to find a degree of political stability and coherence that ruled out the prompt translation of chaos into Communist rule that Stalin and Mao had in mind in the period 1947-1950. Second, the passage of time underlined the depth and urgency of the domestic economic problems of Communist China. Mao was willing to gamble on a vigorous exploitation in Asia of his victory in China, using the period 1949-1952 at home for the relatively easy domestic task of reactivating existing industrial capacity in Manchuria and China. But he did not have the industrial base for the long-sustained campaign of aggression that American and United Nations resistance in Korea forced upon him. By 1952 he had to turn, at first priority, to the basic neglected domestic tasks of economic growth. Third, Stalin died, accentuating the pressures within the Soviet power structure evident before his death which looked to a Soviet external policy geared to the long run, which would leave greater energy and resources for domestic tasks and for meeting the challenge of the technological race in new weapons.

The United States had not clearly perceived the shape and timing of Communist strategy and tactics in Asia before the Korean War; and it failed to measure what it had achieved in impaling the Communists for three years in Korea. But it was one of the costs of the Korean War and its controversies— to the administration and to the nation at large—that, excepting partial mobilization, it made more difficult the effective use of the time that was available —the exploitation of which was the key to Acheson's reply to MacArthur. In the seven years that followed the MacArthur debate of 1951 the nation made remarkably slow progress in formulating an effective policy in Asia and in the other regions gripped by the nationalist revolutions which Moscow and Peking sedulously exploited. To this indifferent performance the confusion, political conflicts, and traumatic memories centering on the Korean War and its settlement greatly contributed.

# PART IV

# THE WATERSHED OF THE EARLY 1950's

### 32.  Intimations of a New Phase

It was round about 1925—six years after the Armistice—that the world ceased to be dominated by forces directly generated by the First World War. Problems and events began to take on their own character, still inseparably linked to the past and to the upheaval of 1914-1918, but evidently requiring new concepts and new men. Something similar, but even more profound, happened after a similar interval in 1951-1952.

Down to 1951 both Stalin and Truman had been dealing with strategic problems of a kind familiar for about a half-century. Stalin, exploiting the disruption and weakness of the postwar world, pressed out from the expanded base he had won during the Second World War in an effort to gain the balance of power in Eurasia: first, turning south and west, in the sequence running from northern Iran through Greece and Turkey, down to the failure of the Berlin blockade in 1949; then, turning to the East, to back Mao and to enflame the North Korean and Indochinese Communists as well as the other Communist parties in Asia.

In effect Stalin and Truman dueled for six years across the truce lines determined by the military and diplomatic outcome of the Second World War, lines which left the balance of power still—but barely still—in the hands of the non-Communist world. There emerged, even, an implicit set of rules for conducting hostilities. When the truce line was crossed, by direct or indirect forms of aggression, the aggrieved party counterattacked with any means he chose, within his own boundaries, if he had the will and resource to do so. The counterattack could be resisted; but the fact of counterattack would not be taken by the initiating party as a justification for enlarging the area of hostilities or for launching major war.

From Stalin's acceptance of Truman's ultimatum on Northern Iran in 1946 to Truman's acceptance of stabilization at the 38th Parallel in June 1951 the haphazard Eurasian truce line of 1945 was mutually respected. Stalin, of course, tested it systematically around virtually the whole periphery of his empire. The United States tested it only once, impulsively, in the drive to the Yalu. But, in the end, the maintenance of this line, and the implicit rules governing action on either side of it, were the basis on which major war was avoided—even if peace was not made—after the Second World War.[1] The post-war truce was thus determined in the spirit, if not the exact terms, of the Stalin-Churchill discussions of October 1944.

By June 1951, however, Stalin had about exhausted the possibility of gaining prompt decisive victory by the quasi-military means he had used in Greece, Berlin, and Korea; the possibilities of promptly applying Mao's takeover technique in the rest of Asia, the Middle East, and Africa were not bright, as the new nations, vulnerable and shaken in the immediate postwar years, began to find their feet; and in Peking Mao knew that, having restored production to prewar levels, it was essential to end large-scale military operations, divert an increased proportion of China's energies and resources to domestic economic growth, and decide on the strategy of his first Five Year plan in a country still 80 per cent peasant. Lastly, Soviet scientists—hard at work since 1945 in the new world of nuclear weapons, electronics, jet engines, supersonic aircraft, and rockets—were beginning to achieve results which put in question Stalin's rather traditionally Russian concepts of ground warfare. It was time for international communism to redefine its problems, its objectives, and its techniques on a longer-run basis. That process was almost certainly seriously undertaken in the summer of 1951.

By mid-1951 the world also looked somewhat different to the West. The decision to fight the Korean War, followed by the commitment of American divisions to NATO, made it reasonably clear that the presence of American power in Eurasia was not transitory. Put to the test, the United States had not reverted to the postwar isolationism which Europeans feared and for which Stalin had been given every reason to maintain at least a reasonable hope. Eisenhower was back in command of an Allied European headquarters, and, at the other end of Eurasia, there was under negotiation with Japan a peace treaty (signed September 8, 1951) which translated the occupation into an alliance which involved a long-run American military commitment.

In May 1947, at a United Europe Meeting in Albert Hall, London, Churchill had said: "What is Europe now? It is a rubble-heap, a charnel-house, a breeding ground of pestilence and hate." These words could not have been spoken four or five years later. As Europe moved along into the 1950's, reconstruction gave way to prosperity. And it gradually became clear, as the 1950's rolled on, that Western Europe and Japan had moved into the stage of growth dominated by durable consumers goods and services which the United States had entered in the 1920's, achieving a sustained economic momentum which Western Europe had not know since 1914. Hesitantly, only half believing, men in Western Europe who had lived from day to day in the late 1940's began to peer ahead and make solid plans for themselves and their societies, notably when the limits of Soviet intentions were tested in the Korean War and found to be short of an immediate invasion of the West. NATO gathered strength and military meaning; skepticism of Monnet's and Schumann's vision of a European Coal and Steel Community gave way to hardheaded acceptance of a reality. Western Europe was recovering sufficient strength to begin to assert itself, to react to and even to begin to define its problems, even though it could not immediately solve them. And something quite analogous was happening a bit more slowly in Japan.

Beyond the persistence of the American commitment in Eurasia and the unexpected resilience of Western Europe and Japan, two new forces began to obtrude on postwar conflict in its latter stages, foreshadowing the central problems of the next stage: the emergence of new military technology, and the acceleration of the nationalist revolutions in Asia, the Middle East, and Africa.

How had the United States dealt with these emergent problems between 1945 and 1952, when they had not yet come to dominate the international scene?

## 33.  The New Military Equation

As the postwar years began, the United States had a monopoly in atomic weapons, means of delivery, and, so far as effective fighter aircraft was concerned, means of defense. In Europe this conditional advantage was promptly countered by the maintenance of Soviet ground forces capable of marching to the Channel virtually without opposition. In Asia the American monopoly was countered by the nature of local Communist guerrilla tactics, which neither politically nor technically offered the United States appropriate strategic targets. Down to the explosion of the first Soviet atomic weapon in September 1949, Western and Communist policies and forces maneuvered against one another within the framework of a stand-off between the United States Strategic Air Command, armed with atomic weapons, and Soviet ground forces.

In the meanwhile Stalin launched a massive effort, employing the cream of a whole generation of scientists and engineers, to catch up with and if possible surpass American military technology in virtually every dimension except aircraft carriers and atomic-powered submarines. The Soviet Union was assisted significantly over a part of this period by the fact that it was able to avoid direct involvement in the Korean War, which, in its most acute phase, absorbed a high proportion of American military energies despite the maintenance of priority for NATO and the problem of deterring Soviet strength in the West. Thus, as the Truman-Stalin duel was being fought to a standstill within the immediate postwar military framework, a new and more dangerous framework of stand-off was evolving which already strongly affected the conduct of the Korean War.

At almost every step, the pace at which the Soviet Union developed capabilities equivalent to those of the United States caught Washington by surprise. By the end of 1952 the Soviet Union was clearly in the process of developing a fusion as well as a fission weapon; it had a substantial stockpile of fission weapons; it had moved through a B-29 bomber stage to the protoype of a first-class jet bomber; it had developed a large first-class jet fighter force which was being woven into a competent radar network, including the beginnings of a night-fighter force; it was dealing with civil defense and dispersal on a serious basis; it was obviously at work at full tilt on a variety of missiles including missiles deliverable from a large modernized submarine fleet.

POSTWAR RESEARCH AND DEVELOPMENT

The American response to emergent Soviet capabilities was colored by the manner in which postwar American research and development were organized. The golden age of applied science and technology in the Second World War did not last. The success of the partnership had depended on at least six factors: the scientific effort was led by bold men having the confidence of the nation's best scientists; the scientists had a powerful central organization in OSRD; both as a bureaucratic threat and in fact the leaders of the scientific effort had access to the President; the leading civilian (Stimson) and soldier (Marshall) in the military establishment were both sympathetic and accessible to new scientific ideas; the OSRD had its own funds to allocate over and above research and development done within the services; and, finally, the arrangement permitted a limited degree of shopping by the scientists as among the services and as between Britain and the United States. This combination was not perpetuated when Americans, even with the greatest good will, sought soberly to institutionalize the relationship between the soldier and scientist for the long pull.

All hands were prepared to agree in 1945 that the link between the scientist and soldier had to be maintained in the national interest; but there was wide disagreement as to how the relationship should be handled. In 1946 the Office of Scientific Research and Development was abolished. Its work passed to the military services and to what later was to become the Atomic Energy

Commission. A Research and Development Board was organized and brought into the Department of Defense after the passage of the National Security Act of 1947. In addition, after four years of essentially sterile debate a National Science Foundation was created in 1950 to evaluate scientific research programs undertaken by agencies of the Federal Government and to support basic research.[1] Despite the existence of the Research and Development Board within the Pentagon and the National Science Foundation, power over research and development devolved after the war into the three services and the AEC where, in fact, the most fruitful relationship between the military and the scientists persisted. The Office of Naval Research, for example, supported basic research on a remarkable scale from 1946 forward.

Above the level of the individual services, however, the voice of the scientist was not often heard except on such melodramatic occasions as the controversy over whether a hydrogen bomb should be constructed. In surveying the postwar experience in 1954, a Congressional subcommittee found it "disconcerting . . . that scientists have not been called in by the Joint Chiefs of Staff."[2] With a few notable exceptions the postwar years saw an elaboration of existing concepts and prior breakthroughs rather than bold new efforts based on a carefully developed national military strategy with clear priorities flowing from it.

The basic reasons for this outcome lay in three forces which tended to dilute the American effort: a complacency generated by the widespread view that the American monopoly in atomic weapons would not be broken until 1952 at the earliest; the inherent tendency of the military bureaucracy in peacetime to limit the authority and freedom of action of civilians within it or connected with it, a tendency not overcome by the political chieftains of the services; and the partial or total withdrawal of first-rate scientists and engineers from government business. And to these factors must be added the fact that over this period the three services could not reach agreement on any coherent strategy from which research and development priorities could be derived. The context of the research and development effort, therefore, remained one of bitter interservice competition.

Thus, at a decisive period, when Russian science was organized in an all-out effort to close the gap between Soviet and American strength, there was a substantial deterioration in the efficacy with which the pool of American science and technology was applied to military problems.

Nevertheless, within the orbit of the three services and the AEC important developments occurred in American military technology and in American thought about the problem of national security. Both the efficiency and flexibility of nuclear weapons were radically increased. After a highly charged debate among the scientists, administrators, and politicians involved, running from September 1949 to January 1950, the development of fusion weapons was ordered by President Truman. At the other end of the spectrum, the California Institute of Technology conducted Project Vista, which in 1951 yielded new conceptions of the use of atomic weapons in land warfare. Its ultimate purpose was to equip NATO forces with weapons capable of countering the overwhelming mass of Communist ground forces by means which might not necessarily involve that wholesale destruction of cities and populations which seemed unavoidable in all-out strategic air attack. In 1949 the Air Force and the Massachusetts Institute of Technology set up an air defense laboratory in Lexington, Massachusetts, and in 1951-1952 there was a series of projects (Charles, East River, and Lincoln) examining aspects of the nation's vulnerability to air attack and the possibilities of air defense. The Lincoln summer project of 1952 led on directly to the work of the committee headed by Mervin Kelly, President of the Bell Telephone Laboratory, whose conclusions, given to the government in 1953, did much to accelerate the development of an early warning system and an organization for continental air defense.

In these three directions, then, there was a clear response to the new problems and complexities raised by the ending of the nation's monopoly in nuclear weapons. In addition, a wide variety of guided and ballistic missile projects were launched on a research and development basis by each of the three services.

THE ARMS RACE AND PUBLIC POLICY

As the Eisenhower administration came into office it was handed a report, prepared in the course of 1952 at the request of the Secretary of State, which surveyed in broad terms the gloomy prospects of the arms race evidently gathering momentum. This report made such recommendations as it could concerning the possibility of negotiating effective disarmament with the Soviet Union and concerning the protection of the nation's interest under the likely assumption that the arms race would continue. Three of the committee's recommendations were: that the nature and dangers of the atomic arms race be fully explained to the American public; that the legislation governing atomic secrets be revised to permit a collaborative military effort with the nation's allies; and that an effective air defense be developed.[3]

Thus, at the end of the Truman administration, as the brutal old-fashioned infantry fighting in Korea and the frustration of the truce negotiations dominated public attention, the major dimensions of the problem of maintaining a nuclear stand-off were being quietly explored by that extremely small group of persons with access to information on both the Soviet and the American military efforts.

### 34. *American Policy and the Rise of the New Nations: 1945-1952*

THE SETTING FOR POLICY

The second force that was increasingly to shape the nation's external environment after 1945 was the emergence from colonialism (or from quasi-colonial status) of a large group of new nations in Asia, the Middle East, and Africa and the struggle of the residual colonial areas to achieve nationhood.

In the immediate postwar years—down to about 1949—the political energies of the peoples in these regions were largely taken up with what might be called local politics: that is, with gaining their independence, with forming central governments, and with defining or arguing about their boundaries. In Asia, the British led the way in 1946 by releasing India, Pakistan, Burma, and Ceylon; and Indonesia gained its sovereignty by the end of 1949. In the Middle East, Israel emerged in 1948 as an independent state; and elsewhere the powers of the European nations in Middle East affairs began a process of dilution. Even China fits this time sequence, its civil war ending in 1949, although its sovereignty was immediately corrupted by Mao's commitments to Moscow. The equivalent stage in Egyptian evolution came with the *coup d'état* of July 1952, which led to the abdication of Farouk and the takeover of power by a corps of army officers. Indochina and French North Africa were, however, still tightly held; and between the Sahara and the Union of South Africa the forces at work looking toward modern nationhood were somewhat less clamorous although clearly gathering momentum.

With independence consolidated as a fact of local politics and international law, politicians in the new nations faced a set of choices closely analogous to those which had been faced by the newly modernized nations of the previous era—for example, the United States at the close of the eighteenth century, Germany in the third quarter of the nineteenth century, Japan in the two decades before 1914. To what extent—or in what proportions—should the surging nationalist energies and aspirations which had made possible the achievement of independence be concentrated on consolidating the political victory of the central government over residual regional powers; on redressing real or imagined external humiliation or in exploiting real or imagined possibilities of external aggrandizement; or in economic, political, and social development at home? The new nations of the mid-twentieth century had to make their decisions on those questions in the context of the emerging struggle between the Communist and free states; and they faced the difficult problem of defining their relationship to that struggle.

The political process and setting in which their choices were made differed markedly from those familiar in Western politics. Out of the struggle against the colonial powers, coalitions had emerged which shared a stake in building modern nations. These coalitions had fought for independence and to replace old interests and institutions, while the mass of illiterate citizens had passively observed the battle or entered into it with sporadic violence. The groups in the new national coalitions were often, however, without a common past—beyond the fact of victory and the memories of struggle in the common cause—and without stable common interests except in the making of a new nation state.

Once the new state was established, a whole array of new and different issues emerged. The institutions for the making and execution of national policy were often weak; and the coalitions were by no means agreed on how and at what pace to proceed with economic and social modernization which often had revolutionary and disruptive consequences for some groups within the victorious coalitions—notably the land-owning interests. In the post-1945 era (as in China of the 1920's and 1930's) there was the additional problem of relations between non-Communists and Communists, the latter having usually played an active role in achieving the nationalist victory. Local politicians thus found it easy and attractive to continue to harness the new nationalism to external objectives if for no other reason than because such objectives formed common ground on which the revolutionary coalition could continue to operate in unity after its old enemy was defeated. Whereas in the United Nations and elsewhere the diplomacy of the new nations placed great emphasis on the tasks of economic and social modernization, and on the desirability, if not the duty, of assistance from the more industrialized nations, the actual mobilization of human energies and local resources on these tasks often proceeded in a desultory way.

The consolidation of domestic power at the center, the attempt to retrieve old national disasters or humiliations, and the waving of the colonial bloody shirt involved more or less familiar military and political maneuvers. They commanded wide support from the political élite and they could be presented in such ways as to stir the memories and emotions of urban populations. The spreading of measures of public health, the diffusion of new techniques in agriculture, the execution of land reform schemes, the building of bureaucracies based on principles of effective performance rather than on family or personal loyalty, and the other inevitable items on the agenda of modernization required that men learn to do things they had never done before; that cultural and social patterns be altered; and, above all, that the balance of political power be shifted from rural to urban groups often at the expense of at least some of those who had helped to make the national revolution.

ELEMENTS IN THE AMERICAN RESPONSE

The regions where the nationalist revolutions gathered momentum after 1945 evidently constituted—in their population, resources, geographic location, and long-run military potential—a determining element in the world power balance. Indirectly, their evolution was bound to determine in large measure the economic and political status of Western Europe in the world arena. Directly, their evolution could throw the balance of military power to communism if they were to fall under the domination of Moscow and Peking. Directly, also, their political evolution—whether they evolved under democratic or totalitarian techniques—could largely determine whether the further development of American democracy would proceed in quasi-isolation or as part of a dominant world system of open societies.

Thus it was the American interest that the great transitional processes go forward in ways which would prevent Moscow-or Peking-dominated governments from gaining power, which would prevent the external projection of nationalism from taking forms which disrupted the strength of the Free World alliance or threatened armed conflict, and which would yield a reasonably steady process of political and social development toward the norms of modern democracy. These required, in turn, among many other conditions, steady economic progress at a rate which exceeded substantially the rate of population increase.

On the one hand, it was the American task to make it as costly and unattractive as possible either for Communists to exploit successfully the complex transitions going forward or for the new nations to project their nationalist aspirations abroad in disruptive adventures. On the other, it was the American task to use its influence and its resources to make it as attractive as possible for the political leaders in the underdeveloped areas to channel their own and their nation's energies into the domestic tasks of modernization.

American policy toward the underdeveloped areas in the postwar years was compounded in varying proportions of these three elements. The first was derived from positive aspects of American political ideology. The second focused on the struggle against Moscow and Peking. The third sought to apply American technical knowledge and capital to accelerate the process of modernization. These three elements did not mesh neatly on all occasions; that is, the criteria for independent democracy, resistance to Communist aggression, and rapid economic growth did not automatically converge.

Ideologically, the United States brought to the colonial and ex-colonial areas and the new nations a broad sympathy for their pursuit of effective independence and a desire to see them develop along democratic paths.

But sympathy for independence and democracy proved an insufficient guide to policy after the war just as it had failed to grip the wartime situation in colonial areas—for example, in North Africa. The struggle with Moscow forced the United States to take into account the consequences of its support of independence for the position of its Western allies who were colonial powers; and the formulas of reconciliation were not easy to find. In addition, the United States had to face the fact that generalized support for independence and democracy did not in itself furnish an adequate answer to the various forms of Communist aggression, direct and indirect, which were mounted in the transitional areas. In effect, American policy tended to set aside or to dilute its ideological touchstones for action in order to concentrate on the struggle with Moscow and Peking, just as it had made the Chinese contribution to the defeat of Japan the overriding criterion of wartime policy toward China.

The third element in American policy consisted in efforts by various kinds of American technicians and advisers to help modernize the societies and economies of the underdeveloped areas. Soldiers, economists, technicians, public administration experts, and other specialists brought their insights to bear on the urgent problems of the underdeveloped areas with varying degrees of effectiveness. And in some cases they were backed by substantial American loans and grants designed to build up the local economy and its armed forces.

## SOME AMERICAN PROBLEMS

In approaching these regions, the nation confronted a problem of peculiar difficulty. The United States could not derive out of its own history any instinctive general frame of reference which closely fitted the status of the transitional areas and nations. In dealing with Western European countries the United States faced societies which had evolved their own forms of organization—political, social, and economic—which, while different from the American patterns, nevertheless bore a close family relation to them. It was relatively easy for reasonably perceptive Americans to find their feet in Europe, to translate what they knew into effective European terms, and to work fruitfully in that setting. But there had been no clear equivalent in American history to the passages through which the underdeveloped areas were moving in the postwar decade. The United States was formed as a culture and a nation by Europeans who came across the ocean in the post-medieval stage of European history. The United States lacked the marks and memories of a traditional society. Americans were, therefore, often baffled and frustrated in the transitional areas by the existence of nondemocratic political practices, by methods of administration in which personal or family loyalty outweighed the criteria of efficient performance, by the presence of military leaders and practices which made the troops the personal appendage of their commanders, by the existence of social values which made able and educated men unwilling to do work that desperately needed doing in the village or factories of their land, and which led promising members of the élite to regard the mass of their fellow-citizens in ways that, to Americans, seemed unfeeling and undemocratic.

Americans had had, of course, a unique opportunity to observe and participate in the evolution of transitional societies. For a century and a quarter the states of Latin America had been going through transitions similar in their general character to those which could be observed in the postwar years in Asia, the Middle East, and Africa. But, protected as they were by geography and the Monroe Doctrine from all but occasional involvement in the world's power struggles, the states of Latin America were permitted to proceed with their transitions at a leisurely pace; and their inevitable periods of vicissitude and crisis only rarely raised issues which seriously touched the American national interest. The whole of Latin America, in a sense, was a pistol pointed at the heart of the Antarctic; and its relatively neutralized power status under the Monroe Doctrine permitted Americans to observe its evolution with only the most casual understanding of the deeper processes at work. Although postwar American efforts in technical assistance owed much to those few who earlier had entered deeply into the Latin American experience, the nation as a whole, and those who effectively made day-to-day policy, had generalized little from the erratic but shapely story of Latin America since its major areas had achieved nationhood in the first quarter of the nineteenth century.

The kind of men who rose to authority in the American diplomatic and military establishments in the period 1940-1952 were quite at home in the problems of alliance with mature states and in the problems of major war. They understood Europe and, in a sense, Japan also. But only a few among them were at home in an Indian village or in advising a Magsaysay on how to deal with guerrilla operations in the countryside; and such invaluable Americans did not always find themselves assigned to critical posts. It is altogether in keeping that high officials in the Department of State are reported to have discouraged Truman from enunciating his Point Four.[1] Although early in 1950 Acheson made two perceptive statements on the attitudes and processes at work in non-Communist Asia, they have an arms-length abstract quality, emphasizing that the United States was prepared to help, but that responsibility and initiative must lie with the local governments.[2] They caught little of the mood of comradeship in which such men as Bowles, Ladajinsky, Stilwell, and Van Fleet worked in the field. Something more was required of American policy than a decent respect for the status of the new nations.

There were required an understanding of the turbulent processes at work in the transition from traditional to modern societies, a human sympathy for the often difficult moods and attitudes these transitions generated, and a sense of shared human adventure. Some Americans from many walks of life and varying traditions—the missionary, the military, the farm extension service, to name only three—did enter deeply into the life and problems of the transitional areas. But at the highest and dominant levels of policy there was a tendency to view Asia, the Middle East, and Africa in rather formal strategic and diplomatic terms.

When the transitional societies became caught up in a world power struggle, where one of the participants had fully developed concepts and strategies for exploiting aggressively the potentialities of the transitional process, the United States was neverthless forced to concern itself deeply with their affairs. Lacking a democratic equivalent to an analysis and an operational strategy like those derived from Lenin's *Imperialism*, American policy tended to polarize around the short-run, relatively familiar tasks of preventing direct aggression rather than around the more difficult and searching problems involved in using effectively the American margin of influence to constrain and encourage the transitional processes toward the norms of progressive, stable democracy. And, since many of the most dangerous forms of aggression involved Communist exploitation of the frustrations in the transitional areas, the United States, focused heavily on immediate and palpable acts of Communist aggression, found itself often outflanked or in danger of being outflanked.

## THE EVOLUTION OF AMERICAN POLICY

Nevertheless, the tasks of economic growth in the new nations gradually rose on the American agenda.

As early as the Bretton Woods Conference of July 1944, the representatives of what were to be later known as the underdeveloped areas had urged strongly that the International Bank be used not merely for medium-term reconstruction but also for long-run economic development. This pressure arose mainly from representatives of the countries of Latin America; but the Latin Americans spoke as well for the incipient nations of Asia, the Middle East, and Africa. In the immediate postwar years the representatives of the latter areas in the councils of the United Nations steadily pressed their case for loans and technical assistance from the richer, more industrialized nations, expressing an increasing resentment at the enormous sums being allocated by the United States to sustain Europe at relatively high standards of welfare while their peoples languished in extreme poverty.

Responding to that pressure, the United Nations Assembly, meeting in Paris in the winter of 1948—shadowed by the most acute and dangerous stage of the Berlin blockade—set in motion the United Nations Technical Assistance program on January 20, 1949. President Truman presented his Fourth Point in his Inaugural Address:

> Fourth. We must embark on a bold new program for making the benefits of our scientific advances and industrial progress available for the improvement and growth of underdeveloped areas.
>
> More than half the people of the world are living in conditions approaching misery. Their food is inadequate. They are victims of disease. Their economic life is primitive and stagnant. Their poverty is a handicap and a threat both to them and to more prosperous areas.
>
> For the first time in history, humanity possesses the knowledge and the skill to relieve the suffering of these people.
>
> The United States is preeminent among nations in the development of industrial and scientific techniques. The material resources which we can afford to use for the assistance of other peoples are limited. But our imponderable resources in technical knowledge are constantly growing and are inexhaustible. . . .
>
> We invite other countries to pool their technological resources in this undertaking. Their contributions will be warmly welcomed. This should be a cooperative enterprise in which all nations work together through the United Nations and its specialized agencies wherever practicable. It must be a world-wide effort for the achievement of peace, plenty, and freedom. . . .
>
> Such new economic developments must be devised and controlled to benefit the peoples of the areas in which they are established. Guaranties to the investors must be balanced by guaranties in the interest of the people whose resources and whose labor go into these developments.
>
> The old imperialism—exploitation for a foreign profit—has no place in our plans. What we envisage is a program of development based on the concepts of democratic fair play dealing. . . .
>
> Democracy alone can supply the vitalizing force to stir the peoples of the world into triumphant action, not only against their human oppressors, but also against their ancient enemies—hunger, misery, and despair.[3]

The precise character of the American national interest in the economic growth of the underdeveloped areas was not made clear in Truman's exposition. He leaned mainly on a combination of humanitarianism and American economic self-interest; he also linked successful economic development to the conditions for peace and the spread of the democratic process. He did not, however, in scale or in urgency elevate the Point Four program to the level of, say, the Marshall Plan or national defense policy.

The importance of the underdeveloped areas of the world to the American interest and the need to meet their powerful aspirations for the modernization of their societies was, however, increasingly appreciated in 1949-1950, as European recovery gathered momentum and the military position there appeared to be stabilized, and while communism moved to victory in China, shaking the fragile foundations of free Asia. Acheson's speeches on Asia of January and March 1950, Gordon Gray's report in November 1950, and Nelson Rockefeller's "Partners in Progress" Report of March 1951 all reflected a gathering awareness of the strategic importance to the United States of long-run development in the underdeveloped areas. And in October 1951 Chester Bowles went to India, plunging wholeheartedly into the adventure of the First Indian Five-Year Plan, transmitting at both ends of the cable line a sense of overlapping interest and commitment.[4]

The Point Four concept was well rooted in parts of the nation's values and tradition. It appealed to the missionary spirit still powerful in the land, and it represented the kind of concrete, constructive response to problems which instinctively caught the nation's imagination. On the other hand, there was no clear general understanding that the Point Four enterprise represented a major aspect of the task of protecting the national interest. It was treated by the Congress as a low priority matter in the first half of 1950; and then it was all but overwhelmed by the Korean War.

The fact of Communist military aggression immediately focused attention on actions designed to hold the line in the short run at the sacrifice of action designed to yield wholesome political and economic change for the longer run. Moreover, the neutralism of many political leaders in the new nations (and their recognition of Communist China)—which could be regarded as reasonably harmless when, for example, Nehru visited the United States in 1949—took on a different, and for many Americans a more sinister, cast by 1951, when the Korean War was at its height. When the issue was put to the test in Congress by the India grain bill (designed to cover the famine of 1951), the loan was granted; but it was clear that the nation found it difficult to pursue simultaneously its immediate interest in frustrating Communist military aggression and its long-run interest in the evolution of successful democratic societies when the two interests did not yield neatly convergent lines of action.

In terms of resources and attention, then, the short-run military aspects of the struggle against communism in the underdeveloped areas rose sharply in priority in 1950-1952. Military aid, which had been well under 10 per cent of economic aid in (fiscal) 1950 and less than a quarter of the total in 1951, was more than two thirds of the total authorization for 1953. And in the underdeveloped areas this aid flowed overwhelmingly to areas of military crisis—to Korea, Taiwan, and to assist the French in the struggle against the Vietminh forces.[5]

The changing pattern of outlays in foreign aid reflected the main directions of diplomacy—that is, the build-up of NATO (including efforts at German rearmament) and the effort to spread the NATO pattern of alliances and bases around the whole periphery of the Communist Bloc. In 1951 NATO itself came to embrace Greece and Turkey; and Yugoslavia was brought bilaterally within the Western security system. Arrangements were made for air bases in Morocco and in Saudi Arabia. Bilateral arrangements were made or expanded with Japan (in the context of the treaty negotiation) as well as with the Nationalist forces on Taiwan and with the Philippine Republic, Australia, and New Zealand.

There were, however, setbacks. The first efforts to negotiate a Middle East regional pact failed; and in the course of 1951-1952 Middle Eastern nationalism in Iran and, to a degree, in Egypt, revealed its powerful anti-Western strain. In the Far East the Indochina conflict worsened; and American relations with Indonesia, as well as with India and Burma, became increasingly distant.

In general, then, American diplomatic and economic foreign policy shifted its course in June 1950 away from the path marked out by Truman's Fourth Point and took as its central task in the following two and a half years the problem of building a structure of alliances calculated to prevent another Korean War. But from about June 1951 Communist strategy and tactics began to concentrate on alternative and less overtly military means for advancing the power and influence of Moscow and Peking. Thus, the one creative and anticipatory dimension in foreign policy was throttled back while the nation continued in its familiar style to institutionalize its emergency response to the last crisis.

### 35. From Truman to Eisenhower

THE RHYTHM OF PUBLIC MOODS DURING THE TRUMAN ADMINISTRATION

The period of 1945-1952 within the United States was one of widely shifting popular moods and attitudes toward the Truman Administration and toward public policy in general. The two low points in public confidence might be designated by the Congressional election of 1946 and the Presidential election of 1952, the peak by the Presidential election of 1948. The downswing which followed Truman's election was interrupted in the latter half of 1950 by a surge of public support for the President in the early stage of the Korean War, but it resumed when the Chinese Communists entered the war and, especially, when Truman relieved MacArthur of his command.[1]

One can observe in the first phase a transition from a sense of relief and achievement at V-J Day to a growing mood of irritation which came to be directed specifically at the price controls and rationing arrangements which were maintained in the postwar years.[2] This was a time of the big steel strike and the meat famine and of a nagging realization that the wartime hopes of stable peace based on continued accord with the Soviet Union would probably not be realized.

Against this background the "Bob Taft 80th Congress" came in.[3] Its main objective was to reverse so far as possible the shift in power to the federal government and toward the interests of the farmer and organized labor which had characterized the years since 1933. The Taft-Hartley Act was the most notable achievement of this limited but purposeful counterrevolution.[4]

This phase was virtually ended by the heightening of international tension in February and March 1947 when Britain placed the Greek and Turkish problems in American hands. Vandenberg took over from Taft as the national effort to rebuild Western Europe overshadowed the domestic scene. From the summer of 1949, however, the nation's confidence that it was successfully dealing with its problems began to give way to doubts and worries in three directions: the full realization of failure in China; the heightened sense of direct vulnerability that began with the Soviet explosion of an atomic mechanism; and the unfolding revelation of past Soviet infiltration and espionage in the American, Canadian, and British governments. The China White Paper was published early in August 1949; the first Soviet bomb exploded on September 23; the Chinese Communist government was formally set upon October 1; the second Hiss trial, ending with his conviction, ran from November 1949 to January 1950. On February 3, 1950, the British announced that Klaus Fuchs had for some years been passing to the Soviet Union information of the highest military importance. It is symbolic of this transition from confidence to growing doubts that Vandenberg fades from his dominant status in the autumn of 1950, not only because of failing health but also because his position of bipartisanship could not be sustained within the Republican Party on the China issue.[5]

Vandenberg was succeeded as the dominant Congressional figure not by Taft but, in effect, by Senator McCarthy. Late in January 1950 McCarthy decided to tie his political destiny to a dramatic personal exploitation of the Communist issue, and on February 9 he made his accusation that the State Department contained either 207 or 57 (depending on source) members of the Communist Party. From that time forward, with a hiatus from about the time of the outbreak of the Korean War to the relief of MacArthur from his command (announced April 11, 1951), the nation was split along new and painful lines.

The failure in China, the indecisive war in Korea, and the Soviet acquisition of weapons which added a new dimension of direct threat to the nation's security were all problems about which the United States could do nothing definitive in the short run. Lacking any satisfactory answer to the questions they raised, a politically significant margin of Americans found it easier to believe that the nation had been betrayed over the two previous decades by the Democratic administration than to accept the hard fact of the increase in the nation's security problems which the intervening course of history implied.

Politically, the new circumstances furnished an opportunity for counter-attack for those who had futilely resisted for many years the trend of domestic policy under Roosevelt and Truman, the trend toward enlarged international commitments, or both. The men derived from the Mahan-Root and Wilson traditions of internationalism who had run the nation's military and foreign policy since 1940 represented ideas, regions, and a set of social values and mannerisms resented in some parts of the country. Oil tycoons in Texas, Midwest isolationists, and anti-British elements of German and Irish descent could be united by McCarthy's crusade.[6] Their cause was aided by the fact that, at the center of the Republican Party, Senator Taft, disappointed by his failure to get the nomination in 1948, could not bring himself to disassociate the Republican Party from a political issue which brought such unlikely but useful converts to the Republican side.[7] Moreover, the combination of McCarthy's treason charge—so explosive to a democratic two-party system—and his tactics of personal blackmail of his Senate colleagues made many Democrats as well as Republicans back away rather than fight back.

Most important of all was the fact that the moderate majority of the electorate was shaken by these events. To a degree the majority lost confidence and sense of direction; and the hard-pressed Truman Administration, its nerve permanently damaged by the Chinese Communist entrance into the Korean War, and dealing with its problems from day to day without any persuasive long-range vision or strategy, could supply neither. Indeed, the Truman Administration was vulnerable to criticism. There had been some Communist infiltration of the government in the 1930's as well as during the period of wartime alliance with Moscow; and this had never been fully revealed although it had long since been corrected. The Soviet acquisition of nuclear weapons had not been accurately forecast, nor had the public been prepared for its consequences. While the debacle in China had long been discounted within the Administration, its tragic fruition was shocking; and no persuasive alternative policy for Asia was set in motion. Moreover, while the Korean truce negotiations dragged on, characterized by what appeared to be inadequate American firmness and purpose, there was a constant reminder that the nation's military policy from 1947 to 1950 was largely responsible for leaving South Korea an attractive target. On every point the Truman Administration could debate legitimately; but in terms of the American political tradition there was a rude political justice in the hard times it faced in 1950-1952.

At the end of June 1951, when, within two days, the MacArthur hearings ended and Jacob Malik announced the Communist willingness to negotiate a cease-fire in Korea along the existing battle lines, the tension eased to a degree. But by that time the forthcoming presidential election had come to dominate the political scene, giving the Republicans every incentive to maintain the mood of political dissatisfaction and insecurity; and the Truman administration, unable to reconstruct the bipartisan majority by which it had conducted military and foreign affairs in the period from the enunciation of the Truman Doctrine to the commitment of American divisions to NATO, could do little more than hold the line and carry forward policies which had been already decided upon.

The last year and a half of the Truman Administration was thus a relatively passive period in American policy and one in which it came to be widely felt that a twenty-year dynasty had come to an end and that it was, indeed, time for a change.

Although no major new national initiatives could be undertaken in such circumstances, within the orbit of Executive Branch operations—and notably within the Department of State, Defense, and the AEC—momentum was maintained. NATO continued to be built up; from January 1950 the development of the hydrogen bomb was pressed forward, with a first successful test taking place in 1952; the NATO concept was extended piecemeal around the periphery of the Comunist Bloc to Japan. Various efforts were made to reassess the situation within the Communist Bloc in the light of unfolding postwar experience and to grope for more positive means for coping with the phenomenon of international communism, which was evidently moving into a new phase of strategy and tactics. Recognizing that indirect forms of power and influence were increasingly important, the Truman administration set in motion a number of studies of psychological warfare, leading to the creation in 1951 of a Psychological Strategy Board; and ambitious and imaginative conceptions of economic foreign policy toward the underdeveloped countries were formulated.

The long-term strategy which emerged from the concurrent deliberations of the Kremlin had three main elements, two of which emerged clearly in the pronouncements of Stalin and Malenkov at the Nineteenth Party Congress of October 1952:[8] first, to encourage the splitting off from the United States of Europe and Japan; second, to encourage the nationalist revolutions of Asia, the Middle East, and Africa in ways which in the short run would disrupt the ties of those regions with the United States and the West and in the longer run would lead to Communist takeover. These first two elements in Communist strategy were defined with the greatest explicitness by the Communist leaders, although their exposition was couched in the theological language of Marxist and Leninist doctrine. The third—to press on at highest priority with the development of nuclear weapons, means of delivery, and means of defense —was left implicit in the exaggerated emphasis given to American and Western European rearmament, to the alleged intention of the United States to launch a nuclear war, and, above all, in the proposed pattern of Soviet economic development with its continued priority in the development of heavy industry and armaments. Well before the Nineteenth Party Congress, the Communist Party programs in the underdeveloped areas had shifted in degree away from military or quasi-military action toward a professed association of communism with peace, local nationalism, and the popular aspirations for economic development—although Communist military operations continued on an increasing scale in Indochina, and they damped down rather than disappeared in Malaya, Burma, and the Philippines. Meanwhile, although the Chinese Communists used the occasion of the 1951-1952 truce negotiations to rebuild and to re-equip their shattered armies on a modern basis, they turned as first priority to the formulation of their First Five-Year Plan, which was officially launched in 1953.

### THE TRUMAN TURNOVER

As the Truman Administration ended, then, the immediate postwar Communist offensive in the West had been contained on the Elbe, West Berlin stood firm, and Tito had defected, permitting a significant strengthening of Europe's southern flank. The Communist victory in China had been consolidated; but the concerted Communist effort of 1947-1951 to exploit that victory and seize decisively the balance of power in Eastern Eurasia had failed, leaving the arc from Japan around to India still in non-Communist hands. Mao had turned to the problem of generating sustained economic growth in China, while Moscow mapped a longer-term strategy for detaching the United States from its Eurasian positions, which had been given added meaning by the build-up of American air bases and the extension of mutual security pacts in Eurasia over the period 1950-1952.

On the other hand, Soviet military capabilities in modern weapons were rapidly expanding, putting in question the existing conception of NATO's military function; and it was becoming increasingly clear that a policy of military alliance focused on the deterrence of further Communist military aggression was a grossly insufficient basis for a policy that would effectively associate the United States and Western Europe with the governments and peoples of Asia, the Middle East, and Africa.

All of this was implicit in the papers and reports passed by the Truman to the Eisenhower Administration at the close of 1952. When, on November 18, 1952, it came time for Truman and his staff to brief General Eisenhower on the state of military and foreign affairs the new Administration would confront, the agenda clearly reflected the fact that the American security problem had radically shifted from that of 1947.[9] The briefing began with atomic energy matters, including, presumably, the relative position of Soviet and American nuclear capabilities (on which the new administration was to receive a special report and recommendations), and then moved on to the following array of problems:

1. *Korea.* The achievement of a truce hinged on the prisoners-of-war issue, which, in turn, centered on the possibility of modifying slightly an Indian proposal and of rallying within the United Nations the support of the neutral states for a resoultion which would not involve forcible repatriation.

2. *Iran.* Inflamed Iranian nationalism led by Mossedegh had produced a running crisis over the period since April 1951, centering on the confiscation of British oil properties, with the evident danger of successful Communist exploitation.

3. *Indochina.* The United States was carrying between one third and one half of the financial burden of a war in a country where the political policy of France made it impossible to rally the local population in effective opposition to the Communist forces.

4. *Foreign aid.* How large an appropriation should be envisaged, and how should aid be allocated as between military and economic categories?

When Truman had taken the measure of his problem in the West in 1947, he had been able to do so with the knowledge that the military problem consisted in so using the American monopoly in atomic weapons and delivery capabilities as to pin down Soviet superiority in ground forces in Europe; and within that framework the central task was to prevent a disintegration in Western Europe which would permit the balance of power to pass into Communist hands. Looking to the East, although Marshall's mission had failed, and although every indication of the fate of Nationalist China was ominous, at least for the moment Truman could set that problem aside.

But six years later, when Truman briefed Eisenhower, the Chinese Communists had completed their victory and emerged as the strongest military power in Asia. Even more important, the nationalist revolution had spread through Asia and the Middle East, creating problems both difficult in themselves and which had an important playback effect on the Western alliance. In NATO the central issue was the terms and pace of German rearmament, then planned within the framework of a European Defense Community which France had proposed but which it could not quite bring itself to accept. But as Acheson reported to Eisenhower on the occasion of the November 18 briefing: "We have been concerned for a long time about the course of action in Indo-China. There was a strong body of opinion in France which regarded this as a lost cause that was bleeding France both financially and undermining the possibility of French-German equality in European defense." Even in the heart of Europe the nationalist revolutions in Asia were a decisive factor.

Between them the two new forces—the weapons of mass destruction and the nationalist revolutions in Asia, the Middle East, and Africa—were beginning to produce an arena of world power different from that which had characterized the first half of the twentieth century: at the same time that ultimate powers of destruction were being rapidly gathered and concentrated in the hands of two states, real political power and influence were being diffused away from Moscow and Washington.

This paradox resulted from the fact that, so long as one major power did not feel it safe or wise to attack the other with nuclear weapons, those weapons were virtually unusable and the major powers had to seek lesser means for the exercise of influence and authority. The proportionality between their military potential and rationally usuable force was violated. Thus Nehru and the neutralists played a key role in the settlement of the Korean War; the struggle in Iran was fought out by diplomacy, economic pressure, and subterranean maneuvering; the war in Indochina was conducted by formations using World War II equipment at best, employing guerrilla and counterguerrilla tactics; foreign aid, military and economic, to underdeveloped areas was becoming a major instrument of strategy.

The Eurasian arena, stretching from Britain to Japan, was widening out to embrace the new nation states of Southeast Asia, the Middle East, and Africa; and these states found that, with the two great powers locked in a tense but self-defeating armaments race, and with the lines from the 38th Parallel in Korea to the Elbe becoming increasingly rigid, there was considerable room for maneuver and influence.

In Moscow and Washington problems of strategy and policy tended to polarize around the two extremes: weapons of mass destruction on the one hand; and techniques of propaganda, economic aid, and other forms of direct but nonmilitary influence on the other. These new circumstances, calling for radical innovation in military and foreign affairs, were evidently about to test once again the viability of the national style as an instrument for protecting the national interest.

# BOOK THREE

*Notes*

## CHAPTER 21. The First Two Stages of Postwar Communist Policy

1. For the significance of the breakdown of the negotiations for German economic unity (nominally on the unified planning of foreign trade) see especially L. D. Clay, *Decision in Germany*, New York, Doubleday, 1950, pp. 120-125.

2. See, notably, V. Dedijer, *Tito*, New York, Simon & Schuster, 1953, p. 322.

## CHAPTER 22. American Military Policy: 1945-1947

1. The analysis of unification presented here is based substantially on the painstaking account of L. J. Legere, Jr., *Unification of the Armed Forces*, unpublished doctoral dissertation, Harvard University Library, August, 1950.

2. Postwar Demobilization, 1945-1950:

### PERSONNEL ON ACTIVE DUTY (JUNE 30)

|      | Total | Army | Air Force | Navy | USMC |
|------|-------|------|-----------|------|------|
| 1945 | 12,123,455 | 5,985,699 | 2,282,259 | 3,380,817 | 474,680 |
| 1946 | 3,031,978 | 1,435,496 | 455,515 | 985,288 | 155,679 |
| 1947 | 1,582,999 | 685,458 | 305,827 | 498,661 | 93,053 |
| 1948 | 1,445,910 | 554,030 | 387,730 | 419,162 | 84,988 |
| 1949 | 1,615,360 | 660,473 | 419,347 | 449,575 | 85,965 |

### BUDGETARY EXPENDITURES BY FISCAL YEAR (IN $ MILLION)

|      | DOD | Army | Navy |  | Air Force |
|------|-----|------|------|------|-----------|
| 1945 | 80,537 | 50,490 | 30,047 | —— | (11,375.4) |
| 1946 | 41,558 | 27,094 | 14,464 | —— | ( 2,519.4) |
| 1947 | 13,727 | 8,022 | 5,705 | —— | ( 854.3) |
| 1948 | 11,092 | 5,671 | 4,297 | 1,124 | |
| 1949 | 11,844 | 5,615 | 4,442 | 1,800 | |
| 1950 | 11,886 | 3,985 | 4,102 | 3,600 | |

3. *Report of the Chief of Staff, United States Air Force to the Secretary of the Air Force*, Washington, D. C., Govt. Printing Office, 1948, p. 13.

4. See, for example, *Annual Report of the Secretary of the Navy for FY 1946*, Washington, D. C., Govt. Printing Office, 1947, pp. 25-26.

5. Truman's two major formal interventions on the unification issue were: his message to Congress of December 1945, and his settlement (in terms which permitted the debate still to continue within narrower limits) of the unresolved issues, as of June 1946.

6. L. J. Legere, Jr., *op. cit.*, pp. 359-361. Legere's conclusions on the pattern of compromise are worth quotation at length:

"Any examination of the compromises effected and concessions granted between 1945 and 1947 leads to the conclusion that the Army gave up much more of its original plan than did the Navy. As an objective conclusion, this is correct, but it is reached too easily; it is the result of simple addition and subtraction, and does not begin to weigh the real consequences of what took place when the National Security Act of 1947 became law. Some did think that the War Department had retreated on a great many issues in order to secure the passage of a law that looked rather anemic compared to earlier Army plans for a tightly integrated, vertical organization including all the armed forces. Those who thought thus could have looked behind appearances; had they done so, three important facts would have stood out, facts which indicated that the Navy had conceded so much (rightly or wrongly) that such gains as it had achieved, in the form of concessions by the War Department, might prove hollow and transitory. These four facts were:

"(1) Unification was law. The period of essentially uncoordinated peacetime planning and activity of the War and Navy Departments was over. The law may only have been a beginning, but it was a beginning which the Navy had opposed and which the Army had favored.

"(2) The power of the Secretary of National Defense was still subject to different interpretations. All the general qualifying phrases in the thesaurus could not prevent a strong-willed Secretary from exercising considerably more control over the operating departments than the Navy believed would be in the national interest.

"(3) Roles and missions of the armed forces were set forth in an executive order. Regardless of the initial allocation of functions, the President could change them by merely writing a new order, and the Secretary of National Defense might prevail upon him to do so.

"There was a fourth fact, initially somewhat obscured, which also indicated the extent of the Navy's concessions. It was in protest against the granting of this concession that the naval nonconformists—Towers, Radford, Oftsie, Crommelin, and the others—had appeared at the eleventh hour before the House Committee on Expenditures in the Executive Departments. This fourth fact was that the sort of separate air force created by the unification act ran counter to everything the Navy believed about airpower. If it was logical for the new Air Force to include air units whose combat missions would figure exclusively or primarily in the exercise of landpower, it was equally logical for that Air Force to covet the air units—especially those land-based—whose combat missions would figure exclusively or primarily in the exercise of seapower. No matter what the executive order said, many and probably most naval fliers were convinced that sooner or later the Air Force would try to control everything that flew, or, for that matter, everything that moved through the air. Because of their representations presented to Congress, certain broadly phrased protective clauses were written into the law as passed, but the danger was not over.

"The danger was not over because, as has been pointed out, roles and missions, general and specific, could not be written or maintained in a vacuum. They only gained significance after the most realistic and comprehensive evaluations of the nature of future wars, short-range and long-range evaluations couched in general and specific terms of reference. The naval officers opposing a separate air force feared that an earth-water-air approach to waging war would result in an unbalanced and otherwise unsound national defense organization."

7. *Ibid.*, p. 313.

8. W. Millis (Ed.) with the collaboration of E. S. Duffield, *The Forrestal Diaries*, New York, Viking, 1951, p. 153.

## CHAPTER 23. The Surrender of Eastern Europe: 1945-1946

1. For a definitive examination of this process, see the study directed by J. E. Cross, *The Soviet Takeover of Eastern Europe*, Cambridge, Center for International Studies, Massachusetts Institute of Technology, 1954. See also, for a brief summary, W. W. Rostow, *The Dynamics of Soviet Society*, New York, Mentor, 1954, Chap. 9.

2. Communist takeover tactics were based on seven Soviet assets which have been summarized as follows:

"It can be broadly said that the Communist leaders counted heavily on the following factors at every stage of takeover of Eastern Europe:

"(1) The confusion and destruction that followed in the wake of the war.

"(2) The presence throughout the region of Soviet military forces in overwhelming power.

"(3) The overt position and recognized authority of Soviet officials. There were many of these throughout the area serving on Allied Control Commissions and other bodies.

"(4) The cadres of the national Communist Parties. Many of these parties were small, but their membership was made up of either Russian trainees or the hard-bitten survivors of the Nazi rule.

"(5) The complete absence of any effective allied assistance or intervention on the non-Communist side. The speed and thoroughness of the United States disarmament in the immediate postwar period gave the Communists an effective guarantee that they would be able to work unhindered.

"(6) The Communists' clear and positive objective for their whole movement, i.e., the seizure of absolute power. Their tactics and to some extent their methods varied in different places and at different times, but the process of takeover was never aimless or drifting.

"(7) The willingness to use physical force without regard to future popularity or public support. Early in the process of takeover the direct intervention of the Russian Army in such matters as the arrest of Polish Home Army officers and the campaign against Dimitrov in Bulgaria demonstrated that in the last analysis true power lay with the Communists." (J. E. Cross, *op. cit.*, Introduction, pp. 4-5.)

3. Public opinion polls over the period 1945-1946 show that a substantial American majority was prepared to keep troops in Europe, Japan, and even China; that the rate and terms of discharge from the service were judged fair; that a rapid shift occurred toward reliance on U.S. strength rather than the U.N. for defense; that suspicion of Soviet intentions, never low, rapidly increased. On the other hand, most politicians took the view that the public clamor for demobilization was irresistible. For a discussion of the evidence for both views see N. Boardman, *Public Opinion and United States Foreign Policy, 1937-1956*,

Cambridge, Center for International Studies, Massachusetts Institute of Technology, 1958.

4. See J. F. Byrnes, *Speaking Frankly*, New York, Harper, 1947, Chaps. 6-8.

5. *Forrestal Diaries*, p. 124.

6. J. C. Campbell, *The United States in World Affairs, 1945-1947*, New York, Harper, 1947, pp. 72-73.

7. H. S. Truman, *Memoirs*, Garden City, N.Y., Doubleday, Vol. II, 1956, p. 95. See also J. M. Jones, *The Fifteen Weeks*, New York, Viking, 1955, pp. 48-58.

8. Arthur Bliss Lane, *I saw Poland Betrayed*, New York, Bobbs-Merrill, 1948, p. 195.

9. The origins and general character of this proposal were reported by the Alsop brothers in the *New York Herald Tribune* of Wednesday, April 24, 1946.

10. In 1946, Yugoslavia, lying along Austria's southern border, was, to all appearances, the most obedient student in Stalin's Eastern European school.

11. The proposal was, however, not entirely without result. It contributed directly to the negotiation of an Economic Commission for Europe in the United Nations discussions in London which proceeded in parallel to the treaty negotiations in Paris of the spring and summer of 1946; and to the lines of thought and advocacy which, a year later, helped yield the Marshall Plan. (See J. M. Jones, pp. 241-244.)

## CHAPTER 24. The Split of Germany: 1945-1946

1. For Germany policy in this period, see, especially, Byrnes, *op. cit.*, chap. 4 and pp. 187-194; B.U. Ratchford and W. D. Ross, *Berlin Reparations Assignment*, Chapel Hill, Univ. North Carolina Press, 1947; L. D. Clay, *Decision in Germany*, New York, Doubleday, 1950; and the Department of State, *Germany 1947-49, The Story in Documents*, Washington, D.C., Govt. Printing Office, 1950.

2. Quotation from L. D. Clay, pp. 121-122.

3. Eisenhower, *Crusade in Europe*, New York, Doubleday & Co., 1948, p. 458.

## CHAPTER 25. The Emerging Concept of Unity in Western Europe: 1945-1946

1. The following table is presented (with an account of its sources) in J. C. Campbell, *op. cit.*, pp. 378-379.

## CHAPTER 26. Chinese Civil War: 1945-1946

1. The agreement between the Communists and the Nationalist government to concentrate on the common enemy and to accommodate their respective policies to this purpose was incorporated in a series of exchanges and manifestos in 1937, the upshot of which was the following four promises of the Communists:

"1. The *San Min Chu-I* (Three People's Principles) enunciated by Dr. Sun Yat-sen is the paramount need of China today. This party is ready to strive for its enforcement.

"2. This party abandons its policy of overthrowing the Kuomintang of China

PRINCIPAL CREDITS EXTENDED BY U. S. GOVERNMENT
JUNE 30, 1945—DECEMBER 31, 1946
(MILLIONS IN DOLLARS)

| Country | Export-Import Bank Loans | Lend-Lease Credits | Surplus Property Credits | Total |
|---|---|---|---|---|
| U.K. | — | 590 | 60 | 4400 |
| British Commonwealth | 5.7 | 26 | 12 | 43.7 |
| Austria | — | — | 10 | 10 |
| Belgium | 100 | 56 | 49 | 205 |
| Czecholsovakia | 22 | — | 50[b] | 72 |
| Denmark | 20 | — | — | 20 |
| Finland | 40 | — | 15 | 55 |
| France | 1200 | 420 | 300 | 1950.9 |
| Greece | 25 | — | 45 | 93.7 |
| Hungary | — | — | 15 | 15 |
| Italy | 25 | — | 160 | 205.4 |
| Netherlands | 310 | 63 | 20 | 493 |
| Norway | 50 | — | 10 | 75.9 |
| Poland | 40 | — | 50 | 90 |
| U.S.S.R. | — | 244 | — | 244 |
| Total Continental Europe | 1832 | 783 | 724 | 3529.9 |
| China | 66.8 | 48 | 15 | 129.8 |
| Netherlands Indies | 100 | — | 100 | 200 |
| Philippine Islands | — | — | — | 75 |
| Saudi Arabia | 25 | — | 2 | 27 |
| Turkey | 28 | — | 10 | 40.8 |
| Others | — | — | 47.8 | 47.8 |
| Total Asia | 219.8 | 48 | 174.8 | 520.4 |
| Brazil | 46 | 2 | 8 | 65.4 |
| Chile | 47 | — | — | 47 |
| Mexico | 37 | — | — | 37 |
| Others | 8 | — | 1.5 | 13.6 |
| Total Latin America | 138 | 2 | 9.5 | 163 |
| Other | 9.5 | — | 123.5 | 133 |
| Grand Total | 2205 | 1449 | 1103.8 | 8790 |

by force and the movement of sovietization, and discontinues its policy of forcible confiscation of land from land-owners.

"3. This party abolishes the present Soviet Government and will enforce democracy based on the people's rights in order to unify the national political machinery.

"4. This party abolishes the Red Army, reorganizes it into the National Revolutionary Army, places it under the direct control of the national government, and awaits orders for mobilization to share the responsibility of resisting foreign invasion at the front."

Despite their ambiguities, these promises were judged by Chiang Kai-Shek to be at least formally acceptable under the conditions he faced. On September 23, 1937, he issued this statement.

"The Manifesto recently issued by the Chinese Communist Party is an outstanding instance of the triumph of national sentiment over every other consideration. The various decisions embodied in the Manifesto, such as the abandonment of a policy of violence, the cessation of Communist propaganda, the abolition of the Chinese Soviet Government, and the disbandment of the Red Army are all essential conditions for mobilizing our national strength in order that we meet the menace from without and guarantee our own national existence.

"These decisions agree with the spirit of the Manifesto and resolutions adopted by the Third Plenary Session of the Kuomintang. The Communist Party's Manifesto declares that the Chinese Communists are willing to strive to carry out the Three Principles. This is ample proof that China today has only one objective in its war efforts."

These quotations are from *United States Relations with China with Special Reference to the Period 1944-1949* (White Paper on China), Washington, D.C., Govt. Printing Office, August 1949, pp. 50 and 51, respectively.

2. White Paper on China, *op. cit.*, p. 97.

3. This position has been so widely misunderstood that it is worth quoting Davies' own formulation as of Oct. 9, 1944:
"The Communists are in China to stay. And China's destiny is not Chiang's but theirs.

"In this unhappy dilemma, the United States should attempt to prevent the disaster of a civil war through adjustment of the new alignment of power in China by peaceful processes. The desirable means to this end is to encourage the reform and revitalization of the Kuomintang so that it may survive as a significant force in a coalition government. If this fails, we must limit our involvement with the Kuomintang and must commence some cooperation with the Communists, the force destined to control China, in an effort to influence them further into an independent position friendly to the United States. We are working against time because, if the U.S.S.R. enters the war against Japan and invades China before either of these alternatives succeeds, the Communists will be captured by the U.S.S.R. and become Soviet satellites." (White Paper on China, *op. cit.*, p. 573.)

4. White Paper on China, *op. cit.*, p. 70.

## CHAPTER 27. The American Response in Europe: 1947-1952

1. H. S. Truman, *op. cit.*, Vol. II, p. 106.

2. See notably J. M. Jones, *op. cit.*; H. B. Price, *The Marshall Plan and Its Meaning*, Ithaca, N.Y., Cornell Univ. Press, 1955; H. S. Truman, *op. cit.*, Vol. II; E. F. Goldman, *The Crucial Decade*, New York, Knopf, 1956. Also, of course, for early stages, the *Forrestal Diaries*, and *Vandenberg Papers*.

3. For published references to this conversation see L. Clay, *op. cit.*, p. 153; and Jones, *op. cit.*, pp. 222-223.

4. See, especially, J. M. Jones, *op. cit.*, Chaps. 4-7.

5. For the relation of the ECE to the early phases of the Marshall Plan see especially, D. Wightman, *Economic Cooperation in Europe*, London, Stevens & Heineman, 1956, Chap. 2.

6. J. M. Jones, *op. cit.*, p. 283.

7. See Acheson's retrospective memorandum on the breakdown of the Paris Conference quoted Price, *op. cit.*, p. 28; also Goldman, *op. cit.*, p. 76.

8. At Paris Molotov did not even do the one thing which might have troubled if not split the West: that is, insisted that the European recovery program be handled through the United Nations Economic Commission for Europe, then meeting concurrently in Geneva.

9. The concept of "weak" or "strong" Secretariats in an international organization (and even within a national government, for example, the National Security Council) is reasonably precise. The distinction centers on the Secretariat's right to initiate studies and to initiate policy proposals. It is this power, for example, which mainly distinguishes the formal status of the United Nations Secretariat from that of the League of Nations, although this power has only been weakly developed and sporadically used in most U.N. activities. When this right is granted, the Secretariat assumes a position both of potential power and responsibility, despite the fact that only sovereign governments can decide that a given policy will be pursued. It can matter greatly to the outcome of an international meeting whether a secretariat places in negotiation a proposal around which a majority—usually a majority of weaker states—can rally. Without such proposals initiated by a secretariat, paid to think in terms of the collectivity, the major powers dominate the negotiation. The position of a strong secretariat is also one of grave responsibility because its status can easily be reduced and its influence vanish if it places in negotiation a series of proposals that prove unacceptable. A secretariat has no power except the quality of its staff work and its ability to judge maturely what might be accepted by the group if ably and perspicaciously presented.

With the power of initiative granted, it is possible to attract into an international secretariat men of higher quality and greater enterprise than in a weak secretariat. In the latter case the role of the Secretariat is to collect information, to perform narrowly secretarial functions, and to prepare only those papers which are directed by the collective decision of the governments.

10. *Economic Survey of Europe since the War*, Research and Planning Division, Economic Commission for Europe, United Nations, Geneva, 1953, p. 239.

## CHAPTER 28. The Political Background of Military Policy: 1947-1950

1. Kennan was the most steady advocate in this period of the primacy of the limited war problem, his analysis of Soviet policy leading him to the view that Moscow would be exceedingly cautious about risking major war.

2. *Forrestal Diaries*, pp. 374-375.

3. F. L. D. Clay, *op. cit.*, pp. 343-357; and *Forrestal Diaries*, pp. 387-388.

4. *Forrestal Diaries*, p. 389.
". . . The Finletter and Brewster reports had fostered the notion that by increasing expenditures on Air, 'There would be no necessity for UMT.' Actually —and it was a weakness in the administration position—UMT was . . . scarcely a more relevant power than Air expansion to the pressing immediate need, which was for some readily available forces, not to fight a possible future third world war but to deal on the ground at that time with the 'various potentially explosive areas,' as Forrestal put it, out of which alone the danger of a future world war could come."

5. For an able account and analysis of this explosive passage see P. Y. Hammond,

*Missions of the Services,* Twentieth Century Fund Study of Civil-Military Relations (preliminary edition, mimeographed). Hammond concludes:

". . . Clearly, then, the Navy's major difficulties came from the economy program of the Truman Administration which kept all three of the services on short rations (measured by their own standards), and forced them to adopt strategic concepts which, by stressing strategic air power, were unfavorable to the Navy. While economy measures tended to cut the Navy disproportionately more than the other services, the disproportion might have been much greater, particularly if the only strategic plan regarded as feasible under the budget ceilings of the Truman Administration—air retaliatory deterrence—was made the basis of all forces planning in the military establishment. In this light, the Navy's choice of the Air Force for the object of its criticisms, rather than the military budget itself, made some sense. Ultimately an attack aimed at the Air Force and strategic air power would probably have the same effect as an attack upon the level of military expenditure set by the Administration, for it would present the strategic considerations which made necessary larger military expenditures; and it would not place the Navy in the highly disadvantagious position of criticising its civilian superiors."

6. For a detailed account of the background and substance of this reappraisal, as well as the complex bureaucratic politics which accompanied its evolution see P. Y. Hammond, *NSC 68,* Twentieth Century Fund Study of Civil-Military Relations, (preliminary editon, mimeographed).

CHAPTER 29. The Military Services and Policy-making: 1947-1950

1. *Forrestal Diaries,* pp. 513-514.

2. It should be noted that although the ruthless execution of military policy within Truman's budget constraint is associated with the fifteen months when Secretary Johnson presided over the Pentagon, Forrestal's view of the budget problem was distinctly ambivalent. (*Forrestal Diaries,* pp. 536-537.) Louis Johnson's view was reflected in the following statement made during the MacArthur Hearings: "You would conclude, if you read Stalin's books, and what Stalin said, that he doesn't look to a clash of arms, that he expects America to spend itself into bankruptcy." (*Military Situation in the Far East,* Hearings before the Committee on Armed Services and the Committee on Foreign Relations, U.S. Senate, Washington, D.C., Gov't. Printing Office, Washington, D.C., 1951, p. 2627.) This powerful rationalization for low American military budgets (usually linked to alleged statements of Lenin) runs through the thought of both the Truman and Eisenhower administrations, virtually dominating the latter down to early 1957. There is no scrap of serious evidence that it ever represented Communist policy.

3. *Forrestal Diaries,* pp. 390-393. The second JCS conference of 1948, at Newport in August, resolved to a degree the question of air force monopoly of atomic weapons and strategic air functions but advanced no further on the basic issues of policy.

Forrestal's notes on the Key West meeting of the Joint Chiefs of Staff (11-14 March, 1948) catch the flavor of the argument and the issues on which the professional military were concentrated.

"Forrestal prepared some terse 'Notes for Friday—Opening of Meeting,' which he later entered in his diary. They are sketchy, but they clearly show the searching significance which he saw in the seemingly technical question of 'roles and missions.' 'We must be guided,' the notes began, 'by the National Security Act, but I don't want the impression that we are engaged in legalistic discussions.' The Navy, they continued, would keep its own air power but would have to realize that budget limitations might compel it to 'make-do' with help from others; that it would, for example, have to give Air Force crews training in anti-submarine work and the close support of amphibious landings. The notes go on:

*11 March 1948*                                        *Notes for Friday*

"3. There should be certain studies inaugurated now looking for reciprocal use of personnel in the event of emergency. For example, I doubt if the Navy will require the number of pilots that were in training at the end of the last war. *Question:* Could any of these be made available to meet deficiencies of the Air Force?

'4: Question: What is being done about joint amphibious training operations between Army and Marines and Navy, so that techniques and tactics will be identical?

'5. Question: Are there any plans for the use of Marine commanders with Army units on tactical maneuvers?

'6. Function of strategic bombing is the Air Force's.

'7. The Navy is to have the Air necessary for its mission, but its mission does not include the creation of a strategic air force.

'8. Both services, that is, Navy and Air Force, have to give much more thought and help to the third department, the Ground Forces, who are the catch-all for the unwanted and unglamorous jobs.

'9. The mission of the Navy which was inescapable in the Pacific war was the knocking out of enemy-held land bases which were unreachable by land-based Air. I should like to see some study given to the possibility of passing surplus Navy air power into the Air Force when such missions are no longer necessary. For example, the closing phases of the Japanese. . . .

"They seem not to have answered all of Forrestal's penetrating questions, but by Sunday noon (March 14) they had arrived at certain 'broad, basic decisions.' The diary summarizes them as follows:

'1. For planning purposes, Marine Corps to be limited to four divisions with the inclusion of a sentence in the final document that the Marines are not to create another land army.

'2. Air Force recognize right of Navy to proceed with the development of weapons the Navy considers essential to its function but with the proviso that the Navy will not develop a separate strategic air force, this function being reserved to the Air Force. However, the Navy in the carrying out of its function is to have the right to attack inland targets—for example, to reduce and neutralize airfields from which enemy aircraft may be sortying to attack the Fleet.

'3. Air Force recognizes the right and need for the Navy to participate in an all-out air campaign."

4. H. S. Truman, *op. cit.*, Vol. II, pp. 124-126.

5. P. Y. Hammond, "Missions of the Services," pp. 74-75.

". . . Limited war was an important part of the State Department conception of national strategy in the summer of 1949.

"But limited war had no comparable place in the strategic thinking of the Joint Chiefs of Staff. During the fall of 1948, when the fiscal 1950 budget was under preparation, the Joint Chiefs had maintained that if the President's defense budget ceiling were not lifted the military establishment would be capable of only a hard air strike from the British Isles in case of war. With budget prospects even dimmer in the summer of 1949 than nine months earlier, the military establishment remained committed to this strategic plan. The full-scale retaliatory air strike, whether or not it could itself end a war with the Soviet Union, could not be wasted upon a minor Soviet aggression. It would have to be reserved for a large-scale Soviet aggression, and might do no more than give the United States time to mobilize for total war. Furthermore, if the United States were prepared to fight only this kind of war, it would have nothing to offer a military ally in Western Europe except liberation following conquest—a prospect uncomfortably close to annihilation.

"All of these facts were pointed out to the Joint Strategic Survey Committee, a strategic planning appendage of the Joint Chiefs of Staff, by members of the Policy Planning Staff of the State Department. Kennan, then Director of the Staff, argued for two highly mechanized and mobile divisions to fight the 'brush fires' which he anticipated in containing Russia. Others on the staff thought that additional forces would be needed, but all stressed the capability of fighting limited wars to contain Russia and help protect America's allies in Europe.

The rejoinder of the Joint Strategic Survey Committee was simple and unanswerable: while the recommendations of the Policy Planning Staff were quite persuasive, and in general already familiar to the Committee, the budget made their implementation impossible."

### CHAPTER 30. The Korean War: Its Military and Political Conduct

1. In addition to familiar published sources see, on the origins and conduct of the Korean War, P. Ogloblin, "The Korean War: A Background Paper," Cambridge, Center for International Studies, Massachusetts Institue of Technology, 1958; B. F. Mason, The War in Korea, (Parts I and II), Harvard University Defense Policy Seminar, 1956-1957.

2. The rationale, scale, and constitution of the effort at partial mobilization are reflected in the Secretary of Defense's semiannual report for the period ending June 1952, looking back over the two years since the Korean War began.

"In June 1950, with the communist attack against the Republic of Korea, the American people decided to rebuild their military strength. Two years later the United States had 3,636,000 men and women under arms—an increase of nearly 2,200,000 during the period. . . .

"Throughout the past two years the highest priority has been assigned to the requirements of our armed forces in Korea.

"The basic objectives of our rearmament program were announced early in the Korean conflict. They remain the same today. Briefly stated, they aim to provide reasonable defensive strength as a deterrent against war, to furnish protection against disaster in the event of such a war, and to establish a mobilization base which can be rapidly expanded in case of need. The military programs to achieve these objectives have been agreed upon after repeated careful consideration of world conditions. They are within limits that the United States should be able to sustain for as long a period as necessary.

"A possible alternative to these objectives would have been to create and maintain a large military establishment with vast stores of munitions and constantly to replace, in quantity, older weapons and equipment with the latest designs as they become available. This policy was discarded as contrary to our national tradition as well as our national interest. Its cost in manpower and taxes would have seriously disrupted our social and economic system.

"We reached the manpower goals established for the close of fiscal year 1952 increasing the personnel strength of the armed forces two and a half times in the space of 2 years and the combat efficiency of fighting units to a marked degree. The Army has grown from 10 divisions and 11 regimental combat teams—all at less than peacetime manning levels and without operational support units—to a force of 20 divisions and 18 regimental combat teams, the great majority of which is combat-worthy. The Army's military personnel increased from nearly 600,000 to almost 1,600,000. The Navy expanded its personnel from less than 400,000 to about 800,000 and its warships from 200 to 400. It doubled the number of its big carriers and added seven carrier groups to its air arm. The Marine Corps increased from 75,000 men to more than 230,000 organized into 3 divisions and 3 air wings. The Air Force grew from 48 groups to 95 wings on the way to its goal of 143 wings and was manned on June 30, 1952 by 980,000 officers and men as compared to a little more than 400,000 two years earlier."
(Department of Defense, *Semiannual Report of the Secretary of Defense*, Jan. 1-June 30, 1952, Washington, D.C., Govt. Printing Office, 1952, pp. 1, 3.)

3. For more extended discussion of the Korean War in the context of nuclear weapons see R. E. Osgood, *Limited War, the Challenge to American Strategy*, Chicago, Univ. of Chicago Press, 1957, especially chaps. VII-IX and H. Kissinger, *Nuclear Weapons and Foreign Policy*, Harper, New York, 1957, pp. 43-51.

4. Before the end of the Korean War the United States learned even more directly, through the build-up and training of the Republic of Korea army, that Asians could quickly be developed into competent troops handling modern weapons with skill.

5. The most obvious apparent exception to this dictum is the use of jet fighters. In the setting of the air operations in Korea, however, this transition was not of great significance; and, in any case, the Messerschmitt 262 had flown operationally before the end of the Second World War in Europe.

CHAPTER 31. The Korean War: Political Decisions, The Debate, and a Summation

1. J. F. Byrnes, *op. cit.*, pp. 226-229.

2. H. S. Truman, *op. cit.*, Vol. II, p. 325.

3. M. Bundy (ed.), *The Pattern of Responsibility*, Boston, Houghton Mifflin, 1952, p. 200.

4. *Ibid.*, p. 189.

5. H. S. Truman, *op. cit.*, Vol. II, p. 371-372

6. M. Bundy, *op. cit.*, p. 280.

7. *Ibid.*, p. 288. Acheson's statement on this basic issue is worth quoting in full: "I should like to deal briefly with the . . . proposition that we may need to take extreme risks now because time may not be on our side. I believe this is wrong.

"The basic premise of our foreign policy is that time is on our side if we make good use of it. This does not necessarily mean that time must bring us to a point where we can match the Soviet Union man-for-man and tank-for-tank.

"What it does mean is that we need to use the time we have to build an effective deterrent force. This required us to create sufficient force-in-being, both in the United States and among our allies, to shield our great potential against the possibility of a quick and early onslaught, and to ensure that our allies will not suffer occupation and destruction. And back of this shield we need to have the potential that would enable us to win a war.

"This is the measure of the force we need; as we approach it, we approach our objective of preventing war.

"Can we do this? I believe we can. We and our allies have the capacity to out-produce the Soviet bloc by a staggering margin. There is no doubt about that. Our capacity to produce has been set in motion and is rapidly getting to the point where its output will be vast and its effect significant.

"There is also the critical factor of our will. The future belongs to freedom if free men have the will to make time work on their side. I believe the American people and their allies do have the will, the will to work together when their freedom is threatened. This is the ultimate source of our faith and our confidence. A free society can call upon profound resources among its people in behalf of a righteous cause."

8. *Military Situation in the Far East*, Hearings before the Committee on Armed Services and the Committee on Foreign Relations, U. S. Senate, Washington: p. 84. G.P.O., 1951.

9. The cutting edge of MacArthur's position—and his most persuasive rhetoric before the Committee—was that a decent settlement in Korea would be impossible unless the war were enlarged. Although his position—and those of his supporters—had many other dimensions, the Communist offer to negotiate a truce around the 38th Parallel, brought about by the defensive victories of April-May, 1951, relieved to a degree the acute tension of the nation.

## CHAPTER 32. Intimations of a New Phase

1. The Indochina settlement of 1954, splitting the country on the 17th Parallel and the passivity of the Eisenhower Administration in the face of the East German, Polish, and Hungarian uprisings of 1953 and 1956 carried forward this common law set of rules, as did Mao's acceptance of American intransigence over Quemoy and Matsu in 1955. The first major break in the line came with American acquiescence in the Communist arms deals with Egypt and Syria, in 1956-1957.

## CHAPTER 33. The New Military Equation

1. On this phase of the postwar evolution see, notably, D. K. Price, *Government and Science*, New York, New York Univ. Press, 1954, chap. II.

2. *Organization and Administration of the Military Research and Development Programs*, Twenty-fourth Intermediate Report of the Committee on Government

Operations, 82nd Congress, Second Session, Washington, D.C., Govt. Printing Office, 1954, p. 23.

3. For the origins, membership and (unclassified) conclusions of this committee, see *In the Matter of J. Robert Oppenheimer, Transcript of Hearing before Personnel Security Board*, Wash., D.C., April 12, 1954, through May 6, 1954, U. S. Atomic Energy Commission, Washington, D.C.: Govt. Printing Office, 1954 p. 95.

CHAPTER 34. American Policy and the Rise of the New Nations: 1945-1952

1. E. Goldman, *op. cit.*, pp. 93-94.

2. One of Acheson's speeches was given before the National Press Club in Washington on January 12, 1950; the other on March 15, before the Commonwealth Club in San Francisco. For a summary and extracts see M. Bundy, *op. cit.*, pp. 191-200.

3. For the origins of this passage in Truman's Inaugural Address, see Truman, *op. cit.*, Vol. II, pp. 226-239; and Goldman, *op. cit.*, pp. 93-95.

4. For Bowles' role in persuading Nehru to base the Indian First Five Year Plan substantially on village development, and the origins of this concept in pre-Communist Chinese experience, see C. Bowles, *Ambassador's Report*, New York, Harper, 1954, pp. 196-203.

5. W. S. Salant has made the following calculation of the breakdown of foreign aid for the calendar years 1946-1953:

FOREIGN AID IN CURRENT PRICES

| Year | Total | Military Grants | All Other |
|------|-------|-----------------|-----------|
| 1946 | 5044 | 69 | 4975 |
| 1947 | 6609 | 43 | 6566 |
| 1948 | 5218 | 300 | 4918 |
| 1949 | 5859 | 210 | 5649 |
| 1950 | 4166 | 526 | 3640 |
| 1951 | 4661 | 1470 | 3191 |
| 1952 | 4983 | 2603 | 2380 |
| 1953 | 6300 | 4251 | 2049 |

W. Reitzel, M. A. Kaplan, and C. G. Coblenz, *United States Foreign Policy, 1945-1955*, Washington, D.C., Brookings Institution, 1956, p. 483.

CHAPTER 35. From Truman to Eisenhower

1. G. Gallup, *Public Opinion News Service*, January 12, 1953.

2. For an excellent evocation of public moods over the postwar decade, see E. Goldman, *op. cit.*

3. See W. S. White, *The Taft Story*, New York, Harper, 1954, especially Chap. 6.

4. E. Goldman, *op. cit.*, pp. 56-57, summarizes the domestic performance of the 80th Congress as follows:

"When the actual record of the Congress began to emerge in 1947, it proved an assault on the legislation and the tendencies of the Half-Century of Revolution. The practical political basis of the session was a deal between Southern Democrats and right-wing Republicans, which meant the end of any hopes for civil-rights

TRUMAN POPULARITY

| | Approve | Disapprove | No Opinion |
|---|---|---|---|
| July 1945 | 87% | 3% | 10% |
| October 1946 | 32 | 53 | 15 |
| March 1947 | 60 | 23 | 17 |
| April 1948 | 36 | 50 | 14 |
| January 1949 | 69 | 17 | 14 |
| January 1950 | 45 | 40 | 15 |
| June 1950 | 37 | 45 | 18 |
| July 1950 | 46 | 37 | 17 |
| December 1950 | 36 | 49 | 15 |
| February 1951 | 26 | 57 | 17 |
| June 1951 | 24 | 61 | 15 |
| August 1951 | 31 | 57 | 12 |
| November 1951 | 23 | 59 | 19 |
| February 1952 | 25 | 62 | 13 |
| April 1952 | 28 | 59 | 13 |
| June 1952 | 32 | 58 | 10 |
| November 1952 | 32 | 55 | 13 |
| Today (January 1953) | 31 | 56 | 13 |

legislation. The two most important laws passed were the Taft-Hartley Act, which weakened the power of the unions, and a new income tax formula that reduced the disproportion of taxes on high incomes. (The bill cut the levies three per cent for families with incomes of $2,400 or less; eight per cent for those in the $10,000 bracket; fifteen per cent for the $20,000 a year class; and forty-eight to sixty-five per cent for the group over $100,000). The structure of government aid to farmers was attacked by cuts in funds for soil conservation and for crop storage. The Congress refused demands for federal help in the form of more public housing, strong price controls, extended social security, or aid-to-education. Both what was done and what was not done in the field of immigration legislation reflected distaste for immigrants of southern and eastern European origins. Over the whole session hung wrathful counter-revolution. "T.R.B.", the New Deal columnist of the *New Republic,* was as accurate as he was melancholy when he wrote: 'This Congress brought back an atmosphere you had forgotten or never thought possible . . . Victories fought and won years ago were suddenly in doubt. Everything was debatable again.' "

5. See, notably, *The Vandenberg Papers,* especially Chap. 27.

6. For three assessments of the strands in American political life to which Macarthy appealed, see R. Hofstadter, "The Pseudo-Conservative Revolt," *The American Scholar,* Winter 1954-55; T. Parsons, "Macarthyism and American Social Tension: A Sociologist's View," *Yale Review,* Winter 1955; and E. Goldman, *op. cit.,* pp. 113-132.

7. See, notably, White, *op. cit.,* "The Sad, Worst Period," Chap. 7.

8. For the texts of Stalin's professorial "Economic Problems of Socialism in the USSR", and Malenkov's speech, see the *Current Digest of the Soviet Press,* October 18, (special supplement) and the issues of November 1, 8, and 15, 1952.

9. For an account of this briefing, see notably, H. S. Truman, *op. cit.,* Vol. II, pp. 515-521; and R. J. Donovan, *Eisenhower: The Inside Story,* New York, Harper, 1956 pp. 12-17.

BOOK FOUR

# THE
# EISENHOWER ADMINISTRATION
# AND ITS CRISIS

# PART I

# INTRODUCTION

### 36. The Three New Issues

In January 1953 the Eisenhower Administration took over in Washington. Stalin's death was announced on March 6. The new regimes in Washington and Moscow confronted a world which, having been wracked by six years of indecisive cold war, appeared to be settling down on the lines of demarcation which had emerged—a fact dramatized by the completion of the Korean truce negotiations in July. Meanwhile, however, the pace of change in military technology was accelerating and the nationalist revolutions were gathering momentum in the southern half of the globe, bringing to decision long-term problems new to the twentieth century. A new look was evidently required in military and foreign policy; and there were fresh dispositions to be made in domestic affairs as well.

In the course of 1953 the men in Washington and Moscow crystallized their conceptions of what was required at home and abroad; and for almost four years the two great powers went about their business, working out those conceptions to their logical conclusions. American and Soviet policy over this interval were both largely determined by specific decisions taken in the course of 1953; for those first moves had the special power over later events that characterizes the early dispositions made in fluid situations. Then, starting with the Suez crisis, late in 1956, the results of the interaction between the two sets of policies clearly emerged; and a protracted crisis occurred in the West.

The domestic problems and considerations which bore upon American and Soviet political leaders differed radically; but Washington and Moscow faced three common issues in dealing with the world arena of power. How should military force be reorganized in the light of fusion weapons and the possibilities of long-range missiles? What position should be adopted toward the governments and peoples of Asia, the Middle East, and Africa as they pressed forward to assert themselves on the world scene and to modernize their societies? In the light of these two new elements, each of which profoundly affected the status of Western Europe, what policy should be adopted toward that area, which had entered a new phase of economic growth, achieving a momentum unknown for forty years.

The chapters that follow examine successively how these three issues were dealt with within the Communist Bloc and in the United States down to 1956 and then consider the nature and evolution of the crisis in the West which emerged in the period 1956-1958.

Like the international crises of the late 1930's and the late 1940's, the crisis of 1956-1958 was initiated by the military and foreign policy of the enemies of the West. The story of that crisis is, again, a story of intimate interaction—in this case of interaction between Moscow and Washington, even though their relationship was complicated by interventions of increasing assertiveness from Peking and Bonn, London and Cairo, Warsaw and Paris, Tel Aviv, Caracas, et al. But, since the making of military and foreign policy is never wholly divorced from domestic affairs, to understand the crisis of 1956-1958 it is necessary to turn first to the situation which unfolded within the Communist Bloc after Stalin's death.

# PART II

# THE NEW COMMUNIST OFFENSIVE

## 37. *Policy Within the Communist Bloc*

POST-STALIN SOVIET POLITICS

It was the essence of Stalin's rule that he made it extremely difficult for power to pass into a single pair of hands. The keystone of his system had been a personal grasp on all the instruments of Soviet power.[1] Stalin's authority permitted him both to intervene intimately and directly at any level in the chains of command of the bureaucratized instruments for the handling of power which had emerged in the 1930's under his guidance and to avoid a disproportionate accretion of power to any single bureaucratic organization or subordinate.

The decisive instrument of Stalin's rule was the secret police. He used the secret police not merely as an instrument for control over the Soviet population as a whole but also to control his immediate subordinates and the chains of command which they administered. The Soviet Union under Stalin was not merely a police state; it was operated, quite technically, by police politics.

Stalin's successors, each with personal control over a piece of the machinery, were confronted, therefore, with the choice of engaging in life-and-death struggle for control over the police apparatus or forming some kind of collective system in which power was shared and there was agreement to prevent the secret police from being used as an instrument against one another. They chose the latter course. The secret police remained, of course, a prime instrument of control over the Soviet population. Despite certain moves to put the whole range of its operations on a less arbitrary basis, ample loopholes were left—notably with respect to the elastic concept of "espionage"—for the arbitrary secret use of the police power over the Russian peoples. Thus, although police politics was radically reduced after 1953, the Soviet Union remained after Stalin essentially still a police state.

This was the system which emerged in the course of 1953, confirmed by the liquidation of Beria, whose limited but considerable grip on the secret police he evidently sought to extend. The constitutional basis for the system lay in placing the secret police under a Committee on State Security announced in March 1954; the ideological basis for the system was enunciated at the Twentieth Party Congress in February 1956, when Stalin's one-man rule was denounced, and, in effect, oligarchical rule of a sort was proclaimed in its place.

Within this framework Khrushchev, starting in 1953, conducted a systematic effort to rehabilitate the role of the Communist Party apparatus as the center of organization, power, and policy within the collective leadership system. Building on his base in the Party, Khrushchev moved forward in 1954 to a position of joint status with Malenkov; and he then openly debated with Malenkov on the following issue: Should the Soviet Union cut back its ground forces radically and sharply increase output of consumers goods, relying increasingly on its emerging nuclear weapon delivery capabilities with strategic air power and missiles; or should it continue to maintain large ground forces, with modernized air support, for atomic combat? Khrushchev evidently lined up with the Red Army. In 1955 Malenkov was demoted and replaced by the figurehead Bulganin; and Khrushchev continued to fill as many places as possible with his own men, including places in the Central Committee, the classic procedure of bureaucratic politics within a dictatorship.

In 1957 he felt his position strong enough to assert himself in three directions: against Malenkov to the left, against Molotov and Kaganovich to the right, and against Zhukov, an indispensable agent in Khrushchev's rise, who had been systematically diminishing the Party's role in the armed forces and otherwise asserting himself as a political figure. The removal of Zhukov was followed by no significant changes in the structure of military command or in leading personnel.

Politically, with the exception of the light-stepping Mikoyan, Khrushchev at mid-1958 stood alone among the major figures of Stalin's old entourage. There was, however, no evidence that Khrushchev had been able to recapture the secret police as an instrument of personal power; and, above all, the armed forces, although put back to studying Marx and Lenin, still apparently controlled their ammunition dumps and thus held an ultimate veto power within Soviet society.[2]

Outside the area of high politics and the control over policemen and guns, the new disposition of executive authority released many new trends in thought and aspiration within Soviet society in the post-1953 period—from the Presidium's Secretariat, to the university students, down to the millions of Soviet citizens in forced labor. The immediate operational effect, however, was to bring to bear on the making of Soviet policy at home and abroad younger and fresher minds whose views had been suppressed by the heavy-handed rigidity and omnipresence of Stalin in the postwar years. In many ways the years after 1953 have been a golden period for the generation of technicians, soldiers, and bureaucrats whom Stalin educated and trained to operate a modern industrial and military system but who had worked under severe restraint and inhibition as well as human fear so long as Stalin was alive.

## THE EASTERN EUROPEAN SATELLITES

In Eastern Europe Stalin's successors faced a difficult aspect of his heritage; for since 1949 Stalin had clamped on the satellites rigid and imitative institutions which demanded that Moscow take increasingly direct responsibility for day-to-day administration. Essentially, the Soviet Presidium in 1953 sought to extend to the satellite empire a version of the limited diffusion of power which they had begun to bring about within the Soviet Union.

In the short run, the new policy could be developed inside the Soviet Union with reasonable confidence; for within the established Soviet elite there was a sufficient mixture of loyalty to nation and loyalty to the system which had made them to hold the Soviet structure together without the application of terror to the elite. In the short run, de-Stalinization almost certainly increased the loyalty of the bureaucratic and technical Soviet elite to the system as a whole. But four flaws in Soviet policy quickly emerged when Stalin's successors sought to extend their system of limited diffusion of authority to Eastern Europe.

First, nationalism, which by and large is the major cohesive force within the Soviet Union, proved disruptive when given scope in the satellite states. In the postwar decade Moscow totally failed to build any stable sentiment—ideological or national—for attachment between the peoples of Eastern Europe and Russia.

Second, the Communist political and military elite developed in the satellite areas in the postwar decade were only superficially loyal to Moscow and, when put under pressure, proved to be committed to degrees of nationalism incompatible in the long run with the notion of a new Communist Commonwealth led from Moscow.

Third, the limited but real de-rating of secret police power, which in the Soviet Union had thus far led only to relatively harmless expressions of dissent, led men in the satellite areas to undertake seriously—at the risk of life—to alter the circumstances of their rule. Despite the evidence of June 1953 in East Germany and of June 1956 in Poznan that no Western aid could be expected for revolt in the satellites, the Poles, putting Lenin's 1917 tactics into reverse, won back control over their army and secret police and were able to face down Khrushchev on the night of October 19-20, 1956—a major turning point in modern history which triggered the tragic Hungarian revolt.

Fourth, the course of events in Eastern Europe, and notably in Poland, was colored by an underlying crisis in agriculture. The application of Communist methods had permitted high levels of investment and rapid increase in industrial output after 1948. But collectivization and collections by the state in agriculture damped output. The satellite governments of Eastern Europe found themselves increasingly in difficulty in trying to meet the food requirements of the expanding cities and of an expanding foreign trade. The solution available to Russia—of subsidizing collectivized agriculture with heavy investment in the form of machinery and chemical fertilizers, as well as the opening of new acreage—was not available to the smaller states of Eastern Europe. Thus in Poland Moscow faced the difficult choice of seeing collectivization supplanted by an incentive system that virtually freed the farmer of political control or subsidizing Polish agriculture indefinitely. The problem was heightened because of Tito's limited but still substantial success in restoring agricultural productivity—a success achieved, in effect, by abandoning collectivization. These developments, posing grave doubts about the longer future of communism, lay behind much of the ideological controversy of 1958 which extended from East Germany to Communist China.

### THE CHINESE TAKE-OFF BEGINS

The year 1953 was also important in Communist China; for the first Five Year Plan was then launched. The whole process was conceived in terms of Communist theology as "the transition to socialism" and modeled closely on the policies of Stalin's First Five-Year Plan, although, from the beginning, the Chinese Communist industrialization effort was explicitly linked to "modernization of the armed forces."

The story begins with the Sino-Soviet economic negotiations, which ran from late in 1952 to September 1953, the upshot of which appears to have been a detailed plan of Sino-Soviet economic cooperation and trade looking ahead to the period 1957-1959. The plan apparently included provision for: maintaining a substantial level of trade between China and the Communist bloc with some limited Soviet credits; maintaining a high level of Soviet technical assistance to Chinese industry; a concentration of Soviet assistance around a group of 141 plants to be reconstructed or built; detailed scheduling of deliveries in both directions; detailed scheduling of Soviet deliveries of military equipment to China in exchange for Chinese exports to the Soviet Union.

The limited scale of Soviet credits and the ardent ambitions of the Chinese Communist leadership decreed that the first Five Year Plan would be conducted in a setting of austerity, a theme fully developed in Peking's propaganda by September 1953, when the limits of external assistance had been defined.

In the autumn the pace of nationalization of private industry was accelerated and a parallel move toward agricultural collectivization was foreshadowed. Whereas collectivization proceeded at a moderate pace in 1953-1955, grain collection at government-decreed prices was strictly enforced, raising acute difficulties on the rural scene, which, however, Mao's enormous control system could easily contain. In mid-1955 Mao decided to press on to virtually total collectivization—a decision taken against considerable opposition within the Chinese Communist Party and in the face of considerable evidence of peasant dissidence of a kind likely to affect agricultural productivity. But Mao was heartened to go forward by a bumper harvest and the conviction that without collectivization his control over China would be dangerously dilute.

In the process of industrialization, the Chinese Communists made rapid progress in the period 1953-1958. The Manchurian industrial base left by the Japanese—although damaged by Soviet reparation withdrawals—provided a useful foundation. The powerful control system erected in 1949-1952 served to harness the substantial technical talents within China, to acquire for the state a high proportion of agricultural output, and to permit a high level of investment including certain types of agricultural investment where tightly mobilized masses of labor could be effective. Soviet technical assistance and credits, though limited, were helpful; the intimate tie to the Communist Bloc permitted long-term trade agreements which provided reliable flows of industrial equipment and missing raw materials. The Chinese peasant, however, like farmers everywhere under Communist rule—and still about three quarters of the Chinese population—managed to sustain a dangerous passive sabotage of productivity which even Mao's compulsively detailed control of the Chinese villages could not fully suppress. The control system was, however, capable of maintaining order and of mobilizing adequate agricultural supplies in the hands of the state over the first decade of Communist rule. Without question, the First Five Year Plan had at last firmly set China as a nation on the path of self-sustained economic growth, although the fate of communism was still tied intimately to the unresolved question of whether Communist techniques could yield a sufficient increase in agricultural output to permit the Chinese take-off to proceed under the political and social auspices under which it was launched.[3]

In the years 1953-1958, then, Communist leadership confronted within the Bloc a series of difficult challenging situations: the pressures to diffuse executive power within the Soviet Union, the problem of acute political dissidence and agricultural sluggishness in Eastern Europe, and the problem of economic growth in China. Each reflected problems threatening to the essence of communism in the long run; and none was wholly solved either by Stalin's successors or by Mao in these five years. On the other hand, Communist leadership exhibited sufficient tactical vigor and determination to prevent any of these problems from erupting into uncontrollable crisis; and it reserved a sufficient margin of energy, talent, and resources to pursue simultaneously a military and foreign policy geared to the potentialities of the two great revolutions at work on the world scene.

## 38. Soviet Military Policy

### STALIN'S MILITARY DOCTRINE: 1945-1953

The shape of the Soviet response to the new military technology has become tolerably clear in the past several years.[1]

From the moment at Potsdam in July 1945 when Truman told a well-informed Stalin that the United States had successfully tested a nuclear weapon, the Soviet Union adopted a posture of studied poise. While work proceeded at highest pitch within the Soviet Union on nuclear weapons, Soviet military doctrine continued to rely on ground forces with tactical air support; and Stalin steadily reaffirmed the view—a mixture of the dogmas of a Communist and a Russian ground force soldier—that nuclear weapons had in no way fundamentally altered the "permanently operating factors" which determine the outcome of war: the stability of the rear, the morale of the army, the quantity and quality of divisions, the army's weapons, and the organizing ability of the commanding officers.

In diplomacy, the Soviets refused to entertain seriously any system for international control of nuclear weapons while the American monopoly held and they were at a tactical disadvantage. In psychological warfare, through peace movements and other devices, by heightening the widespread sense of horror at the destructive possibilities of the new weapons, they maintained maximum political pressure on the United States not to bring to bear its monopolistic advantage.

There was virtually no overt change in the Soviet posture between September 1949, when the first Soviet nuclear weapon was exploded, and Stalin's death.

### THE H-BOMB AND THE BALLISTIC MISSILE

Stalin's death evidently released within the military bureaucracy, as elsewhere within the Soviet structure, ardent debate in which Stalin's pronouncements were no longer taken to be sacrosanct. And the debate was accompanied, if not in fact initiated in its most serious phase, by the successful explosion of a fusion weapon in August 1953.

Fusion weapons suddenly opened up new possibilities in the field of long-range missiles. Soviet experts, like those in the United States, had been working since 1945 with German technicians and their V-2 rocket. The V-2 had proved capable of hitting the London area regularly with a one-ton warhead from a range of 150-200 miles. Undoubtedly, the V-2 had been considerably refined in both countries in the period 1945-1952. The Soviet research and development effort was probably somewhat more substantial over these years, among other reasons because the intermediate ballistic missile—the first major stage beyond the V-2—was immensely significant for Soviet strategy since it could strike at American bases around the periphery of the Communist Bloc. It is clear that down to 1953 Moscow also pursued at the research and development level a major effort to create the long-range aircraft required for a modernized Soviet Strategic Air Command.

In short, during the first eight postwar years, Soviet military authorities left open the possibility of developing delivery capabilities for weapons of mass destruction in the field of both long-range aircraft and ballistic missiles. But until the fusion bomb was created, the long-range ballistic missile appeared as a relatively limited instrument of war. This was so primarily because the aiming error of rockets was so great and the destructive range of fission weapons so limited that damage to chosen targets was problematical. Thus the vastly enlarged area of destruction of the H-bomb, once it could be reduced in size to fit the nose cone of a rocket, elevated the military status of missiles. In the course of 1953 the long-range rocket for the first time thus became a weapon of self-evident and urgent operational interest.

There is much published evidence that during 1953 the Soviet authorities made a fundamental decision to proceed at full tilt with the development of intermediate- and long-range ballistic missiles.[2] At the same time, the pace of development of the Soviet Strategic Air Command was reduced. This was done despite the fact that in the Bison and Bear the Soviets had already developed what appeared to be first-class bombers and that in the whole of their aircraft industry they had exhibited a capacity to match at least the development of new American types.

A Ministry of Defense Production charged with the production of missiles was set up in 1953; a special Committee on Space Travel, at the highest scientific level, was set up in 1954; and the ablest minds in the four most relevant fields of basic science evidently turned with increased operational emphasis to the missile problem—fluid dynamics and heat transfer, fuel chemistry and combustion, structures and materials, electronics and communication theory.

In the course of 1954 the field of missiles technology invaded the Soviet engineering curriculum on a large scale.

This strategic decision—substantially to throttle back the long-range bomber—undoubtedly appealed to Russian minds for several reasons. In the first place, although the Soviet Union had developed long-range aircraft and a long-range bombing force, it had not developed a strategic air command on anything like the scale of the American forces. Moreover, the experience of the Second World War had not given the Russian air force experience in long-range mass flying, targeting, and navigation. Further, the American base structure and the air defense system rapidly building in North America during 1953 seemed to forecast a more or less permanent Soviet disadvantage. The Soviets may thus have felt that in relying for nuclear weapon delivery on a strategic air command they would be moving in behind a more experienced force and would be bound to remain somewhat inferior in this area. They may have felt in relation to the American Strategic Air Command somewhat as the Germans felt in relation to the British Navy in the first half of the twentieth century.

On the other hand, there was no reason to believe that the Soviets were in any way behind the United States in missiles: Russia had a distinguished history of scientific contributions to rocketry reaching back to Czarist times and had used short-range rockets extensively in the Second World War; the fundamental talents in the relevant fields of basic science and engineering were evidently available; and the missile business was in some of its dimensions an extension of artillery, in which Russia had traditionally excelled. Moreover, the whole enterprise appeared to provide a way of bypassing an enemy's main strength.

It is possible that Malenkov, believed to have been the political overseer of the Soviet missile program since 1947, had a large hand in the decision to proceed at full speed with the intermediate- and long-range ballistic missile. In any case, it fitted well the policy which he was then pursuing—one of allocating increased resources to light industry and consumers goods.

REVISIONS IN POLICY AND DOCTRINE

The 1953 decision to proceed at highest priority with missile development did not, however, settle post-Stalin military policy. The question arose: To what extent should the Soviet Union come to rely on the offensive and retaliatory power of ballistic missiles as opposed to modernized ground and naval forces? It is evident that in the course of 1954 the Soviet Union went through a major policy struggle in which the military fought against what they regarded as an excessive commitment of Malenkov to rely in the future on the ability to deliver nuclear weapons with ballistic missiles. Khrushchev openly argued against Malenkov on the balance of light versus heavy industry, in favor of the latter. And this abstract debate concealed an argument on the scale of military budget and, especially, on the scale of allocations to fields other than nuclear weapons, delivery capabilities, and defense against air attack. In the end Krushchev, backed by the Soviet military, won and the Khrushchev, Zhukov, Bulganin team took over.

In 1955, then, Soviet military policy consisted in a balanced program designed to produce as soon as possible intermediate- and long-range ballistic missiles; to modernize substantial if somewhat reduced infantry, artillery, and tactical air forces for atomic ground combat; to modernize the Soviet navy, at the expense of older vessels, notably to increase submarine missile delivery capabilities and to extend and refine air defense. And this program was pursued without major change down to 1958, drawing off at least 20 per cent of the Soviet gross national product.

### THE IDEOLOGICAL DEBATE

In typical Communist style, these issues of budgetary allocation and military substance were accompanied by a contrapuntal ideological debate of high abstraction designed to set a new theoretical frame for Soviet military policy.

First, the question arose: Had Stalin's "permanently operating factors" been changed by the nature of modern war? In a now famous article in *Military Thought* in November 1953, Major General Talenski asserted that planners should abandon the "permanent operating factors" as the only correct basis for military organization and should recognize the primacy of technical military factors operating equally on the capabilities of Soviet forces and on those of its possible enemies. This politically "naked" doctrine, closely tied to the temporarily successful effort of the Soviet armed forces to free themselves from Communist Party influence as well as from secret police control in the period 1953-1957, was soon opposed by Marshall Vasilevskii in *Red Star* in February 1954. But a latent theme in the original Talenski article, in which he had argued that modern techniques could settle the outcome of a war in short order, whatever the "permanent factors," was fully vindicated in 1955. And with Zhukov's elevation as Defense Minister in February 1955 the importance of surprise in modern warfare was accepted in the Soviet Union. Marxist dogma had hitherto converged with Russian history to deprecate the importance of surprise—Marxism, with its emphasis on underlying economic and sociological factors, and Russian history, with its memories of long, slow, bloody salvation, after severe initial setbacks, through geography and the Russian peasant mass.

While the possibility of destructive surprise attack was being absorbed into Soviet military doctrine, a second even more explosive ideological issue was debated and briefly exposed in public controversy. In March 1954 Malenkov suggested that "civilization"—not merely "capitalism"—might be at stake in a Third World War. This view would have radically altered the classic Marxist-Leninist vision of communism triumphing in the wake of cataclysmic battle generated by the death throes of capitalist imperialism; and, perhaps more important, it might have lessened the nerve of Communists in facing the test of will implicit in the arms race. Malenkov recanted in April; but it is evident that, having examined the destructive possibilities of modern weapons, the Soviet leadership has not been prepared to portray a Third World War as an incident of unvarnished opportunity for communism. And at the Twentieth Party Congress there was some considerable hedging on the "inevitability" of war.

This doctrinal position probably conforms to the following evaluation: that the Soviet Union will count essentially on the extension of its power by means short of major war; but major war initiated by Moscow is not to be excluded if (1) the Soviet Union should generate so decisive a technological advantage over the United States as to judge it possible to take out United States retaliatory power at a blow; or if (2) the Free World position in Eurasia should so degenerate—and the Communist position so expand—as to make it possible to take out the isolated fortress the United States would then be.

In short, the Soviet New Look of 1953-1955 did not exclude the possibility of future major war, but it did not make major war a necessary condition for the expansion of Soviet power. And throughout this period Soviet ground forces were retrained and re-equipped to fight a limited war—short of mutual destruction with airborne H-bombs—with tactical atomic weapons. Soviet military policy thus embraced the full spectrum of possible levels of combat.

INTERIM SOVIET POLICY

In the interval between the Soviet decision to give first priority to producing a missile delivery system to the time that operational tests were successfully completed—that is, from the end of 1953 to sometime in 1956—Moscow pursued a policy designed to minimize the possibility of major war. The missiles were not in place, the Soviet bomber force was under limited development at best, and American delivery capabilities remained very substantial. Thus the Indochina clash was settled on reasonable terms and the Summit Conference of July 1955 was sought and consummated.

From the Soviet point of view, the mood of relaxed tension generated at the Geneva Conference of 1955 had two major purposes. The first was to spread tranquility in the West and, in particular, to allay anxiety concerning the Soviet maneuvers in Asia, the Middle East, and Africa, which were beginning to accelerate at just this time. The second purpose was to encourage the West to diminish the attention and outlays devoted to the arms race at just the stage when the Soviets were pressing hard and hopefully to close the gap in weapons of mass destruction and to modernize their ground forces as well. The published Soviet military budget of 1955 was increased from 18 to 19 per cent of the Soviet GNP; American military outlays for 1955 were reduced from 12 to 11 per cent of the American GNP. Malenkov, sponsor of a Soviet policy which would have concentrated more acutely on the strategic use of weapons of mass destruction, lost. Those in Washington who held to a similar policy won their point.

In the course of 1956 the Soviet testing of missiles was sufficiently far advanced and successful to begin the era of missile diplomacy. The first threatening references to the Soviet use of missiles came from Khrushchev in his visit to Birmingham in April 1956; and similar threats lay behind the series of notes addressed to the lesser of the NATO powers in 1956. The most important threat came during the Suez crisis; and Moscow was undoubtedly heartened to find that both Washington and London may have been moved in some degree by this threat, in combination with other Soviet military moves in the Mediterranean, to hasten the withdrawal of British and French troops from the Suez area. Whatever the influence of these threats on Washington, London, and Paris, Moscow was extremely successful in spreading the view that they had been effective.

Against a background of increasing reports of successful Soviet tests of ICBM's, the first satellites were launched on October 4 and November 3, 1957. These had a profound psychological and political effect on the world scene for at least three distinct reasons. First, they confirmed for all to see what had been firmly known by only a small group in the Western world: namely, that the Soviet Union had fully closed the gap and in fact, for an interval at least, had outstripped the United States in an extremely important means of delivering nuclear weapons over long distances. Second, specifically, the capabilities inherent in the Soviet satellite were widely understood to mean that the United States was foreseeably, if not immediately, vulnerable to direct attack for which no means of defense existed, an attack that could bypass Western Europe. Third, and perhaps most powerful, the Soviet performance confirmed the image, long cultivated by Communist propaganda, that in the decisive area of science and technology the Soviet Union was outstripping the complacent old front-runner—an image of tremendous importance in Asia, the Middle East, and Africa.

### 39. Soviet Policy in the Underdeveloped Areas

THE DISRUPTIVE EXPLOITATION OF NATIONALISM

Communist policy toward Asia, the Middle East, and Africa was shifted onto a new long-term basis between the time that truce negotiations began in

June 1951 and July 1953, when the Korean War was brought to a close. The essence of the new policy lay in the perception that the aspirations of the peoples and governments of Asia, the Middle East, and Africa could be turned to the purpose of Soviet power without the direct application of Communist military force.

Since 1953 the immediate objective of Communist policy in the underdeveloped areas has been to exacerbate the potential areas of friction between new nations on the one hand and the United States and the West on the other. Communist policy has sought to maintain an atmosphere of enflamed anticolonialism in Asia, the Middle East, and Africa and to concentrate the limited political energies of the new states on such problems as Kashmir, West Iran, and Israel. In some areas that policy not only has promised generally disruptive effects in the non-Communist world but has also struck directly at the political foundations of American air bases and at raw material supplies essential to the West. In the longer run, Communist policy in the underdeveloped areas has been designed to weaken or dilute the efforts of the new nations in the direction of economic and social modernization and to prepare the seed-bed for ultimate Communist takeover.

In a sense the whole of post-1953 Communist policy toward Asia, the Middle East, and Africa has been based on analogy with the successful Communist experience in China since 1920. There, too, ardent Chinese nationalism was diverted to military tasks: first, by the protracted Communist insurrection after 1927, and then, increasingly, by the Japanese; and in time, as the popular hopes for material and social progress were progressively frustrated, the local Communists could build a political base for guerrilla operations and rise to power on unfulfilled human and national ambitions.

### THE ROLE OF TRADE AND AID

Just as it proved possible for Moscow to pursue in the 1920's and 1930's a policy of limited support for Sun Yat-sen and Chiang Kai-shek while encouraging the Chinese Communists toward power for the longer pull, Moscow has found it possible since 1953 to conduct a program of expanded trade and lending with the new nations; and, since the Communist Bloc is increasingly a deficit area in foodstuffs and raw materials, and since it could sometimes trade obsolescent military equipment for useful commodities, these arrangements could be made to pay.

The Soviet economic offensive began in 1953 when the new Soviet leaders launched a general program for expanding East-West trade. Between 1952 and 1956 the Communist Bloc trade agreement network with the underdeveloped areas—which initially touched only Afghanistan, Iran, and Egypt—extended to Argentina, India, Greece, Lebanon, Uruguay, Iceland, Burma,

Yugoslavia, Syria, Yemen, Pakistan, and Indonesia.[1] At the same time, the Sino-Soviet Bloc began to participate with great energy in the trade fairs of the Free World.

While East-West trade expanded, the proportionate share of trade between the Communist Bloc and the Free World as a whole remained relatively limited, never rising much above 3 per cent. Nevertheless, the post-1953 trade expansion had certain important political consequences. First, although the over-all level of trade between the Communist Bloc and the Free World remained low, trade with certain nations was sufficiently high to constitute a significant source of leverage. In 1956 more than 20 per cent of the trade of Afghanistan, Iceland, Egypt, Yugoslavia, and Burma was with Communist Bloc countries; 17 per cent for Turkey; 12 per cent for Iran. Second, the Soviet trade program reinforced the image sedulously cultivated after Stalin's death that the Soviet Union was ending its isolation and emerging as a self-confident world power in the normal peaceful business of international life. Third, the Soviet willingness to purchase the raw materials and foodstuffs produced in the underdeveloped areas on a stable trade agreement basis and to provide counter-part goods by barter agreement often seemed attractive to nations worried by the fluctuation of raw materials and foodstuff prices in Free World markets, by currency difficulties in the purchase of imports, and by commodity surplus problems. In the latter category, for example, the Communist Bloc was able to make politically influential deals for Ceylon rubber.

In 1954 the Soviet Union, in addition to expanded trade, began to offer credits and technical assistance to certain selected nations in Asia, the Middle East, and Africa. The scale and spread of Communist Bloc credits (1957)[2] and technical assistance agreements (1956)[3] was fairly impressive.

Credit terms granted have been easy by international standards. Soviet loans usually run from ten to thirty years with interest rates at 2 or 2½ per cent. Certain loans—as in the case of Yemen—have been without interest. Moreover, the conditions of repayment permitted in Soviet loan agreements have taken the form either of commodities normally exported or local currency to be used for Soviet purposes within the country in question.

The distribution of these credits and their scale suggest the variety of Soviet purposes they were designed to maintain. In Afghanistan, exploiting the cross-purposes of Free World policy in the Indian peninsula, the Soviet Union has been able to become the major supplier of capital, technical assistance, and military supplies in a region of historic strategic importance. Moscow's aim is obviously to move gradually toward direct military and political control over the classic gateway to India. In Egypt a high proportion of Communist aid took the form of arms, a move designed both to exacerbate the tensions within the Middle East and to give Russia a position of general leverage over Egyptian policy. The Soviet arms loan was obviously a prime instrument in the events which led to the Suez Crisis of November 1956. The Soviet credit arrangements with Yugoslavia were designed to begin the process of weaning Yugoslavia back into the Soviet orbit and to reverse the consequences of what was evidently judged to have been Stalin's inept handling of the Yugoslavs in 1947-1948—a process subject to many vicissitudes. In India, Soviet aid has been purely economic. It has been on a scale sufficient to support the image of the Soviet Union as an authentic friend of India, to support the build-up of popular attachment to the Soviet Union and to the Communist cause, while maintaining, in the short run, friendly relations with Nehru and the Congress Party. Soviet aid in India has not been on a scale, however, to fulfill the acute foreign exchange requirements of the Second Five Year Plan, on the frustration and failure of which Indian Communists are evidently counting heavily.

In general, then, the Soviet Union has placed its credits in the underdeveloped areas selectively, with an eye to concrete specific advantages both short- and long-run in character. Like Soviet military policy as developed after Stalin's death, Soviet economic policy toward the underdeveloped areas has the earmarks of a program developed step by step for the long pull.

The Soviet program of expanded trade, technical assistance, and credits in the underdeveloped areas has been conducted against a background of policy and propaganda designed to impress the governments and peoples of these areas with the rapid growth in Soviet military and technological strength vis-à-vis the United States. It is altogether typical of this strategy that when Khrushchev and Bulganin barnstormed through India in 1955 a fusion weapon was test-exploded in Central Asia.

### MOSCOW AND PEKING IN THE UNDERDEVELOPED AREAS

The victory of communism in China, the impressive role of the Chinese Communist forces in the Korean War and in support of the Vietminh operation in Indochina, and the leading part played by Chou En-lai at the Bandung Conference of April 1955 raised the question of whether Communist China might assume the role of political leadership in Asia, the Middle East, and Africa on behalf of the Communist Bloc as a whole.

The purposeful offensive in trade, technical assistance, and loans from Moscow and the assertive peregrinations of Soviet leaders in 1955-1958 served to affirm that Moscow in no way intended to turn Communist leadership over to Peking in these decisive regions. Russia remained a major power in Asia, pressed hard into the Middle East, and began to prepare the way for the exercise of power and influence in Africa. The enormous relative advantage of the Soviet Union and its Eastern satellites over Communist China in resources, trading potential, and technicans has been brought to bear at a time when the economic requirements of Communist China might have absorbed a much higher share of the Communist Bloc's exportable surplus than has been made available to it.[4]

However much Peking may dislike this firm assertion of Soviet primacy within the Communist Bloc—even in Burma, Indonesia, and the other areas close on to Chinas' borders—the hard facts of relative military and economic power at this period of history have been accepted. In the meanwhile Peking has maintained its own ties and apparatus of influence in North Korea, North Vietnam, Malaya, Indonesia, and elsewhere, undoubtedly awaiting a day when its proportionate role in the Communist partnership will expand, and hastening that day by applying with skill its bargaining leverage over Moscow to extract not only capital and technical assistance but also modern weapons and high ideological status within the Communist Bloc.

THE SOVIET OFFENSIVE IN PERSPECTIVE

As foreshadowed by the themes of the Nineteenth Party Congress of October 1952, the Soviet Union mounted in 1953 a major offensive designed to exploit to its own ends the problems, aspirations, and moods of the peoples and governments of Asia, the Middle East, and Africa, with excursions into Latin America as well. This offensive was designed to expand Soviet power and influence without the use of military force. The ending of the war in Indochina was, in fact, an important element in the strategy, making more persuasive the image of Communism's peaceful and constructive purposes. The whole operation was based on an assessment which identified the major areas of Asia, the Middle East, and North Africa, excepting Japan, as at a stage of history similar to that in China in the 1920's and exploitable by roughly parallel means over a roughly similar time span.

The offensive has been specifically designed to embarrass and weaken the United States and Western Europe to the maximum in the short run and to lay the basis for Communist takeover in the long run. It has been pursued by a mixture of diplomatic, economic, political, and cultural devices as well as by exploiting such leverage as the local Communist parties could bring to bear. Soviet military policy—projecting the image of increasing virtuosity in science and technology as well as in powers of destruction—served to reinforce the Soviet claim to be regarded as the future leader of Asia, the Middle East, and Africa.

This soft strategy in the underdeveloped areas undoubtedly raised some interesting and difficult questions in Moscow and Peking.[5] Could Communist takeover be envisaged without the massive use of force? After all, it took the combination of civil and external war to lay the basis for the Nationalist disintegration in China; and Communist power had never been achieved elsewhere without major hostilities or physical occupation except in Czechoslovakia, where the threat of occupation operated. And, if force were required to climax the disintegration process envisaged in the new nations, how would the prospective victims then react—and how would the United States? Although these questions could not immediately or easily be answered, the prospects for embarrassing the West and for such limited gains as the political disruption of base areas were sufficiently attractive in 1953-1958 for Moscow to proceed in good heart.

### 40. Soviet Policy Toward Western Europe

Soviet policy toward Western Europe since 1953 has been to encourage European complacency about Soviet intentions while the foundations of Western European strength and influence and the foundations of the North Atlantic Alliance were gradually eroded by the consequences of Soviet military policy and of Soviet policy in Asia, the Middle East, and Africa. Whereas Europe was the primary focus of Stalin's offensive (like the Kaiser's and Hitler's), Europe has been increasingly a secondary objective in Krushchev's hopes and plans.

Immediately after Stalin's death Moscow launched a whole series of pacific gestures, some of which were designed to have a special impact on Western European thought. In a speech of March 16, 1953, before the Supreme Soviet, Malenkov made peace central to the posture of the new regime; and starting at the end of March, the Chinese Communists, backed by Molotov, accepted the United Nations offer to exchange sick and wounded prisoners. Moscow launched discussions with Britain on air safety along the approaches to Berlin; a visit of American newspaper editors to the Soviet Union was organized; Soviet delegates put on a particularly businesslike performance at the East-West trade meetings of the United Nations Economic Commisison for Europe in Geneva. A new willingness to expand contacts between Soviet and Western bureaucrats and intellectuals was indicated; and, above all, there was a massive demonstration of professional good fellowship by Soviet diplomats at a variety of points where they were in contact with the external world.

All this stirred a powerful desire in Western Europe to enter promptly into negotiation with the Soviet Union on the abiding issues of Germany and the control of armaments; and in the summer of 1953 this desire was strongly enhanced by the explosion of the first Soviet fusion weapon.

For the first time since 1949 the four Foreign Ministers were finally brought together in Berlin at the end of January 1954. The three Western Ministers, fearful of some new Soviet flexibility, found Molotov's position on Germany absolutely unchanged. There was every indication that Moscow was prepared to sit tight on the line of the Elbe. The one substantial result of the conference was to force a commitment from the West to meet in April, along with Communist China, on the issues of Korea and Indochina. And over the four subsequent years, at no point did the Soviet Union indicate a willingness to conceive of a German settlement on the basis of free elections. Biding its time patiently against the day when Adenauer would be removed from the scene and Soviet nuclear capabilities would alter the military meaning of NATO, Moscow held out to the West Germans the possibility of a bilateral settlement on the condition that West Germany disassociate itself definitely from the West and accept the East German government as a negotiating partner.

In the meantime, Soviet policy counted on damaging Western European interests, while avoiding the appearance of overt aggression, by maintaining attritional pressure through its association with disruptive forces in Asia, the Middle East, and Africa: on France, in Indochina and North Africa; on Britain, in Malaya and, to a degree, in Cyprus and Greece; and, above all, by its exploitation of the explosive potentialities in the Middle East. This policy paid immediate dividends by increasing the resistance of the bedeviled and overextended French to West German rearmament and by yielding damage to Anglo-American relations, as well as to the oil supply of Western Europe, in the matter of the Suez crisis.

The troubles imposed on Western Europe and on American relations with Western Europe by Communist policy in Asia, the Middle East, and Africa merged with the radical change in the Western European military position as the Soviet main strength shifted from its ground forces poised on the Elbe to a massive delivery capability in weapons of mass destruction. Churchill sensed this change almost immediately upon the explosion of a Soviet fusion weapon in the summer of 1953 and actively sought a summit meeting to see whether the historic convergence of this capability with the aftermath of Stalin's death might make possible a less dangerous form of coexistence. Soviet strategy, however, had been set. In each of its major dimensions—the development of modern weapons, the encouragement and exploitation of disruptive forces in Asia, the Middle East, and Africa, and the attrition of the North Atlantic tie—it moved forward step-by-step.

The limited but real tactical success of Soviet policy down to 1958 was not due primarily to its character or to the skill of its execution. The phase 1953-1958, like the sequence of the Second World War and the events of the early postwar years, is a story of interaction—essentially, of interaction between Moscow and Washington. The Communist strategy, developed in rough outline in 1951-1952, given energy and substance in 1953, and worked out in detail over the following five years, yielded substantial results because American military and foreign policy was not geared to deal with it.

# PART III

# THE EISENHOWER FIRST TERM

### 41. The "Great Equation"

THE REPUBLICAN TAKEOVER

The changes in Moscow in 1953 shifted power to men determined to assert themselves in their release from an overbearing parental figure, anxious to experiment, looking to the future. In Washington the center of gravity of the new American Administration came to rest on men and views focused on the past. Those who gained authority in Moscow in 1953 were reacting against what they regarded as the overly rigid and inflexible policy of Stalin in the postwar years; those who gained authority in Washington were reacting against the changes in American policy engineered over the two previous decades by their predecessors.

Specifically, those who dominated the Republican Party looked to a reduction in the role of the federal government in American life as the necessary condition for retaining the sort of society to which they were attached. For twenty years, in political impotence or active opposition, they had watched the absolute size of federal expenditures rise—first, during the New Deal, then during the Second World War, and finally during the Korean War. Not only had they watched with disapproval and fear the extension of federal powers, along with the expanded welfare and control functions of the state, but also, at times of war and rapid rearmament, they had seen and felt the related dangers of inflation and direct administrative control over prices and raw materials. Above all, it was the aspiration of a substantial group of Republicans to undo these believed evils when political power was regained, and to move American society back toward an older balance between government and private capitalism—and in a wider sense, between government and private life—which they found more congenial.[1] They were convinced that minimum essential American interests could be protected with diminished direct responsibility and at less cost. Further, many Republicans had convinced themselves that the nation's costly military and foreign policy—including the Korean War—was the result of incompetent meddling in the world rather than of an inescapable if belated effort to protect straightforward American interests. With authentic passion, they sought to cut the federal budget, to reduce the scope of federal power in the economy, and to reduce the nation's commitments on the world scene.

Thus in December 1952, when key members of the new Administration gathered for three days on the cruiser *Helena* with Eisenhower en route from Korea, the central task was defined in terms of "the great equation"—how to equate minimum needed military strength with maximum economic strength. Wrestling with this definition of the problem, objectives were defined in the following two categories.[2]

> *In economic policy*: To remove controls as rapidly as possible. To bring down the cost of the federal government by a rigorous extirpation of wasteful and unnecessary services and by removing the government from areas and functions that properly belong to the free market. Thus to balance the budget as soon as possible. To curb excessive credit.

> *For the national security*: To liquidate the Korean War at once, accepting the stalemate. To proceed with a thorough-going examination of the military establishment and of the strategic estimate, as the matter of topmost priority on taking office, in the expectation that great savings would result. Eisenhower made a strong point on the rapid obsolescence of weapons as a result of technical breakthroughs and insisted that military forces and strategy must be reshaped around these new weapons for what he called "the Long Haul."[3]

In human terms this definition of the task emerged from the interplay of three views within the Eisenhower team. First there was the view of what might be called the midwest Republicans. They were not isolationists in the sense that they sought to reverse radically and promptly the existing national commitments beyond the hemisphere; but their minds were strongly colored by isolationist images and conceptions from the past. They did not accept with sympathy and understanding the sequence of modern history which had engaged the United States so deeply around the whole periphery of Eurasia and on the European continent itself. The names of Mahan, Root, Hughes, and Stimson evoked little if anything in their memory or experience.

Second, there was the view of the eastern Republicans who were in part linked to the internationalist Republican tradition but either were committed to respect the midwestern view or shared in some measure its economic presuppositions.

Third, there was the view of the liberal Republicans—mainly responsible for Eisenhower's nomination—who felt that the Truman administration had become sluggish, unimaginative, and excessively defensive in dealing with the nation's military and foreign policy problems and who looked to new programs and initiatives. Although they were eager to explore ways of protecting and advancing the national interest at reduced cost, in their hearts these men did not doubt that the nation could spend more on external affairs without risking capitalism and democracy.

While much of the rhetoric of the Eisenhower first term was fashioned from the conceptions of the third group, the framework of policy was set by the first, holding as they did what Lenin might have called "the commanding heights" within the Executive Branch: Treasury, Defense, and the Budget Bureau. And within these conflicting dispensations of language and money, the second group sought day-to-day compromises which would prevent the gap from becoming overt or excessive.

When the full Cabinet gathered in the Hotel Commodore in New York on January 12, 1953, to hear the President-elect read the draft of his first Inaugural Address, the central themes for discussion were the budget and the rate at which it could be reduced, given the position in which it was left toward the close of the Korean War, and the appropriate timing for the removal of the price and wage controls placed on the economy during the Korean War.

In retrospect, two things are clear about the Administration's conception of the Great Equation. First, "maximum economic strength" was viewed primarily as the maximum degree of freedom for the private sectors of the economy, minimum tax revenues, and hopefully, a relatively stable price level. Other concepts of economic strength occasionally entered into the Administration's thought, e.g., the notion that high levels of output in, say, aluminum, required for the civilian economy, also increased long-run military potential. But, operationally, "strength" was normally equated with minimal administrative intervention by the government over the economy and with reduced taxation.[4] Second, the assumption was initially made that the new military technology would cheapen the costs of military defense. This was a somewhat static conception, in which a kind of once-for-all substitution of nuclear weapon delivery capabilities for manpower was envisaged. This view did not embrace a realistic vision of the costly succession of new weapons systems—each leaving a prompt trail of obsolescence—which was just over the horizon.

Once in power, certain inescapable facts of the world arena in which the nation lived and operated and certain inescapable requirements of national security were respected. But in the formative months, when policy wavered in the councils of the Executive Branch, there was Taft to remind them of the meaning of the Republican victory.

> The President opened the meeting with a statement on foreign affairs and the new military policy. When he had finished, there were explanations of

the new budget and national defense by Humphrey, Dodge, and Kyes. All three pointed out that although the new administration had been in office barely three months, it was already giving a new direction to Federal spending. A beginning, at least, they said, had been made in reducing Truman's budget estimates.

The full import of their words was nevertheless that heavy military spending would continue, that more deficits lay ahead and that the first Republican budget would be out of balance. When this hit Robert A. Taft, he went off like a bomb.

The sedate discussion was rent by his hard, metallic voice. Fairly shouting and banging his fist on the Cabinet table, Taft declared that all the efforts of the Eisenhower Administration to date had merely produced the net result of continued spending on the same scale as the Truman Administration. Unless the inconceivable step of raising taxes was taken, he said, the new budget—the budget for the fiscal year 1954—would carry a large deficit. He denounced the budget total as one that exceeded 20 per cent of the national income, a limit Taft thought high enough.

The President was taken aback as Taft barked out a prediction that the first Eisenhower budget would drive a wedge between the administration and the economy-minded Republicans in Congress and drag the party to defeat in the 1954 elections.

"The one primary thing we promised the American people," he shouted, "was reduction of expenditures. Now you're taking us right down the same road Truman traveled. It's a repudiation of everything we promised in the campaign."

Taft said that he could see no prospect of future reductions so long as emphasis was placed upon military preparedness for which, he said, funds could be spent without limit.[5]

Thus in 1953, as the nation was confronted by the expensive consequences of the revolutionary forces at work in weapons technology and in the underdeveloped areas, its policy was controlled by a powerful and purposeful thrust to reduce the size of the Federal budget.

### 42. Military Policy

STRATEGY AND THE BUDGET

The shape of the Eisenhower Administration's military policy was derived directly from its conception of the Great Equation. The main characteristics of the new strategy were also defined aboard the *Helena*.

A new approach to the economics of national strategy had begun to take root in [Eisenhower's] mind in the course of his Pacific voyage. Part of the germinal idea was supplied by John Foster Dulles, who had accompanied Eisenhower on his *Helena* trip. From his negotiations of the Japanese peace treaty, Dulles had developed the rough outlines of the concept that later became known as the "massive retaliation" doctrine. It was Dulles' theory that all that was militarily required of small nations on the Soviet periphery was indigenous forces strong enough to put down indirect aggression in the form of Communist fomented internal upheavals and screening forces that could hold off external attack long enough to make the aggression clear-cut. So long as the Communist Bloc could not count on a rapid overrunning of peripheral positions Dulles reasoned that the deterrent power of the US atomic advantage would restrain Soviet adventurism.

Eisenhower was impressed by this idea, and in a long conference at Honolulu with the Navy's foremost strategist, Admiral Arthur W. Radford, then Commander-in-chief of the Pacific Fleet, the logic of the underlying strategic economics began to emerge. Secretary of Defense-to-be Charles E. Wilson had already nominated Radford as his choice for the next Chairman of the Joint Chiefs of Staff, and Radford, in his analysis of the general strategic situation, stressed a point that had already been worrying the President. It was that US power was dangerously overextended; too large a fraction of the US power in being had been drawn, as in the Far East, into exposed positions where it could be too easily pinned down. Radford argued for concentrating US striking power as a central reserve within or near the North American continent, depending upon our allies to hold the front lines, and counting, in the event of war, upon superior US mobility for the rapid outward deployment of that reserve along the more profitable axes of counter-attack.

These propositions accorded with Eisenhower's own strategic views.[1]

It will be noted that the Dulles and Radford positions summarized above were not identical. The Dulles doctrine, taken as stated, would have confined the American contribution to the threat and ability to counterattack with atomic weapons, virtually relieving the United States of commitment to prepare to fight on the ground. The Radford doctrine would have envisioned some kind of mobile strategic reserve. This ambiguity—concerning the scale and character of a strategic reserve—proved to be of considerable consequence over subsequent years.[2]

The question of over-all strategy was subjected to one further major re-examination before, as it were, the books were closed and definitive budgetary dispositions made. As a result of a discussion in the White House solarium on May 8, 1953, three study groups were set up to articulate and defend alternative strategies.

The broad choice obviously lay among three general courses of strategy. Course A was to continue on with the Truman containment doctrine. Course B was to draw a line around certain threatened areas—Formosa, Southeast Asia, the Middle East—and to serve notice on the USSR that a violation of these lines would invite general war. Course C was for the US to pass over to the initiative and subject Russia to intense political and economic pressure.

Eisenhower's method of resolving the dilemma was characteristic. Cutler was instructed to set up three different task forces to examine the feasibility of the different postulates. Each was to be led, on the President's order, by a fervent 'advocate.' Interestingly, the expert nominated to present the case for Course A—containment—was its author, George F. Kennan, one-time director of the State Department's Policy Planning Staff. An Air Force general and a Navy admiral were given the briefs for the other strategies. The famous Lieutenant General "Jimmy" Doolittle, a vice president of Shell Oil and an independent and courageous thinker whom the President has since used in many like inquiries of the highest importance, was made chairman of still another group of thinkers who laid down for each task force the bounds of the problem it was to study. The task forces then disappeared into the secluded precincts of the National War College and for several intense weeks they each developed their case for the competitive strategies.

In July the case for each of the three possible courses of action was presented by the individual task force commanders, in turn, to the President and his advisers. From the development of US policy, thereafter, it is fairly self-evident that the strategic course finally decided upon was a compromise of A and B; more containment, but with gaping holes in Southeast Asia and the Middle East to be plugged with new strategic alliances. (This became Foster Dulles' job.) Out of the total study also came a strong recommendation that US military policy be reshaped around atomic weapons.[3]

The strategy of the Eisenhower administration thus emerged with three key operating objectives: to maintain the power to deter Soviet military strength with American nuclear delivery capabilities while shifting an increasing proportion of American striking power to nuclear weapons; to complete the ring of military alliances around the Communist Bloc; and to shift an increasing proportion of the burden for maintaining ground forces on to Eurasian allies. The three dimensions of this strategy defined the hard core of policy not only in the Department of Defense but also in the Department of State and in the foreign aid agencies (MSA and the ICA) over the four subsequent years.

Although presented in somewhat different terms, this strategy represented an effort to tidy up, to institutionalize, and to fix for the long pull the programs evolved in the Truman administration. There was the same primary reliance on the retaliatory power of the Strategic Air Command which had dominated the pre-Korean War days; there was a rather mechanical extension of the device of military pacts to Eurasian states outside NATO, backed by military and economic aid programs, which had marked the latter months of the Truman administration; and there was the same fixation in Europe on German rearmament within a multilateral framework which had marked American policy when Soviet intentions were reappraised after the outbreak of the Korean War.

The evolution of national security policy is roughly reflected in Table 3, showing expenditures from 1950 through 1958 (fiscal years).[4]

Since the national security budget over these years was presented on an

TABLE 3. FEDERAL BUDGET EXPENDITURES ON NATIONAL SECURITY, 1950-1959
(*in billions of dollars*)

| Budget Expenditures: | 1950 | 1951 | 1952 | 1953 | 1954 | 1955 | 1956 | 1957 | 1958 | 1959 |
|---|---|---|---|---|---|---|---|---|---|---|
| Major national security: | | | | | | | | | | |
| 051 Direction and coordination of defense | 10 | 12 | 13 | 15 | 12 | 13 | 14 | 14 | 21 | 215 |
| 052 Air Force defense | 3,600 | 6,349 | 12,709 | 15,085 | 15,668 | 16,407 | 16,749 | 18,363 | 18,441 | 18,736 |
| 053 Army defense | 3,987 | 7,469 | 15,635 | 16,242 | 12,910 | 8,899 | 8,702 | 9,063 | 9,043 | 8,880 |
| 054 Navy defense | 4,103 | 5,582 | 10,162 | 11,875 | 11,293 | 9,733 | 9,744 | 10,398 | 10,640 | 10,913 |
| 055 Other central defense activities | 192 | 353 | 379 | 394 | 452 | 481 | 582 | 602 | 716 | 830 |
| 056 Development and control of atomic energy | 550 | 897 | 1,670 | 1,791 | 1,895 | 1,857 | 1,651 | 1,990 | 2,300 | 2,550 |
| 057 Stockpiling and defense production expansion | 438 | 793 | 966 | 1,008 | 1,045 | 944 | 588 | 490 | 565 | 422 |
| 058 Mutual defense assistance: | | | | | | | | | | |
| military assistance | 130 | 991 | 2,442 | 3,954 | 3,629 | 2,292 | 2,611 | 2,352 | 2,200 | 2,200 |
| defense support | — | — | 1,987 | 1,467 | 967 | 1,463 | 1,184 | 1,143 | 945 | 885 |
| Proposed civilian personnel pay adjustment (proposed supplemental) | — | — | — | — | — | — | — | — | — | 205 |
| Total, major national security | 13,009 | 22,444 | 45,963 | 51,830 | 47,872 | 42,089 | 41,825 | 44,414 | 44,871 | 45,836 |
| International affairs and finance: | | | | | | | | | | |
| 151 Conduct of foreign affairs | 198 | 190 | 142 | 150 | 130 | 121 | 120 | 157 | 193 | 201 |
| 152 Economic and technical development | 4,442 | 3,506 | 598 | 493 | 543 | 498 | 431 | 542 | 1,133 | 973 |
| 153 Foreign information and exchange activities | 35 | 40 | 99 | 106 | 91 | 100 | 111 | 133 | 141 | 139 |
| Total, international affairs and finance | 4,674 | 3,736 | 839 | 749 | 765 | 719 | 662 | 832 | 1,468 | 1,312 |

institutional rather than a functional (or program) basis, it is difficult to isolate some of the major changes in the allocation of resources for security purposes—for example, consolidated outlays on air defense, missiles,[5] and research and development. Certain principal features, nevertheless, stand out: the Korean War bulge; the rise of the Air Force budget relative to those of the other services; the successful Navy acquisition of new functions through its ability to deliver nuclear weapons from aircraft carriers, missile ships, and, foreseeably, nuclear-powered submarines; the budgetary hard times experienced by the Army; the high level of post-Korea defense assistance and defense support; the low level of allocations for economic and technical development.

And perhaps, above all, one can observe in these figures the ardent hopes and dour intent that the security budget decline meeting defeat in the face of stubborn facts as the drop after the Korean war gives way to a slow, reluctant rise in fiscal 1957, a budget formulated toward the end of 1955.

### CONTINUITY: PRE-KOREA AND POST-KOREA

The military budgets and figures in the post-Korea period give a limited and somewhat misleading insight into the character of the forces that were at work on the nation's security position. The administration apparently concluded that it was unsafe to return to a pre-Korea military establishment, setting its new sights at a level of forces about 80 per cent of the Korean peak. The Army, which had been more greatly enlarged than the other services to deal with the Korean War, bore the brunt of the 20 per cent over-all post-Korea cutbacks. The Air Force continued its steady tendency to expand relative to the other services. By the close of 1954 it had 121 active wings, almost three times its pre-Korea peak; and, as compared with early 1950, the Navy had about doubled, with something like 11,000 ships in operation. As a first approximation one might say that the nation had simply concluded that the scale of its preparedness before Korea had been faulty, and that what was required was that the nation maintain on a stable basis a military establishment about twice the size judged necessary in 1947-1950.

Indeed, in some respects the nation did treat the Korean War as if it were a temporary, extremely painful, but relatively normal incident in a continuing security crisis like, for example, the Berlin airlift; and, having dealt with it, the nation returned to a kind of normal semimobilized military posture, with special emphasis on measures designed to avoid a repetition of the Korean experience.

As one reads the reports of the Secretaries of Defense, Army, Navy, and Air Force in the period 1953-1956, a considerable degree of continuity with the period 1947-1950 emerges. Secretary of Defense Wilson, in accents hardly to be distinguished from those of Johnson, discusses the dilemma of defending the nation without bankrupting it over the long pull. Wilson merely applies a higher but equally arbitrary budgetary measure for the maximum price the nation "can afford" for military security. The Secretary of the Army reports with barely concealed pain the gallant manner in which he has overseen the cutting back of divisional strength in order to save money, finding occasion, nevertheless, to reaffirm the dictum that the infantryman will never be superseded (even in the new age of tactical atomic weapons, including the army's cannon). The Secretary of the Navy emphasizes the nation's continued reliance on control of the seas (as well as the Navy's increased virtuosity with devices designed to maintain the Navy's position in the age of atomic weapons); while (with an increased acknowledgment of the importance of air defense) the Secretary of the Air Force reports the build-up of the Strategic Air Command and the decisive importance of the American capability to deliver an overwhelming retalitatory atomic blow against its possible enemy.

### THE NEW SITUATION

Nevertheless, beneath the surface of slightly modified continuity in concept and of simple enlargement in scale there was a radical difference in the American military position pre- and post-Korea. The Soviet hydrogen bomb was exploded in August 1953, roughly one month after the signing of the Korean truce; and this event symbolizes the two respects in which the post-Korea phase has a special character. It was marked, first, by an open acknowledgment by political leaders and the professional military that the new weapons of war could, if delivered, by themselves bring about not merely a military decision but also, in some sense, permanent damage to the societies attacked. The scientists' postwar assertions to this effect and the layman's instinctive sense that war had changed its character at Hiroshima became an increasingly acknowledged technical and political fact both in the Soviet Union and in the United States. And that fact profoundly affected the political and psychological mood of peoples everywhere.

Simultaneously, this period was dominated by a second major characteristic —an acceleration of the race in new weapons brought about, on the American side, by the evidence of a progressive narrowing in the gap between Soviet and American technology in the key weapons of atomic war, notably in the ballistic missiles race. From 1945 to 1953 Soviet and American scientists and technicians absorbed the German V-2 and began to move beyond on their own at the level of research and development. In both countries the effort accelerated in 1953, moving from about 1955 into a phase when operational ballistic missiles of medium and long range became first a planning and then a foreseeable production reality. These developments had profound implications for air defense, the deterrence and conduct of limited war, and the meaning of secrecy both within the United States and as between the United States and its major allies. They also colored the nation's basic psychological and political—as well as military—relations with the governments and peoples of Asia, the Middle East, and Africa, as well as of Europe. The situation evidently called for important innovational steps over the whole range of military and foreign policy.

### THE PENTAGON ADMINISTRATIVE SETTING

The nation's performance in the tasks of military innovation was strongly colored in the years 1953-1957 by the character of administration in the Department of Defense. Following the doctrine that the Pentagon primarily needed more efficient and businesslike management, the Secretary of Defense was drawn from the nation's largest business firm. Along with Humphrey, Dodge, and Weeks, Wilson "formed the hard core of the 'hard-money,' cut-spending-to-the-bone school of thought; with them a balanced budget and lower taxes had become almost a point of personal honor."[6] Although Wilson lacked (and was not expected to acquire) any profound grasp on the strategic problems of the nation, it was believed that he would bring to bear the skills of a hard-handed, experienced administrator. Large savings in procurement were expected to follow.

An extensive re-examination of the Pentagon organization was undertaken in 1953 by a committee on defense organization. Its recommendations, largely accepted, placed in the hands of the Secretary of Defense increased (or less ambiguous) powers. Wilson's administration emerged, however, with some forty civilian assistants at the level of assistant secretary or secretary. Their appointment was designed to make sure that all aspects of policy were screened through civilian minds imbued with the Administration's budgetary objectives. It proved impossible to recruit and to hold a substantial proportion of able men in these posts. As a result, virtually all aspects of Department of Defense business were complicated and slowed down at a time when the character and pace of decisions in the field of research and development profoundly affected the course of the arms race.

The administrative characteristics of Wilson's period at the Pentagon bore with special weight on the process of innovation. Wilson himself lacked any direct experience of the complex process whereby new weapons systems evolved from basic scientific ideas through the graduated stages of research and development into first-line strength. He came from a middle-aged industry—unlike, for example, chemicals or electronics—where the fundamental engineering breakthroughs lay in the distant past; and among the leaders in the automobile industry Wilson was less interested than some in the operational role of basic research.

A second basic weakness in the Pentagon arose from the fact that the Secretary of Defense and his civilian assistants were incapable of developing and imposing an independent concept of strategy sufficiently precise and firm to guide budgetary allocations to the services on the basis of functions performed.[7] The post-1945 tendency of military policy to emerge in the form of budgetary compromises as among the individually developed strategic plans of the three services, achieved after brutal internecine strife, increased. Lacking a substantive grip on the problems of defense, the crude budgetary ceiling remained the last residual method of civilian control.

It may have been hoped in the early days of the Administration that the President, an experienced man of military affairs, would operate in effect as his own Secretary of Defense, with Wilson as an administrative chief of staff; but Eisenhower did not employ such direct exercise of presidential authority except when forced by acute crisis, as, for example, the issue of American intervention in Indochina.

The new Pentagon Administration's inherent weakness in innovation was accentuated to some degree by a deterioration in relations between the government as a whole and the scientific community. The climax of this process was the withdrawal of security clearance to Robert Oppenheimer in 1954 on evidence which had altered in no significant respect since his postwar clearance in 1947. This painful incident, leaving scars on all involved in it, tended to make more difficult a fruitful association of the scientific community with the government—especially at the highest levels of strategic decision—at a period of marked acceleration of innovation in military technology.

Thus a situation which to some extent had deteriorated in the Truman administration, as compared to that during the Second World War, grew distinctly worse.

Such vitality as was maintained in military policy was generated primarily from within each of the three services, which, on the whole, maintained reasonable working relations with the nation's pool of breakthrough talent in science and technology. Hampered by acute budgetary limitations, and subject to a civilian command which was incapabale of designing any coherent general plan, each service struggled to maintain a maximum claim on the budget, notably in those categories to which the Administration was primarily committed—the weapons of mass destruction, the means of delivery, and the means of defense.

In this struggle the Air Force managed to increase its relative status and the Navy to hold its ground, but the Army underwent a steady attrition. As in the interwar years and the pre-Korean War period, budgetary limitations imposed without reference to any coherent military plan led to a disproportionate decline in allocations for basic research and development, the bureaucratic instinct being to maintain overhead establishments and fighting forces in being and to allocate risks to the future—an instinct which converged partially with the operational instincts of the Secretary of Defense.[8]

One strongly stated impression of the Pentagon's operations in this stage—but one well supported by other testimony—is Trevor Gardner's evaluation of the missile program in the spring of 1956, a year and a half before the launching of the first Soviet satellite:

1. The Army, the Navy, and the Air Force, each working on its own parochial guided-missiles program, are vying with each other in an intolerable rivalry.

2. The over-all missiles program is smothering in an administrative nightmare of committees and subcommittees competing with each other for influence and appropriations.

3. The ICBM project, which two and a half years ago was given a top-priority status, now shares top priority with many subsidiary missiles projects and the result is that there is no such thing as "top priority."

4. The executive personnel of the missiles program is notable for its preponderance of management experts recruited from private business, and for its poverty of full-time scientists who qualify as missiles experts and know what they're talking about.[9]

The Wilson administration of the Pentagon, characterized on the one hand by an obsession with budgetary objectives and on the other by a stubborn indifference to the significance of basic research and development, did not stop the process of innovation in American military technology; but it slowed that process at a critical time.

AIR DEFENSE

From the moment that the Soviet Union acquired atomic weapons and capabilities for delivering them, American military planners had been concerned with the problem of defense against air attack on the United States. After three years, and after study by a considerable array of expert panels, the decision was made in the course of 1952-1953 to develop an extensive system of continental air defense including the erection of a distant early warning line in the far north. But it was a decision made only after an extremely bitter debate.

Since the basic objective of the Strategic Air Command and of American military policy in general was to deter the Soviet Union from risking all-out war, it could be argued that, so far as deterrence was concerned, air defense added little to the American position. Even a very expensive air defense might not prevent the penetration of attacking bombers and the delivery of a substantial number of atomic weapons against the United States. Those who viewed the matter in this light argued not only that a concentration of attention and resources on air defense would add only marginally to the protection of the United States but also that it would draw resources away from the real goal, which was the continued deterrence of all-out war by a steadily enlarged and improved Strategic Air Command. They held, in short, that extra resources added to offensive power had a vastly greater positive effect on the nation's security than the application of these resources to air defense, their underlying assumptions being that air defense would have no significant deterrent effect, that the resources and energy going into air defense would compete with those available to SAC, and that a massive defense effort would generate in the public mind an incorrect concept of the problem of security.

Dominant elements in or associated with the Air Force sponsored a series of attacks on air defense advocates on the grounds that they were Maginot Line-minded and insufficiently tough in the face of the Soviet threat.

This was an unfair and misleading assault, but it stemmed from very real fears which had their roots in the Pentagon obsession with budgetary considerations. Those responsible for the Air Force felt that an increase in allocations for air defense would inevitably result in decreased (absolute or relative) allocations for the Stratgeic Air Command. Almost without exception, advocates of air defense took the view that it ranked second in American military priorities to the maintenance of the striking capability of SAC. But there was an honest fear among Air Force leaders that the existing Defense Department administration was incapable of allocating the limited relatively fixed pool of military resources in such a way as to give to these two Air Force functions, attack and defense, first and second priority. They felt that the proposed air defense system would have the effect of weakening the build-up of SAC, the maintenance of whose capabilities they regarded as the prime requirement for the nation's security.

The advocates of air defense, besides arguing that, with sufficient expenditure (and the new scientific possibilities for defense unfolded by Project Lincoln), a considerable degree of protection might be afforded, offered three arguments to support the view that air defense was an integral part of the deterrence process.

First, air defense was required to minimize the likely damage to American air bases and was therefore an instrument for helping to guarantee that the United States would maintain a capability for decisive counterattack.

Second, air defense acquired a more general deterrent importance if it could achieve the capability of holding damage from surprise enemy air attack within limits which would still leave American society with sufficient resources and organization to recover and, particularly, to maintain the continuity of attack with SAC and with other necessary instruments of war.

Third, there was a case for air defense on psychological grounds. The whole power struggle short of all-out war, including the most correct formal diplomacy, was being conducted in the shadow of atomic war. If the nation felt that it lay unprotected in the face of Soviet attack and that its only satisfaction in a major war was likely to lie in the knowledge that the Soviet Union might be equally devastated, the nation might be bluffed into accepting a series of limited setbacks which in the end would add up to the loss of the balance of power in Eurasia and, in effect, to clean-cut American defeat. In short, the maintenance of the nation's deterrent power was judged to hinge in part on avoiding a popular sense of complete exposure to enemy attack.

In the end, these three distinct but related considerations triumphed.

The decision to create an air defense against Soviet bombers had an important organizational consequence. Aspects of air defense lay in the hands of the Army and Navy as well as the Air Force, and the logic of this fact led to the setting up of a functional task force, the Continental Air Defense Command, directly under the Joint Chiefs of Staff. This innovation, which faced the fact that modern technology did not break down along old service lines —each with a natural element to control—stimulated thought on how the Defense Department might be reorganized; and it influenced the many proposals for military reorganization presented in 1958, which looked to operational task forces as the prime instrument for organizing national defense.

### LONG-RANGE MISSILES

The decision to proceed with a major air defense organization against attack by bombing aircraft was made at a time when the potentialities of long-range ballistic missiles were beginning to emerge, and they were expected to be operationally significant by about 1960.

Unlike the Soviet missile effort, which was placed under the unified control of a special ministry, the American effort was undertaken on virtually a competitive basis by the three services, whose enterprises were only loosely coordinated when they were coordinated at all. The missiles programs, perhaps more than any other, suffered from the policy and administrative outlook of the Department of Defense over the period 1953-1958. The technical form this disadvantage assumed was a markedly longer lead time in American than in Soviet military technology; that is, the period from invention to operational strength was relatively extended in the United States. Assuming the availability of high scientific and technological competence, this interval is substantially determined by the way decisions are made. As Dr. Karman pointed out in the context of the missile program:

> A great deal of so-called lead time is taken up in persuading the next higher command to proceed with a project. For example, the Air Force scientific

office may give out a research contract. But after the research is completed, it may take as long as two years to persuade the responsible command to build a prototype.[10]

While attitudes towards basic research and the administrative process undoubtedly slowed the American missile effort as compared to that of the Soviet Union, it should also be noted that the position of the Soviet Union and the United States with respect to missiles was not wholly symmetrical. Two factors in particular would in any case have made it somewhat more difficult for the United States than for the Soviet Union to launch an all-out drive for ballistic missiles of long and medium range. First, there was the existence of the Strategic Air Command. Here was a force in being whose capabilities were being expanded with the acquisition of new aircraft, which was currently doing the job of deterring major war, and which, from all estimates, was likely to continue to do it for some years. 1960—the expected earliest operational date for long-range ballistic missiles—seemed far away in 1953. Thinking along such lines tended to inhibit American planners from plunging without reservation into long-range missiles because of their commitments to an older weapons system. Meanwhile, the Soviet Union enjoyed the same kind of advantage in this area as that exploited by the German over the French army between the wars in adopting *blitzkrieg* tactics—the advantage of starting (in the particular area of long-range nuclear weapons delivery) more nearly from scratch.

A second factor may have made it more natural for the Soviet Union than for the United States to move wholeheartedly into the missiles field. For the Soviet Union, lacking a mature Strategic Air Command, and anxious to increase the vulnerability of Western Europe and of American bases around the periphery of the Communist Bloc, the development of missiles of intermediate range—in fact, of virtually any range over the V-2's 150-200 miles—represented a significant net military advantage.[11] This meant that it made good sense to move out from the V-2 to missiles of gradually increasing range. And there is every reason to believe that this is precisely what the Soviet missile project did. The IRBM, with a range of about 1500 miles, must have seemed peculiarly attractive to Soviet planners since it would bring virtually the whole range of Free World strength in Eurasia within range of attack. Thus, although the ICBM involves immensely more difficult (and in some respects quite different) problems than the IRBM, the Soviet Union was able to approach the ICBM against the background of an extremely solid effort at the level of the IRBM, which by 1956 had already become an important weapon in Soviet diplomatic and psychological as well as military strategy.

To the United States—a distant island off the continent of Eurasia—the ICBM was evidently an extremely important weapon for the long run; but, from a narrow national perspective, the IRBM was not, unless one were to assume the very marked Soviet lead which, in fact, did emerge. The IRBM was, of course, a weapon of great significance for the nation's Eurasian allies; but in making costly dispositions of scientific talent and resources, under severe budgetary pressure, it was easy for Americans to slight the IRBM stage; and, in turn, this meant that the decision to go for the extremely complex ICBM was more difficult and riskier than it would otherwise have been.

In the up-shot, then, American rocketry made large strides in the period 1953-1958 on a diffuse basis; but it fell several years behind the Soviet effort. Budgetary policy, attitudes towards research and development, concepts and methods of administration, and the inherent nature of the American, as opposed to the Soviet, strategic position all played some part in the outcome; but information is not now sufficient to weigh with confidence the role of each of these factors. One thing may be said, however, with confidence. There was a gross failure of understanding and imagination concerning the worldwide political and psychological consequences of permitting a substantial Soviet lead in medium and long-range ballistic missiles and concerning the quite specific consequences of such a development for the maintenance of unity, morale, and effective American leadership within the North Atlantic alliance.

### INFORMATION AT HOME AND ABROAD

Military policy and diplomacy in 1953-1956 were affected also by the essentially negative response of the Eisenhower Administration to two major moves recommended to it soon after assuming power.[12] In order to explore the problems and feasibility of international armaments control under circumstances where the Soviet Union had developed full nuclear capabilities, Acheson appointed a special committee in 1952 which worked in secret down to the turn of the year.[13] Three of its major conclusions were incorporated, with official permission, in an article by Oppenheimer in *Foreign Affairs* of July 1953.[14]

This paraphrase of the Committee's conclusions argued first that the American public be more fully informed of the character of the arms race which was developing, including the foreseeable capabilities for mutual destruction. The first requirement, Oppenheimer said,

> . . . is candor—candor on the part of the officials of the United States Government to the officials, the representatives, the people of their country. We do not operate well when the important facts, the essential conditions, which limit and determine our choices are unknown. We do not operate well when they are known, in secrecy and in fear, only to a few men. . . . Many arguments have been advanced against making public this basic

information. Some of these arguments had merit in times past. One is that we might be giving vital information to the enemy. My own view is that the enemy has this information. It is available to anyone who will trouble to make an intelligent analysis of what has been published. Private citizens do not do this; but we must expect that the enemy does. It is largely available by other means as well. It is also my view that it is good for the peace of the world if the enemy knows these basic facts—very good indeed, and very dangerous if he does not.

There is another source of worry—that public knowledge of the situation might induce in this country a mood of despair, or a too ready acceptance of what is lightheartedly called preventive war. I believe that until we have looked this tiger in the eye, we shall be in the worst of all possible dangers, which is that we may back into him. More generally, I do not think a country like ours can in any real sense survive if we are afraid of our people.

As a first step, but a great one, we need the courage and the wisdom to make public at least what, in all reason, the enemy must now know: to describe in rough but authoritative and quantitative terms what the atomic armaments race is. It is not enough to say, as our government so often has, that we have made "substantial progress." When the American people are responsibly informed, we may not have solved, but we shall have a new freedom to face, some of the tough problems that are before us.

The second recommendation—which correctly foreshadowed the implication for NATO of Soviet missile delivery capabilities—was for increased technical collaboration within the alliance, including the giving of essential information to Canada and certain European allies:

There is also need for candor in our dealings with at least our major allies. The Japanese are exposed to atomic bombardment; and it may be very hard to develop adequate countermeasures. Space, that happy asset of the United States, is not an asset for Japan. It is not an asset for France. It is not an asset for England. There are in existence methods of delivery of atomic weapons which present an intractable problem of interception, and which are relevant for the small distances that characterize Europe. It will be some time at least before they are relevant for intercontinental delivery. These countries will one day feel a terrible pinch, when the USSR chooses to remind them of what it can do, and do very easily—not without suffering, but in a way that the Europeans themselves can little deter or deflect.

There have been arguments for technical collaboration with the United Kingdom and Canada; these have often appeared persuasive. There have been arguments for military collaboration with the NATO governments, and with the responsible commanders involved. General Bradley and General Collins both have spoken of this need, partly in order to explain to our allies that an atomic bomb will not do all things—that it has certain capabilities but it is not the whole answer. This is surely a precondition for effective planning, and for the successful defense of Europe.

Yet there are much more general reasons. We and our allies are in this long struggle together. What we do will affect the destiny of Europe; what is done there will affect ours; and we cannot operate wisely if a large half of the problem we have in common is not discussed in common. This does not mean that we should tie our hands. It means that we should inform and consult. This could make a healthy and perhaps very great change in our relations with Europe.[15]

These recommendations were not lightly set aside, but they were, in fact, both rejected.

The question of undertaking a program of expanded public information on the arms race was debated on and off within the administration during most of 1953.[16] In the end, "Operation Candor," as it was called, was converted into the Atoms for Peace proposal presented by the President before the United Nations Assembly on December 8, 1953, immediately after the Bermuda Conference. This constructive initiative, although accompanied by ample indications of the capabilities for mutual destruction inherent in the new weapons, did not provide the American public an adequate insight into the evolving shape of the arms race and its implications both for American military security and American diplomacy. That gap was not filled until the outpouring of evidence and reports after the successful Soviet launching of its satellites in October-November 1957—and then it was not adequately filled.

The reasons advanced within the Administration for deflecting the original purpose of Operation Candor are by no means wholly clear from the public record. They certainly included the view that frank authoritative report on the race in modern weapons might frighten the American public and lead to either despair or pressure for desperate action. They certainly included the view that the facts were likely to stir irresistible pressure for an expansion of the military budget judged by the Administration to be incompatible with the good health of the economy and the basic institutions of the society.

But there was more than these *ad hoc* arguments reflected in Robert Cutler's authoritative exposition of the Administration's view.

> Since mid-1953, some people high in our Government were favoring the formal release to the American people of more facts as to the effect of the atomic weapons. This course was pressed by some scientists. The thesis was that the American people could take bad news: officially apprised of facts already speculated upon in the press, they would be more self-reliant, more understanding, more ready to bear the costs of defense. This thesis was today's version of the World War II concept that the best soldier was the best informed soldier. Things progressed as far as the sketching out of an operation known as CANDOR.
>
> But other and, I think, wiser counsels prevailed. We had fallen into the error of thinking rather exclusively of but one of the unseen audiences . . . the American people. It was safe enough to tell them of the then deficiencies in our continental early warning system and in our ability to defend against atomic attack. Surely, the American people could take it. But we had failed

to count fully the other costs: the resulting alarm to our allies and to the neutrals, the deepened despair of the subjugated peoples, the glee in Moscow—perhaps even an intensified risk of attack upon a homeland that was then deficient in defense.

. . . There is another seamlessness in our complex world: the fabric of our national defense. Perhaps the most potent argument against public disclosure of secret projects or of short-falls (which inevitably always exist) in any one aspect of our national defense is that such disclosure build up a Potomac propaganda war to rectify that defect or over-finance that project. But if you devote larger resources to one area of national defense, you are apt to imbalance the rest.[17]

The basic assumption here is that it was both possible and wise to conduct military policy within a democracy which was caught up in a life-and-death struggle and which was committed to lead half the world without informing Americans and the citizens of allied democracies what it was they faced and without sharing with them the character of the choices being made in their name.

Similarly, the Administration rejected the proposal to seek in the Congress to change the terms on which information might be supplied on atomic weapons to the nation's major allies. Those who opposed this course argued that a rigid denial to others of what were regarded as the nation's secrets was essential to national security;[18] and the opposition carried the day. This view was significantly altered only in 1957-1958—and then only with respect to Britain—despite the evidence that much information classified in the United States was already in the hands of the Soviet Union; in spite of the predominant view among scientists that in certain important areas secrecy was vastly less important than the pace at which information and concepts were translated into usable weapons; despite the nation's evident need for strengthening in research and development in military technology which Western Europe could afford on a partnership basis; and despite the evidence (already painfully familiar to Eisenhower in 1953 from his SHAPE experience) that denial to NATO of knowledge of atomic weapons was helping cause a most serious corrosion of the Alliance.

## LIMITED AND BRUSHFIRE WAR

The second great issue for military policy raised by strategy of the Eisenhower Administration was the issue of limited war, that is, of war limited consciously in three dimensions—terrain, weapons, and objectives.

As the Soviet Union evidently acquired major capabilities in atomic weapons, means of delivery, and means of defense, it became increasingly likely that the two great powers would succeed in making it mutually irrational to employ their full nuclear strength. Nevertheless, it was clear that there would still be situations where Moscow and Peking might seek to expand their area of control by military means under circumstances where it would be against the American interest to employ fully the retaliatory power of SAC. Indeed, precisely this had happened in the Korean War. The initial military conception, crystallized out on the *Helena* from the somewhat divergent reflections of Dulles and Radford, was not only that the United States would encourage nations around the periphery of the Communist Bloc to expand their own military forces but also that the United States would concentrate a reserve of some kind against the possibility of limited war. To a degree this policy was implemented; but the reserve which emerged was mainly an air and naval force overwhelmingly committed to the use of atomic weapons and capable of intervening with military and political success only under extremely narrow circumstances.

The Radford reserve conception (as opposed to pure "massive retaliation") posed a searching test of thought and policy about the future of the Army. In the first postwar decade the official doctrine of the American Army was centered not around a reserve force at instant readiness for limited combat but around the classic possibility—rooted in Hamilton's and Washington's prescriptions—that the United States might become involved in a major war to be fought with very large infantry and artillery formations. According to that doctrine the function of the Army was to maintain in being a limited professional establishment which was geared for rapid expansion. That is, the Army establishment was to be essentially the nucleus for large-scale mobilization. This had been the nation's—and the Army's—experience not only in the First and Second World Wars but also, to an important degree, in Korea. This was a conception quite different from that of a mobile reserve prepared to move promptly in support of local forces at any point around the periphery of the Communist Bloc where these allied forces might be challenged by Communist military strength.

Quite apart from the possibility of another substantial if limited engagement such as Korea, there was the possibility of limited war of a lesser order: that is, engagements fought against local native Communist or Communist-dominated armies rather than against organized formations which had entered non-Communist areas across frontiers. In fact, a good deal of the Free World's post-1945 military experience had been with what came to be called brush-fire wars. This was the case with the Greek civil war, the British struggle against the guerrillas in the Malayan jungle, and Magsaysay's successful deflation of the "Huk" (Hukbalahap) insurrection in the Philippines. In addition, the American role in rebuilding the armed forces of South Korea and (after the Geneva Conference of 1945) of Southern Vietnam, as well as helping earlier to strengthen the Italian militia, reflected an awareness of this form of internal military invasion. The American participation in these enterprises—shot through with nonmilitary problems, and conducted with nonnuclear weapons—was undertaken, however, on an emergency basis as special jobs. They were not officially conceived as a major long-range function of the American military.

Two factors in the post-1953 period, however, tended to justify fresh thought and planning for brushfire war. In the first place, there was the disconcerting experience in Indochina, where, despite the American warning in 1953 that an increase in Communist supplies to the Vietminh after the Korean truce would be taken as a hostile act, the United States watched impatiently while the French, backed by American money and diplomacy, failed to deal with the expanded Vietminh effort and were forced at the Geneva Conference in 1954 to surrender to communism the northern half of the country. A political policy capable of making American intervention effective was lacking; a naval and air task force armed with nuclear weapons was an instrument of doubtful effectiveness; and a mobile Army-Marine force organized to operate effectively on the ground did not exist. Events in Indochina clearly represented a pattern which, if repeated on a sufficient scale, could lose the balance of power in Asia, the Middle East, and Africa.

Second, a contemplation of the problems and risks of crossing frontiers with Soviet or Chinese Communist formations gave many professional soldiers little confidence that such engagements could be limited. Thus, as the American military examined the possible patterns of Soviet aggression, they came to conclude that the Free World might be challenged by the progressive erosion of the political and social fabric of various areas through subversion, and that such development might be climaxed by limited military operations in which it would be the American interest to take a hand. The problem of brushfire war, at the lower end of the spectrum of force, evidently could not be solved by aircraft carriers launching aircraft armed with nuclear weapons.

The concept of limited war gained force for another and more parochial reason. As the Army came to re-examine its functions after the development of fusion weapons, it came increasingly to accept the idea that, should all-out war come, there would be a relatively small role, if indeed any role, to be played by infantry; and if, in addition, one assumed that major ground-force engagements on the European continent were tantamount to major war and that a major engagement against China would be primarily a function of naval and air power, a serious question arose as to the nature of the Army's combat mission—if indeed a mission still existed. The younger and more enterprising among American ground force soldiers turned their thoughts to this residual, limited kind of engagement. While Ridgway's unsuccessful efforts to maintain the Army were still couched mainly in the classic mold—envisioning the possibility of large-scale ground force operations—Maxwell Taylor's period as Chief of Staff (starting in July 1955) saw an increasingly explicit acknowledgement that the central mission of the Army might well be in limited engagements of either the Korean or brushfire variety.

Ironically, during the first postwar decade the Marine Corps, the American military formation classically suited to this form of enterprise, was not in a mood to contemplate this job as its principal mission. In the course of the island war in the Pacific the Marines had undertaken major ground force operations and had developed from regimental to divisional units. They had clung to their new status in major ground force engagements and to their new organizational structure as both the symbol and substance of a relative rise in stature in the military hierarchy. Marine organization was a major technical issue in the unification debate of 1945-1947; and the Marines gained their point. Having won its new status, the Marine Corps was not eager to rethink and regroup in terms of the limited, awkward problems of guerrilla operations and the smaller military units involved in them. In terms of institutional Marine history, this was regarded as a retrograde step. Only in 1958 did Marine thought and training begin to reflect seriously the probable primacy of brushfire operations on the Marine agenda.

The work going forward in the field of brushfire war was mainly at two levels. First, in the armed forces journals, the war colleges, and the higher staffs the issue of brushfire was widely studied and discussed; and the problem received considerable public attention in 1957-1958. Second, within the Army there was considerable effort made to develop the kinds of equipment and operating tactics necessary for limited engagements of this kind. The Eisenhower administration, however, faced with the unyielding and costly pressure of the race in new weapons, continued to cut Army allocations and, down to 1958, never wholeheartedly accepted the necessity for deterring or preparing to fight limited engagements of the brushfire order with a highly mobile task force.

Moreover, there persisted in the development of brushfire war concepts and tactics a missing element—an understanding of the role of nonmilitary factors in the military outcome. Since brushfire wars can be mounted only in areas where there has been for some time a progressive deterioration in the fabric of organized society, the process of winning a brushfire war involves the development of an effective and appealing political program in addition to appropriate military operations. The connection is not merely abstract and ideological; it is technical. Brushfire wars are civil wars fought in small units over the homeland of the citizenry concerned. If the average citizen is sympathetic to one side or the other, he can render invaluable military service

—supplying food and intelligence, resisting actively or passively the side to which he is opposed. It is difficult if not impossible to win a brushfire war against the sentiments of the average citizen without an overwhelming occupation force. The basis for any sensible military doctrine lay, then, in the political and psychological setting in which military operations would be conducted.

More than that, of course, the first lesson of brushfire war is that it is the prime duty of civil foreign policy to be so conducted as to prevent the creation of conditions which make its outbreak possible. The outbreak of a brushfire war in the Free World is a *prima facie* evidence of a prior failure in civil policy. It was this lack of forehandedness which determined the French and American failure in Indochina; and it was the belated merging of appropriate political, psychological, economic, and military policies which made possible the Free World's victories in Greece and the Philippines as well as the salvage of southern Vietnam in 1954-1958.

As of 1958, then, a mobile American reserve capable of justifying the disengagement of American ground forces in Eurasia had not yet been created. The nation did not opt for pure "massive retaliation"; and elements for such a reserve force capable of dealing with brushfire operations existed within the Navy and the depleted Army. But the nation did not fully face up to the requirements for and the implications of an instrument to deter, and if necessary to prosecute, limited war;[19] and it did not link its diplomacy and economic foreign policy to the problem of deterring such wars. This fact continued to affect the whole cast of national policy in Asia, the Middle East, and Africa.

### 43. Policy in the Underdeveloped Areas

PREVENTING THE LAST WAR

The primary objective of American policy in Asia and the Middle East in the period 1953-1956 was to reduce the American burden in cost and manpower of holding the line around the periphery of the Communist Bloc. Although there was increasing evidence of the new Communist strategy and tactics in the underdeveloped areas, the Administration continued to base American policy on the assumption that the primary danger was a recurrence of the type of invasion launched against South Korea in June 1950; and the avoidance of another direct engagement of American ground forces was central to the Administration's domestic political strategy as well as to its foreign policy. The American government after 1953 became deeply committed, in effect, to defend the national interest within the limit that no American rifleman again fight in Asia.

The principal method for deterrence was to extend the pattern of bilateral and regional military alliance created in Europe by the Truman Doctrine and NATO to those other areas where Communist military aggression might occur and which had not been brought within the orbit of direct American alliance in the latter days of the Truman Administration. In the Middle East a pact of mutual defense between Turkey and Pakistan was signed in May 1954; and the United States became directly linked to Pakistan when SEATO was set up in September 1954 in the wake of the Geneva Conference on Indochina. The Baghdad Pact was negotiated with American support but under British leadership early in 1955, linking Iran and Iraq to Turkey and Pakistan. Bilateral security relations between the United States and Japan, provided for in the Japanese Peace Treaty, were consolidated in a Mutual Defense Pact in March 1954, and Formosa was linked to the United States by a mutual security pact in 1955. The mantle of explicit American military commitment was thus spread over a vast new area; and these nations were offered American military aid to enlarge and modernize their armed forces.

The application of the military pact formula to the Middle East and the Far East yielded less satisfactory results than in Europe at an earlier time. The indifferent outcome stemmed from four fundamental differences between conditions in Europe and in the rest of the non-Communist world.

First, in those portions of the Middle East and in the SEATO area where multilateral pacts were attempted very little sense of regional solidarity or purpose existed. Behind NATO lay the experience of the Second World War and of SHAEF as well as of a long shared historical experience. Moreover, the presence of Russian troops massed on the Elbe was a powerful focus of attention. In 1947-1951 even the most nationalistic Western Europeans felt a sense of threat and of common danger; and, quite apart from the Soviet threat, deep European currents were running against nationalism, looking toward Europe as the symbol around which the spiritual, political, and economic energies of the continent should rally. No such regional focus suffused the efforts at coordinate regional defense in the Far East or the Middle East. On the contrary, in the Middle East they cut directly across the drive toward Arab regional unity, where the motivating impulse was not anti-communism.

Second, the primary Communist threat in the period 1953-1956 was not one of overwhelming ground force attack but rather one of ideological and economic attraction, of subversion, and, possibly, of guerrilla warfare. Neither formal American bilateral pacts nor regional military pacts eliminated the key danger; indeed, they tended to mislead the governments and peoples concerned, including the American people, as to where the danger lay and how it should be headed off or handled.

Third, the nature of the American military commitment in these peripheral regions was ambiguous. In Europe, the United States in 1951 made a historic commitment of four divisions to the mainland. There was no equivalent commitment in SEATO to the Asian mainland. On the contrary, American military thought was read in these regions to indicate an intention to rely wholly on American naval and air attack should the Chinese Communist ground forces move across their frontiers. In the face of the American reluctance with respect to serious ground force commitment on the Asian mainland—and the unsettled ambiguity as between the concepts of "massive retaliation" and a ready, mobile ground force reserve—the diffidence of certain of the Asian powers with respect to reliance on SEATO was understandable.

Fourth, American support for NATO followed upon and was combined with a major economic program designed to assist Europeans in meeting their nonmilitary aspirations. Technically and politically, NATO would clearly have been impossible without the prior and concurrent application of the Marshall Plan. In Asia and the Middle East, where nonmilitary aspirations lay at the core of the revolutionary process, American political policy appeared to focus almost exclusively on the new nations' relations to Communist military power (and their overt diplomatic position in the Cold War) rather than on their domestic political and economic evolution or on their local and regional ambitions, which generally bulked much larger on the local political scene than the threat of Communist invasion.

The Korean War had, then, a curious, paradoxical effect. The success of the American Eighth Army and its associated forces in the spring of 1951 in decimating the massed attacking armies of Communist China convinced Moscow and Peking that the military phase of the exploitation of postwar instability was about at an end and that a sharp shift in tactics toward diplomacy and ideological competition was called for. On the other hand, the heavy casualties, indecisiveness, and controversies of the Korean War launched the United States into a protracted phase during which, with almost obsessive single-mindedness, American diplomacy and resources were devoted to creating the kind of military arrangements around the periphery of the Communist Bloc which were judged most likely to discourage a second Communist venture along the lines of the Korean War. (Although it is clear that Communist policy had shifted prior to 1953 toward softer forms of aggression in Asia, the Middle East and Africa, and although it is clear that Moscow had every reason to maintain a soft policy until its missile delivery systems had matured, it is still possible, of course, that the ring of pacts helped to confirm in Moscow the correctness and to maintain the stability of that policy over the period 1953-1958.)

The somewhat contrary lessons drawn from the Korean War by the two sides yielded a situation, dramatized by the Twentieth Party Congress in Moscow in February 1956, in which the Communist world appeared to be concentrating on the extension of power and influence by persuasion while the United States appeared to be trying to hold the balance of power in Eurasia by military means against a military threat that did not then exist— a state of affairs which appeared to characterize the Communist and American performances for the bulk of the period 1951-1956.

In fact, of course, Communist policy had by no means divorced itself from the use of force even in the short run. Appearances were a not wholly accurate measure of a reality which included the rapid build-up of Soviet strength in missiles, modernization of its ground forces for atomic combat, and the continued application of force by guerrilla operations and subversion based in part on Communist arms shipments. Nevertheless, American policy in these years was not devoted to generating in the underdeveloped countries the kind of attitudes and activities best calculated to frustrate post-1951 Communist policy.

SOME PROBLEMS OF MISDIRECTED EFFORT

The cast of American policy toward the underdeveloped areas created certain specific difficulties both within the nations prepared to negotiate pacts with the United States and within those unprepared to do so.

Within the pact areas the existence of the American military tie and of the commitment to expand local military forces led to a focusing of scarce administrative talent, political energies, and local resources in ways that did not assist the development of the economy and the modernization of the society as a whole. Moreover, since American resources were available to subsidize these military and political alliances, the incentive to face up to the many difficult local conditions required to generate self-sustaining growth was reduced.

The military pacts had a further subtle but powerful consequence. Since the flow of funds from abroad is an extremely important business, especially for a poor country, there was a tendency for politicians, soldiers, and civil servants to rise in stature on the local scene in relation to their functions in negotiating and distributing American aid; but the kinds of men most suitable for handling a military aid program were not necessarily those most suitable—or best trained and motivated—for organizing and directing policies of political, social, and economic modernization. Although, because of the dollar subsidy, countries like Korea, Taiwan, Southern Vietnam, and Pakistan could struggle along from year to year without facing self-evident economic crisis at home or a foreign exchange crisis abroad, the short-run avoidance of crisis concealed the fact that more fundamental economic, social, and political measures required for modernization were not being taken, or were being taken more slowly than the long-term conditions for stability and progress required.

In the absence of any clear economic criteria for loans and grants, an implicit acceptance of a kind of diplomatic blackmail grew up both in Washington and in certain allied foreign capitals. It became habitual for the local governments to put pressure on Washington for increased loans or grants on the grounds of an alleged increase of local Communist pressure, in order to counter a real or alleged trade or loan offer from Moscow or Peking, as a *quid pro quo* for voting with the United States in the United Nations on a difficult issue, and so on. In the Department of Defense there developed a dangerous vested interest in the continuance of military aid and even in its expansion. It was useful to ship out as military aid obsolescent equipment rather than to junk it. This permitted for some years a form of bookkeeping magic (in which the equipment was valued at different points at original and depreciated cost) yielding supplemental funds for the Department of Defense. A substantial proportion of what appeared in the budget and in American politics as military aid flowed in fact into the domestic American military establishment.

Military aid over these years had one further weakness. There was a strong incentive to build in the underdeveloped areas military units modeled on American World War II establishments. If, indeed, the nature of the threat faced in these areas was most likely to be an overt crossing of frontiers by modernized Communist formations (as in the case of Korea in June 1950), such establishments might well prove to be the optimum local formations to have available. On the other hand, they might prove to be inappropriate in equipment, organization, and training if the major military threat proved to be guerrilla operations; and it was the latter that increasingly appeared the more likely source of danger as time passed.

The areas in Asia, the Middle East, and Africa which drew the bulk of military and economic aid from the United States after 1953 represented, however, only a small proportion of the total area and population still part of the non-Communist world. Although it is difficult to derive accurate estimates of the distribution of aid by countries for these years, it can be estimated, by way of example, that for the fiscal year 1955 military aid and that form of economic aid going as "defense support" to nations linked to the United States in military pacts accounted for about 86 per cent of total aid allotments, the bulk of assistance going to Indochina, Korea, and Taiwan, with smaller grants to Pakistan, the Philippines, and Thailand. Thus only 15 per cent or so of aid was available to countries outside the framework of military pacts, including such major and strategically important nations as Egypt, India, and

Indonesia. In the latter nations the bias of American policy created frustrations and local political difficulties which manifested themselves in various forms.

### THREE CASES: INDIA, INDONESIA, EGYPT

India was not only the largest nation of the Free World, with a population approaching 400 million, but also the Asian state most advanced on the road to modernization. It had launched a First Five-Year Plan in 1952; and, in general, Nehru and the Congress Party had succeeded in focusing a high proportion of nationalist energies and sentiment on the tasks of modernizing Indian society. On economic grounds India was the area where American grants and loans were most likely to be used productively; and, of the major nations of Asia, the Middle East, and Africa, it was most likely to produce results capable of challenging the ideological pretensions of communism as a unique instrument for rapid, effective modernization. But these criteria did not control aid allocations in 1953-56. Although aid to India was continued over these years, it was never on a scale capable of associating the United States effectively with the main directions of Indian domestic politics and national aspirations. Moreover, the problem of American relations with India was greatly complicated by the decision to enter into a military pact with Pakistan in 1954. The primary American objective was to strengthen Pakistan against Communist invasion; but the view in Karachi was more directly focused on the balance of force within the Indian peninsula, and notably on the bargaining leverage of Pakistan vis-à-vis India on the question of Kashmir. Thus tensions between Pakistan and India were increased; pro-American elements within India were put at a grave political disadvantage; and Pakistan felt cheated to discover that the existence of the American pact did not lead automatically to American diplomatic support in the matter of Kashmir or even to very large economic aid.

The problem of American policy toward the Indian peninsula was, under the best of circumstances, not easy or simple. There was something to be said for a degree of military support for Pakistan and for close alliance. But without substantial and sustained support and encouragement for economic development in both Pakistan and India, divisive issues were heightened and potentialities for amelioration of tensions in that area were not exploited.

The problem of India's relation to American policy was increasingly dramatized in 1956-58 by the Indian commitment to proceed with a relatively ambitious Second Five-Year Plan the success of which—and with it, perhaps, the success of the experiment of democracy in India—was likely to depend substantially on whether or not much expanded supplies of foreign exchange would be made available to India from abroad.

Both in symbol and substance the problem of India represented throughout these years a test of the nature of American objectives in Asia, the Middle East, and Africa. Here was a nation committed on the one hand to avoiding any overt military alliances with the major contending powers in the Cold War, committed to pursue a policy of neutralism often to the embarrassment of immediate American objectives; on the other hand, here also was a nation committed to struggle against communism within its own borders and to modernize its society by means of consent. The cast of the Eisenhower Administration's strategy made it impossible for the United States wholeheartedly to throw itself behind the Indian effort down to 1958.

Like India, Indonesia also opted for diplomatic neutralism and the avoidance of military alliance with the United States, but as a society and a political system Indonesia was not nearly so far advanced as India on the road to modernization. Moreover, Indonesian history, social structure, and culture made it somewhat more difficult for Indonesia than for India to focus the attention of the political elite on the problems of economic growth and social modernization. Indonesian trade and finance and its modern industrial activity were substantially in the hands of the local Chinese population or of those Dutch who remained behind after the achievement of Indonesian independence. Finally, Indonesia faced the searching problem of maintaining political unity in an island state in which overpopulated Java, which contained the capital, was relatively rich and contained the major exportable surpluses of the nation. It was evident that, if unity were to be maintained and a political distintegration costly to American and Western interests avoided, Indonesia would have to focus its postliberation nationalism on the common tasks of modernization in which, perhaps, a Java backed by international support would be able to offer the outer islands capital assistance in the development of their ample resources. It is altogether possible that forces within the Indonesian political and social system would have forestalled such an outcome. In any case, the nature of American policy toward the underdeveloped areas prevented the United States from playing any significant role in thwarting the progressive deterioration which proceeded in Indonesia down into 1958.

Similarly, the overriding priority accorded in Washington to the development of a military and diplomatic defense against the Communist Bloc prevented the development of a policy in the Middle East capable of heading off the crisis which exploded at Suez in 1956. The United States did not have a policy which might have committed Nasser in the period immediately after his takeover of power in November 1954 so overwhelmingly to the domestic development of Egypt that it would have been difficult for him simultaneously to have entered with such disruptive vigor into the alternative outlet for the Egyptian nationalist spirit—that is, into the exploitation of Soviet-American rivalry to advance the Egyptian claim to regional political leadership.

## THE PERSISTENT DILEMMA OF COLONIALISM

The Eisenhower administration, like those which had preceeded it since 1941, faced the inescapable dilemma of a nation allied to colonial and ex-colonial powers on the one hand but also linked, by historic instinct and current interest, to the fate of the nations newly emerged from colonialism and to regions still under colonial control. There was—and there is—no simple formula for American policy capable of leading the nation out of this dilemma except that the United States use such power and influence as it can bring to bear to temper the clash over colonialism and to anticipate crises before they come to dominate and distort the international scene. Generally, this re-quires the release of the colony from its metropolitan ties earlier than may seem wise by objective criteria of "preparedness," earlier than is likely to be easily acceptable to the colonial power. Over the period 1953-1956 this difficulty was faced on a major scale in Indochina, French North Africa, Cyprus, and, in a sense, with respect to Egypt and the Suez Canal, regarded by many Egyptians as a colonial institution before its seizure in July 1956.

What can be said in general about this problem was that the United States under the Eisenhower administration continued to be no more forehanded in using its power and influence to prevent these situations from coming to acute crises than it had been in previous years; and that the military cast of its diplomacy and foreign aid programs in Asia, the Middle East, and Africa tended to heighten the colonial issue in those nations not allied to the United States by military pacts.[1]

### THE TWO STRATEGIES IN PERSPECTIVE

The application to the underdeveloped areas of the strategy derived from the Great Equation led the United States to pursue, then, a policy of short-run military and political alliance designed to frustrate direct Communist military aggression. In the period 1953-1956 this policy was applied with single-mindedness and vigor at a time when Communist policy had shifted to tactics of longer-run erosion in which the alleged Communist association with peace, economic progress, and nationalism could be contrasted with alleged American militarism, indifference concerning local economic development, and colonialism. The nations not allied to the United States in military pacts proved particularly vulnerable to these tactics; and it was to these that the bulk of Soviet economic aid funds was directed.

In Asia and the Middle East, Communist policy sought to leap-frog the ring of bases around the bloc by increasing its influence, for example, in Indonesia, Afghanistan, Egypt, and Syria; and that policy succeeded to a substantial degree—although nowhere did it reach the stage of complete

Communist takeover. Communist tactics included an important role for military force; but that role in a sense outflanked on both sides the main military strength the United States sought to build in the underdeveloped areas in this period. On the one hand, Communist policy relied on a background of mounting Soviet strength in weapons of mass destruction; on the other hand, it included the execution of guerrilla and other subversive operations which were beyond the ability of the infantry divisions built under American guidance to control.

Thus, as the nationalist revolutions gathered force and purpose in the southern half of the globe, the Eisenhower administration in its first term viewed the underdeveloped areas narrowly in terms of the military policy derived from the Great Equation. The nation's difficulty in dealing with societies in the transition from traditional to modern, growing structures— dramatized by American relations with Nationalist China during and after the Second World War—persisted. The insight symbolized by Truman's Fourth Point, the Gordon Gray Report, and Bowles' performance in India was largely ignored. The old American problem of relating and balancing military and nonmilitary objectives persisted in a peculiarly acute form.

### 44. Policy Toward Western Europe

A MOMENT OF SUCCESS

In Europe, American strategy as crystallized in 1953 called above all else for the achievement of a substantial West German contribution to European defense within a framework calculated to guarantee that German military strength be used only for commonly agreed purposes. In this respect, the Eisenhower administration carried forward the policy of pressing for German rearmament formally initiated at the NATO meeting of September 1950, accepting, as had the Truman administration, the supplementary French proposal that the German ground forces be woven into an integrated European Army through a European Defense Community. French willingness to proceed with German rearmament on these terms waned, however, in 1952- 1953; and in December 1953 Dulles felt it necessary to threaten an "agonizing reappraisal" of American policy toward Western Europe if the EDC arrangements were not promptly consummated.

Nevertheless, in the wake of the failure of the foreign ministers to progress toward German unity it did prove possible during 1954 to find an agreed framework for a measure of German rearmament. This was done not within the orbit of the fully integrated EDC, but within the looser, British-inspired Western European Union—an arrangement made possible by Eden's commitment to station permanently on the continent four British divisions and a tactical air force. This agreement was ratified by the European states before the end of 1954, despite a major Soviet effort of warning and threat. A German army began to be raised; and the major immediate objective of American policy in Western Europe over the previous five years was apparently achieved.

More than that, over the period 1953-1956 Western Europe evidently moved out of the phase of reconstruction and beyond a prosperity that might be attributed to the Korean War boom into rapid growth and increased material prosperity. Further, the forces making for the economic and political unification of Western Europe advanced beyond romantic idealism and organizational structure of doubtful substance into a phase of serious business, diplomacy, and politics. But these years, which saw come to fruition three major dimensions of American postwar policy toward Western Europe—self-sustained prosperity, serious movement toward unity, and a common defense embracing a substantial German contribution—saw also a progressive deterioration in the North Atlantic tie. This happened because the old transatlantic policy formulae, derived from the threat of Soviet ground forces and Western European Communist parties in the immediate postwar years, were rendered inadequate by the impact on Western Europe of the revolution in weapons of mass destruction and the surging forces at work in Asia, the Middle East, and Africa which neither American nor Western European policy proved capable of harnessing to the common interest and purpose in the period 1953-1956.

THE DESCENT FROM LISBON

The meeting of the NATO Council in Lisbon in February 1952 had been, perhaps, the high point in NATO policy in its first phase, when all Western eyes were fastened on the Soviet ground force potential mounted in East Germany or on the ground force reserves to the rear. It was then agreed that 50 divisions, half active, half in reserve, might be developed for NATO by the end of 1952; 70 at the end of 1953; 97 by the end of 1954. These goals were, undoubtedly, overambitious, given the realities of Western European politics; and to some degree they represented promises to Washington that the Western European governments felt were subject to review. But a build-up of ground forces on even a lesser scale, woven in with excellent tactical air and naval forces and backed by a Strategic Air Command flying from bases in the NATO areas as well as from the United States, began to provide a somewhat new conception of NATO's military meaning. Europe's ground forces might not be able alone to meet and defeat a fully mobilized ground attack by the Soviet Union; but, on the other hand, NATO was clearly a force which could obstruct a march from East Germany to the Channel. Its capabilities would evidently demand a major further mobilization of forces in

East Germany by the Soviet Union before an attack could be contemplated, thus giving important warning to the United States and the West. And, with the build-up of German forces then envisaged, it was not impossible even to regard NATO as potentially a serious deterrent to Soviet ground force strength quite aside from its link to SAC, notably if the United States were prepared to mobilize and ship gound force units rapidly after a Soviet attack was launched. In short, NATO as it appeared to be developing in 1952 was something more than a permanent plate glass window which if broken would guarantee SAC assault. It was becoming a force seriously to be reckoned with even if it was still something less than a match for the Soviet ground-force potential.

From the high-point at Lisbon the build-up of NATO and the vision of its meaning were changed by three converging circumstances, all of which altered in European eyes the likelihood and the urgency of the threat represented by the Soviet ground forces.

First, notably after the beginning of serious negotiations looking toward a Korean truce, it became reasonably clear that in Asia as in Europe the Communists were entering a new phase in which military aggression was likely to play a lesser role than in the recent past. The themes enunciated at the October 1952 Nineteenth Congress of the Communist Party, Stalin's death and its evidently absorbing domestic aftermath within the Soviet Union, and the increasingly explicit emergence of a policy of competitive but less overtly belligerent coexistence (based in many European eyes on the acceptance in Moscow of the irrationality of major war) all progressively reduced the sense of urgency which, from the Prague *coup* of February 1948 to the Chinese Communist entrance into the Korean War, had provided the somewhat ambiguous military but extremely real political foundations for NATO.

This sense of diminished aggressive force from Moscow was strengthened by economic and political attitudes in Western Europe. The building of NATO under the Lisbon Plan would have been expensive. The European peoples, having dealt successfully with the immediate postwar problems, were anxious to enjoy the fruits of the prosperity which was emerging in 1953-1956, a prosperity rooted in the diffusion of durable consumers goods to levels of the population which had hitherto found them beyond their reach. Moreover, Europeans were by no means convinced that their own efforts in NATO had very much to do with war or peace, and, especially, with the outcome of major war should it come. In part this was a technical judgment which viewed NATO as merely an elaborate and costly device for involving the United States (and Britain) automatically should Moscow move troops across the truce lines on the continent and which judged the American Strategic Air Command as the only serious Western instrument of deterrence or of war. In part it reflected a sense of impotence in a world apparently dominated by the two postwar giants equipped uniquely with large stockpiles of atomic weapons. At the time of the airlift, the Prague *coup*, and the Korean War, Western Europe bestirred itself; but it lapsed back when the threat diminished under persistent economic and psychological pressures. And when knowledge of the power of fusion weapons spread out to the continental European populations, that knowledge deflated the sense that their military destiny lay in their own hands, a conviction which had begun to re-emerge tentatively in the period 1947-1952.

The third factor that altered the Lisbon Plan was the arrival of a period of atomic plenty in the United States and the consequent rapid development of tactical atomic weapons. The idea developed that NATO's mission—psychological, military, or both—could be achieved by a substitution of atomic weapons for manpower. The decision to proceed in NATO on the basis of atomic weapons was explicitly made in December 1954 and slowly applied in the following years.

Whatever the realism of the new tactical concept, it was, indeed, new. Infantry warfare historically had been conducted over the centuries around the concept that ground would be gained by the bodies of men, assisted as best they might by the equipment which the technology of their day could provide, including cavalry, tanks, and tactical aircraft. But down to the surrender of Japan, infantry remained the queen of battle, moving in on foot to take the ground and consolidate victory. In tactical atomic warfare, for the first time, the area effects of the weapons permit ground to be gained by weapons. The role of men is to move in and consolidate the areas cleared of the enemy by atomic explosions. It was on this new basis that NATO proceeded to develop in the course of 1955-1956, although the scale and quality of forces required to make good even this more economical conception were increasingly hard to come by as the Soviet diplomatic peace offensive developed after the Geneva Conference of 1955.

LIMITED NUCLEAR WAR IN EUROPE?

Meanwhile, Moscow too was reorganizing its ground forces around the new tactical atomic weapons. Two great armies faced each other across the face of Europe, each with components armored with atomic weapons of enormous power capable of flexible tactical use. Could these armies fight a limited war? Was an engagement between them short of direct attack on the great cities of Europe, Russia, and the United States thinkable? Was limited war in Europe a rational conception?

By and large, the answer was no. The Korean War remained limited because it was possible and more or less rational for both sides to fight for limited objectives in a limited area with limited weapons. In Europe a limited objective was difficult to define, once major ground units were engaged. The loss, say, of West Germany to the West or of East Germany to Moscow was tantamount to decisive loss of the balance of power in Western Eurasia. The fringe of Western Europe would be almost impossible to hold with Western Germany and the Ruhr in Soviet hands; and the erosion of the Soviet empire in the East would be virtually inevitable if East Germany should be conquered by the West. There is no real stopping place short of the Channel in one direction or the Curzon line in the other if the line at the Elbe is broken by military force.

Could the area of combat be limited? This would be difficult in two senses. Europe is so densely populated that it would be extremely difficult to attack even the most legitimate tactical targets—airfields, river crossings, troop concentrations, supply and transport centers—without destroying major population centers. For the continental European the distinction between limited and all-out nuclear war was likely to be somewhat academic. It would also be difficult to limit the terrain of battle in a second sense. A minimum condition for success in ground warfare under European circumstances is tactical control of air over the battlefield. One could not count in Europe on maintaining the curious common-law agreement governing the use of air power which emerged in Korea, in which the United Nations were, in effect, given tactical air supremacy, challenged mainly by fire from the ground, in return for not attacking the fighter bases from which aircraft flew against United Nations heavy bombers. Such an implicit agreement was unlikely to work because tactical air control was likely to be vastly more effective against the modern armies engaged in Europe than against the Chinese Communist forces with their limited logistical support. Thus in Europe the odds are strong that the air battle would stretch back from the battlefield to the sources of aircraft supply; that is, back to Paris, London, and the American factories in one direction and back to Leningrad, Moscow, and the Urals in the other.

What about the limitation of weapons? If the stakes of battle were hard or impossible to limit, and the terrain as well, it is difficult to see how or why the side most severely pressed would not invoke its most effective weapons to avoid what it regarded as a situation tantamount to total defeat. If Moscow faced the loss of East Germany and its whole Eastern European empire, and if Western tactical power seriously threatened to control the whole European area back to Soviet cities, why should Moscow not invoke its strategic air force or its missiles?

By and large, then, the odds were that substantial ground force combat in Europe was tantamount to all-out nuclear war.

On the other side, of course, it might be argued that there had been two limited tests of military strength in Europe—Greece and the Berlin airlift. But Greece was a peninsula, and Soviet forces carefully avoided contact there; and the forces engaged in both sides in the Berlin test of will and strength were carefully limited. A clash between NATO and the Soviet armies of the East would be something quite different.

What then, was the military rationale for NATO in 1956? It was still necessary, of course, to maintain in Western Europe some form of ground force structure embracing American units that would guarantee as nearly as anything could that Moscow would have to regard an attack on any NATO member as equivalent to an attack on the United States. Only thus could Western Europe feel assured of the protection of the American retaliatory capabilities incorporated in the Strategic Air Command. This concept could not, however, justify the large establishments of conventional forces, expensive in manpower and resources, so long as limited nuclear war in Europe was regarded as unlikely or even unthinkable.

### LIMITED NONNUCLEAR WAR IN EUROPE?

As thoughtful men contemplated this situation, seeking to minimize the possibility that the use of military force would at any stage appear realistic and attractive to Moscow, another conception emerged. Perhaps, after all, it was argued, the full implication of nuclear stalemate might be that large Western European ground forces, not relying on nuclear weapons, had a function to perform. What was the case?

First, reliance on NATO as a device to trigger the application of the American Strategic Air Command became increasingly unrealistic as Soviet delivery capabilities grew. Therefore, Moscow might be tempted to use its ground force strength against Western Europe, relying on its nuclear strength to deter the application of Amercian nuclear strength. It followed that Europe required a substantial nonnuclear force to make this alternative unattractive.

Second, if serious negotiations were to be pursued with Moscow looking to the control or elimination of nuclear weapons, the West would require much larger conventional forces than it could muster in the mid-1950's to negotiate honestly with Moscow or to maintain its security in an international arms control agreement. In short, in pursuit of peace as well as in the deterrence of war the West was relying too heavily on nuclear arms.

Third, the historical record since 1945 showed clearly that when the West was confronted with a military challenge it did not, in fact, reach for its nuclear weapons; on the contrary it sought *ad hoc* to fashion a limited response, appropriate to the form of the challenge, which would minimize the likelihood that the conflict would expand. If that would, in fact, be the nature of the Western response to a show of Soviet force in Europe, there might be wisdom in thinking before the event in terms of nonnuclear force rather than in terms of the exchange of fusion weapons.

As the 1950's wore on, this line of thought gathered advocates, but as of 1958 it had nowhere yet become official policy in the West.

## LIMITED WAR OUTSIDE EUROPE?

Still another mission for NATO was conceivable. Could not a substantial NATO establishment be regarded (like the American Army in the post-Ridgway period) as a task force to deter or to prosecute limited war outside Western Europe? There had, indeed, been such engagements involving Western European powers since 1945: in Indochina, Malaya, Cyprus, and North Africa as well as in Korea. But there was every reason to believe that any effort to make the NATO force an instrument for the conduct of operations in Asia, the Middle East, and Africa would only make a bad situation worse. Among the NATO powers themselves there would certainly be disagreement over the conditions under which their forces would be permitted to operate against any threat other than the Soviet armies; and such a policy—raising, as it immediately would, the image of an army designed to hold colonial positions—would not generally be welcome outside Europe. Unless a United Nations framework could be agreed upon, as in Korea, it seemed wiser for the deterrence of limited war in Asia, the Middle East, and Africa to be a matter of individual rather than NATO action.

## THE DETERRENCE OF MAJOR WAR?

Finally, of course, it would have been possible in the period 1953-1956 for the European nations to have played a major part in the arms race in nuclear weapons, means of delivery, and means of defense. Here the secrecy provisions of American atomic legislation and the failure of the Eisenhower administration in 1953 to act on the advice to seek its alteration cut deep. The Western Europeans were left almost wholly dependent on the United States for the deterrence of Soviet attack and denied a chance to participate in the scientific and engineering adventure as well as in the costs of maintaining a common deterrence system. At Lisbon, Europeans could feel they were acting to control, to a degree, their own destiny by increasing the costs to Moscow of a ground force invasion of the West. As the threat from the East took the form of fusion weapons and missiles, Western Europe was reduced to the status of a second-class ally, denied access to the serious weapons of war; and this occurred at a time when Western Europe was rapidly recuperating as a society (as well as an economy) from the Second World War—when dignified partnership was increasingly the only politically and humanly tolerable basis for the North Atlantic tie.

PRESSURE FROM THE SOUTH

While the nature of American legislation and policy made it impossible for NATO to focus on the most urgent common military danger, the political unity of the North Atlantic alliance was endangered from another quarter. As the nationalist revolutions gathered strength in Asia, the Middle East, and Africa—at a time when the apparent danger of direct Communist military aggression had receded—the pursuit of the lesser aspirations of the new nations and colonial areas rose in priority. The Pakistani increasingly thought of Kashmir rather than of the threat from the North; the Egyptians began to project their weight into North and Central Africa and toward the formation of an Arab bloc; the issue of colonialism in French North Africa came to a head; the Baghdad Pact became essentially a move in Free World power diplomacy rather than a ground force deterrent against Communist military strength. This assertion of felt national interests further weakened the coherence and effectiveness of NATO. Except for the 1954 crisis over EDC (closely woven into French military commitments in its colonial empire), the great crisis of NATO came over one form or another of colonialism and its aftermath: Indochina, Algeria, Cyprus, and, finally, Egypt and the Middle East.

NATO was created in a transient mood of consensus that one job was worth doing in common—building a reasonably effective deterrent against preponderant Soviet ground force strength. Older common traditions and wider common purposes made NATO possible; but its operational content was limited. In the period 1953-1956 NATO could play only a marginal role in deterring nuclear war; and it split sharply when Europe confronted the manifestations of rising nationalism in Asia, Africa, and the Middle East. Some constructive relationships of Europe with the underdeveloped areas persisted or were developed—in parts of the residual African colonies south of the Sahara, in the British Commonwealth and the Colombo Plan, and in certain German and Italian trade and credit initiatives. But these were almost wholly bilateral enterprises outside the NATO context.

AN ALTERNATIVE TO COLONIALISM?

Given the American preoccupation with building and financing military alliances around the periphery of the Communist Bloc, why did not Western Europe on its own seek to create a new constructive relationship with the peoples and nations of Asia, the Middle East, and Africa? Why, with or without American participation, did Europeans not convert the OEEC, if not NATO, into an instrument for creating a noncolonial relationship with these regions with whose destiny that of Western Europe remained intimately tied?

In part, the answer appears to lie in the asymmetry between the acquisition and giving up of colonial empires. Once the flag is raised and the colonial relationship becomes encrusted by the memory of generations of men and women who have worked under the banners of nationhood and Christianity, as well as private advantage, it becomes a matter of national and human pride that the relationship be maintained. It was an extraordinary *tour de force* (based on the vitality in Britain of a strong anticolonial as well as imperial tradition) that permitted Attlee to surrender India, Burma, and Ceylon when he did. A measure of irrationality generally surrounds the final stages of colonial relationships and makes each loss an event of disproportionate pain and significance in metropolitan politics. One or another of the European states was chronically ill of the colonial sickness in these years, as the process of disengagement shifted from Indochina through Suez, Cyprus, Algiers, and Indonesia. Against this background powerful emotional as well as institutional vested interests led the European nations to continue to put much of their investable resources—including technical assistance—into what remained of their empires.

Put another way, it would have taken strong American leadership to persuade Western Europe to focus its attention on building constructive common relations with the new independent states instead of concentrating disproportionately and to the bitter end on the old bilateral ties. The peculiar psychological processes of colonial disengagement combined with the failure to create an alternative vision and policy for relating the industrialized nations of the Free World with the underdeveloped areas made Western Europe peculiarly vulnerable to Communist policy in the period 1953-1956. France, Britain, and the Netherlands each went through painful private crises which weakened the fabric of the North Atlantic tie, while the bilateral enterprises of Germany, Italy, and Japan—freed of the colonial problem by defeat—were a less substantial and less constructive force than they might have been if the creation of a Free World alternative to colonialism had ranked high on the agenda of American policy.

## 45. Dealing with the Soviet Union

The sporadic process of negotiating with the Soviet Union toward the objective of a definitive peace was never completely broken off from 1945 forward. With the emergence of fusion weapons in 1953 and the acceleration of the arms race, these negotiations took on a heightened importance to human beings everywhere. The question of negotiation with Moscow became in itself an important diplomatic issue, and the pressure on the American government to seek an end of the arms race and a European peace never wholly let up between 1953 and 1958.

The efforts of the Eisenhower administration to negotiate a settlement with the Soviet Union must be set against the background of the nation's evolving conception of communism over the years and, especially, the American sense of the kind of society communism had produced in the Soviet Union—the degree of its unity, the long-run purposes of its rulers, its weaknesses and its capabilities.

### AMERICAN VIEWS OF THE SOVIET UNION

Over the three decades between the October Revolution and Truman's acceptance of a state of Cold War the nation's view of the Soviet Union and of the purposes of its leaders varied widely.

From the beginning to the end, the predominant American view was a mixture of two elements: profound ignorance and a vague conviction that the Soviet Union was an evil dictatorship dedicated to the destruction of the basic values and institutions of Western civilization. This fixed—and by no means inaccurate—image did not, of course, exhaust the range of American attitudes and perspectives on the Soviet Union. There was, for example, widespread apathy about the Soviet Union in the 1920's except for a small group of Americans fascinated by the "Communist experiment." Essentially as a depression measure, the Soviet Union was recognized in 1933 in order to encourage the expansion of American foreign trade. And in the 1930's the drama of the first two Five-Year Plans, against the background of Western economic crisis, stirred a wider interest and a somewhat enlarged sympathy; but this mood was radically altered by the Soviet purges, the Soviet-German pact, and Soviet policy during the early stage of the Second World War, notably the invasion of Finland.

Within the United States government and in American intellectual life a very few men knew a good deal about the Soviet Union. By a kind of minor miracle, the Foreign Service produced a number of men of remarkable perception and scholarship in Russian affairs, notably George Kennan and Charles Bohlen. In the universities, Gerroid T. Robinson at Columbia and Michael Karpovich at Harvard carried forward the study of Russian history and began to apply to its Soviet phase the most refined tools of Western research, producing the beginnings of a second generation of scholars. In addition, there was a steady flow of books and articles by journalists, expatriates, Communist sympathizers, naive and enthusiastic observers of the Soviet scene, and—especially after 1929 when Stalin declared himself for the policy of "Socialism in one country"—by disappointed former members of the Communist movement.

Despite these elements of study, reporting, advocacy, and polemics, it is fair to say that when the Second World War came, solid knowledge of the workings of Soviet society, the evolution of Soviet policy, and of the relation of the Soviet phase to the rest of Russian history was confined to a handful of American citizens. The Second World War accelerated the development of this knowledge, because, among other reasons, most of the younger men equipped to deal with the Russian language were put to work under forced draft in various agencies of the government, notably in the Research and Analysis branch of the Office of Strategic Services, over which Professor Robinson presided, permitting not the slightest dilution of scholarly standards. And after the war, at Columbia and Harvard, the training of scholars in the Soviet Union—both for work in government and for teaching—accelerated remarkably.

## THE INITIAL COLD WAR ASSESSMENT

In the meanwhile, Stalin's postwar posture clarified; and by 1946, both inside and outside the government, an appreciation of the status of Soviet society along the lines of George Kennan's "X" article—"The Sources of Soviet Conduct"—represented something of a consensus among the widening—but still statistically small—group concerned with the gathering struggle against Stalin's purposes. That view regarded the Soviet Union as an effective working society, capable of offering to those within it a mixture of positive incentives and terror sufficient to yield effective military and economic performance. It accepted as fact a level of Soviet investment high enough—and with sufficient organizational skill—to assure that the Soviet Union would continue to grow as an industrial economy. It accepted as fact the built-in hostility of Soviet leaders toward the non-Communist world and their operational intent to extend their power as far as their own strengths and weaknesses and the resistance of the outside world would permit. It accepted also the fact that Soviet society was undergoing a series of internal changes away from the social and political norms of the 1920's and early 1930's; but the timing and significance for the external world of those changes and the degree to which they would prove consistent with the maintenance of communism was a matter of some debate. Finally, there was agreement that Moscow was likely to be reasonably cautious in the use of Soviet military force in pursuit of its expansionary postwar objectives. It was on the basis of some such assessment that the Truman counteroffensive was launched early in 1947.

## THE REVISION OF 1949-1950

The Soviet acquisition of atomic weapons by September 1949 revealed an intent and a capability to apply the new technology with a swiftness somewhat beyond that which most observers had held likely; and a change began to take place in the American assessment of Soviet purposes. The notion of a generalized but militarily cautious program of aggression toward the non-Communist world gave way to the conception that the Soviets might be engaged in a systematic build-up of modern military strength, looking toward a showdown which might come when the curves of Soviet and American military capabilities crossed—a date estimated to be round about 1952. An estimate of this kind was incorporated in NSC 68, completed in the spring of 1950, which might well have led to a substantial enlargement of the American military effort even if the Korean War had not intervened.

Against the background of Stalin's and Mao's military adventure in Korea, the concept of a possible Soviet timetable of military expansion spread; and this notion, quite different from the vision of the Soviet Union incorporated in the original containment doctrine, persisted down to the time when it became clear that both the Soviet Union and Communist China were prepared for a Korean truce.

### THE ASSESSMENT OF SOVIET SOCIETY 1951-1953

In the interval that followed—roughly from June 1951 to March 1953—a fresh assessment of Soviet society and its future was made both within and outside the government. That assessment benefited greatly from the gradual fruition of the analyses, based in part on interviews with Soviet defectors in Germany, conducted by the emerging younger generation of American experts on the Soviet Union. These men, trained in the fields of sociology, psychology, anthropology, and economics, united what could be learned from books and documents with what could be learned from carefully structured interviews with former Soviet citizens.[1] The conclusions fitted, in general, both the less formal perceptions of Kennan and Bohlen and the insights of the best older scholars. They permitted, however, a more systematic and complete picture of how a modern bureaucratic society had emerged in the Soviet Union out of the dynamics of the prewar Five-Year Plans, the Second World War experience, and the postwar Soviet efforts at reconstruction and expansion of external power. Specifically, they confirmed the likelihood that the Soviet Union was not operating on a fixed timetable for the achievement of world domination but was engaged in a systematic effort to maximize its external power within the limits imposed by the need to cope with its internal problems on the one hand and with the resistance met in the external world on the other.

In the year or so preceding Stalin's death there were widespread efforts to achieve a new vision of where Soviet society was headed and what influence the removal of Stalin was likely to have. There was obviously a problem for both social scientists and policy-makers in speculating on the relationship between a massive bureaucratic structure, with evident momentum of its own, and the extraordinary concentrated power of one ruthless man. What would his withdrawal from the system mean? Those professionally concerned with this issue disagreed significantly in their predictions—as well as in the confidence with which they were prepared to predict; but there was virtually universal agreement that the Soviet Union as of the early 1950's was a complex societal structure in which there were many built-in resistances to radical change as well as some potentially explosive frictions. On the whole, the weight of professional analysis fell to the view that Stalin's death would release certain limited changes—backed by forces which the dictator had hitherto suppressed—without radically altering the contours of Soviet society or the content of the Soviet external objectives.

## THE ELEVATION OF PSYCHOLOGICAL WARFARE

The effort to clarify the prospects for change in Soviet society interwove with an effort to develop more mature conceptions of psychological warfare. As the years of Cold War rolled on, it became evident that some part in the conflict was being played by the American impact on the minds and attitudes of men and women in other societies, including Communist societies. When the Soviet Union acquired nuclear weapons, and the possibilities of a stand-off in major weapons became more real, the psychological element in the struggle rose in priority.

Simultaneously, a technical problem arose when in 1949-1950 the Soviet Union invested major resources in jamming American radio broadcasts to Russia and Eastern Europe.[2] This crisis led to *Project Troy*, an analysis of the technical, psychological, and political problems of communication from the United States to the Communist world.[3] On the nontechnical side, what emerged from *Project Troy* and the studies that succeeded to it was a somewhat paradoxical conclusion: that the essential American task in psychological warfare was to project a clear, consistent image of its purposes and policies that would match what in fact the nation did from day to day. From this conclusion flowed few suggestions for new psychological tricks but, rather, the recommendation that the national government find better means for coordinating the flow of policy and action among the various arms, military and civil, which in fact dealt with the outside world. The problem of psychological warfare came to be conceived primarily as the task of making and executing a policy that would dramatize the areas of overlap between the purposes of the United States and other nations.

Thus the Psychological Strategy Board, created in 1951, gave way, under the Eisenhower Administration, to the Operations Coordinating Board.[4] In addition, the role of special adviser to the President on the psychological impact of national policy was maintained during the first Eisenhower term.[5]

## THE INITIAL POSTURE OF THE EISENHOWER ADMINISTRATION

President Eisenhower evidently had other responsibilities in the period preceding his assumption of authority than to follow the development of a more mature image of the dynamics of Soviet society and a more mature conception of the nature and limits of psychological warfare. Nevertheless, three elements in his experience and policy converged to make him look toward the possibilities of change in Soviet society and toward a negotiation with the Soviet Union of a peace settlement.

First, like most Americans in the Control Council in Berlin in 1945-1946, he had seen something of the generation of modern soldiers and technicians who had matured during the Five-Year Plans and the Second World War. While these men were obviously the instruments of Stalin's policy, they exhibited in human and professional interchange the existence of values and manners quite different from those of the dedicated professional international revolutionary; and they left among Americans, including Eisenhower, a sense that Soviet society might evolve in time into something different from what it appeared to be under Stalin—difficult, but more livable in terms of American interests.

Second, this tempered optimism about the potentialities for change converged with Eisenhower's appreciation of the terrible destructiveness of the emerging new weapons. As with most professional soldiers, Eisenhower's understanding of the capabilities for destruction in nuclear weapons, as compared with the weapons of the Second World War, made him regard a major war as not only an irrational undertaking but almost unthinkable. He deeply believed that the nation would have to look to nonmilitary instruments to protect its interests; and this conclusion directly influenced his interest in psychological warfare.

Third, the commitment of the new Administration to seek a substantial reduction in defense outlays, combined with the drawing to a close of the Korean War, made it logical to conceive of a test of Moscow's purposes by the new Administration.

Thus it was natural that Eisenhower should not be reluctant to consider the possibility of negotiations with the Soviet Union centered about the question of the control of armaments.

Dulles, on the other hand, approached the question of negotiation with the Soviet Union with the question of Germany uppermost in mind. Following the strategy of the Truman administration, he wished to avoid any serious negotiation with the Soviet Union until the West could confront Moscow with German rearmament, within an organized European framework, as a *fait accompli*. Moreover, he greatly respected the negotiating skill of Molotov and feared that negotiations might yield only one of two bad results—either an open break with the Soviet Union which would heighten international tensions, or superficial agreements that would lead to a letdown of effort in the West while Moscow carried forward its military and political programs at full throttle.

Despite these reservations, the new Administration was put under immediate political pressure—notably from abroad—to enter into early high-level negotiation with Moscow. And as early as February 25, 1953, Eisenhower stated that he would be prepared to meet Stalin half-way on the condition that the nation's allies were fully informed of the issues under discussion. Then, with Washington undergoing the confusion of a new Administration, with the Korean truce negotiation at a tense stage, and with the Soviet press suffused since mid-January by as ugly an official mood as had been since the purges of the 1930's (centered about the alleged "doctors' plot"), Stalin's death was announced on March 6.

A certain amount of staff work had been done in Washington on what might be done in the case of Stalin's death; but nothing clear or firm had been crystallized out at high levels in the government. The possibilities were roughly these: to do nothing and wait; to undertake various forms of direct pressure on the Soviet empire—nonmilitary, military, or both; to initiate forcefully from Washington negotiations looking towards a definitive settlement of the major outstanding issues.

An aggressive exploitation of the possible confusions and schisms in Moscow was rejected. It was the universal judgment of those seriously concerned with the analysis of the Soviet Union that aggressive American actions at this juncture would minimize the likelihood of any serious change in Soviet society or Soviet policy conducive to the American interest. Specifically, it was judged that, on simple nationalist grounds, Russian ranks would be closed in the face of external aggression or the threat of aggression. Conversely, it was felt that the possibility of change in Soviet society and policy would be maximized if the Soviet leaders were convinced that, while the United States would resolutely oppose any further Soviet aggression, there would be no American attempt to exploit, militarily or otherwise, the possible confusion following the dictator's death.

Whether or not this view was judged valid, the new Administration, for the multiple reasons suggested earlier, was anxious to explore the possibilities of peace; and it was in no mood to increase the range of its military commitments. Having agreed that aggression was to be avoided, something of a debate arose as to whether the United States should sit tight or strongly seize the diplomatic initiative. After a typical passage of Washington turbulence, a compromise emerged in the form of the President's speech of April 16, made before the American Society of Newspaper Editors, in which Eisenhower defined his peaceful purposes, but without commitment or pressure to negotiate. He listed, nevertheless, the ample agenda of major issues that lay before Moscow and Washington: Korea, Indochina, Austria, Germany, the international control of armaments.

### THE COURSE OF NEGOTIATION AND CONCEPTION, 1953-1958

Despite Dulles' reservations, the pressures for negotiation mounted from every direction in the course of 1953—notably after the Soviet fusion explosion of August—and a foreign ministers' conference was held in January 1954. By that time, Soviet post-Stalin strategy in military and foreign policy had been firmly developed, involving a maximum effort in missiles and other modern weapons and the soft offensive in Asia, the Middle East, and Africa. The North Atlantic alliance was to be left to wither under the indirect impact of these two efforts.

The major conferences of 1954 and 1955 reflected this Soviet strategy. In January 1954 Molotov left the Soviet position on Germany rigidly frozen, somewhat to the surprise of Western diplomats who expected and feared a more attractive flexibility; but Molotov used the occasion successfully to arrange the summer conference on Indochina. That conference, in turn, was used to settle the Indochina war and to clear the way for a massive worldwide peace offensive which was climaxed by the Summit Conference.

The conference of heads of state in July 1955 came at an important moment in the unfolding of post-Stalin Soviet strategy. Earlier in the year Khrushchev had won his fight with Malenkov, Zhukov had taken over the Defense Ministry, and the Soviet military budget had been expanded. There was, moreover, every indication in Washington before the conference that, across the whole front of modern military technology, the Soviet Union was closing the gap with the United States at a pace that promised to give it a position of primacy in the foreseeable future unless the scale and character of the American military effort were radically altered. Diplomatically, the conference was preceded by a Soviet tidying up in Europe; Austria (where the Soviet zone of occupation had never been converted into a Communist state) was released, spreading the conviction of Soviet peaceful intentions; ardent efforts were made to bring Yugoslavia back into Moscow's fold; and, in reply to the launching of West German rearmament in the Western European Union, the Warsaw Pact was created, giving an appearance of East-West symmetry for diplomatic bargaining purposes. In Asia, the Bandung Conference, with Chinese Communist participation, had strengthened the neutralist mood in the spring of 1955; and, as the July meeting occurred, the United States was already aware that a Communist arms offer had been made to Egypt, opening the Soviet Middle East offensive.

Dulles' misgivings about the Summit Conference were unconcealed; and before the event there was in Washington little doubt that the Soviet purposes at Geneva would be threefold—to expand and strengthen the popular view that Moscow's purposes were pacific, to continue to minimize the chance of an American-instigated war over the narrowing time interval of Soviet disadvantage, and to produce a mood in which the United States and the West in general was likely to cut its military budgets and turn to domestic affairs. In short, Moscow's purpose was correctly understood to be not the relaxation of international tension but the relaxation of Western efforts, both military and diplomatic.

Against this background, the American delegation at Geneva sought and achieved two objectives:[6] first, to project effectively the American intent and will to pursue peace, which had come widely to be questioned in the post-Stalin period; and second, to test the seriousness of Moscow's peaceful posture. Both purposes were simultaneously accomplished by offering a spectrum of American proposals ranging from cultural exchanges to the hard and serious proposal for mutual aerial inspection as a preliminary step looking toward the effective international control of armaments.

As an exercise in short-run international politics and diplomatic exploration, the conference was a thoroughgoing American success. The President effectively projected to the world his peaceful intentions, and it was established that the Soviet Union was unprepared to move forward with respect either to the control of armaments or a German settlement. If there were any doubts about the meaning of the Geneva Conference, they were settled by the October 1955 meeting of foreign ministers, which proved peculiarly barren; and in the meantime the Egyptian arms deal had been successfully negotiated by Moscow, opening a new and not wholly pacific phase of events in the Middle East. But while the Summit Conference cleared the way for the formulation of an American policy capable of coping with the post-Stalin phase of Soviet strategy, it did not produce that policy. The short-run advantages of the President's performance at Geneva were accepted; but policy was not changed in the light of the clear and ominous evidence of Soviet intentions.

In the course of 1955, however, the issue began to be seriously joined within the Administration on whether or not a radical increase in American outlays for both military and foreign aid was required: increased military outlays to outmatch the evidently accelerating pace of Soviet developments in missiles and other modern armaments; foreign aid to associate the American interest with the constructive ambitions of underdeveloped nations unwilling to join with the United States in military pacts. Month by month, the evidence steadily mounted that the Soviet Union was conducting both a military program of rearmament and a political offensive in Asia, the Middle East, and Africa for which existing American dispositions were inadequate in both direction and in scale.

A number of factors contributed to make the Administration's reaction to the gathering evidence sluggish. Among these was a tendency to put excessive weight on the consequences for Soviet military and foreign policy of the changes taking place in Soviet domestic society and in the satellite empire. In the spring of 1955, for example, Cutler assessed the situation as follows:

> It is not at all partisan to say the recent completion of the Western European accords and treaties is a transcendent triumph for our diplomacy. As I have said before, Western Europe is the golden prize; not Korea, nor Vietnam, nor even Japan can compare with the industrial might, the skilled capabilities, and the free heritage of Europe. And Western Europe has stayed on the free world's side—without a shot, without a bomb.
>
> The events culminating in this diplomatic triumph have mightily stirred the Kremlin cauldron. Stalin dead, Beria dead, Malenkov sinking, the Soviet agricultural program askew, the satellites still yearning to be free, the burdensome drain of Red China's war-making demands . . . I do not mean to overplay or draw false hopes; but I believe that something is rotten—and it is *not* in Denmark.
>
> This is the time, then, to give rein to diplomacy.[7]

And in the fall of 1956 this view was immensely strengthened by the Polish and Hungarian upheavals.

As a purely intellectual matter it was exceedingly difficult to cast up the balance between the momentum of Soviet military and foreign policy and the elements of corrosion and change in the Soviet domestic base and in its satellite empire. There was, nevertheless, a systematic tendency for those most deeply concerned about the implications for the United States of an enlarged military and foreign aid budget to give excessive weight to the inhibiting effects of possible disruptive change in the Soviet empire. The initial budgetary obsession of the Eisenhower administration remained. And this tendency was joined to a deeper, almost cultural reluctance to accept the evidence that Russia had moved to a stage of mature capabilities in modern science, technology, and production. As one privileged observer of the scene later put it:

> First, a national security program, both in terms of content and timing, must be directly geared to an estimate of the power, stability, and future growth of the USSR. Second, the estimate developed during the past summer [by the Gaither Committee] was drastically different from that then employed as

the basis of our security planning. From these two points, the dilemma of the Administration may be posed: either the picture of the threat has to be reduced so as to bring into conformity with existing plans and policies or the plans and policies have to be enlarged to accommodate the new estimates of the threat.

It is fascinating and sometimes discouraging to watch this interplay at work. This is not the time or the occasion to treat with the enormously complex problems of evolving weaponry and military strategy. It is, I believe, highly relevant to observe the way we have refused to believe the evidence we have had, or have downgraded its importance when we have believed it. The capacity of the human race for self-deception is more considerable than we care to admit.

First of all, we start out with an enormous difficulty in believing that a non-Western society could ever really become our equal in technological matters. It was almost an article of faith that advanced technology was the monoply of the United States and Western Europe though we admitted a rather odd aberration on the part of the Japanese. But when a non-Western society is also Communist, then our powers of belief in technological equality are very limited indeed.

So evidence has to be very strong to swim upstream against this current. Every fact that reduces the Russian dimension has, therefore, a far easier time in getting itself accepted.

But then if the evidence has successfully bucked these currents it runs head on into other facts that have already arrived and secured a lodgment.

The most tenacious of these is the belief that the number one danger is domestic inflation, not Russian military power. Adherents to this view are almost always prone to minimize the Russian capability because to do otherwise would be to expose their left flank to unanswerable pleas for increased federal budgets. There would seem to be an almost direct correlation between our view of the stability of the Russian regime and our view of appropriate federal fiscal policy.

This is not a failing confined to those in high circles. Sam Lubell, in a most interesting piece in the Columbia University Forum, has shown that a random sample of the American public reacts exactly the same way. After a number of interviews even an old veteran like Lubell was astonished to discover that:

"Those whose concern with unemployment led them to favor more government spending voiced considerable more alarm over sputnik than those who are untroubled by the fears of economic recession or who were eager to see taxes reduced. The belief cherished by so many journalists that one has only to give the people the facts and the people will lead the way did not seem at all justified."

But Lubell missed a point. The people could not for security reasons receive all the facts and they had not received all the facts they could have received. Furthermore, there had been so little public education and discussion of Russia that they would not have been able to decide what the real facts were nor their importance. Facts become facts only when they help validate and are validated by the whole context of our knowledge.[8]

Thus, although the nation's knowledge of the structure and motivations of Soviet society increased remarkably over the period 1953-1958, there was a tendency within the highest levels of the government—and to some degree, throughout American society—to underrate the capabilities of the system and the united will of its leaders to mobilize its human and material resources to expand Soviet power on the world scene; and there was an unwillingness to acknowledge the nature of the post-Stalin strategy and its potential effectiveness in the face of existing American military and foreign policy.

More fundamentally, there was repetition of a wartime and immediate postwar error; that is, a failure to appreciate the profound interconnection between Moscow's and Washington's dispositions. During and immediately after the Second World War responsible Americans asked: What is Stalin up to? They did not ask: What must we do to make continued Big Three unity the only realistic alternative open to him? Similarly, the Eisenhower administration did not appreciate the extent to which Soviet policy was directed to the openings afforded by American dispositions. Post-Stalin Soviet policy was based on a systematic effort to exploit the American reliance on the Strategic Air Command and an air defense system geared to manned aircraft; on an American approach to Asia, the Middle East, and Africa based on military pacts focused against Communist ground forces; and on the concept of a NATO built around conventional forces backed by American nuclear weapons knowledge of which Europeans were denied. The Eisenhower administration did not face up to these direct connections between Soviet action and American policy.

THE DIALOGUE OF THE SCIENTISTS

The creation of fusion weapons by the United States and the Soviet Union in 1953 led directly to a new dimension in Soviet-American relations—a quiet dialogue of increasing political maturity among the scientists. Eisenhower's proposal of the Atoms-for-Peace program before the United Nations in December 1953 launched this phase, leading as it did to the remarkable Geneva Conference on atomic energy in 1955. There the scientists of the United States and the Soviet Union met with others; and, within clearly drawn lines of security, they exchanged information and came to know one another as human beings.

That confrontation had a good deal in common with other meetings of Soviet and American professionals since 1945. Men whose lives are devoted to a specialized field of work—be they soldiers or housing experts—tend to have much in common. They have read the same books, undergone a similar technical apprenticeship, revered the same pioneer innovators in their field; faced similar day-to-day problems; developed within their societies similar friends and enemies of their professional causes. They have, in short, a good deal to talk about.

With the atomic scientists all of this was heightened. On both sides of the Iron Curtain their careers and their personal lives had been radically transformed by the translation of the basic insights of modern physics into new weaponry, the revolutionary implications of which they had been forced to expound to a generation of professional military men and politicians. And the problem of communication among them was eased because a considerable proportion of the Soviet scientists were men whose family and cultural roots were middle class, not very distant from the common matrix of pre-1917 European life.

In the course of 1955 it became clear from the increasingly sophisticated texture of Soviet diplomatic positions on the subject of armaments control that the complexities of the world of nuclear weapons were beginning to penetrate into the Soviet government; and the dialogue of the scientists, hitherto confined to the peaceful uses of atomic energy or conducted through the veil of diplomatic negotiation, was enlarged between 1955 and 1958 by informal meetings and by the Geneva negotiation of the summer of 1958 on the possibilities of monitoring atomic tests.

The existence and extension of the dialogue of the scientists was not accidental. It was a conscious act of policy on the part of the Soviet and American governments. The American government had been committed since 1945 to accept a radical degree of armaments control on the condition that virtually free inspection was permitted within the Soviet Union. An armaments control system can never be completely secure; but it can be given a high degree of security if even a relatively few technically competent inspectors can move about with the kind of freedom traditionally accorded bank inspectors. The dialogue thus afforded Washington useful soundings on the Soviet view of how atomic weapons might be controlled and, particularly, on whether the hitherto rigid Soviet view of the inspection problem might be undergoing change.

While the Soviet scientists evidently were enjoying in human and professional terms their re-entrance into the essentially international world of science, the purposes of the Soviet government, as of 1958, were more narrow and specific. At the minimum, the intelligence possibilities of the dialogue undoubtedly appealed to Moscow in much the same way as it appealed to Washington. But Moscow was also evidently exercised about the spread of nuclear weapons beyond Britain, the United States, and the Soviet Union—including their spread to China; and it was seeking ways of limiting this diffusion of nuclear strength which would inevitably complicate Soviet political and military strategy and dilute its effective power. It was possible, but less evident, that the Soviet Union sought to eliminate the possibility of surprise attack and, even, to stabilize the arms race at a less costly level. But whatever Moscow's objectives, they were sought down to mid-1958 by means which would not involve free inspection, with all its consequences for the workings of Soviet society and Soviet policy.

As the dialogue proceeded among men who understood better than others the extraordinarily narrow range within which atomic weapons could rationally be used, it gradually came to rest on the ultimate issue: while American society was so structured as to permit acceptance of free inspection, Communist societies confronted virtually revolutionary change if free inspection was installed. While much in Soviet and American behavior in the arms race appeared to be symmetrical—like two sides of the same coin—at bottom lay this fundamental asymmetry which no amount of professional *camaraderie* could conceal. And no amount of ingenuity short of free inspection was likely to produce a more secure method for ending or controlling the nuclear arms race than the maintenance of a capacity for mutual destruction which could not be wiped out at a single sudden blow. The foreseeable development of solid-fuel, mobile, long-range missiles promised to provide the major nuclear powers with a destructive capacity virtually impossible to locate and attack as a blow; although it also opened up an endless race in antimissile defense. Nevertheless, the accelerated development of the mobile long-range missile appeared the most rational course until Russian political leadership was persuaded that free inspection was more acceptable than the expensive, dangerous stalemate which shielded Soviet society and Soviet military and foreign policy from the need for radical change.

The changes in Soviet thought and policy necessary to accept free inspection could not be brought about by Soviet scientists; but should the world find its way safely through the second half of the twentieth century, the dialogue of the scientists will have played a part.

# PART IV

# THE CRISIS OF 1956-1958

### 46. The Underdeveloped Areas

Between the events at Suez of November 1956 and the events in Iraq, Jordan, and Lebanon in July-August 1958 each of the major dimensions of American military and foreign policy came to crisis. In point of time, this rolling crisis began with the interplay of American and Soviet policy in the underdeveloped areas. These areas yielded a series of situations dangerous to the American interest in 1956-1958, among them political disintegration in Indonesia and Burma, the actue foreign-exchange shortage of India, the dangerous allied cross-purposes in Cyprus, the war in Algeria, and increasing turbulence in American relations with Latin America. But the Middle East was the dominant regional area of trouble. There the crisis began to unfold in its most acute form with the Israeli invasion of the Sinai Peninsula on October 29, 1956.

THE MIDDLE EAST: THE BACKGROUND IN GENERAL

Like the other underdeveloped areas, the Middle East presented, in addition to the endemic problem of domestic modernization, a range of local conflicts. The most acute of these centered around Israel. There was, first, the question of its continued existence; and, if its existence was implicitly conceded, there remained the questions of its permanent boundaries, the Arab refugees, the joint use of Middle East water resources, Israeli access to the Suez Canal and the Gulf of Aqaba, and, finally, of normal commercial, diplomatic, and cultural intercourse with the Arab world.

The Eisenhower administration, through the tripartite declaration of 1950, inherited a policy of backing Israel firmly. In general, the Eisenhower administration sought to shift somewhat the unequivocal nature of the American commitment to Israel in order to gain flexibility in dealing with the Arab world. It did not, however, move resolutely to resolve the specific issues in contention. These may well have been impossible to resolve, but the Administration did not devote to their resolution the energy and resources devoted, for example, to the building of the Baghdad Pact. Moreover, the main thrust of American policy in the Middle East—military defense against Soviet invasion—did not create an environment within which those issues were most likely to lose their central place in regional politics and come to lend themselves to resolution.

Thus, in the end, the effort to loosen the American commitment to Israel simply weakened the confidence of the government in Tel Aviv without gaining significant capital in the Arab world.

In addition to the problems of Israel and of organizing military strength against the Soviet Union, the Middle East presented the following issues:

1. The acceleration of nationalism and nationalist ambitions which assumed a greater importance for the peoples throughout the area than the objectives of a rigid anti-Communist and anti-Soviet policy.

2. Beyond nationalism, the gathering movement for regional unity and the conflict between Arab and non-Arab Moslem groups for regional leadership, centered, respectively, about Egypt and Turkey.

3. An increased interest in economic development and the growing pressure to direct an increasing proportion of oil revenues to this end.

4. The continued acute dependence of Western Europe on Middle East oil and on its regular secure transport through the Suez Canal.

The pursuit of a single-minded American effort to mount military force in the Middle East vis-à-vis the Soviet Union led over the period 1953-1956 to a crisis in United States-Israeli relations; to Soviet penetration of the area via trade, loans, and arms; to the emergence of a movement toward regional unity which was focused against, rather than in harmony with, long-range American interests; and to an oil supply crisis which acutely damaged American relations with Western Europe for some time.

THE SPECIAL PROBLEM OF EGYPT

Properly speaking, the Middle East crisis of 1956 centered on Egypt.[1] In that context the story began to take shape in the autumn of 1951 when Egypt, its emergent nationalism humiliated by the Israeli victory of 1948, turned against Britain and abrogated the 1936 treaty which had guaranteed the British military position in Egypt. In July 1952 Egyptian officers executed a *coup d'état*, Farouk left for Capri, and Naguib appeared as the new Egyptian head of state. As British-Egyptian relations worsened, Dulles undertook early in 1953 a role of conciliation, his aim being to maximize the chance that the new Egyptian leadership, having been conciliated with respect to British "colonialism," would join the Western Alliance against the Soviet Union while Britain and the United States organized regional military bases alternative to Suez.

It soon became evident, however, that Naguib and his colleagues were intent on objectives other than military alliance with the West against the Communist Bloc. They looked broadly to economic, political, and social modernization at home; to the pursuit of leadership in the Arab world designed, among other things, to give Cairo access to oil revenues; and to revenge for the debacle against Israel of 1948. All of this required in Egyptian eyes a policy of at least apparent disassociation from Western alliance—the normal posture of states newly freed from what they regarded as colonial ties. An anti-Western policy had a special local dimension; for the new coalitions of younger soldiers and intellectuals were contesting for power in the Arab world with older groupings, more heavily weighted with landowners' interests, historically associated with the West.

The only realistic alternative open to the United States under these circumstances was to accept the formal international neutralism of the new Egyptian government and to use every incentive and restraint available to induce the ardent new leadership to concentrate Egyptian energies on the tasks of domestic economic development which, in the face of the extraordinarily high rate of population increase, justified, in all conscience, single-minded Egyptian attention. But this course was not adopted; and in 1954 Dulles turned away from Egypt to concentrate on the building of a military alliance system in the Middle East.

In April 1954 the Turkish-Pakistani pact was signed. This evident challenge led Moscow to issue warnings to Iraq and Iran against completing the northern tier. In terms of Middle East regional politics, the northern tier threw Western weight behind non-Arab leadership and stirred Cairo to look to new means not only to prevent its isolation in the Middle East, but also to accelerate its drive to grasp the leadership of the whole Arab world. Meanwhile the British agreed to shift their main base to Cyprus, announcing a willingness to withdraw from Suez on July 28, 1954.

NASSER, ARMS, AND WATER

In November 1954 Nasser replaced Naguib, and a complex quadrilateral poker game began between Cairo, Moscow, London, and Washington; for the limited but real overlap of interest between Cairo and Moscow was evident, given American and British intent in the northern tier. Thus, while the United States and Britain rounded out the Baghdad Pact in the early months of 1955, the basis was laid for a Soviet-Egyptian *rapprochement*. In June, just before the Summit meeting at Geneva, Washington received word that a deal to exchange Communist arms for Egyptian cotton was in the making. Although Egypt was unwilling to join in military alliance with the United States and the West, bilateral agreements for both arms and economic assistance from the United States had been explored indecisively in 1955. In fact, in the week preceding the announcement of the Egyptian arms deal with the Communist Bloc in September 1955 there were reports that the United States had agreed in principle to sell Egypt arms; but the negotiations failed, and the deal was made via Czechoslovakia.

At this point American diplomacy faced three choices: to use full pressure short of military attack to halt the arms deal, to ignore but neutralize Nasser, or to enter into competition with Moscow for influence in Cairo. Essentially, the third choice was initially made. For almost a year American diplomacy sought to keep Egypt from entering too deeply and irreversibly into relations with the Soviet Union; but it did so under circumstances in which Nasser's bargaining position had been increased by the arms deal. From September 1955 forward, therefore, the American-Egyptian negotiations were shot through with self-evident blackmail. In the fall of 1955, for example, it was rumored that the Soviet Union would offer to build the Aswan Dam, the key instrument for enlarging Egypt's effective acreage and food supply. In evident response, Washington began to explore more urgently the possibilities of Western financing for the dam. In the meanwhile, however, Egypt pursued actively its efforts to counter the Baghdad Pact by an Arab Defense Pact embracing Egypt, Saudi Arabia, and Yemen; and Nasser interested himself actively as well in African affairs both in North Africa and south of the desert. In May 1956 Egypt recognized Communist China; in June British occupation of the Canal ended, followed immediately by Shepilov's descent on Cairo. And on July 19, 1956, the American offer to aid in the building of the Aswan Dam was withdrawn.

There is some indication that in July 1956, since Moscow was not then prepared to make so long-term and substantial a commitment to assist the Egyptian economy as the Aswan Dam would have required, Nasser was willing to accept the American offer of aid on the Aswan Dam. But at just this moment, against the background of some opposition from Senators representing cotton-producing states and from those incensed with Nasser's recognition of Communist China, the American offer was withdrawn.

Thus the United States, having assumed in 1953 major Western responsibility for dealing with Egypt in its new phase, had first failed to create a military ally, then failed to fashion a relationship outside military alliance which would associate important aspects of Egyptian ambitions with the West, via economic development, and finally permitted to develop a process of Egyptian double-dealing between Moscow and Washington which, in the showdown issue of the Aswan Dam, Dulles chose not to play through to the end.

So far as the Senate was concerned, there is reason to believe that if Dulles had chosen to play resolutely the Aswan Dam card—in the hope that this long-run commitment of Egyptian energies and constructive association with the United States would gradually deflate the Egyptian danger—he would have been backed. But for reasons still not wholly clear, the American offer was withdrawn in the form of a virtual personal challenge to Nasser, in effect ending the awkward interval of two-way Egyptian blackmail and inviting Nasser to do his worst.

EVERYONE DOES HIS WORST

For Nasser's worst, Washington was not prepared. The next stage of the Suez Crisis opened with Nasser's speech on July 26, announcing the nationalization of the Suez Canal, incorporating some of the most impassioned xenophobic rhetoric of the century directed against the United States. With the canal nationalized—and control of the oil traffic removed from Western hands—the economic interests of Europe, and especially Britain and France, came into play as a new urgent dimension.

From the point of view of London and of Paris, the United States had assumed, from roughly the time of Dulles' visit to Naguib in May 1953, a direct responsibility in the Middle East for a policy which required simultaneously the building of the northern tier pact and the pacification of Egyptian nationalism. Having failed to guide Egyptian nationalism constructively, and having disengaged from Nasser's game of two-way blackmail, the United States was expected by London and Paris to block Nasser forcefully and protect their vital oil supply. The French hoped at least for American support in limiting if not ending what they regarded as Egypt's disruptive role in Algeria.

Instead, American diplomacy reverted to the mood in which the British base at Suez had been liquidated—that is, a mood of gradually persuading Western Europe to disengage and to cut its losses.

Step by step the Western defeat unfolded: a foreign ministers' conference in July, the Users' Conference of August, the Menzies mission in September, and the setting up of an almost impotent Users' Association in October. The final dilution of the Users' Association agreement in September, which made the paying of canal tolls to the Association permissive rather than mandatory and which ruled out any American show or use of force, struck the British and French governments hard. The Users' Association, built on real economic interests with some foundation in international law, appeared a promising and orderly place on which to stand if resolutely backed. In the upshot, the British and French came to feel, rightly or wrongly, that the leader of the Western alliance not only had failed to protect their vital interests but also had not honored its pledged word.

Technically, the difference between London and Paris on the one hand and Washington on the other was simply on the question of whether the use of force against Nasser to preserve Western rights in the Canal was justified and wise. From July 26 forward the British and French never wavered in their formal reservation of the right to invoke force. Washington held that, given the tactical nature of the problem of seizing and holding a long canal, the use of force would be ineffective; and, further, that it would only worsen an already dangerous situation in the Arab world. But this (almost certainly correct) judgment could have been persuasive to British and French leaders (harried in Cyprus and Algeria as well as by the Canal crisis) only if the United States had produced a plan for protecting the oil flow to Western Europe by nonmilitary means. Thus the progressive sterilization of the Users' Association—and the belief that Dulles had practiced diplomatic salami tactics on his closest allies—struck with peculiar psychological force.

On October 25, a military pact linking Syria, Jordan, and Egypt having been announced four days before, the Sinai campaign was launched, almost certainly with the cooperation of the French and the knowledge of the British. In Israel the moment was chosen not simply in the light of the move toward Arab encirclement but also—and mainly—to end the nerve-wracking *fedayeen* border raids. The French, already embroiled in the *cul-de-sac* of Algeria, were similarly prepared for extreme risk. The British—hardest hit by the oil situation, with Eden ill and withdrawn to a somewhat private vision of his problem, including the faith that Washington would preserve a more or less benevolent neutrality—acted equally in terms of short-run desperation. And the whole atmosphere was colored by the turmoil in Poland and Hungary and, at a crucial stage, by the re-entry of Soviet troops into Budapest.

### THE SUEZ CRISIS: SOVIET EXPLOITATION AND INITIAL AMERICAN RESPONSE

Up to the point when Egypt was attacked the crisis had represented the successful use of Soviet diplomacy and aid to heighten and complicate a situation in which American and Free World policy had failed to deal in an orderly way with either the strategic requirements for containing the Soviet Union or the aspirations of Arab nationalism. On November 5, however, as Anglo-French paratroop battalions were dropped in the Port Said area, Moscow announced its determination to use force to "crush the aggressors and restore peace in the Middle East." In addition, Moscow implied that long-range missiles might be used against Western Europe, a threat planted by Khrushchev in Birmingham in the previous April; and reports flowed into

Washington and London which suggested the possibility that Soviet forces were moving by air across Turkey into Syria.[2]

There appears to be no doubt that these Soviet military gestures had a profound effect in Washington, where it was believed also that the Polish and Hungarian crises may have induced in Moscow an irrational desperation. The fear of direct or indirect Soviet military action certainly strengthened the America determination to force not only an immediate cease-fire but also a virtually unconditional withdrawal, softened at the insistence of the Senate in the case of Israel. With the United Nations expeditionary force in place and the Gulf of Aqaba more or less guaranteed, the armed expeditions were withdrawn by the end of December.

## THE MIDDLE EAST CRISIS OF 1956 IN PERSPECTIVE

Here was a region with immense variety in history, culture, and stages of modernization, emerging to a sense of nationhood and common regional interest in a setting of Cold War struggle and containing resources as well as military positions of first-class importance to external powers. Set in the midst of the area was Israel, whose existence, boundaries, population, and future economic relations with the region posed a peculiarly tough set of issues—issues reaching into those areas of irrational human commitment that do not accommodate easily to the give and take of sensible politics and diplomacy. Moreover, most of the Middle Eastern states were in that early stage of transition from traditional to modern status when political life is peculiarly fluid within the controlling élite and external infiltration and influence are relatively easy to bring about. The inner political life of the Middle East was dominated by a struggle between the older leaders, rooted in the land, often with old ties to the West, and new coalitions of younger soldiers and intellectuals, based mainly in the cities, controlled by a will to assert the nationhood of the Arab world. It was to be expected that the local emergent political leadership would seek to advance their own immediate interests as opportunity offered; and it was not to be expected that a smooth transition wholly consonant at all stages with American and Western interests would occur.

The existence of crisis in the Middle East in 1956 is not to be taken in itself, then, as evidence of failure or fault in American diplomacy. Given the complexity of the forces at work, the nature of certain key personalities, and the limits of American influence, it is impossible, even with hindsight, to chart a course of American policy which would necessarily have prevented the crisis of 1956. Nevertheless, three things can be asserted in regard to the American policy actually pursued.

First, the Eisenhower administration was irresolute in asserting its will to face down Soviet military threats and, especially, Soviet military infiltration of the area. The Middle East was an area of prime Western economic and military interest. That fact was understood in Moscow and confirmed after the Second World War by Stalin's acceptance of Truman's ultimatum of 1945-1946 in Northern Iran. The Soviet acquisition of influence and power in Egypt and Syria in 1956-1958 and American acceptance of the Communist right to ship arms into the non-Communist world was the first major break in the truce lines of the Cold War, leaving aside the special case of China, where civil war had already been joined in 1945.

Second, the Eisenhower administration, while shifting its position in directions calculated to make it easier to gain confidence in the Arab world, failed to seek at high priority a resolution of the Arab-Israeli issues the settlement of which were a condition for regional stability.

Third, the Eisenhower administration failed to hold out steadily the offer of substantial long-term loans and technical assistance to those nations willing to concentrate their energy, talents, and resources on domestic economic development. Although it can by no means be asserted that the existence of such an offer in 1954 and early 1955 would have channeled Egyptian energies predominantly in this constructive direction, many close observers of the Egyptian scene at that stage believe the possibility to have been real and substantial. But an American policy organized around the problem of military pacts to the virtual exclusion of any other major strategic goal clearly failed to test this possibility. Moreover, on a wider plane, the lack of an American economic development policy in these years made it impossible to offer a constructive matrix within which Arab ambitions for regional unity might have developed.

It was to be expected that Moscow would seek to leap-frog the northern tier pact and otherwise make efforts to extend its power in the region; but it was essential for minimum stability in the Cold War struggle that the American reaction be swift, firm, and effective—not least because once a Soviet foothold is gained, as in Egypt and Syria, its removal is not only difficult but also involves a greater loss of Soviet prestige than if it had never been established—a problem to be avoided, if possible, at a time of precarious nuclear stalemate.

### THE MIDDLE EAST REVISITED: 1958

In the wake of the Suez crisis Moscow pressed its advantage mainly by consolidating a position of political, military, and economic influence in Syria—a position short of complete takeover, but still an impressive extension of authority; and by continuing to lend support to Nasser's leadership of Arab nationalism despite evidence that Nasser sought increasingly to ensure that

Cairo rather than Moscow would remain the unchallenged center of Arab politics.

Nasser himself was temporarily deflected by four factors arising from the Suez crisis: the Egyptian defeat in the Sinai, leading to the presence of United Nations forces on the Israeli frontier; the economic strains imposed by Western freezing of his funds abroad; the threat to the neutralist balance between East and West he had sought to maintain which was represented by the increased direct Soviet influence in Syria; and the American willingness to apply counterforce against any direct Soviet military intervention, a willingness asserted late in the course of the Suez crisis and confirmed in the Eisenhower Doctrine.

The Eisenhower Doctrine of 1957, with its dual offer of military and economic aid, did not, however, yield a prompt resolution of the Middle East crisis or even a change in the trend of events. It failed partly because it was addressed so substantially to the remote or nonexistent problem of a Soviet military invasion, and partly because the American approach to economic development in the Near East and the whole posture toward Arab nationalism incorporated in the Doctrine was not attractive enough— or politically powerful enough in its effect on Arab and world opinion—seriously to deflect Nasser from his goal of virtually unilateral power in the Arab world.

In one direction Nasser did conciliate the West. The Canal was run with impeccable efficiency, and a settlement of the rights of the Suez Canal owners was negotiated.

On the other hand, the drive to extend Egypt's influence beyond Syria gradually accelerated. In particular, Nasser addressed himself to the problem of removing four major stumbling blocks to his dominance of the Arab world: that is, the residual western influence in Saudi Arabia, Iraq, Jordan, and Lebanon. If those countries could be brought within his orbit by a rise to power of the new coalitions of soldiers and intellectuals, the oil sheikdoms at the head of the Persian Gulf would be put under great pressure and the dream of control by Cairo of the oil revenues would be close to reality. In effect, American policy within the framework of the Eisenhower Doctrine sought to contain Nasser's outward thrust by holding the four areas in a state of relative independence with respect to Nasser, through alliance with older political groupings.

As Cairo recovered from the shock and strain of the Suez crisis, Nasser mounted a sustained program of subversion, armed infiltration, and psychological pressure and succeeded in focusing Arab nationalist feeling around the rupture of the residual links of formal alliance to the West. His campaign, converging with the thrust of local forces Nasser did not wholly control, yielded a sharp change in the policy of Saudi Arabia, the overthrow of the Iraq government, and, in its wake, the imminent danger of collapse in Jordan and Lebanon. To avoid this debacle, the British and American governments sent troops into Lebanon and Jordan in July 1958 at the request of the threatened governments.

Articulating his moves with this Nasserite thrust, Khrushchev sought urgently a high-level meeting of the heads of state, hoping to bring Britain and the United States to the bar as opponents of nationalism, invoking once again the threat of missiles and "volunteers," thus combining a posture of dominant strength and association with a popular movement. When this tactic did not immediately succeed, however, Moscow drew back from a heads-of-state meeting at the level of the United Nations Security Council, which was the formula the West had finally accepted. The issue was then brought before a special meeting of the United Nations Assembly, a move which offered a moment of tactical respite to the United States in which the direction of American policy could be altered from a position of poise, at American initiative.

This transient opportunity was seized. The Eisenhower adminstration, after a passage of creative effort not seen in Washington for some years, conducted in the disarray of fast-moving crisis, attempted a new approach to the problem of Arab nationalism along the following lines. First, to reaffirm and extend the American commitment to support the Baghdad Pact in the wake of Iraq's probable defection, thus seeking to isolate the problems of the Arab world from those of the non-Arab Moslems to the North, and foreclosing the possibility of a Soviet move to press for total neutralization of the Middle East. Second, to seek United Nations support for continued Lebanese independence under the less Western-oriented but, hopefully, stable government which emerged from the 1958 crisis. Third, to buy time to permit a resolution of the Jordan crisis. Fourth, to create a United Nations stand-by force which would represent an alternative to British and American power in resisting Nasser's effort to acquire authority in the region, where the will to resist the wave of pressure might exist. Fifth, to begin an approach toward an arms moratorium between Israel and the Arab world which might frustrate Moscow's arms deal tactic, reduce mutual fears within the region, and, conceivably, set the stage for a definitive settlement. Sixth, to offer substantial economic assistance to the Arab world, including the possibility of acquiring oil revenues for regional economic development if Arab nationalism was prepared to divert an increased amount of attention and energy to formulating and executing seriously the tasks of modernization. The whole program was framed by the demonstration, in Lebanon and Jordan, that the United States and Britain were not prepared to abandon positions on the Free World side of the World War II truce lines in the face of Soviet missile and "volunteer" threats.

This was the policy Eisenhower enunciated before the United Nations Assembly on August 13, 1958. It represented a balance among the elements in the nation's policy which many had sought without success to introduce before the Suez Crisis as well as during and after the formulation of the Eisenhower Doctrine a year and a half earlier.

The new approach to Arab nationalism represented an acceptance of the fact that the policy followed since 1953 towards the nationalist revolutions in the southern half of the world would not suffice. The focus of the new policy was not the threat of Communist ground force invasion of the Middle East; it was, rather, the direction which the nationalist ambitions of the Arab world should assume. The role of the Soviet Union was recognized not as threatening invasion but as corrupting the course of Arab nationalism with images of power capable of rendering the West impotent and with offers of arms, trade, and diplomatic support for Arab nationalism's most disruptive ambitions. Above all, an unmistakably authentic offer of substantial and sustained economic assistance was made to Arab nations hitherto hostile to the West and barely neutralist.

The fate of these proposals lay in a future beyond the range of this book. They hinged on a change in the direction of Arab nationalism on which diverse forces were at work.

Nevertheless, with time, persistence, toughness, and a sense of history it was possible that, out of the elements in the August 13 speech, the world might, despite Moscow's strategy of diversion, ride out the initial explosive phase of Arab nationalism and see it turn to its ultimate mission of completing the preconditions for take-off and launching the Near East on the path of sustained growth under circumstances which would not foreclose the possibility of a progressive democratic development of the region.

On one point, however, the consequence of Eisenhower's speech of August 13 was reasonably predictable. It acknowledged that what the United States was prepared to do for the Arab movement in its most disruptive phase the United States must be prepared to do in Latin America, Asia, and Africa as well. The criterion that economic aid should be primarily an instrument of support for those joined with the United States in military alliance against the Communist Bloc was, after a long dominance, definitely altered. The objective of economic assistance as a means for supporting the emergence of independent states, focusing their ardent nationalism increasingly on the modernization of their societies, had been enunciated under circumstances likely to commit the United States over a long future; and in the context of American economic foreign policy since 1953 this was a radical departure.

### POLICY TOWARD ECONOMIC DEVELOPMENT

The rigidity of American economic policy toward the underdeveloped areas in the period 1953-1956 was due to a persistent conflict within the Eisenhower administration which the President was not prepared firmly to settle. In the Administration's initial strategic dispositions economic aid had only one clear purpose—to assist the nation's Eurasian allies to maintain deterrent forces on a scale sufficient for the United States to cut down its own ground forces and concentrate on weapons of mass destruction, their means of delivery, and the means of defense against them. In accordance with this view, the American economic aid organization was renamed the Mutual Security Agency; and several forms of economic assistance were placed under military categories on the assumption that Congress would support military but not economic aid.

Nevertheless, some within the Executive Branch understood the importance of associating the United States with the positive and constructive objectives of the underdeveloped areas via economic aid. In 1953-1954 Stassen and others, including Bowles' successor in India, advocated an expansion of the economic aid program to non-Communist nations unwilling to join in military pacts. In mid-1954, however, at a stage when concrete proposals to this end were being formulated and seriously considered in Washington, the opponents of this view succeeded in displacing Stassen with Hollister, a man explicitly dedicated to the reduction of foreign aid; and Herbert Hoover, Jr., of similar persuasion, moved into the position of Undersecretary of State and was granted by the Secretary of State guidance of economic foreign policy. These men and their like-minded colleagues in the Treasury, the Budget Bureau, the White House staff, and elsewhere in the government controlled American economic foreign policy over the period down to 1957 and retained considerable influence thereafter.

What was their case? Their argument generally centered on these points:

1. The expanding pressures for military outlays in the arms race made it essential to cut back on programs of lesser importance to the national interest; and programs of economic aid to nations not militarily allied with the United States belonged in that category.

2. There was no evidence that economic assistance to such nations brought the United States any benefit in the Cold War struggle. On the contrary, those nations appeared to take pride in asserting their diplomatic independence, often to American embarrassment; and it was, if nothing else, undignified for the United States to appear to be seeking borrowers for its money, notably under circumstances of neutralist behavior.

3. Since many of the so-called uncommitted nations were, at least verbally, socialist, and democracy was unlikely to survive under a regime of state ownership, they were to be written off as ideological as well as military allies.

4. Aside from India, few if any of the underdeveloped areas had the adminstrative and technical talent, the social overhead capital structure, and the political and social will to use more capital effectively. Those that did have these preconditions could get capital from existing international sources; in those that did not have them American grants and loans would be wasted.

These were by no means trivial arguments. An answer to the first of these points required a willingness to face an expansion in the federal budget; an answer to the second required an alternative view of the nature of the American interest in the underdeveloped areas; an answer to the third required an alternative view of the relation between democracy and capitalism and, especially, a more hopeful and dynamic view of the future prospects for private enterprise as the new economies acquired momentum; an answer to the fourth required the concept of the offer of substantial long-term American aid as an incentive to mobilize the preconditions for the effective absorption of capital.

The debate was conducted in and out of the government; and the advocates of enlarged long-term economic aid very gradually won ground. The concept of long-term economic aid was finally aired in 1956; after a remarkable Senate examination of the foreign aid problem, a Development Loan Fund was created on a small scale in 1957; in 1958 it began to make loans and its funds were modestly expanded. Equally significant, in 1958 some $290 million was raised in Washington to prevent too radical a cut-back in the goals of the Indian Second Five-Year Plan; and an amendment to the Mutual Security Act was passed by the Senate (but not taken up in the House of Representatives) designed to guarantee adequate and sustained support on an international basis for the Indian economic development effort.

Although the debate may have been fruitful, notably the Senate examination conducted by the 85th Congress, the heart of the matter was the quiet withdrawal from the Washington scene in 1957 of those who had ardently opposed programs of economic aid over the previous three or four years and their replacement by men of cautious but different views. This simple fact was reinforced in 1958 by the mounting evidence of Soviet reliance on economic policy as an instrument to extend its power and influence in the underdeveloped areas, by a radical deterioration in relations with Latin America centered in part on economic policy, and then by the Middle East crisis of the summer of 1958.

Additional aid in itself could not alter the nation's relations with the nations of Asia, the Middle East, Africa, and South America; nor could additional aid in itself cope with the complex Soviet offensive in those transitional areas. The availability of American resources for economic development rather than merely military purposes was a necessary but not sufficient condition for an effective policy toward the underdeveloped areas. Nevertheless, the evolution of the economic aid debate in the United States— both inside and outside the government—and the evolution of the government's policy over the period 1953-1958 provide a significant index of the direction and pace of change in the nation's view of the nature of its interest in these regions.

The Administration began to confirm in action what had long been part of its formal rhetoric: namely, that the United States had a direct interest in the survival and development of independent democracy in nations in the underdeveloped areas quite aside from whether these new nations were prepared to join the United States in military pacts. In pace and scale, however, the dispositions of the Eisenhower administration in economic foreign policy fell far short of the minimum sums necessary to achieve the objectives its rhetoric proclaimed. After some four years of debate within the Administration and outside, and the emergence of a remarkable consensus among the leaders of the nation's public opinion, American policy toward economic development remained grossly inadequate to its strategic purpose of offering a powerful constructive incentive to nationalism or to its tactical purposes of maintaining an adequate rate of growth in the Free World economy and coping with the Soviet economic offensive.

## 47. Military Policy

### SPUTNIK: THE ADMINISTRATION VIEW

There is no clear analogy in American history to the crisis triggered by the launching of the Soviet earth satellite on October 4, 1957. This intrinsically harmless act of science and engineering was also, of course, both a demonstration of foreseeable Soviet capability to launch an ICBM and a powerful act of psychological warfare. It immediately set in motion forces in American political life which radically reversed the nation's ruling conception of its military problem, of the appropriate level of the budget, and of the role of science in its affairs. The reaction reached even deeper, opening a fundamental reconsideration not only of the organization of the Department of Defense but also of the values and content of the American educational system and of the balance of values and objectives in contemporary American society as a whole.

This reaction occurred despite the predominant views within the Executive Branch. The Administration had known for several years that the Soviet

Union was certainly ahead of the United States in ballistic rocketry. It had made an explicit decision to separate the American earth satellite program from military rocket development; and it had discounted—without great imaginative insight, but discounted nevertheless—the likelihood that the Soviet Union would launch an earth satellite ahead of the United States. For at least two years, various groups inside and outside the Executive Branch had warned not only that the Soviet Union was ahead of the United States in ballistic missiles but also that it was rapidly closing the gap over a wide range of military technology and modernized order of battle; and that Soviet momentum, set against the existing scale and pace of American military activity, would yield in a relatively short time a general Soviet military superiority over the United States.

The Administration view was affected by a frame of mind which tended to discount this judgment on the pace of the arms race while formally acknowledging it. Nevertheless, the likelihood of Soviet superiority in several major dimensions was in the end accepted by those with ultimate authority in the Executive Branch essentially on the ground that, even without general military superiority, the United States had in being and under development sufficient forces to continue to make irrational the overt Soviet use of military force. And, indeed, it could be argued that since the demobilization of 1945-1946 American security had been maintained not by a general superiority over the Soviet Union but by a sustained ability to retaliate with nuclear attack. The ability to maintain with selective instruments the capability of massive retaliation with nuclear weapons, rather than general superiority over the Soviet Union, continued to be regarded as the correct touchstone for American military policy. The strength of the reaction to the Soviet launching of an earth satellite was, therefore, regarded at the highest level in the Administration as a manifestation of "mass hysteria."

## THE INITIAL PUBLIC REACTION

But the Administration reckoned without two elements in the nation's reaction, one popular and the other confined to a knowledgeable but influential minority.

The American public had not been prepared for the military policy implicit in the Eisenhower administration's posture, that is, an acceptance of Soviet equality or even superiority in certain of the most modern capabilities for the use and delivery of nuclear weapons. In a sense this was the first major cost of the failure to execute and to sustain Operation Candor. If the President had clearly and regularly explained before the event the evolution of the arms race and why the Administration was prepared to see the Soviet Union outstrip the United States to a degree in missiles and other branches of modern military technology, why the launching of an earth satellite was not in itself of military significance aside from the known Soviet lead in ballistic missiles, and why current and future planned American military capabilities would suffice to protect the nation's interest, it is possible that his policy would not have been so seriously questioned in 1958.

A popular acceptance of existing policy under such circumstances would not, however, have been assured even with the President's great prestige brought to bear. Reliable facts on the relative military position of the two great powers would then have been available and brought responsibly to public attention. A major political debate might well have been opened, the outcome of which could not be predicted. The Administration had feared since 1953 that a full airing of the facts of the arms race would lead to an irrepressible demand for an enlarged military budget. Given the nation's image of itself in relation to the world, it is doubtful if a military position of second rank in new weaponry would have been explicitly accepted as the foreseeable end of national policy.

Nevertheless, the initial strength of the popular reaction to the Soviet demonstration of a capability equivalent to the launching of an ICBM was compounded both of surprise at the fact and determination to alter the evidently shifting balance of military power. The public could not believe that the Administration's policy could have been what it was; and the initial Administration reaction of blandness to the launching of an earth satellite was taken to be something different from the essentially honest view that it reflected.

### THE ÉLITE REACTION

Of equal if not greater importance was the development that lay behind the Gaither and Rockefeller Reports. Over the previous three years there had spread, by a curious and subtle process, both a knowledge of the essential military facts and a consensus on the directions in which the Administration's policy ought to be changed. Leading businessmen, scientists, labor leaders, lawyers, foundation officers, soldiers, journalists, professors, and unemployed politicians of both parties had begun to acquire a sufficiently firm and confident grasp on the facts to challenge the Administration's policy and to formulate an alternative.

The problem of security classification of military facts was not the essential difficulty in crystallizing an independent view; for Congressional hearings combined with the lack of inhibition of the American press radically narrow the range of true secrecy for those who wish to establish the facts. The problem was to assemble a sufficiently complete picture of the emerging military position of the United States vis-à-vis the Soviet Union for responsible, experienced men to feel confident in challenging the views of those publicly charged to look after the nation's interests. Despite what appears to be cavalier criticism from the sidelines, there is, in fact, a widespread and creditable diffidence among responsible men outside goverment to believe that they know better what ought to be done in military and foreign policy than those bearing day-to-day responsibility—even when those bearing responsibility are their political opponents. But in the period 1955-1957 there spread through the ranks of the American elite—the responsible leaders of the grass-roots private voluntary groupings and institutions which are the basis of the nation's social organization—a growing uneasiness; and, in the end, the outline of an alternative national security policy was formulated and was ready for presentation at the end of 1957.

How did this come about? First, a considerable number of citizens had been drawn into advisory groups by the government on particular national security questions and given access to at least a portion of the evidence available on the relative military position of the United States and the Soviet Union. These groups systematically emerged from their tasks urging an enlarged American effort. They derived from the facts recommendations for policy different from those drawn by the highest Administration officials. Second, by various devices—ranging from Congressional hearings to the annual strategy seminars at the Army, Navy, and Air War Colleges—the three services made available estimates of the situation and recommendations for policy at variance with the Administration's official view. No one of these occasions or devices was in itself decisive; but they had a cumulative effect within the circle of those outside the government deeply concerned with security affairs. Third, the Council on Foreign Relations in New York kept a substantial group of men from this circle quite professionally briefed in military and foreign policy matters; and, to a degree, similar independent examinations of military policy were being conducted at universities and elsewhere throughout the nation. Finally, of course, the more normal process of a free politics and a free journalism had exposed facts and issues for debate which, while ineffective in themselves in causing a shift in national policy, had helped create a climate of latent uneasiness which the Soviet launching of an earth satellite appeared to justify. The Symington Hearings of 1956 played, for example, an important preparatory role in the post-satellite military crisis.

In different ways these converging processes came to a head in the Gaither Report and in Rockefeller Panel Report II. From press accounts it would appear that those who prepared the Gaither Report had been assembled in the summer of 1957 to examine the question of whether the nation should invest large resources in the construction of shelters which would protect its citizens against fallout in case of nuclear attack. Like all men engaged on a specific problem in a complex general context, their first apparent impulse was to conclude that the narrow question could be answered only if they had before them a total picture of the present and foreseeable Soviet threat and of American dispositions, current and prospective, to meet that threat. By a process not yet known to this historian, they managed to act on this impulse and brought the camel into the tent.

Thus by early October 1957 they had assembled from official sources an estimate of the total military situation and an array of recommendations for national security policy as a whole alternative to those on which the nation had been operating. Although the Gaither Report has not been made public, it is evident that its authors recommended a radical increase in military expenditure in a good many directions, and that it challenged the Administration view that the United States could maintain effective deterrence of Soviet military strength at the existing level and organization of the nation's military effort. In the wake of the launching of the second Soviet earth satellite, this view was laid before the National Security Council, an occasion of some historical moment since it represented in effect a charge by one wing of the Republican Party (symbolized, for example, by Lovett, McCloy, and Foster) that those in command had not met adequately their first responsibility to the nation over the previous several years.

## THE ELITE CONSENSUS

The substance of the consensus which had been developed on military policy in the two previous years was published shortly thereafter as the first in a series of reports prepared under the initiative of Nelson Rockefeller.[1] Rockefeller had resigned early in 1956 from the post of special assistant to the President, evidently after a battle centered on the adequacy of the military and foreign aid budgets.[2] He turned in private life to organizing a general review of American problems and policies, domestic and foreign, looking ahead some years. Members of the six Rockefeller panels included men actively engaged in an advisory capacity to the government as well as some with recent governmental experience and generally well-informed laymen. There was some overlap between the membership of the Gaither and the Rockefeller groups;[3] and highly professional staff work was available to those panels which touched on military affairs.

Their conclusions are worth quoting in summary as a reflection of the precision with which a consensus had been reached outside the government on issues normally inaccessible to the democratic process unless the Executive Branch makes them so:

It is the judgment of the panel that prepared this report that all is not well with present US security policies and operations. The over-all US strategic concept lags behind developments in technology and in the world political situation. Defense organization is unrelated in major ways to critically important military missions. Systems of budgets, appropriations, and financial management are out of gear with the radically accelerating flow of military developments. The United States system of alliances must be adapted to constantly changing strategic requirements. The United States is rapidly losing its lead in the race of military technology.

We are convinced that corrective steps must be taken now.

We believe that the security of the United States transcends normal budgetary considerations and that the national economy can afford the necessary measures.

In brief, the conclusions of the panel are:

I. The world knows that we would never fight a preventive war. But we and the rest of the free world must be prepared to resist any one of three types of aggresion: all-out war, limited war, and non-overt aggression concealed as internal takeover by coup d'etat or by civil war.

II. In order to deter aggression, we must be prepared to fight a nuclear war either all-out or limited.

III. At present there are major shortcomings in our posture for both all-out war and limited war. Our retaliatory force is inadequately dispersed and protected. Our active and passive defense is insufficient. Moreover, we lack mobility and versatility for limited war.

IV. Basic changes in our defense organization are recommended to correct the inefficiency and duplication of effort growing out of interservice rivalry.

a). The military departments should be removed from the channel of operational command.

b). All of the operational military forces of the United States should be organized into unified commands to perform missions which are called for by our strategic requirements.

c). The Chairman of the Joint Chiefs of Staff should be designated Principal Military Adviser to the Secretary of Defense and the President.

d). The staff of the Joint Chiefs of Staff should be organized on a unified basis and placed under the control of the Chairman.

e). All officers above the rank of Brigadier General or equivalent should receive their permanent promotions from the Department.

f). The line of operational command should be from the President and the Secretary of Defense to the functional commanders through the Chairman of the Joint Chiefs of Staff in his capacity as Principal Military Adviser.

g). The line of logistic command should be from the President through the Secretary of Defense to the Secretaries of the three military departments.

h). The Secretary of Defense should be given direct authority over all research, development and procurement. He should have the right of cancellation and transfer of service programs together with their appropriations. He should also be given a direct appropriation for the conduct of research and development programs at the Defense Department level.

V. We must strengthen the regional groups of nations, not as an alternative to the United Nations, but as its complement in line with Article 51 of the Charter.

VI. The United States must make a concerted effort to meet the joint security requirements of all partners in the alliances in which we participate by contributing to the development of a common strategic concept, by assisting in the re-equipping of allied forces by fostering political cohesiveness and by economic and technical cooperation.

VII. We must pool with our allies in NATO scientific and technical information, and provide them with nuclear weapons and delivery systems.

VIII. Civil defense must be part of our over-all strategic posture. A program must be undertaken to include a warning system and fall-out shelters.

IX. We must face the fact that a meaningful reduction of armaments must be preceded by a reduction of tensions and a settlement of outstanding issues that have divided the world since World War II. At the same time, concrete proposals to limit such wars as might be forced on us should be introduced into negotiations on reduction in forces. Even if the Soviet Union should reject our proposals, a unilateral declaration might be given a strong incentive to follow suit.

X. Starting immediately, defense expenditures must be increased substantially over the next few years. Testimony indicates that current deficiencies in our strategic position require additional expenditures each year of approximately $3 billion for the next several years. This does not include necessary increased appropriations for mutual assistance and for civil defense. Because we must maintain our present forces as we go into production on new weapons, such as missiles, the cost of military programs will continue to rise until at least 1965.

Specific recommendations include the following:

a) Aircraft procurement to modernize existing units be authorized into the 1960's while pressing for the most rapid development of operational intermediate Range and Inter-Continental Ballistic Missiles.

b) The SAC base structure be made less vulnerable to surprise attack through dispersion and other protective measures.

c) An accelerated research and development support be provided for such key programs as missiles.

d) Additional troop transport be authorized in the form both of modern aircraft and ships.

e) The program of equipping both surface and underwater ships with missiles of various types be accelerated and additional funds for anti-submarine defense be provided.

f) Military pay scales be raised to retain skilled officers and men.[4]

Point by point, Rockefeller Panel Report II was a public rejection of the concept of the Great Equation and the specific policies which the Eisenhower administration had built upon it over the previous five years. The report rejected the notion that a healthy recognizable American society required for the maintenance of its institutions a rigid limitation of budgetary expenditures.[5] It rejected the concept that an ability to retaliate with nuclear weapons was a sufficient deterrent to Soviet strength. It rejected the continued denial to NATO of information about nuclear weapons and the weapons themselves. It rejected the notion that existing dispositions were sufficient to maintain American retaliatory power over the foreseeable future. It rejected the pattern of administration which had emerged during the previous five years in the Department of Defense, including the priority for and methods of handling research and development.

The professional clarity with which these positions were articulated and the ability to get virtual unanimity on them in a group as diverse as the almost fifty signers of the Panel II report are to be understood only in the light of the process which had preceded that report over the previous three years.

In a sense, a representative group of leaders from both political parties had formed a kind of shadow Cabinet in opposition. With the help of experts inside and outside the government, they had done their homework on the nation's security problem; and they were able to persuade a kind of Senate, made up of leaders from a wide range of American private institutions, to back this alternative program against the President. It is doubtful that unanimity around anything like such a program could have been achieved without the Soviet launching of the earth satellites; but the ground was well laid. There was already a substantial body of highly responsible American citizens prepared to commit themselves to an alternative program when the demonstration of Soviet capabilities was made.

It was, once again, the existence of a massive body of evidence which had been carefully analyzed before the event which permitted a unanimous report to emerge from Senator Johnson's Preparedness Sub-Committee in the Senate on January 7, 1958, with its fourteen-point program.

### THE ADMINISTRATION'S RESPONSE

In the Pentagon itself, a new Secretary of Defense, McElroy, took over a few days before the launching of the first Soviet satellite; and he moved with some vigor to begin to undo certain of the key decisions made over the previous year with respect to the military budget and research and development. Senator Johnson's Sub-Committee could list seven major actions by McElroy designed to accelerate the missile and satellite programs and to enlarge the work on new weapons. The budgetary limitation on defense was, to a degree, temporarily lifted; Killian was brought to the White House as a public guarantee (as well as, in fact, to ensure) that research and development would be conducted in ways which scientists and engineers regarded as most conducive to the development of new weaponry; and the arms race proceeded with its American end operating under new concepts and under relatively new management.

Finally, the missile issue, dramatizing the extent to which the new technology bypassed the land-sea-air distinction on which the three services were built, brought the question of Pentagon reorganization to a head. As with other aspects of military policy, a consensus had developed outside the government on the main lines which a reorganization of the Department of Defense should take. That consensus embraced three fundamental points: the need at the apex of the Department of Defense for improved centralized staff work in terms of the nation's security problem as a whole; the recommendation that the triservice task force conception, applied to continental air defense, be extended, with the task forces operating directly under the Secretary of Defense (and Joint Chiefs of Staff) rather than under the three services; and that the powers of the three services over operations, research and development, and promotion (to general and flag officer rank) be reduced.

By mid-1958 the sense of urgency endemic six months earlier was greatly deflated. The President had thrown his weight behind the consensus only with respect to the reorganization of the Pentagon; and there he gained from the Congress something of what he asked. But military expenditures when corrected for price increases were expanded little if at all. And with earth satellites no longer a novelty, the foreseeable military threat they symbolized—which had deeply shaken the members of the Gaither and Rockefeller Panels—was increasingly lost from view; that is, the threat that sometime after 1959 the Soviet Union might well have a substantial ICBM threat capable of obliterating SAC bases, which, combined with developments in air defense, might leave the United States and the Free World without a meaningful capacity to retaliate against Soviet military strength for the first time since 1945.

The Administration had, on the whole, successfully resisted the pressures for expanded and accelerated military programs of attack and defense. It was estimated officially that "the defense budget had been affected less than 2 per cent since the Russians announced the possession of intercontinental ballistic missiles and successfully launched the first earth satellite."[6] Nor had the Administration responded to the plea that a highly mobile task force for the deterrence of limited war be created. The sluggish flow of American troops into Lebanon, against no opposition, demonstrated that airlift was grossly inadequate, but no steps were taken in 1958 to create it.

In part this extremely limited budgetary reaction reflected the fact that new weapons were still in a research and development stage, incapable of large-scale production. In part, however, it reflected a willingness of the Administration to continue to accept risks with the nation's security in the interests of economy beyond those advised by any of the nongovernmental groups which had examined the nation's security problem over the previous four years and by its own military advisers.

It was, of course, possible that the nation would survive "the gap"—that is, the interval between a substantial Soviet delivery capability with ICBM's and the development of an equivalent American capability; for there was a second gap to be reckoned with, the gap between a degree of Soviet superiority and that degree of superiority in delivery capabilities and air defense which would make rational an all-out attack on the Free World's retaliatory power. Even without a substantial ICBM force there were ways of maintaining sufficient retaliatory power, invulnerable to a single blow, to continue to make a Soviet assault irrational. All was not lost; and it was not to be ruled out in mid-1958 that the United States could emerge in the 1960's with a mobile solid-fuel rocket force that was secure. But it was clearly going to be an uncomfortably close thing; and it had, in no sense, been a necessary risk to run.

## 48. NATO

### THE HERITAGE OF SUEZ

The issues of conflict which arose between the United States and its Western European allies in the period 1956-1958 derived from the course of events in Asia, the Middle East, and Africa on the one hand and from the changing character and balance of the arms race on the other. The cross-purposes within the alliance came to focus, respectively, in the Suez Crisis of 1956 and in the post-sputnik NATO meeting of December 1957. The consequences of Suez strongly colored the situation faced in NATO a year later.

With respect to the British, the Suez affair produced a crisis with three dimensions. First, the West as a whole suffered defeat, but the British effort to deal with the problem outside the Anglo-American alliance ended, quite particularly, in debacle. Second, the manner in which the most acute stage of the crisis was handled by Eden had even deeper effects within Britain. He operated outside the common-law limits of British government practice, bringing into his councils only a portion of the Cabinet, the civil service, and the military. Moreover, the military operation was executed with inadequate force and decisiveness. The image projected by this performance both to Britishers and to the world was out of keeping with the good order, poise, and competence with which British affairs were traditionally conducted. Finally, of course, the unreliability of the United States as an ally, from London's point of view, on an issue of highest importance to British welfare shook confidence in the Anglo-American alliance as the unique foundation for the British world position and in the capabilities of American leadership of the Free World in general.

Although a good deal of resentment was focused on the role of the United States in this affair, more fundamentally the Suez crisis dramatized for Britons the extent to which the old image of themselves and their relationship to the world as a first-class power might no longer hold. Such reflections had been endemic since the end of the Second World War; but the Suez crisis crystallized out a sense of national limitation, frustration, and decline.

For France, the impact was somewhat different. The French had suffered in the Second World War a national humiliation and soul-searching through which Britain had not passed. In the postwar period the French had been seeking to re-establish a position of influence and authority rather than to hold on to a wartime image of effective performance. Impaled on the almost insoluble problem of Algeria, they had less to lose psychologically in the Suez venture than the British. Thus the setback of the Suez venture was less of a shock than it was in Britain. Moreover, having made more direct common cause with Israel, the French could take greater comfort than the British from the Sinai affair and from the limitation it placed, even temporarily, on Nasser's freedom of action and influence.

Nevertheless, for both the French and the British the development of a situation where they felt impelled to act desperately and outside the orbit of the tie to Washington in order to protect primary interests which Washington was not prepared to defend forced a general re-evaluation of the Free World alliance and the American role within it.

The other states of Western Europe, being less directly involved with Suez or its consequences, were more dispassionate observers of the scene. They were, nevertheless, shaken by the extraordinary disarray of the Western alliance and its inability to cope effectively with the forces set in motion by the interplay of Soviet strategy and the nationalist revolutions at work in the world arena.

SUEZ TO SPUTNIK

In the year following the Suez crisis some limited progress on the road back was made. The United States and Britain began to reform the lines of policy built on the Baghdad Pact; and, although the Eisenhower Doctrine worked no magic in the Middle East, Saudi Arabia was kept for a time from definitive commitment to Nasser, and the oil continued, after relatively brief interruption, to flow through the canal to Western Europe.

Meanwhile, however, the Soviet incursion into Syria was, to a degree, consolidated, and the French, with the existence of large-scale oil deposits confirmed in the northern Sahara, struggled like men in a nightmare to bring their policy in Algeria to a resolution.

There was, then, no quick regeneration of the vitality of the Atlantic Alliance after the Suez crisis. There were no new lines of policy or action capable of reversing the impact on Western interests of the nationalist surge as guided and deflected by Soviet policy.

The major constructive response to the Suez crisis took the form of an acceleration of Western European plans to create a common market, a move so powerful in its potentialities that the British proposed the link to a free trade area. In fact, the decision to proceed with a common market and the opening of negotiations to create a related free trade area preceded the Suez crisis, and, in general, the movement toward European unity in the postwar decade had many converging sources. But frustrations in dealing with the aspiring new nations on the one hand and with Washington on the other undoubtedly contributed to the acceleration of European union in 1956-1958.

NATO AFTER SPUTNIK

When, in the autumn of 1957, the sputnik crisis arose, some of the intensity of feeling of a year earlier had drained away; and within the European governments the outcome at Suez was read by cooler heads as definitive evidence that major action in military affairs outside the orbit of agreement with Washington was a dead end.

The impact of the satellite launchings in Western Europe was both psychologically and militarily somewhat different from the impact in the United States. The Soviet capability to launch an earth satellite signaled a foreseeable capability to launch an ICBM, a Soviet weapon system directed against the United States rather than against Western Europe. Western Europe had been living over the previous year and a half under an explicit threat of Soviet attack with IRBMs to which the counterdelivery capabilities of the American Strategic Air Force—and to an increasingly significant degree RAF Bomber Command—were the only serious deterrents. While the Soviet satellites dramatized for Western Europe the fact of rising relative Soviet capabilities, they did not radically alter the existing perspectives on their security problem except to this degree: the sputniks to some extent shook their confidence that, whatever its inadequacies an an ally, the United States would maintain in the future a sufficient capability in retaliatory power to continue to hold the Soviet Union in check.

More narrowly, however, an important military problem was posed by the Soviet display: namely, that the Soviets might have an operational ICBM capability for some time period before the United States had acquired it. Conceivably, this might lead to an acute vulnerability of American air bases as well as continental United States, and leave the Free World without the shield of an effective retaliatory instrument.

This possibility led promptly to an American desire to mount in Western Europe IRBM bases which would extend the Free World's retaliatory capability. In both the United States and Western Europe it was apparent that, for an interval at least, a prudent American policy required the Western alliance and the IRBM range bases it afforded. In addition, the evident pace of Soviet military technology led Washington to reconsider its policy of secrecy with respect to atomic matters and to propose measures which would not only give Europeans increased access to nuclear weapons but also expand the possibility of European contribution to research and development in nuclear weapons.

For European politicians, the American proposals to tighten the alliance in these two respects—IRBM bases and a drawing of Europe closer into the world of nuclear weapons—posed a serious problem; for they came at a time when popular forces in Europe were restive with American leadership and, more fundamentally, eagerly seeking alternatives to the nuclear arms race, which hung like a sword of Damocles over Europe's head. There was lively political pressure to explore the possibilities of a high-level negotiation with the Soviet Union which initially almost took the form of ultimatum. Moreover, Western European political leaders as human beings could not wholly resist enjoying, to a degree, an American discomfiture which gave them an increased bargaining weight within the alliance.

Thus the NATO meeting of December 1957 yielded a limited and delayed result. The British alone were prepared forthwith to set up joint IRBM bases. An expansion of joint research and development was arranged within the limits of American law, but a radical change evidently awaited Congressional action. And an American willingness to explore the coordination of economic development programs in the underdeveloped areas, expressed in his opening statement by the President, was set aside, awaiting clarification of the Administration's own proposals and action on them in the 1958 session of Congress.

NATO clearly survived the cumulative shocks of Suez and the sputnik crises and, more than that, the serious issues on which the development of a joint Western policy toward the new weaponry and the underdeveloped areas were raised. But the response at Paris was, like that in Washington over the previous weeks and months, slow moving. There was no clear-cut program around which the energies of the alliance could be mobilized and the persistence of ultimately common interests could be dramatized.

Moreover, behind the confusion and moods of the NATO meeting of December 1957 lay three issues of substance which colored European thought.

First, if IRBM bases were granted in order to retain Western retaliatory power over the interval of possible Soviet monopoly in the ICBM, and if the alliance were tightened for this purpose, where would the alliance stand when the United States had created its own ICBM capabilities plus a capability to launch the IRBM from nuclear-powered submarines? Was a more intense commitment to the North Atlantic Alliance justified on these relatively short-period grounds?

Second, was it not necessary, in any case, for Western Europe to develop its own IRBM capability and thus have a retaliatory power vis-à-vis the Soviet Union independent of decisions made in Washington or in which Washington had to concur? Would Washington be prepared to risk hideous damage to American society in order to face down a Soviet ultimatum directed at (say) West Berlin, Paris, or London? Was it fair and wise to confront any third nation with this kind of choice?

Third, what, in fact, were the possibilities of a degree of mutual Soviet and American withdrawal from the heart of Europe? Was there any safe way to experiment with the line of thought incorporated in Kennan's Reith Lectures and the Rapacki Plan?

Thus, in the wake of the Soviet launching of the earth satellites, the specific military and political formulae on which the North Atlantic Alliance had been created between 1949 and 1952—formulae which had been steadily eroding over the previous five years—were being subjected to critical analysis—wise and wishful, irrational and distraught. By the late winter of 1957-1958 no consensus in concept or program had yet emerged. Nevertheless, NATO still stood. The issues for joint Western decision, long implicit in the technological and nationalist revolutions and in the Soviet strategy for their exploitation, had, at long last, been raised.

And, as 1958 wore on, in several dimensions the West began to act on these issues, or, at least, to think about them in new ways. The vague but powerful impulse for an urgent summit meeting gave way to working negotiations with Moscow centered about the conditions for the cessation of H-bomb tests and for a reduction in the danger of surprise attack. The issue of restructuring the Free World economy on a cooperative basis, to provide increased trading reserves as well as expanded loans for the underdeveloped areas, was raised with increasing clarity on both sides of the Atlantic. Britain and the United States moved toward a military cooperation based on a sharing of nuclear information more complete than any arrangements since 1945. And France, with De Gaulle in power, was at last wrestling with its unresolved problems— from Algeria to H-bombs and housing.

In 1956-1958 a turning had clearly occurred in the affairs of the North Atlantic, as it had in American policy toward the underdeveloped areas and in American military dispositions. It was by no means yet clear, however, that the new attitudes would yield actions and programs of sufficient bite and pace to master the problems with which the United States and the West were confronted.

## 49. The Crisis of 1956-1958 in Perspective

It is possible to view American public policy over the past thirty years as a historical sequence of crisis and response. In each instance the nation faced a gathering set of problems with which existing policy could not effectively deal. The pressure of these problems gradually increased, and the evidence of inadequacy compounded until a quite clearly defined moment or interval of crisis arrived when the need for a radical change in direction was accepted by a substantial majority of the electorate as well as by those who bore political responsibility. There followed a sustained burst of action, initiative, and innovation focused around the new problems as they were defined at the moment of crisis. This phase of initiation lasted a few years, yielding a new set of policies that became institutionalized. A condition of relative stability followed until the positions which resulted from the response to the previous crisis revealed themselves, in turn, to be inappropriate; and a new cycle began.

The first of these crises centered about the Great Depression after 1929. The turning point in policy occurred in 1933. The response was the New Deal, the principal contours of which were settled by the end of Roosevelt's first term, to be altered in only minor respects over the subsequent twenty-two years.

The second crisis centered about the threat posed by Hitler and the Axis, the menace of which gathered strength from about 1936 forward. The turning point came with the Fall of France and the American commitment to see Britain through. The basic lines of policy—embracing a shoot-at-sight policy in the Atlantic, Lend-Lease, support for the Soviet Union when subjected to German attack, priority for victory in Europe, and unconditional surrender—were all in effect by early 1943; and the war was fought and the postwar arrangements made around these commitments.

The third crisis centered about Stalin's and Mao's post-1945 efforts to convert the wartime positions gained by the Communists into decisive victory in Eurasia by means short of major war. The turning point in Europe came with the Truman Doctrine early in 1947, in Asia with the response in 1950 to the invasion of South Korea. These two responses yielded a complex structure of military alliances committing the United States around the whole periphery of Eurasia. They thus not only shaped the military and foreign policy of the Truman administration but also governed Eisenhower's first term. In 1953-1956, however, the nation's problems were shifting swiftly away from the 1947-1951 pattern, and the policies built in response to the events of those earlier postwar years became progressively less effective, yielding the fourth crisis.

The crisis of 1956-1958 centered about the new problems posed for the United States and the Free World by the pace of Soviet development of the new military technology and by the disruptive consequences of Communist exploitation of the revolutionary forces at work in Asia, the Middle East, Africa, and Latin America. That crisis, gradually shaping up in the period 1951-1956, began to come to a head at Suez in November 1956. It erupted in a different dimension a year later after the two Soviet earth satellites were launched, and then again in the Middle East in the summer of 1958.

The pattern of political response to the first three of these crises was strikingly uniform. Against the background of a spreading sense in the American public and among its leaders that a change in the direction of public policy was required, the President formulated and explained his view of the problem and presented his program. With Presidential prestige and leadership firmly committed before the public to new lines of action, Congress acted. In the case of the New Deal, the political base for action lay in the heavy Democratic majority achieved in the election of 1932; in the foreign policy crises of 1940, 1947, and 1950 the President moved on the basis of a bipartisan coalition, symbolized, in the first two cases, by the roles of Stimson and Vandenberg. In 1950, although the initial intervention of Truman in Korea could be regarded as having bipartisan support, bipartisanship did not survive Truman's policy after the Chinese Communists entered the war.

The crisis of 1956-1958 had a great deal in common with its three predecessors; but both the external challenge and the American response were less sharp than they had been on the previous occasions. The military challenge took the form not of military attack but of gathering evidence of Soviet primacy in certain new weapons and of Soviet pace in their further development that might yield a later mortal threat to the nation. The political challenge took the form not of definitive loss of Free World territories but of the progressive decline of cohesion in the Free World that might yield later definitive gains for Communism. The piecemeal and muted response to the challenges occurred because the power of Presidential leadership was not fully committed around a clear-cut course of action. Put another way, the leadership within the Executive Branch did not fully agree concerning the character of the crisis that was faced; and there was even disagreement as to whether the nation faced a major crisis. In fact, the President used a part of his influence to deflate the nation's sense of urgency in the face of the flow of events. Outside the Executive Branch many of the bipartisan elements which had operated in 1940, 1947, and 1950 were once again in active coalition; but the President did not choose to base his position firmly upon them. Nevertheless, the American political process, in its widest sense, did recognize the existence of crisis and slowly fashioned a response of sorts.

The course of events in 1956-1958 broke up the rigid dispositions which had been built over the previous years around the Great Equation of 1953, and a major shift occurred in the personnel of the Eisenhower administration. One after another, the major figures who had been identified with the fiscal, military, and foreign policy of the Eisenhower first term left the scene and were replaced by men less committed to the old policies and to the ideology of the Great Equation even if not wholly in harmony with the consensus which had developed outside the government.

There is no evidence that the Old Guard was replaced as a conscious and purposeful act of initiative by the President. From outside the government, at least, it appeared as if an instinctive sense had emerged that times were changing, that the old frames of mind no longer were relevant, that the old lines of policy could no longer be held. The new men were generally less wedded to the notion that the overriding criterion of policy should be a stable, if not declining, Federal budget. And in the areas of greatest contention the new men were prepared for larger outlays in defense and larger outlays for foreign aid to nations not joined to the United States in military pacts. Their entrance into the governmental process in the course of the crisis undoubtedly contributed important degrees of initiative and responsiveness which had not been present.

But the heart, the command center, of the Eisenhower administration appeared to be relatively unaffected. The President himself appeared less prepared, on the whole, to formulate and execute new policies in response to the crisis than many of his subordinates and, probably, even the Congress. He moved in small steps, cautiously, in the wake of events.

The military budget initially presented to the Congress by the President in January 1958 was, when corrected for price changes, lower than that for the previous year; and the Congress voted more funds than the President had requested. The foreign aid proposals placed before the Congress represented an exceedingly modest movement forward toward economic (as opposed to military) programs when compared to the legislative action of the preceding year; and they were even more modest than the previous year's Executive proposals. In every dimension one could observe a somewhat reluctant acceptance of the fact that previous formulae and dispositions were inappropriate, and the external consensus operated in many subtle ways—through the Congress, the new administrators, and by other means—to press policy, budgetary and otherwise, into new molds. But without a vigorous, personal Presidential leadership and conviction, the process was slow-moving, limited, and without articulated direction. The nation as a whole was responding to its crisis; but the Executive Branch was, for a long time, in the middle rather than at the head of the parade.

To understand the Administration's muted response to the crisis of 1956-1958 it is necessary therefore to examine directly the inner character of the Eisenhower administration.

# PART V

# AN INTERIM SUMMATION

## 50. *The Eisenhower Administration: Its Special Character*

THE PROBLEM TO BE EXPLAINED

The Eisenhower administration came to power at a moment of revolution in world affairs requiring radical innovation in military technology and with respect to the nation's and the Free World's relations with the underdeveloped areas. Innovation in those two key areas of the national interest required, in turn, innovation in the North Atlantic alliance.

The reality of the problems posed by those issues was evident in the agenda passed to the Eisenhower administration by Truman; and staff work in the early years of the Eisenhower administration confirmed their central place and generated proposals to deal with them. But in none of the directions indicated did the Administration undertake any determined new action in the Eisenhower first term; and the Administration's reaction to crisis centered on those issues in 1956-1958 was, by previous American standards of executive leadership, exceedingly sluggish. What determined this performance?

This result arose from a political fact and from a method and concept of administration, both of which appear to have been rooted in the personal operating style of the President.

RIGHT-WING DOMINANCE: 1953-1956

The political fact was that the posts from which the shape of military and foreign policy were determined in the Eisenhower first term were held by men from the conservative wing of the Republican Party. Eisenhower's victory at the Republican Convention of 1952 was, like Willkie's in 1940 and Dewey's in 1944 and 1948, a clear-cut victory for the liberal, international element in the Republican Party. The motives of an electorate in a landslide victory are difficult to disentangle. One can always adduce more reasons than one needs to explain the outcome. Nevertheless, there is little doubt that Eisenhower's believed military competence and his apparent dedication to the maintenance of an American position of Free World leadership were fundamental to the swing of a high proportion of the independent vote. When the Cabinet was formed, however, positions dominating policy were held by men obsessed with the problem of reducing the Federal Budget rather than by those Republicans who felt that the Truman administration had, in its later years, been too rigid and incapable of making fresh dispositions to cope with the new forces emerging on the world scene.

Put another way, when the first Republican administration in twenty years came to power, no major post was held by a representative of the continuous line running from Root through Stimson to the substantial group of experienced internationalist Republicans which had widened out well beyond the East Coast during and after the Second World War.[1]

John Foster Dulles, with his long ties to the internationalist tradition, appears to be an exception to this judgment. He seems, however, to have viewed his role in the Eisenhower first term as that of advocate for the Republican Party and for whatever positions were crystallized out of the interplay of its leading political figures; that is, he did not regard his function as that of an active political representative for one wing of the party except on such extreme issues as the Bricker Amendment. And there is some evidence that he shared to a degree the budgetary obsession of some of his senior colleagues. An exceedingly high proportion of his effort was devoted to the process of negotiating personally the military pacts which were designed to reduce the burden of ground force support on the military budget and on the American military establishment. The nature of this central task explains why he could operate so substantially on his own, with so little integral connection with the Department of State as a whole. In short, Secretary Dulles performed consistently within the limit with which he took office: namely, that he remain acceptable to Senator Taft and to the wing of the Republican Party that Senator Taft represented.[2]

The outcome was an administration which, as nearly as one can judge, differed in its balance from what the decisive marginal group of American voters had expected. They had expected an administration conservative perhaps in domestic policy, but under the leadership of a great internationalist general who had come to the nomination supported by the internationalist wing of the Republican Party in a dramatic, closely-followed convention, and who had been elected by the swing to him of a great wave of independent voters either willing to see a more conservative domestic policy or prepared to accept such a policy as a cost for a vigorous and flexible foreign policy and a military policy fully adequate to the challenge represented by the Soviet acquisition of nuclear weapons. With relatively minor exceptions, the domestic policy of the Eisenhower first term reflected an acceptance—whole-hearted, reluctant, or enforced by the political process—of the New Deal and the Fair Deal; and this was an important fact in American domestic history. But in military and foreign policy the weight of the Republican right wing revealed itself as unexpectedly and disproportionately powerful. Despite the departure of the key right-wing figures of the first term, despite the attrition imposed by the political process on the Republican right wing in the Senate, the deference of the Administration to its views continued down to 1958 on many important issues.

## DECISION BY BUREAUCRATIC CONSENSUS

This political fact converged with the concepts of orderly administration which were applied by the Eisenhower administration—notably in the Pentagon under Wilson and in the staff work processes leading to the formulation of policy within the National Security Council, where the concept developed that policy should be made by achieving an acceptable consensus among all those operationally responsible for, or even legitimately interested in, the outcome.

The interdepartmental committee was no new feature on the Washington scene in 1953. In the Eisenhower first term, however, it came to hold a place of authority, if not sanctity, which differed significantly from its place in the organization of the Washington bureaucracy in the previous two decades. The Administration seemed to feel that it was of the nature of the democratic process that decisions be made in a form which left all parties feeling that their interests were adequately reflected in the result. Secretary of Defense Wilson, for example, speaking before the National War College in June 1957, justified the existing organization of the Department of Defense in the following terms:

> The problems created by the current international situation and by our rapidly advancing technology require the thorough consideration of all possible points of view and alternative courses of action. Any other course might be fatal to the security of our country and would be contrary to the traditions to which we adhere.
>
> Our government is a government of checks and balances. The President cannot do certain things without checking with the Congress. Within the Executive Branch, policies are coordinated with all the Departments concerned, and decisions are reached after all have had their say. We follow the same procedure within the Department of Defense. . . .
>
> The final decision will not always completely satisfy everybody concerned. In an organization composed of people working for a common purpose, decisions are accepted in the knowledge that they were reached after full

consideration of all points of view and a realization that the decisions can
be reconsidered at any time if new facts are discovered which bear upon
the problems.

I would like to clearly go on record with all of you that I believe the present
organization of the Department of Defense is sound.[3]

This extension of what was regarded as the democratic political process
into the heart of the federal bureaucracy had two consequences, both of which
radically slowed the pace of innovation and damped the government's responsiveness to new situations. First, it was exceedingly time-consuming and
caused, by the sheer weight of bureaucratic process, inordinate delay. Second,
since those participating in communal decisions represented operating arms
of the government, they brought to the process of policy-making the operator's
incvitable opposition to change. It is instinctive to men charged with day-to-
day operating decisions to resist innovations; and governments which have
successfully solved problems of drastic change have required strong leadership
at the top.

But more than sluggishness was implied in this procedure. Compromise
decisions reached within the interdepartmental committees assumed forms of
language in which ostensible agreement concealed unresolved ambiguities.
Men could leave the table in apparent agreement; but their departments could
go on doing just what they had been doing before. Such ambiguous policy
formulations left the ultimate making of decisions in the hands of those near
the apex of power in the hierarchy; and there the prevalent view, shaped by
the Great Equation, was strongly resistant to change and to any increase in
expense. Thus, when new proposals did manage to survive trial by committee,
they were quite easily nullified by those with effective operating control at high
levels. In the end it was not the bureaucratic consensus but the budget that
controlled policy.

EISENHOWER'S CONCEPTION OF LEADERSHIP

To say that the performance of the Eisenhower administration can be
explained by a convergence of the political balance of the first term and
certain concepts of administration weighted disproportionately to the *status
quo* is to pose a problem rather than to solve it.

Under the American Constitution, the President of the United States bears
inescapable and personal responsibilities. More than that, it is something of
a miracle of American life and of bureaucratic structure that the personality
and operating style of the President manage somehow to touch and to suffuse
the way business comes to be conducted even in the most humble and remote
corner of the massive federal enterprise. Washington under Roosevelt, Truman, and Eisenhower bore intimately the marks of three distinct and different

men. The problem is, then, why did Eisenhower lend himself to a distribution of political power which gave such heavy weight to the Republican right wing; and why did he sponsor a form of administrative technique which tended radically to reduce the innovational capacity of the American political process? Later historians will have better data and the advantage of more distant perspective than the contemporary observer. Nevertheless, something may be said on the basis of the record as it is known in the summer of 1958.

It is evident that Eisenhower carried over from his military experience quite particular concepts of leadership and of organizational principle.

These may be documented from Eisenhower's own writing, from his personal statements, and from friendly and privileged published accounts of his wartime and Presidential experience. They may be summarized as follows:

1. The leader's central responsibility is to give continuity to the institution he is charged to lead by articulating its abiding values and ensuring, to the degree possible, that day-to-day decisions are made in such a way as both to maintain institutional continuity and to conform to these abiding values.

2. The leader should refrain to the maximum from imposing on institutions his own judgments as to appropriate specific courses of action. Within the limits of continuity and loyalty to broad first principles, the leader should seek to create a consensus by mutual persuasion and negotiation in which the diverse interests and perspectives arising from the differing tasks and functions of a complex modern institution are brought into harmony.

3. When, after the process of persuasion and negotiation is exhausted, the necessity emerges for the leader's decision, he must resolutely take final responsibility; but he should do so in forms of decision which, to the maximum possible, continue to reflect the conflicting interests and views embedded in the institution.

4. When a course of strategy is embarked upon and understood throughout the organization, it should be persevered in unless an overwhelming case for change builds up.

5. Primary responsibility for day-to-day policy must be with those charged with operational tasks; and they must bear also the responsibility for achieving a maximum degree of mutual accommodation. The duty of an operating staff is to bring to the leader the minimum number of issues for decision; and, when access to the leader becomes necessary, they should come with either an agreed course of action or clear-cut, well-staffed alternatives.

6. Institutionally, the leader should have a strong chief of staff, capable of forcing a resolution of the maximum number of decisions short of action by the leader and of screening rigorously the issues brought to his attention for action.

Regarded as a whole, a system of organization based on such principles not only gave great scope to those holding operational command over sectors of the institution but also permitted strong purposeful operators to achieve disproportionate influence below the level of the leader.

STAFF AND COMMAND

These conceptions of leadership and organization were, evidently, the product of a military career—but of a particular kind of military career. Eisenhower was almost exclusively a staff officer. He never intimately commanded units in combat; and for a professional soldier this was a most serious matter. Eisenhower described the "hard blow" that assigned him to the War Department in December 1941.

> "The Chief says for you to hop a plane and get up here right away. Tell your boss that formal orders will come through later." The "Chief" was General Marshall and the man at the other end of the line was Colonel Walter Bedell Smith, who was later to become my close friend and chief of staff throughout the European operations.
> This message was a hard blow. During the first World War every one of my frantic efforts to get to the scene of action had been defeated—for reasons which had no validity to me except that they all boiled down to "War Department orders." I hoped in any new war to stay with troops. Being ordered to a city where I had already served a total of eight years would mean, I thought, a virtual repetition of my experience in World War I. Heavyhearted, I telephoned my wife to pack a bag and within the hour I was headed for the War Department.[4]

Eisenhower's climactic military experience was to preside at some distance from operations over a complex allied enterprise in which he exercised ultimate command not only over men in his own profession whose military experience was wider and more direct than his own but also over men whose operational skill he greatly respected. There was, during the war, a revealing exchange between Eisenhower and Patton, reported by Butcher:

> Interesting to hear Ike and Patton talk Army personalities. General Ike dislikes officers who feel they have fulfilled their responsibility when they simply report a problem to a superior and do not bring the proposed solution with them. Patton says he doesn't necessarily want a smart staff; he wants a loyal one. He says he has a sixth sense and can guess the intentions of the enemy better than a staff of G-2.[5]

Eisenhower did not build his career on faith in an operational sixth sense. Out of a combination of personality and his experiences in the positions to which he was assigned, Eisenhower came to place the views of his staff, notably when the staff achieved agreement, above his own instinctive judgment about the course operations should take. The theme—"once an action has been taken by his staff, Ike ordinarily supports it . . ."[6]—runs strongly through his career. When during the war there was conflict which could be resolved only at the level of his leadership—as in 1944 between Spaatz and Tedder, and later between Bradley and Montgomery—he found whenever possible compromise forms of resolution which gave to each a part of what he demanded.

Projected into the many-faceted role of the office of the President, these principles of leadership and organization raised problems. The President stands in a series of inescapable major relationships—to the Executive Branch of the government, to the Congress, to his political party, and to the nation as a whole. In each of these relationships Eisenhower's operating style gave a particular form and character to his administration.

### STAFF DIRECTOR IN THE EXECUTIVE BRANCH

With respect to the Executive Branch, Eisenhower was able to find and to install a kind of chief of staff for domestic affairs in the person of Sherman Adams;[7] and over an important range of issues Adams was able to fulfill functions closely analogous to his predecessors in Eisenhower's experience—Bedell Smith, Clay, and Gruenther.[8]

In military and foreign affairs, however, no equivalent post or function emerged. The Secretary of State's limited conception of his political role and technical task ruled him out as the operating coordinator of diplomacy, military affairs, economic foreign policy, propaganda, and the other arms which constitute the nation's instruments for dealing with the world. None of the White House staff carried the political and administrative weight to fulfill such a function, conflicting as it would with the jealously guarded prerogatives of the Secretaries of State and Defense on the one hand and the Joint Chiefs of Staff on the other. The activities of the National Security Council were remarkably enlarged and invigorated under the guidance of Robert Cutler in his two phases of responsibility; but its methods of discussion, negotiation, and drafting, while capable of raising issues for decision, could not perform the powerful function of intermediate level decision-making and screening of issues for the President which a Chief of Staff might have performed. The result left great but not always well-coordinated powers in the hands of the cabinet officers.

With respect to the major cabinet members, Eisenhower sought and found men who conformed to his conception of able technicians—the equivalent, in his experience, of first-class army commanders.

There is no doubt that after the electoral victory of 1952 (in addition to finding men acceptable to Senator Taft, or at least noncontroversial as between the wings of the Republican Party) Eisenhower looked for successful operators. Humphrey and Wilson commended themselves on this score as men skilled in business affairs, Adams as a professional politician, John Foster

Dulles as a man trained and eager since boyhood to protect and advance American interests by the skills of traditional diplomacy.

By a mixture of accident and design these men, aside from their apparent administrative and operative skills, all accepted or were prepared to accept the concept of the Great Equation as the basis for national security policy. Thus, with a broad strategic understanding reached on the *Helena* and at the Commodore, and confirmed and consolidated after the Solarium review of alternatives, the Eisenhower first term proceeded in good administrative order, with Humphrey overseeing the budgetary limit, Wilson administering the shift to nuclear weapons, Dulles arranging the requisite diplomatic and military alliances. Humphrey, in particular, was a key figure, as budgetary limit and control were the essence of the strategy that became fixed. He is reported to have told Eisenhower that "he had only one request. When anyone talks to you about money, will you ask him if he has seen George?"[9] And, roughly, that request was honored.

With the administration's broad strategy determined, day-to-day control over military and foreign policy devolved into the hands of strong departmental chieftains; and the Executive Branch, its institutions for adjustment and change relatively weak and unresponsive to innovational pressures from below, pursued in military and foreign policy a remarkably consistent course over its first four years.

When difficult issues arose which the machinery of negotiation could not settle within the Great Equation, the President acted firmly on the principle that ultimate decision rests with the leader. In the final phases of the Korean truce negotiations, during the Dienbienphu crisis in Indochina, and in finding and making the formula for Quemoy and Matsu, Eisenhower acted personally. At the summit conference at Geneva of mid-1955 he finally accepted and projected effectively the proposal for aerial inspection. And again, in the face of the second Middle East crisis of 1958, when Washington at last found a balanced consensus, he delivered with force and evident conviction his speech before the United Nations Assembly.

The Executive Branch under Eisenhower was, however, more rigid and sluggish with respect to innovation than under Roosevelt's technique of personal control by overlapping authority; and it was considerably less capable of innovation than under Truman's sporadic but powerful initiatives backed and followed through in detail both by the President and by the small group of like-minded administrators in military and foreign affairs who emerged as Truman's principal subordinates. In 1953-1958 Washington was not a town in which men rose in the ranks on the basis of their vigor in pressing forward new initiatives.

### THE DEFERENTIAL SOLDIER AND THE CONGRESS

With respect to Congress, Eisenhower's concept of leadership led to an attitude of marked conciliation and deference. He actively resisted the notion of chronic conflict between the Executive Branch and Congress; and he was affronted and deeply disturbed when immediately upon assuming office he faced the challenges of the Bricker Amendment and of McCarthy. It is possible that Eisenhower's general dedication to the concept of consensus achieved by accord—rather than by political struggle—was reinforced by an Army officer's habit of deference to the legislative branch which traditionally controlled the Army's purse-strings and much else. In any case, the White House officer charged with the Congressional relations, General Persons, had made his career in the War Department as Congressional liaison; and he undoubtedly carried over into the White House attitudes and inhibitions inappropriate to strong Presidential relations with Congress in the American political system.

Notably in the House of Representatives, but to an important degree in the Senate as well, the member of Congress is forced to look to local and regional issues as the basis for his political position. Since military and foreign affairs on the whole are bound to intrude on many local and regional interests which the congressmen must respect and take into account, a powerful and sustained advocacy, taken to the public with full Presidential prestige and backed by all the direct and indirect political leverage the President can bring to bear, is generally required to move the legislative body along the paths required to protect the national interest.

Eisenhower did not appear to understand the extent to which the Congress must count on a degree of Presidential assertion and even conflict to find a basis for supporting an effective military and foreign policy. Thus the friends of the President's policies in Congress were often left with an inadequate base on which to legislate what was required. Conciliation, deference, and a sharing of responsibility were not enough.

### THE RELUCTANT PARTY LEADER

Within the Republican Party once again there was a clash between the imperatives of the President's political position and the concept of leadership Eisenhower brought to office. It had been evident since 1940 at least that a Republican president, when he came to office, would face the task of shifting the balance of power within the Republican Party. There was a marked lack of symmetry between the Republican Party as a Congressional and national organization and its character as reflected in the national conventions after 1940. To professional politicians Eisenhower's victory at the 1952 convention and then in November was a major palpable fact. They assumed that a candidate with a party and national mandate of the kind accorded Eisenhower in 1952 would move swiftly to shift the balance of power in the Republican Party, placing his supporters in key posts. Given the formidable weight of the Republican right wing in the Congress, this would not have been easy for any politician, no matter how skilled, purposeful, and prepared for bloody combat. But the effort was never seriously made. Conciliation within the Republican Party, much as it stood, emerged as Eisenhower's basic position. Eisenhower sought to preside over the two wings of the party in much the same mood as he had once brought British and American officers together in SHAEF—with strong compulsions to minimize overt conflict. This worked to the advantage of the right wing. The powerful but hitherto disorganized elements of the Republican liberal wing were not vigorously unified in 1953. Taft's power in the Congress was uncontested. Although he moved in his last months to assist the President in several important ways, the Eisenhower Republicans in the Senate were quickly reduced to a place of trivial influence; and none achieved or maintained high status in the Executive Branch. The fate of Eisenhower Republicans in the Eisenhower administration recalled the dictum of Leo Durocher about the Darwinian process in professional baseball: "Nice guys end up in last place."

It may have been that to Eisenhower, with his ingrained concept of the continuity of institutions and the limited conciliatory function of leadership, the notion of restructuring a major national institution—the Republican Party—in the image of his private values and purposes was abhorrent. He may have seen his duty to be to preside over the best consensus which the structure and interests of the Republican Party as he found it could yield by negotiation.

In any case, Eisenhower was systematically bedeviled, notably until the Democratic victory in the Congressional elections of 1954, by the unresponsiveness of the Republican Party to his temperate and conciliatory exploitation of his victory and party powers. Time, the trend of public thought, and the attrition of the election returns did, indeed, produce significant changes in the Republican Party between 1952 and 1958. But, despite many favorable voting trends, it failed to evolve persuasively in the directions which might have permitted it to achieve majority status; and down to 1958 the continued conservative weight in its organization contributed to the stultifying of the Executive Branch initiative in military and foreign policy.

THE PRESIDENT AND THE PUBLIC

In his relations to the public Eisenhower concentrated on one important function of the President which was wholly congenial to his style: namely, the articulation and projection of the unifying principles and moods of the nation.

As head of state for all the people, he executed with conviction the roles of ceremony; and in this dimension he was aided by the personal reticence and inhibition of his conception of leadership. But the image of Eisenhower as national leader was never identified with strong positions on divisive issues. Thus Eisenhower shunned where possible the President's function of advocacy of new measures.

The Executive Branch, the Congress, and the two political parties are organized institutions. With respect to these, Eisenhower's style suggested lines of approach which, while not necessarily the most appropriate or effective in achieving his own and the nation's purposes, nevertheless yielded a clear-cut organizational result. But a President's relationship to the public on concrete issues of policy requiring education and innovation is a subtle, personal, instinctive thing. No staff work can tell a great political leader when to place a new major issue on the national agenda, how to articulate it, how to set the stage for programs and action. But unless the President performs this function in the American political system it is likely to be done late and clumsily.

Eisenhower presented many issues to the nation in his first five and one-half years of office, but, with the major exceptions of the Atoms-for-Peace program,[10] the reorganization of the Pentagon, and the Middle East program of 1958, he drew back from the role of policy innovator.

EISENHOWER IN INTERIM PERSPECTIVE

In terms of the criteria of the national interest applied throughout this book, and with the benefit of hindsight, failures emerge in all three of the administrations examined.

Roosevelt's approach to the Second World War, an approach colored by elements from Wilson and Mahan, led to somewhat superficial views on the inner problems of Eurasia, notably, with respect to the Polish and China questions and, in general, with respect to the approach to Stalin most likely to maximize the chances of postwar peace and stability.

Truman in his first two years did little to prevent the slide into Cold War, and he was ineffectual in preventing an exceedingly radical demobilization. Moreover, in 1947-1950 he permitted an American military posture to emerge which made the Communist attack on South Korea exceedingly attractive to Stalin and Mao.

Nevertheless, both Roosevelt and Truman were responsive to the views of those who led the bipartisan internationalist coalition in American life. They were active in their response to the emergence of concrete problems and crises; and once problems and crises were perceived within the Executive Branch, they were active in alerting and leading the American public and the political process in the widest sense.

Eisenhower, while no more forehanded than his predecessors in avoiding crisis, failed to respond promptly and actively when crisis came. He was unresponsive to the bipartisan internationalist coalition which, in a sense, he was chosen to lead and which certainly elected him. He was sluggish in response to new problems defined within the Executive Branch, and he virtually rejected the President's role of personal leadership and innovation in the political process until inescapable circumstances and strong pressures within his staff persuaded him to act. Each of these three dimensions of failure may be linked to the conception of organization and executive responsibility which he brought to the office of President—the conception of a professional soldier who clung to the habits of staff director, in which position he had greatly excelled.

Eisenhower's style as President, taken as a whole, was admirably geared to situations in which the nation could solve its problems and protect its interests by slow, gradual change in the classic American manner. It is wholly understandable that his popularity was high during his first term and that he was re-elected by an overwhelming majority. After the turbulence, strain, innovation, and frustration of the 1940-1952 period, it was comforting to believe that the struggle with the Communist world could be institutionalized and operated on a steady, orderly basis, along not unfamiliar lines, under the command of a well-poised leader with competent subordinates, demanding limited public sacrifice and little of the pain of fresh thought and concept. And the acceptance and consolidation of the welfare state, the gradual deflation of McCarthy, the maintenance of full employment, and the image of a relaxed, unexcited leader, patently anxious to respond to the interests of as many segments of the community as possible, was powerfully appealing. Finally, the projection of Eisenhower as a President competent in military affairs but also dedicated with unmistakable fervor to the active pursuit of peace rounded out the image of a widely popular national leader. In a world evidently full of danger the nation could feel that Eisenhower's institutionalized administration of affairs left its citizens more free to concentrate on their private affairs and the enjoyment of the satisfactions of a rich society than had been possible for more than a generation.

From 1955 forward, evidence multiplied that with respect to the arms race, the underdeveloped areas, and NATO the position and policies of the Eisenhower administration were losing touch with the problems on which the nation's security depended; and there was an extraordinary gap during the election campaign of 1956 between the popular conception of the nation's position on the world scene and the view within the Executive Branch and among those outside the government who were more or less professionally knowledgeable in military and foreign affairs. There can have been few elections which reflect less credit on the democratic process than the uncandid projection and the self-indulgent public acceptance of the slogan of Peace and Prosperity in 1956.

But the deterioration of the American and Western position did not take the form of major and palpable crisis until Suez; and, since it was difficult to believe that Eisenhower and his administration would cling as rigidly to their course in the face of the new situation as they did, the public image of the Eisenhower first term was not immediately broken. Moreover, the Democratic campaign of 1956 did not systematically and persuasively clarify what had been happening to the nation's position over the previous four years. But from the Suez crisis forward, the image was broken step by step; and the nation—and its political process—came face to face with the real issues without the intermediary of a strong purposeful Executive Branch.

Eisenhower's personal operating style, then, can be linked directly to the political balance and administrative method of his first term and to the limited and sluggish response of the Executive Branch to the crisis of 1956-1958. It was a style admirably suited to a time when slow change in existing formulae and institutions would suffice. It was inappropriate to a phase in the nation's history when rapid, vigorous adjustment to a quickly changing environment was required to protect the nation's interest.

There is an element of loss, if not even of tragedy, in this story. Eisenhower had a quick, clear understanding, human insight, and a wide experience of the nation and the world by the time he came to the office of President. The instinctive direction in which he reacted to situations and the lines of policy he would personally have chosen to pursue were in many ways different from those taken by his administration.

There is ample reason to believe that as early as 1953 he was troubled by a budgetary pressure that came to rest on security outlays;[11] that he understood the importance of economic support for underdeveloped nations not allied to the United States in military pacts; that he believed the Department of Defense should be unified, with a strong staff at its apex. It is clear that he fully understood from the beginning of his term that NATO required for its continued vitality a wider collaboration with the United States in the development and use of nuclear weapons. He was evidently restive with the balance of power within the Republican Party and with its failure to assume a more steady and responsible internationalist position.

But he did not build his policy on these instinctive views and understandings. For whatever reasons—diffidence, uncertainty, or inner conviction—Eisenhower did not impose his own insights, his own sense of direction on the nation's policy. He remained loyal not to his views of substance but to his principles of administration. He decided, in effect, only when his immediate subordinates could not. He maintained, with respect to Humphrey, Wilson, and Dulles, the kind of relationship he had built during the war with Alexander, Montgomery, and Bradley—a relationship in which, within the agreed strategy, the field operator was given maximum scope and the leader confined himself to making the residual decisions that were brought to him in terms of the alternatives posed by a staff process he did not dominate or control.

In part, Eisenhower as President was imprisoned by the initial political and strategy dispositions he made—from the time of the Republican convention down through the Morningside Heights meeting with Senator Taft to the selection of his Cabinet, the days on the *Helena,* and beyond through the first year of office. In part he was imprisoned by a conception of leadership and administration which forced him systematically to give precedence to the consensus developed in the institutions around him—created by men of his own choosing—over his own instincts about the course policy should take. No President in the past century came to office under circumstances and with a mandate which less required such self-abnegation.

The ultimate consequences for the nation of Eisenhower's method cannot now be measured. The crisis of 1956-1958 arose directly from the initial dispositions made by the Eisenhower administration; but of its nature that crisis was a less clear-cut affair than those of 1941, 1947, and 1950. Enemy troops did not cross frontiers; nor did enemy bombs fall on American territory. As of 1958 it is not yet inevitable that the United States and the Free World stand defenseless in the face of Soviet ICBM's at some point in the future, or without effective recourse in the face of limited military assault; nor is it yet inevitable that India, Indonesia, and Egypt go the way of China; nor is it yet inevitable that the United States and Europe fail to recapture a basis for joint initiative in military, economic and political affairs. The events from Suez to sputnik to the foreign exchange crisis in India to the Middle East crisis of 1958 were a warning of dangerous trends. The outcome hinges in part on decisions taken within the Communist Bloc; but it will mainly depend on what Americans do or fail to do from the present forward.

# BOOK FOUR

*Notes*

### CHAPTER 37. Policy Within the Communist Bloc

1. For the full development of this view, see the author's *Dynamics of Soviet Society*, New York, Norton and Mentor, 1954.

2. The author's view on the relation of the Soviet military to political power remains much as expressed in the *Dynamics of Soviet Society*, pp. 227-228.

"There is little doubt that the Soviet armed forces were, in fact, invoked to bring Beria down and that they have succeeded to the secret police in certain key security functions within the Soviet Union.

"This is a new and dangerous development from the point of view of Communist political power. Is there not the danger that, with the police weakened, the armed forces might not seize control of the country? Technically it is altogether possible that this could now be done. If it is true that the Soviet armed forces now command their own ammunition dumps within the Soviet Union—a function allocated by Stalin to the secret police—then indeed they hold the power of political decision.

"On the whole, however, Malenkov and his political colleagues can feel reasonably secure under these circumstances. They will undoubtedly still maintain an intensive degree of party and secret police control in the middle and lower levels of the armed forces; but they can, within limits, rely on more substantial elements of stability. The Soviet military leaders are, after all, top Soviet bureaucrats, created by the Soviet system, with every stake of status and material reward in its survival. It is certain that they have disliked Stalin's suspicious and denigrating system of control over them. It is likely that they have disagreed with aspects of his internal and external policy. But they are not, as a group, revolutionists. Nor are they Bonapartists, with inflamed nationalist ambitions. They are bureaucrats, with large salaries, and material rewards, high status, and a rather conservative desire for personal and national security. These are likely to be satisfied under the present distribution of power within the collective leadership.

"The danger the armed forces present to the stability of the post-Stalin system lies in the questionable stability of the system itself. Any move for the resumption of effective one-man rule must envisage a reduction in the policy-making prerogatives now shared by those who head the several bureaucracies. It must envisage, in particular, the re-creation of effective control over the armed forces, with a withdrawal of the privileges and powers acquired since Stalin's death. An attempt to withdraw these powers may, indeed, lead the armed forces to exploit the *de facto* authority implicit in the present positions it holds within Soviet society. Only in this negative sense, then, can we now envisage a military *putsch*— as a reaction to a political effort to re-impose a Stalinist relation between the political executive and the armed forces, probably by action of a rejuvenated secret police under new management."

It should be noted that this view is by no means universally accepted among experts on the Soviet Union.

3. In the overpopulated areas of Asia increases in output depend, essentially, on two devices: irrigation which permits double-cropping, and the application of chemical fertilizers. Technically the problem of adequate Chinese agricultural output over the whole period of its take-off (say, 1953-1970) hinges on the application of chemical fertilizers on a large scale. China had pressed irrigation far forward well before the Communist take-over. Significant increases in agricultural output could be attained between 1949 and 1958 by some additional irrigation measures, by the use of better seeds and insecticides, and by the re-establishment of internal order. As of 1958 there was some evidence that the Chinese Communists, dourly committed to collectivization, were, in fact, turning to the massive use of chemical fertilizers.

## CHAPTER 38. Soviet Military Policy

1. See notably, W. R. Kintner, "American Responsibilities in the Nuclear Age," Prize Essay 1956, *United States Naval Institute Proceedings*, March, 1956; H. Kissinger, *Nuclear Weapons and Foreign Policy*, New York, 1957, Harper, Chap. 11; and H. Dinerstein, "The Revolution in Soviet Strategic Thinking," *Foreign Affairs*, XXXVI (January), 1958, pp. 241-252; and *The Soviet Military Posture as a Reflection of Soviet Strategy*, Rand Corporation, Santa Monica, California, January 15, 1958, monograph P-1258.

2. The author is much indebted to conversations with Professor Leon Trilling of M.I.T. for the analysis of Soviet missile decisions in 1953.

## CHAPTER 39. Soviet Policy in the Underdeveloped Areas

1. See Council for Economic and Industry Research, "Foreign Assistance Activities of the Communist Bloc and their Implications for the United States," a study prepared at the request of a Special Committee to Study the Foreign Aid Program, United States Senate, Washington, D.C., Govt. Printing Office, March, 1957, p. 7. Also, K. E. Knorr, *Ruble Diplomacy: Challenge to American Aid*, Center of International Studies, Princeton University, November 16, 1956; and the Department of State study released January 4, 1958.

2. Study prepared by the State Department on Soviet Economic Aid Campaign in the Mideast and Orient, *The New York Times*, January 4, 1958, p. C4.

3. "Foreign Assistance Activities of the Communist Bloc and their Implications for the United States," a study prepared at the request of a special committee to study the foreign aid program, United States Senate, by the Council for Economic and Industry Research, Washington: March 1957, p. 12.

4. Peking's resentment of Moscow's allocation of loans may form part of the backdrop to Chinese Communist pressure in 1958 for a "hard line."

5. In an effort to capture the nature of Communist reservations and difficulties with the soft offensive in the underdeveloped areas the author wrote and circulated

the following (only partially prescient) memorandum in Molotov's name on February 29, 1956, in the wake of the Twentieth Party Congress.

TOP SECRET<br>
(Not a Government Security<br>
Classification)

TO:　　My Presidium Colleagues
FROM:　V. Molotov

Now that the Twentieth Party Congress is over I wish to warn my colleagues of the danger that confronts us as a result of our actions. I speak freely because, as is well known, I accepted the collective decision, denounced my own previously stated views, and joined in an effort which, I cannot conceal from you, I still regard as right-wing adventurism.

Let me recall the arguments we have had over the past few years and which came to a head before the Congress.

Certain of our Comrades took the following view:

1. In prolonged reaction to the Korean war the United States was devoting its efforts overwhelmingly to developing a ring of military pacts.

2. These pacts were unpopular as well as ineffective. The peoples of the countries concerned wanted peace, economic development, and increased national development and stature.

3. Therefore, it was time to make serious movements to associate ourselves with these emotional sentiments and outflank the Americans.

I led those—numbering I may say the more experienced among us in these matters—who took a contrary view. We held the following position:

1. The tactics proposed would strengthen existing bourgeois governments, give these nations time to organize themselves, and promote a protracted stage of bourgeois development.

2. The influence we would gain by such tactics would be superficial and could not be translated into a serious acquisition of Communist power.

3. The necessary Popular Front tactic within these countries would make impossible the development of infiltration and guerrilla tactics which alone promise success in these regions.

4. We could be drawn into economically costly competition at a time when our resources are badly needed for military and economic purposes within the Soviet Union.

The only hope that could be offered was that without American assistance, these countries, with their silly bourgeois methods, would fail in their economic plans and turn to us.

I repeat that we regarded the proposed tactics as a denial of every lesson of our collegial experience, from Lenin's October victory to our diplomatic triumph at Geneva in 1954 in the matter of Indo-China. Our movement has never before confused the superficial symptoms of power and influence with its substance. In the end, power is a matter of physical control; and the proposed policy in no way promises physical control. On the contrary, it makes more difficult the problem of acquiring physical control.

As you well know, no one of those advocating the proposed policy was able to explain to us how we move from economic pacts and flowers around the necks of our colleagues to the serious acquisition of power. But our clever and flexible colleague Mikoyan settled the matter with his two famous propositions:

1. What is bad for the United States is good for the Soviet Union;

2. Mikoyan can make a profit out of Soviet economic aid.

These two superficial, I might say almost cosmopolitan, concepts settled the matter; and we all went in together to enunciate the doctrines of the Twentieth Congress: prolonged coexistence, popular front, and all the rest.

Why do I now return to these painful matters, having accepted manfully the collective decision? I do so because now I believe we shall see the Americans spring the trap upon us. We are now deeply committed to these high-flown positions and policies. Every day we pursue them, we strengthen in some measure non-Communist governments over whom we have no real control. As long as the Americans continue their present policies we can no doubt influence these governments to act in our interest. But are the Americans committed to their silly concentration on military pacts? Are their ruling circles (who can blame changes on such absurd excuses as elections and a mercurial public opinion)—I ask you—

are their ruling circles incapable of changing their economic foreign policy? And if they do, what reliable controls do we have over these Asian and Middle Eastern governments to insure that, once strengthened, they will not again switch their allegiance to the American Bloc?

We have known all along that the margin of success or failure in the Indian Second Five Year Plan was a matter of a few billion dollars in foreign exchange. This news excited even some of our colleagues. You recall it was only with the greatest effort that I managed to persuade some of our colleagues from making that Plan a great success for Nehru by lending him this money. But do you think the Americans, having feigned stupidity in this matter, are incapable of making the offer now, after we are committed to this right-wing adventurism? The money means little to them; and if they prolong the automobile boom in the United States by borrowing on the 1957 model, as that great expert on American capitalism, Mikoyan, was telling us, they will need to make foreign loans next year to keep full employment.

And so also in Indonesia, Burma, Pakistan, and—mark my words—in the Middle East as well.

We are playing with bourgeois tricks, Comrades; and we will get burned. We have been led into a trap. The Americans will soon be coming with money and technicians and missionary interest in these wretched areas; and the people there will be glad to see them back. India will be getting Goa with American support and with all the more credit because of Dulles' cleverness. We shall soon have to return to the true principles of Lenin and Stalin—yes I say Stalin—and we had better begin to think about what is then to be done.

*February 29, 1956*

## CHAPTER 41. The "Great Equation"

1. The view that the degree of governmental intervention in the economy could be radically reduced, consecrated by many years of political campaigning, received what was regarded as reinforcing postwar evidence by several prominent members and advisers to the new administration who had shared in making postwar occupation policy in West Germany and Japan. The rapid revival of those two economies after currency reform under regimes of high interest rates without extensive direct government control was taken to suggest that a policy of domestic economic freedom in combination with a wise use of fiscal and monetary instruments would suffice also in the United States. And, aside from this recent experience, the notion had gathered strength in the postwar years, in Europe as well as in the United States, that the potentialities of fiscal and monetary policy, as opposed to direct government intervention in the economy, had hitherto been underestimated.

2. For a relatively full account of the initial approach of the new Administration and its initial dispositions, see C. J. V. Murphy, "The Eisenhower Shift," *Fortune,* January, February, March, and April 1956; also R. J. Donovan, *Eisenhower, The Inside Story,* New York, Harper, 1956, Chaps. 1, 2, and 4; White, *op. cit.,* Chaps. 14-19; and Goldman, *loc. cit.,* Chap. XI, especially pp. 236-243. Murphy's articles and Donovan's book are to be regarded as virtually official administration accounts of the evolution of policy, based as they are on materials made available uniquely to the authors.

3. Murphy, *loc. cit.* (January), pp. 86-87.

4. There circulated widely in the Eisenhower administration and in Congressional and business circles outside the doctrine that the prime objective of Moscow's policy was to force the United States to "spend itself into destruction." Lenin was often cited as the source of this view of Communist strategy. It will be

recalled that a similar view had been expressed by Secretary of Defense Johnson in the Truman administration. After research over some years the author has been unable to establish any serious basis for such a Communist view of the democratic world.

5. Donovan, *op. cit.*, pp. 108-109.

## CHAPTER 42. Military Policy

1. Murphy, *loc. cit.*, March 1956, pp. 111-112.

2. Radford's conception of a mobile strategic reserve, while distinguishable from total reliance on "massive retaliation," appears to have embraced mainly the use of naval and air power for limited war purposes and differed, therefore, from the larger conception of a mobile Army reserve advocated, for example, by Maxwell Taylor.

3. Murphy, *loc. cit.*, p. 232.

4. The *New York Times*, January 14, 1958.

5. In presenting the budget for fiscal 1959, the Administration gave retrospective figures for outlays on missiles as follows: 1955, $1.2 billion; 1956, $1.7; 1957, $3.0; 1958, $4.3; and 1959, $5.3.

6. Murphy, *loc. cit.*, January 1956, p. 206.

7. See, notably, W. R. Kintner, J. Coffey, and R. Albright, *Forging a New Sword*, New York, Harper, 1958, pp. 127-138.

8. The Secretary of Defense was less concerned than the three services with the maintenance of basic establishments, and significant budgetary cuts were applied to those establishments which lowered the fighting power of apparent front line strength.

9. Trevor Gardner, "Our Guided Missiles Crisis," *Look*, May 15, 1956, pp. 46 ff.

10. T. von Karman, "Can US Win Missile Race?," *U.S. News and World Report*, November 15, 1957, p. 52.

11. The author owes this wholly speculative but persuasive point to a conversation with Dr. Jerrold Zacharias.

12. The third recommendation of this committee—for expanded air defense—was in fact, accepted—a recommendation in which this committee was by no means alone in 1952-1953.

13. In addition to Robert Oppenheimer, the committee included Vannevar Bush, McGeorge Bundy, Allen Dulles, Joseph Johnson, and John Dickey.

14. R. Oppenheimer, "Atomic Weapons and American Policy," *Foreign Affairs*, Vol. 32, July 1953, pp. 530-532.

15. *Ibid.*, pp. 532-533.

16. Donovan, *op. cit.*, pp. 184-193. See also John Lear, "Ike and the Peaceful Atom," *The Reporter*, January 12, 1956.

17. Presented in a talk called, "The Seamless Web," published in the *Harvard Alumni Bulletin* of June 4, 1955, p. 665.

18. Quoted Lear, *op. cit.*, p. 12.

19. Essentially three military issues remained unresolved in 1958 in the field of limited war: the question of organizing a task force capable of uniting Navy, Army, and Air Force elements; the appropriate scale of the Army establishment for this purpose; and, above all, the question of adequate air lift.

## CHAPTER 43. Policy in the Underdeveloped Areas

1. For a view of how an alternative economic aid program might diminish and soften the colonial issue within the Free World, see M. F. Millikan and W. W. Rostow, *A Proposal—Key to an Effective Foreign Policy*, New York, Harper, 1957, pp. 39-42.

## CHAPTER 45. Dealing with the Soviet Union

1. The project to develop interview material as well as to achieve a coherent analysis of Soviet society from all sources was sponsored by the Air Force from 1950 forward. For a summary of findings and listing of materials generated in this remarkable effort, see R. A. Bauer, A. Inkles, and C. Kluckhohn, *How the Soviet System Works*, Cambridge, Harvard Univ. Press, 1956.

2. For an account of the evolution of American policy in this field and its vicissitudes, see, especially, E. W. Barrett, *Truth is Our Weapon*, New York, Funk & Wagnalls, 1953.

3. *Ibid.*, pp. 18-23.

4. Two of the major constructive acts of the first Eisenhower administration arose from the initiative of the special advisers: C. D. Jackson, who fathered the Atoms-for-Peace program; and Nelson Rockefeller, who developed the President's proposal for international aerial inspection, made at Geneva in 1955. In addition, C. D. Jackson returned briefly to Washington in August 1958 to serve as architect of the President's speech on the Middle East before the United Nations Assembly.

5. For an authoritative account of the evolution of the concept of psychological warfare in the United States see W. H. Jackson, "The Fourth Area of National Effort in Foreign Affairs," a speech. Jackson was chairman of a committee which surveyed the problem of psychological warfare in 1953. A key paragraph in its report follows:

"The directive which created the Psychological Strategy Board assumes that in addition to national objectives formulated by the National Security Council, there are such things as 'over-all national psychological objectives'; PSB is indeed charged with the formulation and promulgation of these. The PSB directive also speaks of 'psychological policies' and the Board has been working to develop 'a strategic concept for psychological operations.' We believe these phrases indicate a basic misconception, for we find that the 'psychological' aspect of policy is not separable from policy, but is inherent in every diplomatic, economic or military action. There is a 'psychological' implication in every act, but this does not have life apart from the act. Although there may be distinct psychological plans and specific psychological activities directed toward national objectives, there are no 'national psychological objectives' separate and distinct from national objectives."

6. For a brief account of the elements entering into the American position at Geneva, including the origins of the aerial inspection proposal, see R. Donovan, *op. cit.*, pp. 343-351.

7. R. Cutler, "The Seamless Web," Harvard Alumni Bulletin, June 4, 1955, p. 664.

8. J. A. Perkins, "A Wider Public for Area Studies," address delivered at the Tenth Anniversary of the Russian Research Center, Harvard University, January 30, 1958. Mr. Perkins was a member of the Gaither Committee, which reviewed national security policy in the latter half of 1957. See also A. W. Dulles, "The Soviet Challenge," speech before the Conference on "America's Human Resources to Meet the World Scientific Challenge," Yale University, February 3, 1958.

"History is full of examples where the high standard of living countries—placing emphasis upon those things which make the rounded, developed and cultured human being with leisure for a broadened life—have failed to comprehend the extent and nature of external threats from the Spartas which have concentrated on military might. All you need do is read your history from the Greek and Roman days right down to England and France before World War II, or even our own history.

"A free people such as ours seem to require at periodic intervals dramatic developments to alert us to our perils.

"Some people seem to think that this shock treatment should be replaced by a continuous process of indoctrination which could and should be furnished by government officials. I am somewhat doubtful as to the efficacy of this.

"Most Americans seem to be from Missouri. Seeing is believing. By and large, the press does a good job in this field. Its sources of information are wide and varied. Jeremiads from government leaders are generally regarded as tinged with political or budgetary motives. It was only by orbiting our own *Explorer* that an effective answer was made to the American people as to our own technical competence in the missile field. No amount of speech making would have done it.

"Recently it has been hinted that *if* only the Central Intelligence Agency had been believed, everything would have been well. This is flattering but a great oversimplification. There never has been a time in history to my knowledge when intelligence has had as clear an opportunity to get its views over as it has had in this country in recent years. The National Security Act of 1947, creating the Central Intelligence Agency, has given Intelligence a more influential position in our government than Intelligence enjoys in any other government of the world. If in our government, intelligence estimates have not always had the impact that in the light of hindsight they may have deserved, responsibility must be shared by the intelligence producer. We have the chance to sell our wares.

"No intelligence appraisal could have had the impact of a Sputnik.

"Maybe it was necessary that over the last decade in our relations with the USSR, we had to have a series of political, economic and military Sputniks—costly as some have been—to keep us periodically alerted to our dangers, though once a particular crisis is over, we quickly forget the past."

## CHAPTER 46. The Underdeveloped Areas

1. For a more detailed account and analysis of the evolution of the Middle East crisis see J. Clarvoe, *The Middle East Crisis of 1956*, Center for International Studies, Massachusetts Institute of Technology, Cambridge, Mass., 1958.

2. For a quasi-official account of the impact and response to these Soviet threats, see especially, C. J. V. Murphy, "Washington and the World," *Fortune*, January, 1957.

## CHAPTER 47. Military Policy

1. *International Security: The Military Aspect*, Report of the Panel II of the Special Studies Project, Rockefeller Brothers Fund, Garden City, N. Y., Doubleday, 1958.

2. For references to the intra-administration struggle involving Rockefeller, see Donovan, *op. cit.*, p. 67.

3. The basic data on the shape and pace of the arms race developed by the Operations Research Office of Johns Hopkins University were, for example, made available to both groups. See interview with Ellis O. Johnson, *U.S. News and World Report*, January 31, 1958, pp. 50-55.

4. *International Security: the Military Aspect*, pp. 62-64.

5. In the military debate of 1957-1958 the following positions on the military budget can be distinguished. The position of the President's 1958 budget, in which the absolute level of real military expenditures was held about constant; the Rockefeller Panel position, in which military expenditures were to be enlarged progressively by increments of about $3 billion per year, which would keep the proportion of military expenditures to GNP roughly constant, with an expanding economy; the O.R.O. position, which suggested an increase of about $15 billion; and the Gaither Report position, reported to be somewhere between the O.R.O. and Rockefeller Panel recommendations. See Ellis Johnson interview, *loc. cit.*, pp. 53-54.

6. Jack Raymond, "U.S. Limits Arms Build-up Despite Sputnik Challenge," *The New York Times*, July 5, 1958, quoting "an authority at the Pentagon."

## CHAPTER 50. The Eisenhower Administration: Its Special Character

1. Stassen's post as Chief of the Mutual Security Agency was an exception, at an intermediate level; but his relatively prompt removal from a post involving expenditures underlined the dominance of the right wing where power really counted.

2. Historians may find a degree of mutual misunderstanding and lack of full communication in Dulles' posture within the Administration. While Dulles appeared to take his task to be the loyal advocacy of the policy which emerged by concensus within the Administration, with its heavy right wing bias, the President may have looked to Dulles, notably during his first term, to supply an active counterweight to the right-wing position of Humphrey, Wilson, Hoover, etc.

3. Quoted, W. R. Kintner, *et al.*, *op cit.*, pp. 8-9. In replying to a suggestion that the National Security Council might be a more effective instrument if equipped with a staff independent of departmental connections, J. T. Noonan, Jr. argued the case for policy-making by committees of operators, concluding: "The committee, odious as it is, is the democratic way of structuring a government." "The Astronomer and the Gondolas," *Harvard Alumni Bulletin*, September 28, 1957. For other expressions of the bureaucratized concept of decision-making which dominated these years, see Dillon Anderson, "The President and National Security," *Atlantic Monthly*, January, 1956; R. Cutler, "The Development of the National Security Council," *Foreign Affairs*, XXXIV (April), 1956; R. Bowie, "Analysis of our Policy Machine," New York *Times Magazine*, March 9, 1958.

4. Dwight D. Eisenhower, *Crusade in Europe*, New York, Doubleday, 1948, p. 14.

5. H. C. Butcher, *My Three Years With Eisenhower*, Simon & Schuster, New York, 1945, p. 47.

6. *Ibid.*, p. 729.

7. For a brief description of Eisenhower's "institutionalized Presidency," see E. S. Corwin, *The President*, New York, New York Univ. Press, 1957, pp. 299-305.

8. When, in 1958, Adams found himself in political trouble Eisenhower sought to keep him at his post precisely on the grounds of operational need that determined his decision in the equally difficult wartime decision about General Patton when he, too, was in bad trouble. Eisenhower, *op. cit.*, pp. 179-183.

9. Quoted in E. F. Goldman, *The Crucial Decade*, New York, Knopf, 1956, p. 240. At second hand, the author has heard Humphrey's dictum reported as: "Anyone in this government who spends money works for me." Whatever the text, the fact was that, in his vigorous use of his powers within the Great Equation agreement, Humphrey exercised enormous influence in the Eisenhower first term over military and foreign policy.

10. For the vicissitudes of the Atoms-for-Peace program and the determined advocacy of the few men who, in fact, brought it to fruition, see John Lear, "Ike and the Peaceful Atom," *The Reporter*, January 12, 1956.

11. One of the problems most difficult to solve about the Eisenhower administration on the basis of existing, partial evidence is the degree to which Eisenhower personally believed (or came to believe) that an expanded federal budget was an overriding threat to the nation's welfare; that is, whether in his dour support of the Great Equation down to 1958 he was reflecting a consensus on what the Republican party (or the American people) would accept or also projecting a personal judgment. There is scattered evidence for both views; and later historians may be able to trace a shift in Eisenhower's thought on this crucial point.

BOOK FIVE

# PROSPECTS AND PROBLEMS

# INTRODUCTION

### 51. *Probing the Future*

The concluding chapters of this book peer ahead a little, and, in broad terms, they prescribe. Both prediction and prescription are dangerous occupations—notably for the historian.

Prediction is dangerous because the large number of forces at work in historical situations permits many outcomes consistent with their existence; and the role of accident, including the magical (or satanic) accident of individual personality, adds a dimension calculated to humble those who grasp too arrogantly at the future. Nevertheless, history unfolds within limits which give it a rough shape and continuity;[1] and, among the forces operating at a given time, the correct identification of those with the controlling power permits a degree of accurate prediction. The challenge to the historian and to the participant in public affairs is to make that identification.

But why prescription? The object of this book is to clarify what the nation has recently experienced against the sweep of its longer past in such a way as to permit more effective action in the future. Assuming a degree of validity in the way the story has been told, the reader may and will draw his own lessons for American policy and action; but it is also fair for him to ask: Having exploited the advantages of hindsight, having applied private criteria of value and national interest, what, in the author's view, then follows?

There is another reason for posing this question. The nation's action at home and the efficacy of its actions abroad are inescapably linked. Whether acknowledged or not, whether explicit or implicit, American public policy from the beginning of national history has been suffused by one concept or another which related external problems and objectives to domestic objectives and concerns. Today this relationship shapes the national budget; it strongly influences policy toward education; it touches even so local a matter as the still unfolding drama of the Negro in American society. And there is every reason to believe that the interconnection between external and internal arrangements will become more intimate in a world where time and space are every day more compressed.

There may be some virtue, then, in an exercise that brings into the open a view of what the basic forces appear to be which will shape the nation's external environment; what choices the nation confronts in seeking to ensure the security of American society; where, out of its own history and dynamics, American society appears to be heading; and, on one view of the national interest, what the nation's agenda is as Americans seek to reconcile their country's security with their conception of a good life.

The inquiry begins with an effort to define the basic forces on the world scene which will set the limits within which each nation will seek to fashion its destiny.

# PART II

# THE DIFFUSION OF POWER

## 52. *The Future of the World Arena*

### THE THREE BASIC FORCES

Three forces are conspiring to create in the second half of the twentieth century a world arena in which the affairs of nations are more intimately interacting than in the past and, simultaneously, one within which power is progressively diffused. Those forces are the accelerated technological revolution in communications, the revolution in weapons of mass destruction and means of delivery, and the revolutionary movement toward modernization in Asia, the Middle East, Africa, and Latin America. Thus the forces which began to assert themselves as dominant on the world scene in the early 1950's are judged to be long term in character.

They simultaneously enlarge the world arena, press the nations towards greater interconnection, and diffuse power because their effects are mutually reinforcing. Old concepts of sovereignty are broken down not only because men can fly in a relatively few hours to any point on the globe; not only because mass communications transmit the news so swiftly; not only because minimum military security demands degrees of international coordination—whether in Cold War or organized peace—never before confronted; but also because the evolution of the underdeveloped areas is both dependent upon and reacts upon the more advanced societies of the world in most intimate ways. Similarly, the diffusion of power is taking place not only because the weapons of mass destruction are rationally almost unusable in a situation of stand-off; not only because new and ardently sovereign nations are being created out of the revolution in the underdeveloped areas; but also because modern means of communication produce new degrees of political interdependence.

John Von Neumann wrote: "Soon existing nations will be as unstable in war as a nation the size of Manhattan Island would have been in a contest fought with the weapons of 1900."[1] The violation of time, space, and scale which underlies this vivid appraisal of modern military technology extends to the nonmilitary relations among nations as well.

### THE DIFFUSION OF POWER IN THE SHORT RUN

In the 1950's there was something artificial, something of a *tour de force*, about the bargaining leverage the smaller nations brought to bear against the two great nuclear powers. With Tito's successful defection from Stalin's control in 1948, the smaller powers began to exploit increasingly two elements in the world position: the military stalemate, which made the great powers anxious to avoid major war, and the fact that they occupied strategic positions where each major power sought to maintain or increase its influence or to deny influence to the other power. Under these special circumstances, the smaller powers have been able to behave in relation to the major powers in ways quite disproportionate to the relative military strengths and industrial potentials involved. And so long as the Soviet Union and the United States maintain relative positions in the arms race which rule out major war as irrational (or they do not make common cause), the paradox of unusable force in a situation of Cold War competition should continue to give the smaller powers disproportionate freedom of choice and action.

This does not mean, of course, that the small power can always succeed in asserting its interest against a major power; the major power can bring to bear under certain circumstances its ground force capabilities, for example, as Moscow did in Budapest in 1956. And there are many channels of influence and authority the United States can bring and has brought to bear within the non-Communist world. The point is that the interplay of major and minor powers in the context of a stand-off arms race in nuclear weapons gives the minor powers a bargaining position disproportionate to their industrial capacity and military potential which they are progressively learning to exploit.

### THE DIFFUSION OF POWER IN THE LONG RUN

In the long run, the diffusion of power will acquire a more solid base; for it is as sure as anything can be that, barring a global catastrophe, the societies of the underdeveloped areas will move through the transitional processes and establish the preconditions for take-off into economic growth and modernization. And they will then continue the process of sustained growth and move on to maturity; that is, to the stage when their societies are so structured that they can bring to bear on their resources the full capabilities of modern technology.

The nations and regions presently regarded as underdeveloped stand at quite different points along this path. In Africa south of the Sahara there are traditional societies barely touched by modernization which face long periods of transition before the political, social, and economic preconditions for economic growth are established. A few, like Mexico, Brazil, Argentina, and Turkey, are in the process of self-sustained growth. In between, Pakistan, Indonesia, portions of the Middle East (including Egypt, Iran, and Iraq), and many of the nations of Latin America are quite far along the road toward the completion of the preconditions. Although the time of their take-offs cannot be firmly predicted, the beginning of take-off in these more advanced transitional societies, given the strength of the forces making for modernization throughout the world, should not be delayed much beyond a decade from the present.

But something more definite even than this may be said about the future of the underdeveloped areas; for the two most populous nations of the world—India and China—are already launched on the take-off process. That historical moment can be dated from about 1952, when the Indian and Chinese Communist First Five-Year Plans were launched. In something like a half-century from now the power of compound interest, combined with the passage of three generations in a growing society, will have brought them both not necessarily to high levels of consumption but at least to the stage where the tricks of modern industrial production and technology will be at their command.

This we can say, then, with some certainty: round about the turn of the next century—say, 2010—China and India, with a population between them of about two billion souls, will have joined the ranks of the mature industrial powers. They face many vicissitudes over the coming decades. Political democracy, for example, is not yet secure in India; nor is communism in China. But they will certainly modernize their societies over the next half-century. What is at stake is the kind of societies they will be at home and the kind of objectives they will pursue abroad.

It is, therefore, as sure as anything can be that the central international problem for the future is the organization of a world community in which the United States, Western Europe, Japan, and Russia are joined by powerful industrial states in Asia, Latin America, the Middle East, and Africa— in about that order; and that, within something like seventy-five years, the bulk of the presently underdeveloped areas will have attained economic maturity.

Just as the orientation of France, Germany, Russia, and Japan to modern industrialization restructured the world arena of power as it existed in (say) 1815, yielding the problems and conflicts of the first half of the twentieth century, so, again, the further spread of the industrial revolution is setting a new frame for international politics and power. The world arena which expanded from the old British-dominated maritime fringe to embrace the northern Eurasian line from London to Tokyo (with the United States in strategic reserve) is now becoming for the first time in man's history truly global, with industrialization spreading in the southern belt from the Philippines west to Peru.

## SOME MILITARY IMPLICATIONS

One facet of this process is that the capacity to manufacture and to deliver nuclear weapons will spread widely unless armaments are brought under effective international control. That capability will spread first in Western Europe; but it is likely to come to the underdeveloped areas even before full industrial maturity is achieved because of the high priority that the newer nations are likely to accord this objective. And the weaving of nuclear weapons into the orders of battle of the present nonnuclear powers is likely to occur at a still earlier stage, since, so far as the non-Communist world is concerned, tactical nuclear weapons constitute a means of raising the power of defense against the overwhelming weight of Communist ground force establishments.

Compound interest will continue to do its work in Russia, Europe, Japan, and the United States. Their gross national products will rise, and their virtuosity in modern weaponry will increase if the arms race continues. But so long as the military stalemate is maintained, this process is likely to add little to their capacity to use military force rationally. Some increase in rationally usable force may emerge as limited war capabilities develop and the antagonists feel their way toward common-law rules that permit some clashes of force to occur without spiraling into an unwanted exchange of all-out nuclear attack. But so long as each side is believed capable of shielding a substantial delivery capability from sudden decisive nuclear attack, the use of force by the major industrial powers is likely to remain rational only over a narrow range. And beyond the requirements of security policy, the bulk of the increase in output is likely to be channeled into consumption—or increased leisure—even in the Communist states.

Thus the most likely prospect—ruling out both major war and the organization of an effective system of arms control—is for the newer industrial states to narrow the gap between their own military capabilities and those of the existing industrial powers.

The central fact to which all nations must accomodate their policies, then, is the likelihood not only that the enlarging world arena will become more intimately interconnected but also that the centers of effective power within it will increase in number.

## 53. *The Future of Communism*

TACTICAL SUCCESS

On the evidence of the period 1953-1958, it would appear that the new circumstances within the world arena might well work to Communist advantage. The Soviet leadership, notably after Stalin's death, was quick and vigorous in designing a strategy which accepted the central importance of the new weaponry and of the nationalist revolutions in the underdeveloped areas; and that strategy achieved for the Soviet Union important tactical gains in Asia, the Middle East, and Africa as well as enlarged international prestige.

Looking out on the world in mid-1958, Khrushchev could radiate an authentic pride in the success of the Soviet missile threat on the Anglo-French Suez expedition a year or so earlier; he could look with condescension on deflated American pride in the field of missiles and earth satellites. He could, almost as a matter of ultimatum, seek to rule out a discussion of Eastern Europe from the Summit agenda and accept the international costs of executing Nagy and Maleter. He could observe the disarray of NATO and the discomfiture of Western politicians pressed from below to negotiate, at almost any cost, with the Soviet leadership. He could observe in the Middle East a situation of chronic danger to Western interests which Soviet policy could exploit at small cost and with little risk; he could play an effective marginal role in the disruptive civil strife within Indonesia and Burma; he could observe the Indians returning from Washington with credits grossly inadequate to their task, with a significant number of their countrymen wondering aloud whether the Communist model for economic development might not, after all, be necessary in India. And he could look ahead to the disruptive forces gathering strength south of the Sahara in Africa as promising a further field of application for well-tested Communist tactics.

Looking back over the transformation since 1953, there were even deeper bases for Soviet confidence. The confused top leadership left by Stalin's death had been transformed, with little bloodshed and minimum public disorder, into a somewhat more limited dictatorship which permitted the Soviet state machinery to operate with continuity and, perhaps, increased efficiency; and, although many problems of stable executive authority remained for the future, Khrushchev in particular could view the outcome of the political sequence of 1953-1958 with at least interim satisfaction.

Economically, the Soviet state had been able to enlarge the flow of income to consumers while maintaining a full 20 per cent of Gross National Product available for military purposes and a sufficient level of investment to maintain a high, if decelerating, rate of over-all economic growth. Although no real solution had yet been found to the problem of low productivity in agriculture, time had been bought by opening up the dry lands of Kazakhistan; Khrushchev was willing to risk the break-up of the machine tractor stations, which had served as the basis of rural power and control for over two decades, in an effort to increase productivity; and there were still untapped possibilities in the increased application of chemical fertilizers. There was no reason to believe that a mature Soviet economy could not continue to pay the high price necessary to get its food from a collectivized system.

In terms of social structure and institutions, the Soviet regime had been able to make a variety of adjustments to the desires of the new generation of bureaucrats, technicians, scientists, and intellectuals, making their life less oppressive and humiliating than it had been under Stalin, without serious short-run loss of state and Party control; and when a political threat appeared to arise—as in the case of Zhukov—that threat was removed without immediate consequence to the stability of the regime. Even in Eastern Europe, where the corrosion of the Communist position was most severe, the crushing of the Hungarians without Western *riposte* had numbed and cowed the citizens of Eastern Europe for the time being at least. Enthusiasm for Russia and communism Khruschev could not create in the satellite empire, but he was prepared to settle for an apathetic acceptance of Soviet power as the only perceivable alternative.

Nevertheless, beneath the surface of tactical success and of the authentic confidence reflected at the Twentieth Party Congress of 1956 by the top Soviet leadership, the evolution of the world arena posed a searching set of problems for Soviet policy; for the forces at work both on the world scene and within the Communist Empire were working against that centralization of power which lay at the core of modern communism. Post-Stalin policy had checked those forces, found ways of exploiting them for the short run, or made concessions to them; but it had not eliminated them. Khrushchev had, for a time, improvised a remarkably successful set of moves at home and abroad; but their foundation was uncertain. Moscow faced a profound dilemma—a fact undoubtedly impressed on Khrushchev by neo-Stalinist pressures from Peking and from elements within the Soviet leadership.

COMMUNISM AND THE CENTRALIZATION OF POWER

The dilemma of communism in the second half of the twentieth century arises from a clash between the diffusion of power and the underlying nature of communism itself. Early in the twentieth century Lenin perceived that the majority of the Russian working class was prepared to follow the banners of democratic socialism, seeking piecemeal improvements of welfare and a Western type of political system rather than the violent revolution followed by a dictatorship of the proletariat which he envisaged. Lenin faced the choice of accepting the gradualist impulses of the Russian working class or acting against its impulses, in its name. Lenin (and communism thereafter) chose the latter course. He rejected a role of influence for the Russian Communists in a diffused power situation. He accepted the break with the Russian social democrats and accepted minority status for the Communists as early as 1902, when he published *What Is To Be Done*, stating in effect that the Communists swimming against the tide of history must be a conspiratorial, disciplined minority, seeking and holding power against the will of the majority.

This policy was transferred from the realm of the struggle for power against czarism into a technique for ruling the Russian peoples in the aftermath of the November Revolution of 1917. The Constituent Assembly was suppressed; the czarist secret police was reorganized and enlarged as a basic instrument of Communist rule; the opposition within the Communist Party to the emerging bureaucratic dictatorship was suppressed by force at Kronstadt; and the posture of controlling and manipulating the Russian peoples, while holding the keys to power within the small co-optive elite of the Communist Party, became fixed.

There has been a strong subsequent continuity in the interplay between the Communist leadership and the Russian peoples. The Russian peoples have looked steadily to improvements in welfare, to release from the fears and pressures of a police state, to a peaceful communal relation with the external world. The leadership has countered by maintaining a system of rigid state control and constraint on consumption which it has justified by pointing to the hostility of the external world. The ultimate triumph of communism on the world scene and high levels of consumption for the Russian peoples have been held up as the distant vision and rationale for unrelenting effort, discipline, and sacrifice. Lenin found the formula of external danger useful at the time of the Civil War and the allied intervention; and, at every stage since, when the pressures for release in the domestic society gathered force, a new version of external danger has been evoked to rationalize a postponement in the day when the normal human desires of the Russian peoples could come to dominate the domestic and foreign policies of the government in Moscow.

The specific touchstones for change in communism are, therefore, change in the policy which looks to indefinite expansion of the power wielded from Moscow—the obverse of the image of a hostile world projected to the Russian peoples; change in the policy which abnormally constrains the standard of consumption of the Russian peoples; and change in the system of centralized dictatorial power backed ultimately by a secret police. It is, of course, possible to envisage radical alterations in the policy and domestic institutions of Russian society which would move in these directions still under the name of communism. Gomulka's Poland and Tito's Yugoslavia are shot through with elements quite inconsistent with Lenin's and Stalin's communism; and post-Stalin Russia has been wrestling to accommodate itself to similar forces while maintaining the essence of Communist rule. Moreover, the process of moving from dictatorship to a system of ordered, diffused power—in the West and elsewhere where it has occurred—has been complex, passing through many intermediate stages.

Thus, in examining now the relation between the present cast of Soviet external and domestic policy in the light of the longer-run forces operating upon it, the criterion is not whether communism as a name will be abandoned; it is not whether, full blown, a parliamentary two-party system of government will promptly emerge; it is, rather, whether the linked policies of external expansion, of abnormal repression of consumption, and of centralized police state rule will be significantly and progressively altered.

## THE PROBLEM OF CONTINUED EXTERNAL EXPANSION

First, then, the diffusion of power in the world arena in relation to Communist external expansion. The objective of continued external expansion derived, in the first instance, from the Marxist notion that at the appropriate historical stage socialism would succeed to capitalism on a worldwide basis. Lenin added the corollary that the Russian Communist Party was to be the active purposeful instrument for bringing about this inevitable result.

The merger of a sense of world ideological destiny with an operating conspiracy was, however, quickly modified after November 1917 in two respects. First, the goal of external expansion was made subject to the limitation that it not interfere with the maintenance, consolidation, and security of the Communist base in Russia. Second, the concept of Communist expansion was subjected to the *proviso* that communism outside Russia itself be subjected to intimate and direct control from Moscow. Long before Stalin proclaimed the priority of achieving "socialism in one country," the international Communist movement had been made a direct reflex of Moscow's military and foreign policy. What evolved, therefore, was not a master-plan for Communist world domination as the unique focus for the policy of the Soviet state but a fixed, institutionalized posture in military and foreign affairs looking to the expansion of the direct power exercised from Moscow within the limits set by the need to devote energy and resources to the domestic base and by the opposing strengths and weaknesses faced in the external world.

Despite interwar Communist setbacks in Central and Eastern Europe and in China, Stalin was able to emerge from the Second World War with the balance of power in Eurasia almost in his grasp. And when the postwar strategy was checked by the sequences leading up to the Berlin airlift and the Korean War stalemate in the spring of 1951, his successors could still look ahead to a victory meaningful in Communist terms which might assume any one of these forms, or several in combination:

1. An advantage in military technology over the United States sufficiently great to make rational a sudden decisive nuclear assault on American retaliatory power.

2. A fragmentation of the North Atlantic alliance, leading to the withdrawal of American forces from Europe and, in particular, the drawing of West Germany into a form of neutralized unity which would permit later Communist takeover.

3. A substantial limited war, in which the Soviet advantage in ground forces would be exploited and American nuclear capabilities neutralized by Soviet missiles, to permit, say, the acquisition of direct Communist power in the Middle East or in some other decisive strategic area.

4. A progressive victory of communism, by means and a sequence similar to that in China over the period 1920-1949, in Asia, the Middle East, and Africa.

Different degrees of probability and risk attached to each of these roads to victory; and the rationality of each depended on the nature of American and Free World policy. Nevertheless, over the period 1953-1958, it still remained within the bounds of reason for the Soviet leadership, looking ahead over, say, the next decade, to remain loyal to the notion that virtually total power, exercised from Moscow, might be acquired.

But there was a darker side to Soviet prospects.

First, military victory was a very long shot to play and extremely expensive to boot. It was one thing to get ahead of the United States in missiles, but quite another to develop a sufficient advantage to make a decisive Soviet assault rational. Soviet military doctrine and military policy were altered to take this possibility into account. The concept of "pre-emptive attack" is an extremely lively notion in the Kremlin's thought; but it is evidently not the unique basis of Soviet policy.

Second, looking further ahead, it was most unlikely that Moscow could in fact maintain direct dominance over the two billion men and women in the mature China and India which were bound to emerge in the foreseeable future. Put another way, Communist ideological victory in Asia, the Middle East, and Africa in the next decade or so—even if achieved—was by no means synonymous with the exercise by Moscow over the long pull of effective control over those parts of the world. Even in the 1950's, powerful centripetal forces were pressing within the Communist empire; and although they could be held in check for the time being, they were evidently bound to grow. On such occasions as the Twentieth Party Congress, it was possible, and perhaps comforting, to identify the ideological success of communism with the objective of Moscow's policy; but, in fact, Moscow had long since come to identify acceptable communism only with movements it could directly control. The postwar experience of Tito, the quick draining from Polish communism of much of its ideological content after October 21, 1956, and the state of affairs in Hungary revealed during the revolution of November undoubtedly confirmed the Kremlin in its old skepticism of Communist movements it could not directly control. And the evident assertiveness of Mao in the summer of 1958 undoubtedly helped dramatize this problem in the minds of the Soviet leaders.

In short, even optimistic ideological prospects for communism in Asia, the Middle East, and Africa might offer thoughtful Russian Communists only cold comfort at a time when the possibility of long-run direct control of those areas was in doubt. A world full of Titos represents nightmare for the Kremlin, not triumph.

Third, even if the objective of spreading communism—with or without firm Moscow control—was accepted by the Kremlin, the problem of repeating the China sequence of 1920-1949 in the rest of Asia, the Middle East, and Africa was not as easy as it may sometimes have looked. It was quite possible to score tactical gains, notably in the context of American and Free World policy of 1953-1958; but it was a quite different matter to translate the discomfiture of the West into definitive Communist takeover. Many of the regions of greatest interest in the underdeveloped areas were awkward or inaccessible to Communist military strength; and even limited military operations carried the danger of uncontrollable nuclear involvement. Moreover, the political leaders of the new nations were jealous of their sovereignty and not wholly naïve. They were quite willing to exploit Moscow's diplomatic and economic support to gain objectives against Western interests, or to increase their bargaining power in the West; and this, to Moscow, was usefully disruptive of the non-Communist world in the short run. But in the longer run it was not easy to envisage how Communist takeover could occur unless Soviet or Chinese Communist military strength could be brought to bear. A society in transition from traditional to modern status can wallow around shapelessly for some time without falling under Communist control unless a technique is devised and executed which permits the Communists to gain and hold the commanding heights of power within it. In the case of China itself, the convergence of a major prolonged civil war and the disruption caused by Japanese invasion were required to create the conditions for takeover; and, even then, a different cast of nationalist leadership in China might have prevented this result.

There was nothing in these difficulties to justify the slightest degree of complacency or slackness on the part of the West in dealing with the problems of Asia, the Middle East, and Africa; and nothing so hopeless in the Communist effort as to justify its immediate abandonment, since, in any case, it was yielding such acute immediate embarrassment to the United States and the West. Nevertheless, the difficulties of takeover combined with doubt that control by Moscow could be maintained made the prospects in Asia, the Middle East, and Africa somewhat less attractive strategically than they might appear tactically.

Fourth, the prospects for communism within the Eastern European satellites were by no means wholesome. Poland's economic crisis in 1956 had put to Moscow the choice of permitting Gomulka to free the Polish peasant from the political and social as well as economic constraints of collectivization or of subsidizing Polish agriculture for the indefinite future as Soviet collectivized agriculture was subsidized. The choice was initially made for Gomulka's formula, cheaper in the short run, but with explosive potentials both in Eastern Europe and China—potentials which appeared increasingly to exercise the minds of Communist leaders in mid-1958. And elsewhere in Eastern Europe as well the prospects for anything more than a prolonged Soviet military and political occupation of the area receded.

Fifth, the evolution of postwar Western Europe—with its renewed economic momentum as well as the emergence of an impressive unity on the continent—day by day belied the canons of the Marxist historical sequence. Specifically, the rapid re-emergence of Germany posed a major problem of both power and ideology. Western Europe could be, to a degree, impressed if not cowed by Soviet military strength; and under certain circumstances it might even be successfully destroyed or invaded or neutralized. But its resurrection from the Second World War—even more marked than the post-1918 revival—was an affront to Communist expectations; and if military force was to be ruled out as an instrument for dealing with Western Europe, a most serious dilution of Moscow's power prospects on the world scene was in prospect.

Barring a cataclysmic military conclusion to the process, then, the long-run forces at work on the world scene posed a searching question for Soviet leadership. They placed in doubt, even if current tactics were successful, either the vision of a world directly controlled from Moscow or, even, a world made up predominantly of independent Communist states.

### THE RUSSIAN NATIONAL INTEREST

In terms of Russian interests these forces justified a quite different course of policy; for they promised not only a world where power would flow away from

Moscow but also a world which at any time might start an unwanted major war and a world where the maintenance of the existing position required that the heavy costs of a frustrating arms race be borne. A different course of policy would require, however, that the notion of Moscow-controlled world domination be explicitly abandoned; that an effective system of international arms control be established in cooperation with the United States; and that Russia accept status as one among a group of major nation states, seeking its security by multilateral arrangement on the world scene.

But a fundamental adjustment of Russian strategy to the facts of life of the second half of the twentieth century had not yet occurred by 1958; and it had not occurred because such an adjustment required a basic alteration in the cast of Soviet policy with respect to the Russian peoples.

THE LINK BETWEEN EXTERNAL AND INTERNAL COMMUNIST POLICY

The reason for this link between external and internal policies may be perceived by considering the two central issues on which the end of the Cold War depends: the granting of political freedom to Eastern Europe in exchange for a European armaments and security agreement, and the creation of an effective international system of nuclear arms control.

The freeing of Eastern Europe is difficult to contemplate not primarily because it would threaten Russian military security but because it would involve open acceptance of an ideological defeat with enormous consequences for both the Soviet offensive in the underdeveloped areas and for the survival of communism in Russia. It would be hard to stop the dismantling of Communist systems at the Curzon Line, whatever the tactical virtuosity of the Soviet leadership in finding ways to alter the cast of Russian society within the framework of existing institutions. Similarly, the fundamental inhibition on Soviet acceptance of collective security arrangements in the field of atomic weapons is that they would inevitably induce radical changes within the Soviet Union itself. The Soviet government would have to admit to its own people that their security was dependent on the maintenance of accord with the non-Communist world; it would have to permit international inspectors to roam the Soviet Union on a scale and with a freedom that would make Russia virtually an open society in Western terms; and it would release Russian resources from military use to a degree which would necessitate radical increases in the Soviet standard of life, converting the level of welfare of the Russian peoples into the central operative issue of Soviet politics.

These considerations take on a special importance—and, in a sense, hopefulness—in the light of the forces already at work in Soviet society; for, despite the tactical success of Soviet rule at home in 1953-1958, the dynamics of Russian history is pressing Soviet society away from the conditions of Communist rule and in the direction of those required for an abandonment by Moscow of its aggressive stance towards the rest of the world.

## THE PROBLEM OF EXPANDING WELFARE

Economically, Russia had attained in the 1950's the status of a mature industrial power. Technically, if its leadership chose, Russia was able to offer its citizens high and expanding levels of consumption: better quality food, ample housing, and even that revolutionary vehicle, the mass automobile. Soviet literature and, to a degree, Soviet politics strongly reflected the pressures welling up from Soviet society to expand the level of consumption beyond the narrow circle of the elite which had already begun to enjoy the amenities and gadgetry of a mature industrial society.

This pressure was not merely psychological. It arose also from the need to supply incentives to the kind of well-educated technicians and to the skilled or semiskilled worker on whom the Soviet system increasingly was coming to depend. Even the Soviet soldier was changing from the brave peasant into the highly capitalized technician of modern warfare, who had to be trusted with extremely complex equipment in dispersed operations requiring a wide range of personal responsibility in the making of decisions. As the Soviet economy moved to maturity it became less and less rational to treat its working force as a peasant or unskilled mass; and the emerging working force required an environment of relatively high welfare to do its jobs properly. To some degree, this pressure was met after 1953 by increased allocations to consumption from the annual increment in Soviet GNP; but down to 1958 there was ample evidence that the pressure to turn the great modern economic machine of Russia to consumption had not been relieved by Soviet policy.

Russia as a society was certainly ready and anxious for the age of durable consumers goods and services; but so radical a shift to consumption would not only obtrude on the conduct of Soviet military and foreign policy but also create difficult problems for the maintenance of the political and social base of Communist rule in Russia. The Soviet top leadership is almost certainly haunted by the vision of Soviet society fully possessed of a model T-Ford or a Volkswagen. The mobility, privacy, and expectations set up in a society caught up in the automobile age posed problems for the maintenance of secret police control, for the maintenance of a political system whose rationale hinged on endless struggle with a hostile external world, and for a military and foreign policy which required so high an allocation of income for non-consumption purposes. In the post-1953 years, the spread of television served as a stopgap, urban housing was somewhat improved, and the food supply was enlarged at great cost. Consumption could expand along those politically safe paths for some time to come; but the ultimate problem for communism posed by higher levels of consumption in Russia had not been solved.

What lies behind this assertion? Why, precisely, should there exist a conflict between expanding levels of consumption and communism as it has existed in Russia? Surely, the commonsense conclusion would be that the Communist regime would be more, not less, secure if it could offer its peoples progressively higher standards of life.

If the problem were one of popular unrest, the commonsense conclusion would indeed hold; but the problem of Communist rule in Russia has never been one of controlling popular unrest. Lenin's tactical insight—that a purposeful disciplined minority could seize and hold power against the majority by controlling the keys to urban power—was tragic but quite correct. So long as the ruling elite remains unified in organization and purpose, the powers of police control, combined with selected incentives, can maintain the rule of the minority; for the average among human beings is not brave in the face of a unified purposeful state organization. Rather, he takes its powers as a fact of life beyond his control and makes the best private dispositions that he perceives to be open to him. And within contemporary Russia this framework of passive acquiescence is strongly reinforced by strands of national pride and the opportunities for individual achievement and expression offered by the Soviet system. There is no reason to believe that communism within Russia is threatened by popular revolt.

The problem posed by expanding levels of consumption for Communism is to maintain on the one hand the rationale for a policy of external expansion and, on the other, the conditions for a system of secret police control at home.

Communism has been essentially a form of permanent organization of society at war. Effort, sacrifice, and discipline have been demanded in the name of an unending struggle. Once the stage is reached where it is acknowledged that expanding levels of consumption may be enjoyed—not promised but actually delivered on a mass basis—then the expectations of further expansion become legitimate, both for the elite and the public; and it also becomes legitimate to question whether the balance being struck between consumption and nonconsumption outlays is correct, and whether the distribution of increased consumption within the society is fair. The case for a society structured and motivated for war is thus weakened once the commitment is made to translate increased consumption from status as a future goal into a current, spreading reality.

This dilution of policy away from the tasks of external expansion is likely to be strengthened by the nature of a high consumption modern economy. Once the commitment is made to the mass automobile—which is likely, at some stage, to become crucial to the expansion of Russian consumption levels—further commitments follow: in road-building, gas stations, the type and location of housing. Vested interests—both popular and bureaucratic—emerge which demand that the process of diffusion be pressed on until a high proportion of the working force is lifted from the immobile life of the urban tenement to the more mobile and fragmented life of suburbia, centered on the one-family house.

But even more than this is involved. The age of durable consumers goods and services brings with it changes in social life which alter the technical and psychological problem of secret police control. Communist techniques of mass organization and surveillance have hitherto been based on the economy with which a centralized, relatively immobile urban population may be kept in hand. Historically, the basis of Communist social control has been the extremely narrow range permitted private life and private communication; and there is little doubt that in contemporary Russia, where the progressive constriction of housing space was one of the most marked features of Soviet rule, a desire for an expansion in the range of privacy is one of the most deeply felt human sentiments. Should Soviet society move on, then, to the form of mobile metropolitan life typical of the United States and increasingly typical of Western Europe, the balance between freedom and certainty of control would be altered in ways which, while difficult to calculate precisely, would move Soviet society away from the patterns and texture of the Communist past.

Taken by itself, too much should not, of course, be made of this argument. The age of the mass automobile can evidently be postponed in Russia for some time; and the resources of surveillance and control with modern technology are, unfortunately, ample. There is nothing in this line of thought which justifies a simple prediction that Russian communism will be unstrung by the mass automobile or by any other single factor. It is, nevertheless, a fact that the constraint of consumption in the Soviet Union has served not merely to permit abnormally large resources to be allocated to military and investment purposes but also to maintain a psychological, political, and technical setting which eased the problems of conducting an aggressive policy abroad and of managing a police state at home.

THE DIFFUSION OF DOMESTIC POWER

The problems posed by the continued expansion of Russian consumption levels converge in their consequences for Communist rule with the trend toward the diffusion of political power within the Soviet system. This trend has been contained but not halted by Khrushchev's rise to political power and the reassertion of an enlarged role for the Communist Party among the arms of the Soviet bureaucracy.

Khrushchev holds the dual posts of Party Secretary and Premier; but as of the summer of 1958 there was no evidence that he had made the secret police his personal instrument or recaptured from the army control of its ammunition dumps; and there was still reason to believe that, should he attempt to recreate the essentials of Stalin's system, strong resistance would be encountered within the Soviet elite. Powerful vested interests emerged after 1953 for maintaining "legalism"—notably as it applied to those high in the Soviet system. The police state may not be under serious challenge in Russia; but a return to police politics would be a different matter.

It was still to be established, in short, whether the centripetal forces in Soviet society built up as that society matured and released by Stalin's death could be recentralized. And if they were not recentralized, they promised to yield in time an oligarchic political system radically different from that which Lenin had created and Stalin had personally mastered in his time, and with which Khrushchev sought to maintain continuity.

This slow, erratic erosion of the old political bases of communism proceeded at the level of ideology as well. During the period 1953-1958, notably among the younger age groups in the Soviet population, degrees of communication and discussion of alternatives developed which, while they in no way immediately threatened the safety of the Soviet state, posed a grave problem for the future.

The Soviet top leadership continued to consist of Stalin's old henchmen, men in their sixties whose roots and formative experiences lay in the building of the Soviet state and economy in the 1920's and 1930's. The brief period of Malenkov's premiership in 1953-1954 had revealed the existence of forces seeking quite radical change in the Soviet state and its policies. These were, evidently, checked. From 1953-1958, Khrushchev had threaded his way to political primacy by balancing successfully the men and the issues in such a way as to combine elements from the views of both older and younger men, shucking off potential rivals from both sides along the way; but there is every reason to believe that, as the younger men shaped by the war and postwar years come to power, they will be drawn further along the paths leading Russian society to higher levels of welfare and consumption and to greater decentralization and diminished arbitrariness in the exercise of political power. They will find it more congenial to build policy around the interests and capacities of the Russian national state than around the old Marxist-Leninist concepts and Stalin's operational formulae, the relevance and vitality of which have steadily diminished.

As broad directions of change implicit in the interplay between the dynamics of the world arena and the dynamics of Soviet society, these observations on the diffusion of power can be made with some confidence; but there is, of course, no guarantee that they will work themselves out step by step, peacefully, to yield a Russia come to terms with a world of quasi-independent nation states, devoting itself primarily to the human welfare and more humane political order of Russian society. History offers little basis for confidence that such a transition will be smoothly accomplished; and the memories of interwar fascism in Germany, Japan, and Italy should be fresh enough to warn that the triumph of Russian nationalism over communism does not automatically guarantee a peaceful resolution.

And the hard fact is that in both foreign and domestic policy Khrushchev is pursuing a course wholly consonant with old Soviet strategic objectives while ably adapting them to the new forces at work on the world scene and in Soviet society.[1] And, if one did not peer too far ahead, the goal of world domination could be regarded as closer and more possible of attainment than at any previous period in Communist history; and the continued apparent concentration of power in Khrushchev's hands appeared to make it possible to conceive of a political dictatorship which reorganized for its own purposes the centripetal forces in Soviet society. A showdown between short-run and long-run forces in Soviet politics and in Soviet society had been avoided or postponed.

All that can be said with confidence about the future is that Soviet policy in the period 1953-1958 had not yet come fully to terms with those forces whose influence and power over events—at home as well as abroad—were most likely to grow with the passage of time. But in this, policy-makers in Moscow were by no means alone.

### THE FUTURE OF COMMUNIST CHINA

Something of the same conclusion emerges with respect to Communist China. There too, in the period 1953-1958, an interim strategy was drawn up and executed with vigor which, for the short run, fulfilled the interests of the top leadership and conformed to old Communist images of how things should evolve in the post-takeover stage. A Sino-Soviet alliance was set in motion and operated at every level; industrialization was launched in China on the model of Stalin's two Five-Year Plans of the 1930's, and impressive economic results were achieved; and a joint policy toward the non-Communist world was pursued which, if it did not yield a prompt seizure of the balance of power in Asia, granted a flow of tactical gains which at least justified persistence along the lines as worked out by Mao and Stalin in the winter of 1949-1950 and modified in the post-Korea war phase of 1951-1953.

Nevertheless, Communist China faced problems, both proximate and remote, which threatened the presuppositions on which the Communist regime in Peking was built. At home Peking confronted the unresolved problem of how to generate the regularly expanding supplies of foodstuffs that would be required as China industrialized, with a population increasing at something like 2 per cent (or 12 million souls) per annum. Industrialization radically increased the demand for food not only for the increasing population but also for two other purposes: to feed the even more rapidly expanding urban population, and to earn the foreign exchange necessary to buy imported machinery and industrial raw materials, the requirements for which normally expand sharply in the early stages of industrialization.

Through 1958 the problem of enlarging the amounts of agricultural output in the hands of the state had successfully been met, partly by exploiting certain limited possibilities for an immediate increase in output, but mainly by increased efficiency in collection. There was no evidence that the agricultural sector had developed the sustained momentum required to fulfill Chinese agricultural requirements for the long pull; and there was much evidence that the Chinese peasant was reacting to collectivization as had the peasants of Russia and Eastern Europe before him. There were developing within China elements for precisely the kind of agricultural crisis which Tito had faced and surmounted and which in 1956 had permitted Gomulka to come to power in Poland. In Yugoslavia and Poland, however, the solution required a shift in the balance of economic development away from heavy industry combined with a revision in political and social as well as economic policy toward the peasantry. This solution Mao had examined and rejected in 1955. But in 1958 the Chinese harvests were good, there was still the card of chemical fertilizers to play, the aging group of Long March veterans was still in full command, and the arrogant confidence projected from Peking was well grounded.

Over the longer run China faced the problem of its relations with the Soviet Union. Struggling along at the earliest stage of industrialization without atomic weapon capabilities of its own, anxious to play an active and expansionist role on the world scene, Peking's alliance with Moscow represented for the moment an admirable solution to its problem. And Peking was learning how, within that alliance, to maximize its bargaining position despite its military and industrial inferiority. But just as men in Moscow in their more reflective moments looked forward with some puzzlement to the implications of Chinese industrial maturity, the Chinese Communists undoubtedly contemplated with some pleasure the increased degrees of authority they might exercise on the world scene in the future—without, however, very clear notions as to what policies they might then pursue.

COMMUNISM IN PERSPECTIVE

To sum up, when projected into the longer future, the prospects of the Communist Bloc as of 1958 looked somewhat different from what they would if they were assayed in terms of the present and more immediate future. The military and diplomatic momentum of the Soviet Union, the primacy of Moscow's power within the Communist Bloc, the evident potentialities for tactical exploitation of the transitional societies of Asia, the Middle East, and Africa were offset by the limited usefulness of the new weaponry as long as the nuclear stand-off was maintained; by the likelihood that power would be progressively diffused away from direct Moscow control both within and outside the Communist Bloc; and by forces making for the diffusion of power within Soviet society, the Eastern European satellites, and even Communist China which, if permitted to work themselves out over a substantial period, could radically modify communism. Khrushchev was able for a time to weave the diverse elements at work within the Communist Bloc into a thoroughly possible program of action. But, like Tito and Gomulka, he could not state candidly where current opportunism was likely to lead communism. As Djilas discovered, the articulation of such projections within the Communist Bloc was dangerous.

But to base day-to-day policy on very long-run considerations and objectives is quite abnormal for working politicians; and there was every reason for the Soviet top leaders to "live it up," in Khrushchev's phrase, exploiting the ample opportunities offered to them by the state of the world and by the deficiencies of American and Western policy, and to let the long run take care of itself. Moreover, from their point of view there was practical good sense in not ruling out too soon the possibility of world domination. The course of future history depended in part on how the other nations of the world reacted to the new forces at work on the world scene; and the Soviet Union appeared to be accommodating itself to these forces more actively and successfully than its rivals.

Nevertheless, somewhere in the back of their minds the Communist leaders were aware that they looked out on a world where communism as a creed was disintegrating in the satellites and in the West, if not within the Soviet Union itself; where nuclear capabilities were spreading into the hands of new nations with increasing freedom of action; where a continental European coalition centered on a powerful Germany was rapidly emerging; where the Nassers and Nehrus seemed to be using Moscow at least as much as Moscow was using them; where compound interest was bound to yield in a time relevant to their grandchildren, if not their children, mammoth new industrial states which Russia could not control. Some Russians may have even begun to define an alternative: namely, to exploit the transient primacy of the Soviet Union and the United States to create a system of armaments control so solid and secure that it would guarantee a world of reasonable and orderly politics by the time the new nations came to maturity. This would not be a world dominated by Americans, by Russians, or by both, but a world in which even-handed rules of armaments were applied to all. But it would also be a world in which Moscow abandoned the effort to maintain its security by the direct political and military control of Eastern Europe; and it implied profound changes in the nature of Russian domestic politics which would shift the locus of attention to human welfare and human freedom away from the old imperatives of a society endlessly at war with the world.

In 1958 it was too soon to expect Russian policy to be built on such a vision.

## 54. The Future of the Underdeveloped Areas

As the diffusion of power proceeds, the central choice for Moscow is either to continue to pursue the goal of unilateral domination and hope for the best or to exploit the transient phase of Soviet-American power dominance to alter the terms on which the diffusion of power works itself out. For the peoples and nations of Asia, the Middle East, Africa, and Latin America the central problem is quite different; and it differs among them according to the stage of political and economic modernization which has been reached.

For a relatively few areas, notably in Africa, the immediate overriding issue is to achieve political independence. For others, which have not yet established the preconditions for take-off, the problem is to find a way of organizing nationalism and nationhood in such a way as to reconcile the ambitions for the effective assertion of sovereignty on the world scene, for the creation of modern and efficient central government at home, and for economic progress. India, and a few other nations which have moved into the take-off, face the somewhat different problem of maintaining economic momentum and of dealing with the political and social growing pains which inevitably accompany economic expansion.

Looking ahead, thoughtful men in these nations—as in Communist China —must perceive that their status, responsibilities, and choices on the world scene are likely to be very different a half-century from now from what they are at present. For the time being, however, the management of the birth, infancy, and adolescence of new modern nations, in the context of a major power struggle which offers grave dangers as well as opportunities for shrewd bargaining, constitutes an ample agenda. With the exception of a few leaders and groups who feel that they have no future unless a major war occurs between the Soviet Union and the United States, the instinct of political leadership in these areas will be to continue to exploit, as opportunity offers, the possibilities of diplomatic, economic, and military assistance by the major powers; to preserve and consolidate their independence; and to move toward modernization of their societies. Whether the newer nations are formally joined to the United States in military pacts or not, whether they are postured toward overt anticommunism or neutralism, their operating horizons are likely to be local and regional, their interest in larger affairs mainly focused on the problem of achieving momentum and regular economic growth.

Until a society is moving forward persuasively year by year and its citizens feel themselves to be an effective part of a growing national organism, a wide and dangerous gap exists between the aspiration for progress and the perceived reality. The evidence of history and contemporary experience is that political and social frustrations are not created primarily by envy, that is, by a wide gap in levels of income between societies or even within societies. Such frustrations are created by men coming to perceive that, although progress is a realistic possibility, their own national progress is either not taking place or is taking place more slowly than they believe it might.

It is this latter gap which raises the central domestic choice for the under-developed areas. Shall they persist with some version of the political method of consent; or should they opt for the fully centralized dictatorial techniques of communism? To what extent should the advantages of human freedom and a system of more or less diffused authority be surrendered in the interests of a more rapid rate of modernization? The question is likely to be answered on strictly pragmatic grounds; that is, on the basis of whether the method of consent and of association with the industrialized areas of the Free World in fact yields substantial and regular movement forward; for communism is not a form of social organization which emerges naturally from the imperatives of modern industrialization. It is a pathological form of modern state organization capable of being imposed by a determined minority on a transitional society frustrated and disheartened in its effort to complete the movement to modernization by less autocratic methods.

The issues of domestic policy, centered about the choice of method for modernization, are likely to dominate political life in the underdeveloped areas for some time. The predictable long-run role of enlarged power and responsibility on the world scene, although foreshadowed by the occasional attempts to consolidate the neutrals and to bring to bear against Washington and Moscow a form of effective restraint, is a relatively remote matter. They seek now and in the more immediate future a world environment which will permit them to grapple with their own local problems with maximum freedom; and, where the influence of the Cold War cannot be eliminated, they seek to manipulate the forces it sets in motion to their own advantage.

## 55. The Future of Western Europe and Japan

### THE BACKWARD LOOK

While Moscow maneuvered with skill, energy, and optimism in 1958, as if its current tactics were consistent with a long-run strategy of world domination, Western Europe and Japan went about their business with conceptions of the future more limited and more pessimistic than were necessarily implied by the future of the world arena and their own potentialities within it. Moscow was, in a sense, projecting forward a rate of increase in its power and influence on the world scene which was unlikely to be sustained; the views of Western Europe and Japan were clouded by an image of progressive decline which was likely to prove equally misleading.

In different ways, the major nations of Western Europe (as well as Japan) had each made in the past their unilateral bids for regional if not global primacy, based on the achievement of industrial maturity; each had failed through defeat in war or the attrition of empire. Meanwhile, the United States and Russia had surged to a competitive dominance dramatized by their virtuosity with weapons of mass destruction. In the shadow of the Second World War and the postwar decade, it was not difficult for Europeans to draw for themselves a future analogous, for example, to the provincial retreat of Sweden from its brief interval of glory in Europe. Japan, its role in the Free World limited largely to its military tie to the United States, shadowed by the Soviet Union and Communist China close by, concentrated mainly on domestic issues.

In Britain, fresh from a remarkable performance as a major power in the Second World War, the transition to what appeared second-class status was peculiarly painful; but there was an equivalent in many European and Japanese minds for the bitterness reflected in these lines from *Punch*:

> When Britain first at Heaven's command
> Arose from out the azure main
> She scarcely foresaw how NATO planned
> To plunge her right back in again.
>
> Cool, Britannia, beneath the nuclear wave;
> While the bigger, bigger nations misbehave.[1]

### RENEWED MOMENTUM

At home, both Western Europe and Japan exhibited remarkable, sustained economic momentum after the phase of immediate postwar reconstruction had passed. Their new surge of growth was based on the spread in mass markets of durable consumers goods and services. The diffusion of new levels of consumption was accompanied by high rates of expansion in the lighter industries of advanced technology the growth of which had been stimulated by the military requirements of the Second World War.

Population tended to shift in such ways as to ease the problem of economic growth. In Italy and Japan there were remarkable declines in the birth rate which reduced or promised foreseeably to reduce the burden of overpopulation; while in the rest of Western Europe there was some tendency for birth rates to rise, giving a degree of lift to the growth process.

Sociologically, the elevation of standards of consumption and the new expectations set in motion by the spread of durable consumers goods and services lent a touch of "Americanization" to the scene in both Western Europe and Japan, which indeed were entering wholeheartedly into an economic stage similar to that of the United States in the 1920's.

DEPENDENCE AND FRUSTRATION

As economic health returned, the peoples and governments in these more advanced industrial areas began to grope towards some new, more substantial, and more independent status on the international scene. The miracle of recovery from war, of renewed economic growth, of relatively steady full employment, of expanding levels of consumption—all, indeed, authentic miracles looked at from the perspective of 1945 and the fifteen years of crisis and destruction which had preceded—lost their magic. Men and women lifted their heads to look out on a dangerous, frustrating world within which it was difficult to define a destiny for their nation and their children worth striving for which lay within the compass of national policy to bring about. The immediate postwar phase of status under a more or less benevolent American protectorate no longer sufficed; and American policy remained rigidly fixed in a cast which neither gave scope for enlarged European and Japanese action nor dealt successfully with current problems. Down to 1958, no persuasive image had emerged around which energies and policies could be rallied except for the movement toward unity on the European continent, dominated by the remarkable resurgence of a Germany left relatively free of the burdens of armament.

In the meanwhile these nations dealt individually with a set of frustrating problems as best they could. First, the momentum of their economies, with the new built-in commitment to expand consumption, combined with the costs of defense, led to chronic inflationary pressure and balance-of-payments difficulties; and, lacking an agreed economic strategy in the Free World, there was little basis on which politicians could appeal persuasively for restraint on consumption levels. Second, the powers which still held colonial possessions or which had major interests in the transitional areas were chronically bedeviled by the pressures arising out of the national revolutions in Asia, the Middle East, and Africa; and again, lacking an agreed Free World approach to the problems of transition from colonialism, Britain, France, and the Netherlands were each left to wrestle with the consquences of the disruptive events arising from the colonial past. Third, the nature of the arms race in nuclear weapons, combined with American secrecy legislation about atomic matters, made it extremely difficult for political leaders to define either a military strategy or a position toward the Soviet Union that was possible, sensible, and persuasive to their electorates.

The concept of a Free World allied to and led by the United States was formulated in the early postwar years. Then the fundamental problems of Europe and Japan were economic recovery and military defense against the nonnuclear threat of Communist military strength. But the working policies of the Free World had not been revised to meet the issues raised by the emergence to dominance in the 1950's of the new revolutionary forces in both weaponry and in the transitional areas. Thus, at just the stage when psychologically, politically, and economically, Western Europe and Japan were prepared to undertake increased responsibility on the world scene—to be something more than the protected charges of the United States—no framework within which to assert these possibilities was created.

THE RANGE OF CHOICE

The choices now open to Western Europe and to Japan constitute a kind of spectrum ranging from a fully revived and active Free World, with a major role for the United States, to total retreat from world power and responsibility, if not subservience to Moscow. Along this spectrum the following possibilities might be defined.

First, to make new policies in association with the United States which would better meet the common requirements for military security, for dealing with the underdeveloped areas, and for exploring in reasonable order and safety the possibilities of more peaceful accommodation with the Communist Bloc. Second, to attempt to achieve a world policy along these lines by consolidating their own strength and acting independently of Washington. Third, to execute, with or without American participation, a kind of fighting withdrawal from Asia, the Middle East, and Africa, maintaining to the last ditch positions of unilateral advantage but accepting the likelihood that the newer nations of the non-Communist world would be essentially hostile to the older industrial nations if not positively under Soviet control. Or, finally, to look forward to some form of accommodation with Communist power which, while accepting its world primacy, would maintain maximum areas of independence and freedom of action. For both Western Europe and Japan, however, no serious choice can be made until the nature of American dispositions in the face of the new problems of the world arena can be assessed; for, although their power had markedly revived in the postwar decade, the role of the United States remains for the foreseeable future a major factor in the equation which will determine their possibilities and their status on the world scene.

Whatever the course of events, it is evident that a clarification of the nature of the world arena and of the choices it offers is required. In both Western Europe and Japan the change in the shape of the world arena has tended to be identified with a shift of power out of their hands. It is one thing to face a future which is viewed as passing power from London, Paris, and Tokyo to Washington and Moscow. It is a quite different—and more heartening—matter to regard the transition as one to a world where no one or two powers will dominate but where a great many considerable powers must find the terms of accommodation as virtual peers.

It is true that Europe and Japan will not recapture positions of great unilateral influence; but the world of diffused power could offer them an extremely substantial role of responsibility and leadership. Barring a major war, nuclear power will either spread in such a way as to give these powers some command over nuclear weapons, or nuclear weapons will be brought under effective international control. In either case, the peculiar sense of impotence imposed on them by the bilateral arms race of 1953-1958 is likely to be a transient phenomenon. Beyond that, there is the possibility—foreshadowed by the British Commonwealth structure, the Colombo Plan, and the groping bilateral enterprises of Japan, Germany, and other Western European states —of building constructive associations with the new nations to supplant the old imperial ties the days of which, where they still existed, were obviously numbered, but the severance of which step by step was so extraordinarily painful.

As of 1958, however, neither of these potentialities had yet been made central to the common policy of the Free World. Western Europe and Japan moved along from day to day in a mood of increasingly energetic frustration, which could not be resolved until the United States decided what to do; for, while the postwar years had seen a remarkable gathering of strength and confidence in Western Europe and Japan, the problems they confronted on the world scene were too big to be handled except in coalition with the United States. America's allies were in a position to ask for an enlarged voice in the making of a common policy, and they could bear a higher proportion of the costs and responsibilities of common action; but they could not safely dispense with the American connection.

## 56. American Policy and the Future

THE RANGE OF AMERICAN CHOICE

The nature of the emerging world arena decrees that the United States must either grapple actively with the forces developing within that arena or effect one form or another of withdrawal. One can conceive, specifically, of four levels of American policy.

*First, a policy of unilateral disarmament and passive resistance.* The nature of the new weapons and the instability of the arms race have led many Americans to examine—and a few to prefer—the risks of Communist domination to the risks of destroying a large part of the human race. Such a Ghandian policy would renounce the American use of nuclear weapons for any purpose and declare the United States and the Free World an open city. At its most hopeful, this policy would count on the moral and psychological power of such an act to lead to a parallel transformation in the policy and outlook of the Communist Bloc; but it would accept the consequences of whatever Moscow would then choose to do in preference to the believed risks of the current situation.

*Second, a policy of armed withdrawal to the American continent.* This objective—the proximate goal of current Soviet strategy—would, from the American point of view, be based on the creation and maintenance of a system of nuclear deterrence independent of alliances or overseas bases—a technical possibility offered, perhaps, by the development of the ICBM and the nuclear-powered submarine armed with a solid-fuel IRBM. From a national base thus armed, the United States would endeavor to maintain its influence in the rest of the Western Hemisphere or at least continue to enforce the Monroe Doctrine. The nation would, in effect, leave the fate of the Eastern Hemisphere to the interplay of the forces at work in its various regions. It would return to the concept of an America seeking to fashion its national destiny independent of the world scene.

*Third, a policy of limited withdrawal to the level of alliance with Western Europe and Japan.* With this objective, the United States would cease its efforts to influence the outcome of the nationalist revolutions in Asia, the Middle East, and Africa. It would concentrate on maintaining sufficient strength and unity in the industrialized portions of the non-Communist world to continue to fend off—or to deal on acceptable terms with—the Communist Bloc, the emerging new nations, or both in combination if current Soviet strategy should succeed.

*Fourth, a revived policy of Free World partnership.* The goal of such a policy would be to initiate and to maintain active programs, embracing both the older and newer nations of the non-Communist world, which would ultimately leave no realistic alternative open to Moscow except to seek external security on collective terms.

The policy of unilateral disarmament is to be ruled out as a serious alternative because there is no reason to believe it could be accepted and carried through. There is nothing in the cultural and historical heritage of the people of the United States or of the other nations of the Free World which would lead them to prefer unilateral surrender to individual or national death. Put another way, the forces set in motion by the effort to execute such a policy are more likely to lead to instability and a nuclear war than persistence in efforts to live with the nuclear arms race while seeking its ultimate transformation into an international system of arms control.

Both policies of armed withdrawal—the second and third alternatives—would impose problems on the United States so acute that neither appears stable for the long pull. The nature of modern weapons and the world's increasing economic, political, and psychological interdependence make it unlikely that either of these policies could successfully protect the national interest. Under the assumption of complete withdrawal, for example, the maintenance of the Monroe Doctrine under the conditions of the second half of the twentieth century would prove exceedingly difficult. Neither Canada nor Latin America is likely to follow the United States into isolation; nor could they be easily coerced. Whatever the technical possibilities of mobile solid-fuel missiles in maintaining the retaliatory capacity of an isolated society, the nonmilitary forces at work in the world are making isolation increasingly an unrealistic conception. In the case of limited withdrawal as well, it would prove exceedingly difficult to maintain a Free World in which the Japanese islands, distant from the United States and Western Europe, faced not only Communist China and the Soviet Union but also a Communist or otherwise hostile Southeast Asia. Similar but somewhat less acute problems would exist in maintaining the viability of a Western Europe cut off from constructive associations with Asia, the Middle East, and Africa.

Militarily, it would be exceedingly costly—if, indeed, possible at all—to maintain a secure nuclear retaliatory capacity if the resources and bases of the rest of the world were available to an American enemy. In both cases of withdrawal, moreover, the costs of defense and the costs of acquiring or substituting for imported commodities would endanger the level of welfare, quite possibly requiring the imposition of quasi-permanent direct government controls over the American economy and over the economies of those nations still associated with the United States.

Equally important, the quality of American society would be gravely affected in two respects by policies of withdrawal, whether sought or imposed. With the balance of the world's power in the hands of an enemy or potential enemy, the United States would become a defensive garrison state, the American people living under chronic siege conditions. The national and ideological failure implied by withdrawal would damage, if not destroy, the historic sense of world responsibility and mission which in different forms has given an important dimension to American life and policy since the origins of the nation.

## THE BEST OPTION

It is clear, then, that the optimum policy still open to the United States is the fourth: that is, actively to use the nation's real, if limited, margin of influence on the course of history to yield with the passage of time a multipolar world held in order by effective international control of armaments, its individual societies structured around their own versions of government by consent. There is no guarantee that such a policy will succeed. The forces at work on the world scene are only partially susceptible to influence by American policy. The nation may at some stage be required to face, for a time at least, some version of a policy of withdrawal. But, as of 1958, the national interest requires, and the state of the world arena does not yet rule out as beyond the nation's reach, the fourth course of action.

## THE MAIN HEADINGS OF POLICY

It would be inappropriate to the purposes of this book to describe in detail the content of an appropriate military and foreign policy consonant with this optimum course of action. Its main headings, however, are clear enough.

First, to continue to make war, major or minor, irrational for the Communist leadership. The United States must continue to develop and protect its nuclear retaliatory capacity by a substantial and persuasive margin. Given the fact that American policy has permitted a gap to open between Soviet and American capabilities in long-range missiles, the maintenance of an effective and persuasive retaliatory capacity in the next several years will demand an imaginative and determined effort to maintain the capacity to penetrate Soviet defenses with less advanced weapons systems. In addition the United States must succeed in avoiding situations where it would appear rational for the Soviet Union or Communist China to employ their ground force preponderance on the assumption that the United States had no usable countervailing force and that the nuclear strength of the United States and the Free World could be held in check by Soviet nuclear strength. In part, the creation of this kind of deterrence is a matter of building and maintaining forces capable of conducting limited war, including especially the capability of prompt and substantial airlift. In part, it is a matter of projecting before the event the nation's will and determination to face down blackmailing threats of the kind which were applied during the Suez and Iraq crises, the success of which evidently impressed the Soviet leadership

Second, the creation of a policy in Asia, the Middle East, Africa, and Latin America which will maximize the chance that the nationalist ambitions of these areas will be turned predominantly toward the tasks of domestic modernization, and thus create a secure long-run foundation for their independence. This requires that ample economic resources be made available both as an incentive for local politicians to adopt a constructive course and to assist the nations and regions of these areas to move into the process of self-sustained economic growth without recourse to Communist or other totalitarian political methods.

Third, the bringing into effective and responsible partnership of Western Europe and Japan in both military and economic policy. The attitudes and formulae of 1947-1950 are no longer appropriate to the Free World alliance. Responsibilities and costs must be more equally shared. Just as peace must be sought, the alliance must be rebuilt by recognizing and exploiting the diffusion of power which has been proceeding since 1945. Militarily, this requires that the more advanced industrial nations of the Free World be permitted to contribute to research and development in weaponry; to the maintenance of nuclear deterrence; and, within the range that their capabilities can be effectively used, to the deterrence of limited war. With respect to the underdeveloped areas, this policy requires that the economic development efforts of the Free World be organized in systematic association and on a scale capable of offering sufficient external aid to move the nations of the underdeveloped areas through the preconditions and take-off processes. And the development of these new long-term capital flows must be linked to a fresh effort to increase the size and stability of the Free World's commercial reserves. Politically, an alternative to colonialism must be built between the industrialized and underdeveloped parts of the Free World; and, against such a background of constructive communal association among peers, the residual colonial problems must be dealt with at sufficiently early stages to avoid that kind of wracking crisis that comes when the literate elite within the colonies decides that the prompt achievement of independence is an overriding priority.

To execute such an American policy requires that certain harsh choices be faced. Notably the United States and the rest of the Free World must be prepared to face down Communist military incursions, including the Communist supply of arms in circumstances of civil or regional conflict in the Middle East and Southeast Asia. The truce lines inherited from the Second World War must be steadily protected from direct and indirect assault, whatever the nature of the threats mounted against them. Without Soviet confidence that the West will continue to defend these lines, there is no basis for peace in either the short run or the long run.

Fourth, while thus blocking, by a mixture of military deterrence and creative policy, all the major routes for the extension of unilateral power which are now implicit in Soviet policy, the United States must hold out to those in power in Moscow—and to those who may be in power over the next generation, and to the Russian peoples—a vision of the kind of world the United States seeks and the place of dignity and responsibility within it which Russia could have when divested of its present ambitions. Never losing the initiative, always ready with concrete proposals, a running dialogue—or, if necessary, a monologue—with the Russians must be maintained which makes clear not only what the American objectives are beyond the day-to-day tactics of cold war but also what specific steps and stages the United States proposes to take to achieve them.

Something like these four items are the agenda for the next creative phase in American military and foreign policy.

### THE GREAT ACT OF PERSUASION

In essence, the whole enterprise would constitute an act of persuasion. Its objective would be to persuade those who may be responsible for Soviet policy that the only realistic alternative left open to them by the course of history in Russia and by the emerging contours of the world outside is to accept status as a major responsible state in a multipolar world. Forces within Soviet society are now moving in directions which could with the passage of time make this choice increasingly easy for Russian leaders; and forces operating on the world scene which tend to the diffusion of power could be organized in such ways as to make this choice appear the residual rational alternative for Moscow.

The alteration in the vision of themselves and of the world that is required of the Russian leaders is drastic; and men do not often make their choices in terms of long-run trends unless these trends are translated into vivid, recurrent, inescapable day-to-day reality. In the years 1953-1956 the United States and the Free World let a dangerous gap open between the way the world looked in the short run and the way the world would tend to look in the longer run —if it were not destroyed. The task imposed on the United States by the nature of the national interest is to close that gap, and, by costly, sustained, and creative exertion, to execute the act of persuasion which might yield for the first time in history a global arena of power within which the threat of war had been radically reduced, if not fully eliminated.

### BEYOND THE COLD WAR

Although the forces at work in the world arena make thoroughly possible— not inevitable, but possible—the emergence in the foreseeable future of an international system of diffused power within which the use of major military force is ruled out by international agreement, the task of defending the American interest would by no means end at that stage. The best prospect that can be discerned is that the dangers and risks inherent in the nuclear arms race and the pursuit of world domination would be reduced.

With the great act of persuasion still to be accomplished, and the processes by which it might be brought about—and their consequences—by no means predictable, it is not highly profitable to peer too far ahead. Nevertheless, it is certain that even in a world more or less freed of the danger of atomic war —freed even of the danger of international communism as we know it—the national interest could be threatened. It could be threatened by a democratic failure in the underdeveloped areas, by limited wars, or by new schisms in the world as dangerous, perhaps, as that caused by communism—for example, a split along color lines. Above all, as a possible result of some combination of these three, the United States could be threatened by the emergence of a new coalition which felt it both safe and profitable to violate the assumed armaments control agreement.

In order, therefore, to protect the national interest, the United States would have to prevent in the more advanced areas the emergence of new aggressive coalitions seeking to seize and maintain ideological leadership in the transition of Asia, the Middle East, and Africa to modern status. It would have to maintain a flexible range of military capabilities short of all-out war and the understanding and will to use them. It would have to create and develop policies to prevent major conflicts from developing either within the major regions of the world or between the underdeveloped areas and the industrialized areas. In short, the nation would have to continue to play an active, leading role in a worldwide coalition which shared its essential interests, including especially its interest in maintaining an arms control system.

There is, thus, nothing in the foreseeable prospects of the world arena that justifies the postulation of a time when the United States might without excessive risk divert its attention from the external world and return to a new isolation. The situation which marked the nineteenth century is not likely to recur; that is, the constellation of forces at work in the world arena is not likely to surround American society with an environment which protects the American interest without steady and substantial American attention and exertion.

In a curious way the problems of the 1950's—with military force largely sterilized by the nuclear stand-off—foreshadow much in the world of diffuse politics stripped of the grosser forms of power which the world at best will confront. Taken all in all, the American problem in the stage of diffused power, within a world arena which is for the first time truly global, appears less dangerous, even if more complex, than the problem of dealing with the three direct bids for European hegemony of the first half of the twentieth century. It is also a problem congenial to American political gifts—if the nation cultivates and develops them in this new setting. American society is, after all, built on the proposition that, within ordered limits, the diffusion of power is the basis for human liberty. American domestic political skills and social habits are accommodated to achieving order and direction from situations of diffused power, where regional, class, cultural, and economic interests clash and intertwine in complex patterns. If the nation can evoke and sustain the best in its own instincts and experience, it ought to do reasonably well in a world where history is likely to impose a larger version of continental politics as the working basis for international life.

The grim test of surmounting the arms race without major war or destruction and the transition in the objectives of communism lies more immediately ahead; but the arts required in the stage beyond are already needed to deal successfully with current threats to the national interest.

# PART III

# THE DYNAMICS OF AMERICAN SOCIETY

## 57. The Domestic Base

The tasks of military and foreign policy which emerge from the assessment of the nation's choices in confronting the world arena fall on American society at a quite particular stage of its evolution. The attitudes and actions required to execute them will in part converge with and in part clash with those required to fulfill the domestic goals and aspirations of the American people. The performance of the United States both abroad and at home will reflect the interweaving of efforts both to protect the national interest and to pursue the good life. It is necessary, therefore, to assess how American society has changed in recent decades and what fundamental forces are at work within it which are likely to set the terms and the limits of the national performance on the world scene.

Between 1940 and 1958 two processes which for a half-century and more had posed the central questions for American social and political life came to a stage of at least interim resolution—suburbanization, based on the spread of the automobile, and the evolution of the welfare state.

There was a resumption in the first decade after World War II of the pattern of economic and social evolution which had taken shape in the 1920's and an acceptance of the political adaptation of the 1930's. The set of institutions and public attitudes crystallized in the first phase of the New Deal were consolidated; and, in the end, they were accepted by both political parties and by a substantial majority of the public as the appropriate matrix of mid-twentieth century American life. The rise of real income and the progressive diffusion of durable consumers goods and services did not cease as the postwar decade came to an end; nor were the problems and contours of the welfare state once and for all settled. But just as the forces on the world scene were moving away from prevailing American images during the early 1950's, something of the same appears to have been taking place in domestic life; and by 1956-1958 a relatively new set of issues for American economic

443

and social life, and for politics as well, began to define and assert themselves.

## 58. Recent Patterns of Change

### VALUES AND THE SETTING FOR ACTION

The changes in domestic life and in the patterns of action of individual American citizens during the postwar decade raised a question: Had the emergence of American society to a stage of tightly organized urban life, accompanied by high and secure levels of consumption, brought with it a change in American values?

This is not an easy matter to sort out; for human action, being a choice among perceived alternatives, is determined by the interplay between human values and aspirations on the one hand and, on the other, by the setting in which men and women seek to make these values and aspirations effective. The setting determines the range of choice available.

Changes in the setting of a society result, however, from the flow of past action; that is, they reflect the past interplay between values and the environment in which those values expressed themselves. At any particular period, therefore, the setting of a society is not simply a material, objective fact determined merely by external circumstance; it reflects both sides of the equation, both sides of the market.[1] It is thus exceedingly difficult to establish for any society the extent to which changes in its setting are the product of objective factors external to human values and aspirations as opposed to the cumulative (if partial) influence of values on past action; and it is equally difficult to establish whether changes in human action are due to shifts in values or to shifts in the choices which the setting of a society allows its citizens.

Accepting the inherent complexity of this interaction, it is nevertheless useful to consider first the changes in the setting of American society as it evolved from 1940 down to the mid-1950's and then to explore changes in action and performance which may reflect an authentic change in values, a change in the alternatives open to Americans, or some combination of both.

### CHANGES IN THE ECONOMIC SETTING

The major changes in the economic setting of American life in the recent past are familiar enough and may be briskly summarized.

The heavy unemployment of the 1930's was dissipated during the war years; and, although there were postwar recessions at roughly three-year intervals, following a rhythm of inventory fluctuation at least a century and a half old, an environment of relatively full employment was maintained, imparting to the postwar years a gradually gathering sense of security with respect to employment.

The rise in employment and the more or less regular increase in productivity built into American economic institutions yielded a rise in real income per head and per family. Real income thus defined rose sharply during the war years and continued slowly to rise in the postwar decade. Average (mean) personal income per family or unattached individual after taxes, at 1956 prices, increased from $4520 in 1947 to $5050 in 1955.[2] Changes in the structure of the working force and the nation's progressive tax structure combined to shift an expanding proportion of the population into middle-class income levels, where the ownership of a single-family house and an automobile was the normal expectation. In 1955, 59 per cent of American families or unattached individuals had annual incomes (before income tax) of more than $4000.[3]

The movement from rural to urban life proceeded; and within urban life there was a surge to the more distant suburbs, a shift which moderated during depression and wartime years but then resumed at an accelerated pace. By the mid-1950's about half the population of metropolitan areas were living in suburban areas, as opposed to about one third in 1940.

How did Americans dispose of their rising real incomes? With respect to consumption, at periods of peace and full employment the pattern of relative expenditures followed a path of change reasonably consistent with the previous four decades. Increasing relative amounts were spent on transportation, recreation, medical care, and insurance. Outlays on household equipment and operation fell away slowly; the percentages expended on clothing, housing, private education, religion, and private welfare fell away somewhat more sharply. The proportion spent on food, liquor, and tobacco, although falling in the post-1945 years, remained higher than in the prosperous 1920's. And within the universal human categories—food, shelter, and clothing—there was a shift toward more expensive and various forms of consumption away, as it were, from the old staples.

The changing level and pattern of American expenditures yielded a relative shift in the working force into services and government, as opposed to manufacturing and the older related activities.[4]

In a sense, the most important change in the pattern of consumption was the remarkable rise in the birth rate, begun about 1940. Americans began to behave as if they preferred the extra baby to the extra unit of consumption. During the war years the birth rate rose from 18 per 1000 to about 22. This was judged at the time—and, to a large degree, it certainly was—a phenomenon of resumed full employment and of early wartime marriages. In the postwar years, however, the level of births moved up and stayed at about 25 per 1000, yielding a rise in the population, as well as changes in the age structure of the population, with implications reaching far into the future. An official forecast of American population made in 1946 estimated that the American population would reach 165 million in 1990; that figure was, in fact, passed within a decade.

As real income rose and full employment was maintained, the availability of personal service declined; and services tended to become commercialized where they were not thrown back on to the family itself. Although the American housewife—with more children, more gadgets, and fewer services—led an extremely hardworking life, the decline of the average working week yielded some increase in leisure—for men, at least—reflected in a sharp expansion of outlays on recreation: from horse and dog racing and pinball machines to motorboats, paperbound books, long-playing records, and do-it-yourself workshop equipment.

The pillars of the postwar boom lay in housing, automobiles, durable consumers goods, and in the industries and services related to them. In resuming in the post-1945 decade a prosperity based on the rapid spread of the automobile and the suburban one-family house which had marked the 1920's, the economy was strongly supported by the backlog of housing and durable goods demand unfilled during the war years. The filling of the wartime gap, however, concealed some natural deceleration in these categories, as higher proportions of the American population achieved a middle-class level of life and the amenities that went with it. The output of refrigerators, washing machines, vacuum cleaners, and electric toasters, for example, began to decline in the early 1950's; and although air conditioners, dryers, and home freezers were at an early stage of their diffusion, the extent to which full employment and growth could continue to be built on the regular expansion in the older categories of consumption came into question.[5]

The progressive acquisition of certain major durable consumer goods is reflected in Table 4.[6]

As the impulses from the housing, automobile, and durable consumers goods industries waned somewhat after 1955, a surge in commercial construction and in outlays by state and local governments carried the economy forward until the recession of 1957-1958. That recession bears a family resemblance to the one begun in 1929; but within the American economic and political structure and in the nation's international economic position there were many factors that promised to yield a sequence less catastrophic than that of 1929-1932.

CHANGES IN THE SOCIAL SETTING

Three other slow-moving but powerful forces were meanwhile altering the social setting of American life: a spread of bureaucratic experience, a rise in the educational level, and an increase in social homogeneity.

The proportion of the total working force employed within large-scale units increased. So far as the economy as a whole was concerned, this phenomenon

TABLE 4. DISTRIBUTION OF DURABLE CONSUMERS GOODS IN AMERICAN FAMILIES

| Year | Per cent of All Families Owning Automobiles[a] | Per cent of All Wired Homes With[b] | | | | | | |
|---|---|---|---|---|---|---|---|---|
| | | Television Sets | Refrigerators | Freezers | Vacuum Cleaners (floor) | Electric Washers | Dryers (electric and gas) | Air conditioners |
| 1946 | | — | 69.1 | — | 48.8 | 50.5 | — | 0.2 |
| 1947 | | — | 71.2 | — | 49.5 | 63.0 | — | 0.2 |
| 1948 | 54 | 2.9 | 76.6 | 4.3 | 51.7 | 67.4 | 0.4 | 0.3 |
| 1949 | 56 | 10.1 | 79.2 | 5.2 | 52.8 | 68.6 | 0.7 | 0.4 |
| 1950 | 60 | 26.4 | 86.4 | 7.2 | 56.5 | 71.9 | 1.4 | 0.6 |
| 1951 | 65 | 38.5 | 86.7 | 9.3 | 57.7 | 73.5 | 2.4 | .8 |
| 1952 | 65 | 50.2 | 89.2 | 11.5 | 59.4 | 76.2 | 3.7 | 1.4 |
| 1953 | 65 | 63.5 | 90.4 | 13.4 | 60.5 | 78.5 | 5.1 | 2.6 |
| 1954 | 70 | 74.1 | 92.5 | 15.1 | 62.2 | 81.3 | 6.6 | 4.0 |
| 1955 | 71 | 76.1 | 94.1 | 16.8 | 64.3 | 84.1 | 9.2 | 5.6 |
| 1956 | 73 | 81.0 | 96.0 | 18.0 | 66.7 | 86.8 | 11.9 | 7.6 |

a SOURCE: Board of Governors of the Federal Reserve System. Note: Data relate to ownership of an automobile by some member of the family early in each year. Data are not available prior to 1948.
b SOURCE: McGraw-Hill Publishing Co. (Electric Merchandising).

turned out to be a consequence mainly of the shift of labor out of agriculture rather than of any marked tendency toward increased concentration in American business. Since 1929 the proportion of agricultural to nonagricultural employment has fallen from more than 25 per cent to less than 10 per cent.

Within industry such comparable statistics as are available indicate that the proportion of wage earners in the largest 5 per cent of manufacturing establishments rose modestly: from 55 per cent in 1914 to 62 per cent in 1947.[7] But the trend in manufacturing does not apply to business as a whole because of the vitality of small business units in other sectors, notably retail trade and services. The independence of these small units is, however, often compromised by their links to the great corporations, as in the case of automobile dealers.

Government greatly expanded. The Civil Service rolls of the federal government rose from about 600,000 in 1930 to about 2,400,000 in 1955; and the armed forces have remained mobilized at something like ten times their level of the 1930's. Cumulatively, about 20 million American men have known the round of military life.

More than that, important branches of American industry as well as university and intellectual life became partially linked to the government's military programs, pressing the framework of federal bureaucracy far out into the society.

By and large, then, the experience of life and work within a large-scale organization became increasingly typical of American society.

The dynamics of the national commitment to popular education extended rapidly toward the end of the nineteenth century into secondary and higher education. Its broad consequence can be seen in the relative educational status of enlisted men in the First and Second World Wars.[8]

TABLE 5. RELATIVE EDUCATIONAL STATUS OF ENLISTED MEN,
WORLD WAR I AND WORLD WAR II

| | Percentage of Total Enlisted Men | |
|---|---|---|
| Years of Schooling | World War I | World War II |
| Grade school | 76.7 | 30.9 |
| High school | | |
| 4 years | 4.1 | 23.3 |
| 3 years | 2.7 | 11.2 |
| 2 years | 4.8 | 10.9 |
| 1 year | 6.3 | 7.8 |
| College | | |
| 4 years | 1.2 | 3.6 |
| 3 years | 0.9 | 2.0 |
| 2 years | 1.5 | 4.0 |
| 1 year | 1.8 | 6.3 |
| Total | 100.0 | 100.0 |

Stouffer data on education by age group, in a more recent national sample,[9] are shown in Table 6.

TABLE 6. EDUCATION BY AGE GROUP
(IN PER CENTS)

| National Cross-section | 21-29 | 30-39 | 40-49 | 50-59 | 60 and over |
|---|---|---|---|---|---|
| College graduates | 8 | 10 | 9 | 7 | 4 |
| Some college | 14 | 10 | 9 | 9 | 6 |
| High school graduates | 40 | 33 | 20 | 14 | 13 |
| Some high school | 24 | 23 | 24 | 20 | 13 |
| Grade school | 14 | 24 | 38 | 50 | 64 |

Veterans' benefits and the high level of postwar incomes have carried this process forward with wide-ranging consequences covering the whole realm of public taste, opinion, and manners.

There has been a parallel maturing of American intellectual life marked, for example, by a sharp increase in the American contribution to theoretical concepts in both the physical and the social sciences. This trend toward virtuosity in theory was certainly accelerated by the intellectual immigration from the European continent of the 1930's and probably by the intrusion into American academic life of certain war and postwar problems of public policy. But the development appears to have been implicit in the aspirations and intellectual values of the generation of American scientists who came of age between the wars and who reacted along a broad front against the extreme empirical bias of their elders.

In the pre-1914 years, immigration to the United States was running at the rate of about one million per year. It fell away in the 1920's and became a thin trickle in the 1930's. The process of adjustment to the predominant goals of American life and culture steadily proceeded, generation by generation; and it broke down or strongly diluted those groupings in American life based on racial or national origin which for a time formed enclaves of non-American cultures. To this process was added the industrial revolution in the South of the past two decades, which also produced changes in the direction of national uniformity.

There was, then, a marked increase in the social homogeneity of the American population. However, this broad trend left the problem of the social status of the Negro in a special category, felt, perhaps, with peculiar acuteness as other minority problems became less sharp and as the average economic and educational level of the Negro rose and with it his level of aspiration.

Abstracting, then, from the Second World War and the international involvements of the post-1945 years, American society appeared to have found in the early 1950's a distinctive moving equilibrium in which certain of the old processes—notably the open frontier and a large flow of immigration—

were supplanted by the dynamics of an industrial growth oriented increasingly to durable consumers goods and services and to the migration to the suburbs. Having gradually thrashed out a resolution which narrowed the conflicts between industrial private capitalism and the other values of political and social democracy, Americans found themselves a suburbanizing nation, increasingly at work in large bureaucracies, with a new security of employment, rising levels of welfare, rising standards of education and of intellectual sophistication, and an increased social and political homogeneity.

### THE CONFLICT AND CONVERGENCE OF EXTERNAL INFLUENCE

The setting of post-1945 American society is a product not only of forces arising from the sweep of domestic history but also of their interplay with forces arising from protracted engagement in the world arena of power since 1941.

Basically, the nation's new international status set in motion forces which ran directly counter to the directions decreed by the dynamics of the domestic society. The nation emerged after the Second World War in a position (and with the evident desire) to cultivate a rather attractive domestic garden. And it had reached a stage of economic, social, and political development where a uniquely comfortable life under conditions of relatively low political and social tension was probably possible. At just this stage, American society was required to take active measures to protect the security of the nation against forces and methods for which it was not well prepared; and it has lived since 1945 under a foreseeable threat of direct, catastrophic assault from nuclear weapons, a threat made increasingly real after September 1949. It has had to allocate not only large resources but also a substantial proportion of the energy and talents of the nation to maintain minimum national security. An America come to terms with the welfare state at high and rising levels of real income and an America which was the fortress base of the West in an intense Cold War shadowed by nuclear destruction has made, indeed, a curious mix.

Nevertheless, in its impact on American society the Cold War has converged with many of the trends built into the nation's domestic dynamics at the same time that it has set up important countertrends and tensions.

The scale of the military budget has made it easier to maintain full employment but posed more sharply than would otherwise have been the case the problem of inflation control in a political and social democracy of diffused authority.

The scale and the ramified industrial and intellectual activities of the military establishment have accentuated the trend toward bureaucratization.

The workings of the Selective Service, combined with the social values built into the military establishments and veterans' benefit legislation, has accelerated the trend toward social homogeneity, toward higher average levels of education, and (via veterans' housing) toward suburbanization.

The imperatives of the arms race in new weapons and, to a degree, the problems of policy-making in relation to societies which do not share American values and institutions have stimulated the development of both the natural and the social sciences, encouraging the practical application of higher order abstractions than would have been demanded if American science had continued to be oriented toward the concerns of a more isolated domestic society.

The cumulative effect of overseas experience during the Second World War, of occupation duties, and of the Korean War, and the narrower but powerful experience of work by Americans in overseas aid and information programs, have radically increased the knowledge and awareness of the world outside the United States; and the flow of international news, punctuated by a series of major crises, has carried this awareness deep into the society in all regions of the country. Although knowledge and awareness are by no means to be equated with sympathy and a sense of common interest, isolationism has been powerfully diluted by these intrusions of the world on American life.

The existence of chronic national emergency has led to the development of an elaborate system of personnel security by the federal government. Given the scale of the national security effort and the administrative techniques of the personnel security program, the lives of millions of Americans have been touched in one way or another by this dimension of national policy, quite aside from that phase of the postwar experience when personnel security issues became embroiled in national policies.

The drawn-out and intractable nature of the struggle with the Soviet Union —including the frustrations of the Communist takeover in China, the indecisive outcome of the Korean War, the nation's impotence in the face of the Hungarian revolt, the Soviet lead in missiles—has imposed a sense of limitation on the nation's old image of itself, a limitation which has been accepted with greater or less maturity and which has touched the nation's domestic life at many points with elements of escapism, with a tendency to search for scapegoats, with simple worry, and with much thoughtful, responsive effort as well.

## 59. Have American Values Changed?

Against the background of the changes in the setting of domestic life, there emerged in the early 1950's an extensive literature focused around this question: Have American values and aspirations been undergoing important change?[1]

The emergence of this analytical material on American society reflected a remarkable development of societal theory in American intellectual life. Since this development was relatively new, and comparable studies had not been systematically made in the American past, it is difficult to establish whether the attitudes and values established in American society in the post-1945 decade were, in fact, new or only newly documented. Many of the characteristics isolated by recent analysts as typical of American society—for example, a tendency to conformity in manners and opinion on issues of public policy— were observed by Tocqueville in the 1830's. Moreover, the fields of sociology, social psychology, and anthropology are at an early stage in their separate (and coordinate) development; and their analytical terms and tools are not yet so structured as to permit wholly unambiguous conclusions to be drawn or communicated.

Nevertheless, there emerged a wide range of agreement that Americans were making choices among the alternatives they perceived to be open to them in terms of objectives which differed from the prevailing concept of what American objectives had hitherto been; and many thoughtful observers noted a definitive shift of American society away from the values of the Puritan ethic. A useful summary of the believed shift in values is that of George Spindler.[2]

It came widely to be believed, then, that Americans were adapting themselves to the new setting of their society in ways which diminished the pursuit by individuals of the goals of personal material success in favor of conformity to organizational and group objectives on the one hand and, on the other, to the cultivation of the immediate satisfactions and privates values offered by a rich society.

Something of the same judgment about American society was reflected in the work of American novelists who treated the Second World War not primarily as a clash between humane civil values and the brutal facts of organized violence but as a problem of the individual's relation to a massive bureaucracy. In different ways this was true, for example, of *From Here to Eternity, Mr. Roberts, The Caine Mutiny,* and *Guard of Honor.* Each of these works dramatizes the clash between the individual personality and the unfeeling requirements of a massive military organization which, in a higher interest, must deal with the individual virtually as a statistical unit; and each, in its way, made the case for the primacy of the organization and its communal purposes. And as the novelists turned to the issues of the postwar world, once again the theme of the individual personality in relation to bureaucracy emerged—often in relation to the bureaucratized structure of modern American business. Even where the hero withdraws to a degree from the demands of successful organizational activity—as in Sloan Wilson's *The Man in the Grey Flannel Suit*— the case for the individual expressing his creativeness through his role in a group, and within the terms set by a large institution, is strongly made.

| TRADITIONAL VALUES | EMERGENT VALUES |
|---|---|
| *Puritan morality* (Respectability, thrift, self-denial, sexual constraint; a puritan is someone who can have anything he wants, as long as he doesn't enjoy it!) | *Sociability* (As described above. One should like people and get along well with them. Suspicion of solitary activities is characteristic.) |
| *Work-Success ethic* (Successful people worked hard to become so. Anyone can get to the top if he tries hard enough. So people who are not successful are lazy, or stupid, or both. People must work desperately and continuously to convince themselves of their worth.) | *Relativistic moral attitude* (Absolutes in right and wrong are questionable. Morality is what the group thinks is right. Shame, rather than guilt-oriented personality, is appropriate.) |
| *Individualism* (The individual is sacred, and always more important than the group. In one extreme form, the value sanctions egocentricity, expediency, and disregard for other people's rights. In its healthier form the value sanctions independence and originality.) | *Consideration for others* (Everything one does should be done with regard for others and their feelings. The individual has a built-in radar that alerts him to other's feelings. Tolerance for the other person's point of view and behaviors is regarded as desirable, so long as the harmony of the group is not disrupted. |
| *Achievement orientation* (Success is a constant goal. There is no resting on past glories. If one makes $9,000 this year he must make $10,000 next year. Coupled with the work-success ethic, this value keeps people moving, and tense.) | *Hedonistic, present-time orientation* (No one can tell what the future will hold; therefore, one should enjoy the present—but within the limits of the well-rounded balanced personality and group.) |
| *Future-time orientation* (The future, not the past, or even the present, is most important. There is a "pot of gold at the end of the rainbow." Time is valuable, and cannot be wasted. Present needs must be denied for satisfactions to be gained in the future.) | *Conformity to the group* (Implied in the other emergent values. Everything is relative to the group. Group harmony is the ultimate goal. Leadership consists of group-machinery lubrication.) |

This recurrent contemporary theme, which identifies the central issue of American society as the individual's relation to bureaucracy and which counsels a high degree of respect for the imperatives of bureaucratic order and continuity, was indeed new to the national literature, in which the classic heroes had for the most part a strong touch of defiant anarchism about them. It differed radically both from the protest of the individual against the values of

the marketplace which dominated so much of American writing in the prosperous 1920's and from the wider ranging protests against the values and institutions of capitalism which characterized much creative writing of the de-
pressed 1930's.

The question has been raised as to whether the shifts in the objectives pursued by Americans can be correctly identified with a change in basic American
values, notably if those values are defined at a high level of generality. Some
commentators would argue the possibility that fundamental American values
have not altered but that the setting of American life has altered the objectives
open to Americans in such ways as to make the pursuit of the old values in
terms of the old objectives impossible. Winston White, for example, following leads from Talcott Parsons, points to the institutionalization of business
management, of risk-taking, and of innovation as having eliminated some of
the classical areas in which the lonely, purposeful individual might find effective expression.[3] He thus poses the problem of distinguishing the extent to
which a change in action is determined by a change in the available alternatives
on the one hand or by a change in values on the other. Moreover, much depends on the level of abstraction at which values are defined.

Basic values become deeply embedded in a society only over very long
periods of time, over which they appear to gather legitimacy by yielding a
flow of acceptable solutions to individual and community problems;[4] and it
is, perhaps, too soon to know whether in some long-run sense the context of
American life will be such as to alter permanently the old emphasis on the
optimistic individual pursuit of goals and achievements external to the private
sphere of life.

The conception of American society accomodating itself neither to the exploitation of a physical frontier nor to the possibilities of applying modern
industrial technique to its basic resources but rather to the potentialities of expanding consumption raised an even more fundamental question. What would
happen to the quality of American society if hedonism and security were to
supplant individual striving and adventure in a challenging physical environment as the norms of American experience? Put another way, were Americans
(and human beings in general) capable of maintaining a life consistent with
the oldest values out of the Western past if that life did not require that men
work hard? Are human beings, in the large, capable of building an ordered
and satisfying life centered about the pursuits of leisure and the cultivation
of peace of mind? Could a large population live within the kind of environment that was emerging in the United States in the early 1950's, where the
challenges and possibilities to the individual were reduced—or altered out of
the traditional context of frontier, farming, and the marketplace—without the

nation becoming a bore to itself and to the world? Would the devil make work for idle hands?[5]

At just the time when these issues were being defined with increasing clarity and were receiving a kind of official sanction in the conduct of the Eisenhower first term—when, to many, peace and prosperity seemed to have been successfully institutionalized—the setting of American life began to change. The problems of what might be defined as secular stagnation of the spirit (as opposed to the economy) appeared to be at least postponed.[6] The changes which asserted themselves in 1956-1958 by no means made irrelevant the questions posed by the postwar social analysts and novelists; but they suggested that the nation faced, both in its domestic dynamics and in its changing relation to a changing world, a set of challenging problems the response to which might modify for a time at least the emergent conception of the consumption-oriented, group-minded, complacent America of the early 1950's which had institutionalized all of its problems except the use of leisure and the attainment of peace of mind.

## 60. The Domestic Crisis of 1956-1958

The national mood was altered in 1956-1958 by a series of independent events: the crisis over school integration and, notably, the events at Little Rock in the autumn of 1957; the severity of the recession of 1957-1958; the re-evaluation of the American educational system, its purposes and values, induced both by the competition of the rising school age for placement in college and by the emergent Soviet lead in missile technology; and, finally, the increasing evidence that the nation had been living off its social overhead capital not only with respect to schools but also with respect to its urban areas, roads, railroads, water supply, and in other directions as well. In combination with the running crisis in the nation's international position, these factors yielded—perhaps only for an interval—an atmosphere markedly different in the spring and summer of 1958 from what it had been two years earlier.

With respect to segregation, outside the South, Americans had generally welcomed the Supreme Court's decision of 1954. It may have been received, however, as the measure of progress already made in the nation's long evolutionary struggle with the Negro problem rather than as the opening of an extremely complex and difficult new phase. The nation as a whole only gradually became aware of the depth of feeling stirred in the South by the desegregation decision and by the expectations of further social change to which it gave life. In the limited areas where the decision was executed, there was nothing automatic about the result; local organization and local leadership at the highest levels of good sense and statesmanship were required. And where desegregation was postponed or frustrated, the primitive strength of the emotions which still surrounded the Negro problem were revealed with uncomfortable clarity to the nation and to the world. There was nothing to justify complacency in that revelation—only the definition of a new and extremely challenging as well as potentially disruptive phase in the nation's old problem.

If Little Rock gave a generation of Americans a moment of apparent second sight into the emotional setting of the Civil War, the recession of 1957-1958 faintly evoked the moods of the Great Depression a quarter of a century earlier. A depression which raises unemployment to 5 million directly touches the lives of about 18 million persons; and it shadows the lives of those placed on short time as well as those who feel that they too may be laid off.[1] Briefly, at least, some of the corrosive consequences of this form of breakdown in the social fabric could be glimpsed again: heightened tension between management and labor; heightened tension between white and Negro workers; the anger of the younger worker who, due to seniority rules, was often the first to be laid off; and a general turning inward toward domestic problems, with evident costs to the nation's international position.

Fundamentally, however, the situation was vastly different from that of the 1930's. Built-in stabilizers strongly cushioned the down-swing: a tax system which automatically cut tax payments rapidly—by almost 50 per cent—with the fall of income; substantial unemployment benefits and farm income supports; and the virtually automatic easing of interest rates and terms of credit supply, including mortgage rates. More than that, intellectual and political attitudes toward the problem of unemployment had altered out of all recognition in the previous quarter century. Unlike the situation in 1929-1933, there was almost unanimous agreement that an unbalanced federal budget was a necessary and proper instrument for bringing the country back to full employment. Differences concerned the method by which the federal budget should be unbalanced, the scale of an appropriate deficit, and the optimum timing of a tax cut, if any.[2]

While the desegregation issue and the recession raised new versions of old and essentially familiar national issues, the emergent problem of education was being defined in terms of issues relatively new to the national (but not necessarily the local) scene.

In education, as in military policy, the launching of the Soviet earth satellites crystallized out and heightened a controversy which had been building up for some years, posed by the rising pressure of population of school age, the rise in education costs, and the shortage of teachers. To these elements was added the shock of competitive failure in the missiles race, which became widely associated with a failure of the nation's educational system.[3]

The main elements in the position which emerged in opposition to the educational *status quo* could be summarized in some such terms as these:[4]

1. The intellectual life and the quality of intellectual excellence would have to be accorded a higher prestige and be more truly cherished by the society if the nation's talents were to be channeled and developed along the paths necessary to protect the nation in the world into which it was emerging. In particular, it would be necessary to allocate disproportionate educational resources to students of first quality.

2. In addition to the need to develop to the highest pitch the best young minds, education as a whole should be given a greater rigor and should be less diluted with courses of an empirical character designed to give the student merely enlarged factual knowledge about the workings of his society.

3. In order to develop and maintain an educational system of this kind in the face of the population increase already under way, the nation would have to offer its teachers both more money and more social status; and it would have to invest vastly increased resources in school buildings and other physical facilities for education.[5]

The most revolutionary aspects of the debate on education in 1957-1958 were the open emphasis on quality and the affirmation that it was legitimate in American society to allocate unequal amounts of public resources to the children of equal citizens. Both ran counter to the strong egalitarian strand in the nation's tradition. On the other hand, there was something familiarly American about the new emphasis on intellect in the post-sputnik era. The nation behaved a little like a business firm confronted by competition from an unexpected source and in an unexpected dimension: if brains were the pay-off, then it would be necessary to cultivate brains. Thus, in his major initial reaction to the launching of the Soviet earth satellite, Eisenhower elevated the President of Massachusetts Institute of Technology to a high post in the White House; and hardened bureaucrats in Washington were soon muttering of the new hegemony of physicists in succession to high business executives.

The changing moods of 1956-1958 and the altered terms of public discourse and controversy are difficult to assess. Were they a mere transient ripple on the rising tide of complacency and secular spiritual stagnation; or did they signal a major turning point? It was certainly true, for example, that, although the crisis in the South over desegregation had been sobering, a good deal of care was likely to be exercised by all hands to avoid a repetition of Little Rock. Strong forces would seek to keep the struggle within bounds, its irrational core concealed or repressed. It was not impossible, at least, that the school desegregation issue would be shifted from the area of acute and searching national crisis to a process of slow, piecemeal local change.

It was also clear that a good deal of the mood of the first half of 1958 would alter when unemployment began persuasively to fall off and the upward march of high and expanding levels of national and family income was resumed. It might even emerge that, having conquered the recession of 1957-1958, which had been a more searching affair than its three postwar precedessors, the nation would become truly confident that it could determine the level of employment. Moreover, should the international situation remain relatively stable, should the Middle East and Far East crisis of 1958 be contained and slowly resolved, should Moscow neither undertake military aggression nor exhibit any further relative improvement in its technological prowess, the impetus to thought and action in American education stirred by the sputnik crisis might wane; and the whole matter of educational improvement might fall back to the old indecisive level of politics in the local communities.

It is, in short, possible that the troubled, questioning mood of 1956-1958 might prove to be a relatively transient phenomenon.

## 61. Prospects for the Future

### TWO INESCAPABLE IMPERATIVES

However transient the mood of 1956-1958, there were at work in American society two forces generated from the dynamics of the war and postwar years which were not to be denied—whether the response to them was energetic, well-articulated, and strongly guided by political leaders; or sluggish, piecemeal, and reluctant. The first of these forces was the rise in population brought about primarily by the sharp increase in the birth rate since 1940; the second was the increasing claims on the nation's resources for social overhead capital. Between them they promise to alter the setting of American society significantly for a decade at least, quite aside from the possibility that other domestic or international forces might press in the same direction.

During the early 1960's the rise in the birth rate will yield a rising rate of family formation certain to increase the demand for housing, the standard household package of durable consumers goods, and social overhead capital. The expansion of the working force which will come about as the children of the 1940's go to work will be outpaced, however, by the expansion of the population as a whole. From the mid-nineteenth century to about 1940 the proportion of the working force to the population regularly increased. The reversed trend of recent years is likely to continue for a time, with each worker supporting, as it were, an increased number of both older and younger dependents, as suggested in Chart I.

A number of unpredictable factors will determine precisely how this shift in the size and age structure of the population will be borne; but the presence of these changes at the heart of American society is likely to alter for the time being the notion that hours of work are bound progressively to decline,

Chart I

Percentage Distribution of Population by Dependent
and Working Age Groups, 1850-1950, with Estimates
for 1960.

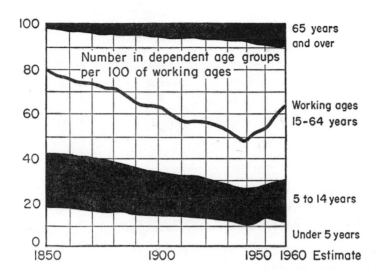

Chart II

Per Capita Expenditures on Public Works

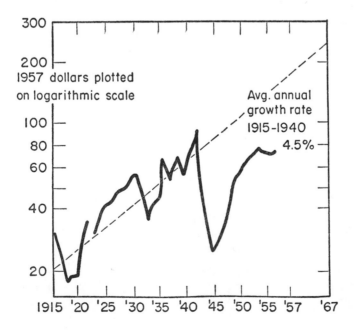

that retirement at 65 is an overriding objective, and that a regular rise in private consumption per head is somehow automatic and a necessary condition for a decent national life.

This suffusion of national life with a touch of austerity in the private sector will be strengthened to the extent that the nation faces and meets its accumulating bill for social overhead capital. The post-1946 decade saw a remarkable rise in outlays for housing and automobiles. Leaving aside the modest role of the government in the housing boom, these activities could be conducted through the private sector. Meanwhile, however, roads, schools, and the urban areas (whose taxable revenue was drained away by the flow to suburbia) were grossly neglected. In a vivid chart, the Report of Panel IV of the Rockefeller Special Studies project caught and measured roughly the extent to which the nation had been living off its previously accumulated social capital in certain major directions. (See Chart II.)

If the nation is to retrieve this gross lock of balance, a radical relative shift in resources in favor of social overhead capital is required. And this, too, could put pressure on the level of private consumption per head.

> "In the period 1915-1940 per capita expenditures in constant dollars on schools, roads, waterworks, and other public works rose at an average annual rate of 4.5 per cent. In this manner, Federal, state, and local governments provided the public assets needed by a growing economy.
>
> Expenditures dropped sharply in 1932 and 1933 and, despite a massive effort by the Federal government, did not regain their previous rate until 1936. This experience shows that public works programs are slow to get underway.
>
> Despite the sharp increase during the past decade, per capita expenditures on public works are no higher than they were two decades ago. Moreover, they have leveled out in the past few years. And total public works expenditures have lagged behind the growth of total national output—the ratio to GNP decline from 4.5 per cent in the late 1930's to 3 per cent now."

Rockefeller Report IV estimated that the nation's minimum bill for social overhead capital (given the likely rate of increase in national security expenditures over the next decade) will permit only a 2 per cent per capita increase in consumption to be maintained if GNP increases regularly at 4 per cent per annum; a 5 per cent growth rate in GNP would be required if social overhead capital is to be built up to high levels and the nation's "normal" 2 per cent increase in consumption per capita is to be maintained.[3]

Aside from dramatizing the strategic importance of the growth rate in determining the outcome, the Rockefeller Panel IV calculations make clear how pressure on the level of private consumption is likely to be exerted by forces making for the simultaneous expansion of both national security outlays and social overhead capital.

SCIENCE, TECHNOLOGY, AND PRODUCTIVITY

The degree of strain imposed on private consumption by other requirements of the society comes to rest in part on the rate at which productivity will increase. Many factors determine the course of productivity, including elements as elusive as the will to work and the competence of managers. Among them, however, are the flow of new technology emerging from the expanding pool of basic science and the rate at which it is brought to bear in the economy.

Recent developments in electronics have enlarged the possibilities of what is now called automation; and recent developments in nuclear science and engineering promise cheap power at some future stage. It is, of course, impossible to predict with confidence what will unfold from the intensive work now going forward in electronics and nuclear engineering over the long future. Over a shorter span—of, say, ten years—automation will certainly be extended, shifting the proportions between men and capital and, especially, increasing the requirements for skilled workers in factory and office. Automation should contribute to the maintenance of recent productivity increases of, say, 3 per cent per annum;[4] but it is not likely to yield a dramatic further rise in the productivity rate.

For the United States, with its still relatively cheap supplies of coal, gas, and oil, nuclear power based on fission is likely to supply over the next decade only a small proportion of total energy. If and when the problem of fusion power is solved, the United States and the world may well have a cheap and inexhaustible source of energy. But in itself, fusion power is unlikely to bring about an economic millennium.[5]

The expansion of research and development is proceeding, of course, on a much wider front than these two dramatic areas. Between 1920 and the mid-1950's the nation's research and development expenditures had regularly risen from something like .1 per cent of the gross national product to about 1 per cent, the latter figure representing outlays of about $4 billion a year.[6] The industries which had led the way in industrial research earlier in the century—chemicals, electricity, and aircraft (including missiles)—retained their leadership. But the conception that industry must systematically organize the innovational process was becoming generally applied. A continuation of this trend, increasing the outlay on research and development at a rate of about 10 per cent per annum, will almost certainly be required to maintain the post-1945 rate of increase in American productivity.

Despite the accelerating development of science and technology, the nation will have to run hard to stay where it is. This speculative judgment flows from the following considerations: consumers are spending increasing amounts on services, where research and development can make only a limited contribution; similarly, the construction industries, mainly involved in the expansion of social overhead capital, are not among those which have exhibited a capacity to develop rapid increases in productivity;[7] and, finally, large resources (including research and development resources) will continue to be allocated to military purposes.

Thus, although science may provide in the future many unexpected breakthroughs which will permit resources to be used with unforeseen efficiency, there is nothing in the pattern of current trends to justify the view that Americans will be suddenly relieved by modern science of the need to strive and to make difficult choices in fulfilling the multiple objectives of American society.

## SOME PROBLEMS OF AUSTERITY AND AFFLUENCE

It is possible to conclude with reasonable confidence, then, that the dynamics of American society in the period 1940-1956 yielded two situations liable to impose a somewhat more austere environment for private consumption in the decade or so to follow. First, the quiet, unexpected choice of postwar Americans for enlarged families over enlarged stocks of durable consumers goods and services—a decision which reflected at the margin a rejection or dilution of material objectives—is having and will have profound material consequences. Second, an unbalanced extension of private consumption since 1940 has left the society with an enormous backlog of social overhead requirements at precisely the period when population and family formation increases are about to enlarge current requirements for social overhead capital. And while the progress of science and technology should make it possible for the nation to meet these burdens without either skimping on national security or suffering a sharp reduction in private living standards, no magical release from the pressure on the nation's resources is in sight. Political economy will remain the art of dealing with scarcity.

From these limited conclusions on the nation's setting over the next decade or so, there follows a further conclusion on the nature of domestic politics.

The acceptance—reluctant, resigned, or eager—of the essentials of the New Deal and Fair Deal by the Eisenhower administration brought a phase of American political history to a close. The recurrent national debate over the appropriate balance between the interests of private property and the interests of the private citizen was by no means ended. The heirs of Cotton Mather, Hamilton, McKinley, and Coolidge as well as the heirs of Roger Williams, Jefferson, Jackson, Wilson, and Franklin Roosevelt are still likely to be identifiable. Nevertheless, the nation's life is likely to be dominated by a clash between somewhat different elements in the individualist-utilitarian creed than in the decades since the Civil War. The great affairs of domestic policy—education, health, water supply, the rebuilding of the cities, the control of inflation, the provision of adequate social overhead capital for a bulging population—are, in a curious way, community rather than special interest or regional issues. The problems of allocating resources between private and public sectors, which have traditionally dominated state and local politics, appear likely to be elevated to the national levels. In its politics as in its social life and communications, the nation is likely to become increasingly a continental township. Desegregation is, in one sense, a special case—a stage in a long, slow, familiar, painful, ongoing process. But its solution—like the solution to the other major domestic issues—requires an extraordinary concert of effort by the majority in each community, an effort which could not be conceived of as realistic until quite recent times.

What if anything may usefully be said of the longer future, assuming that nuclear disaster is avoided and that there is regularly at least a 3 per cent annual increase in GNP?

At some stage, surely, the level of armaments expenditures will have to decline as a result of mutual satiety or as a result of an effective arms control agreement. The resources available for nonmilitary outlays would then increase. As Gerhard Colm has said: ". . . demobilization would not create an entirely new problem but would add to the problem which we have to meet anyway in an economy of increasing productivity."[8] It can be demonstrated that, say, a halving of military outlays over the next decade would pose problems in maintaining full employment of a relatively modest order. Put another way, there can be envisaged increases in personal consumption, private domestic investment, foreign net investment, and in government outlays for purposes other than security adequate to maintain full employment in the less armaments-ridden world of (say) 1965. Colm exhibits the possible consequences of a 50 per cent decline in security outlays in Table 7.

In the long run, however, the problem of increasing wealth and leisure—the threat of secular spiritual stagnation—surely becomes central to organized

TABLE 7. Gross National Product: Calendar Year 1956 and
Alternative Projections for 1965
(billions of 1956 dollars)[9]

| Item | 1956 | 1965 | Change between 1956 and 1965 |
|---|---|---|---|
| Gross national product | 412.4 | 584.0 | +171.6 |
| National security expenditures | 41.6 | 20.0 | − 21.6 |
| Personal consumption | 265.8 | 395.0 | +129.2 |
| Private domestic investment | 65.3 | 91.0 | + 25.7 |
| Foreign net investment | 1.4 | 4.0 | + 2.6 |
| Government purchases, other than for national security | 38.3 | 74.0 | + 35.7 |

societies which have internalized growth. Will the devil make work for idle hands and men find ways of destroying sufficient capital, while not destroying the planet, so that they can continue to build their lives on active material striving? Will human beings regularly reimpose Malthusianism: that is, create a sufficient rise in the birth rate to avoid the horrors of universal plenty and excessive leisure? Will men find in outer space a frontier sufficiently expansive and rewarding to put off the day when the relative marginal utility of real income becomes dangerously low? Or will the human race find in a life of expanding leisure and repose, combined with the irreducible challenges and drama of carrying forward the species, sufficient inner frontiers to maintain a tolerable life?

The state of society in the United States and in parts of Western Europe during the 1950's was such as to justify the posing of these questions; and, to a degree, they are likely to continue to lurk as a real element in the lives of portions of the population in the more advanced societies. But with American society under increasing pressure and challenge from forces arising out of both the world arena and its own dynamics, the question of secular spiritual stagnation seemed for the time most relevant to current decision among the less urgent of the nation's problems. American society was not yet quite as affluent as it looked.[10]

# BOOK FIVE

*Notes*

### CHAPTER 51. Probing the Future

1. For a more spacious discussion of this theme, see the author's *British Economy of the Nineteenth Century*, Oxford, Clarendon Press, 1946, Chap. VI, "Economic Factors and Politics: Britain in the Nineteenth Century."

### CHAPTER 52. The Future of the World Arena

1. J. von Newmann "Can We Survive Technology," *Fortune*, June 1955, p. 106.

### CHAPTER 53. The Future of Communism

1. One problem, implicit with much of the future, did appear to trouble Moscow in mid-1958; the foreseeable emergence of fourth, fifth, and sixth nuclear powers. It was almost certainly a desire to suppress this form of diffusion of power which led Moscow to exert pressure to stop H-bomb tests and to negotiate technically in Geneva on the problem of test surveillance. It is likely that Moscow is as troubled by the prospect of H-bombs in Chinese Communist hands as it is by their development in France, Germany, Japan, or Sweden. The Soviet desire is, apparently, to forestall this development but to continue the Cold War in its other dimensions; that is, there was no evidence in mid-1958 that Moscow was yet prepared for a thorough-going system of international arms control. It is almost certainly true, however, that the implications of the spread of nuclear power are most likely to dramatize in Communist minds the whole question of the future of communism in a world of diffuse power and may play a large part in ultimate Russian acceptance of status as a nation state in a multi-polar world within an international system of arms control.

### CHAPTER 55. The Future of Western Europe and Japan

1. Paul Dehn, *Punch*, March 19, 1958.

### CHAPTER 58. Recent Patterns of Change

1. In economics, demand and supply can be regarded as independent variables only in the short period; but in the long period they emerge as interdependent, thus posing almost insuperable obstacles for long-period economic analysis by classical, equilibrium methods. For further discussion, see the author's *Process of Economic Growth*, Oxford, Clarendon Press, 1953, pp. 4-7, and 38-48.

2. *Economic Report of the President*, transmitted to the Congress, January 23, 1957, Washington, D.C., Govt. Printing Office, p. 106, Table D-7.

3. *Ibid.*, Table D-8.

4.     NUMBER OF WAGE AND SALARY WORKERS IN NON-AGRICULTURAL
ESTABLISHMENTS, 1940, 1956
(*in millions*)

|  | 1940 | % | 1956 | % |
|---|---|---|---|---|
| Manufacturing, mining, construction, transport, and public utilities | 16.0 | 50 | 24.9 | 48 |
| Trade, finance, and service | 11.9 | 37 | 19.8 | 38 |
| Government | 4.2 | 13 | 7.2 | 14 |
| *Total* | *32.1* | *100* | *51.9* | *100* |

Source of figures: *Economic Report of the President*, transmitted to the Congress, January 20, 1958, Washington, D.C., Gov. Printing Office, p. 140, Table F-22.

5. A similar question underlies S. H. Slichter's view, expressed in an address at the annual meeting of the Associated Industries, March 3, 1958:

". . . the automobile industry will be meeting increasingly severe competition from many sources during the next several years. The growing competition being met by automobiles is shown by the fact that between 1953 and 1957 personal consumption expenditures increased by 21.6 per cent, but outlays for new cars, used cars, and parts increased by 18.9 per cent. Between 1953 and 1956 (the latest date for which detailed figures are available), when spending for new and used automobiles increased by 11 per cent, many important kinds of personal expenditures increased far faster:

| | | |
|---|---|---|
| Elementary and secondary education | 55.1 | per cent |
| Higher education | 47.7 | " |
| Barber shops and beauty parlors | 47.7 | " |
| Interest on personal debt | 37.2 | " |
| Boats and pleasure aircraft | 35.0 | " |
| Privately controlled hospitals and sanatoriums | 31.0 | " |
| Telephone and telegraph | 29.2 | " |
| Foreign travel | 28.4 | " |
| Medical care & hospitalization insurance | 21.8 | " |
| Electricity | 21.4 | " |
| Physicians' fees | 16.1 | " |

". . . Probably the greatest competitor of the automobile industry (and of many industries) will be children."

6. *Economic Report of the President*, 1957, pp. 110-111.

7. A. D. H. Kaplan, *Big Enterprise in a Competitive System*, Washington, D.C., The Brookings Institution, 1954, p. 70; and, in general, Chap. III, for a survey of evidence on changing business scale. See also E. S. Mason, "The Apologetics of 'Managerialism,'" *The Journal of Business of the University of Chicago*, January 1958, pp. 1-2.

8. J. F. Dewhurst, *America's Needs and Resources*, New York, Twentieth Century Fund, 1947, p. 302.

9. S. Stouffer, *Communism, Conformity, and Civil Liberties*, Garden City, N. Y., Doubleday, 1955, p. 92. On the correlation between "tolerance" and level of education, see especially Chap. 4 (pp. 89-108) and the conclusion summarized on p. 236.

## CHAPTER 59. Have American Values Changed?

1. For an excellent analytic summary of this literature, as well as perceptive judgments on the problem of changing values, see C. Kluckhohn, "Have There Been Discernible Shifts in American Values During the Past Generation?," a chapter in E. E. Morison (ed.), *The American Style: Essays in Values and Performance*, New York, Harper, 1958.

2. G. Spindler, "Education in a Transforming American Culture," *Harvard Educational Review*, Summer, 1955, quoted by C. Kluckhohn, *loc. cit.*

3. Winston White, "Are American Values Changing?," an unpublished paper. Also Talcott Parsons, "A Tentative Outline of American Values," an unpublished paper.

4. For further discussion of this conception, see the author's *British Economy of the Nineteenth Century*, Oxford, Clarendon Press, 1948, Chap. VI, especially pp. 133-137.

5. See, notably, D. Reisman, "Consumption for What?" *Bulletin of Atomic Scientists*, April, 1958. For the author's evocation of this issue in a foreign policy context, see M. F. Millikan and W. W. Rostow, *A Proposal—Key to an Effective Foreign Policy*, New York, Harper, 1957, pp. 149-151.

6. The parallelism between spiritual and economic secular stagnation is, for an economist, legitimate. The assumptions of diminishing relative marginal utility and of diminishing marginal productivity are the twin pillars of formal economics. The concept of secular economic stagnation is simply an extension of the classical economist's prognosis of diminishing marginal productivity; while the concept of spiritual secular stagnation implies that, as real income rises, the value of additional increments falls, relative to leisure—and that man fails to fashion a spiritually satisfying life with so high a proportion of his time uncommitted to the pursuit of income.

## CHAPTER 60. The Domestic Crisis of 1956-58

1. A Roper poll (*Boston Sunday Globe*, July 20, 1958) found that about one third of American families were directly affected by the slump of 1957-58: 10 per cent had members of the immediate family out of work; 22 per cent suffered a decline of income.

2. There were, roughly speaking, three schools of thought in the first half of 1958 on how the recession should be handled. One school argued that full employment would be reattained by a prompt expansion in government outlays for military purposes, foreign aid, and domestic social overhead capital, leaving the tax level fixed. This view was based on the judgment that governmental expenditures for security and other purposes had been unnaturally constrained in previous years and that the existence of substantial unemployment (like the large pool of unemployed on the eve of the Second World War) gave the nation the opportunity to restructure its flows of enterprise in more appropriate balance and with minimum friction. Moreover, this view held that the problem of rallying political support for programs of foreign assistance would be eased if government outlays for social overhead capital at home were simultaneously increased. The case for foreign aid had been made difficult in the early part of 1958 by the Ad-

ministration's proposed budget which, while asking for an increase in foreign aid, reduced outlays on domestic irrigation and other social overhead projects.

A second, more short-run view argued that the appropriate method for bringing the nation back to full employment was to expand income in the hands of the public by some form of tax cut, which was taken to be the most prompt, sure, and administratively simple device for raising the level of effective demand and employment. Some advocates of this position did not recognize the legitimacy of the view that outlays on social overhead capital had been inadequate over the previous decade and that the opportunity of depression should be taken to move in new strategic directions. Others of the tax-cut school shared the view that social overhead capital was acutely in deficit, but held that the route to full employment via increased government outlays was likely to be too slow to end the recession as promptly as the situation required.

The Administration's position in the early spring of 1958 appeared to be an extremely cautious version of the second view. Knowing that pressures for expenditure in the Congress combined with falling tax revenues were, in any case, opening up a large deficit in the budget, the Administration was anxious not to widen that deficit further. To men still caught up in the budgetary concepts which underlay the *Helena* decision, the notion of a budgetary deficit of some $15 billion, created in cold blood, was hard to take. On this view, it made sense to await the possibility that an upswing might begin without a tax cut. Delay also commended itself on the grounds that if, in the end, a tax cut were to be required, it should be put into effect only when the persistence of unemployment had begun to bring prices down, reducing the chronic inflationary pressure within the economy which had survived even quite heavy unemployment.

3. The Soviet missiles lead was caused not by failures in the American educational system—yielding relatively too few scientists and engineers—but by a method of administering military research and development in the post-1945 years, and notably in the period 1953-1957, which grossly misused and misallocated the existing, available pool of creative talent in science and engineering. This judgment would not exclude the possibility that continued pace in Soviet education accompanied by continued failure to solve the problems in American education might yield in time results costly to the national interest.

4. See, notably, "The Pursuit of Excellence," *Education and the Future of America*, Special Studies Project Report V, Rockefeller Brothers Fund, Garden City, N. Y., Doubleday, 1958.

5. The Rockefeller Panel on education suggested that the proportion of national product going to education would have to rise from 3.6 per cent to 5 per cent over the coming decade, which would more than double outlays (at constant prices) between 1955 and 1967. *Ibid.*, p. 34.

## CHAPTER 61. Prospects for the Future

1. Quoted, Dewhurst, *op. cit.*, p. 64.

2. Quoted, *The Challenge to America: Its Economic and Social Aspects*, Special Studies Project Report IV, Rockefeller Brothers Fund, Garden City, N. Y., Doubleday, 1958.

3. The following tables are quoted from The Special Studies Project Report IV, *ibid.*, pp. 8, 71, 72.

Table I

Projections of Federal, State and Local Government Expenditures
(billions of 1957 dollars)

| | 1957 Actual | The Range of Estimates for 1967 | |
| --- | --- | --- | --- |
| | | Low | High |
| National Security | $46.0 | $60.0 | $70.0 |
| Defense Dept. | 39.0 | 49.8 | 55.9 |
| Military aid | 2.3 | 3.0 | 4.5 |
| Economic aid | 1.7 | 2.7 | 3.7 |
| Atomic energy* | 2.1 | 3.0 | 3.9 |
| Other | .9 | 1.5 | 2.0 |
| Education (including school construction) | 13.0 | 24.0 | 30.0 |
| Welfare | 20.0 | 38.5 | 45.0 |
| Social insurance and public assistance | 15.5 | 31.0 | 36.0 |
| Health (incl. hospital construction) | 4.5 | 7.5 | 9.0 |
| Public works (except schools and hospitals) | 9.5 | 20.5 | 27.0 |
| roads** | 4.8 | 10.5 | 12.0 |
| water supply and disposal | 1.3 | 2.7 | 3.5 |
| urban renewal | 0.7 | 4.0 | 7.0 |
| other | 2.7 | 3.3 | 4.5 |
| Other | 25.5 | 27.9 | 31.0 |
| agriculture | 4.7 | 2.0 | 2.0 |
| veterans | 4.9 | 4.9 | 4.9 |
| administration and operation | 15.9 | 21.0 | 24.1 |
| Total Government cash expenditures | $114.0 | $170.9 | $203.0 |

* Includes expenditures by the Atomic Energy Commission on civilian projects.
** $10.5 billion estimate for 1967 is based on current legislation.

Table II

billions of 1957 dollars

| | 1957 | 1967 | |
| --- | --- | --- | --- |
| | | GNP at 3% Growth rate | GNP at 4% Growth rate |
| Gross National Product | $434 | $583 | $642 |
| less low estimates for Government Purchases of Goods and Services | 86 | 127 | 127 |
| less Gross Private Investment to support growth | 67 | 100 | 112 |
| leaves available for Consumption | 281 | 356 | 403 |
| Annual Growth Rate of Per Capita Consumption | | 0.8% | 2.1% |

TABLE III

BILLIONS OF 1957 DOLLARS

| | 1957 | 1967 | |
|---|---|---|---|
| | | GNP at 4% Growth rate | GNP at 5% Growth rate |
| Gross National Product | $434 | $642 | $707 |
| less high estimates for Government Purchases of Goods and Services | 86 | 153 | 153 |
| less Gross Private investment to support growth | 67 | 112 | 123 |
| leaves available for Consumption | 281 | 377 | 431 |
| Annual Growth Rate of Per Capita Consumption | | 1.4% | 2.8% |

4. R. H. Ewell, "Role of Research in Economic Growth," *Chemical and Engineering News*, July 18, 1955, p. 2982. The average rate of increase in American productivity has risen from 1.25 per cent in 1910-1920 to 3.00 per cent in 1946-1953, averaging over the whole period 2.14 per cent.

5. Although it would not in itself bring about the millennium, John von Neumann's vision of energy as free as "unmetered air" would, indeed be a radical contribution to productivity:

". . . fission is not nature's normal way of releasing nuclear energy. In the long run, systematic industrial exploitation of nuclear energy may shift reliance onto other and still more abundant modes. Again, reactors have been bound thus far to the traditional heat-steam-generator-electricity cycle, just as automobiles were at first constructed to look like buggies. It is likely that we shall gradually develop procedures more naturally and effectively adjusted to the new source of energy, abandoning the conventional kinks and detours inherited from chemical-fuel processes. Consequently, a few decades hence energy may be free—just like the unmetered air—with coal and oil used mainly as raw materials for organic chemical synthesis, to which, as experience has shown, their properties are best suited." (*Fortune*, June, 1955, p. 107.)

6. *Ibid.*, pp. 2981-2982. By 1956 the figure had leaped to $6.4 billion, reflecting a rise in the costs of research and development combined with a radical increase in government outlays, notably for the missile program (National Science Foundation, *Review of Data on Research and Development*, Number 10, May 1958).

7. There is no reason, of course, why concerted and imaginative efforts might not yield radical increases in productivity in the generally sluggish construction industries.

8. G. Colm, "The Economic Implications of Disarmament," *Illinois Business Review*, July 1957, p. 7.

9. *Ibid.*

10. The argument presented here shares with that in J. K. Galbraith's *The Affluent Society*, Boston, Houghton Mifflin, 1958, an emphasis on the lack of

balance between private consumption and social overhead capital in contemporary American society. It differs, however, in its assessment of the implications of changes in population and the working force. While sharing the judgment that it is necessary to examine the composition of the nation's output—not merely the rate of increase of GNP—it is the author's view that a rapid and steady rise in GNP will, in fact, be necessary if the nation is to meet the multiple claims of security and the good society at home. There is nothing in the present argument which would justify, for example, the complacent acceptance of protracted periods of substantial unemployment, no matter how comfortably cushioned by increased benefit payments.

# THE AMERICAN AGENDA

# PART I

# THE AMERICAN AGENDA

## 62. The Tasks of American Society

It is clear that protection of the American national interest and the maintenance of the historic purpose and quality of American society impose for the
forseeable future a set of tasks different from those to which the national style
has had to accomodate itself in the past. Having identified the central problems of foreign, military, and domestic policy, it is necessary to identify those
new tasks.

What must the nation do to cope with its foreign, military, and domestic
problems? For a time at least, and quite possibly for a substantial period, the
United States must maintain large and regularly expanding outlays in support
of military and foreign policy; and if the nation's effort at deterrence is to be
successful, this must be done without the goad of active military hostilities.

Similarly, the nature of foreseeable military and foreign policy problems requires rapid anticipatory innovation by the national government without the
stimulus of major crisis; for major crisis in a world of nuclear weapons immediately places in jeopardy the nation's interests if not its survival; and other
forms of crisis, such as might occur in Central Europe and in certain regions
of Asia and the Middle East, could yield extremely dangerous results reversible,
if at all, only at great cost and over long periods.

Moreover, American policy must be geared to processes of change within
Communist societies and within the transitional societies of Asia, the Middle
East, Africa, and Latin America which cannot be read off by simple analogy
from American life and experience but require widespread vicarious understanding of human beings, institutions, and problems formed in settings vastly
different from contemporary United States.

And the whole effort at dealing with the world must be maintained at a
delicate point of balance between ready military strength and patient
diplomatic flexibility which avoids either the self-indulgent position of un-

controlled aggression or that of slothful illusion that peace has been attained or can be attained without effort, sacrifice, and change.

The importance of military and foreign policy problems and the scale of their impact on American domestic life are not likely to diminish until the arms race is liquidated; and this condition will place steady and historically unnatural burdens on the two-party system, on the democratic process, and on the life of a free society as a whole.

In military and foreign policy matters the nation is thus confronted with the problem of doing well and regularly things which it has done in the past only convulsively at moments of acute and palpable crisis. It must do these things, if it is at all possible, without the release of energies, the sharp definition of problems, and the easy convergence of interests afforded by major crisis; and it must do what is necessary in ways which do minimum damage to the quality of domestic life.

These tasks emerge at a time when the dynamics of American domestic society appear to be imposing at least a decade of strain on the nation's resources in order to meet the consequences of the changing size and structure of the American population and of the accumulated national bill for social overhead capital; and at a time, also, when the pace of scientific and technological development places skill in innovation in domestic life at a premium almost as high as in military and foreign policy.

To formulate and act on policies which will enable the United States to perform these tasks—simultaneously protecting the nation's external interests and the quality of its domestic arrangements—American society must shift the balance of its common life in moral, philosophic, administrative, political, and economic dimensions. The national interest cannot be defined, projected, or acted on effectively without a reassessment of the place of moral purpose in American public policy; the problem of anticipation and of pace in innovation cannot be solved without change in American philosophical, administrative, and political method; the mobilization of resources to do the jobs that must be done requires change in American economic thought and practice.

These are the themes of the chapters that follow.

### 63. Moralism, Morality, and the National Interest

#### THE CHALLENGE TO MORALISM

The nation found in its first century of national life a distinctive way of reconciling the universal problem of ideals and special interests in public policy—a style marked by the ritualistic articulation of moral purposes and goals as if they reflected somewhat more of total reality than they did, combined with sensitive and subtle systems of compromise which were institutionalized where possible but remained largely unarticulated. Strained by various crises in the nation's history, altered in significant respects by the nation's military and foreign policy problems of the first half of the twentieth century, this element of the national style nevertheless persisted down to the end of the Second World War and beyond, leaving marks on both domestic and external policy.

The nation's post-1945 military and foreign policy tasks have placed this method of dealing with the problem of public morality under sustained pressures not unlike those confronted during the Civil War. Communism (like slavery in the South) has posed two distinct but subtly related threats to the national interest: a direct threat to the nation's miliary security, and an ideological threat with implications both for the nation's military security and for its survival as an open society. Quite aside from the possibilities of direct sudden nuclear assault on American territory, the balance of power in Eurasia could be lost to the United States by the movement of Soviet or Chinese Communist ground forces; and, equally, it could be lost if, in hope or despair, men and women in the decisive regions of Eurasia should turn to communism or, in apathy, let the Communists take over as a believed solution to problems which could not be solved within the orbit of the democratic processes and the alliances of the non-Communist world.

The conduct of American military and foreign policy has thus required and will continue increasingly to require related but distinctive courses of action designed both negatively to deter Communist military strength and constructively to defeat its challenge as an ideology and as a method for making the transition from a traditional to a modern society. The task has been complicated because the techniques and attitudes of mind necessary to deal with the threat of military aggression did not neatly converge; indeed, they have often clashed with those necessary to deal with the ideological threat of communism.

But this is not all. There has been a further complication, which is bound to increase in importance if the great act of persuasion is to be brought to pass: namely, that Americans must strain to understand with intellectual and moral humility the complex processes taking place in the Communist Bloc. They must continue to negotiate with the Soviet government and maintain a widening area of sympathetic human communication with Soviet citizens. How does one sustain simultaneously the conception of mortal enemy and potential fellow citizen of a crowded and increasingly interdependent panet? Again, to find a similar dilemma, one must reach back in American experience to the Civil War, when men of the North and South fought to the death knowing that somehow they or their children would have to find the terms of moral, political, and human accommodation.

Put another way, the central persistent fact about the problem of dealing with Communist strategy and methods in the context of modern weapons and the spreading nationalist revolutions is that it denies to the United States the opportunity to react to national threat in the style with which the nation had become in the past century most comfortable—that is, a clean and total switch from peace to a war which could be fought with the widespread conviction that both interests and ideals neatly overlapped. The nation is forbidden, in its own interest, a convulsive once-and-for-all resolution; for the nature of modern weapons and the strength of the enemy have eliminated total crusade as a realistic solution to the military problem; and the ideological problem of communism is, in large part, inaccessible to the use of military force. In consequence, the nation has faced and continues to face a sequence of dangerous but not definitive crises which force it to explore the character of its abiding interests, the limits of its power, and the nature and limits of its idealism.

There has been in authority in this generation no Lincoln to pose clearly for Americans the nature of the nation's moral dilemma and the inescapable problem of balance and relationship between national interests of power and ideology. Moreover, the problems of the fast-changing world arena after the Second World War did not lend themselves to the institutionalized solutions which America often applied at home. A stable unification of the insights of Mahan and Wilson—the equivalent of a Lincolnian policy for America in relation to the world of mid-twentieth century—has not been easy to achieve, to maintain, and to apply from day to day.

### THE THREE DIMENSIONS OF CHALLENGE

In at least three major directions the nation's military and foreign policy problems are pressing American society to come to terms with the problem of public morality in less evasive terms.

First, the nation has been forced to contemplate the role of force as a measured instrument of foreign policy. The acceptance of the fact that Americans might have to die for limited objectives of a political or strategic nature and not simply in a once-for-all moral crusade has not come easily. The misunderstanding and frustrations of the Korean War have not even now been completely dissipated. Nevertheless, there has been a widening acceptance of the relationship between military force and international politics, and an increasing candor in the search to discipline the inescapable conflict somewhere between all-out nuclear war and a peace that could not yet be attained.

Second, the nation has been forced to consider in new terms the meaning of its commitment to the democratic process, notably in dealing with the underdeveloped areas of Asia, the Middle East, Africa, and Latin America, but also in relating its outlook and policy to the mutations of communism in Yugoslavia and Poland and to the processes of change going forward slowly and irregularly in the Soviet Union.

The instinctive effort to apply in the transitional areas the moral and institutional canons of American democratic practice yielded a series of frustrations and failures. Starting with Chiang Kai-shek and the China problem, the nation has been forced, for example, to face the fact that societies with which alliance is needed in the national interest may stand at stages in their own history which do no offer as a realistic possibility the immediate creation of democratic regimes on the Western model; and it also has been forced to learn that allies whose policies are built simply on the concept of a shared enemy and who are inefficient in moving toward the constructive objectives of their societies become weak allies. Equally, the nation has been forced to face the fact that formulae for policy and for the building of institutions derived from American experience—formulae weighted virtually with moral sanction in American eyes—did not necessarily meet the needs or solve the problems of construction in such transitional societies. And, given the American tradition, it has been a fundamental moral shock to find decent men who share many Western humane values soberly assessing the virtues of communism as they understand it as against what they consider the weaknesses of democracy as an instrument for modernizing transitional societies.

In addition, the impact on the world of the slow, private American struggle to bring the Negro into status as a first-class citizen has held up a disturbing mirror of the nation's life. It has added weight to those forces among white Americans whose moral uneasiness (as well as the steady pressure of special interest among Negroes) has kept American society moving in directions which would bring American ideals and American practice closer together; but it has also induced in some an instinctive movement to withdraw from a world which compounds their fears and sense of guilt.

In short, the struggle of power and ideology in Asia, the Middle East, and Africa has challenged the instinctive assumption that democracy in the American image was automatically and everywhere the wave of the future and morally right.

Third, the nation has confronted the challenge represented by the military, economic, diplomatic, and intellectual success of Soviet society and by its ability to maintain itself as an ongoing system. That society is one in which political power centers in a co-optive self-perpetuating dictatorship based on the threat and reality of secret police power, a society whose leadership appears to deny every fundamental value of Western and American life. And yet its performance in military technology, in over-all rate of economic growth, and in quality as well as scale of scientific effort exhibits a pace which threatens to outstrip the performance of free, democratic, and virtuous America. This is the most direct of contemporary assaults on the moral foundations of American life. It raises not simply the question of whether the United States may be defeated in war—hot or cold—but also the question of whether the principles of social organization which lie at the heart of the American conception of its nationhood are correct; for in one essential dimension, Americanism as an articulated creed has consisted in the faith that virtue and success converged, and that this convergence was a model and guide to humanity at large.

How serious a matter is all this? How profound are these shocks to the American verbal image of itself, its power, and its virtues? What are the lessons to be drawn?

### THE PROBLEM OF AMERICAN RHETORIC

It is first necessary to distinguish the extent to which the challenges of the post-1945 world are challenges to the moral bases of American life from the extent to which they are merely a challenge to American rhetoric, to the nation's ritualistic articulation of its principles to itself and to the world.

Within the United States and the Western Hemisphere, for example, America had long since accepted the legitimacy of force as a limited tool of political policy: against the Indians for almost three hundred years, in the Mexican War, in the post-Civil War occupation of the former Confederate states, and in various Latin American affairs. Similarly, the puzzlement of American democracy, its formulae, and its articulated experience in relation to underdeveloped areas outside the Anglo-Saxon tradition is at least as old as John Quincy Adams' excessive pessimism about the future of the Latin American states.[1] Although Americans have talked occasionally as if the methods and institutions developed out of American history might be universally applied in detail, the abiding sense of world mission in the United States has been a broadly based matter related to the basic values of humane democratic societies rather than to specific institutional detail. And, as many European comentators noted, as far back as pre-Civil War America, the nation's boastfulness about its virtue and strength was closely linked to an old provincial sense of inferiority with respect to Europe, not least in the areas of intellectual virtuosity and diplomatic skill.[2]

Americans have been distinctive not because they believed their virtue and power were unique but because their nationality was built on the explicit commitment to strive toward certain ideal goals and because the vision of their future remained youthfully uncircumscribed, full of vague hopes, a powerful optimism, and a sense that there would be time and occasion to correct error. Doubts and self-criticism have been, in fact, as typical of the American style as boastful rhetoric.

Nevertheless, to some degree, the revealed limitations of American virtue and strength in the post-1945 years are a serious affair in American history. They are serious, in the first place, because men are always taken in a little by their own magic. It has been said that the only sure victim of propaganda is the propagandist.[3] The nation's style in moralistic articulation which has served a vital function in building a unified American society out of exceedingly diverse, pluralistic elements left, nevertheless, some residue of bland belief. This belief was not challenged by the normal dualism built into the nation's method for making its domestic compromises; and the ultimately successful outcomes of the Civil War, of the absorption and taming of industrialization by the democratic process, and of the First and Second World Wars—each of which was accompanied at the time by stages of profound introspective doubt—permitted the image and the method to persist.

The nation's style for articulating its purposes was one thing when the United States was a favored backwater in the arena of world power—or even when it stood as the strategic reserve of the West, to be thrown into battle only under circumstances of extreme danger; but it is a quite different matter when the nation stands as the sole effective antagonist to a powerful enemy whose actions are closely related to American words as well as American actions, and when the United States stands also surrounded by nations whose basic interests—indeed, whose survival—depends on what the United States does or fails to do as an ally. Under such circumstances, the extension beyond the nation's shores of its private dualism yields a result quite different from the result at home. Under circumstances of global responsibility and authority, the American moralistic style is a source of disturbance to the world and a cost to the national interest. The nation's manner of dealing with traditional moral dilemmas has ceased to be a private affair.

## THE PROBLEM OF MORAL PURPOSE

But there is even more substance to the problem than that. For the challenge to American society offered by its environment is not a verbal but a real challenge. The nation is challenged by the nature of the problem of power in an age of nuclear weapons; by the nature of and the prospects for the democratic faith in the context of the revolutionary ambitions of Asia, the Middle East, Africa, and Latin America; by the nature of the capacities and of the processes of change within the Soviet Union and the Communist Bloc as a whole; and by the foreseeable emergence of a world environment of diffused power containing a good many major, industrially mature societies of which the United States will be only one. These, the central substantive issues around which the future of American society in its world setting will depend, pose questions which touch directly the moral bases of American life as well as its method of articulation.

Is the United States capable of fixing and acting on a more mature and somber view of the relationship between ideals and the facts of power, a balance elevated to high drama by the nature of modern weapons? Is it capable, while maintaining effective military strength, of playing a role of initiative in moving toward a liquidation of the arms race and the creation of an effective system of arms control when, at last, opportunity offers? Is it capable of accepting a widened, less parochial view of the nature of the democratic process—as a matter of degree and direction of change, rather than of absolutes linked to contemporary American institutions—and of associating itself effectively with the processes at work in Asia, the Middle East, Africa, and Latin America? Is it capable of altering the disposition of its talents, energies, and resources in such ways as to deal with the Soviet challenge while, at the same time, exploiting the possibilities of change for the better in Soviet society and while also avoiding the dangers of becoming a mirror image of the enemy?

The essential change required is that the nation strip off elements of illusion and self-indulgence which have been permitted it by the course of its history. Excepting the Civil War, the domestic evolution of American society was rendered extraordinarily easy. There was no deeply rooted feudal heritage to overcome. The balance between its resources and its population permitted initially high and steadily rising standards of welfare. Its initial endowment of social values and institutions accommodated well to the problems of commercial and industrial enterprise and to the problem of converting a fringe of Eastern colonies into a continental community. On the world scene the nation was permitted in the nineteenth century, by the accidents of the world power structure, to achieve its hemispheric objectives with the expenditure of little blood or treasure; and in the first half of the twentieth century, time, distance, and allies twice permitted it the illusion of total victory at relatively little cost. Even the Second World War was fought with rising levels of income per head, due in part to the accident of heavy unemployment at the time of the war's outbreak.

The nation for a century and a half was granted an illusion denied its citizens; namely, that major advantages could be achieved without proportionate effort and sacrifice.

Now the cushions are gone. The world arena is unlikely to grant the United States anything for nothing. To cope with the nation's problems a new candor is required, a fresh assessment of national purposes, and a mobilization of the human and physical resources to achieve them. Few would

quarrel with Acheson's assessment of the "ultimate sin" for the United States
at this stage of history.

> On one thing only I feel a measure of assurance—on the righteness of con-
> tempt for sanctimonious self-righteousness which, joined with a sly worldli-
> ness, beclouds the dangers and opportunities of our time with an unctuous
> film. For this is the ultimate sin. By representing that all is done which needs
> to be done, it denies to us the knowledge that we are called upon for great
> action; and denies to us, too, the chance to "give a sample of our best, and
> . . . in our hearts . . . feel that it has been nobly done."[4]

In finding the moral basis for the performance required of it the nation
must return, in a sense, to the origins of its national life. Its formative values
are rooted not in the soil of the Western Hemisphere but in the merger
of religious concepts brought mainly from nonconformist Britain and concepts
of political organization derived from Britain and France of the seventeenth
and eighteenth centuries; and these two proximate roots, both moral and
political, go back directly into the common Mediterranean heritage. The
mixture of Puritanism and the Enlightenment on the rich soil of the American
continent did, indeed, yield a distinctive version of the Western tradition with
a special optimism, a particularly acute concentration on the possibilities of
material progress. But behind the American creed there is a more universal
set of beliefs the essence of which lies in some such propositions as these:
that all human beings, standing equal before God and the law, are to be
accorded respect in and for themselves; that the individual, in a world of both
good and evil, is charged actively and responsibly to struggle to express
his unique personality in terms of social as well as private good; and that
societies, while protecting themselves against the reality of human weakness
and evil, should in their organization be tilted toward the hopeful assumption
that a responsible citizenry will be able to exercise an increasing range of
functions by freedom of individual choice.

American life was founded in optimism, but not in a facile optimism. The
possibility of good was balanced by the recognition of the reality of evil and
of the need for active striving. The goal of liberty was balanced by the recognition that responsibility was necessary, that a society based on individual freedom of choice could work only if the pursuit of individual advantage was
tempered by a willingness of the individual to find a part of his destiny in
terms of communal purposes. The possibility of progress was balanced by a
humility which recognized human frailty, imperfection, and the possibility of
failure—a humility which suffused much American humor. This recognition
of the somber side of the nation's adventure touched all its great enterprises
—from Washington's incredibly difficult struggle to maintain a Revolutionary
Army in being and the making of the Constitution, through Lincoln's Civil

War leadership and the long ardent struggle to harmonize the values of a humane life with the imperatives of industrialization, down to the soberly weighed use of atomic weapons to end the Second World War and the painful exercise in collective security in Korea.

More than that, the texture of life for the individual American was in no way exempt from the fundamental struggles and anxieties of men and women everywhere. Food, shelter, and clothing were, it is true, a little easier to come by for Americans than for others; but the round of life for the American farmer, the frontiersman, the immigrant in the cities, while, perhaps, touched with a special hope for the future and for the fate of the children, was simply a portion of the human condition.

American rhetoric has tended, then, not only to strip the nation's expressed creed of its recognition of the moral dilemmas which men must face, to render it incommunicable and provincial, to rob it of its universal connections and meaning; it has also forestalled the development of a stable and serviceable definition of the national interest comprehensible to Americans, understandable to the world, and capable of being linked to what in fact the nation must do from day to day. At its core, the problem of defining the national interest is a problem of balancing and relating abiding considerations of power and idealism. It is the problem of avoiding either a performance excessively dominated by considerations of power and military force the rhetoric of which is suffused with an excessive moralism, or a performance promising in its rhetoric but failing in substance to deal with the concrete issues on which a solution to real problems depends.

If the dynamics of the world arena is correctly assessed in this book, American life will be linked in increasing intimacy to that of other peoples as multiple forces operate to end the privileged sanctuary within which the nation has come to maturity over the century and a half of its corporate existence. Both the nation's fate as a part of this community and the possibility of seeing the world through until the time when such a closely knit world community might emerge in reasonable order hinge, in part, on shucking off the special comforting illusions which the sanctuary encouraged and finding a new, more steady, and balanced moral position.

To protect the national interest in the foreseeable future requires that the nation not abandon but, in fact, build on its old sense of world mission in respect to the democratic faith. To do what must be done, however, requires that the searching moral presuppositions of that faith be confronted afresh and understood; for only then are they likely to suffuse the nation's public policy with the requisite force and vitality and relate American society effectively to a world society of which it will be increasingly a regional segment.

## 64. *Theory, Fact, and Public Policy*

To understand the national interest, Americans must establish afresh what are the moral bases of the common life. To communicate national purposes, Americans must find a rhetoric of greater clarity and candor. To build and execute policies capable of protecting the national interest, Americans must enlarge and apply more effectively their capacity to innovate. The capacity to innovate is no more nor less than the measure of a society's ability to deal with a changing environment, its ability to avoid going down to defeat or decay in the style and with the policies to which it has become accustomed.

In one dimension the process of innovation depends on how men look on the world about them and order what they see; that is, it depends on their philosophic style, on what kinds of theories they use and how they relate those theories to the problems they confront.

### THE EVOLUTION OF THE NATIONAL PHILOSOPHIC STYLE

The generation of eighteenth-century men who founded the nation was part of an international philosophic tradition of considerable sophistication which placed a high premium on formal thought and its precise articulation. However hardheaded and pragmatic the Founding Fathers were as working politicians, they were notably unembarrassed in the face of abstraction. And they brought the facts they perceived into an orderly relation to the abstractions which framed their thought.

As the nation moved forward into the nineteenth century, however, it developed a more distinctive style, acutely empirical, geared to facts and to the job in hand on the unfolding American scene. American empiricism was joined to a tendency to seek order among the perceived facts by loose generalizations. This splayed approach to the universal dilemma of theory and fact concentrated at the two extremes of the spectrum of abstraction, with the intermediate connections left vague—or not examined.

The predominant American way of looking at and dealing with the world linked naturally with elements of the German intellectual and educational tradition of the nineteenth century and helped the nation to emerge with universities devoted to high degrees of specialization, training their men narrowly in rigorous empirical exercises, the conclusions of which were hastily drawn (often in the short last chapter of doctoral theses) by the method Tocqueville long before had identified as distinctively American: the method of explaining "a mass of facts by a single cause."

This method marked, for example, the institutionalist school which began to emerge as the special American contribution to the analysis of society in the first quarter of the twentieth century. The United States was in the midst of an effort to assess the transitional process through which it was passing and to establish what should be done to mitigate its evils. As Riesman has pointed out, the kind of thought represented by Thorstein Veblen and Alvin Johnson "was, along with the Sherman Act and the Wobblies, a response of a once rural society to the changes brought about by industrialization— changes that could not be understood simply through analyzing their exchanges and transactions, by following the flow of goods and credits."[1] A similar philosophic bias shaped, for example, Beard's economic determinism, the frontier thesis school of American history, and Wesley Mitchell's passionate empirical investigations.

In natural science, too, from the Morrill Act forward, Americans in dealing formally with physical reality were, with a few notable exceptions, mainly engineers rather than scientists. The first generation of American scientists to emerge in the twentieth century, moving beyond skillful engineering, were, like the institutionalists, strongly empircal—for example, Michelson and Millikan who, without actively rejecting the relevance of theory, made their mark by imaginative, energetic experiment.

Between the wars, the balance of American intellectual life began to shift away from this empirical and experimental pattern. That shift appears to have resulted from several converging forces. For one thing, the younger generation of scholars, born into an amplitude of statistics and descriptive monographs, behaved in the eternal manner of a new generation: they took for granted what they had and began to devote themselves in higher proportion to what was missing in American thought, that is, to formal theory.

In this development the economists were strengthened between the wars by the rise in the influence of the British school. In the other social sciences, the theories of Freud, Weber, and Durkheim gave to American thought about society a stimulus parallel to that of Pigou, Keynes, and Robertson in British economics.

In addition to such new transatlantic influences and the natural contrariness of a new generation, the Great Depression and Hitler played a role in shifting the balance of American intellectual life. The Great Depression obviously violated the continuity of American institutional development. It was an unexpected event, not to be understood by a simple examination of facts or a projection of slow-moving trends. Moreover, the British in particular had been developing between the wars, in response to their chronic problem of unemployment, theoretical structures which were immensely helpful. The Great Depression thus stirred up in economics and the social sciences generally a wave of new theoretical speculation. Hitler's contribution was even more direct. His policies drove or detached from Europe a substantial number of scholars who, whatever their particular intellectual tradition, brought into the heart of American universities a respect for theoretical concept and virtuosity.

Thus, before the Second World War, there was a vigorous development of theory and theorists in the social sciences directly linked to intellectual developments in Europe.

There was a similar process, under somewhat different stimuli, in the natural sciences. Large numbers of the newer generation of the interwar years—the postexperimentalists—traveled and studied abroad, where they were caught up in the excitement of the revolutionary development stemming from the work of Rutherford, Einstein, Bohr, and the others. The new physics was, in a sense, the equivalent of interwar monetary and income analysis for the new generation of economists. And in the 1930's American natural science—even more than social science—was strengthened by the inflow of Europeans seeking refuge.

The America that entered the Second World War was thus reinforced by the presence in the society of a good many European theorists, some of whom were of first quality, plus a younger generation in both the social and natural sciences trained in, comfortable with, and respectful of theoretical constructs. In many dimensions—from the Manhattan Project to the administration of the war economy, from the development of radar to the design of the Bretton Woods institutions, from the choice of strategic bombing targets to the psychological testing of officer candidates—this new generation of American theorists left their mark. In the various wartime enterprises, men were effective in part because they were intelligent, strongly motivated, and adaptable; but the relative success of the nation in rapid innovation during the Second World War was in part also due to the fact that the qualities of the good theorist were brought to bear on new practical questions.

The empiricist, the student of institutions, and the engineer may well be the best men to work out the next stage in a process of gradual piecemeal change; but the theorist, used to constructing and manipulating radically different models of reality, can enormously accelerate the innovational process. It is out of new ways of looking at things that new questions are posed; and it is through posing new questions that problems are solved. By the nature of his profession, the man trained to deal with abstractions thus often finds himself reasonably at home in practical situations of rapid change.

## THE INTELLECTUAL IN THE BUREAUCRACY

Contrary to a widely held view, the intellectual continued to occupy an elevated public role in American life in the postwar years. In industry there was a radical enlargement of funds available for research; and a new high status came to be accorded not only the natural scientist and engineer but also the economist, the psychologist as personnel expert, and the sociologist or social psychologist willing to apply his skills to market research and labor relations. American business had come to take an increasingly explicit view of its relation to the economy and to the whole society of which it is a part. Industrial economists examine long-period trends in population, income, and tastes, seeking to deduce the trend in demand for their firm's output and, thus, the appropriate rate of investment. They study their firm's relations to the public and to the political process in much the same way.

The American business firm is no longer an atomistic unit concentrated on the current behavior of its prices and its costs, guessing as shrewdly as it can its future prospects, making relatively simple profit-maximizing decisions, with its only communal concern to ensure that its officers keep out of jail. It is a self-conscious unit in a complex, interacting society, trying to understand how to exploit its environment, trying to influence (if not fully to determine) its own technological, social, and political setting. This new role has required business men to deal with the world about them with increased intellectual sophistication; and this, by and large, they have done.

There has been a parallel revolution in the institutions and attitudes of the national government, notably in national security policy. During the Second World War (quite aside from the atomic bomb) all three military services found that the natural scientist, the economist, the psychologist, and even the psychiatrist had important uses. And the post-1945 soldier retained a new degree of respect for the intellectual and the theorist, reflected, for example, in the remarkable elevation in the quality and level of military education. By the mid-1950's the Federal government had become the sponsor of intellectual effort, basic and applied, on a mammoth scale, providing about half the funds for research and development in industry in 1956 (about $3 billion) and a high proportion of university research funds as well.

The nation's intellectual structure and balance have thus changed in directions which should permit the society to deal with its environment in more responsive ways, transcending more swiftly than in the past the limits imposed by a vision of reality focused on a static or slowly changing *status quo*.

Despite the existence of an underlying trend which fits the nation's requirement, two major issues of intellectual organization and balance remain: the synthesis of thought around the solution to concrete problems of public policy, and the cultivation of intellectual excellence.

INTELLECTUAL SYNTHESIS AND PUBLIC POLICY

The first issue arises because major problems of public policy do not break down according to the formal categories of departmentalized knowledge, and because they violate the old separation between the study of human and natural behavior.

To understand something of the dynamic forces at work in the Soviet Union or in the transitional societies of Asia, for example, the conventional discipline of economics, of political science, and of what have come to be called the behavioral sciences are all helpful; but their insights are only partial. Moreover, each field of study has acquired vested interests as well as a logical momentum leading to increasing degrees of specialization. The initial American concept of the graduate school and the nature of the task of seeking new knowledge by orderly methods combine to fragment what is known. And this appears to be as true of the natural as of the social sciences:

> Our knowledge of nature is in no true sense common knowledge; it is the treasure of the many flourishing specialized communities, often cut off from one another in their rapid growth. Never has our common knowledge been so frail a part of what is known. Natural science is not known, and probably cannot be known, by anyone; small parts of it are; and in the world of learning there is mediation in the great dark of ignorance between the areas of light.[2]

On the other hand, in dealing with the external world the nation acts not in relation to an economy, a political system, a social structure, or a culture; it acts in relation to whole men and whole societies whose behavior the nation seeks to influence. Who shall bring to bear on the nation's policy what organized but fragmented knowledge affords?

The predominant tradition in American academic life has not encouraged scholars to undertake the task of unifying knowledge in such ways as to relate to public policy. The intellectual specialist is encouraged from his graduate school apprenticeship forward to stay within the terrain marked out by the discipline in which his competence is vouched for in doctoral working papers. As a professional and a citizen he may answer questions relating to public policy when asked; but it is left to others both to pose the questions and to organize the answers around the issues of public action. A gap thus emerges between the specialized form which professional knowledge assumes and the unified judgments about men and societies which, implicitly or explicitly, must underlie acts of public policy; and the professional social scientist is not generally encouraged to close that gap.

Those charged to fill this gap—the governmental staffs—are, in a sense, the professional mediators between the worlds of politics and intellectual life. But they, too, are generally products of overspecialized disciplinary training; and they tend to be organized and administered in fragmented ways which frustrate the process of linking the segments of knowledge to each other and to the problems they are meant to illuminate and help to solve.

Thus the problem of intellectual synthesis tends to be thrust disproportionately on those who bear political responsibility.

If, in fact, the intellectual problem of making policy consisted merely in collecting and ordering information in answer to clear-cut questions, the gap between the intellectual and the maker of policy would not be serious; but one major form of intellectual contribution to public policy is, or should be, to redefine the problem, to expand the range of alternatives that are perceived to be open, to pose new questions. It is out of the intermediate and higher ranges of abstraction that new ways of looking at things emerge which embrace but transcend what is already known; and it is from new ways of looking at things that new paths for action emerge. To help define these paths, the intellectual must be prepared to enter, to a degree, into the world of operational choice. But he must do more than descend from time to time from the ivory tower; within the ivory tower, he must go further than his professional code now requires or permits in making the intellectual synthesis on which political choice ultimately must rest.

The problem of intellectual synthesis is not limited to the social sciences. The issues of public policy which the nation confronts include some problems which require that the insights of the natural and social sciences be intertwined. In designing a strategy to deter or to prosecute limited war or to move forward the negotiation of armaments control, such issues as the nature of modern weapons, the meaning which would attach to their use in different societies and different diplomatic circumstances, and the political and psychological consequences of alternative methods of arms inspection must be intimately related to each other. While the frontiers of knowledge within the natural and social sciences are progressively extended by increasingly specialized techniques, the scientist must strain not only toward higher degrees of unity within his area of knowledge but also toward developing and maintaining an expanding range of sympathetic discourse between the social and natural sciences.

If American intellectual life is to contribute to the making of more effective public policy in relation to other societies, the sciences in America must thus change the proportions of their effort. They must allocate more time and talent to unifying knowledge in ways which bring to bear what is known and perceived on the concrete problems of public action. And this need not either vulgarize the quality of intellectual life nor force it to concentrate on applied rather than basic research. It is, in fact, from basic research that the truly new ways of looking at things—and new courses of action—mainly derive.

In the end, public policy and intellectual life are linked by the fact that they are, in different ways, high exercises in the world of ideas. As Santayana said:

Practical men may not notice it, but in fact human discourse is intrinsically addressed not to natural existing things but to ideal essences, poetic or logical terms which thought may define and play with. When fortune or necessity diverts our attention from this congenial sport to crude facts and pressing issues, we turn our frail poetic ideas into symbols for those terrible irruptive things. In that paper money of our own stamping, the legal tender of the mind, we are obliged to reckon all the movements and values of the world.

In public life a version of Gresham's law operates: bad thought drives out good. And in a period of rapid change intellectual currency depreciates quickly and automatically with the passage of time. Under such circumstances the intellectual has a special and positive responsibility to help maintain the value of his society's conceptual currency.

The generalization of scientific knowledge and its application to concrete problems of public policy is, of course, not a job for all scientists, nor even for some scientists all the time. The pursuit of knowledge requires many men doing many different things. As Vannevar Bush has written:

There are those who are quite content, given a few tools, to dig away unearthing odd blocks, piling them up in the view of fellow workers, and apparently not caring whether they fit anywhere or not. Unfortunately there are also those who watch carefully until some industrious group digs out a particularly ornamental block, whereupon they fit it in place with much gusto and bow to the crowd. Some groups do not dig at all, but spend all their time arguing as to the exact arrangement of a cornice or an abutment. Some spend all their days trying to pull down a block or two that a rival has put in place. Some, indeed, neither dig nor argue, but go along with the crowd, scratch here and there, and enjoy the scenery. Some sit by and give advice, and some just sit.

On the other hand there are those men of rare vision, who can grasp well in advance just the block that is needed for rapid advance on a section of the edifice to be possible, who can tell by some subtle sense where it will be found, and who have an uncanny skill in cleaning away dross and bringing it surely into the light. These are the master workmen. For each of them there can well be many of lesser stature who chip and delve, industriously, but with little grasp of what it is all about, and who nevertheless make the great steps possible.

There are those who can give the structure meaning, who can trace its evolution from early times, and describe the glories that are to be, in ways that inspire those who work and those who enjoy. They bring the inspiration that all is not mere building of monotonous walls, and that there is architecture even though the architect is not seen to guide and order.

There are those who labor to make the utility of the structure real, to cause it to give shelter to the multitude, that they may be better protected, and that they may derive health and well-being because of its presence.

And the edifice is not built by the quarrymen and the masons alone. There are those who bring them food during their labors, and cooling drink when the days are warm, who sing to them, and place flowers on the little walls that have grown with the years.

There are also the old men, whose days of vigorous building are done, whose eyes are too dim to see the details of the arch or the needed form of its key-stone; but who have built a wall here and there, and lived long in the edifice, who have learned to love it and who have even grasped a suggestion of its ultimate meaning; and who sit in the shade and encourage the young men.[3]

There is no single path to knowledge. A high proportion of scientific effort must continue to be expended at specialized margins of knowledge, not least because it is out of insights derived from such narrow, intense investigation that new general concepts are often derived. Nevertheless, the requirements of American society appear to demand that the boundaries among the intellectual disciplines on which the great academic bureaucracies are built be systematically transcended, and transcended in ways that permit knowledge to be brought to bear with greater efficiency around the major issues of public policy.

### THE SCARCITY OF THE FIRST RATE

A second unsolved problem arises from the relationship between the innovational process and the cultivation of intellectual excellence. While expensive equipment and an adequate supply of competent technicians appear essential for many forms of research and development, it also appears to be the case that the indispensable element in the creative process is quality, an extremely scarce ingredient.[4] There is every reason to believe that first-rate intellectual quality is distributed at random within a large population. In other words, American society contains at any given period a limited number of human beings with first-rate intellectual gifts. One problem of a society whose interest requires rapid innovational pace is, then, to organize itself so as to offer in its prevailing values and institutions the incentives which will lead men of such natural gifts to develop and to use them in the common good.

In recent years the problem of American education has received exhaustive re-examination—from school buildings and teachers' salaries to the balance of the curriculum and the valuation American society places on the world of ideas. It is evident that an educational system in a democracy must serve many purposes other than training for the life of the intellect. The modern American educational system was shaped mainly around the values and needs of a society whose primary concern was to create citizens trained to play a productive role in the economy and to adjust themselves to life in the round of American democratic institutions. And these objectives must be maintained and continue to draw a high proportion of educational resources.

The selection and development of intellectual talent did, indeed, have their place. For some Americans the innate attraction of intellectual life was irrestible. For others, the professional development of intellectual virtuosity was a chosen route to higher social status. Moreover, cultures from abroad which cherished the world of ideas and of intellect more than the prevailing average norms of American society entered the stream of the nation's life. And, whatever the weight of the pragmatic criteria imposed on American education by the special imperatives of an expanding, isolated society seeking to socialize its young to the standards of American behavior, the criteria of intellectual life universal to the Western tradition were never wholly submerged. Nevertheless, it is only in quite recent times that the cultivation of intellectual excellence has come to be considered a matter of legitimate national policy, related directly to the national interest. And this new emphasis is proper; for the nature of American problems makes costly and dangerous the diversion, dilution, and wastage of first-class intellectual talent on the scale which, for a century and more, was acceptable.

In placing on the national agenda the two intellectual problems outlined here—synthesis related to public policy, and the cultivation of excellence—it is important to recognize that their solution does not run counter to trends already at work. The United States has ceased to be a society in which intellectual life is dominated by gadgeteering, a society either incapable of generating new abstract concepts or awkward in their use. While the marks of the older style are still easily to be observed, there has been a major change in the past quarter-century. The generalization that Americans derive their basic science and fundamental innovations—intellectual and otherwise—from abroad requires substantial modification, as does the view that the marketplace drains and dissipates the best minds. About half of the Nobel Prize winners in science since 1945 have been Americans. Nevertheless, the performance of American society in the face of its innovational problems since 1945 suggests that the pace of change should be accelerated in the common interest; for the nation's success in dealing with the world it confronts is to be weighed not against the criterion of whether the underlying trends in American society are in the appropriate direction but against the criterion of whether the nation solves its problems. Set against this hard measure, the state of American intellectual life offers no ground for complacency.

### 65. Bureaucracy, Innovation, and the Individual

The need for higher orders of intellectual synthesis and the need for the cultivation of excellence which arise from the nation's enlarged innovational requirements have this in common: they place a new premium on individuals and on the expression of individuality in the context of public organization and public problems. Intellectual excellence of the first order is the gift of a few among millions; the act of synthesis is a creative experience uniquely achieved. The need to cherish them in the common interest sets up imperatives which, while consonant with certain old American values, run counter to modes of thought and organization which have come to develop in a society much of whose business—even its intellectual and artistic business—is conducted by large-scale bureaucracies.

### THE EVOLUTION OF THE NATIONAL BUREAUCRATIC STYLE

Lacking a national history which stretched back to the Middle Ages, American society began without substantial bureaucratic elements. In the early decades of national life, continuity with European forms of organization existed only in the professional military establishments and in such minimum essential parts of government as tax collection and the post office. In the nineteenth century, units within the national and state governments were generally small; and the problem of relating staff to line and policy to operations could generally be overcome by the presence of a single politically responsible figure.

American industry confronted the problem of scale somewhat sooner than American government, and it exhibited early a tendency which has persisted to the present day: that is, a combination of abundant use of capital and acute specialization of labor. Americans took with special vigor to Adam Smith's propositions about pin manufacture. There is a continuity from Eli Whitney's innovations in mass production down through Taylor's doctrines of scientific management and beyond—a continuity stemming from the fact that the balance between population and resources in the United States made labor expensive, capital relatively cheap, and capital-intensive methods therefore profitable. At the operating level—of a machine tool layout or an assembly line—the nation has steadily exhibited a gift for economy and efficiency.

When industry began to take a firm grip in the textile towns of New England in the 1820's and 1830's, there began to emerge a classic pattern of development and administration which has continued in many sectors of the American economy until very recent times; indeed, it is still to be observed in certain young industries.

The key to the successful industrial development of New England was the perception of one man—Francis Cabot Lowell[1]—that the problem of costs on the New England scene could be solved in such a way as to meet British competition, at least in certain grades of cotton textiles. Basic technology he could import illegally, and he could find here the ingenuity to manufacture the machines, conduct maintenance, and make the necessary modifications; power he could find in the flow of New England streams; and a labor force he could develop by giving to the unmarried daughters of New Hampshire and Massachusetts farmers a decent human setting in the Lowell dormitories. On the basis of these initial insights, Lowell, the team he assembled, and their successors created a viable industry which, decade by decade, continued in a process of extension.

Problems of innovation did not cease. Machinery had to be improved, cyclical fluctuations weathered, the labor force shifted on to an immigrant labor basis, and adjustments made to changing tastes. But with a market initially large in scale, expanding in both population and in real income per head, the task of American industrial growth remained one of vigorous extensive exploitation of an initial perception about how profit could be made. So it was, for example, with Rockefeller's insights into how the national petroleum market could be corralled, with Henry Ford's concept of the cheap, mass-produced automobile, with Eastman's Kodak, and so on.

In short, the creative insights out of which various key sectors of the American economy took their start were not historically the product of large-scale staff organizations. On the contrary, they arose from the head of a single man or from the consensus of an exceedingly small group. Large-scale units emerged in consequence of the correctness of the initial insight, the vigor with which it was translated into reasonably efficient process, and the powerful upward lift of the American economic environment.

Despite the use of research as a new industrial dimension in certain industries, it has remained true down to quite recent times that the really substantial innovations could originate in this private way, they could be pioneered on a small scale, and they could yield massive institutions operating subsequently—at least for some time—by processes requiring relatively minor innovation.

The central problems of American business administration arose not from the need to innovate but from the scale of operations and from the need to coordinate their various phases. The railways were the formative national experience in these dimensions of bureaucracy.

Just before the Civil War, when the railway networks stretched out from the East to consolidate half a continent, their problems produced the perceptive observations of Henry Varnum Poor.[2] He saw clearly that the separation of ownership from management and the obsession of management with profit possibilities arising from railway extension, financial manipulations, and the monopolist's relative freedom to raise rates left management grossly inefficient, the ablest operating men profoundly frustrated, the run-of-the-mill operators reduced to meaningless routine jobs. In examining the problems of morale and leadership in large-scale units, and the requirements for systematic organization, efficient internal communication, and public information, Poor anticipated much of the approach as well as the substance of latter-day American administration experts.

And the railway was later joined in its influence on administrative concepts by two other elements in the nation's experience: the Army in peacetime and the efficient machine shop, from the lessons of which the whole field of scientific management arose. All three forms of enterprise share the problem of using men whose talents can be assumed to be only modest; and the answer in each case was the orderly meshing of their efforts in closely defined, highly specialized tasks.

In government as in industry, for the bulk of national history, innovation could be centered in the hands of a relatively few individuals or in small homogeneous groups. Until well into the twentieth century, for example, the pace and content of diplomatic life allowed the President, the Secretary of State, or both together to handle personally all major issues. More than that, the scale of government permitted day-to-day administration to be in fairly direct control of the same men who made policy. At the turn of the century the Department of State had a staff of less than one hundred, its routine operations under the direction of a Chief Clerk with direct access to the Secretary. Excepting the Civil War period, the other Cabinet departments were also small, and staff work could be centered in the hands of a man or a few men. Government bureaus and commissions did emerge in the latter years of the nineteenth century with regular, recurring military and civil tasks, but they were relatively small in scale and limited in authority; and they settled down to the quiet life of well-entrenched bureaucracy. The permanent officer corps of the Army and Navy were in effect moderate-sized clubs of men and their families, bound together by ties of personal intimacy, common academy backgrounds, and a common unfolding experience.

In the early years of the twentieth century, however, at just about the time when American industry was beginning to face on a wider front the kind of administrative problems the railways had already confronted for some decades, the national government also came face-to-face with the question of large-scale administration. In the aftermath of the Spanish-American War, for example, the size of the permanent Army and Navy roughly quadrupled as compared to its average post-Civil War level. And the trend toward increase in scale within the government has continued as a powerful trend down to the present, almost irrespective of the policies of the various administrations.

The answer that was found to the problem of scale in government was to break the jobs down into clearly defined, specialized professional categories, structured in vast hierarchical pyramids.

## THE AMERICAN THEORY OF ADMINISTRATION

The major question Americans came to pose in their formal consideration of the administrative problem was this: How shall an existing large-scale operation faced with fixed or slowly changing problems be made to work efficiently and without corruption?[3] This remained the central focus of thought on administration down to Herbert Simon's sophisticated analysis:

> The theory of administration is concerned with how an organization should be constructed and operated in order to accomplish its work efficiently. A fundamental principle of administration, which follows almost immediately from the rational character of "good" administration, is that among several alternatives involving the same expenditure the one should always be selected which leads to the greatest accomplishment of administrative objectives; and among several alternatives that lead to the same accomplishment the one should be selected which involves the least expenditure. Since this "principle of efficiency" is characteristic of any activity that attempts rationally to maximize the attainment of certain ends with the use of scarce means, it is as characteristic of economic theory as it is of administrative theory. The "administrative man" takes his place alongside the classical "economic man."[4]

The virtues and deficiencies of Simon's view are precisely those of the neat formulations of classical economic theory: they illuminate the efficiency conditions in static processes; but growth and major structural change are assumed to occur as the result of forces outside the analytic system. And the great question is never posed: To what extent do the short-run imperatives of administrative order clash with the innovational requirements of long-run survival? For, once established, large-scale units face the problem of generating out of their own structures new innovations capable of maintaining their vitality. As a basic point of departure, modern administrative theory is no more appropriate to the process of innovation than short-run Keynesian income analysis is to the process of economic growth.

The problem of innovation and change is, indeed, treated to a degree by American administrative analysts; but it tends to be subsumed in a rather abstract way in the concept of "the choice among alternatives," just as modern economic theory assumes that entrepreneurs choose the most profitable techniques available from a given "state of the arts." This is a gross evasion; for the very heart of the decision-making process is the posing of the alternatives. Innovation—creativeness—consists in thinking up an alternative which hasn't been thought of before. The good executive knows that one of his major tasks is to ensure that all the conceivable alternatives are explored and available to him, not merely those which his operating subordinates or staff men think up, agree upon, and regard as appropriate to place before him.

By making the act of decision the center of the job—and deflating the problem of formulating alternatives—concepts of the administrative process emerge which are attuned, at best, to modest, slow-moving innovation. When, for example, Simon and his colleagues treat such issues as "the growth of administration," "how problems give rise to administrations," and "the strategy of planning," their examples derive from American domestic life in which innovations are seen to arise from a slowly accumulating sense of an unresolved problem, gathering popular momentum until a political consensus is reached and action is taken. Subsequently, the planning process is seen as the projection out to the future of familiar ongoing processes and trends. The classic American table of organization for staff work consists of a hierarchy of specialized experts, each surveying a sector of operations, passing his recommendations for marginal change upward to be considered by the responsible executive in his "choice among alternatives." There is no perception—until very recent years—that the definition of alternatives in a rapidly changing field for action is, in itself, a powerful creative act most unlikely to be generated by specialized bureaucrats.

INNOVATION BY BUREAUCRACY: THE UNSOLVED PROBLEM

The cumulative national experience and American thought about it have left this central problem unsolved: How shall change be instituted to meet new circumstances in large-scale units which, because they are committed to comparatively static standards of efficiency, limit the capacity of those relatively few creative men capable of innovation and leadership?[5] In dealing with this problem, the nation is inhibited in both business and government by the following characteristics of the national style:

1. An empirical approach that tends to discount the reality of problems defined by imaginative projection of trends until the problems have reached a stage so acute that they obtrude on the field of vision of responsible operators: in government, over the incoming cables, or voting shifts in the electorate; in business, on current income accounts; in war, by initial defeat in the field.

2. A related tendency to organize staff work on highly specialized lines which make difficult the development of an over-all view of the problems confronted by any major institution.

3. In consequence of overspecialization, the tendency to overman staff work units in such a way as to minimize the amount of time available to any responsible figure for coherent thought and reflection, and to dilute the insights and views of knowledgeable specialists as they pass upwards through bureaucratic hierarchies.

4. A tendency, in the interests of organizational cohesion, to accord all

units in an organization a voice in major decisions touching their area of operation.

5. As a result, fundamental policy decisions which take the form of compromise among responsible operators, strengthening the inertia innate to any large-scale unit.

Under these circumstances, the concept of a high executive has ceased to be that of the creative innovator or forceful leader and has become that of the negotiator of successful compromise.[6]

In domestic politics the process of innovation is powerfully checked and governed by the sensitive market of the polling booths; and in business by the equally powerful pressures of competition and profit margin shifts. In both areas the rate of innovation required for the vitality and quality of American society is certainly increasing; but it can be handled tolerably well by the processes of institutionalized innovation which have been evolving when strengthened by enlarged political staffs, outside trouble-shooters, efficiency experts, and idea men.

In military and foreign policy, however, neither the domestic political process nor the competitive marketplace of power operates sensitively until acute crises have arisen; and the character of innovation required to deal with reality is more radical.

The two great institutions designed to synthesize a view of national problems in security and foreign policy—the National Security Council and the Joint Chiefs of Staff—have been in their first decade of life essentially committees of operators. There the bureaucratic chieftains meet, each freighted with large vested interests to protect, each biased heavily toward the *status quo*—as, indeed, operators must be. Under such circumstances these institutions have been unable to survey in a systematic way the horizons of the national position and formulate policies which effectively unified day-to-day operations.

High-level policy has tended to emerge in one of two forms: either as general statements so broad that operators could go on doing what they were doing and interpreting policy statements as they wished, or as tough practical compromises, allocating money or other scarce resources, in which the pattern of policy is much less important to the outcome than the bargaining weight of the negotiators.

What is the result? Policy-making has consisted in a progression of reactions to major crises. Having failed to define, to anticipate, and to deal with forces loose in the world, having tried merely to keep the great machine of government ticking over from day to day in the face of issues even operators could not ignore, at last the problems either never recognized or swept under the rug came ticking in over the incoming cables. Then, at last, the reality of the matter was recognized, but at a time when the options were narrowed. Emergency efforts—often bypassing all the bureaucratic machinery created to deal with national affairs—were hastily launched; and these became the working norms of policy until the next crisis came along. As a first approximation it is quite accurate to say of any moment over the period 1940-1958 that current military and foreign policy was a bureaucratized version of that created *ad hoc* to deal with the last crisis.

The nation has thus far been saved because Americans do not respect tables of organization nearly so much as would appear. A battalion in the field, a firm in trouble, or the White House at a moment of national crisis has its decisions made for it by the few men who really matter and who are rallied round for the occasion by the responsible officer who seizes personal command. Everyone knows that the vitality of even the largest of institutions hinges on a few key men. But the nation has found it difficult to acknowledge that the qualities of a few men matter so much when institutions are designed or their workings formally described.

### THE CHARACTER OF A SOLUTION

How can the quality of individual creativeness be woven back into the fabric of a society much of whose business must continue to be conducted by great bureaucratic structures embracing and seeking to organize coherently many highly specialized skills? There is, of course, no simple answer. The struggle between staff and line, between the inertia of operators and the perception of the need for change, will go on; but the balance can and must be tilted in ways which favor the process of innovation.

Each institution will have to fight out its own battles, find its own improved balance. There are, nevertheless, four things which can usefully be said in general.[7]

First, the reality of the problem should be recognized. The notion that American society is competent in the field of administration must give way to a skeptical analysis of the extent to which the pace of innovation is sacrificed to essentially static concepts of order. The problem of inevitable conflict between the canons of order and those of creative change must be accepted as one which can be resolved only by uneasy, endless struggle and balance.

Second, staff structures should be re-examined on the presupposition that they are likely to be too large, burdening the ablest men with tasks of human organization and manipulation to the point of diluting their knowledge of the substance of problems and their time to think.

Third, within staff administration, the role of the committee as an instrument for defining alternatives and arriving at decisions must be reviewed. The checks and balances which must inevitably operate when many factors and interests bear on a given decision cannot be eliminated even if that were desirable. But individual men can be assigned responsibility to formulate the alternatives and to propose an answer to problems, bearing with that assignment the responsibility of consulting legitimately interested parties. The essential point is this: the performance of the same individual as the member of a committee bearing a dilute communal responsibility and his performance when faced with an unambiguous personal assignment to do a job is remarkedly different.

Fourth, in industry as well as in government, the technique of decentralization of operating function appears capable of further extension. In the end, in all bureaucracies the unity and the coordination of parts must be achieved; but it well suits a nation constructed politically by making an art of federalism to find new and economical ways of maintaining unity on minimum essential issues while still permitting large areas of responsibility and choice to elements within the large organization.

The argument here, then, is that, although large-scale organizations inevitably place the individual in a setting different from that of a farmer who owns his own land, the man who sets up his own small business, or even the scholar writing his book alone in the library, the loss of connection between what a man does and the larger purposes of the organization of which he is a part has been excessive. It is not beyond the wit of man to devise better ways of reconciling the imperatives of large-scale organization with those personalized challenges and incentives on which the best human performance depends.

In Washington, aside from new administrative procedures and balances like those going forward slowly in the Pentagon, a change of spirit is required. The individual human beings in the great bureaucracies must be encouraged to think, to throw out new ideas, to debate openly. The illusion that the nation's affairs can successfully be handled by negotiating minimum consensus in layer after layer of interdepartmental committees must be broken. The government must recapture a sense that creation is something the nation badly needs; and that creation is a job of individuals backing their play with integrity. This spirit must suffuse the whole apparatus from the Office of the President to the lowest GS-5.

The interdepartmental machinery of negotiation and consensus will continue to grind along. Bureaucracy will not end. But its processes must be made to grind on something other than departmental vested interests and the precompromised views of men anxious above all to avoid controversy and trouble.

A systematic counterattack on prevailing administrative theory, bureaucratic structure, and organizational spirit appears to be in order, not only to salvage for American citizens a wider range of individual responsibility and expression but also to give increased play to those forces of creation and innovation on which the survival of American society—as well as its quality—increasingly depend.

## 66. Innovation, Leadership, and the Democratic Process

Although ideas and administrative methods shape and limit the character of public policy, the political process decides in the end what shall and shall not be done. It is necessary therefore to consider what changes in the democratic process in the United States might yield an American performance better able to cope with the problems arising from the nation's external environment and its domestic dynamics.

In treating military and foreign policy this book has mainly proceeded in terms of recurrent patterns of American performance. Behind those patterns lay certain persistent national habits of thought, ways of acting, and balances of political interest and outlook. Thus far this book has touched upon the politics of military and foreign policy only at occasional points—for example, the bipartisan isolationism of the 1930's, the political setting of demobilization after the Second World War, and the political balance of the Eisenhower administration during its first term. Here the political process must be approached directly.

### A DILEMMA OF DEMOCRACY

The dilemma of democracy in military and foreign policy is a familiar theme. On the one hand, the natural bent of man is to be concerned first of all with his income, his health, his family;[1] and a political system based on the principle of one man, one vote, must reflect not only the primacy of these proper homely concerns but also the fact that military and foreign affairs are likely to interfere with their pursuit. On the other hand, military and foreign affairs cannot be indefinitely the private domain of a skilled elite group; since, in the end, blood and treasure are at stake, Congress—and the whole democratic process—must finally decide. And if its hand is forced by the use of Executive power, the democratic process finds ways of passing judgment after the event.

The dilemma has yielded over a long period a distinguished literature reflecting concern for democracy's fate in military and foreign affairs—from Tocqueville and Bryce to Lippmann and Kennan. The pessimistic view dramatizes the gap between those at the apex of government—knowledgeable in the affairs of the world, sensitive to limitations on national power and the legitimacy of interests other than their own—and the mass of citizens—ignorant, apathetic, preoccupied, their instinctive provincial nationalism systematically enflamed by mass media and by politicians whose first and overriding interest is to get themselves elected by such an electorate.

The problem of effective military and foreign policy performance in contemporary American democracy is real enough; but it is neither as simple nor as insoluble as the pessimistic view would suggest.

## LEADERSHIP AND DEMOCRACY

Both the complexity of the problem and the basis for relative optimism lie in the nature of the process of leadership in American society.

Why, in general, are leaders required in a democracy, and what do they do? Why does not the interplay of individuals pressing their special interests against the resistance of other special interests suffice?

Leadership is required for two reasons. First, democratic thought has always acknowledged—if sometimes grudgingly—that all men are not equally gifted in the special tasks—ultimately in the art—of handling the affairs of the community; nor are they equally drawn to communal affairs. Second, and quite aside from natural endowment and interest, the handling of communal affairs requires a knowledge of special areas of fact and of situation which all cannot know equally. In social and political organization—as in virtually all else done in a modern society—specialization is required.

In assuming special powers of decision in communal affairs the leader must look in three directions; and if he is to be successful, he must harmonize what he sees. First, he must perceive—if possible, he must anticipate—the urgent new problems faced by the community which require for their solution change in method or in communal policy. Second, he must examine alternative solutions to those problems and throw his weight behind those which are both effective and in harmony with the constitutional and moral rules of the community. Third, he must persuade the community that the proposed course of action is correct and organize its energies effectively around that course of action in such ways as to maintain his mandate.

On this view the leader in a democratic community must be an innovator— the man who perceives new problems and organizes technical solutions for them; he must be the protector of the community's long-run continuity, the keeper of its historic values and institutions; and, finally, he must combine the talents of educator and short-run political tactician. This is a considerable task; but in a modern democratic society multiple facets of leadership are everywhere to be observed in successful organizations, including those formally outside the political process.

The successful businessman is not merely an automaton making rational market calculations. He is the leader of his firm, peering ahead to understand its future problems of technology and markets, carrying with him not only his board of directors but also his managerial staff and his labor force, harmonizing his decisions not only with the legal but also with the moral values of the society of which his firm is a part. Similarly, the successful labor leader must concern himself not only with the current and foreseeable agenda of problems affecting labor's real income; he must also carry along both his immediate constituency, the rank and file, and the more distant but still powerful constituency of the American community.

These three dimensions of the task of bringing about change by consent within the continuing values and constitutional rules of American democracy —dimensions of innovation, continuity, and persuasion—exist equally for the President and for the leader of the most modest communal organization within the society.

### THE TRIANGULAR PROCESS OF POLITICAL INNOVATION

How does leadership operate in solving new problems at the level of national policy? As a crude first approximation, one can view the innovation of policy by the federal government as a triangular process. The President goes to the voters with his definition of the nation's problem and with his proposed solution broadly outlined. With the weight of the national interest thus strengthened in the electorate, Congress is encouraged to act in a less parochial way than the local and regional pressures and responsibilities which bear upon it generally decree. Something like this process, with the President as innovator and educator who sets in motion the reduction of the inhibiting pressures upon and widens the area of choice open to Congress, can be seen to apply, for example, in the political history of Lend-Lease, the Truman Doctrine, and, more recently, the foreign trade and aid legislation of 1958.

A classic form of this relationship emerged from the discussion between Truman and the Congressional leaders on February 27, 1947, when the latter were presented the dour facts of the threat to Greece and Turkey and of the inability of Britain further to carry the burdens of military and economic support. After the recitals of Truman, Marshall, and Acheson:

> A profound silence ensued that lasted perhaps ten seconds. It was broken by the voice of Senator Vandenberg. Slowly and with gravity, Vandenberg said that he had been greatly impressed, even shaken, by what he had heard. It was clear that the country was faced by an extremely serious situation, of which aid to Greece and Turkey, although of great importance, was only a part. He felt that it was absolutely necessary that any request of Congress for funds and authority to aid Greece and Turkey should be accompanied by a message to Congress, and an explanation to the American people, in which the grim facts of the larger situation should be laid publicly on the line as they had been at their meeting that day.[2]

Vandenberg was the leader of the Congressional majority in foreign affairs, and his party confidently expected to place its man in the White House the next year. Truman, the President only by succession, had seen his party lose control of the Congress a few months earlier. Nevertheless, the leader of the Senate in foreign affairs, at the height of his powers, knew that only the unambiguous voice of the President could create a setting in which the job could be done.

The triangular relationship is not, of course, quite as simple an affair as this example would suggest. In each of the three dimensions of leadership there is a complex interaction between the presidency and the other institutions of the nation. The problems requiring new national policy are not necessarily defined in the President's head. They may be forced on his (and the nation's) attention by events in the world so obvious and threatening that it would be politically dangerous for the President to fail to make new policy. A problem may be brought to the President's attention by one of his principal advisers. The act of initiation may come from outside the Executive Branch—through the controversy of the two parties, from the Congress, or from informed and even excited elements in the public.

Similarly, staff work—the exploration of alternative solutions—will certainly be conducted not by the President alone but through his interaction with the various institutions of the Executive Branch. In foreign and military affairs the President's freedom of action and, indeed, his vision of what alternatives are open to him will be limited and colored by views and interests of the Department of State, the three military services, and the Department of Defense. At any moment in time the President may be able to influence the great bureaucracies only marginally. Moreover, the President's definition of the situation he confronts in the world—and thus, by implication, the roads of action open to the nation—will be profoundly affected by the intelligence picture drawn for him by the CIA and by those others charged with informing him. Often an extremely important, if not decisive, role in the definition of alternative solutions may be played by special Presidential commissions or by other groups outside the normal machinery of the Executive Branch. And, finally, the Congress, despite its limitations in the conduct of staff work, has played in many domestic issues a role of greater importance than the Executive Branch; and it has demonstrated increasingly that on occasion it can do so in foreign affairs as well.

Finally, the process of persuasion in a democratic community is a vastly more complex and interacting affair than the picture of the President as teacher and advocate of the communal position would indicate. Not only does political leadership at every level play a part, but also the world of mass communications, voluntary associations, and determined private individuals.

In short, no matter how positively the President interprets his constitutional responsibilities as communal leader, no matter how "strong" or "weak" he is in the parlance of American constitutional history, the leadership process in modern America is diffuse and many-sided, embracing the activities of a whole spectrum of governmental and nongovernmental institutions.

In a phase of American history when both external and internal problems require increased communal effort and accelerated innovation, there is thus a *prima facie* case for strengthening the leadership process in each of its major dimensions: the Executive Branch, the Congress, and the instruments for informing and organizing public opinion.

### STRENGTHENING THE OFFICE OF PRESIDENT

Under the Constitution the President, both in his person and in his office, must be the central figure in any consideration of leadership in national policy. It is the President, above all, who must identify and if possible anticipate urgent new communal problems; it is the President who must generate the staff work which will yield the array of alternative solutions open to the community. Moreover, he must play an important role in making the community aware of its problems and in persuading it to support effectively the course of action which he regards as both effective and in harmony with the community's constitutional rules and values. Notably in military and foreign policy, but also to an important degree in major domestic issues, the President must be—in fact as well as symbolically—the community's mind and voice if the community is to function effectively.

The nature of the office of President offers much common-law latitude in the exercise of leadership; and the most important prescription reduces to the assertion that the leadership possibilities of the Presidency be vigorously employed. Beyond such observations—of undoubted truth but limited utility —there is a range of possible measures which might strengthen the quality of the staff work available to the President and a few changes in law which might usefully enhance his constitutional powers.

As for staff work, it is essential to recognize, however, that each President will have his own operating style and must be left considerable freedom in organizing the Executive Branch to his private taste. It was wholly legitimate for Roosevelt to work by orchestrating the ardent overlapping efforts of many diverse personalities and branches of the government; and for Truman to surround himself in military and foreign affairs by a small like-minded team (mainly) of Yale men and West Pointers; for Eisenhower to build the quasi-military staff structure which he found congenial. There are many potentially useful changes in the organization of the federal government which should be regularly considered in the light of emerging experience and changing problems; but even such vital changes as strengthening the staff of the National Security Council, restructuring the Department of Defense, and widening the permanent civil service in the various arms of foreign policy should not obscure the fact that in its most important dimensions the performance of the Executive Branch will depend on the person of the President and a few key men around him.

Constitutionally, it might prove useful to permit the President the right of item-veto; to grant him the possible additional political leverage that would go with the repeal of the 22nd Amendment to the Constitution forbidding a third term; and it is evidently essential to continue to fight off restrictive Constitutional amendments along the lines of the Bricker proposal. But the extraordinary powers of the President and the many directions in which they must simultaneously be exercised make his job, in the end, one of personal artistry, coming to rest on qualities of insight, mind, and character beyond the range of political science or the field of public administration.

## LEADERSHIP AND THE CONGRESS

The most important things to be said about the Congressional role in the triangular process also transcend concrete prescription.

There is, first of all, the abiding problem of legislatures in democracy which is rooted in the fact that congressmen, generally speaking, are elected on the basis of local and regional issues. Foreign and military affairs are, essentially, an intrusion on what they regard as higher-order business; and when local or regional pressures do become directly enmeshed in foreign or military affairs (as with racial groups, tariffs, or local military establishments), they are more likely to obstruct than to advance the national interest.

In addition to the fundamental lack of convergence between Congressional and Executive Branch responsibilities and outlook on foreign and military affairs, there are additional problems of Congressional organization that make difficulties for American democracy in its military and foreign policy performance. There are rarely united party positions within the Congress on military and foreign policy; and there is, therefore, rarely a single party leader with whom the Executive Branch can negotiate with confidence. The Executive Branch and Congressional leaders must construct a special *ad hoc* coalition, drawn from both parties, to carry through each major piece of legislation. Moreover, the separation of policy-making from the appropriation process adds exhausting strains and hazards to the process of Executive Branch advocacy before the Congress. Finally, the seniority rule in the election of committee chairmen adds an element of Russian roulette to the leadership process in military and foreign affairs.

When all this is said—when the Congress is enjoined to organize itself in a more responsible way in military and foreign policy matters—the fact nevertheless remains that the Congressional performance since 1940 has generally matched that of the Executive Branch. The Executive Branch has been in trouble when it lacked a clear-cut united policy in which it deeply believed, or when it has not adequately done its homework. Members of Congress are, in the end, responsible American citizens who, although they bear the special professional responsibility of seeking re-election in local and regional constituencies, are as a group most unlikely to behave irresponsibly when the nature of responsibility is made clear to them by a firm and well-presented Executive Branch policy followed through with force. And their electorates tend to give them a considerable latitude, notably if a strong case on a given issue has been made to the public by the President.

The character of the Congressional performance in military and foreign affairs has been significantly shaped in recent years by deeper political forces: the attrition imposed by the electorate on the old-style right-wing Republican isolationists, the emergence of a new isolationism in parts of the Democratic South, the outlook, competence, and strategy of the majority and minority leaders in the Senate and House of Representatives. Of their nature, these factors of historic trend and the accident of personality do not lend themselves to easy prescription; they merely complicate or ease a task of Executive leadership which, on the basis of recent experience, is bound to be difficult but is by no means insoluble.

MILITARY AFFAIRS: AN AREA OF CONGRESSIONAL WEAKNESS

Nevertheless, a major problem for the democratic process remains in military affairs—a problem of knowledge and of Congressional responsibility. In foreign affairs the knowledgeability of the Congress has markedly increased in postwar years. Both the Senate and the House of Representatives contain men who are remarkably well informed and who are relied upon to lead their parties and the Congress as a whole in major matters of foreign policy. On some issues the Congress has demonstrated that it is capable of acts of initiation previously associated with the legislative branch only in domestic policy. In military affairs, however, the problem of secrecy has converged with the continuing split of the three services to make the self-education of the Congress more difficult. It is an extraordinary fact that the largest item in the national budget is voted annually by the Congress with only a minimal knowledge of what is involved. The defense budget has been purposefully designed as a virtually impenetrable document, in no way presenting clearly the nation's military policy and the programs which are designed to implement it. This ambiguity has been the inevitable result of the negotiatory process by which the military budget is achieved in the Executive Branch. It is understandable that most Congressmen confine themselves to assuring that the local air base, army camp, or naval establishment will be maintained. A few members of Congress manage to grasp hold of one aspect or another of military policy in the larger sense; but the average level of knowledge and professional concern is low.

In short, the process of leadership in military policy at the Congressional level is peculiarly weak. Congressional weakness is obscured in the short run by the willingness of Congress to go along on matters of national security, partly because most congressmen regard it as unrewarding to take strong independent positions on major military matters until the nation has worked its way into a crisis so unpleasant that it appears safe for the party in opposition to exploit it. This is not the democratic process at its best. In a world caught up in revolutionary military change, with the nation facing all manner of danger, it is unwise for American democracy to proceed with its legislators in a fog of ignorance, apathy, and irresponsibility about military matters.

## GOVERNMENT AND THE PUBLIC

The process of leadership should be improved at many points in the Executive Branch and the Congress; but the most important area of potential political innovation lies in the relations between government and the public. Contrary to the literature of pessimism on this problem, it is by no means automatic that those with greatest access to detailed knowledge in military and foreign affairs will arrive at an intelligent consensus; it is by no means true that they face merely the difficult but straightforward task of persuading an ill-informed public to follow their agreed course of policy. In some matters —for example, foreign aid in the period 1953-1958—the major inhibition to action lay not in public opinion but in intractable unresolved differences within the Executive Branch.[3] Nevertheless, the most fundamental long-term problem for a democracy whose survival requires an expensive, active, and rapidly changing military and foreign policy lies in the general area of what is usually called public opinion.

One way of posing the problem of strengthening the relations between the political leadership and the public in these more remote matters is this: Can the nation—as a steady part of the national scene and performance—do what has been successfully done in the past two decades only at moments of acute crisis in foreign relations?

The essence of what was done on occasions such as the Lend-Lease or Marshall Plan debates is precisely the opposite of what one would deduce from the literature of pessimism on democracy and foreign affairs. The key to successful action lay not in insulating a knowledgeable élite from popular pressure but in a widespread sharing of responsibility for the nation's decision. The President and the Executive Branch responsibly laid before the public the problem the nation confronted, the facts bearing upon it, and the choices that appeared open. The President personally committed himself concerning the broad direction in which a solution was to be found. The Congress held extensive hearings, permitting all manner of opinion to be expressed, fixing public attention on the problem in hand over a considerable period. Finally, the extraordinary substructure of private associations which characterize American life was galvanized into taking positions and making them felt in the political process. Out of this complex, apparently disorderly process— wholly different from the image of a single wise leader charting his course and an obedient public following along—three things happened. First, a responsible view of the problem was presented to the public, with the President himself vouching for its urgency and for the general character of the decision required of the nation. Second, a wide range of representative and trusted communal and group leaders did their homework and said their piece—not only congressmen but also business, labor, and farm leaders, churchmen, professors, and the rest. Third, a public, informed to the limit of its absorptive capacity, with every opportunity for communication open, evidently reached a majority consensus, and its assent was registered by a Congress which had been hard at work on its own but with a sharp eye for the emergent balance of grass-roots thought.

The lesson to be learned from these successful exercises is that when the political process is widened out from the Executive Branch and the Congress and the public is brought into the arena of decision—notably through those men and women who lead the voluntary associations—the capacity of the nation to act boldly and strongly in foreign affairs has been increased, not diminished. The public needs, of course, to be responsibly informed on major issues of military and foreign policy as they arise. There is no substitute for a strong President and competent Executive Branch staff work; but political leaders need to be reminded of the intelligence and of the capacity for action and sacrifice of the American electorate when it is brought into a position of responsibility.

### THE STRUCTURE OF PUBLIC OPINION

This relatively optimistic conclusion is based not merely on the record of public performance at its best over the past two decades but also on the character of public opinion in relation to military and foreign policy.

Public opinion in military and foreign affairs is often discussed in one of two ways: as if it were an inflexible undifferentiated mass phenomenon out-side rational guidance, or as a phenomenon easily manipulated by experts in mass communications. In fact, American public opinion in military and foreign affairs is a complex, flexible, but shapely phenomenon, in which the influence of the following specific factors must be taken into account.

*The President's capital.* In one sense there is no clear-cut public opinion in military and foreign affairs until the President has taken his position. The President is endowed with a considerable capital fund; that is, the American public is inclined to give him a considerable latitude and to be influenced significantly by his assessment of external events and their meaning for the national interest. This latitude varies with many factors; it was, for example, great for President Truman at the outbreak of the Korean War but much narrowed by the end of 1951. Nevertheless, while the American public is not inclined to follow blindly the President's lead, his view is a powerful element in the equation which determines public opinion. The President's role can also operate negatively. The press, the experts, and even Congress can become quite exercised about a military or foreign policy problem; but if the President chooses to remain passive, action is unlikely unless a crisis as inescapable as the fall of France, Pearl Harbor, or the attack on Korea occurs. And, if the crisis is not such as to demand immediate military action, the President, within limits, has the power to deflate the mood of the electorate, as Eisenhower did after the Suez and sputnik crises of 1956 and 1957. To a significant if limited extent, then, public opinion in military and foreign affairs is a function of what the President wishes it to be.

*The 60-25-15 split.* On the other hand, American public opinion is not a blank slate. The President faces a public whose general attitude is strongly affected by recent memories and by strongly held general views. Out of the experience of this generation of Americans—involving the bankruptcy of inter-war isolationism, the Second World War and, then, protracted Cold War— a rather consistent and recurrent pattern of public attitude towards international affairs has emerged. Broadly speaking, one can expect about 60 per cent of the American public to take what might be called an "internationalist" position, about 25 per cent an "isolationist" position, and about 15 per cent a "don't know" position. These figures vary from issue to issue, but something like this breakdown in basic attitudes appears to exist, increasingly independent of party allegiance and of region. This does not mean that 60 per cent of Americans wish actively to become more involved in the world and its affairs. On the contrary, there is ample evidence that Americans remain reluctant in assuming international responsibility. What these recurrent poll figures do demonstrate is that a substantial majority of Americans will support military and foreign policy measures when they become convinced that they are absolutely necessary for the maintenance of the nation's world position; and a substantial majority will shy away from positions they believe associated with an isolationist retreat or an abandoning of major alliances.

*The range of knowledge, concern, and confidence.* Within the 85 per cent or so prepared in most polls to express a view on military or foreign affairs there is, of course, a range of knowledgeability, of seriousness of interest, and of confidence of judgment. Some portion of the American public is truly and regularly impervious to military and foreign affairs: ignorant, unconcerned, and apathetic. But at a time when young men are subject to draft and taxes are as high as they are in support of the nation's security policy the number of persons truly apathetic about military and foreign policy is smaller than some analyses might lead one to believe. In Presidential primaries and elections of recent years it is clear, for example, that the public may not have made its choice in terms of specific military and foreign policy issues—lacking confidence in its information and judgment—but it made an over-all assessment of the candidates in relation to their believed competence in these areas; and these over-all assessments were powerful in determining the outcome.

Beyond a widespread public concern with the nation's external position— perhaps, simply, a chronic uneasiness—there are varying degrees of knowledgeability and, especially, of confidence of judgment within the American public. In domestic affairs the average citizen sees the impact of national policy in terms of the familiar round of his life. He not only knows the essential facts; he also sees what they mean in terms of situations and values with which he is at home. In military and foreign affairs the citizen—even the interested and knowledgeable citizen—can only rarely feel confident that he has a sufficient grasp of the situation to make a responsible assessment. He remains an outsider in these important and expensive matters, an observer of the Washington insider, even if his newspapers and magazines, his radio and TV programs are full of pieces of possibly relevant information and opinion. Under these circumstances, short of a major crisis, or short of some special effort by the President to focus his attention, the typical American citizen will read his paper, listen to the news, absorbing more or less information as his background, taste, and intelligence dictate, but remain an essentially passive figure—friendly, suspicious, hostile or neutral, in his attitude toward current policy—lacking a sense of involvement or of personal responsibility.

To this static portrait an important dynamic element must be added—the rising average level of education. Interest, knowledge, and concern with foreign policy are positively correlated with schooling; and the average level of education is regularly increasing in the United States. One can, then, anticipate with confidence a progressively more knowledgeable and responsive public in international affairs.

*Three special groups.* In addition to the citizen whose information is derived essentially from the mass media there are three small special groups within the American public who can play a special role in the formation of public opinion on specific issues of military and foreign policy—the outside expert, the semiprofessional, and the leader of voluntary associations. The expert in military and foreign affairs outside the government is probably a less powerful influence on the general public than he would like to believe he is; or, put another way, his power is exercised more by catching the attention or influencing the thought of those with direct political responsibility and power than in influencing public opinion at large. The expert columnist or author in the field of military or international affairs has, on the whole, a small audience, the most important elements of which may prove to be members of the Executive Branch or the Congress.

He may, however, have significant impact on a second special group, the semiprofessionals. Every substantial community in contemporary America contains a small group of citizens—usually men and women otherwise distinguished by their competence and sense of civic responsibility—who maintain an active interest in international affairs and who are, on the whole, well-informed. These people participate in the regional Councils on Foreign Relations; lead the work in the Foreign Policy Associations and the relevant committees of the League of Women Voters; write the surprisingly thoughtful and mature editorials to be found in newspapers from coast to coast; speak the wise Sunday sermon on international affairs; teach the foreign policy courses in colleges and high schools; or simply continue to assert their interest and responsibility as individual citizens of a democracy whose fate is caught up in a treacherous world arena.

Then, finally, there is the group of responsible leaders of business, labor, farm, religious, and other groups who do not specialize in international affairs but who are prepared, when occasion demands, to do their homework and to take public positions. This group is exceedingly important in achieving a national consensus; for its members often stand closer to the individual citizen and his interests than elected officials. Their responsible assent in measures of military and foreign policy is a two-way signal of some power. It is an important reassurance to their special constituents that the measure is necessary for the common good; and it is a message to the Executive and the Congressional branches that when the issue is clearly explained, public support is likely, and it is politically safe to proceed.

There are two general observations to be made about these special groups within the American public.

First, because of special knowledge, experience, or judgment they cannot be persuaded to support a line of public policy unless the case is fully, honestly, and persuasively made. Neither as individuals nor as special groups are they in anyone's pocket. Second, the members of these special groups are getting to know one another. One facet of the rapid evolution of an American continental community is that leaders in special segments of national life are being brought together to consider major foreign and domestic problems. Businessmen and professors, labor leaders and churchmen, farm organization executives and foundation officials gather now as a matter of course from every part of the country on one occasion or another. As a result, there now exists as never before the physical and human possibility of thrashing out rapidly a nationwide consensus among those outside the government who can play important roles in leading the community toward agreement and action in military and foreign affairs.

## FOUR PRESCRIPTIONS

American public opinion in military and foreign policy reflects, then, attitudes ranging from a minority's apathy to a majority's continuing but not necessarily well-informed concern. It is broadly committed to uphold the nation's world position of power and responsibility. It is prepared to respond to the President's lead and accord him important degrees of flexibility, notably when his case is well made and presented with conviction. It has available a vast and regular flow of information, but only a small proportion of the public feel sufficient confidence in what they know to take firm positions on specific issues without further guidance; the public looks for guidance not only to the President and to other political leaders but also to trusted local communal leaders, to the leaders of voluntary associations with whom they are connected.

If this assessment is correct, what steps might be taken which would yield a more regular sense of public commitment and responsibility in military and foreign affairs and permit the nation to pursue a more forehanded policy, one more likely to cope with problems before they develop into dangerous crises?

The essentials appear to be these:

First, the President should use more fully and regularly his unique power to focus public attention on major problems of military and foreign policy. This should be done not only when the Executive Branch wishes urgently to take fresh action but also when major issues are evidently just over the horizon. The President should be prepared to focus attention and to stimulate public discussion even before he and the Executive Branch as a whole have matured a clear policy position.

Second, the Executive Branch should adopt and sustain in military as well as foreign affairs a policy of candor. Information should be denied the public on grounds other than aid or comfort to the enemy—narrowly defined—only under the most rare and special circumstances, if ever. The public must be trusted, and the natural tendency of Washington to underestimate the public's wisdom and good sense endlessly combated.

Third, whenever possible, issues should be presented to the public in the same terms as they are dealt with within the Executive Branch; that is, in the form of a tripartite statement of a factual situation, an array of alternative policies, and the case for the specific alternative chosen. A more effective public opinion requires not only the availability of more authoritative information but also a sense of sharing in the choice of alternative courses of American action.

Fourth, the President and the Executive Branch should actively encourage voluntary groups of all kinds to study specific major issues of military and foreign policy, to examine the policy choices open to the nation, and to make their recommendations. Under no circumstances, however, should the relationship between the government and such groups be regarded as one of a channel for propaganda. The objective is the quite different one of inducing a widening range of Americans to share the experience of examining alternative policy positions on the basis of responsible information.

The capacity of the political process to innovate can be increased by changes in law, Executive Branch administration, Congressional procedure, and the policy of government toward public information and public opinion. In the end, however, it is essential for a democracy to recognize the irreducible basis for leadership and innovation—private and personal courage. New courses of action always bring unpredictable factors into play and incur risk. There is no way to avoid taking steps in the dark, for which there is no prescription other than the reply to those who hesitated in Holland to make the pilgrimage to Plymouth:

> It was answered, that all great and honorable actions are accompanied with great difficulties and must be both enterprised and overcome with answerable courages. It was granted the dangers were great, but not desperate. The difficulties were many, but not invincible. For though there were many of them likely, yet they were not certain. It might be sundry of the things feared might never befall; others by provident care and the use of good means might in a great measure be prevented; and all of them through the help of God, by fortitude and patience, might either be borne or overcome.[4]

## 67. The Political Economy of a Continental Community in a Time of Protracted Crisis

### RESOURCE ALLOCATION IN A DEMOCRACY

If the United States is to deal with its foreseeable problems, something more is needed than a clarification of the national interest based on a redefined moral position; something more, even, than those shifts in the balance of American intellectual life, administrative method, and political process which would increase the nation's capacity to deal with its external environment by a technique other than innovation by crisis. In the end, the execution of public policy in the right directions and on the requisite scale demands that enlarged resources be allocated for the common defense and for the common welfare at home. The task is, moreover, not only to release adequate resources for public purposes but also to provide a domestic economic setting sufficiently secure and acceptable so that the nation's political energies are not disproportionately diverted inward, away from the tasks on the international scene. Finally, the nation must seek to organize the domestic economy in ways which do not excessively narrow the range of private choice and private initiative; for the preservation of these characteristics is essential to the quality of the society.

In narrower economic terms the question may be put: How can American democracy learn to make a more appropriate division of real resources among the requirements for national security, the requirements for maintaining and developing social overhead capital, and the requirements for expanding private consumption? And this process of allocation must, if possible, be reconciled with the answer to a second question: How can American democracy learn to maintain relatively full employment without either chronic inflation or excessive direct government administation of the economy?

These two questions, centering on the process of resource allocation and on the pursuit of a balanced path which skirts the dangers of excessive unemployment, chronic inflation, and expanding direct government control frame the contemporary and foreseeable problem of political economy in the United States.

### SOME COSTS OF MISALLOCATION

The nation has paid a heavy price in the past three decades for its failure to reconcile successfully these conflicting imperatives. The burden of a good deal of the analysis presented in this book is that at crucial stages in recent history the nation failed to make an allocation of its resources appropriate to the protection of its external interests and the quality of its society.

In the 1930's it failed to develop a policy capable of moving the economy back to full employment; and the fact of severe depression helped reinforce other influences making for an isolationism that permitted the threat of the Axis to attain the dimensions that it did, leaving a Second World War as the only realistic alternative open for the protection of American and Western interests. Moreover, the nation failed, until late in the day, to undertake a program of rearmament appropriate even to an isolated posture; and, in part, this reluctance to allocate increased resources to defense stemmed, as in Great Britain at the same time, from belief that the institutions and workings of the private economy would be damaged by an adequate defense program.

In 1945-1946 the nation dismantled its military apparatus with dangerous haste. It did so in part because it sought the satisfactions of an economy devoting its resources overwhelmingly to private consumption freed of direct government controls over the commodity and labor markets; and the resulting shift of resources away from defense—and the isolationist cast of mind and policy it communicated—almost certainly contributed to Stalin's decision to pursue forthwith a policy of vigorous Communist expansion short of major war.

Moreover, even after Truman's counterattack on Stalin was launched in the spring of 1947, the three following years saw even those most concerned with the problem of national security torn by fears of what a military budget expanded beyond $15 billion might mean for the future of capitalism and democracy in America. In 1948 Forrestal recorded as follows his view of the Truman Administration's dilemma:

> Our biggest headache at the moment, of course, is the budget. The President has set the ceiling at 14 billion 4 against the pared down requirements that we put in of 16 billion 9. I am frank to say, however, that I have the greatest sympathy with him because he is determined not to spend more than we take in in taxes. He is a hard-money man if ever I saw one, and believing as I do that we can't afford to wreck our economy in the process of trying to fight the "Cold War," there is much to be said for this thesis of holding down spending to the absolute minimum of necessity. . . .[1]

Here, with its consequences for the American ground force establishment— which bore the brunt of budgetary constraint—was the basis for the Communist attack in Korea.

From its very beginnings the believed conflict between the imperatives of a relatively free economy and the requirements for public outlays, notably in defense, shaped the policy of the Eisenhower Administration. And the dispositions in military and foreign policy which followed from the Great Equation helped directly to yield both the rolling crisis of 1956-1958 and the sluggish response to it.

Finally, it was the clash of military outlays and social overhead outlays within arbitrarily determined budget ceilings that largely accounts for the development of the nation's enormous deficit in the latter. The puzzlement of Eisenhower, expressed as early as 1953, was never resolved:

> The President then proceeded in so many words to pose this question: "If balancing the budget was everything, why should only the military programs on which the security of the country depended be sacrificed? Why shouldn't

the sacrifice be spread through veterans' benefits, the farm program, and grants-in-aid to the states"—obligations, he said, which had been assumed at a time when the country was not under compulsion to spend heavy sums for security?

Eisenhower made it very clear to the Cabinet that he was not suggesting abolition of such programs. The point he was making was that if great reductions had to be effected, it would be better to institute them almost anywhere else than where they would strike vitally at national security.[2]

In part, the systematic failure of the American political process to yield adequate allocations for public purposes has stemmed from a lack of clarity and consensus concerning the national interest and the threats to it, and from a consequent failure to assess in time the dangers the nation faced. In part, however, it has derived from problems arising directly from the economy itself and from the concepts Americans have come to apply to the economy.

### THE DUAL SYSTEM OF ALLOCATION

An important part of the difficulty arises from the clean separation traditionally made at a time of peace between the world of private choice (for allocating income left after taxation) and public choice (for deciding the level and uses of taxation). Theoretically, the decision made by the community through its representative legislative bodies on the level and uses of taxation should reflect the will and considered judgment of the majority. Under a system of elective government there should be no objective grounds for complaint that the system does not work; only, perhaps, personal disagreement with the majority view.

There are, indeed, significant imperfections in the representative process in American democracy which bear on the level and uses of taxation. For example, many state legislatures are grossly overweighted with sparsely populated rural areas and their interests; the interests of the Negro citizen are grossly under-represented in parts of the South; local government revenues depend heavily on the property tax. Such flaws in the democratic process have played an important role in the creation of the social overhead deficit.

But in an economy at full employment, several general factors operate to distort the mechanisms of decision even when the democratic process functions sensitively. First, one major way the community can constrain inflation is to constrain public expenditures. While monetary devices are available to check the level of demand in the private sector, they are usually applied late in the game. At best, the range of their influence is limited, and, during the upswing, their effect is likely to be erratic and clumsy. The consequences of excessive ardor and optimism in the private sector thus tend automatically to set in motion forces tending to constrain the level of government outlays.

Specifically, under full employment, an increase in government outlays raises the specter of direct government control in the allocation of resources as well as the specter of accelerated inflation. It is precisely these two fears—the fear that increased public outlays will accelerate inflation and/or lead to increased direct government administration of the economy—which have inhibited dedicated, patriotic men from advocating over the past decade military and social policies they would otherwise have supported.

Why under such circumstances does not the classic prescription work? Why are political leaders unprepared to advocate a rise in taxation? Why was Forrestal, as he surveyed his task, confronted in his mind with the choice of risking external danger or risking the wreck of an economic system the freedom of which he regarded as essential to the quality of American life? Why was Eisenhower forced to look to reduced social welfare and social overhead outlays as an alternative to dangerously inhibited levels of military expenditure?

The answer appears to lie in the convergence of several different forces. First is the fact that the choice between private and public expenditure assumes in the public mind an abstract, general form which obscures the content and purpose of public outlays. The issue of higher taxes is difficult to relate precisely to the concrete programs which require increased expenditure. It is politically and psychologically difficult to compare at the margin the relative values of the extra dollar privately spent and the extra value—in national security or public welfare—to be derived from an equivalent expansion in public outlays. The calculus takes the form of a crude clash between the total claims of the state against the individual family budget. In that familiar form, the public budget suffers grave psychological disadvantages, as all politicians know.

Second, the existing level of taxation acquires a degree of acceptability as citizens accommodate themselves to its burdens. Familiarity breeds not contempt but stoicism. It is not too difficult to maintain an existing tax schedule; but a palpable national (or local) crisis is generally required to make a rise in taxes politically acceptable. The tax rate is, therefore, generally insensitive to the gradually changing requirements of the public sector; and this leads politicians, except under unusual circumstances, to work out the pattern of public outlays within ceilings determined by what the existing tax schedules—the arbitrary product of the last acute crisis—will yield at existing levels of income.

Third, there has grown up in recent years, in limited but influential circles, a conviction that the stability of capitalism and its institutions is likely to be endangered by federal outlays of greater than a certain specific proportion of gross national product, often taken as 25 per cent. Although a point of danger evidently exists at some level, the point is certainly elastic and probably higher than 25 per cent. This bogey has, nevertheless, contributed to a mood which has led some men in authority to feel that a decline in outlays in the public sector is an important, if not even an overriding, goal of public policy. In this form—that is, a compulsion to seek a reduction in relative outlays for public purposes as an objective transcending the society's protection or the quality of its public services—the doctrine is, indeed, irrational; and it has proved costly to the national interest.

The case for an approximate ceiling on public outlays in relation to gross national product was quite reasonably put as follows by Senator Taft:

> In short, even though the United States has the greatest production in the world, there is a definite limit to what we can do. We cannot and should not proceed on the theory that war will begin tomorrow. All-out mobilization can only be undertaken when war is certain.
>
> WE SHOULD STRIVE TO LIMIT FEDERAL EXPENDITURES DURING THE EMERGENCY TO ABOUT 75 BILLION DOLLARS
>
> It is hard to set any exact figure beyond which the Federal budget should not go. Marriner Eccles, in an article in *Fortune* magazine, November 1950, estimated that seventy-five billion dollars is a possible federal tax. Roswell Magill, writing in the *Saturday Evening Post* of August 1951, also indicates his belief that we cannot tax more than 75 billion a year without inflation. Any general increase in prices might justify a higher tax burden in dollars. My own view is that in President Truman's estimate of Federal expenses in fiscal year 1952 of seventy-one billion dollars we have almost reached the limit to which the Federal government in peacetime should undertake to expend in a single year, unless the emergency is so great as to justify a deliberate policy of inflation and loss of liberty.[3]

The gross national product was running at about $300 billion when Taft set his $75 billion limit for the Federal budget. Although it is possible to debate Taft's proportions, there is evident sense and legitimacy in conceiving of some limit to public outlays in times short of an all-out military effort. The claims of the private sector and the workability of its institutions form an integral part of a free society which requires that a balance be struck between the degree of acceptable risk in national security and the degree of acceptable strain on the essential institutions of a democratic society. In political practice, however, Taft's essentially rational approach has tended to become lost in an almost blind drive to reduce the proportion of outlays in the public sector. The dynamic arithmetic of the problem disappeared from sight, and a decent sense of proportion was lost. Righteousness seemed to lie in a simple brute opposition to any expansion of public outlays.

The result in recent years has been a progressive decline in the public claim on resources in relation to gross national product:

TABLE 8. GOVERNMENT PURCHASES OF GOODS AND SERVICES

| | 1. Total Gross National Product | 2. Total | 3. Federal | 4. State and Local | Col. 2/ Col. 1/ | Col. 3/ Col. 1/ | Col. 4/ Col. 1/ |
|---|---|---|---|---|---|---|---|
| | (billions of dollars, 1956 prices) | | | | | | |
| 1952 | 367 | 84 | 58 | 26 | 23% | 16% | 7% |
| 1953 | 382 | 92 | 65 | 27 | 24 | 17 | 7 |
| 1954 | 375 | 82 | 52 | 30 | 22 | 14 | 8 |
| 1955 | 402 | 80 | 48 | 32 | 20 | 12 | 8 |
| 1956 | 412 | 80 | 47 | 33 | 19 | 11 | 8 |

Total federal spending (including expenditure for transfers, grants-in-aid, and interest, which do not absorb resources) of about $72 billion for (calendar) 1956 should be compared, for example, with the $100 billion which would have been permitted even under Taft's cautious formula.

THE DIRECTIONS OF REMEDY

In which directions is remedy to be found? Is the United States doomed by the nature of its economy and its thought about its economy to constrict its outlays for security and for social overheads in favor of private outlays? In the allocation among defense, loans to underdeveloped areas, schools, and high-powered automobiles, must luxurious private transport inevitably win?

The concrete issues which will determine the nation's answer to these questions reduce to the following:

1. *The continuity of output, income, and employment.* The maintenance of relatively full employment and a widely shared sense that employment is secure have a number of consequences which bear on the nation's willingness and ability to allocate increased resources for communal purposes. In the first instance, the maintenance of full employment yields cumulatively a higher level of production and a larger volume of goods and services to be distributed for all uses than output under conditions of fluctuating employment. Although output may climb back to the old trend-line after an interval of unemployment, a substantial part of the loss is permanent. For example, the cavalier handling of the recession of 1957-1958 lost the nation at least $40 billion in production.

So far as public outlays are concerned, tax yields are, of course, closely related to the level of income; and here, too, a substantial part of the tax loss due to lapses from relatively full employment are permanent.

Psychologically, moreover, a period of unemployment if at all protracted, creates a general sense of insecurity at home and diverts the energy, attention, and concern of all branches of the government (and of the public as well) away from the problems of maintaining the nation's external interests. On the other hand, a sense of assurance about employment provides a base of confidence and poise from which the nation can, if it chooses, face up to its external challenges.

To a degree, the material and psychic consequences of unemployment can be mitigated by unemployment insurance if it is adequate in scale and continuity; but this mitigation can be effective only for short periods. The effect of protracted unemployment on a man and his family—as a form of rejection by the society—is a powerful corrosive force, private and public; and it is likely to remain so unless American values and attitudes radically change.

There are certain potential effects of the relative level of employment which run in contrary directions. Chronic full employment can, for example, breed a complacency which encourages failure to assess properly the dangers and challenges of the external world. At a time of unemployment, moreover, foreign aid can be presented as an anti-recession measure although the lowering of tariffs is generally made more difficult. And, if Lubell's assessment is correct, in the wake of the Soviet launching of earth satellites, the degree of alarm expressed and the willingness of American citizens to contemplate enlarged military budgets was positively correlated with the fear of unemployment.[4]

On balance, however, the lesson of modern experience strongly suggests that the maintenance of a high degree of continuity in output, income, and employment is an important potential constructive influence on external policy. It provides political leaders a backdrop of national confidence and security against which they and the nation as a whole can contemplate other common problems and the solutions to them. Fluctuations in employment are, of course, inevitable and necessary, if only to assist the shift of resources from one use to another, as the structure of the economy changes; but a high premium attaches to making recessions short and shallow.

2. *The rate of growth.* In over-all terms, as the Rockefeller Project Report IV dramatizes, the extent to which a clash will occur among outlays for national security, social overhead capital, and private consumption depends on the rate of growth. Although the essence of the problem lies in a reallocation of resources, the degree of difficulty confronted by the nation and the degree of sacrifice required to achieve the desired result depends on maintaining a high over-all rate of growth.

In the past, conflicts of interest within the society were mitigated by a rapid increase in available resources. Harrowing beggar-thy-neighbor struggles over the allocation of resources were unnecessary when all could share to a degree in the expansion of communal income. The Rockefeller Report IV suggests that to meet the community's needs and to maintain its rate of growth in private consumption the gross national product must rise over the next decade at 5 per cent per annum, as opposed to the 4 per cent which marked the best postwar performance. Whether the momentum of the American economy can be increased to yield a regular 5 per cent increase per annum depends on many factors, among them the rate at which innovations are introduced, the extent to which the tax structure encourages the reinvestment of profits, and the composition of output itself; for the increase in output associated with a given amount of investment varies widely in the different sectors of the economy.

While a 5 per cent rate of expansion is not an impossible goal, and while a rate of growth which would provide for the maintenance of the existing average rate of expansion in private consumption per head is, evidently, the optimum solution, it would be unwise for Americans to face the problems of the next decade without preparing to contemplate an increased degree of austerity; that is, a decline in the rate of increase, or stagnation, of the private consumption level or, even, an absolute decline in private consumption per head. The possible and even likely challenges that Americans will have to face from abroad and the evident need for redressing the balance in the social setting and quality of American life at a time of rapid increase in family formation are unlikely to be successfully faced by a people who have set as an overriding condition that private consumption per head regularly increase at past rates.

3. *The composition of output.* The essence of this argument comes to rest, then, on the composition of output rather than on its over-all rate of growth. The workings of the economic and political system have resulted in recent years in allocations for national security and for social overhead capital that are too low. Put another way, the nation has been taking risks with the national security, and, for example, with the education of its children and youth, which it would not take if the choice were put to it in a different setting.

When as a community the nation has found itself pressing against the limit of its resources, it has not sat back as a family to examine all current outlays and decide which might most easily be foregone. The re-examination has been primarily confined to only one part of national outlays—the 25 per cent or less of gross national product which passes through the hands of governments—local, state, and federal. The private sector was regarded as sacrosanct except for that form of extra taxation called inflation.

Arthur F. Burns thus reflects the frame of mind automatically brought to public policy in recent years when the requirements for public outlays were, by any objective standards, rapidly increasing for both security and domestic purposes:

It is true that federal spending increased much less rapidly than did the nation's total expenditure after 1954. It may justly be held, however, that there was a need for special restraint on the government's part at a time when the rest of the economy was displaying extreme exuberance.[5]

This view stems directly from Burns' concept of what the nation seeks from its economy: ". . . a high and stable rate of employment in relation to the labor force, expanding production, improvement in living standards, and a reasonably stable consumer price level." These are insufficient criteria. They derive directly from the problem of the interwar years in Europe and the American depression of the 1930's. They are misleading at a time when American society is surrounded by a sea of troubles and when its domestic welfare requires substantial expansion in overhead capital. It is not enough to accept the quasi-Keynesian view that public outlays must be accommodated, in some compensatory way, to the degree of exuberance in the private economy. The composition of output directly matters as well as its level and rate of growth.

There is a further reason for looking afresh at the composition of output as well as at its level. If the view of modern American economic history which runs through this book is correct, the nation is approaching a point where the diffusion of durable consumers goods and services and the migration to the outer suburbs can no longer be relied upon to the same extent as in the periods 1920-1929 and 1946-1957 to provide a steady basis for full employment. This is not a matter on which dogmatism is justified; but it is altogether likely that, if the American economy were freed of its external burdens and responsibilities, military and otherwise, the American people would rather have increased leisure at this stage of history (say, a four-day week) than the indefinite extension of each family's complement of durable consumers goods. Leisure has, of course, its economic consequences, to be seen already, for example, in the radical increase of outlays on travel and on horse- and dog-racing. But it is important to be alert to the possibility that the maintenance of full employment and regular growth itself may hinge on a different balance of outlays and production than in the recent past; and at this moment and over, say, the next decade both the nation's international context and the quality of its domestic setting make increased public outlays and production conducted at a full five-day week (at least) a better solution than a premature lapse into the three-day weekend.

The issue for the American agenda is then, how to shift the focus of national politics from the problems which have obsessed the nation since the Civil War—problems of income distribution, security, and power as among social classes embraced in the sweep from the Grangers to the acceptance by the Eisenhower administration of Keynesian economics—to the issues of communal survival and communal development which are, in fact, now and foreseeably central to the nation's life and its welfare.

The nation must come to survey as a community the total pattern of its outlays so that a marginal increase in the public sector is not forced necessarily to compete against some other item of public expenditure. Public expenditures are, of course, not sacred. A searching re-examination of public sector commitments must regularly be undertaken; but the nation must learn to conduct its affairs so that an increase in public expenditures is not automatically viewed in itself as a threat to the fundamental institutions of the society.

Although the development of some such attitudes and perceptions is essential to bring about the shift in the composition of output required in American society, the task itself comes to rest on the political process—indeed, at the most sensitive of all points in the political process, the system of taxation.

4. *Taxes.* Does this whole argument come merely to a plea for higher taxes? Not necessarily; but increased taxation may well be required.

An increased rate of growth at sustained full employment might yield both the requisite resources and the requisite tax revenues (with existing tax schedules) to do the job. And, if necessary, there are ways other than taxation to constrain private consumption and release resources for the public sector without either inflation or direct government administration of markets. The nation has acquired, for example, a considerable experience in manipulating the rates and terms of mortgages and installment credit. There are even more subtle tools available to the society which may be illustrated with respect to the most obvious marginal item in American private consumption, that is, the large automobile.

In classic terms of the individualist—utilitarian calculus, if the public budget required expansion, the proper course would be to tax income or consumption or some specific consumption items of inelastic demand (like salt, beer, or cigarettes) and let the consumer exercise his freedom of taste and choice over what was left. If the individual citizen prefers to use his income after taxes for a large automobile, whose business is it but his? It is evident, however, that public taste in automobiles is not simply a matter of private individual judgment. The whole social setting of the nation—advertising, the behavior of political and other leaders, the mood on the street—has in recent times encouraged an extravagant outlay on transport. Moreover, it is difficult if not impossible for the citizen to measure the cost to the society—in forgone alternatives—of current transport methods, including the costs in roads and urban parking space. The wisdom of large cars is a legitimate communal issue and belongs on the public agenda. A systematic public reappraisal of present private transport methods might lead the nation to alter the pattern of its demand for automobiles even without a horsepower tax or some other fiscal device.

But when these and other possibilities for shifting resources from private consumption without higher taxes are all arrayed, the possibility of using taxes to transfer resources from the private to the public sector should, nevertheless, be faced. Higher taxes are likely if for no other reason than that a good deal of social overhead capital must be generated at the level of state and local governments where, respectively, the rural-urban imbalance and the limitations of the property tax must be faced. Although his case against progressive taxation is by no means definitive, nor applicable equally to all regions of the nation, it is distinctly wholesome that Galbraith placed on the national agenda the case for an expanded use of the sales tax.[6]

However fortunate the nation may prove to be in meeting its requirements without higher taxes, it would be most unfortunate to assume that this result will emerge; for the compulsion to constrain public policy within the limits set by existing tax rates has contributed to the nation's dangerous tendency to await serious crisis before facing its problems. Such delay can be dangerous not only in military and foreign affairs but also with respect to education, urban reconstruction, rail transport, and other domestic matters where slowly accumulated deficits become increasingly costly to correct and take time. The crash program is a costly tool of limited efficacy at home as well as abroad.

5. *Inflation and its alternatives.* The attitudes and methods which the nation brings to bear on its determination of the level and distribution of output will also largely determine whether prices tend to rise, remain steady, or fall. In the post-1945 years the nation has suffered mild but chronic inflation. Between 1946 and 1956 the wholesale price level rose 45 per cent, the consumer price level 39 per cent; that is, on average, there was an inflation rate of about 4 per cent per annum. There is wide agreement that the rise in prices was caused by something like these converging factors: a sustained high level of private and public demand unchecked by resolute public action; a tendency of labor unions to compete for the loyalty of their members and the relative status of their chieftains in terms of money wage and other cost-increasing benefits; and the wastage of large resources in war or military outlays, which inhibited the rate of increase of productivity.

Burns states as follows the general walfare case against inflation:

> It is highly important that we try to manage our economic affairs so as to stop the upward drift of the price level. True, a gradual inflation does not carry the horrors of a runaway inflation. But even a price trend that rises no more than one per cent a year will cut the purchasing power of the dollar by over a fifth in twenty-five years, while an average rise of prices of 2 per cent a year will cut the purchasing power of the dollar by nearly two-fifths. Such a slow but

persistent rise in the price level, to say nothing of stronger doses of inflation, is bound to deal harshly with the plans and hopes of millions of people in the course of a generation. We sometimes overlook the fact that consumers, on balance, are the major creditors of our economy, while the federal government, state, and local governments, and business corporations are the debtors. Holdings of liquid assets, combined with equity in life insurance policies and retirement funds, exceed the indebtedness of every income group of our population. The same is true of every occupational group and of every age group except the newly married. Any increase in the price level therefore reaches into the pocketbooks of the great masses of people and, if it continues for many years, it will impoverish substantial numbers who lack the knowledge or the means for a proper defense against inflation. Various worthwhile programs have been developed in recent times for improving the economic status of people who have been left behind by the onrush of progress, and it is desirable that these programs be extended. However, our best efforts in behalf of economic and social reform will surely be weakened, and they may be entirely frustrated, by the tendency of inflation to keep adding to the list of people facing hardship or distress.[7]

The present argument has suggested a further element in the case against inflation as the norm for American society; that is, the tolerance of inflation in the private sectors of the economy sets up extremely powerful forces seeking to constrain public outlays and thus inhibits the nation's performance at a decisive point.

Aside from inflation, there are, broadly, two patterns which can be sought: relatively stable prices, with real income increasing through money wage increases accommodated to increases in productivity; or slowly falling prices with relatively constant money wages, a pattern in which rising real wages are achieved by the passing along of productivity increases through the competitive market process. Historically, rising real wages have generally emerged either from a decline in prices more rapid than the decline in money wages or from a decline in prices under a regime of relatively constant money wages Put another way, it has been only under exceptional circumstances that money wages have been able to keep up with a rise in prices.[8]

In setting a noninflationary objective for public policy there are no *prima facie* grounds in either history or theory for choosing relatively constant prices as a goal rather than, say, relatively constant money wages. As a matter of practice, in the emergent American economy two factors appear to make stable prices with rising money wages the apparently more realistic goal. First, with something like 10 per cent of gross national product allocated regularly to unproductive military outlays, the pace of productivity increase is slowed down, and the economy, at reasonably full employment, will contiue to have an inflationary bias. Second, both private corporations and labor unions have fallen into habits of mind and practice which in the one case strongly resist price decreases and in the other look competitively (as among the unions) to rising money incomes as the index of effective performance.

These arguments from recent experience should not, however, be taken as conclusive. Not only have periods of constant prices been rare in the past but also those intervals when rising real wages resulted, essentially, from falling costs of living were generally marked by an attractive absence of labor conflict.[9] The case for and the possibilities of a regime of relatively constant money wages deserves more attention than they are usually given.

There is, however, no unambiguous and overpowering case for setting relatively constant money wages as a goal rather than relatively constant prices. In setting for itself the objective of non-inflationary relatively full employment, the nation should be prepared to keep an open mind and to experiment; for, whichever goal is chosen or emerges, quite radical changes in outlook and procedure are required in price policy, wage negotiations, and the posture and role of government. The consequences and possibilities of these changes in outlook and procedure cannot now be predicted with confidence.

Basically, like much else the nation must do to protect its interests, the pursuit of a noninflationary policy demands that individuals and groups come to understand better the relation between their interests and actions and the communal interest.[10] The United States is no longer a society whose communal welfare can be assured by the raw interplay of Madison's "factions." To control inflation while maintaining relatively full employment, the nation must generate attitudes and create the forum within which the major groups in the society negotiate agreement to sacrifice real or apparent short-run interests to a clearly perceived common longer-run interest.

As Burns suggests, the amendment of the Employment Act of 1946 to embrace "reasonable price stability" (or decline) is a sensible place to begin; and his recommendations for strengthening the instruments of credit available to the government and the machinery of policy formation itself are clearly germane.[11] His approach would help create a climate within which the price policies of corporations and the wage bargains struck between corporations and unions might take place in a different atmosphere, under different and more insistent public pressures to avoid inflationary arrangements.

In the end, however, a form of mutual assurance as between labor and management must be found. Labor must be assured that management will, in fact, compete in terms of price, and not trap in higher profits the margin released by wage bargains short of the maximum the market position would offer. Management must be assured that labor has not built into its institutional procedures and rivalries automatic pressures for regular increases in money wages which will absorb profit margins if the commitment is made to price competition. This is a bargain almost impossible to strike between

one union and one corporation no matter how big each is; for the single negotiation cannot embrace wage or price increases determined elsewhere in the
economy. Nevertheless, beyond a new national climate and understanding,
the creation of a national forum within which a price-wage treaty is regularly
negotiated and systematically overseen is key to a noninflationary policy and
a major item on the nation's agenda.

It is easy to be skeptical that such an understanding could be brought
about in a society which properly treasures the diffusion of authority in its
economy as in its politics. On the other hand, it is now widely appreciated
that the beggar-thy-neighbor tactics built into the inflationary process ultimately benefit neither capital nor labor and damage the common interest.
Under such circumstances, it should not be beyond the wit of a nation which
has made federalism an art to find a way to harmonize the higher interest of
the community with the continued vitality of its private economic institutions.

In the end, the two questions posed at the beginning of this chapter are
closely related. A nation prepared to face with candor the allocation of its
resources as among, say, missiles, foreign aid, schools, and automobiles will,
by that process, also acknowledge in its fiscal and monetary policy that its
resources are limited; and it will thus tend to constrain inflationary pressure.
Put another way, a part of the problem of inflation arises from the automatic
priority accorded private outlays and the consequent struggle to support
public objectives within whatever limits the exuberance of the private economy permits; and a new way of looking at the allocation problem will also
create a new setting for the problem of controlling inflation. In a larger
sense the two problems are linked because their solution requires in each case
that Americans come to reflect in their public housekeeping arrangements—
still dominated by conceptions and methods derived from the nineteenth
century, the Progressive era, and the years of the Great Depression—the fact
that they are a tight continental community living in conditions of protracted
danger.

### 68. The Future of the National Style

The prescriptions which have emerged from the foregoing analysis would
shift the balance of national performance in relation to the external world;
and they would alter in degree the character of the nation's intellectual life
and education system, its administrative method, its political process, and the
disposition of its resources.

Two questions remain. To what extent would these changes, designed in part to effect a better national performance on the world scene, converge or clash with efforts to maintain and develop the quality of the domestic society? To what extent and in what directions would they change the national style?

### THE INESCAPABLE CONFLICTS AND THEIR MITIGATION

At certain levels there are inescapable conflicts between the imperatives of sustained struggle on the world scene and the values of an open society dedicated to the maximum degree of individual freedom. The existence of such conflicts is not to be taken as an occasion for despair or even regret.

The balance of the communal interest in relation to the external world against private interests at home is not only a universal problem for societies but also a problem present in American life since the nation's founding. And, more generally, man has long been recognized as a social animal whose individuality, in the end, must largely be expressed in terms larger than his unique personality and its private satisfaction. Nevertheless, although conflicts are inescapable, they can take forms more or less costly in terms of the nation's shared values; and one of the tasks of national policy in the widest sense is to minimize their costs.

A personnel security system required to cope with the designs of an avowed enemy is, for example, a cost to human liberty even on the minimum necessary scale and even when administered with wisdom, efficiency, and restraint. A system of classified information which places limitations on the exchange of ideas and restricts the circulation of new knowledge is also a clear cost to liberty, human and intellectual. Above all, an environment in which men must live from day to day with the possibility of instant mass destruction, knowing also that a purposeful enemy is constantly seeking to erode the nation's interests, is a setting which makes fear endemic; and fear inhibits the workings of a society whose institutions are based on wide areas of mutual trust among individuals assumed to be responsible. And the moral strain of making, testing, and holding ready-poised for delivery weapons of mass destruction is at least equally grave for a society whose fundamental chosen goals are humane and pacific.

Some of these costs can be mitigated to a degree.

The current personnel security system was launched under the worst of circumstances—when, for reasons good or ill, some Americans had only recently regarded communism as a potentially constructive force on the world scene, and when the nation as a whole had accepted the Soviet Union as a fighting ally; when substantial espionage had been permitted to occur within the government of the United States and among its allies; and, above all, under circumstances which led some men to introduce the issue into the political arena. As time has passed, the limited dimensions of the security problem have been defined; the massive bureaucratic effort required to assess the backlog of persons concerned has been more or less accomplished; and the issue has substantially lost its political appeal. It should now become possible to make the personnel security system a more limited operation, surrounded increasingly by safeguards which were broken at the height of the security fever.

Similarly, as the capabilities of the enemy in new military technology have become evident, the task of security information has narrowed from one of holding in secrecy a believed unique stock of knowledge to one of protecting a much more restricted flow of new discoveries and their applications. Moreover, it should now be possible to make a more rational calculus between the advantages of secrecy and its costs in reducing the rate of innovation.

In both dimensions of security—human and informational—the nation is now in a position to temper the consequences of being steadily in a state of emergency if not at war.

What of the corrosive force of fear? Here, too, there are things to be done. Human beings are used to the fact of mortality. As a social phenomenon, fear is a matter of knowledge, of confidence, and of participation. Good morale, in units from the family to the nation, stems from facing rather than concealing the dangers confronted; from a sense that all is being done that can reasonably be done to mitigate the dangers; and from an individual opportunity to play a role in reducing the risks of disaster. A sustained public policy of candor, a more adequate military and foreign policy, including actions which make clear that no serious path to peace is unexplored, and enlarged efforts to bring the citizens of the nation into roles of participation are, together, capable of increasing the society's poise and maintaining its commitment to its liberties, its values, and its domestic institutions.

In the end, there are and will be costs—from the minimum inevitable injustices and inhibitions of a security system to the reality of the Gap and the ambiguities about strontium 90; but the democratic creed never promised perfection or nirvana—only a way of dealing with the alternatives that time and place may offer which respected the possibilities and dignity of individual human beings.

## THE DEMOCRATIC MISSION

Nor did the nation's creed ever offer either an end to striving or the vision of democracy as a unique national blessing. From its origins the United States, having created out of its European heritage a concept of working democracy, felt within itself—and was felt by the world to have—a larger mission. And this fact gave to the nation's tasks and challenges a powerful constructive cast. In Asia, the Middle East, Africa, and Latin America are new nations passing through decisive transitions which, in their essence, raise the question of whether societies based on the diffusion of power and the concept of the responsible individual can solve their problems. From one end of the Communist Bloc to the other, beneath the surface of confidence and conformity, there are the stirrings of thoughts and pressures which make not unthinkable a transition toward the norms of democratic practice. In Western Europe and Japan, older advanced societies, having found their feet after a terrible war (and for Europe, after four decades of shock and strain and the destruction of old images), are still caught up in problems and dilemmas which place in jeopardy the democratic conception.

The American interest requires that the nation seek actively to influence the outcome of these historical sequences. It lies outside the power of the United States to impose solutions; but at every point, what the nation does or fails to do will affect the outcome, in some cases profoundly, in others, only at the margin.

Here one can conclude that the effort to protect the nation's external interest—and the searching test of the meaning and contemporary relevance of the democratic faith it involves—could reinforce the historic domestic values of the society.

### THE NEW INDIVIDUALISM

What, then, of the requirement for increased pace in innovation, for learning to deal with problems with a higher degree of anticipation, for avoiding innovation by crisis? The shifts in thought, administrative method, and the political process which appear to be required would, on the whole, strengthen the role of the individual and of individual creativity in American society. There can be, of course, no return to a world of small Jeffersonian farms and individual family firms. The nation's life is committed, beyond recall, to large complex units of organization and to specialized functions for the individual within them. There are, however, both the national need and the possibility of making American institutions more flexible, more responsive to the insights which individuals perceive and to the initiatives they may be prepared to launch based upon them. There is the need and the possibility for enlarging the area of individual responsibility within bureaucratic structures and for thinning out the vast encumbering machinery Americans have tended to erect on analogy with the efficient machine shops and assembly lines which shaped administrative thought in the first half of the twentieth century.

In intellectual life there is the need and the possibility of freeing the individual from the fragmented professionalized areas of knowledge and encouraging him to confront whole living problems directly; for there is correctable human waste in the bureaucracy of American intellectual life as in the overly rigid structures of government and business.

In education as well there is the need and the possibility for balancing the concern for the individual and his social adjustment, which in the last half century progressive thought brought to American schools, with an increased emphasis on the expression of individuality in the form of creative intellectual performance at the highest level.

And, above all, there is the need and the possibility of widening the area of individual and group participation in the political process, notably with respect to military and foreign policy.

There is, then, a wholesome irony to be exploited. The fact that American society is caught up in a sustained communal challenge to its survival could yield a resurgence of individuality and of personal responsibility. It could inspire a new individualism which would fight against a narrowing of the political process at decisive points and against bureaucratized forms and methods of thought which stultify the performance of the tasks of innovation the nation confronts.

There is, in short, the need for a heightened degree of individuality in many directions in the service of the national interest. The quality of diversity which has long distinguished American society needs extension, not constraint.

### THE ALLOCATION OF RESOURCES

The question finally arises: Is there inescapable loss in the fact that so large a volume of the nation's resources must be used in unproductive military outlays? The simple answer is, of course, yes.

If the nation were to be relieved of the need to put something like 10 per cent of gross national product into security outlays, the conflict between private consumption and social overhead capital would be relieved, if not ended. Should the arms race be brought to a halt, there is little doubt that there would emerge a widespread consensus that a substantial part of the savings should be put into education, urban reconstruction, low income housing, and the like.

There are, in the most direct and sensible meaning, inescapable real economic costs in the Cold War.

Moreover, the need to strain for new devices and methods for avoiding inflation and the other inhibitions which a semi-garrison economy imposes on private institutions are, in the normal way of looking at things, a nuisance, if not worse.

But there is a larger and more general question involved. The foreseeable strain on national resources dramatizes and heightens the nature of the connection between the pursuit of individual advantage and larger human and social purposes. In the world of the nineteenth century, for example, those who worked on farms and in factories struggled toward a decent life for themselves and their families; and in America, as everywhere, the struggle for a living absorbed a high proportion of the energy, talents, and nonmaterial motivation that men could bring to the round of life. Those who undertook acts of leadership and innovation in the economy found in their roles not only the possibility of wealth but also the adventure of risk-taking, of power, and of rising in social status. The economists' notion that a free competitive market economy could operate to common advantage on the basis of the interplay of private judgements of private advantage was approximately correct; but it was correct not because men were motivated solely or even predominantly by economic advantage. It was correct because in the pursuit of their living and of profit men were seeking means to ends which transcended material reward—whether it was the future of their children or the prestige and status that went with a home in Newport, or the simple human adventure of construction. As Keynes has said:

> If human nature felt no temptation to take a chance, no satisfaction (profit apart) in constructing a factory, a railway, a mine or a farm, there might not be much investment merely as a result of cold calculation.[1]

In the contemporary setting of American life brute poverty is no longer the central problem, social mobility and economic security have been increased, social status is less uniquely associated with wealth, and even the responsible decisions within the private sectors of the economy have come increasingly under professionalized management. It is wholly fair, then, to raise the question as to whether a reduced rate of increase in consumption levels due to the requirements for protecting the community is to be regarded as an unmitigated cost.

Are there not compensations for those who produce for the national defense or for the farmer whose surpluses may alleviate famine in India? Is it wholly a loss for Americans to be forced to debate, as they will have to debate, whether their schools are more important than the horsepower of their automobiles? Is it necessarily a cost for the leaders of unions to be forced to contemplate the relationship between their rivalry and the problem of inflation, and for responsible industrial managers to be forced to reopen the question of whether competition via advertising rather than price is the proper course for capitalism and the society as a whole? In short, the intrusion of social dimensions on private economic decisions might, to a degree, heighten the sense of larger purpose in economic activity which, in another day, was provided by the personal struggles and triumphs or participation in the creation of a mature industrial society on this continent.

These are truly unanswerable questions at the present time. They hinge, in fact, on an issue posed and set aside in an earlier chapter: that is, on whether the United States and other rich societies, freed of the challenges of poverty and external danger, will at some future time prove capable of making a good life; or, if and when the old challenges are surmounted, they will suffer secular spiritual stagnation.

What can be said with confidence is that a society unwilling to accept the costs and inconveniences of a somewhat reduced rate of increase in consumption is unlikely to solve the problems which the nation now confronts.

## THE FUTURE OF THE NATIONAL STYLE

Now, finally, the future of the national style. In what respects is the drift of American society, interwoven with the imperatives arising from the world scene, transforming each of the three central elements initially identified as comprising the American household?

It is a major theme of this book that the century after 1815 saw the elaboration of an American style distinctive in its balancing of universal dilemmas. The evocation of moral and idealistic goals helped give a sense of nationhood to a sprawling continent full of diverse peoples; but this active commitment was, as it was bound to be, partial. It was linked to social and political practice which incessantly hammered out compromise solutions—wise or merely shrewd—to conflicts of interest and value, solutions by no means wholly consonant with the nation's articulated standards.

The challenge of exciting material problems yielded a philosophic style empirical in method and narrowly pragmatic in its solutions. At the same time, this approach to reality was joined to the habit of spacious generalization which universalized without great reflection or refinement what could be perceived on the American scene.

Finally, the continuity of the American experience in all its dimensions permitted the drama of the nation's physical maturing to unfold by gradual change remarkably consonant with the "magnificent image" of its purpose and meaning articulated at the nation's birth. But this extraordinary operational success confirmed the nation in methods of articulation, thought, and action which relied excessively on the *ad hoc* solution to the practical problem framed by the implicit assumptions of life on the American scene. American society elevated uniquely the virtues of the operator, the manipulator of the concrete ongoing process, rather than the man of reflection.

From Hay's Open Door notes at the turn of the century through Wilson's performance at Versailles, Hoover's isolationism, and Franklin Roosevelt's and Stimson's conception of *noblesse oblige* as an instrument for taming Stalin, to the Eisenhower administration's mixture of moralism and obsessive concentration on the building of military pacts—for more than a half-century now, various strands in the classic national style, representing one dimension or another of the nation's private habits and experience, yielded results which failed adequately to protect the national interests. The environment which the nation faced and the problems it raised for solution were systematically misunderstood when viewed parochially from the setting of American life.

As of the summer of 1958, Americans live in a world where moralism serves the nation ill in its relations to the world and in its vision of itself; where the rate of increase in material output is an insufficient measure of the society's performance, even its economic performance; where the operator's simple empiricism, combined with heavy immobile staff procedures for innovation, fails to keep pace with the challenge of the environment; and where even the image of inevitable American success is clouded.

The agenda developed in the preceding five chapters would shift the balance of the national style and the performance that flows from it in ways presumed to permit the nation's external interest to be better protected, the quality of the domestic society to be improved, and the conflicts between the two objectives to be minimized where they are inescapable. And American society and its policy would appear in fact to have been moving in each of the directions of suggested change in response to long-run forces given increased scope and expression by shocks of the crisis of 1956-58: from the somewhat expanded military budget to the noisy debate on education now reaching down to the PTA's; from the accretion of scientists to the White House staff to the boom in small cars; from the reorganization of the Pentagon to the limitation of billboards on the new highways; from the Senate's anticipatory concern with the fate of India to an advertisement offering engineers work in a firm guaranteeing no "togetherness"; from the popularity of a book on limited war to the slow by steady recent rise in social overhead capital outlays of state and local governments.

If the sole relevant criterion were the underlying direction of change, then it would be possible to say with confidence that the American style is responding in ways necessary to deal successfully with the nation's environment. But, as with other organisms, the fate of societies is determined by the pace as well as the direction of adaptation. Societies have lost their stature or suffered disruption and defeat not only because they preferred to go down in the style to which they had become accustomed but also because they could not alter their style fast enough to cope with the problems presented by their environment. In no major dimension of national policy can it now be said that the pace and scale of the American response to its problems is adequate when the magnitude of those problems is objectively assessed; and this is true whether one looks at military outlays, the pace of military research and development, the capacity to deter limited war, the scale of lending to underdeveloped areas, the building of courses of common action in the Western alliance, the rate of development of first-rate intellectual talent, the reconstruction of the cities, the state of the nation's transport system and water supply. The errors and weaknesses of the nation's enemies may permit an inadequate military and foreign policy to suffice; but there are no objective grounds for building policy on this assumption.

Luck is not wholly an accidental factor in history; but it ill becomes a great nation which intends to maintain its stature to build its policy on the assumption of luck.

The national style towards which the nation has been shifting is distinctively different from that of the nineteenth century. Viewed historically, the nation has at last come to the end of the nineteenth century. It is at last freeing itself from conceptions, methods, and illusions which were appropriate to the tasks of building a mature industrial society on the democratic principle in an empty continent permitted isolation by the accident of a peculiar power structure in the world arena. The style appropriate to that era has lingered on in many forms, not only because the minds and habits of men are formed in their youth but also because the role of strategic reserve for the West, which the nation transitionally filled in the first half of the twentieth century, required only sporadic and limited engagement with the world and made return to the times before 1914—the implicit standard of "normality"—not unthinkable.

Now, brutally and directly and in every dimension, the nation is caught up in a world where its military power, diplomatic influence, and ideological conformation are explicitly, relentlessly under challenge from the Soviet Union; a world whose military and communications technology, whose economics and politics, leave the United States no protecting cushion; a world which day by day is giving birth to substantial new powers whose time of technological maturity is measurable and with whose fate the destiny of American society is inextricably bound up.

While the United States must free itself of much in its style and performance which characterized the nineteenth century, there is at least one strand from that era it should cherish and continue to develop—namely, the capacity to throw itself into the solution of problems with energy, zest, and confidence. The problems of the present and future are more complex than those of the past. Their definition and the isolation of useful areas for action are more difficult tasks. But in the end, neither the nation nor the world as a whole can afford to see lost the operational vigor which has distinguished the American style over the past century and a half.

Moreover, in contemplating the trends in American society, there may be comfort in recognizing that there is at least a family resemblance between the emergent national style and that of a still earlier time in the society's life. The moral maturity and candor required now are not unlike those that characterized the generation that made the nation in the late eighteenth century; and so, also, with its ease in dealing with abstraction, its respect for science, its intense curiosity and search for intellectual synthesis, its lively sense of connection with currents of thought and politics which transcend the American scene. Even Hamilton's mercantilist view that government should be an active and positive instrument in shaping a free economy to social ends has its relevance.

And there is one strand from the past to which, above all, the nation must look in facing both the immediate challenge of communism and the longer tasks which lie beyond in the world of diffused power—a strand also rooted in the eighteenth century: the sense of democratic mission.

The transcendent quality which has long suffused American life and which still gives it a special worth is not the opulence of its resources or any other local dimension of the society, its structure, or its institutions. That special quality is the conviction that the adventure of America has a meaning and relevance for the world as a whole. Having been blessed with a rich and handsome physical endowment, protected for a century from the pressures and strains of the world arena, permitted by its allies the luxury of a further half-century in the role of strategic reserve with limited responsibilities, now the nation faces the test of its worth and of the meaning of its history.

Will the United States mobilize the strength, will, and imagination to bring about the process of persuasion in the Communist Bloc which, by denying all other alternatives, would permit without major war the gradual evolution and release of the forces for good within it? Will the United States mobilize the strength, will, and imagination to bring about the emergence of the new nations in Asia, the Middle East, Africa, and Latin America as congenial open societies in a world structured for order rather than for racial and ideological hostility and nuclear anarchy? Will the United States mobilize the strength, will, and imagination to hold firm, with a new common understanding and new lines of common action, the Western coalition and the links to Japan on which both historical transitions depend?

The role of the United States in determining the outcome of the world's history over coming decades will, of course, be marginal; and success cannot be assured. Moreover nations, like people, are complex units, seeking many objectives simultaneously; and the round of American life will be taken up with many matters other than these. Nevertheless, an outcome consonant with the hopes of the world's peoples cannot be brought about unless American public policy perceives its mission in such terms, dedicates itself to that mission, and acts upon that dedication with a substantial proportion of its energies, talents, and resources. It is equally clear that a United States which failed to undertake the mission in high seriousness would be in default to the best within it and to the generations of striving men and women who, while bringing America to its present material and military eminence, never lost faith in its larger meaning and purpose.

The United States, child of the Enlightenment, favored adolescent of the nineteenth century, powerful but erratic youth of the first half of the twentieth, must now confirm its maturity by acting from the present forward to see the values of the Enlightenment—or their equivalents in non-Western cultures—survive and dominate in the twenty-first.

# BOOK SIX

*Footnotes*

## CHAPTER 63. Moralism, Morality, and the National Interest

1. *The Selected Writings of John and John Quincy Adams*, (ed., A. Koch and W. Peden), New York, Knopf, 1946, p. 319.

"So far as they were contending for independence, I wished well to their cause; but I had seen and yet see no prospect that they would establish free or liberal institutions of government. They are not likely to promote the spirit either of freedom or order by their example. They have not the first element of good or free government. Arbitrary power, military and ecclesiastical, was stamped upon their education, upon their habits, and upon all their institutions. Civil dissension was infused into all their seminal principles. War and mutual destruction were in every member of their organization, moral, political, and physical. I had little expectation of any beneficial result to this country from any future connection with them, political or commercial. We should derive no improvement to our instiutions by any communion with theirs. Nor was there any appearance of a disposition in them to take any political lesson from us. . . ."

2. In some ways the American reaction to the (real or believed) fruits of the Soviet educational system and to the (real or believed) cleverness of Soviet diplomacy and psychological warfare is simply a renewal of old American attitudes towards an older, more astute, more devious Europe.

3. The author owes this aphorism to Gunnar Myrdal, who created it or derived it from an unknown source. See also, F. M. Cornford, *Microcosmographia Academica*, Cambridge, England, Bowes and Bowes, 1908, who defines propaganda as "that branch of the art of lying which consists in very nearly deceiving your friends without deceiving your enemies."

4. D. Acheson, *Power and Diplomacy*, Cambridge, Harvard Univ. Press, 1958, p. 137.

## CHAPTER 64. Theory, Fact, and Public Policy

1. D. Riesman, *Constraint and Variety in American Education*, Garden City, N. Y., Doubleday Anchor Books, 1958, p. 71.

2. R. Oppenheimer, "An Inward Look," *Foreign Affairs*, XXXVI, January, 1958, p. 217.

3. Vannevar Bush, "The Builders," *Techonology Review*, February, 1955, p. 178.

4. The author for some time in the period 1955-1958 asked the following question of knowledgeable men: "How many persons have—intellectually and administratively—been responsible for the development of the major weapons evolved in

the United States since 1940?" The answers ranged between 35 and 160, in part due to differing definitions of "responsible"—a concept difficult to delimit in this context.

### CHAPTER 65. Bureaucracy, Innovation, and the Individual

1. For the human ideological, and technological setting of Lowell's innovating act see, for example, C. L. Stanford, "The Intellectual Origins and New-World-liness of American Industry," *Journal of Economic History*, XVIII, March, 1958.

2. This passage is based directly on the work of A. D. Chandler, Jr. See, especially, "Henry Varnum Poor, Philosopher of Management, 1812-1905," (Ed. W. Miller), *Men In Business*, Cambridge, Harvard Univ. Press., 1952; and *Henry Varnum Poor*, Cambridge, Harvard Univ. Press, 1956, especially Chaps. 6 and 7.

3. The military have had, historically, a special problem which reinforced the tendency to build administration around closely defined specialized routines; namely, that in time of war, it has to be assumed that any given person might be removed at any moment as a casualty, and that the system had, therefore, to be geared to run tolerably with mediocre men, thrown up by chance, in any given post.

4. See, for example, H. Simon, *Administrative Behavior*, New York, Macmillan, 1948, pp. 38-39.

5. For a classic exploration of this problem, see E. E. Morison, "A Case Study of Innovation," *Engineering and Science Monthly*, April 1950.

6. Compare, for example, D. Eisenhower, *Crusade in Europe*, Garden City, N. Y., Doubleday, 1948, pp. 74-76, on the task of a modern military commander and M. Newcomber, *The Big Business Executive and the Factors That Made Him, 1900-1950*, New York, Columbia Univ. Press, 1955, pp. 20-23, on the functions of a modern business executive.

7. For analysis and prescription along these lines, see E. E. Morison (Ed.), *The American Style*, New York, Harper, 1958, chapter by George Kennan and the commentary on Kennan's essay by Richard M. Bissell, Jr.

### CHAPTER 66. Innovation, Leadership, and the Democratic Process

1. A Roper Poll published in the *Boston Globe* of April 7, 1957 sought to establish what American men and women most worried about. The replies centered overwhelmingly on money, health, and children—in that order—with children a source of slightly greater anxiety among women than men. In a similar vein, Al Capp identified the three basic comic strip themes capable of universal communication as death, love, and money, in a television broadcast of May 25, 1958.

2. J. M. Jones, *The Fifteen Weeks*, New York, Viking, 1955, p. 142.

3. It is to be noted that Walter Lippmann's *The Public Philosophy*, Boston, Little, Brown, 1955, derived its impetus from observations on the politics and diplomacy of Western Europe in the period 1933-1939. There, too, it is arguable that the schism which immobilized the West was more a split within the political élite—as between those willing to face down Hitler and those fearful of its con-

sequences—than a split between a wise and united élite and an uninformed apathetic public.

4. *William Bradford, Of Plymouth Plantation, 1620-1647*, Ed., S. E. Morison, New York, Knopf, 1953, p. 27.

### CHAPTER 67. The Political Economy of a Continental Community in Time of Protracted Crisis

1. W. Millis (Ed.) *The Forrestal Diaries*, New York, Viking, 1951, pp. 536-537.

2. R. J. Donovan, *Eisenhower, The Inside Story*, New York, Hope, 1956.

3. R. Taft, *A Foreign Policy for Americans*, Garden City, N. Y., Doubleday, 1951, pp. 72-73. As an outer limit, Taft (p. 71) indicates that, at a time of no major hostilities, he would regard 40 per cent of gross national product for total public outlays (including state and local expenditures) as excessive and bound to result in inflation.

4. S. Lubell, "Sputnik and American Public Opinion," *Columbia University Forum*, Winter, 1957.

5. A. F. Burns, *Prosperity Without Inflation*, New York, Fordham Univ. Press, 1957, p. 40. For a further explicit statement of this point of view, see pp. 75-76.

6. J. K. Galbraith, *The Affluent Society, Boston*, Houghton Mifflin, 1958, especially pp. 315-320.

7. A. F. Burns, *op. cit.*, pp. 20-21.

8. See, for example, W. Layton and G. Crowther, *An Introduction to the Study of Prices*, London, Macmillan, 1938, Appendix E, pp. 271-275. Also, P. Douglas, *Real Wages in the United States 1890-1926*, Boston, Hougton Mifflin, 1930.

9. Such intervals were sometimes marked by disproportionate decline in income and discontent among farming groups; but this is not a necessary condition for a regime of falling prices and constant money wages.

10. For a more detailed statement of the author's position on the underlying changes required for the pursuit of a non-inflationary policy in a democracy, see, *The Process of Economic Growth*, Chap. 10, especially pp. 228-235.

11. A. F. Burns, *op. cit.*, pp. 66-88.

### CHAPTER 68. The Future of the National Style

1. John M. Keynes, *The General Theory of Employment, Interest and Money*, New York, Harcourt, Brace, 1936, p. 150.

# THE NATIONAL INTEREST

NOTE: The concept of the national interest which runs through this book is so central to the author's judgments that it appears worth while to state it explicitly, permitting the reader to isolate the author's presuppositions for critical examination.

A DEFINITION

It is the American interest to maintain a world environment for the United States within which American society can continue to develop in conformity with the humanistic principles which are its foundation. This definition, in terms of the progressive development of the quality of American society, would, of course, include the physical protection of the country; but the protection of American territory is viewed essentially as a means to a larger end —the protection of a still-developing way of life.

The operative meaning of this definition derives from the geographic position of the United States. For no substantial period in the nation's history has the American interest been automatically assured by geographic isolation. Contrary to a mythology which still strongly affects American attitudes and the nation's performance, the American interest has been chronically in danger from the late eighteenth century forward. This danger arose and continues to arise from the simple geographic fact that the combined resources of Eurasia, including its military potential, have been and remain superior to those of the United States—Eurasia being here defined to include Asia, the Middle East, and Africa as well as Europe.

The United States must be viewed essentially as a continental island off the greater land mass of Eurasia. Various combinations of power in Eurasia have been and remain a potential threat to the national interest. American independence was achieved in the eighteenth century only because Americans could exploit a conflict between Britain and France. A united Britain and

France could have stifled the American Revolution. During the nineteenth century the nation expanded and consolidated American power on the North American continent and in the Western Hemisphere by exploiting the power conflicts of Eurasia; and in the twentieth century the United States has been thrice placed in jeopardy, and instinctively sensed that jeopardy, when a single power or combination of powers threatened to dominate Western Eurasia, Eastern Eurasia, or both.

There is, then, much in the whole sweep of American history which denies the notion of an America safely isolated by act of God and geography; and there is nothing fundamentally new in taking the American relationship to the power balance in Eurasia as central to the nation's security problem.

### THE DUAL AMERICAN INTEREST IN EURASIA

If the problem of the national interest is viewed as a question of protecting not only the nation's territory but also its basic values as a society, it follows that the United States has two distinct but connected interests in Eurasia. Since the combined resources of Eurasia could pose a serious threat of military defeat to the United States, it is the American interest that no single power or group of powers hostile or potentially hostile to the United States dominate that area or a sufficient portion of it to threaten the United States and any coalition the United States can build and sustain. But under modern conditions of communication, there is a second threat to the nation's interest. Whatever the military situation might be, a Eurasia coalesced under totalitarian dictatorships would threaten the survival of democracy both elsewhere and in the United States. It is, therefore, equally the American interest that the societies of Eurasia develop along lines broadly consistent with the nation's own ideology; for under modern conditions it is difficult to envisage the survival of a democratic American society as an island in a totalitarian sea.

### THREE CLARIFICATIONS OF THE AMERICAN IDEOLOGICAL INTEREST

This proposition must be immediately clarified in three respects.

First, the United States need not seek societies abroad in its own image. The United States does have a profound interest that societies abroad develop and strengthen those elements in their respective cultures that elevate and protect the dignity of the individual as against the claims of the state. Such elements of harmony with the Western democratic tradition exist in different forms everywhere; and they have been strengthened by the attractiveness of the Western democratic example at its best, notably by the example of British parliamentary government, the American Revolution, and the values on which American society was erected. But the forms of legitimately democratic societies can vary widely.

Second, the democratic process must be viewed as a matter of aspiration, trend, and degree, not as an absolute. The value judgments which underlie the political, social, and economic techniques of Western societies might be summarized as follows:

1. Individual human beings represent a unique balancing of motivations and aspirations which, despite the conscious and unconscious external means that help shape them, are to be accorded a moral and even religious respect. The underlying aim of society is to permit these individual complexes of motivations and aspirations to have their maximum expression compatible with the well-being of other individuals and the security of society.

2. Governments thus exist to assist individuals to achieve their own fulfillment, to protect individual human beings from the harm they might do one another, and to protect organized societies against the aggression of other societies.

3. Governments can take their shape legitimately only from some effective expression of the combined will and judgments of individuals on the basis of one man, one vote.

4. Some men aspire to power over their fellow men and derive satisfaction from the exercise of power aside from the purposes to which power is put. This fundamental human quality in itself makes dangerous to the well-being of society the concentration of political power in the hands of individuals and groups even where such groups may constitute a majority. *Habeas corpus* is the symbol and, perhaps, the foundation of the most substantial restraint —in the form of due process of law—men have created to cope with this danger.

From Plato on, political scientists have recognized that men may not understand their own best interest, and, in particular, that they may be short-sighted and swayed by urgent emotions in their definition of that interest. As between the individual's limitation in defining wisely his own long-run interest and his inability wisely to exercise power over others without check, democratic societies have broadly chosen to risk the former rather than the latter danger in the organization of society, and to diminish the former danger by popular education, by the inculcation of habits of individual responsbility, and by devices of government which temper the less thoughtful political reactions of men.

From this definition the democratic element within a society emerges as a matter of degree and of aspiration. The pure democratic concept is compromised to some extent in all organized societies by the need to protect individuals from each other, by the need to protect the society as a whole from others, and by the checks required to protect the workings of the society from man's frequent inability wisely to define his own long-run interest. Even when societies strive for the democratic compromise, the balance between liberty and order which any society can achieve and still operate effectively, and the particular form that balance will take, are certain to vary. They will vary not only from society to society but also within each society in response to the state of education of its citizens and the nature of the specific problems it confronts as a community at different stages in its history.

It is evident that some present societies have not had and do not now have the capability of combining effective communal action with a high degree of what is here called the democratic element. Both history and the contemporary scene offer instances of governments in which the balance of power is heavily in the hands of the state rather than in the hands of the individual citizens who comprise it.

The legitimate American ideological interest is not that all societies become immediately democratic in the degree achieved in the United States or Western Europe, but that they accept as a goal a version of the democratic value judgments consonant with their culture and their history and that they move toward their realization with the passage of time.

Now a third clarification of the American ideological interest. Since the American interest does not require that all societies at all times accept democratic values and move toward their achievement, the nation is concerned not with total ideological victory, somehow defined, but with the balance and trend of ideological forces in Eurasia. Therefore, the application of the limited, but real, margin of American influence on the course of other societies can and should be selective. Given the nation's geographic circumstance, its history, and the quality of its society, the American interest demands, in a sense, that Americans be crusaders; but the American ideological crusade must be tolerant, long term, and directed toward areas of importance where the nation's margin of influence may be effective. The United States is concerned not with absolutes but with the direction of political trend in Eurasia.

CURRENT THREATS FROM EURASIA

In more specific geographic terms, it is a persistent interest of the United States that no single power or power grouping militarily dominate either Western or Eastern Eurasia.

In Western Eurasia the threat of such an outcome is posed by the possible absorption within the Soviet empire of East Germany and Eastern Europe. The threat would become a reality should West Germany be drawn into the Soviet power orbit; and the threat would be made acute by the ideological defection of Italy, France, or both. In the East the threat of such an outcome is posed by the close alliance of the Soviet Union and Communist China. In

Asia there are two major centers of power, Japan on the one hand and India on the other, the latter being key to the complex stretching from Indochina around to Pakistan. In Asia the threat to the American interest would become virtually a reality should either Japan or India be lost to the Free World.

At the present time the intentions and capabilities of the Communist Bloc pose two threats to the United States—a military threat and an ideological threat. These threats are clearly related; the ideological loss of India, for instance, would raise important military problems; the military loss of northern Indochina has raised important problems of ideological orientation throughout Southeast Asia. But the two American interests are not and should not be considered identical. The time necessary and the kind of effort required to cope with the military threat are likely to differ from those required by the ideological threat. The military threat to South Korea was dealt with in a few years; defeating the ideological threat to South Korea may prove a creative Free World task for a generation.

## THE INTERWEAVING OF POWER AND IDEOLOGICAL INTERESTS

If this view of the American interest is correct, the debate which has been proceeding in the United States over recent years as to whether the nation's interests should be defined in power terms or in terms of the ideological principles to which American society is attached is a somewhat misguided debate. This is so in two respects.

First, if the essential American interest is to preserve a world environment within which its chosen form of democratic society can persist and develop, then the nation's stake in the ideological and political balance in Eurasia is as legitimate as its interest in the military balance of power in Eurasia. Two national efforts, one military and the other political, interacting intimately, must go forward together as part of a total effort to protect the interests of American society.

There is a second sense in which the debate appears misguided. It appears to be a characteristic of American history that this nation cannot be effective in its military and foreign policy unless it believes that both its security interests and its commitment to certain moral principles require the nation to act. From the Spanish-American War to the present, the nation has acted effectively only when both strands in its interest were believed to be involved—in the Spanish-American War itself, in the First and Second World Wars, in the effort to reconstruct and defend Western Europe in 1947-1950, in the early phases of the Korean War.

When idealism alone seemed to be the basis for the positions taken, the nation did not back its play, as, for example, in Wilson's ideological formulation of the American interest at Versailles. Equally, the nation has not been effective when confronted with situations where its power interests might be involved but where a persuasive moral basis for American action was not present. The notion of American imperialism, popular in certain American circles at the turn of the century, died quickly when it confronted the abiding American instinct in support of political independence in the case of the Philippines and elsewhere. Similarly, a major reason why the United States was ineffective in the Indochina crisis of 1954 was that it was then extremely difficult simultaneously to deal with the Communist menace and to disengage from French imperialism in that area; and in the summer of 1956 the United States was gravely inhibited in dealing with Nasser because, among other reasons, his claim to national sovereignty over the Suez Canal had a certain resonance in the American image of its historic meaning on the world scene as the friend of those struggling for independence.

The wisdom of American policy in Indochina and at Suez is, of course, debatable. Moreover, a nation's belief that its ideals are or are not involved is by no means an unambiguous criterion for performance. Nevertheless, it is unrealistic to expect American society—given its history and values—to perform in terms of pure power criteria.

The components in the American ideological interest can, then, be distinguished and summarized in the following three propositions:

1. The ideological loss of key areas in Eurasia would have major military consequence for the United States.

2. Apart from its military consequences, the ideological loss of the balance of power in Eurasia would, under modern conditions, have major adverse consequences for the quality of American society and for the viability of the humanistic principles which underlie it.

3. Among the qualities of American society threatened by the loss of the ideological balance of power in Eurasia would be the historic sense of American democratic mission on the world scene, present since the nation's founding, which has given to American life much of its moral worth, its distinction, and its forward momentum.

The art of American statesmanship is to formulate and to sustain courses of action which harmonize in specific settings abiding American interests and abiding American ideals, steadily preserving the dual power balance in Eurasia, preventing by forehanded effort the emergence of such crises as those which hitherto have been required to evoke a major American effort at self-preservation.

The requirements of protecting the military balance of power and developing the ideological balance of power will not always converge. Foreign policy is full of painful choices. There may be times when in order to maintain military positions action must be taken which will conflict with the norms of the American ideological interest; and there may be occasions when it will be proper to take military risks to permit movement toward ideological objectives. But in the world of 1958 and beyond there are many more points of convergence than are now being exploited. If the dual character of the national interest—as a democratic island off a potentially threatening Eurasian mainland—is accepted, and if the interrelations of the two objectives are perceived, courses of action still appear open to the United States which will protect and sustain the quality as well as the existence of the nation's life in the face of current and foreseeable challenges.

## THE UNITED STATES AND THE DECLINE OF NATIONHOOD

Among those challenges is the problem of using American power and influence to tame military force by effective international accord; for the nature of modern weapons in a context other than American monopoly is a danger to the national interest sufficiently grave to justify acceptance of important constraints on the nation's sovereignty. Put another way, it is a legitimate American national objective to see removed from all nations—including the United States—the right to use substantial military force to pursue their own interests. Since this residual right is the root of national sovereignty and the basis for the existence of an international arena of power, it is, therefore, an American interest to see an end to nationhood as it has been historically defined.

The pace at which means of communication are now under development argues, further, that the present nations of the globe will move into relations of increasing intimacy and interaction.

Between them, the urgent imperative to tame military force and the need to deal with peoples everywhere on the basis of an accelerating proximity argue strongly for movement in the direction of federalized world organization under effective international law. And, should effective international control of military power be achieved, it might prove convenient and rational to pass other functions upward from unilateral determination to an organized arena of international politics.

It is not easy or particularly useful to peer far beyond the time when this great human watershed is attained. Nevertheless, it can be said that the American regional interest would still continue to embrace elements from the long sweep of the past. Convergent and conflicting relationships of geography, of cultural connection, of economic interest would in substantial measure be simply transferred from a setting where military force enters the equation of negotiation to one of global domestic politics. When the great conference has ended and the freely moving inspectors take up their initial posts from one end of the world to the other and the nightmare passes, the agenda of international politics will look not unfamiliar. Much in the historic relation of the United States to the balance of affairs in Eurasia will remain. There will be, however, a special dimension to global politics with special meaning for Americans—the problem of so conducting the world's affairs as to avoid a dissolution of the federal machinery and civil war.

# AMERICAN PROJECT BOOKS
# AND WORKING PAPERS

## BOOKS

FREEMAN, RALPH E., Editor. *Postwar Economic Trends in the United States.* Harper, 1960.

KINTNER, WILLIAM R., with JOSEPH I. COFFEY and RAYMOND J. ALBRIGHT. *Forging a New Sword: A Study of the Department of Defense.* Harper, 1958.

MORISON, ELTING E., Editor. *The American Style: Essays in Value and Performance.* Harper, 1958.

PEET, HARRIET E. *The Creative Individual: A Study of New Patterns in American Education.* To be published.

ROSTOW, W. W. *The United States in the World Arena.* Harper, 1960.

BATOR, FRANCIS M. *The Question of Government Spending: Public Needs and Private Wants.* Harper, 1960.

## WORKING PAPERS

(Available from the Center for International Studies, Massachusetts Institute of Technology, Cambridge 39, Massachusetts.)

I. "Public Opinion and United States Foreign Policy: 1937-1956." Nancy Boardman Eddy.

II. "Notes on Congress and the National Interest: 1945-1951." Richard W. Hatch.

III. "The Korean War." Peter Ogloblin.

IV. "The Crisis in the Middle East: 1956." Jeannette Clarvoe Tierney.

V. "Some Reflections on Recent Changes in the United States." D. W. Brogan.

VI. "A Note on Changing American Values as Seen in Contemporary Popular Literature." Helen G. Kangieser.

VII. "The Making of Modern America." (2 vols.) W. W. Rostow.

In addition, work has been done within this Project the results of which will merge with other research conducted by the authors and will be published elsewhere. Raymond Bauer explored the concept of the mass communications society; Alfred Chandler, Jr. examined aspects of the evolution of American business administration; Lewis Dexter investigated Congressional attitudes and procedures in handling military policy; Gordon Jensen examined pre-1914 American business reactions to aspects of the Progressive Period; Rowland Mitchell examined the evolution of post-1945 research and development within the government; Gregory Rochlin studied the origins and evolution of Eisenhower's concept and method of administration.

# Index

Acheson Dean G., 210, 239, 257, 276, 483

Acheson-Clayton proposal, 185-187

Adams, John Quincy, 30, 480, 540

Adams, Sherman, 390, 406

Adenauer, Konrad, 219

Administration
American competency in, 500
American science in Second World War and, 60-63
American theory of, 497-498
specialization and, 495-496

Advisory Committee on Postwar Foreign Policy, 125

Aerial inspection, 403

Afghanistan, Soviet aid to, 295

Africa
Communist policy toward, 294-297
nationalism in, 250-258

Agriculture
Chinese, 399, 428
Soviet, 416

Air defense, 249, 312-314
See also Strategic Air Command

Air Force, American, 153, 226-227, 266
attacks on air defense by, 313
budget
(1948-1950), 265
(1950-1959), 307
crisis of 1943, 66-70
demobilization (1945-1950), 265
Korean War growth of, 275
Navy criticism of, 272
strength
(1947), 172

Air Force, strength—*Continued*
(1948), 222
post-Korean War, 308
unification and, 174-175
See also Strategic Air Command

Air power
development of, 64-77, 151-156
expansion of by United States, 223-224
Forrestal on, 226
limitations of, 87
military innovation and, 36-37
national security and, 86

Air War Plans Division, 64, 65-77, 152, 153

Aircraft, Rockefeller panel on procurement of, 372

Alexander, Gen. Harold, 158

Alliances
expansion in Far and Middle East of, 324-329
experience of United States with in Second World War, 77-85

Allied commands, structure of, 80

Allied Control Council, 99, 117, 168, 188, 191-195, 344

Allied High Commission for Germany, 218

Altimeter, 58

American Project (MIT), 551-552

Anders, General, 104

Anderson, Gen. Frederick L., 68, 76

Antwerp, clearance of port of, 73, 82

553